2, 3, 4, 5, 6, 11
12, 13, 16, 17.

EDUCATIONAL PSYCHOLOGY

EDUCATIONAL PSYCHOLOGY

Principles and Applications

John A. Glover, Roger H. Bruning
and Robert W. Filbeck

The University of Nebraska, Lincoln

LITTLE, BROWN AND COMPANY

Boston Toronto

Library of Congress Cataloging in Publication Data

Glover, John A., 1949–
Educational psychology, principles and applications.

Bibliography: p.
Includes index.
1. Educational psychology. 2. Teaching.
I. Bruning, Roger H. II. Filbeck, Robert.
III. Title.
LB1051.G567 1983 370.15 82–17089
ISBN 0–316–31766–7

Library of Congress Catalog Card No. 82–17089

ISBN 0-316-31766-7

9 8 7 6 5 4 3 2

HAL

Published simultaneously in Canada
by Little, Brown & Company (Canada) Limited

Printed in the United States of America

ACKNOWLEDGMENTS

Cartoons © 1982 Sidney Harris.
Photos on pages 23, 36, 97, 179, and 229 courtesy of NETCHE, Inc.

Page 6, top: Arthur Grace/Stock, Boston.
Page 6, bottom: Bohdan Hrynewych/Stock, Boston.

(continued on page 584)

PREFACE

Our book is designed primarily for future teachers, current teachers who are developing their knowledge and skills, and all others who are involved with the processes of learning and teaching from preschool through adulthood. We believe that our book will also be valuable for the general reader—the person who wants to know more about what learning is and how teaching can be made more effective.

Three major objectives guided our efforts: (1) to help our readers understand the science of educational psychology—particularly in its past and present relationships to psychology and education, (2) to describe as clearly as possible what is known about how students learn, and (3) to help our readers translate this knowledge about learning into strategies for effective teaching.

The major theme of our book is the influence of meaningfulness on learning. We believe that the best, most lasting learning occurs when teaching methods and materials match up carefully with students' knowledge. Each chapter in our text is based on this premise and is written to demonstrate how all the diverse skills in educational psychology help teachers, in one way or another, do a better job of presenting meaningful instruction to students. We have taken our theme very seriously by trying to create a scholarly yet highly meaningful text for our own readers.

This text is organized in a logical, contemporary manner. We devote Part One to cognitive psychology—the most rapidly growing area in educational psychology. Chapters in this section are "An Introduction to Cognitive Processes," "Memory and Concepts," "Problem Solving," "Intelligence and Cognitive Development," and "Creativity." We do not, however, lose sight of the important contributions of behavioral psychology to modern educational psychology. In Part Two we devote Chapter Seven, "An Introduction to Behavioral Psychology," to an outline of behavioral psychology. Chapter Eight, "Social Learning and Modeling," reflects the changing nature of behavioral psychology while Chapter Ten, "Classroom Management," contains a wealth of behavioral techniques available to today's teacher. The importance of humanistic psychology is recognized in Chapter Nine, "Motivation," and in Chapter Ten, in which we detail the applications of cognitive, humanistic, and behavioral psychology for the guidance of student behavior.

In Part Three the importance of effective communication in instruction is emphasized in Chapter Eleven, "Instructional Goals and Objectives," while procedures for developing meaningful instructional materials are described in Chapter Twelve, "Task Analysis." Part Four is devoted to measurement and evaluation. Chapter Thirteen is "An Introduction to Measurement," while Chapters Fourteen and Fifteen deal, respectively, with "Teacher-Made Tests" and "Standardized Tests." The final part in our book examines the need for teachers to be able to adapt to changing requirements. We devote Chapter Sixteen, "The Exceptional Student," to the topic of special needs students and Chapter Seventeen, "Reading and Reading Disabilities," to that most critical of all academic skills.

We believe our text fairly and professionally represents educational psychology. Clearly, our emphasis on contemporary cognitive psychology is a departure from most traditional texts, as is our integration of cognitive, humanistic, and behavioral psychology. Our inclusion of an entire chapter on reading is also a departure from traditional textbooks. We believe that all teachers, not only those of the early elementary years, must be able to deal with problems associated with reading. In addition, to make our book more useful and interesting, we have supplemented the basic contents with:

1. chronologies of important events in the topic areas treated in each chapter
2. practice exercises designed to demonstrate the specific knowledge and skills in each chapter
3. detailed lists of applications of the knowledge and skills contained in each chapter
4. clear and informative illustrations
5. an outline at the beginning of each chapter
6. higher order objectives, also at the beginning of each chapter, that focus on important learning outcomes
7. suggested readings at the end of each chapter identifying sources of more detailed information on specific topics of interest
8. a complete glossary at the end of the text

Two of these features deserve additional introduction. A unique aspect of our book is the chronology of important events at the end of each chapter (except Chapter One). The chronologies provide brief historical overviews of important events in the development of knowledge about the topics covered in each chapter. We feel strongly that educational psychology should not be treated in isolation. It is a growing, dynamic science and must be studied in light of its roots and close ties to both psychology and education. The chronologies establish meaningful backgrounds for the course content. Throughout our text, we emphasize the evolving nature of educational psychology and how it has been shaped by its research and applications.

The practice exercises contained in each chapter (except Chapter One) have been field tested on thousands of students over the past few years. Each exercise is keyed specifically to a critical issue or skill and allows you to experience directly the concepts in the chapters or to practice an important skill. We believe you will find the exercises worthwhile and illuminating.

In the development of this text we owe thanks to many, many people—too many to list in this brief space. Special thanks are due, however, to Mylan Jaixen, Senior Editor at Little, Brown, who has seen us through good times and bad and helped and encouraged us all along the way. Also, we are grateful to David Moshman (a developmental psychologist *par excellence*), Royce Ronning (a problem solver if ever there was one), and to John Zimmer (a man who needs no introduction), who each provided excellent feedback on several of the chapters. Special mention goes also to Suzie Sybouts, who typed the several versions of the manuscript, often under extreme time constraints. Her consistant good humor and many valuable suggestions were greatly appreciated.

We also want to thank Sue Warne, our book editor at Little, Brown, for her advice, her critical judgments, and her tolerance. Thanks are also extended to Barbara Flanagan, who greatly improved the quality of the final manuscript, and to the many other members of the Little, Brown staff who helped move this book into print.

We also want to express our great appreciation to a very special group of scholars whose attentions to our manuscript were invaluable. Our reviewers have included: Walter Brown, formerly of University of Washington; Steven L. Christopherson, University of Texas, San Antonio; Richard I. Fisher, Colorado State University; Janice Hayes, Middle Tennessee State University; Wayne Kirk, Winona State University; John Long, University of Rhode Island; Wayne Mollenberg, University of New Mexico; Robert Trimble, University of Missouri, Columbia; and Joan R. Yanuzzi, Indiana University of Pennsylvania. We believe the hours that they spent reviewing various drafts of our manuscript contributed considerably to our ability to reach our goals of comprehensive content and clarity of expression.

We have a special feeling also for the many individuals who appear in the photographs in the text. They include staff and students of: Zeman Elementary School, Everett Junior High School, Pound Junior High School, and Southeast Community College. At these institutions, several individuals must be singled out for their efforts: Dean K. Webb of Zeman School, David Van Horn of Everett School, and Jack Huck and Phyllis Kendall of Southeast Community College. In addition, a large group of photographs was provided by NETCHE, Inc. Jim Danielson of NETCHE arranged for their use and we thank him for his efforts. Thanks are also due to Ken Jensen of the Instructional Design Center at the University of Nebraska and to B & W Labs of Lincoln for their important parts in preparing photographic copy for this book.

Finally, we want to thank our wives, Theresa, Mary, and Lee, and our families for the support we have felt as we worked on the book. Their encouragement and love have helped the three of us see our dream for this text transformed into a reality.

J.A.G.
R.H.B.
R.W.F.

BRIEF CONTENTS

CONTENTS

Chapter Four

PROBLEM SOLVING 86

Chapter Five

INTELLIGENCE AND COGNITIVE DEVELOPMENT 122

Chapter Nine

MOTIVATION 248

Chapter Ten

CLASSROOM MANAGEMENT 278

Chapter Fifteen

STANDARDIZED TESTS 464

EDUCATIONAL PSYCHOLOGY

Chapter One

AN INTRODUCTION TO EDUCATIONAL PSYCHOLOGY

Remember the teachers everybody sought out—teachers whose classes were always full and who made their students work hard but helped them enjoy it? You can be remembered this way by your students, although you may feel that you are still a long way from being such an admired teacher. Research on the skills that effective teachers possess shows that they are not mysterious, magical traits that only a chosen few can hope to have. Most of these skills are straightforward and can be learned through study and practice.

Educational psychology can help you acquire many of the skills of an excellent teacher by focusing on major concerns of teachers—how people learn, how best to help them learn, and how to evaluate that learning (Elkind, 1973). The sentiments expressed by George Miller in a presidential address to the American Psychological Association are especially appropriate at the outset of this book:

> I can imagine nothing we could do that would be more relevant to human welfare, and nothing that could pose a greater challenge to the next generation of psychologists, than to discover how to best give psychology away. *(1969, p. 1075)*

The major purpose of this book is to try to give psychology away to you, to show you how the principles and research methods of psychology can be applied to your teaching. To help you understand more specifically what is being given away, we will first provide you with some information about the way in which educational psychologists view the teaching and learning process.

ABOUT TEACHING

Excellence in Teaching

Everyone knows something about teaching. Parents teach their children. Children teach each other. Adults teach themselves all kinds of things. If everyone knows something about teaching, then, why does anyone need a course in educational psychology? Aren't teaching and learning inevitable, natural processes? If someone knows a great deal about a subject such as history, isn't it a simple matter to teach it?

The answer is yes and no. No doubt, there are a few people who are "naturals" at teaching. They have many of the skills of outstanding teachers even without formal training. By fortunate circumstance—having a parent who is a skilled teacher, for instance—these people have acquired the qualities of organization, personality, and ability to motivate students. Most teachers, however, work hard to obtain these skills. They build on their strengths. They also realistically assess their weaknesses and overcome them. Their teaching is built on a firm base in psychology, and it is as consistent as possible with current knowledge about human learning and development.

Excellent teachers are made, not born. It isn't enough just to suppose that one can teach; an array of demonstrable skills and knowledge is needed to ensure maximal and pleasurable learning for students. We don't trust ourselves to the care of a doctor, lawyer, or dentist if we do not have the utmost confidence in his or her skills. Neither should we assume that children will be entrusted to us if we cannot show our excellence as teachers. None of us wants to be under the tutelage of a teacher who is not highly competent. Consider Socrates' comments about a teacher, Protagoras:

> You are going to commit your soul to the care of a man whom you call a Sophist. And yet I hardly think that you know what a Sophist is; and if not, then you do not even know to whom you are committing your soul and whether the thing to which you commit yourself be good or evil. *(Plato,* Dialogues, *"Protagoras")*

We don't often think about how distinguished teachers acquire and perfect their skills. The best teachers, of course, demonstrate many attributes in addition to teaching skills—a great deal of knowledge about students, enjoyment of students, and knowledge and enthusiasm for their subject matter. Educational psychology is not designed to develop your proficiency in a subject matter area, although the principles of educational psychology certainly can be applied to your own studies, as we demonstrate and encourage in many Practice Exercises. This text does not presume to be able to help you enjoy your prospective students, although as your teaching skills improve so will your enjoyment of teaching and of students. What educational psychology offers you is the psychological knowledge about learners that is necessary to develop instructional skills for effective teaching.

Teaching as Art and Science

Whenever teaching is discussed, an inevitable question is whether teaching is an art or a science. Many people prefer to consider teaching an art because teachers must draw upon individual experiences, emotions, and values that seem to occur outside the province of science (Highet, 1957). Others have focused on teaching as a science in which the critical aspects of instruction are reduced to elements that can be studied by the scientific method (Skinner, 1968). Who is right? Is teaching an art or a science? Teaching is both—an art and a science.

The complex, demanding profession of teaching requires artistry and scientific knowledge. As an art, teaching surely engages the emotions, the values, and, some would say, the souls of all who teach well. Many teachers are as deeply involved in their work—the development of students—as painters, sculptors, and musicians are involved in producing their masterpieces. Good teachers are creative; they solve prob-

Psychology tries to translate human experience into a set of scientific principles.

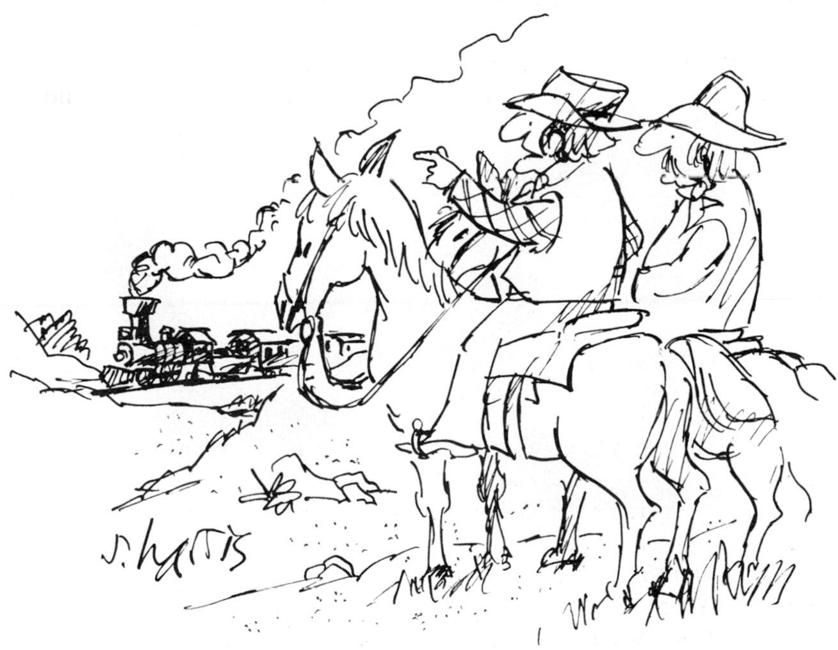

"I love hearing that lonesome wail of the train whistle as the magnitude of the frequency of the wave changes due to the Doppler effect."

Teaching is both an art and a science. A complex, demanding profession, it combines artistry and scientific knowledge.

lems by inventing teaching methods and materials. Education as a science draws upon psychology, sociology, anthropology, ethology, biology, medicine, and many other scientific disciplines to develop effective instruction. Teachers use many of the methods of science, such as hypothesizing, experimenting, and observing outcomes.

Science and artistry are inextricably intertwined in good teaching.

The goal of this text is to help you acquire the skills and knowledge generated by science to complement your artistry, just as a painter uses scientifically derived principles of light, shading, and perspective to produce art forms.

EFFECTIVE TEACHERS

Everyone has experienced good teachers and bad teachers. What are the differences between them? Are effective teachers more intelligent? Are their personalities better suited to teaching? Are some people just born to teach? These are important questions that have been addressed by careful research. The research generally has shown that factors such as intelligence and personality are less important than the skills teachers use in class (see, for example, Good & Brophy, 1978; Good & Grouws, 1979; Brophy, 1982). Research has identified many skills that make a difference in the quality of instruction. Good teachers are able to develop student thinking, manage classrooms effectively, deliver high-quality instruction, evaluate learning, and adapt to changing requirements.

Developing Student Thinking

Perhaps the major goal of education is to develop students' abilities to think. To meet this goal, teachers must understand how thinking (cognition) operates in human beings. The concept of meaningful learning is especially important to the development of student thinking (J. R. Anderson, 1980); effective teachers are able to make learning activities meaningful.

Meaningful learning occurs when students are able to relate new information to what they already know (Moates & Schumacher, 1980). Thus, a knowledge of how new information may be made meaningful to students is critical. This knowledge is gained from first understanding the processes of perception and attention, which determine to a great extent what students will be able to remember.

Another key to providing meaningful learning for students is knowledge of human memory (Klatzky, 1980; Siegler, 1980). Not only must new learning build upon prior knowledge, but students should be able to logically organize their new learning in memory so it is available for continued learning. Curricula are designed so that the information contained in one course builds on prior courses as it lays the foundation for future learning. Teachers should thoroughly understand human memory so their instruction will take advantage of curriculum structure and increase students' mastery of educational goals.

The development of problem-solving skills in students is also

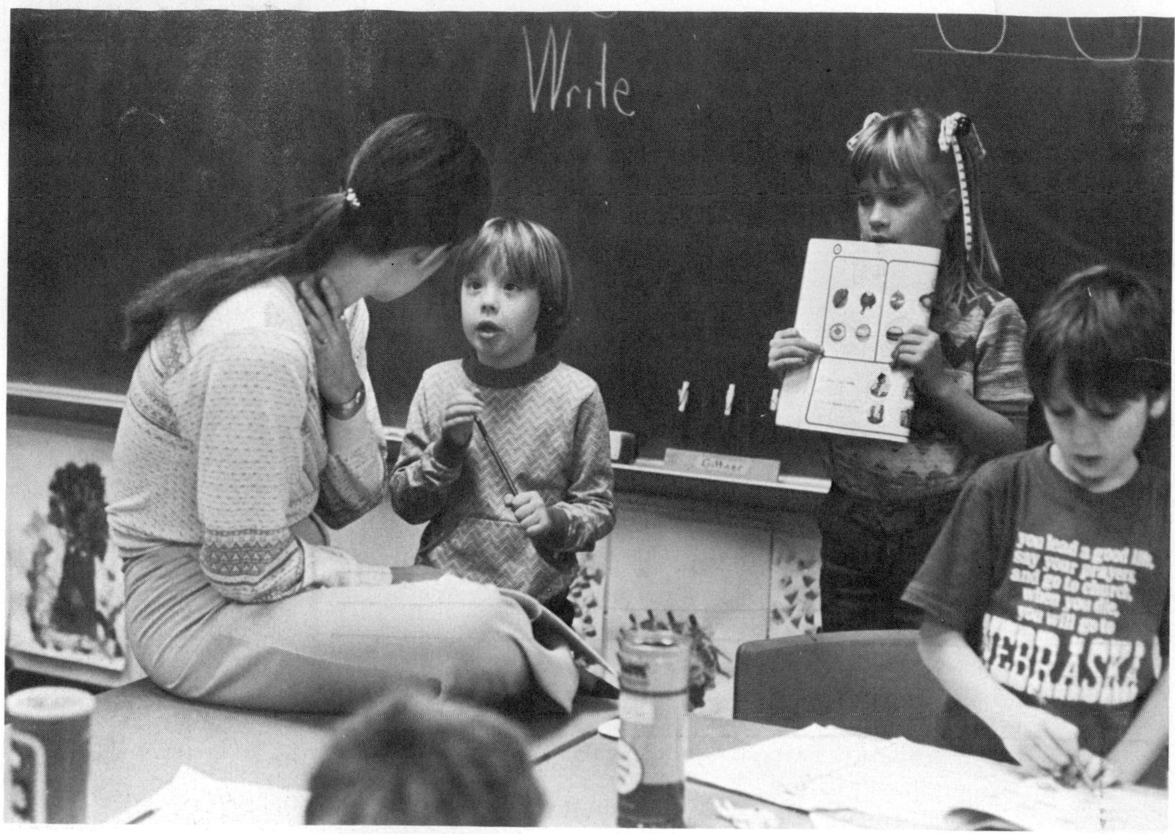

Effective teachers are sensitive to differences in how students think. Like this child, each student has his or her own way of looking at the world.

achieved by effective teachers (Gagné, 1980), who understand the importance of problem solving in modern life and emphasize it in many ways in their instruction. They also foster creative thinking; they understand the conditions that lead to creative thought and arrange learning activities to develop creativity.

Effective teachers are sensitive to individual differences in how students think. One set of differences is in general cognitive ability, that is, intelligence (Hunt, 1978). Another important set of individual differences in cognition is developmental (Piaget, 1976). The logic and reasoning of the typical six-year-old are not the same as those of a nine-year-old. Important changes in thinking continue to take place throughout life at different rates for different people. A third, more general set of individual differences in cognition is known as cognitive style, which generally refers to the characteristic ways in which individuals perceive and deal with information (Messick, 1976). Ineffective instruction seldom takes cognitive differences into account and results in "learning

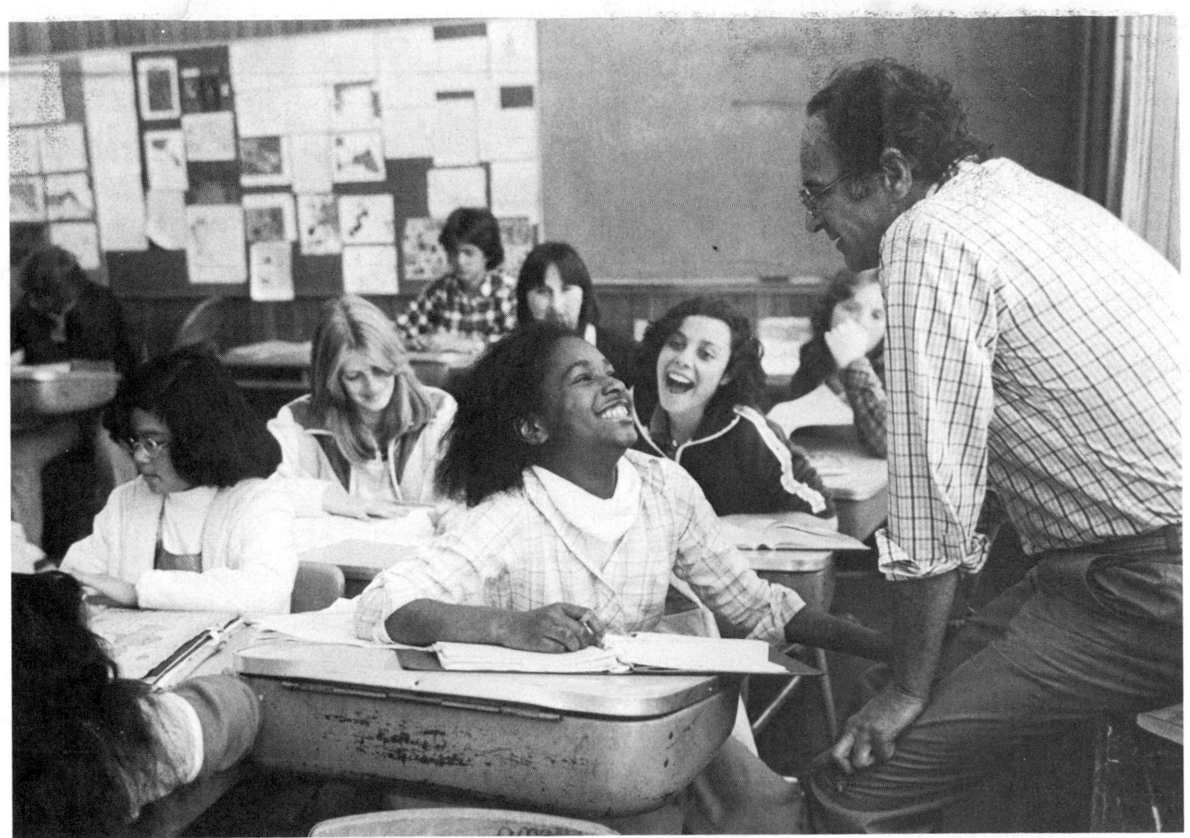

Effective teachers are able to establish rapport quickly.

activities" that are unsuited for many students. Effective teachers, in contrast, are aware of cognitive differences and consider them when planning instruction (see Cronbach & Snow, 1977; Snow, 1980; Wittrock, 1979).

Managing Classroom Environments

Effective teachers have pleasant, organized, and productive classrooms (Good & Brophy, 1978). In contrast, ineffective teachers have difficulty in providing conditions that lead to harmonious and productive behavior. Perhaps the most striking difference between them, however, is the ability of effective teachers to prevent problem behaviors. Effective teachers are highly sensitive to what is happening in their classrooms and are able to head off trouble. They are able to manage many student activities simultaneously and thereby prevent discipline problems. The adage that an ounce of prevention is worth a pound of cure certainly applies to classroom management.

The best teachers also provide excellent role models and help students learn how to work happily, cooperatively, and usefully with others. Unfortunately, ineffective teachers sometimes model undesirable qualities ("blowing up" when frustrated or angered, for instance) and often do not understand their role in helping students learn by imitation and observation. Most people see the school as an arena in which students learn many of the social skills they need to function throughout life. Effective teachers understand the factors that affect social behavior and recognize their role in the social development of their students (Bandura, 1977a).

Effective teachers are able to establish rapport with their students from the beginning. They interact freely and easily with class members, and students perceive them as warm and authentic. They emphasize cooperation rather than competition in their classrooms, which results in more positive learning experiences for their students (Johnson, Skon, & Johnson, 1980; Slavin, 1981). The learning process, rather than its products, is emphasized (Slavin, 1980b). Their important overall goals are to improve relationships among students and to continually nurture the growth of students' self-esteem (Slavin, 1980a).

Excellent teaching motivates students, but poor teaching often leaves students unmotivated to learn. Comprehending the factors underlying motivation and being able to enhance student motivation in the classroom are hallmarks of good teaching. Whether this means building students' self-concepts or developing students' interests, effective teachers have motivation skills.

Delivering Instruction

Objectives:

Effective teachers are able to communicate to students what they are expected to learn. Brophy and Evertson (1976) examined many classrooms, contrasting more effective with less effective teachers. They found that effective teachers were far better organized than their less effective counterparts, clearly informing students what was to be done and how it was to be done. This ability to communicate goals and objectives to students has far-reaching effects. It influences how students prepare for class, what they do in class, and what portions of reading materials they attend to. Clear goals also affect how teachers prepare for and conduct their classes (Good & Grouws, 1979).

The most competent teachers are able to determine where to begin instruction with each student. Brophy and Evertson (1976) point out that effective teachers prepare for instruction at the students' level, provide individualized instruction where necessary, and pace instruction properly. Poor instruction frequently bores good students while it frustrates less able students. The best teachers provide something for everyone—all students are challenged by materials that are suited to their capabilities.

Good teachers are constantly giving thoughtful reactions to what students are doing. Careful feedback like this greatly facilitates learning.

Evaluating Learning

Good instruction is carefully evaluated and constantly adjusted. Students receive relevant and prompt feedback about their learning. Poor instruction, on the other hand, is characterized by inappropriate, irrelevant evaluations of student learning and sometimes by no evaluations at all. Effective teachers possess a whole host of evaluation skills that allow them to determine how well students are learning. This information, obtained from both well-constructed, teacher-made evaluation instruments and standardized tests, helps good teachers adjust their instructional procedures. Student learning is greatly facilitated by feedback received from careful evaluation.

Adapting to Changing Requirements

The role of teachers is changing. They are being called on to perform a wider range of tasks than ever before. Meeting the needs of special students is one critical dimension of their changing role. Another is the increasing recognition that all teachers must be able to provide instruction in reading, the most important of all academic skills. Teachers' roles will continue to change, and effective teachers will meet this challenge by increasing the range of their knowledge and skills.

Handicapped students are often educated in regular classrooms, and effective teachers have adapted their instruction to fit a wide array of individual needs. Poor instruction ignores the needs of individual students, a guarantee that many will never reach their potential. Effective teachers take into account the specific needs of individual learners, including the disabled and the non-disabled. They are able to orchestrate challenging learning experiences for all students (Brophy & Evertson, 1976; Brophy, 1982).

At all levels, attention to reading problems is an integral part of good instruction (Smith, 1978). Good teachers have always recognized that the teaching of reading should not be confined to the early elementary years. If students read poorly—or not at all—they must be taught reading in order to avoid the academic, economic, personal, and social problems associated with illiteracy. Inability to read can be a tremendous disadvantage and can relegate nonreaders to failure in school and sometimes in life as well.

The best teachers are dedicated lifelong learners. Not all teachers are good learners, however. Oscar Wilde reflected the feeling of some people when he wrote: "Everybody who is incapable of learning has taken to teaching" (Wilde, 1904). This skeptical attitude about teachers is, unfortunately, partly correct even today in that some teachers seem to stop learning when they begin teaching. The changing world passes them by and leaves them unprepared to teach effectively. In contrast, excellent teachers keep abreast of new developments in their subject matter areas and continually improve their already outstanding teaching skills. The best teachers are always learning—they are themselves dedicated students.

EDUCATIONAL PSYCHOLOGY AND EFFECTIVE TEACHING

A Definition of Educational Psychology

Educational psychology is that branch of psychology devoted to the study of how humans learn and how they can be helped to learn. Educational psychologists investigate human learning and teaching methods in their research by applying the scientific method to questions educators have about the learning/teaching process. One of the major tasks of educational psychology is conducting research on the most effective ways to teach. In the previous section we listed the skills and the kinds of knowledge effective teachers possess. This list was the product of research by educational psychologists on the differences between effective and ineffective teachers.

Research in educational psychology lies along a continuum from basic to applied, with most falling somewhere in between (Melton, 1959; Wittrock, 1967). Basic research is conducted to answer fundamental questions about the nature of learning or teaching without concern for any direct applications of the results. An example of basic research is an investigation of how finely people can discriminate between different musical tones. The answer is of great interest to many persons and is relevant to the teaching of music but it may not have any direct impact on teachers. At the other end of the spectrum, applied research is conducted to find solutions to actual educational problems. Suppose members of a curriculum committee are developing reading materials for sixth graders and they want to know the best place to insert study questions. A research study designed to answer this question would be directly applicable for these educators and probably for many other teachers as well.

Research at all levels from basic to applied helps us improve education. Principles from basic research are the foundation for much of our current understanding of children's thinking and motivation. Applied studies have often helped the educational community test these principles in complex settings such as reading programs or mathematics curricula. Research at all levels contributes to the theory and practice of education.

There is more to educational psychology, however, than research. Teachers must be able to use research results. Finding out, for example, that mnemonics (memory aids) are helpful for many students doesn't benefit anyone unless teachers learn to use them. So if you ask, "How can educational psychology help me become a more effective teacher?" the answer lies in your ability to learn and employ the skills, knowledge, and principles generated from psychological research. A careful examination of the next few paragraphs outlining the rest of the book will help you see what skills and knowledge you will acquire in your study of educational psychology.

Looking Ahead

The first major part of the book, "Cognitive Psychology Applied to Teaching," is designed to help you attain a broad understanding of human cognition and apply this understanding to teaching. Chapter Two, "An Introduction to Cognitive Processes," introduces you to the study of thinking and provides specific information about the processes of perception and attention. A discussion of short-term memory and a brief history of cognitive psychology are followed by applications of cognitive psychology to teaching.

Chapter Three, "Memory and Concepts," continues the discussion of human cognition. Specifically, Chapter Three describes both historical and current views of memory, with emphasis on the application of memory research to teaching. Concepts, a central feature of memory, are discussed and effective methods for teaching concepts are described. Chapter Four, "Problem Solving," focuses on another major aspect of cognition: how people solve problems. It emphasizes methods by which teachers can help students become better problem solvers. Chapter 5, "Intelligence and Cognitive Development," describes individual differences in cognition from psychometric, information-processing, and developmental perspectives. Chapter Six, "Creativity," closes our section on cognition with a discussion of one of the most important and fascinating concerns of education: increasing the creative abilities of students. After a review of the nature of creativity, the chapter offers a set of guidelines for enhancing creativity.

The next major part of the text, "Guiding and Motivating Behavior," emphasizes the prevention of problem behavior. Chapter Seven, "An Introduction to Behavioral Psychology," provides a thorough description of behavioral psychology, a discipline that views learning from a perspective quite different from that of cognitive psychology. The principles of behavioral psychology are reviewed and applications for teachers are described. Chapter Eight, "Social Learning and Modeling," presents a theoretical perspective, social learning theory, that integrates cognitive and behavioral psychology. We discuss the learning of social behaviors, especially through observation, with particular emphasis on interactions in the classroom. Chapter Nine, "Motivation," surveys several important views of motivation and draws on these theories to present a set of guidelines for motivating student behavior. Chapter Ten, "Classroom Management," draws on the theories presented in Chapters Seven through Nine to describe specific methods of modifying student behavior.

Chapters Eleven and Twelve constitute the next part of the book, "Planning for Meaningful Learning," with a focus on the design of instruction. Chapter Eleven, "Instructional Goals and Objectives," will help you translate broad, educational goals and the principles of cognitive and behavioral psychology into specific statements of your students' abilities. The research on communicating expectations is distilled into a set of skills you will acquire through reading and practice. Chapter Twelve, "Task Analysis," teaches a method for sequencing instruction meaningfully and for beginning instruction at the best point for each student.

The fourth part of our book, "Educational Measurement and Evaluation," is closely related to planning for instruction as well as interpreting the results of instruction. As we have said, good instruction depends on excellent measurement skills. Chapter Thirteen, "An Introduction to Measurement," outlines the concepts, principles, and issues underlying educational measurement. The role of measurement as an essential component of educational decision making is discussed in detail. Chapter Fourteen, "Teacher-Made Tests," applies the principles from Chapter Thirteen to the planning of tests and other measures. It will help you learn to design measurement instruments that will lead to sound decisions about students and provide excellent feedback from them. In Chapter Fifteen, "Standardized Tests," you will learn about using standardized tests in making educational decisions.

The fifth part of the text, "Adapting to Changing Requirements," includes the last two chapters. Chapter Sixteen, "The Exceptional Student," highlights characteristics of the children educators often refer to as "special." Information about a wide range of exceptionalities, from visual impairment to giftedness, is presented along with a description of the mainstreaming process. The topic of Chapter Seventeen, "Reading and Reading Disabilities," is one of the most important academic skills your students will acquire—reading. Your students will have varying levels of reading ability, and some will probably have severe reading deficits. Every teacher should be able to recognize reading problems and help students improve their reading.

A special feature of our text deserves mention here as you consider the contents of the rest of the book. Each chapter closes with a chronology of events that highlights important advances in the history of the area of psychology discussed in the chapter. We present these chronologies to help you tie the contents of each chapter into the larger field of psychology and to aid you in seeing how the knowledge in our field has advanced. We believe that educational psychology should not be studied in isolation from its history. Educational psychology has close ties to both the science of psychology and the field of professional education. We hope that you will take the time to study the chronologies so that you will gain a better understanding of how today's educational psychology is the product of the work of many distinguished psychologists and educators over many years.

SUMMARY

To teach effectively requires both artistry and a knowledge of the principles of effective instruction. Educational psychology is a source of many principles upon which teachers can draw. These principles come from research—both basic and applied—that is conducted to study how people learn and to find the best ways to help them learn. Educational psychology provides both the general principles that underlie all teaching methods and the specific skills that help a person become a more effective teacher. Its ultimate value lies both in its contribution to theory and in its applications, as teachers provide students with successful and enjoyable learning experiences.

Suggested Readings

Clark, P. M. Education and psychology: The relationship question. *Educational Forum,* 1978, *43,* 59–65.

This article provides a brief overview of the relationship between psychology and the field of education. It raises some interesting questions about the proper content of courses in educational psychology.

Glaser, R. Educational psychology and education. *American Psychologist,* 1973, *28,* 557–566.

Robert Glaser has outlined the ways in which educational problems serve to strengthen psychology and also the ways in which the principles of educational psychology can be used to improve educational practice.

James, W. *Talks to teachers on psychology and to students on some of life's ideals.* New York: Holt, 1899.

William James's book is the classic volume describing the application of psychology to teaching. Not only are the ideas in this volume still fresh, but it contains a great deal about the background of our field.

Wittrock, M. G. Focus on educational psychology. *Educational Psychologist,* 1967, *4,* 17–20.

Wittrock's paper provides a definition of educational psychology and the roles it plays in contemporary education and psychology.

Part One

COGNITIVE PSYCHOLOGY APPLIED TO TEACHING

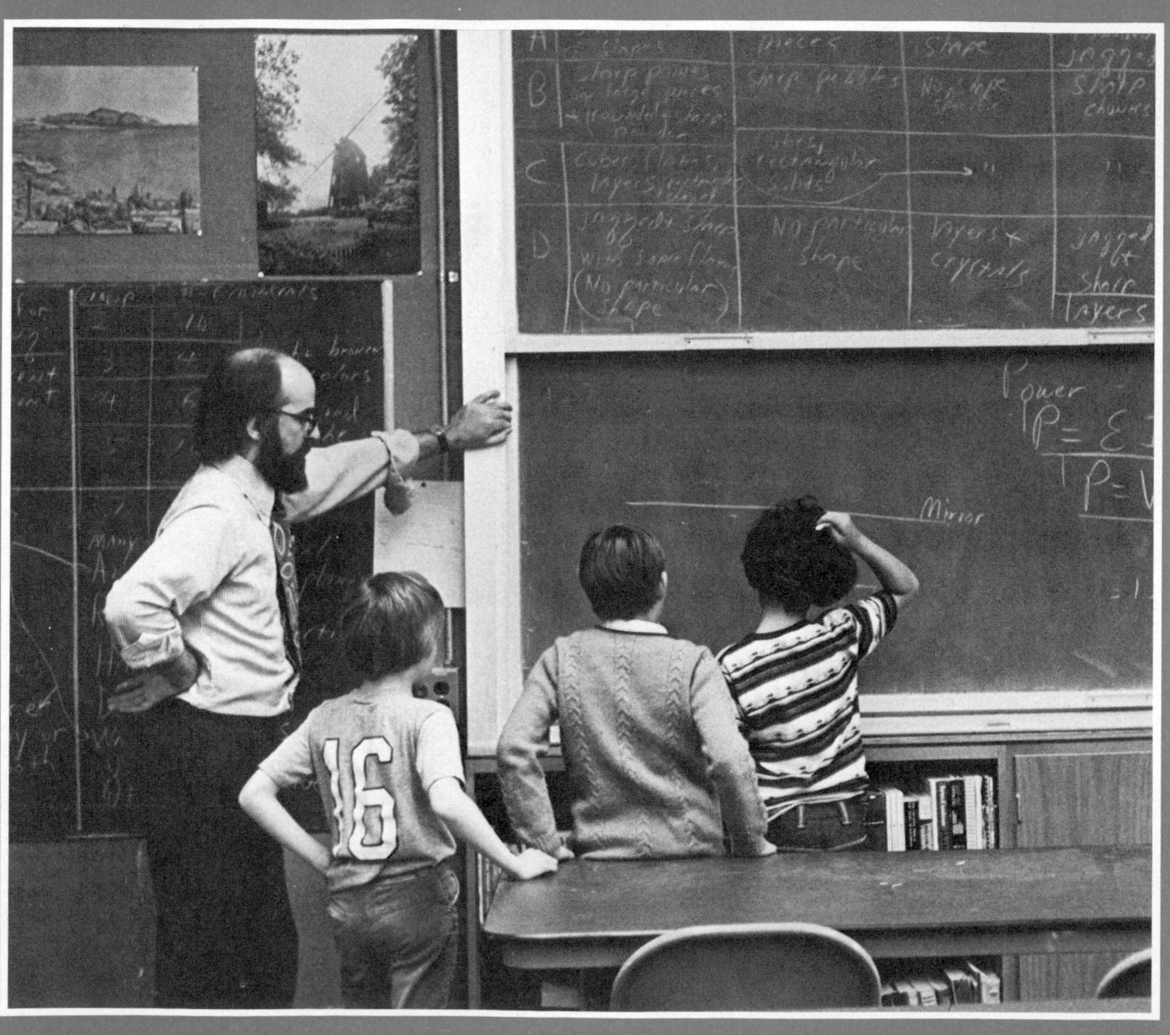

The central issues of cognitive psychology concern the ways in which human beings understand, remember, and use information. Most teachers, of course, have a strong interest in these same topics. The five chapters in this part are devoted to cognitive psychology and its applications to education.

Chapter Two, "An Introduction to Cognitive Processes," provides an overview of the study of human thought, with particular emphasis on a model of human thought and the basic processes of perception and attention. Chapter Three, "Memory and Concepts," is directed to the functioning of human memory and to how teachers can facilitate students' memory for new information. Central to the discussion in Chapter Three is the role of concepts in teaching. Chapter Four, "Problem Solving," addresses a crucial aspect of cognition: how people solve problems. The teacher's role in developing problem-solving skills is described, along with specific guidelines for enhancing students' problem-solving performance.

Cognitive abilities are closely related to the concept of intelligence. Chapter Five, "Intelligence and Cognitive Development," describes three perspectives on intelligence and their use in effective teaching practices. Closely related to both problem solving and intelligence is the ability of students to think creatively. Chapter Six, "Creativity," presents procedures for the development of creative abilities in students.

Chapter Two

AN INTRODUCTION TO COGNITIVE PROCESSES

THE NATURE OF COGNITIVE PROCESSES
A MODEL OF COGNITIVE PROCESSES

— Sense Receptors
— Sensory Registers
— Long-Term Memory
— Working Memory

THE DEVELOPMENT OF COGNITIVE PSYCHOLOGY

— Structuralism
— Functionalism
— Gestalt Psychology
— Contemporary Cognitive Psychology

APPLICATIONS FOR TEACHING
SUMMARY
SUGGESTED READINGS
COMMENTS ON PRACTICE EXERCISES
IMPORTANT EVENTS IN THE DEVELOPMENT OF COGNITIVE PSYCHOLOGY

Just for a moment, take a little trip with us in your imagination. You're standing in front of a floor-length mirror admiring yourself. Suddenly you become aware of a young child standing a little to the side and behind you, looking rather seriously at herself. First she moves one hand and then the other. She stares intently at her mirror image. She then tugs at your sleeve.

"I don't understand it," she says. "Why is it that I'm turned around in the mirror, so that my right hand is my left hand and my left hand is my right hand?" "Hmm . . ." Giving yourself a moment to think, you begin to search your mind for an answer she can understand. You mentally bounce light rays off the mirror. But she goes right on, ". . . but my head isn't at the bottom and my feet aren't at the top! How is it that I'm reversed sideways but not up and down? Why aren't I standing on my head in the mirror?" "Mmmm . . ." you say.

Sometimes a child can ask a seemingly simple question that can momentarily perplex you and force you to think hard to come up with an explanation. Her questions and actions also give us a number of hints about the workings of the child's mind, as she observes herself, does things such as moving her hands to test the effect, recognizes an apparent paradox, and then poses a puzzling question.

The processes of the child's mind—her thoughts, her puzzlings—are generally referred to as ***cognitive processes.*** Cognitive processes include all of the many fascinating functions of the mind—recognition, remembering, self-awareness, thinking, problem solving, and creativity. Your reactions to the child's questions in our story likewise fall into the realm of cognitive processes. As you read the story, you understood the meaning of the sentences and may have imagined the scene. Perhaps you tried to recall certain optical principles from a distant science class. Finally, you may have thought about the problem and about the explanation you would give the child.*

*Actually, the image in the mirror is not "reversed." The reflection is of what is opposite to it at every point on the mirror.

How we think, what and how we remember, and how we solve problems are all cognitive processes that are of great interest to psychologists. These same cognitive processes are crucial to teachers, who are charged with guiding all forms of learning. In fact, many educators would suggest that the primary role of teachers is the development of students' cognitive processes.

In this chapter we introduce you to cognitive psychology, the systematic study of cognitive processes, and we outline a model of human thought that should help you better understand how students acquire, retain, process, and create information. We then develop this model of cognitive processes in detail in Chapters Three through Six. These chapters stress both the research on which an understanding of cognitive processes is based and some applications of the principles of cognitive psychology to teaching.

Objectives

After reading this chapter, you should be able to meet the following objectives.

1. Relate a model of cognitive processes to classroom learning.
2. Translate the major principles of cognitive psychology into a set of instructional procedures in your subject area.

THE NATURE OF COGNITIVE PROCESSES

Mind is something more than a four-letter Anglo-Saxon word.
—*George Miller (1962)*

All cognitive processes are invisible. This fact, though obvious, implies some of the basic problems in the study of cognitive processes. Consider what can be observed when one form of cognitive processing—reading—occurs.

Suppose we have given a student a ten-page essay on the nature of the Rumanian government. The student looks at the title, and we watch as her eyes flick back and forth down the first page. In a few moments she turns the page and we continue observing her as she reads through the essay. Finally, after 10 minutes or so, she announces that she has finished the essay. What happened? What have we seen? We've seen eye movements, hand movements, head movements, and perhaps some movements of the lips. But have we seen any cognitive processes? No. From our observation of this student we still have very little information about any of her mental activities. Did she learn anything? Did

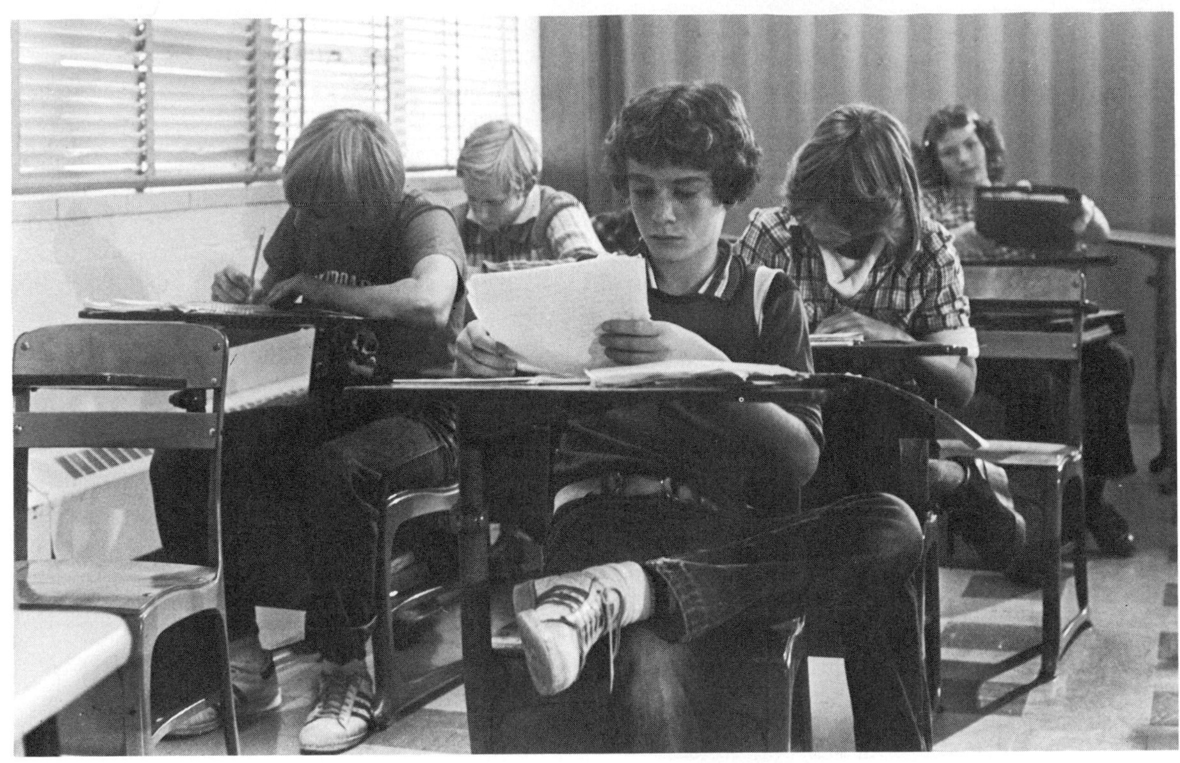

Cognitive processes can never be studied directly.

she comprehend the information? Will she remember any of it this afternoon or a month from now? We simply don't know. Because cognitive processes are not visible, we are forced to use indirect methods to assess them.

Think for a moment about other examples of cognitive processes. Perhaps you have had a roommate who suddenly discovered a method for solving a set of math problems. Maybe you have seen a small child figure out how to open a box. Or possibly you've watched as a person puzzled out the meaning of an unfamiliar term in a textbook. What happened? What did you see? No matter how many examples you consider, have you ever seen anything other than the *results* of cognitive processes? Cognitive processes, whether in reading, solving problems, or listening to a lecture, can never be directly observed. We can only observe the results of these processes—that is, changes in behavior—and make inferences about the processes based on our observations.

In our example of the student who read the essay, we could infer some things about her cognitive processes if her experience (reading) altered her behavior. One way to do this would be to first assess the student's prior knowledge of the Rumanian government by asking her a series of questions. Her answers would constitute behaviors (talking or writing) that we could observe and analyze. After she read the essay, we could ask her the same questions about Rumania. If she could answer the questions that she could not answer before, we would infer that she had learned the answers from her reading. We could, of course, further test her knowledge and determine which parts of the essay she remembered best, which parts she confused with her knowledge of other things, how the writing styles in different sections of the essay influenced her memory, and so on. This procedure—looking at changes in behavior as a result of experience—is the major methodology employed by psychologists and educators who study cognitive processes.

The invisible nature of cognitive processes places researchers in much the same position as astronomers who study black holes. Black holes are believed to be celestial bodies that possess such strong gravitational forces that not even light can escape from them. Astronomers can never directly observe these black holes and thus must try to understand them by studying the effects these invisible objects have on other parts of the cosmos. Similarly, psychologists and educators can never study cognitive processes directly and so have based their studies on the observable outcomes of mental activity.

A MODEL OF COGNITIVE PROCESSES

When scientists wish to understand complex processes, they often attempt to construct a **model** of what they are studying. Constructing a workable and accurate model of the DNA molecule, for example, enabled researchers in biology and genetics to take a major step toward understanding the mechanisms by which genetic information is transmitted. Similarly, cognitive psychologists have constructed models of cognitive processes such as memory. Many of these models picture the human being as an information-processing system (Newel & Simon, 1956) much like a computer. The terms and many of the ideas of computer science, linguistics (the study of language), and information theory (a specialty in mathematics) have been borrowed and reshaped by cognitive psychologists. Models that depict human thought as computerlike have guided the rapid development of cognitive theory and research in recent years. Cognitive psychologists, however, are careful to remember that human beings are not computers (see Jenkins, 1974; Miller & Kintsch, 1980).

In the following chapters, we discuss in detail important cognitive processes such as memory, concept learning, problem solving, and cre-

FIGURE 2–1
An Information-Processing Model of Cognition

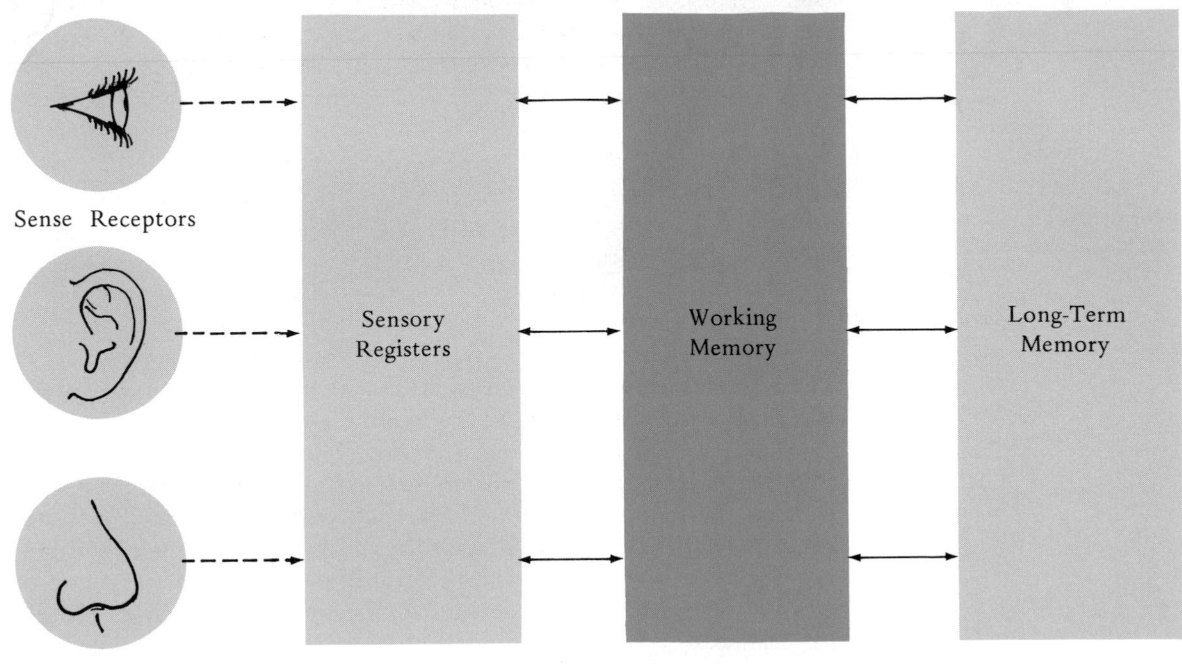

ativity, as well as the collection of high-level cognitive processes that fall under the label of "intelligence." To help you understand how these cognitive processes fit together, we have chosen an information-processing model of cognition as the organizing feature for the next several chapters. The model, which is based on computer models and information theory, is presented in Figure 2–1. As you can see, the model contains several components: sense receptors, sensory registers, a working memory, and a long-term memory. Each plays a vital role in our abilities to process information.

Sense Receptors

Our primary contact with the world and the information in it is through our **sense receptors.** These organs—such as our eyes, ears, and nose—allow us to contact the environment. Each type of sense receptor is sensitive to a particular class of **stimuli** (singular, stimulus), events that can cue or prompt actions on the part of the learner.* A word such as

*Note that this definition of the term *stimulus* is somewhat different from that given in Chapter Seven, in which we take up behavioral psychology.

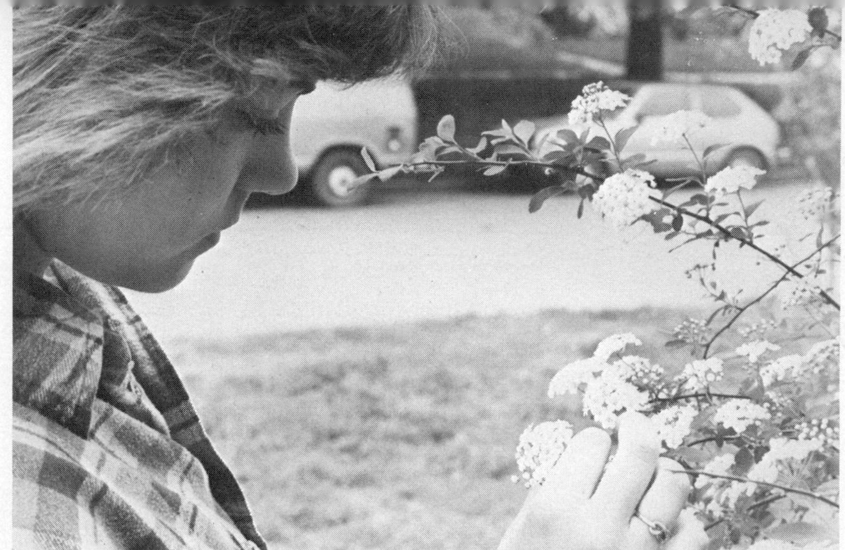

Our primary contact with the world and the information in it is through our sense receptors.

STOP in this sentence is a visual stimulus. It may be a cue for you to take such actions as looking at the word, saying the word to yourself or out loud, thinking about the meaning of the word, or momentarily stopping in your reading. Other types of stimuli are auditory (a spoken word or the sound of a train whistle), olfactory (the scent of a cheeseburger), tactile (the feel of a baseball), and kinesthetic (the feel of your muscles as you write a sentence). Regardless of the type, the sense receptors convey information about stimuli into our information-processing system.

An impairment in a sense receptor obviously has an important effect on how a learner processes information. Children who are deaf from birth, for example, live in an environment in which auditory stimuli play no part. Visual and tactile stimuli are thus especially critical. Some authorities feel that as a result deaf children's cognitive processes have developed quite differently from those of hearing children (see Benderly, 1980). Such differences have important implications for how teachers work with children. Chapters Sixteen and Seventeen explore the implications of sense receptor impairment on learning. Our primary reason for introducing sense receptors here is to show that they are the critical first component in the human information-processing system.

Sensory Registers

One of the most important cognitive processes is **perception.** Perception is more than sensing something in the environment; it is the process of determining the meaning of what is sensed (Moates & Schumacher, 1980). That is, an element of the environment (a stimulus) is perceived when a person can give meaning to that stimulus. The difference between sensing and perceiving a stimulus is analogous to the difference between seeing something (a blur in the corner of your eye, for instance) and knowing what it is that you have seen (a bird flying toward you).

Before a person can determine the meaning of stimuli, a number of cognitive processes must be carried out. Each process takes time, and thus perception is not instantaneous. This fact poses an interesting problem for psychologists who have tried to model cognitive processes. Since the environment often changes very quickly (as when students view a film or listen to directions), many stimuli disappear long before there has been enough time for the processes involved in perception to be completed. This would seem to indicate that the analysis of stimuli would abruptly cease when the stimuli disappear. This doesn't happen, however (at least with most individuals), because human beings are equipped with "holding systems for briefly maintaining a rather complete representation of stimuli so that perceptual analysis can be completed" (Moates & Schumacher, 1980, p. 9). These holding systems are the **sensory registers.**

The importance of sensory registers can be seen in almost every classroom situation. Consider the role of sensory registers as teachers give spoken directions to students. Once an instruction has been given, there is no physical trace of it. Unless words can be briefly maintained in some form by listeners, perception and understanding cannot occur. Imagine the difficulty, indeed the impossibility, of acting on directions if each word disappeared before its meaning could be determined.

There are probably different registers for each of our senses (see Bourne, Dominowski, & Loftus, 1979), and they are all vital to perception, but other components of cognition are equally involved in giving meaning to stimuli. One of those components is long-term memory, a permanent repository of knowledge about the world (J. R. Anderson, 1980).

Long-Term Memory

The permanent repository of information we have accumulated from the world around us is represented as the long-term memory component of our cognitive model. We can recall at will many events from our past, and even in those cases when we are not consciously recalling our experiences, they are affecting our perception. Consider, for example, the following:

Did you see the duplicate word in each triangle? Many readers do not. Because of our prior learning, we usually don't perceive each letter and each word as an individual, separate unit; most readers instead perceive the phrase as a whole. As Goodman (1970) has pointed out, good readers are often likely to make mistakes in their perception of individual words because as they read they predict what a word or phrase will be. Thus, students' perceptions depend to a large extent on what they already know. From the perspective of cognitive psychology, as Ausubel (1960) noted, perception occurs when stimuli become meaningful to students, that is, when students have prior knowledge that enables them to give meaning to new information.

Working Memory

In addition to sense receptors, sensory registers, and long-term memory, the final component of the model of cognitive processes is **working memory,** which guides perception, makes decisions, solves problems, and creates new knowledge. In short, working memory is the part of the model in which thinking occurs. The stimuli in our environment are not always in the same form as is the knowledge of the world that we hold in our long-term memory (J. R. Anderson, 1980). Most readers, for example, have some knowledge of what airplanes are, but their memories obviously do not contain duplicates of real airplanes. What is stored is something very different from a detailed pattern of an airplane. Human memory represents the world symbolically rather than duplicating the environment (Klatzky, 1980).

PRACTICE EXERCISE 2–1
Perception and Cognitive Performance

This practice exercise is a simple one. First we would like you to read the sentence in the box below.

> FINISHED FILES ARE THE RESULT
> OF YEARS OF SCIENTIFIC STUDY
> COMBINED WITH THE EXPERIENCE OF
> MANY YEARS.

Now we want you to count the *F*'s in the sentence. Count them just once. Then turn to page 44 to check your count.

The representational nature of human memory is important to cognition. For human beings to determine the meaning of stimuli in the environment, we "must transform and analyze them so that they can be compared to what is in permanent memory" (Moates & Schumacher, 1980, p. 9). A representational memory permits such transformation, analysis, and comparison. We also regularly encounter different or novel forms of stimuli that only roughly correspond to anything stored in memory. Many of us, for example, have never actually seen a 1938 Cord (a classic automobile), but if we saw one we would quickly determine that we have seen a car and probably an older one. This ability to assign meaning to novel stimuli shows that perception is both active and flexible. Further, it indicates that stimuli are classified and that meaning is assigned to stimuli based on how they are classified.

For our purposes, then, working memory corresponds to what most people call consciousness (Moates & Schumacher, 1980). Our working memory guides the process of transforming and analyzing stimuli to compare them to what is in permanent memory* (Bourne et al., 1979). Working memory can also be conceived of as the component in our model in which decisions about incoming stimuli are made (Hayes, 1978).

Learning cannot occur without perception. Unless meaning can be given to information, no understanding can develop. Stimuli must be recognized, classified, and distinguished from other stimuli for meaningful learning to take place. Until children recognize what a word is and what its boundaries are and distinguish it from other concepts (letters, numbers, sounds), they are likely to have great difficulty learning to read (Ehri, 1978). Many young children simply do not perceive words as units, even though they can combine and recombine them in sentences. As we will see in Chapter Twelve, the process of assessing students' perceptions and planning new instruction so that it builds on present knowledge is a key component of effective teaching.

An important cognitive process that is closely linked to working memory is **attention.** Attention can be defined as "the general distribution of mental activity to the tasks performed by the individual" (Moates & Schumacher, 1980, p. 39). Students are limited in the number of things they can focus on at a given time. A common situation, for instance, might find a student faced with a teacher's explanation of a geometry problem, snow falling outside, thoughts of what to buy a

*The transformation and analysis process is usually referred to as *pattern recognition* (Klatzky, 1980; Lindsay & Norman, 1977). There is a growing body of research in cognitive psychology devoted solely to investigating how this process occurs (compare Klatzky, 1980; Neisser, 1976).

parent for Christmas, a whispered discussion of who's dating whom, and the smell of food from the cafeteria. Obviously, all of these events cannot receive equal attention and so an important question is the student's selection of events for attention. The procedures described in Chapter Ten can help a teacher control distractions in the classroom, but regardless of how carefully a classroom is organized and managed, the selection of what to attend to in an environment is still a cognitive process (Moates & Schumacher, 1980). Consider what happens when a student is carefully taking notes during a lecture. The student selects some of what the instructor says and copies it down, while ignoring or transforming other information. Some questions raised by class members will be carefully scrutinized, and other questions will be largely ignored as the student looks over his or her notes. Even when students are engaged in careful study, they are selectively attending to various aspects of their environment.

The most recent research on attention processes suggests that the selection of stimuli occurs *after* meaning has been assigned to stimuli in the working memory* (Norman & Bobrow, 1975, 1979; Shiffrin, Pisoni, & Casteneda-Mendez, 1974). The importance of establishing attention to learning materials and activities is doubly underscored by the fact that human beings have limited processing resources (J. R. Anderson, 1980). Those materials and activities most likely to be attended to are those to which the learner can assign meaning. Thus, new learning builds on prior learning.

Another component of working memory, **short-term memory,** was regarded by many of the early information-processing researchers (for example, Waugh & Norman, 1965) as a repository for briefly storing incoming information. Although recent conceptions of memory do not place an emphasis on a separate short-term memory, the initial processing, rehearsal, and transfer of incoming information are together regarded as one of the most critical functions of the working memory. If incoming stimuli are not sufficiently processed, forgetting can occur in only a few seconds. Constant rehearsal of new material is often necessary, particularly if there are many separate bits of information. If you are distracted between the time you look up a phone number and the time you dial the phone, for example, you may completely forget the number. Similarly, students trying to take notes may lose their place if

*Broadbent (1958) articulated the first modern cognitive theory of attention and suggested that selection occurs in the sensory registers prior to perception. While his theory is now viewed as too simplistic (see, for example, Moates & Schumacher, 1980), there is no compelling evidence to suggest that his view of attention selection in the sensory registers was totally incorrect (Bourne et al., 1979).

too much information is given to them in too short a time and their short-term memories become overloaded. Once information is transferred to long-term memory, however, it is much less likely to be lost since long-term memory is much less fragile and much more permanent.

In addition to the working memory's function as a short-term repository for new information, it also holds information called up from long-term memory and is the arena in which memories interplay with new information. That is, working memory is where thinking goes on (J. R. Anderson, 1980; Bourne et al., 1979; Mandler, 1975): remembering good times, thinking about the answer to a trivia quiz ("What line proceeds the line 'A woman's work is never done'?"), solving problems ("Let's see, if I brace this board with a brick . . ."), considering alternatives ("Do I want to go to the movies or read another chapter of educational psychology?"), filing away things to be remembered ("I've got to remember to tell Bill to call Bobbie"), analyzing thoughts ("I can't believe I could be so forgetful!"), and creating new knowledge ("Eureka! $E = mc^2$").

As you can see, the overall model stresses the interplay of cognitive functions. Perception depends on incoming stimuli, information in long-term memory, and decisions in the working memory. Attention depends on perception (with all of its constituent processes) and decisions in working memory. Recall of information depends on the working memory and long-term memory but is influenced, of course, by perception. In the same way, problem solving, creativity, and other cognitive processes all result from an interaction of cognitive functions.

As Ausubel (1960) pointed out, a key to all cognitive processing is one highly important concept—meaningfulness. New information is meaningful when it can be related to what is already known. Meaning organizes our perception, attention, short-term memory, long-term memory, and our ability to integrate these components into problem solving and creativity.

THE DEVELOPMENT OF COGNITIVE PSYCHOLOGY

Contemporary cognitive psychology, heavily emphasizing the interplay of cognitive functions and the role of meaningfulness in learning, is a rather recent development in psychology whose origins can be traced to Ausubel (1960), to Bruner (Bruner, Goodnow, & Austin, 1956), and to the publication in 1967 of Ulrich Neisser's influential book *Cognitive Psychology*. Yet today's cognitive psychology has deeper roots than that; it is built on a long history that dates back to the very beginnings of the science of psychology. Cognitive psychology, in fact, can be said to have three distinct histories; an early period of steady growth (1880 to 1925), an intermediate period in which most American psychologists' efforts were in areas outside of cognitive psychology (1926 to about 1960), and a recent period in which advances have been rapid and dramatic (J. R. Anderson, 1980; Bourne et al., 1979; Moates & Schumacher, 1980).

Structuralism

Most historians of psychology pinpoint the origin of psychology as a science at about 1878 in Wurzburg, Germany, when Wilhelm Wundt set up the first experimental psychological laboratory (Boring, 1950; Chaplin & Krawiec, 1974; Schultz, 1975; Wertheimer, 1978). Wundt established his laboratory for the express purpose of studying the structure of consciousness (Schultz, 1975), a goal within the general domain of cognitive psychology. Wundt's psychology, called **structuralism,** had three major aims: (1) to identify the most basic cognitive processes; (2) to ascertain how the elements of thought and thought processes are combined and to determine what laws govern their combination; and (3) to determine the relationship of cognitive to physiological processes (Titchener, 1909). Structuralism was the forerunner not only of cognitive psychology but of all other experimentally oriented schools of psy-

James, Titchener, and Köhler: pioneers of cognitive psychology.

chological thought* (Schultz, 1975). In America, the most well known of the structuralists was E. B. Titchener of Cornell University.

The greatest achievement of structuralism was that it was the first coherent school of thought in psychology. It was replaced, however, by other theoretical perspectives that proved more attractive to most American psychologists. The failure of structuralism, in their eyes, was that its subject matter was extremely specific (the structure of consciousness and nothing else), that it was inflexible in changing to fit new evidence and concerns in psychology, and especially that its method of gathering data (introspection, which involves having experimental subjects report their mental events) was inadequate.

Functionalism

The first school of thought to set itself in opposition to structuralism was **functionalism,**† which was concerned with developing techniques in psychology and education that would be applicable to everyday problems. It was the first truly American psychology and was based on the ideas of William James.‡ James was a genius in the history of psychology, and he cannot be placed into any specific school of thought (Keller, 1937, 1965). James was much less an experimentalist than were the structuralists. He is credited, however, with articulating the first scientific theory of memory, in which he outlined short- and long-term memory processes, well in advance of contemporary theories of memory. His *Principles of Psychology,* published in 1890, was the foundation for functionalist theory.

The objectives of functionalism were to determine "(1) how mental activity goes on, (2) what it [mental activity] accomplishes, and (3) why it takes place" (Keller, 1937, p. 77). In contrast to structuralism, functionalism was a pragmatic, application-oriented psychology. Functionalists were extremely interested in pursuing the educational impli-

*Psychology has tended to develop in such a way that clusters of individuals who share theories and investigative methods have often worked somewhat separately from those with different views. For example, cognitive psychologists and behaviorists (see Chapter Seven) have very different views of what is important to investigate, the nature of thought or observable behavior, respectively. In educational psychology it is important to remain open to both points of view.

†The name functionalism, surprisingly, was coined by E. B. Titchener in his 1898 paper "The Postulates of a Structural Psychology," in which he outlined the differences between the budding functionalist position and his own.

‡William James obtained the funds for a psychological laboratory at Harvard in 1875, but allowed the lab to be closed down after only a few months of operation. Hence, he actually established the first laboratory for psychology but is not given the same kind of credit awarded to Wundt (Murray & Rowe, 1979).

cations of psychology (Carr, 1925). Strongly influenced by Darwinian evolutionary theory, functionalism was "essentially a psychology of the adjustment of the organism to its environment" (Hilgard & Bower, 1975). While functionalism did employ introspection as an investigative method for a period of time, new observational methods quickly supplanted introspection as the major source of data.

Functionalism, centered in the work of John Dewey and James Angell at the University of Chicago, replaced structuralism as the major school of psychological thought in the United States.* Its influence has been long-lived. As Schultz has stated,

> in the United States today, psychology remains definitely functional in orientation, even though functionalism no longer exists as a separate school of thought. Because of its very success, there was no longer any need for it to retain the characteristics of a school. (1975, p. 173)

Today functionalist approaches are extremely important in shaping theories of cognition (Jenkins, 1974; Zimmer, 1979) and in guiding our concepts of what educational psychology should be.

Gestalt Psychology

Between about 1925 and 1955 or 1960, American psychology was dominated by what came to be known as a behaviorist view of psychology or, simply, **behaviorism.** Behaviorism, at least in its early forms, developed in strong reaction to the structuralist and functionalist positions and their emphasis on the study of cognitive processes. Led by John B. Watson, the behaviorists argued that all subjective and introspective data on cognitive processes should be ruled out and that the goal of psychology should be to predict and to control behavior, not to study mental processes (Watson, 1913).

So rapid was the growth of behaviorism and so powerful its influence that its rise ushered in the second phase of the history of cognitive psychology, a dormant phase. The preoccupation of American experimental psychology with behaviorism was not absolute, although compared to behaviorism cognitive psychology was proceeding at a snail's pace in the United States. Psychologists such as Arthur Melton (see Chapter Three) continued to study cognitive processes, particularly memory, but the major new influence in cognitive psychology came, not surprisingly, from outside the United States — from the German school of **Gestalt psychology** (Wertheimer, 1978). Major interests of the Gestalt theorists were in perception and in problem solving.

*Functionalism was never truly a school in the sense that structuralism was; rather, it was a loose aggregation of individuals, such as Dewey, Angell, Harvey Carr (a student of Dewey and Angell), and Robert S. Woodworth (at Columbia), who held common ideas about psychology.

Gestalt psychology, which we examine in greater detail in Chapter Four, was founded by Max Wertheimer, Wolfgang Köhler, and Kurt Koffka in 1912. *Gestalt* in the closest possible English translation means form, shape, or configuration (Lundin, 1972). Gestalt theorists held that psychological experience could not be broken down into elements or pieces that could be studied separately, as the structuralists, functionalists, and behaviorists believed. Instead, experiences are perceived as an organized field of events that interact and mutually affect each other (Bourne et al., 1979, pp. 21–22). Gestalt psychologists argued that people do not perceive or react to individual elements in their environments; rather, they react to their total experiences. The total experience is different and perhaps greater than the sum of the parts.

By 1925, two major Gestalt psychology books had been published in the United States and, ultimately, Wertheimer, Köhler, and Koffka all emigrated to the United States to escape the oppression of the growing Nazi movement in Germany. The impact of Gestalt psychology is such that, as Hilgard and Bower note, "its ideas about human learning have only come to be appreciated and exploited in the past few years" (1975, p. 280). Hilgard and Bower go on to say that the Gestalt psychologists were in fact the intellectual forefathers of a large part of what is today called cognitive psychology. Gestalt psychology no longer exists as a separate school of thought; it has become an integral part of cognitive psychology.

Contemporary Cognitive Psychology

Cognitive psychology has experienced a resurgence in the past two decades, as psychologists have renewed their long-term interests in the mental processes that are critical to teaching and learning. Led by such psychologists as Jerome Bruner and David Ausubel, cognitive psychology clearly entered its modern era with the publication in 1967 of Ulrich Neisser's *Cognitive Psychology.* What does modern cognitive psychology stress? According to Wittrock, "A cognitive model emphasizes the active and constructive role of the learner. . . . Learners often construct meaning and create their own reality, rather than respond automatically to the sensory qualities of their environments" (1979, p. 5). The underlying theoretical perspective of the cognitive approach is that information processing is the most critical human activity. As Smith has stated, the primary function of the human brain is to actively "seek, select, acquire, store and, at appropriate times, retrieve and utilize information about the world" (1975, p. 2).

The continuing influence of functionalism and Gestalt psychology is undeniable (J. R. Anderson, 1980), but events outside of psychology have also provided resources for psychology's renewed interest in cognition. The most important of such events was the development of the

Students actively process information. Here, children not only are learning about magnets but are also acquiring basic skills of inquiry and experimentation.

high-speed computer in the 1940s. Hayes (1978) suggests that computers have had three major effects on the new cognitive movement: (1) computers have served as an information-processing model for human thought; (2) computers can be employed to test cognitive theories through simulations of human thought; and (3) the study of artificial intelligence (such as that of chess-playing computers) became a source of ideas for cognitive psychologists. Additionally, advances in other fields, especially linguistics (Moates & Schumacher, 1980) and information theory in mathematics (J. R. Anderson, 1980), provided new ways of thinking about cognition.

As important as these advances in other sciences were, cognitive psychology would not have reemerged as a strong alternative to behaviorism had it not been for the dissatisfaction among many psychologists with the ability of a purely behavioral psychology to address important issues in such areas as language and problem solving (Moates & Schumacher, 1980). Behaviorism has certainly not lost its influence in American psychology. Nonetheless, many members of the psychological community consider cognitive psychology to be more useful in the study of mental processes central to teaching and learning. Each psychology, cognitive and behavioral, has focused on somewhat different aspects of human activity — cognitive psychology on human mental processes and behavioral psychology on the effects that external events have on the actions of individuals. These interests are not exclusive, of course, and you will find members of both schools of thought holding views compatible with the other position. In educational psychology, in particular, both cognitive and behavioral psychology provide vital information for effective teaching.

APPLICATIONS FOR TEACHING

No psychology, regardless of how interesting, is useful unless it can be related to actual situations and problems. Thus we need to ask, "How does cognitive psychology view the teaching and learning process?" By applying some of the tenets of modern cognitive psychology to the learning process, we can derive a set of statements about students and how they learn best. We will present more detailed applications in Chapters Three through Six where we discuss the major processes of cognition.

1. Students are active processors of information. Students actively process information. They are not sponges or receptacles into which knowledge is poured, but rather relate each new thing they hear or see to what they already know. They classify, make guesses and formulate hypotheses, interpret, and read between the lines.

Suppose that a ninth-grade English class reads the following segment of a poem in a unit on irony.

> "Now tell us what 't was all about,"
> Young Peterkin, he cries;
> And little Wilhelmine looks up
> With wonder-waiting eyes;
> "Now tell us all about the war,
> And what they fought each other for?"
>
> "It was the English," Kaspar cried,
> "Who put the French to rout;
> But what they fought each other for
> I could not well make out.
> But every body said," quoth he,
> "That 't was a famous victory."*

*From "The Battle of Blenheim," by Robert Southey.

Each reader will process the information contained in these lines in his or her own way. Some will have vivid images of young Wilhelmine or of a battle scene. Others may think about the odd names or spend time trying to figure out the meaning of the words *'t was.* Some will begin memorizing the stanzas or will wonder about the author — whether he was English or French, for instance. Still other students will completely reject the idea of learning anything at all from a poem such as this; it simply is not meaningful to them.

As you think about the variety of potential information-processing activities, you should realize that what is learned will depend not only on the actual content but also on what the student already knows and on how the student processes the information received. As a teacher you can influence not only the selection of content, but the latter two factors as well. The effective teacher will choose content that is or can be made meaningful to the student. Learning activities can also be skillfully guided by methods such as questions and role playing so that students learn processes of inquiry as well as the basic information.

2. Learning is most likely to occur when information is made meaningful to students. Psychologists have long made a distinction between types of stimuli. In its most basic form, a stimulus in a learning environment is any event that cues or prompts actions on the part of learners, such as a teacher's instructions to take out a sheet of paper, the distribution of a handout for students to read, or a question posed at the end

of a lesson. On the other hand, the actual interpretation of meaning given to any stimulus must be considered. The instruction to take out a sheet of paper may be interpreted by some students as punishment for poor class recitation; a question from a teacher may stimulate a great deal of thought or only the slightest interest from students, depending on a variety of factors. Cognitive psychologists emphasize that the external stimulus is always given a meaning by the learner.

Several factors determine the meaning of a stimulus for students; some factors relate to the students themselves. Do they have previous interest or prior knowledge in this area? Does the topic match their intellectual abilities or is it too difficult or too easy? Is this topic or problem related to situations they have encountered before? Other factors concern what the teacher does to interest and involve the learners in the topic. Can the teacher relate this topic to something the students are strongly interested in? Can the topic be learned in activities the students enjoy, such as games or projects? Meaningfulness depends on how the teacher handles the topic.

3. How students learn may be more important than what they learn. If you ask some people what education is, they will say that education is the "transmission of information;" that is, each new generation learns information discovered by earlier generations. Cognitive psychologists emphatically disagree with this position.

In a cognitive approach, the greatest empha-

PRACTICE EXERCISE 2–2

Meaningfulness and Learning

As you can see from this chapter, one of the major principles of cognitive psychology is that information is better learned and retained if it is meaningful. If materials, such as a list of words, are not particularly meaningful in and of themselves, most people will automatically do something to make them more meaningful.

To demonstrate this point, we would like you to try a little experiment in memory. You need three or four friends and these words:

Muskrat, blacksmith, panther, baker, wildcat, Howard, Jason, printer, chemist, radish, mushroom, Otto, plumber, pumpkin, chipmunk, Amos, Wallace, parsnip, milkman, druggist, leopard, woodchuck, Adam, grocer, Simon, Owen, lettuce, giraffe, turnip, garlic, rhubarb, typist, eggplant, Noah, zebra, donkey, Gerald, dentist, otter, parsley, spinach, Oswald, weasel, broker.*

To begin the experiment, tell your participants, either individually or as a group, that you will read them a list of words and that they will be asked to recall as many of them as possible. Read the list at a rate of about one word every three seconds. After you finish reading the whole list, tell them to start writing the words they recall as rapidly as possible. You should allow five minutes for recall from the time you tell them to start recalling. Turn now to page 44 for our comments on the results you should see.

*This list is based on a classic study by Bousfield (1953) and the methods of your experiment roughly parallel his.

sis is on the processes of learning. If we can learn how to learn, then we can use these skills over and over. Getting the right answer to a single word problem is not particularly important, from this standpoint, but knowing how to solve word problems is. Knowledge is not especially useful for its own sake; as we know, today's knowledge is quickly outdated. Bruner has said that to be used effectively knowledge must be "translated into the learner's way of attempting to solve a problem" (Bruner et al., 1956, p. 53).

Fourth-grade students, for example, may be studying a unit on the prairie pioneers and the great migration westward in nineteenth-century America. As part of this unit, students may learn that gold was discovered in California in 1848, that the Oto were a Plains Indian tribe, that Father Marquette was a missionary, and that a famous landmark of the Oregon trail was Chimney Rock. While this knowledge may be useful, a cognitive approach would put much more emphasis on helping students to think and to make guesses and hypotheses about why things happened as they did. In short, the goal of the cognitively oriented teacher is to build curiosity, inquiry skills, and motivation to learn more.

Methods of teaching might include questions about which students can venture guesses ("Why did the pioneers travel in large groups in wagon trains while crossing the prairie?"), questions of value ("Were the Indian scouts who worked for the army at Ft. Kearny heroes or traitors to their people?"), and problems requiring the students to design solutions ("Imagine that you and your pioneer family are camped on the prairie on a stormy night in September. You have about three months more to travel before you reach your destination. Lightning strikes several times on the grass-covered hills surrounding you and within moments a huge fire is roaring down on you, driven by terrific winds. The oxen are unhitched from the wagon and you have less than a minute to save yourselves and whatever you can carry into and across a nearby stream. In your group, decide which of the contents of your wagon *must* be saved. Remember, you have less than a minute to save whatever you can, so you will have to decide."). In each case — asking students to guess, to evaluate, or to solve problems — the goal is not to teach facts and figures but to develop students' abilities to think.

Cognitive processes become automatic with repetition. At first, this boy needed to type letter by letter and then word by word. Now, he is typing rapidly, hardly ever thinking about letters or words.

4. Cognitive processes become automatic with repeated use. A variation of the old adage "practice makes perfect" applies to mental processes. Initially, we must analyze stimuli such as words and patterns part by part and piece by piece in order to make sense out of them. Think about children who are just learning to read. Almost every word must be produced by laborious attention to such features as letters and phrases and, often, through a process of "sounding out." Skilled readers, in contrast, very seldom

devote their attention to decoding and to conscious attempts at recognition. Instead their processes of recognition are almost, if not completely, automatic (LaBerge, 1980; LaBerge & Samuels, 1974). Skilled readers pay attention to the content and the meaning of what they read. Only when they are confused about meaning (for example, you read in a dialogue, "Yes, I occasionally suffer from pursy") do skilled readers pay conscious attention to deciphering the meaning of words.

Automatic processing and recognition are processes that can take a long time to develop. Months or years may intervene before students' reading processes become automatic. Some students' reading never does become automatic, and they must always pay attention to decoding. Chess masters who can instantly recognize and reproduce extremely complex patterns of chess pieces on the board are estimated by Simon and Chase (1973) to have spent between 10,000 and 50,000 hours of their lives at a chess board. This obviously is a long time, but it is not out of line with the time many adults have spent practicing their reactions in a variety of physical skills or in reading.

An important goal of education is that information-processing skills not only become accurate, but that they also occur fairly rapidly and at least partly automatically. The foreign-language student who cannot respond automatically to many conversational situations, for example, searching for words and trying to think what to say — is not in a very comfortable position when trying to converse with a native speaker. The goal of much instruction, then, is to produce automatic cognitive processes or, at the very least, a state in which cognitive processes are rapid and communication is fluent.

5. The most enduring motivation for learning is internal motivation. Bruner and his coauthors (1956) captured the motivating qualities of engaging a student's curiosity, interest, and sense of discovery:

> Our attention is attracted to something that is unclear, unfinished, or uncertain. We sustain our attention until the matter in hand becomes clear, finished, or certain. The achievement of clarity or merely the search for it is what satisfies. *(p. 114)*

In the view of cognitive psychology, children are to be regarded as responsible for their own cognitive development. They learn by interacting with the world around them. When experiences confirm their present knowledge, their mental structures become more stable. If new experiences do not fit with their present understanding, however, the understanding must eventually be reorganized to fit the new experiences. Conflict between an old way of understanding and new experiences is the basis for cognitive growth and change (Piaget, 1970a). (This aspect of cognitive development will be explored in detail in Chapter 5.) Not only is this conflict the basis for intellectual growth, it is also highly motivating as children test their present ways of thinking against those of adults.

6. There are vast differences in students' information-processing capabilities. In any classroom, you can expect to observe a wide range of differences in students' abilities to process and retain information. Some students will be excellent memorizers and will be able to learn long lists of facts such as state capitals, spelling words, chemical names, or authors and their works. Others will not retain information easily but may be better at understanding and remembering the sense of what has been said.

One important category of cognitive differences is known as cognitive style. ***Cognitive style*** (Messick, 1976) refers to variations in the ways students approach, process, and remember information. There are an extremely large number of cognitive styles, but they are not equally significant for teachers. One that is particularly important for teaching and learning is ***conceptual tempo*** (Kagen & Kogan, 1970; Zelnicker & Jeffrey, 1976).

In situations in which there is uncertainty about what to do, as in solving a problem, students will react very differently. Some students (impulsives) will plunge right in to cognitive tasks involving memory, discrimination learn-

"The addition is easy—but I tend to be nonverbal, and the apples throw me."

ing, and problem solving and thus make many errors. Others (reflectives) will approach the same problems in an overly careful and cautious way. Reflectives will take much longer than impulsives to complete detailed tasks but they will make fewer errors.

Which approach is better? Jerome Kagen (Zelnicker & Jeffrey, 1976) has pointed out that the analytical approach of the reflective student is well suited for many school tasks. Reading, math, and science, for instance, require detailed analysis for successful performance. For this reason, psychologists generally agreed that modification of extremely impulsive approaches was desirable, and a number of modification studies have been carried out (Meichenbaum & Goodman, 1971).

More recently, however, the evidence seems to indicate that impulsives and reflectives differ mainly on those tasks requiring detailed analysis. On cognitive tasks that require broader information processing, impulsives perform as well as reflectives. Thus, because impulsives' responding occurs quickly, impulsive approaches may actually be superior in some situations.

As a teacher, you should recognize that you will have some students of each type in your classes, with most students falling somewhere in between. If students are either so impulsive that they make many errors on detailed work or so reflective that they take excessive time on cognitive decisions, some intervention may be in order.

Generally, Kagen believes that differences in conceptual tempo are linked to motivation and the standards students have for their performance. Impulsives and reflectives, Kagen believes, are equally capable of detecting detail. When impulsive students are motivated to reduce errors and to slow their pace, their performance can be as effective as that of more reflective students.

In areas directly related to our information-processing model, you can expect students to vary in their ability to pay attention to tasks, in their perceptions, and in their ability to remember information. Some students will be able to work for long periods without distraction, while others may have to be taught to increase their attention to learning materials and activities. (A variety of specific methods for increasing attention are presented in Chapter Ten.) Similarly, you shouldn't expect all students to see things the same way; their perceptions of almost any set of materials or activities are almost certain to vary. Some students will remember your instructions on a single telling, while others may lose even a set of written instructions. The classroom management techniques discussed in Chapter Ten can help you improve students' abilities to carry out instructions or to pay attention to their work, but you still must recognize the reality of large individual differences in cognitive functioning. The subject of individual differences in cognitive processes has long been a focus for many psychologists (see Messick, 1976, for example). In this book, we deal specifically with such intellectual differences in Chapter Five.

PRACTICE EXERCISE 2–3
Applying Principles of Cognitive Psychology

One test for the value of ideas is whether they can be applied. The principles of cognitive psychology will be most valuable if you can apply them to your own teaching.

Listed below are the six major principles of cognitive psychology that relate to instruction. Briefly describe four teaching activities in your subject area and at the grade levels you hope to teach that are based on one or more of these principles. For each activity, indicate the number of the principle (or principles) that most closely relates to the activity.

Principles

1. Students are active processors of information.
2. Learning is most likely to occur when information is made meaningful to students.
3. How students learn may be more important than what they learn.
4. Cognitive processes become automatic with repeated use.
5. The most enduring motivation for learning is internal motivation.
6. There are vast differences in students' information-processing capabilities.

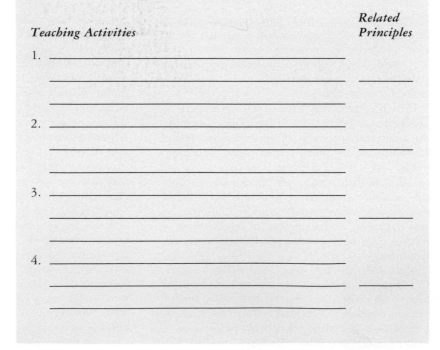

Teaching Activities	***Related Principles***
1. ________________________	
________________________	________
________________________	
2. ________________________	
________________________	________
________________________	
3. ________________________	
________________________	________
________________________	
4. ________________________	
________________________	________
________________________	

Thinking, memory, and problem solving are the major interests of cognitive psychologists. Teachers are also vitally concerned with cognitive processes as they develop these abilities in students.

Cognitive psychology today uses many of the terms of information-processing theory, drawn from computer science, linguistics, and mathematics, to model and explain cognition. Major elements of an information-processing model of cognition are sense receptors, sensory registers, long-term memory, and working memory as well as the processes of perception and attention.

The model pictures human information processing as active and dynamic. Incoming information is related in working memory to already-stored information from long-term memory. Many parts of this modern view of cognition can be traced to earlier concepts of cognitive processes held by the structuralists, the functionalists, and Gestalt psychologists.

In general, a cognitive view of teaching portrays students as active processors of information. Cognitive psychology also recognizes that there are large differences among students in cognitive processing capabilities and, thus, that teachers need to consider each learner individually in planning instruction. A cognitive approach to teaching also is based on the ideas that students learn best if materials are meaningful and that they acquire processes as well as content from their learning. A detailed study of cognitive processes leads to many specific suggestions for teachers, which are outlined in detail in later chapters on memory and concepts, problem solving, intelligence and cognitive development, and creativity.

Suggested Readings

Anderson, J. B. *Cognitive psychology and its implications.* San Francisco: Freeman, 1980.

This book is a good intermediate-level introduction to cognitive psychology.

Jenkins, J. J. Remember that old theory of memory? Well, forget it! *American Psychologist,* 1974, *29,* 785–795.

This classic article, from Jenkins's presidential address to the American Psychological Association, has set the stage for modern studies of cognition.

Moates, D. R., & Schumacher, G. M. *An introduction to modern cognitive psychology.* Belmont, California: Wadsworth, 1980.

This book is an excellent introduction to all aspects of cognitive psychology. It is designed for undergraduates who have had material similar to that covered in this book in Chapter Two.

Neisser, U. *Cognitive psychology.* New York: Appleton-Century-Crofts, 1967.

Neisser's book, along with that of Bruner, Goodnow, and Austin (1956), is credited with marking the onset of contemporary cognitive psychology. Neisser's book was a state-of-the-art text in the late 1960s.

Wittrock, M. C. The cognitive movement in instruction. *Educational Researcher,* 1979, *8,* 5–11.

This brief article, based on a presentation to the American Educational Research Association, provides an overview of the impact of cognitive psychology on instructional practices.

Comments on Practice Exercise 2–1

There are 6 *F*'s in the sentence. Most adults count only three *F*'s on their first try! Why? Perception is the key. As adult readers, we have long since learned to look for the *meaning* of words, phrases, and sentences. The cognitive processes that we use to extract meaning from written materials are so well practiced that they occur almost automatically. We have learned to pay attention to the words that usually carry the most meaning in sentences, particularly nouns and verbs. Prepositions such as the word *OF* are barely attended to, if at all. Cognitive processes relating to meaning are so automatic, however, that they are hard to shut down. Even while concentrating on this easy task, many readers completely fail to see the *F*'s that appear in the *OF*'s. In this task, meaningfulness *interferes* with successful performance.

Comments on Practice Exercise 2–2

As you probably noticed as you read over the list, the words come from four categories: animals, names, professions, and vegetables. The interesting thing about many people's recall of the list is that they tend to recall many of the words in related clusters—not in the exact order they learned the words. This shows that they have been active rather than passive processors of the information you have given them.

More specifically, they already have the concepts of animals, names, professions, and vegetables well learned. Once they recognize that the new learning—the list of words—can be made more meaningful in terms of categories, associations and clustering can take place. Learning is made easier (although this memory task is not an easy one) because the learners have made it more meaningful.

You will also notice differences in recall among your learners. Some will recall more than others, and each person's order of recall will be his or her own. You may also notice that the words at the beginning and the end of your list are somewhat more likely to be recalled. Generally, memory researchers have theorized that words at the beginning are better remembered because they are interfered with less by other words; words at the end are remembered better because they are still being rehearsed in working memory close to the time of recall.

IMPORTANT EVENTS IN THE DEVELOPMENT OF COGNITIVE PSYCHOLOGY

Date(s)	*Person(s)*	*Work*	*Impact*
1878	Wundt	First psychological laboratory	Wilhelm Wundt's laboratory was the site of the first systematic studies of cognitive processes.
1892	Titchener	First school of psychology in America, structuralism	Edward Bransford Titchener established the "study of conscious experience" as the early focal point of psychology.
1878–1909	James	*Principles of psychology; Talks to teachers on psychology and to students on some of life's ideals; Pragmatism: A new name for old ways of thinking*	William James's work was the forerunner of modern cognitive psychology; it formed the basis for functionalism and was strongly opposed to Wundt's structuralism.
1896	Dewey	"The reflex arc concept in psychology"	John Dewey's paper provided the focus for the formation of functionalism. His argument was that psychological activities should not be broken down into parts or elements, but should be considered as a continuous whole.
1912	Wertheimer, Köhler, Koffka	Formation of Gestalt psychology	Gestalt psychology became one of the major building blocks of contemporary cognitive psychology. Gestalt psychology's reaction against the elementarism of other schools of psychology brought forth views of cognition based on the whole of a person's interaction with events.
1914	Lyon	"The relation of length of material to time taken for learning and the optimum distribution of time"	D. O. Lyon demonstrated that meaningful material such as poetry was learned more rapidly than nonmeaningful material such as nonsense syllables.
1913–1956	Watson, Hull, Skinner	The behaviorist movement in American psychology	"The behaviorism program and the issues it spawned all but eliminated any serious research in cognitive psychology for 40 years" (J. R. Anderson, 1980, p. 9).

Date(s)	*Person(s)*	*Work*	*Impact*
1944	Aiken	First functional electronic computer	The development of a functional electronic computer through Howard Aiken's efforts allowed for the possibility of computer models of human cognition.
1956	Bruner, Goodnow, & Austin	*A study of thinking*	Jerome Bruner and his associates wrote the first major text on cognition in contemporary times.
1956	Chomsky	"Three models for the description of language"	Noam Chomsky authored the first contemporary versions of cognitive theories of language. At this time, cognitive theories began to supplant behavioral theories of language.
1956	Newell & Simon	"The logic machine: A complex information processing system"	Allen Newell and Herbert Simon's computer program was the first true exploration of artificial intelligence.
1967	Neisser	*Cognitive psychology*	Ulrich Neisser's text is often cited as the turning point in the formation of modern cognitive psychology. J. R. Anderson (1980) suggests that it was Neisser's text that brought respectability to the field.
1970	Many researchers	Founding the journal *Cognitive Psychology*	*Cognitive Psychology* was the first journal devoted solely to research in cognition.
1974	Jenkins	"Remember that old theory of memory? Well, forget it!"	As a presidential address to the American Psychological Association convention, J. J. Jenkins's paper set the tone for contemporary views of cognition and gave further legitimacy to cognitive psychology.
1978–1979	Wittrock	"The cognitive movement in instruction"	Merlin Wittrock's address to the American Educational Research Association in 1978 and his subsequent paper summarized the growing impact

Date(s)	*Person(s)*	*Work*	*Impact*
			of cognitive psychology on education. His paper also pointed the way to future applications.
1981	Carroll	"Ability and task difficulty in cognitive psychology"	John Carroll, widely respected for his work in cognition, advanced the concept of "elementary cognitive task," performance which is dependent on only a small number of cognitive processes. He points to the possibility of better understanding overall mental ability through intense study of individual differences in the performance of elementary cognitive tasks.

Chapter Three

MEMORY AND CONCEPTS

We all know about memory. Some experiences are easy to remember, even years after their occurrence. Other things, such as all the names and dates students sometimes cram into their heads the night before a test, are often forgotten in a matter of hours. Students "try to remember" many things, including the names of new acquaintances, the phone number of a favorite pizza parlor, twenty French words for tomorrow's quiz, or the formula for nitroglycerin.

As teachers we believe that knowledge should be beneficial to students long after they have left our classes. Educational experiences, regardless of how interesting they are, have little or no use unless they can be remembered and later somehow applied. Effective teachers provide instruction that makes it likely that students will recall important information long after their formal education has been completed. These teachers expect more than just a temporary change in what their students know.

One aspect of becoming an effective teacher is developing an understanding of the nature of human memory. This chapter will provide you with an overview of theories of memory and with a set of teaching applications based on those theories. We will also examine the central feature of human memory, the concept, and discuss the most effective ways to teach concepts.

Objectives

After reading this chapter, you should be able to meet the following objectives.

1. Apply seven guidelines drawn from memory research to your teaching.
2. Determine the defining attributes of a concept.
3. Teach a concept to another person following the steps outlined in the chapter.
4. Teach yourself a concept following the model presented in the chapter and compare the results to your usual approach for learning new concepts.
5. Use the SQ3R method to improve your studying and help someone else use the method to improve his or her studying.

MEMORY

As we saw in Chapter Two, thinking requires the storage of prior experiences in some organized fashion—a memory. Thinking not only includes the perception of immediate happenings in our environment but also prior experiences drawn from memory that influence the way in which we interpret the current environment. In Chapter Two we discussed some important aspects of cognition, including perception, attention, and the working memory. In this chapter we focus primarily on long-term memory, the retention of information over a period of days, weeks, months, and even years.

Researchers in the area of memory have used a wide range of learning tasks in their studies. Some researchers, in order to study memory in its purest state, have emphasized extremely simple learning tasks. These scientists have investigated so-called rote memory—memory for single words, simple pictures, and syllables. Others have focused primarily on higher levels of learning and memory, choosing to study how concepts, principles, and written passages are remembered. They have concentrated on a form of memory in which the information to be learned and recalled is akin to that of most people's everyday experiences. These two traditions have led to different theories of memory and, as we will see, different applications for teachers.

An understanding of memory should help you make better decisions about your teaching methods that will result in improved memory for your students. To help you understand current theories of memory, we will first examine some of the older theories that originated in the early work of the great pioneer of experimental memory research, Hermann

Ebbinghaus (1850–1909). These theories, decay theory and interference theory, were developed and tested mainly through the use of rote-learning methods invented and used by Ebbinghaus.

Decay Theory

The questions of how we remember and why we forget are two sides of the same coin. The questions have been asked for as long as there have been people who remembered and forgot things. One of the first concerns of psychology was memory (Ebbinghaus, 1913) and the earliest psychological theory of memory was the decay theory, which was based on common sense.

The **decay theory** was simple and straightforward: Memories fade (decay) with the passage of time. Memory was thought to be like a photograph left in the sun. At first the image is sharp and clear but the passage of time (plus the sun and rain) gradually fades the picture, until it is not discernible at all. This theory could be tested by two of its predictions. First, the more time that passes after learning some materials, the less well those materials will be remembered. Second, faster presentation rates of material to be learned should result in better memory because there is less time for forgetting. (That is, if it takes an hour to present some information, you have fifty-nine minutes to forget the first part of it; if the same material is presented in ten minutes, you only have nine minutes to forget the first part of it.)

For all its appeal to common sense and simplicity, the decay theory was found to be inaccurate by research done in the 1920s and the early 1930s. Jenkins and Dallenbach (1924), for example, tested decay theory in a study requiring two subjects to learn lists of ten nonsense syllables on two different occasions. After learning the initial list, the subjects were tested after one, two, four, and eight hours. One of the subjects participated during the daytime while the other participated at night. The daytime subject was awake between the time he learned the lists and the time he was tested, going about his normal daily activities. The subject who participated at night slept during these intervals. After this first phase of the experiment was completed, the subjects reversed their daytime and nighttime roles for the learning of the second list of nonsense syllables.

If decay theory were correct, there should have been no differences in forgetting between a subject who was asleep and one who was awake. Forgetting would be governed solely by the passage of time. Another hypothesis, however, was that newly encountered information might interfere with what had already been learned. If this interference theory were correct, the subject who was awake should have forgotten more than the sleeping subject because there are more possibilities of interference in the awake state. The results of both phases of the study very strongly supported the interference theory. The subject who slept in each phase of the experiment remembered about six out of ten of the nonsense syllables, while the subject who was awake recalled only one out of ten.

Jenkins and Dallenbach did not control for time of day. That is, the sleeping subject was tested at night while the subject who stayed awake was tested in the daytime. This flaw, along with the very small number of subjects, served as a hope for the determined supporters of the decay theory until the study was replicated (repeated) and confirmed by McGeoch and McDonald (1931) under better-controlled conditions. More recently, Yaroush, Sullivan, and Ekstrand (1971) extended the Jenkins and Dallenbach results by testing sleeping students after they had learned new information. It turned out that even dreams cause interference: Subjects who dreamed the most forgot the most.

Thus decay theory could not account for common phenomena observed in memory research. Theories that cannot explain what happens in experiments are discarded and scientists must begin to formulate new theories to explain what they witnessed in their research. In this case, decay theory was replaced by the theory that better explained the experimental results—interference theory.

Interference Theory

The phenomenon of one learning task interfering with another is known as **interference.** Interference theories have been with us since Jenkins and Dallenbach's (1924), McGeoch and McDonald's (1931), and Melton and Irwin's (1940) early formulations. Researchers still consider interference theory valid for rapid loss of rote learning of such items as word lists and names, and it has direct implications for classroom teachers. It seems to be less applicable, however, to higher-order learning.

Specifically, interference theory holds that forgetting occurs as time passes because new, conflicting information enters memory and interferes with the original learning. The passage of time is not the important factor. Instead, the amount of interfering information a person processes in memory during a given time accounts for most of the lapse in memory.

We can see how interference theory explains memory loss in an example drawn from everyday experience. Suppose you are enrolled in an American literature course and an American history course during the same semester. Not surprisingly, your professors manage to schedule their first examinations on the same day. Being a typical student, you do a lot of your studying the night before the exams. First you study the literature for several hours and then you study the history. Exhausted, you climb into bed and sleep until ten minutes before your literature test. You dash to the classroom and take the test, working as hard as you can. During the literature test you have several lapses of memory and confuse some of the names and dates from the history course with facts from the literature course.

This case illustrates **retroactive interference***; that is, current learning interferes with prior learning:

Retroactive Interference

> Learn task #1—Learn task #2—Test over task #1. Performance on test is poorer than if only task #1 had been studied.

The results of retroactive interference studies (see Ceraso & Henderson, 1966; Houston, 1966; Koppenall, 1963; Postman, Stark, & Henschel, 1969; Yaroush et al., 1971) reveal that groups given a task between the first task to be learned and the test of the material recall less of the first task than groups given the same first task without the interfering task before testing. Almost all interference studies, unlike our example, have been laboratory studies that used lists of nonsense syllables (such as PAZ, NIC, XOM) paired with nouns as the materials to be remembered. This procedure, which dates back to the work of Ebbinghaus (1913), has been used to reduce possible contamination of the results stemming from the participants' prior knowledge.

Another form of interference, **proactive interference**, commonly occurs in our daily lives; here, prior learning interferes with current learning:

Proactive Interference

> Learn task #1—Learn task #2—Test over task #2. Performance is poorer than if only task #2 had been studied.

Returning to our earlier example of studying for two tests, suppose you had studied the history first, then the literature, and had been tested only on the literature. If as a result you had several lapses in memory, the lapses would be due to proactive interference.

In both retroactive and proactive interference, the similarity of the learning tasks influences the degree to which interference occurs (Ceraso, 1967; Postman & Underwood, 1973). Generally, the greater the similarity of the two learning tasks, the greater the likelihood of interference. If you were to first memorize a list of numbers and then memorize a second list of numbers, for example, interference would be more likely than if you first memorized a list of numbers and then learned a list of names.

*Note that Jenkins and Dallenbach's study (1924) was a study of retroactive interference.

There have been several attempts to explain proactive interference (see Ceraso, 1967; Postman & Underwood, 1973; Underwood, 1957) but none has been able to fully account for the experimental results, that is, to answer the question of why previous learning interferes with the recall of new learning. Nevertheless, the interference theory of memory is still very much alive today even though some of its predictions are not conclusively supported by research.*

Interference theory, while highly valuable for rote learning, has not been demonstrated to be applicable to higher levels of learning. For this reason alone, another theory was necessary to account for how we remember and forget concepts, principles, rules, and other higher forms of learning.

Information-Processing Theory

As we suggested in Chapter Two, information-processing theory came into being both as an alternative to competing theories and as a result of technological advances in other sciences. As you recall, information-processing theory views humans as active processors of information and states that memory cannot be studied apart from what the learner does with new information and how meaningful the information is to the learner. Human beings are seen as information-processing systems similar to computer systems. This view suggests that memory is a process of encoding (or placing into memory) information registered by the sense organs, storing the information, and retrieving or remembering it when necessary. These three processes are common to all information-processing models of memory.

The first process, **encoding,** amounts to the taking in of new information and representing it symbolically in thinking. If we tell you, "Summarize this passage after reading it," you somehow turn both the request and these written characters into a symbolic representation that you encode or place into your thinking. Try it. Read over our instruction and then close your eyes and think about it. The sentence "Summarize this passage . . . " is represented in your mind in some form. You have made some internal symbols to represent the sentence you read.

The next step is **storage.** Items can be stored in our memory for

*Greeno, James, and DaPolito (1971) and E. Martin (1971) examined interference phenomena in experiments that were much more sophisticated than the examples we give in this chapter. It is the inability of interference theories to deal with the phenomena they observed and related issues that have weakened it. Postman and Underwood's (1973) review should be studied by readers wishing further information about the shortcomings and strengths of interference theory.

minutes, hours, months, or even years. We have all had the experience of hearing the first few notes of a song and then recalling an event of many years ago in great detail. How were the sights, sounds, emotions, and words of that event stored? Physiological, perceptual, and memory research is beginning to find some answers to this question. Unfortunately, storage is not yet clearly understood, but we do know

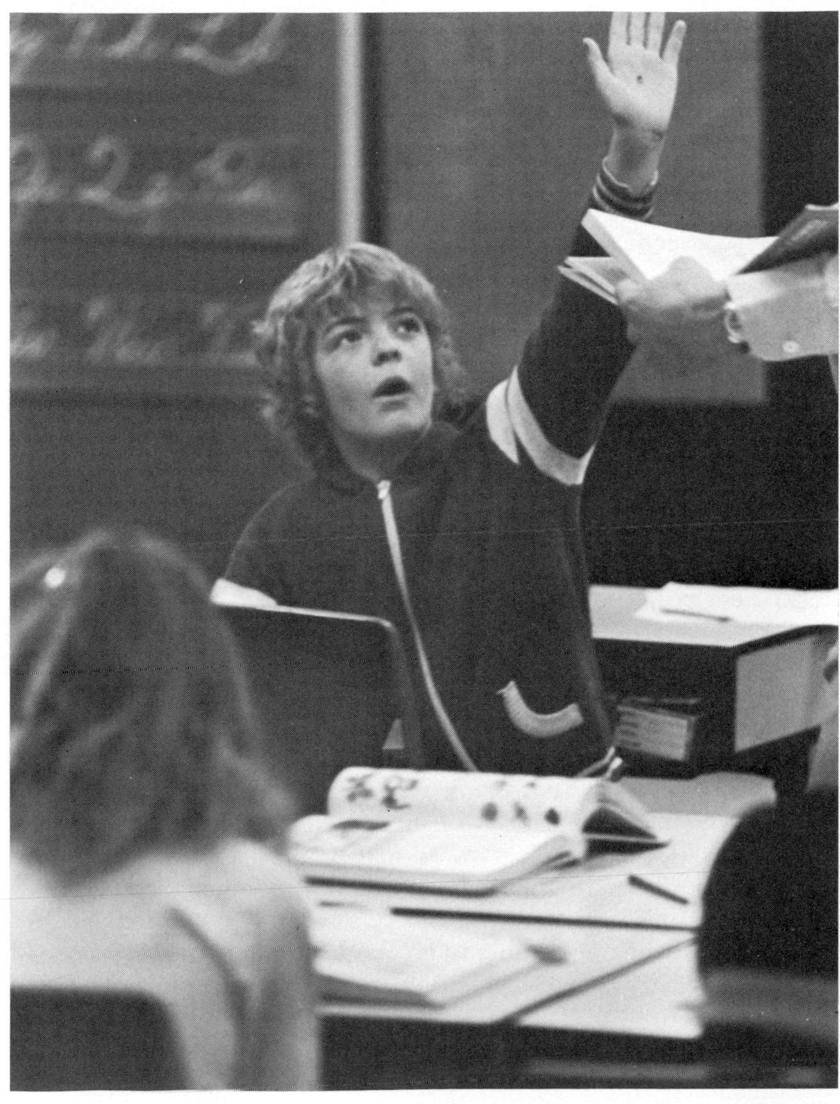

Retrieval is recall of stored information. Volunteering an answer in class requires retrieval of previously learned information.

that many memories are permanent and may be recalled, given the proper cues for retrieval.

Retrieval is the recall of stored information or the recognition of previously learned material. Not all information that is stored is easily accessible. An answer for an examination question may be stored in your memory, for example; you know it's there somewhere but it won't quite come to you. Later, when you leave the test room, you may retrieve the answer.

There is a knotty problem in studying any of these processes independently. Any memory that we choose to study must first be encoded, then stored, and finally retrieved. We can never be sure which of the three processes has had what effect on memory. That is, when you cannot remember something, it is extremely difficult to know if you have had trouble encoding, storing, or retrieving the information. We do know, however, that all three processes must occur in order for memory to function.

Meaningful Verbal Learning

As we saw in Chapter Two, the key to all aspects of information processing is meaningfulness. To be most efficient and useful, new learning must somehow make contact with or be related to information already in long-term memory.

Many definitions of meaningful learning have been proposed by memory researchers. Noble (1952, 1963) defined meaning in terms of associations prompted by a given word. Meaningfulness was determined by the number of associations people could make to a word. The more associations people made, the more meaningful the verbal unit.* Meaningfulness, in turn, predicted ease of learning: "high-meaningfulness" materials were shown to be more easily learned than "low-meaningfulness" materials. From a different perspective, Ausubel (1960, 1961, 1962, 1963; Ausubel, Novak, & Hanesian, 1978) coined the phrase "meaningful verbal learning," which refers to learning from verbal materials that can be related to information learners already know.

In Chapter Two we chose to define meaningful information as new information that learners can tie into their previous knowledge. Our definition is similar to Ausubel's and to recent formulations of J. R. Anderson and his associates (Anderson & Bower, 1973; Anderson et al., 1977). For meaningful learning to occur, the learner must have had past experiences that provide organization and permit interpretation of the new information as it is encountered.

*The word *peach* is likely to generate many more associations (tree, blossom, pie, fuzz, pit) than the word *exiguous*. For Noble, *peach* would be more meaningful than *exiguous*.

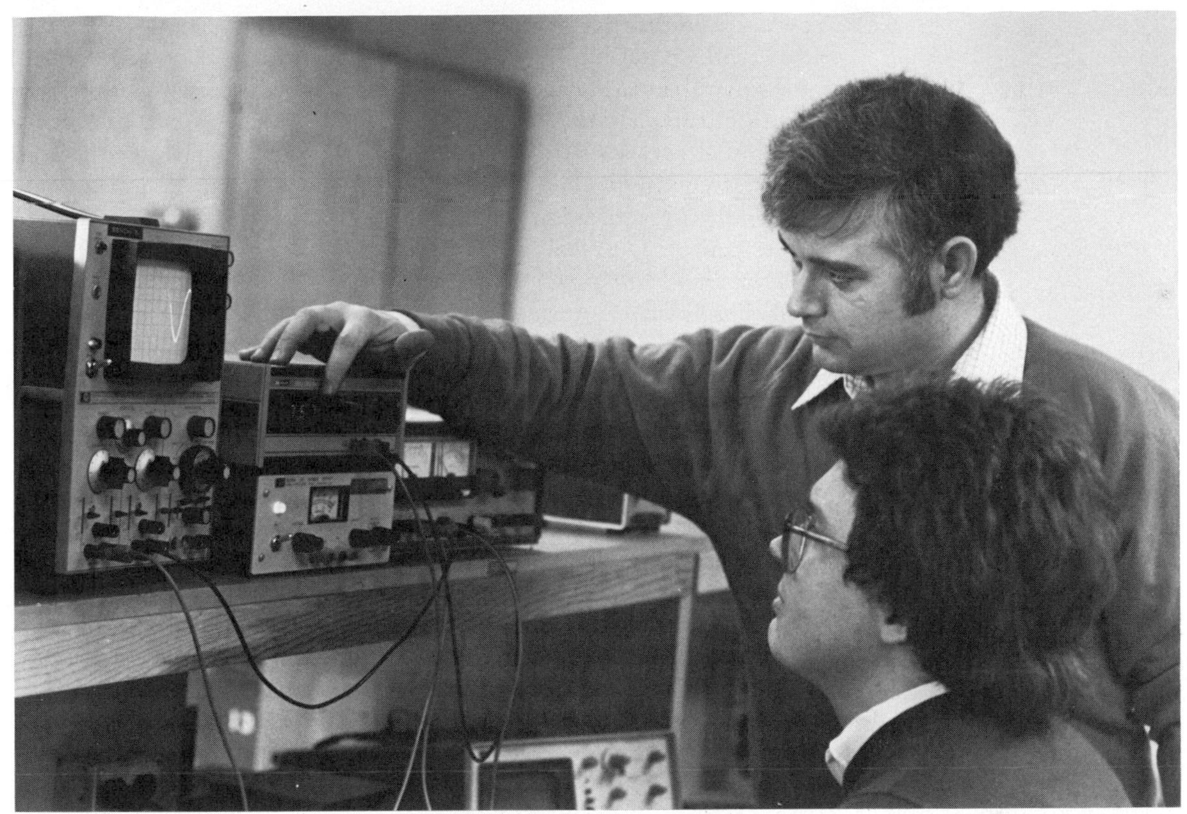

Unless instruction is meaningful, problems are unlikely to be solved.

Some examples will help clarify the notion of meaningful learning. Without paper and pencil, solve the equation $4 \times 7 + 2 = x$ in your head. What do you need to know to be able to solve the problem? Obviously you need to know what x stands for, what + stands for, and what = stands for. Additionally, you must understand 4, 2, and 7. Further, you must be able to outline and follow the steps in both addition and multiplication. Without all this in your memory, the problem would not be meaningful and you could not solve it.

Suppose you are asked to formulate an argument supporting Nathan Bedford Forrest's tactics at Brice's Crossroads. Is this question meaningful? It isn't meaningful unless you know that the question refers to a battle, who Forrest was, what Brice's Crossroads was, whom Forrest fought, what the deployment of Forrest's enemy was, which war was being fought, and on and on. The odds are good that unless you are a Civil War buff you will not find this question meaningful.

If you have ever enrolled in a course for which you did not have the prerequisite knowledge, you have had firsthand experience with information that was not meaningful to you. We can successfully think about problems and issues only if they can be related to ideas we already have stored in our memories.

Materials that initially have little meaning are better learned if they can be related to something meaningful. One well-known approach for relating new material to what students already know is the use of advance organizers (Ausubel, 1960, 1980). **Advance organizers** are abstract, general overviews of new information that are read in advance of the new information. Ausubel takes a cognitive view in his advocacy of advanced organizers, asserting that new information is most easily learned when it can be linked to stable cognitive structures that the learner already has. His theory holds that specific, detailed knowledge (subordinate concepts) is subsumed under existing, high-level cognitive structures (superordinate concepts). According to Ausubel, the advance organizer provides a kind of "scaffolding" or high-level cognitive structure to which the more detailed material that follows can be related. Thus advance organizers are constructed to help learners tie new information into their existing knowledge. Although the concept of advance

"When you're young, it comes naturally, but when you get a little older, you have to rely on mnemonics."

organizers has received some rather strong criticism in recent years (see, for example, Anderson, Spiro, & Anderson, 1978), the idea of employing prefatory material to help make reading materials more meaningful to readers remains a popular one.

Another method for relating "low-meaningful" to "high-meaningful" materials is the use of **mnemonics.** Mnemonics are rhymes, words, or images—anything familiar—that are paired with new information to make it more meaningful (Pressley, Levin, & Delaney, 1981; Paivio & Desrochers, 1981). The rhyme "*i* before *e* except after *c*" is a mnemonic that helps students remember a spelling rule. In much the same way, beginning musicians use the mnemonics *E*very *G*ood *B*oy *D*oes *F*ine and *FACE* to help them recall the lines E, G, B, D, and F and the spaces F, A, C, and E of the treble clef. Teachers often use mnemonics in their instruction (Boltwood & Blick, 1970) and students report that they frequently use mnemonics in learning new information (Morris & Cook, 1978).

Paivio and Desrochers (1981) have pointed out that most effective mnemonics use imagery and that simply advising students to use mental images can give them a powerful mnemonic tool. As Paivio (1971) and Bower (1970) observed some time ago, imagery can significantly enhance recall for many kinds of materials. Several relatively simple but effective systems of mnemonics involving imagery can be learned by students and used for remembering many types of information, particularly lists of items (Neisser, 1982). Three of these are the link method, the method of loci, and the peg or hook method.

In the link method, a person forms an image for each item on a list of items to be learned. Each image is then pictured as "interacting" with the image of the next item on the list. That is, the images are linked in the imagination. In a simple example, if you were trying to remember to buy chicken, cheese, apples, and soup at the grocery story, you might visualize a sequence in which a *chicken* picked up a piece of *cheese,* melted the cheese onto an *apple,* and dropped the cheese-covered apple into a bowl of *soup.* The interactive image makes it likely that the recall of each item will cue the recall of the next item. A great advantage of this method is its simplicity. No external scheme or set of materials needs to be learned.

The method of loci dates back to the ancient Greeks. According to Bower (1970), Cicero attributed the origin of this method to the Greek poet Simonides. Simonides had recited a poem to assembled guests at a large banquet and, following his oration, had been called outside. At that very moment, the roof of the great hall collapsed, killing everyone who remained inside. The corpses were so mangled that not even relatives could identify them. Simonides came forward, however, and was able to name each of the many corpses by their locations in the wreckage of the huge hall. This feat of memory convinced Simonides of a very useful method for remembering: use a set of locations in which you can place images of things to be remembered.

In the modern use of the method of loci, learners first think of a series of ten to twenty well-learned locations (such as points on a path taken daily, rooms in one's house, or locations on a campus) and then "place" each item from the list to be learned at one of the locations. Usually learners are advised to imagine themselves walking and visiting each location in order. On this "walk" each item in the list is visualized as located in one particular location. To recall the items, then, learners are encouraged to "walk" along the path once more and to "look" at each location in order to recall the item placed there. Generally, this method helps learners both in recalling the items and in recalling them in the proper order, since "travelling the path" helps the person recall items in the right sequence.

In the peg or hook method, learners memorize a series of "pegs" on which information can be "hung" as it is learned. Pegs can be any well-learned set of items; the most popular scheme and one often investigated in research is a rhyming peg system (for example, one is a bun, two is a shoe, three is a tree . . .). Each peg is easy to visualize—a bun, a shoe, a tree, and so on.

Once the pegs are memorized, they can be used to help remember a series of items in order. The first step is to form an image of each item interacting with its assigned peg. If the first item on a list were "book," for instance, it might be imagined as sandwiched between the halves of a bun. The second item would be imagined as interacting with a "shoe," and so on through the list.

The success of the method of loci and the peg method hinges on their ability to assist learners in relating the familiar (in the form of a well-learned mnemonic) to the unfamiliar (the items to be learned). A critical factor in using mnemonics successfully is that learners must be completely comfortable with them. Their use must be automatic, or nearly so. There are typically very few problems in obtaining automaticity with the method of loci if the mental walk encompasses familiar locations. For the peg system, however, some effort must be expended to develop a completely familiar and useful mnemonic. If the peg system is not very well learned, it is unlikely that students will find it effective and continue to use it. In mnemonics, as in any skill, practice makes perfect!

As we have stressed here and in Chapter Two, the concept of meaningful learning is central to information-processing theory. When we observe people verbalizing what they remember, it is obvious that hu-

PRACTICE EXERCISE 3–1

Using a Mnemonic

There isn't a better way to make a fair decision about the worth of mnemonics than to try them. For many people, the method of loci is a good starting point because it is easy to use for many different types of information.

We suggest that you try the method for a week. You may want to use it to remember your shopping lists, important compounds in a chemistry class, body parts for physiology (by forming an interactive image of each part and its label and placing the image in the location), or important events in history. Try to do each of the following, in order, to give the method a fair test.

1. Make sure you know your mnemonic well before you try to use it.
2. Take mental "walks" through the locations until you have the order well learned.
3. Place the items to be remembered in the locations, with one and only one in each location.
4. If you study the list of items again, place them in the same locations each time.
5. Use the method with several different types of information.

After using the method for at least a week, make a judgment about how well the method of loci has worked for you. For what kinds of materials was the method most useful? Did you become more comfortable with the mnemonic with repeated use? Are the loci you chose the best for you? After you make changes to suit your needs you should have a versatile and powerful mnemonic to help you in many situations.

man memory is organized into logical and systematic patterns. One way to consider the systematic nature of memory is to think of the information in memory as organized into specific categories that are related to each other. If we ask you what the word *apple* makes you think of, you are likely to respond with words such as "tree," "blossom," and "orchard." It would be unlikely that you would answer "diesel," "pacifist," or "educational psychology." Most people make categorized associations to stimuli. If you are trying to remember the name of a building, for instance, a helpful strategy is to think of the appearance of the building, the last time you were there, and so on. This kind of strategy may help you find the correct category in your memory under which the name of that building is "filed." Later in this chapter, we will discuss one way that psychologists believe such "filing" and organization takes place.

Levels of Processing/ Distinctiveness of Encoding

As with any theory, information-processing theory has been constantly tested, evaluated, and reformulated to account for what is observed in research. As a result, information-processing theory has shifted away from a view of memory as consisting of separate stages of short- and long-term memory. What the learner *does* during learning is now viewed as the critical aspect of memory.

Emphasizing the differences between short-term and long-term stages of memory caused many researchers to commit the same error to which they reacted so strongly in the old interference theory: They had overlooked the most important consideration of all in memory—what the learner does. Melton (1963) argued, however, that the distinction between short- and long-term memory was not particularly important and later suggested that the important thing was how learners reacted to new information (Melton & Martin, 1972). Atkinson and Shiffrin (1968) paralleled Melton's ideas and proposed that the structure of memory was not nearly so important as the things people did while learning.

What the learner does is critical to memory. Learning occurs easily and rapidly as the students work directly with the computer.

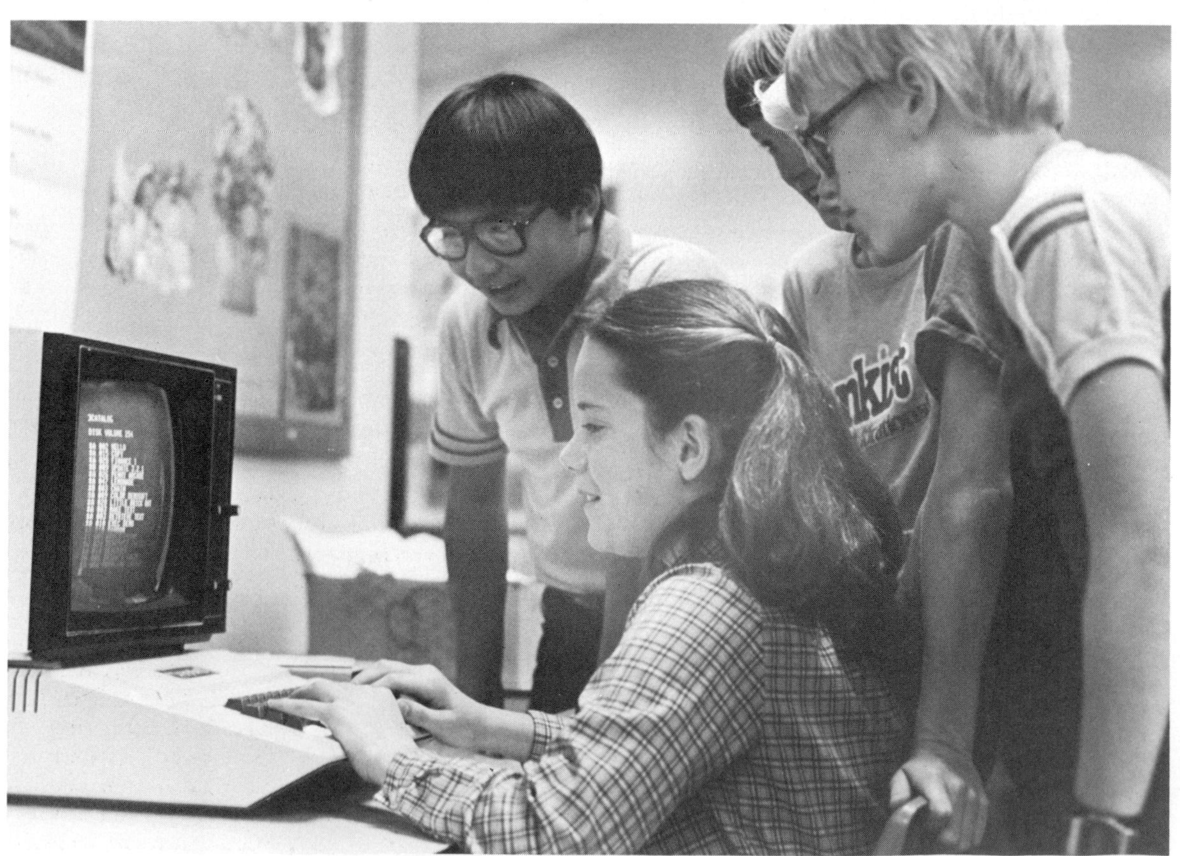

Craik and Lockhart (1972) suggested that memory is a direct function not of structures in memory but of the depth of processing: the more deeply or carefully new information is analyzed by the learner, the more likely it is to be recalled in the future. More recently, researchers such as Jacoby and Craik (1979) and Jacoby, Craik, and Begg (1979) have argued that processing and analysis make events more distinctive and thus more likely to be recalled. That is, the more distinct information is in its context, the greater the probability that it will be remembered.

A particularly well reasoned argument for a "meaning" approach to the study of memory was presented by Jenkins (1974), who pointed out that he and a number of associates had completed well over one hundred studies of memory. He now believed, however, that all of those studies had been in the wrong direction because he had not taken into account what it is people do with new information—he had left meaning out of his studies of memory. He stated,

> Memory is not a box in a flow diagram. What is remembered in a given situation depends on the physical and psychological context in which the event was experienced, the knowledge and skills that the subject brings to the context, the situation in which we ask for evidence for remembering, and the relation of what the subject remembers to what the experimenter demands. *(1974, pp. 793–794)*

In order to understand memory it is necessary to understand all that a person does with new information. Memory cannot be isolated and studied without examining all aspects of the human mind and the actions taken by the learner. It is this continually evolving view of memory, which takes both the material and the learner into account, that allows us to develop guidelines for teaching to enhance our students' memory.

APPLICATIONS FOR TEACHING

By following the seven guidelines we have drawn from research in memory, you can help your students remember new information more effectively.

1. New information must be meaningful. Encoding is the representation of new information in thinking (Hillinger, 1980). Encoding is highly unlikely to occur when the learner has no framework of understanding in which to represent new information. If a teacher reads a passage to a class, those students who don't have a prior understanding of several of its concepts will fail to encode many of its ideas because of their inability to represent the new information.

New information must be given at the learners' levels. Language consistent with the learners' past experience should be used. Saying "aqueous solution" to a third grader rather than "mixed in water" will likely confuse and limit learning. Similarly, the laws of physics, stated abstractly, will be more difficult to learn than if they are stated in terms of everyday experiences that students can use as a framework for encoding the new information.

In general, you should always provide experiences for your students that allow them to translate and express new information in their own words. Asking students to paraphrase ideas is almost certain to help them tie the new information into what they already know. The processing of new information can also be enhanced if students apply it by thinking of examples or by solving problems, either in groups or individually. Role playing may also be used to strengthen ties of new information to what the students already have in their memories.

2. Learners should be active rather than passive. For new information to be remembered it must be rehearsed. You can be assured that rehearsal is going on if your learners are actively involved in a task rather than passively listening or observing. Active learning also means practice. For learning both in and out of school to be effective, learners must practice using new information. Where possible, practice should be free of distractions and uninterrupted.

3. Mnemonics should be used when appropriate. Mnemonics can have a very positive effect on students' recall of information. A great deal of learning in school requires students to commit fairly large amounts of verbal material to memory. Foreign language vocabulary words, names of countries, dates and names in history, and plant phyla, for example, are all essentially rote information when first encountered. Nonetheless, such learning is often critical to successful performance in many classes. By helping students tie new information into existing memory structures through the use of mnemonics, teachers can enhance students' learning and the subsequent memorability of this kind of information.

4. Avoid interference in your class. Give quizzes and examinations at the beginning of the day or the period if you can arrange it. Those teachers who insist on covering new materials during the first part of the period and then give quizzes on old information during the last part of a period are setting up events that almost certainly will result in both proactive and retroactive interference (and frustrated students). Also try to avoid interference with other classes: When possible, do not give an examination on a day when your students must take another examination.

5. Teach your students to "overlearn" information. Many students practice new learning only until they can perform one error-free repetition of the material. If they are learning definitions of several accounting techniques, for example, they may practice until they can recall the list of definitions once without error. This minimum level of learning is extremely susceptible to in-

Point out the implications of remembering new information.

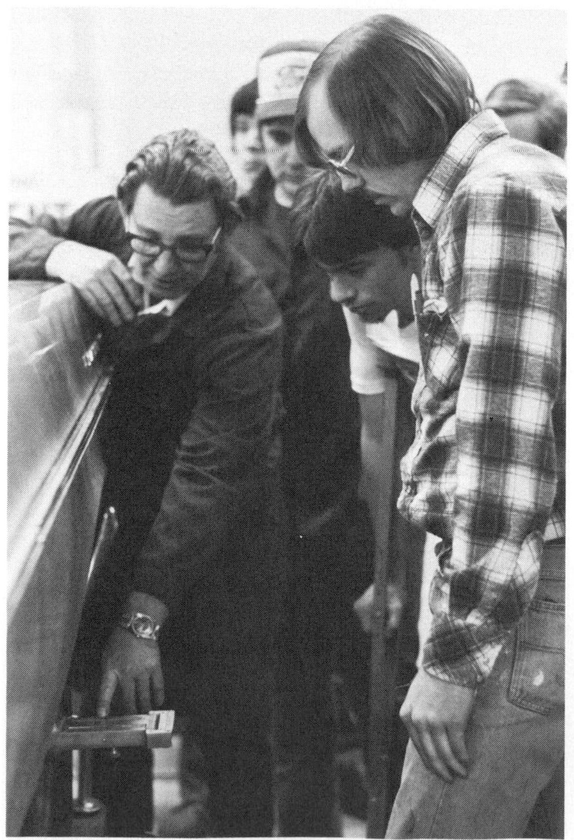

terference. Almost any unexpected occurrence, anxiety, or loss of attention can be catastrophic for recall.

Overlearning is the continued practice of an errorless recitation and can be a great help in reducing interference effects. If learners keep track of how many trials they made to obtain the first errorless recall and then practice the materials that many more times, overlearning is fairly well assured and interference is much less likely.

6. Point out the implications of remembering new information. If students are to remember a series of complex steps for, say, installing brakes in a car, stress the possible outcome if the steps are not correctly remembered. Motivation to remember is a powerful incentive to rehearsing newly learned material.

7. Have students picture where and how they will have to remember information. Pairing learning with the cues students will use to remember helps students organize their memory (Eich, 1980). When the situation arises in which recall must occur, the association of the situation and the information to be recalled is likely to be automatic. Many times information is in memory but simply is not associated properly with the situation at hand. Effective teachers point out those situations in which recall of information is likely to be required.

CATEGORIZING INFORMATION: CONCEPTS

Earlier in the chapter we stated that human memory can be organized in specific categories. One way in which we can think about categories in memory is through the use of concepts. **Concepts** are classes of stimuli (information) that people group together on the basis of some perceived commonalities. Concepts help us reduce the complexity of the world by allowing us to place new information in already existing "compartments" of knowledge. The first time we see an old crop-dusting biplane, for example, we don't have to learn very much about it because we can place it into our memory under the category "airplane"—if we can identify it as an object that is an example or instance of the concept of airplane. Some new information, of course, must be placed into its own category; when this happens, a new concept must be learned.

CONCEPTS

Memory is systematic. One way of thinking about the systematic nature of human memory is to consider the relationships between different concepts. Concepts can be organized into hierarchies; some concepts are more general (animals, for example) and some are more specific (dogs, cats). Two or more concepts can also be related to each other in the form of rules or principles (Gagné, 1977). Consider the following statements:

1. All mammals have four-chambered hearts.
2. Sentences must contain a subject and a verb.
3. All satellites are in orbit.
4. Green plants produce chlorophyll.

Each of these statements is a principle. In the first, the concept of mammal is related to the concept of a four-chambered heart. The second principle relates the concept of sentence to the concepts of subject and verb. The concept of satellites is related to the concept of orbit in the third principle, and the concept of green plant is related to the concept of chlorophyll in the fourth.

The following sections are designed to help you understand concepts and principles and to help you learn how to teach concepts to your students.

Concept Attributes

As we have noted, concepts are classes of stimuli people group together on the basis of some perceived similarities.* These classes of stimuli may be objects (caps, balls, tetrahedrons), persons (lawyers, midgets, clowns), events (parades, picnics, fairs), or ideas (envy, beauty, ambition). People place particular stimuli (examples of concepts) into specific categories as a result of the similarities they perceive. If stimuli do not fit into a given category ("No, that was not an egret we just saw") they are nonexamples of a concept. As we'll see, part of our task in guiding our students' learning is to reduce concepts to the most important similarities so that students can distinguish examples from nonexamples.

These similarities across examples of a concept are called **attributes.** Attributes can refer to size (an ocean is bigger than a pond), shape (a triangle has one shape, a square another), color (oranges are orange, grapes are not), or use (desks are primarily for writing, tables are primarily for eating). Some attributes are necessary to define a concept while others are not. The necessary attributes are known as **defining attributes.** As you begin to identify the defining attributes of concepts on your own, you will find a good dictionary very valuable. Perhaps the best way to explain this idea is to look at a series of concepts.

defining (necessary attributes)

Concept 1: Cup.

What makes a cup a cup? What is "cupness"? Most of us can conjure up a vision of an object that is fairly small, circular on top, designed to hold liquid, with a small handle on it. All of us can imagine a cup and recognize one when we see one. But what are the defining attributes of a cup? Let's look at some attributes of cup to determine what its defining attributes are.

What are cups made of? They can be glass, plastic, ceramic,

*The concepts formed by each individual usually have some unique features. Each person forms concepts and adds to them on the basis of his or her experience. However, in education we try to help students understand concepts in the same way. We might think of dictionaries as standards for defining concepts.

metal, paper, or styrofoam. It seems that the material from which an object is made does not matter in determining whether it is a cup. The material from which a cup is made is an attribute but not a defining attribute.

What kinds of shapes do cups have? Some cups are half spheres, some are squares, some are cylinders, and some have very strange shapes. Shape is an attribute of cups but not a defining attribute.

What about size? Some cups are the size of thimbles. Some can hold as much as a pint. It appears, however, that when an object is much larger than pint-sized it is no longer a cup but is a mug. So size is a defining attribute of cups. Cups must be relatively small.

Does color matter? Cups may be of any color without affecting their "cupness." Color is an attribute of cups but not an important one.

Cups differ from some small glasses only because they are designed to protect the drinker from the heat of the liquid they contain while glasses do not. So the ability to insulate must be a defining attribute of cups.

Do all cups have handles? No. Some do and some don't. Evidently having a handle is not a defining attribute of cups. Use, however, is a defining attribute. Cups, unlike many other objects, are used to hold hot liquids.

We instantly recognize cups but in order to teach the concept we must analyze it. So far we have identified several attributes of the concept "cup" without exactly determining which attributes make a cup a cup. In fact, there is a combination of attributes that, taken together, define the concept "cup." A cup is a small (the attribute of size) drinking container designed for hot liquid substances (the attribute of use). Glasses are like cups but need not be small and need not hold hot drinks. Mugs are typically considered to be larger than cups. So the defining attributes of the concept "cup" are size and use. All the other attributes, including several that we did not list, are not important to defining "cup."

Concept 2: Ring. What makes something a ring? Without listing all the possible attributes of rings we can see that the defining attributes of rings are that they can be affixed to a finger somehow and that they are worn for ornamentation. All the other attributes are unnecessary to defining rings. Color, size, shape, form, materials, and so on are not necessary to define the concept "ring."*

*The concept "ring" could be defined more generally to include washers, targets, and so forth. We have chosen one aspect of the concept because it allowed us to easily describe the attributes that define it.

Concept 3: Pencil. What properties (attributes) must an object have in order to be considered a pencil? We'll define a pencil as a long, narrow object that contains a dry substance used to mark a surface. Only four attributes are necessary to define "pencil": they are used to mark something, they are longer than they are wide, they contain a marking substance, and they have a protective covering over the marking substance. The four attributes will allow persons to place common lead pencils, carpenters' pencils, grease pencils, mechanical pencils, and graphic arts pencils all into the category "pencil."

PRACTICE EXERCISE 3–2
Listing Concept Attributes

We have listed a series of concepts below. Read them and then list the defining attributes of each concept. You may check your responses against ours at the end of the chapter.

1. envelope

2. clock

3. distillation

4. opera

5. referendum

6. over

7. estrange

8. harmony

Types of Concepts

Although there are many kinds of concepts, three are most common: conjunctive, disjunctive, and relational. The concepts we have talked about thus far, those that are defined by common attributes, are **conjunctive** concepts. **Disjunctive** concepts are concepts defined by statements of "either *A* or *B*." A strike in baseball, for instance, is either a ball pitched through a certain zone (one attribute), or a foul ball when there are less than two strikes (another attribute), or a foul tip that is caught with two strikes (another attribute), or a ball that the batter swings at and misses (another attribute). A strike is either *A* or *B* or *C* or *D*. Another example of a disjunctive concept is a point in tennis. A player scores a point when the other player hits the ball out of the boundary lines, strokes the ball into the net, misses a ball hit to him or her, double-faults in serving, touches the net with his or her racquet, and so on. A point is *A* or *B* or *C* or *D*.

Relational concepts are defined by a relationship between two or more of a concept's attributes. Direction and distance are the most common relational concepts. Direction is described by giving a relationship between two or more points (west, thataway), as is distance (about two miles from here). "Over," "under," "beside," and "before" (in fact, many prepositions) are relational concepts.

Relationships Between Concepts: Models of Semantic Memory

We have defined concepts and examined how they are analyzed in order to reduce them to their defining attributes. Before we describe how to teach them effectively, we will examine how they fit into current theories of memory.

Psychologists who study memory typically cast it into two forms, episodic and semantic, although recently some theorists (such as Anderson & Ross, 1980) have argued against this distinction. Endel Tulving (1972, 1979) has used the term **episodic memory** to refer to memories of our personal experiences. Any memories we have about the events in our lives, such as "Yesterday I purchased a new book" or recall of a conversation with a friend, are examples of episodic memory (Franks, Plybon, & Auble, 1982).

Much of what is stored in our memory, however, is not associated with any specific time or place from our past. If you remember the fact that birds fly or that 1816 was the "year with no summer," these memories are not episodic. Memory that is not episodic is referred to as **semantic memory**. Concepts and principles—knowledge not tied to memories of specific events—can be considered part of semantic memory. Much of the learning that occurs in schools involves semantic memory. There are two models of semantic memory that are most relevant to educational theory—network models and set-theoretic models (Loftus & Loftus, 1977; Smith, Shoben, & Rips, 1974).

FIGURE 3–1
A Network Model of Semantic Memory

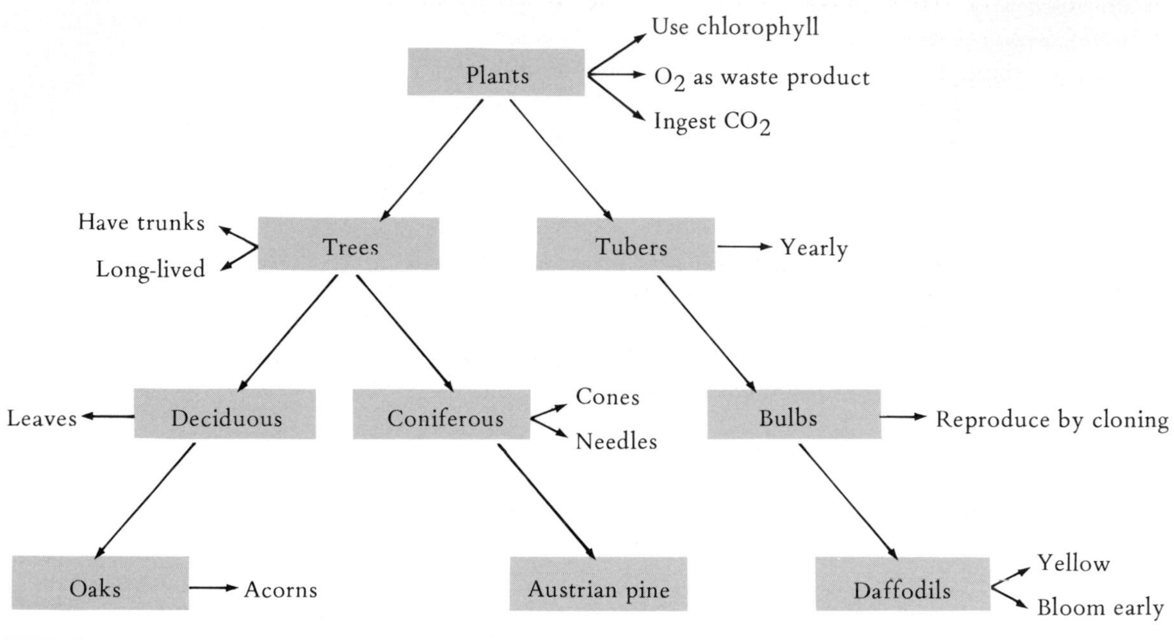

Network Models. Some theorists have suggested that items stored in semantic memory are connected in a giant network. Such network models have been proposed by Anderson and Bower (1973), Anderson, Kline, and Lewis (1977), Collins and Loftus (1975), Collins and Quillian (1969), Kintsch (1972, 1974), Loftus (1973), and Rumelhart, Lindsay, and Norman (1972). Figure 3–1 presents a hypothetical memory structure based on the Collins and Quillian model.

You can see that the concepts in Figure 3–1 are organized in a hierarchy based on subordinate-superordinate relations. The superordinate of "oaks" is "deciduous," the superordinate of "deciduous" is "trees," and the superordinate of "trees" is "plants." You can also see that attributes that define each concept are stored only at the point in the hierarchy that corresponds to that concept. This way of thinking about storage is known as **cognitive economy.** An example of cognitive economy is the placement of "have trunks," an attribute of all trees. It is stored only in the general category "trees" and not in any subordinate items, because all trees have trunks.

To test their model Collins and Quillian performed an experiment in which subjects were required to answer yes or no to simple questions such as the following:

1. Do oaks have trunks?
2. Do oaks lose their leaves in the winter?
3. Do oaks have acorns?

These three questions represent different semantic levels of information contained Figure 3–1. The question "Do oaks have trunks?" can only be answered with information stored with "trees," which is two levels away from "oaks." The answer to the second question can be obtained from information stored at "deciduous," one semantic level away from "oaks." The last question can be answered from the information at "oaks" itself. Collins and Quillian believed that subjects' reaction times to such questions would lead to knowledge about the way information is retrieved from memory. They predicted longer reaction times for information further removed from the semantic level of the concept.

Their findings were as predicted. Reaction time was shortest for questions like number 3, longest for questions like number 1, and intermediate for questions like number 2. Collins and Quillian concluded that subjects who were asked about "oaks," for example, first entered the category "oaks." If the information necessary to answer the question was located there, the response time was short. If the necessary information was at a different semantic level, subjects would still enter at "oaks" but then go up the hierarchy stopping at each level, one step at a time, until they found the answer to the question. This extra processing would account for the longer times necessary to answer questions at semantic levels above or below the entry point.

Set-Theoretic Models. The developers of set-theoretic models (see, for example, D. E. Meyer, 1970) propose that memory is stored as sets of elements such that each set includes all instances of that set and may also include all the attributes of that set. A set such as "cows" may include instances of cows as well as the attributes of cows (they moo, have four legs, and so on). The set idea is best understood by examining Figure 3–2. The set (or concept) "cows" includes the set "Holstein." All Holsteins are cows but not all cows are Holsteins. In the second example, some strikes are fouls but not all fouls are strikes (a foul with two strikes has no effect on the ball-strike count).

The basic process that Meyer conceives for retrieval in his system is

FIGURE 3–2
A Set-Theoretic Model of Semantic Memory

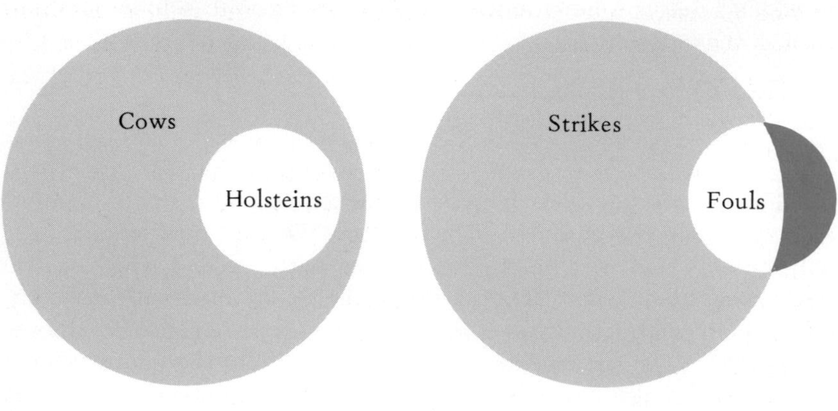

attribute comparison. For example, a question such as "Is a Holstein a cow?" requires a person to determine whether every attribute of "cows" is also present in the concept "Holstein." Meyer found that when subjects were asked to answer true or false to statements using the word "some," they responded more quickly than when they were asked to respond to statements containing the word "all" (some ducks can fly; all ducks can fly). Meyer took this as evidence of the time the subjects spent comparing attributes in memory. He reasoned that statements containing "some" did not require so extensive a search as did statements containing "all."

The process Meyer envisioned for statements containing "all" was as follows (refer to Figure 3–2). A person first retrieves the entire set of categories that intersect (for example, "cows" intersects with "Holstein," "Angus," and so on). For all the categories that intersect, the person makes an attribute comparison between the set (in this case, "cows") and each category ("Holstein," "Angus") until all attributes stored in memory are exhausted. The subject should take more time for this procedure than for processing statements containing the word "some," which only requires a determination of whether the sets intersect.

An Evaluation of Models of Memory. The Collins and Quillian model is based on semantic levels that are thought to represent "givens" in a memory system. Not all researchers have been able to demonstrate that retrieval time corresponds to semantic levels, however (see, for example, Rips, Shoben, & Smith, 1973). This problem has been addressed in several ways (Collins & Loftus, 1975), and individual differences might easily account for the lack of consistent effect observed by semantic levels; that is, not all persons have the same knowledge at the same semantic levels.

The greatest weakness of the set-theoretic model is "hedges," as described by Lakoff (1972). Hedges are statement qualifiers we use to modify many of the things we say. "In a broad sense," "technically speaking," and "on an elementary level" are hedges. Such hedges allow us to make statements like "Loosely speaking, whales are fish." A set-theoretic model cannot account for such a statement because no whales are fish. Set-theoretic models such as Meyer's cannot "explain" how statements like these are made.

We cannot say which model is more nearly correct. What is important for educational purposes, however, is the fact that memory research utilizes concepts, or structures similar to concepts, to describe how semantic memory operates. Of course, the point in our studying semantic memory is to attempt to understand how students organize and structure their knowledge. Insights gained into this process should help you do a better job in one of your major roles as a teacher—helping students master new concepts.

The Teaching of Concepts

The learning of concepts is a lifelong endeavor and guidance is important for learners who must master new concepts. Many methods of teaching concepts have been tested over the years.

Woodson (1974) identified the following seven procedures often used in teaching concepts:

1. Giving a definition of the concept
2. Identifying the defining attributes of the concept for the students
3. Identifying the irrelevant attributes of the concept for the students
4. Giving positive examples of the concept to students
5. Giving negative examples of the concept to students
6. Describing the domain of the concept (for example, telling students that "this concept has to do with size")
7. Giving the students analogies for the concept

Woodson taught a group of students several concepts, each according to one of the seven procedures. The students were tested for mastery in four ways. They were asked to define each concept, to give positive examples of each, to give negative examples of each, and to classify ten new items as positive or negative examples of each concept. The results showed that providing the defining attributes of concepts and giving their definitions were the most effective forms of instruction for all four measures of learning. The least effective means of instruction on all four measures were giving irrelevant attributes and identifying negative examples of the concepts.

Defining attributes of any concept should be made as clear as possible. Here the teacher has a relatively easy job: Some of the attributes of a starfish are there for all the children to see.

APPLICATIONS FOR TEACHING

The six-step process for teaching concepts that we present in this chapter stresses a combination of several of the procedures tested by Woodson.

1. Present the students with a well-prepared instructional objective. As we discuss in detail in Chapter Eleven, the first step in all instruction is the clear communication of what is to be learned.

2. Dispense with all the unnecessary attributes of a concept. As in our examples of the cup, ring, and pencil, only the defining attributes of concepts should be stressed at the beginning of instruction. Take the concept you are going to teach and list all the attributes you think describe it. Then determine which attributes actually define the concept.

3. Help students acquire language that will ensure the meaningfulness of new learning. If the learners do not have the necessary vocabulary to learn the concept, you must first teach the language. New concepts are built on old concepts. Understanding of new concepts (such as "amerce") is unlikely unless the concepts are defined and explained in terms of existing concepts ("amerce" means "to punish").

4. Present the learners with both positive and negative examples of the concept. If you were teaching the concept "reptile," you might present some reptiles (positive examples) and some nonreptiles (negative examples).* You would then point out or ask leading questions to elicit student identification of defining attributes. You would also give students practice with feedback in discriminating defining and nondefining attributes.

The use of many positive and negative examples enables students to differentiate between those things that are classed into a concept and those that are not. It is also very helpful to have students provide examples from their own experiences. This increases students' depth of processing and helps them fit the new information into already existing memory structures.

5. Allow the students to participate actively in the lesson and provide feedback for their responses. Students cannot obtain the best possible practice—trying out their learning to see if it is correct or incorrect—without participating and receiving feedback, which in this case is information about how well they have learned. Students who are not completely sure whether a small furry animal is a mammal need to try out their thinking and to have you react to it.

6. Evaluate the learning of the concept. We are not finished with instruction until we determine how well our students have mastered the concepts. Most instructors hope that students acquire more than just a verbal definition of a concept. Simply defining a word is a low level of concept use. Instead, we expect students to be able to recognize examples and nonexamples of concepts and to use concepts in their thinking. Evaluation should be planned accordingly.

*Positive examples are usually more important than negative examples (E. S. Johnson, 1978). In the case of reptiles, pictures or descriptions are preferable to a room full of animals, although you might be able to obtain lizards or small snakes in the spring and fall. Nonreptilian animals such as goldfish, frogs, mice, and birds can probably also be obtained fairly readily; some of your students may have them as pets.

Examples of Teaching Concepts

Mr. Jones teaches many concepts to his sixth grade students during the year. Let's examine how he taught some of his students the concept of "levee" by following our six-step process.

Mr. Jones started his lesson by providing his students with a set of objectives. Among them was the following: "You will be able to correctly identify eight out of ten objects as levees or nonlevees on your next quiz." Mr. Jones's second step was to reduce the number of attributes of "levee" to the least possible. He did this by defining "levee" as "an embankment raised to prevent a river from overflowing." The attributes were use (preventing a river from overflowing) and form (an embankment). So "levee" was a simple conjunctive concept with two defining attributes.

In order to make sure that his students had the necessary vocabulary to learn the concept, he wrote the words "levee" and "embankment" on the chalkboard and asked the students to pronounce them. All his students could say "levee" very easily. Some, in fact, began to break into songs about levees before he could proceed with his lesson. Stopping the singers, he then spent some time on the term "embankment" to be sure that everyone understood this concept.

To follow the fourth step of the process, Mr. Jones showed the class some large photographs

PRACTICE EXERCISE 3–3

Planning for Teaching a Concept

This exercise consists of two stages: (1) observing concept teaching in one of your classes and (2) planning for your own teaching of a concept. As a first step, we would like you to use the following form and observe concept teaching in a classroom. Any class is acceptable, but it would be best to observe a class in the subject area and grade level you will teach.

1. Type of class and grade level of students:

2. Concept being taught was ______________________________.

3. Was the concept defined? ________ If so, how?

4. What relevant (defining) attributes of the concept were presented?

5. What examples of the concept were given?

   Were they good examples? ______

6. Were nonexamples given? ______ If so, were they helpful? ______

7. From the presentation you observed, estimate the percentage of students who could:

   ______ write a definition of the concept

   ______ recognize almost every example of the concept

   ______ explain the concept clearly to another student

8. Give an overall rating of the effectiveness of the concept teaching you saw:

representing both positive and negative examples of the concept of "levee." As he presented each card he reminded the students that they were looking for objects that were embankments built for the purpose of preventing a river from overflowing. The first picture was a photograph taken of a mound of earth being bulldozed up against a small river. Mr. Jones asked his class if this picture was a levee. The class responded that it was, although several students pointed out that the bulldozer might be building something else and had incidentally piled up the earth along the river. He then held the picture closer to those students so they could see the embankment receding into the distance along the river. They then decided it was a levee. Mr. Jones complimented the class on its responses and went on to describe the process of building a levee. Here he was getting at another instructional objective—the effects of new construction on wildlife habitats.

Mr. Jones then showed pictures of several examples and nonexamples of levees: a dam, a bridge abutment, a bridge under construction,

---

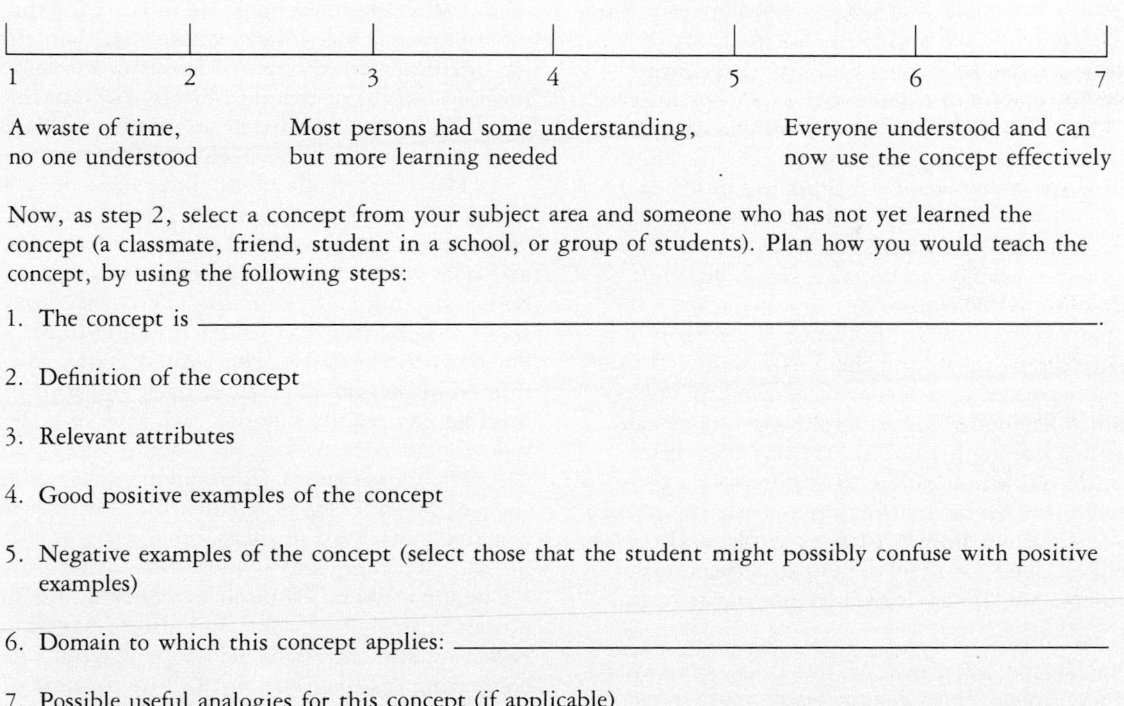

1	2	3	4	5	6	7
A waste of time, no one understood		Most persons had some understanding, but more learning needed			Everyone understood and can now use the concept effectively	

Now, as step 2, select a concept from your subject area and someone who has not yet learned the concept (a classmate, friend, student in a school, or group of students). Plan how you would teach the concept, by using the following steps:

1. The concept is ______________________________.
2. Definition of the concept
3. Relevant attributes
4. Good positive examples of the concept
5. Negative examples of the concept (select those that the student might possibly confuse with positive examples)
6. Domain to which this concept applies: ______________________________
7. Possible useful analogies for this concept (if applicable)

If possible, go ahead and teach the concept. Use the kind of questions you used in your observation of concept teaching to have your pupil give you feedback on how well you presented the concept and how well he or she understood.

sandbag levees, a pier, rock levees, boat ramps, ski ramps, and other assorted constructions along rivers and other bodies of water. He continually had the students respond to the pictures while he provided feedback.* He also asked students to give examples from their own experiences.

Toward the end of the period, Mr. Jones had presented several positive and negative examples of levees in addition to his instruction on ecological concerns. To quickly evaluate student learning, he passed out a brief quiz that consisted of hand-drawn pictures of several positive and negative examples of levees. The students were instructed to label the items as levees or nonlevees. He then had the students score their own papers as he called out the correct responses. He answered a few questions requiring a "judgment call" and then, on the basis of looking over the papers quickly, determined that his class had mastered the concept of levee.

This example is a relatively simple one. It is easy to think of positive and negative examples of levees. Many other concepts are much more difficult to teach and require considerably more effort on the part of the teacher and the learner. A good example can be taken from an adult's self-initiated learning.

Let's suppose that Mr. Jones is a person of many interests, among them astronomy. A budding stargazer and reader of astronomy books, he has decided to build a telescope so he can further pursue his hobby. He has chosen to build a telescope rather than purchase a completed one for several reasons—cost, the chance to learn about how telescopes work, and the general need for involvement in a meaningful project. Mr. Jones, however, has never been exposed to formal instruction in the areas of physics, optics, or astronomy.

As Mr. Jones pores over several telescope catalogs, it becomes apparent that he must better understand several concepts before he can make an intelligent decision about purchasing a telescope kit. Among the concepts he must refine are those of refracting and reflecting telescopes.

Mr. Jones sets an informal objective for himself: "to be able to completely understand refracting and reflecting telescopes." Then he determines the defining attributes of refracting and reflecting telescopes by going to his local library and checking out several books and pamphlets. He then reads through the simplest materials he could find and he determines that a refracting telescope uses lenses to bend and focus light while reflecting telescopes use mirrors for the same purpose. Mr. Jones can see that the defining attributes are the use of lenses or mirrors for forming images of distant objects. He rehearses this information to himself so that he will have it available any time he needs it.

As Mr. Jones reads more about telescopes, he learns many different concepts ("focal length," "resolution," and so on) and with them he builds a broader vocabulary. He sees varied examples of both reflecting and refracting telescopes, from small ones he might consider building to Mt. Palomar, the largest in the United States. He flips from picture to picture, back and forth, until he can readily identify each type of telescope.

As Mr. Jones studies, he frequently asks questions of himself. He is not just the learner—he is actively involved in many other ways as the initiator, teacher, and evaluator of his lesson. He finally evaluates himself by checking his definitions against the books' and also by sketching reflecting and refracting telescope diagrams and comparing his diagrams with those in some of his books. Mr. Jones easily learns the new concepts and after a few more weeks of study he is ready to try his hand at building a telescope. He elects, incidentally, to construct a reflector.

*You should notice that Mr. Jones was doing what all teachers do—blending the teaching of several concepts into one lesson. While the concept of "levee" was being taught he was also describing other waterway constructions and making points about ecological concerns.

ORGANIZING PERSONAL STUDY TO IMPROVE MEMORY

Understanding the process of memory and the process of forgetting allows teachers to adapt techniques to help their students more effectively learn and remember new information. A method of study described by Frank Robinson in his book *Effective Study* (1972) fits well within our current knowledge about memory. Robinson's method has been demonstrated to be successful in helping students above the elementary level learn more effectively. We have found it to be especially effective for independent study assignments such as reading this book. It can be taught to students to improve their memory of what they study and to increase the quality of their learning of concepts and principles. As you look over the steps listed below, you will see that they are designed to help make new information meaningful to students, to keep students actively involved in learning, and to provide occasions for practicing newly learned information.

Step 1: Survey. When any new material is to be learned, the first step is to survey it—to look it over—to familiarize yourself with the objectives of the information to be learned and to determine exactly what your task is and is not. You are seeking to make the task meaningful in the sense in which we have described meaningful learning. You can probably best complete the survey step by looking over the chapter you are about to read and reading its objectives, headings, and summary. This will tie the chapter's information to your past experience.

Step 2: Question. The questioning step helps you become actively involved with the material. As you look over the chapter, convert the headings and subheadings into open questions. Also ask yourself questions about the content: What is the author trying to accomplish with this chapter? How does the information in this chapter tie into things I already know? What experiences have I had that are related to the information in the chapter? The idea is to specify your own objectives as questions and to relate the new materials to what you have already learned. This step greatly increases the meaningfulness of new information and gets you actively involved with it. It also helps you learn to anticipate test questions.

Step 3: Read. The chapter must be read and processed. As you read you should try to answer the questions you formulated in step 2.

Step 4: Recite. As soon as you finish reading a section you should stop and try to answer the questions you asked about it. This active practice helps you give meaning to the passage by stating answers to questions in your own words and relating the material to previously learned information.

Step 5: Review. The review process saves some time because it does not require you to reread all the material you have studied. Rather, you focus on materials related to questions you found difficult and study the difficult portions of the material until you can answer the questions you raised. This step serves as your evaluation of learning and provides additional practice in those places where you need it.

The mnemonic that will help you remember this process is SQ3R: *S*urvey, *Q*uestion, *R*ead, *R*ecite, and *R*eview. Not only can you use this process to enhance your study skills, you can also teach it to others. Your future students can benefit as much from instruction and practice in study skills as you can.

PRACTICE EXERCISE 3–4

Teaching Yourself a Concept

As an adult, you will spend much of your life teaching yourself new concepts. Choose a concept you would like to learn and teach it to yourself following the steps listed below. Place your responses in the spaces indicated. Keep in mind that we seldom learn new concepts out of context; that is, when you are learning new things you will likely learn many new concepts just as Mr. Jones did when he was learning about telescopes.

1. Set an informal objective to master a new concept.
2. Determine the defining attributes of the concept.
3. If you need to learn new vocabulary, indicate what vocabulary you need to learn.
4. Identify several positive and negative examples of the concept. List them here and note how they affect your learning of the concept.
5. Describe specifically how you learned about the concept (other than your reading).
6. What did you do to evaluate the results of your learning? Do you now have the level of understanding of the concept that you need?

SUMMARY

In this chapter we outlined theories of human memory, examining decay theory, interference theory, and information-processing theories. The study of memory led us to a series of guidelines to apply in teaching and studying.

Memory is systematically organized, and the central feature of semantic memory is the concept. Concepts were defined as were their attributes and defining attributes. The way in which concepts are organized in memory was examined by reviewing two models of semantic memory—the network model and the set-theoretic model. A six-step process for teaching concepts was described together with a general study method—survey, question, read, recite, and review (SQ3R).

As we have emphasized in our introduction to cognition in Chapter Two, meaningfulness is a key feature in human memory and concept learning. In Chapter Two we examined the role of meaning in perception, attention, and working memory. Here we devoted our discussion to critical aspects of the repository of knowledge about the world—the long-term memory—that allow people to assign meaning. In Chapter Four we devote our attention primarily to how new and existing information about the world is employed in the working memory. The process we examine is a particularly important one—problem solving.

Suggested Readings

Ceraso, J. The interference theory of forgetting. *Scientific American,* 1967, *217,* 117–124.

While somewhat dated, Ceraso's presentation of interference theory is one of the most lucid descriptions of this theory available.

Craik, F. I. M., & Lockhart, R. S. Levels of processing: A framework for memory research. *Journal of Verbal Learning and Verbal Behavior,* 1972, *11,* 671–684.

This classic article first set out the "levels" position. The ideas in this paper have stimulated a significant amount of research on memory.

Klatzky, R. L. *Human memory: Structures and processes.* San Francisco: Freeman, 1980.

Klatzky's book is an excellent introduction to the study of memory. Her book is highly readable and designed for the beginner yet it provides highly detailed information.

Loftus, G. R., & Loftus, E. F. *Human memory: The processing of information.* New York: Wiley, 1977.

The Loftuses provide an excellent overview of modern views of memory in this book.

Robinson, R. *Effective Study.* New York: Macmillan, 1972.
Robinson's book has long been viewed as one of the best sources of ideas and strategies for improving study. This is an especially good book to use in brushing up on your own study skills.

Answers to Practice Exercise 3–2

1. encloses other objects, nonrigid
2. tells time
3. uses heat, separates chemical substances
4. staged play, major part of story conveyed by song
5. popular vote, decides public issue
6. immediately above another object, not touching other object
7. alienated, removed from
8. agreement, pleasant arrangement

As you can see, the defining attributes of these concepts vary from very simple to moderately complex. If you want to consider one that is really complex, try to obtain your class's consensus on the defining attributes of "love."

IMPORTANT EVENTS IN THE STUDY OF MEMORY

Date(s)	*Person(s)*	*Work*	*Impact*
1885	Ebbinghaus	"Über das Gedächtnis"	First experimental work on memory was conducted by Ebbinghaus. He also developed the use of "nonsense" syllables for learning experiments so that subjects' background knowledge would not affect experimental results.
1890	James	*Principles of psychology*	William James's was the first scientific theory of memory (Bourne et al., 1979). He anticipated later views of short- and long-term memory.
1913	Thorndike	*Educational psychology*	With his law of effect and law of exercise, E. L. Thorndike provided renewed interest in the decay theory of memory.
1924	Jenkins & Dallenbach	"Oblivescence during sleep and waking"	J. G. Jenkins and K. M. Dallenbach provided data supporting the interference theory of memory that began the disproof of the decay theory.
1932	McGeoch	"Forgetting and the law of disuse"	J. A. McGeoch introduced modern interference theory and discussed the effects of retroactive interference from the position of competing responses.
1940	Melton & Irwin	"The influence of degree of interpolated learning on retroactive inhibition and the overt transfer of specific responses"	J. W. Melton and J. M. Irwin discovered "factor *X*" in retroactive interference. Factor *X* was the amount of retroactive interference not attributable to competition between new learning and old learning. Melton and Irwin postulated that factor *X* was an "unlearning" factor; that is, some retroactive interference is due to the actual unlearning of the material.
1949	Mauchley, Ekert, & Von Neuman	First computer with stored programs	This advance allowed psychologists to view memory from the perspective of a computer model complete with working and long-term memories.

Date(s)	*Person(s)*	*Work*	*Impact*
1949	Shannon & Weaver	*The mathematical theory of communication*	C. E. Shannon and W. Weaver developed an information theory that demonstrated that information could be quantified.
1956	Miller	"The magical number seven, plus or minus two"	George Miller studied the capacity of short-term memory. He coined the term *chunk* to "denote that which short-term store can hold about seven of" (Loftus & Loftus, 1977). The chunk, which is anything with a unitary representation in memory, can range in size from a single character (such as the letter *G*) to the gist of a sentence.
1957	Underwood	"Interference and forgetting"	While proactive interference had been observed in research for many years, it was thought to be a minor factor in forgetting. B. J. Underwood's paper demonstrated (through early use of "meta-analysis") that proactive interference was a powerful factor in most memory research.
1965	Waugh & Norman	"Primary memory"	N. C. Waugh and D. A. Norman developed one of the first two-stage (short-term/long-term) models of memory.
1968	Atkinson & Shiffrin	"Human memory: A proposed system and its control processes"	R. C. Atkinson and R. M. Shiffrin provided the first information-processing model of memory that emphasized "control" processes.
1974	Jenkins	"Remember that old theory of memory? Well, forget it!"	A series of studies culminating in a contextualist view of human memory was conducted by J. J. Jenkins and his associates. He postulated that the context of events (including the learner and his or her current state and background) determined the

Date(s)	*Person(s)*	*Work*	*Impact*
			learner's ability to remember. Contextualist approaches are important to current memory theory.
1972	Tulving	"Episodic and semantic memory"	Endel Tulving was the first to formally distinguish between episodic and semantic memories.
1972–present	Craik	Levels of processing/distinctiveness of encoding theory and research	In ways similar to Jenkins, Fergus Craik and his associates broke with the "black box" models of memory and viewed memory from an interactionist perspective. The memorability of an event was determined by its distinctiveness from background information or by the extent to which the meaning of information was processed. With Jenkins's contextualist approach, the levels perspective dominates current views of memory.

Chapter Four

PROBLEM SOLVING

Problems and the search for solutions to them are a part of every person's life. Historically, teachers have aspired to teach their students to "reason," to "think," and to be "responsible citizens." Even critics of schools who want a return to the basics do not dispute these goals. They may differ in how such goals should be achieved, but not on the centrality of these goals for education.

A common theme runs through all these goals: education should prepare students for dealing with their future life conditions. The eminent educational philosopher John Dewey long ago identified this process of "dealing with life conditions" as **problem solving** (1910). He reasoned that living and learning consisted of confronting and solving series of problems and that every human action (including the decision not to respond) represented a choice among alternatives. Dewey and his followers held that if there were no alternatives or choices—that is to say, no problems—then individuals would probably not learn.

Dewey and other adherents to this view pointed out that while each human act occurs in response to a problem, there is great variation in the solutions people devise. Simply, some solutions are better than others. The goal of education in their eyes becomes that of improving the problem-solving abilities of all students.

We have included this chapter to help you provide your future students with learning experiences that will improve their abilities to deal with life's problems—experiences that will develop their problem-solving abilities. We will discuss the importance of problem-solving skill development in the schools, define problem solving, and place it in a context of the intellectual skills that students must develop. We will then briefly survey some historical approaches to problem solving and examine the information-processing approach to problem solving. Our chapter closes with a section on applications from problem-solving research that pulls together information from throughout the chapter to help you develop skills that will enhance the problem-solving ability of your students.

Objectives

After reading this chapter, you should be able to meet the following objectives.

1. Improve the efficiency of your own problem solving.
2. Solve problems using each of the heuristic methods described in this chapter.
3. Develop a strategy for teaching problem solving to your students.
4. Write a description of the process you follow in solving a problem with an unknown number of solutions. Identify the solution paths, problem spaces, and problem searches you utilize.

PROBLEM SOLVING IN EDUCATION

Problem solving has a prominent position in education (Gagné, 1980). Nutrition teachers require their students to construct menus based on several problem situations—restricted diets, restricted funds, restricted energy use, and so on. Science teachers are well known for mixing problem solving into their courses, with laboratory experiments and other methods. Social studies teachers frequently use methods such as political analyses, courtroom simulations, and model legislative situations to get students to react to problems similar to those in the real world. In fact, most curricula now include problem-solving exercises as an important part of students' experiences. These exercises help students learn to apply problem-solving techniques to the kinds of problems they may someday encounter.

Curricula oriented toward problem solving have been widely used in the United States since the mid-1960s. Programs such as Unified Science and Mathematics for Elementary Schools, the Environmental Studies Project, the Wisconsin Project, the Productive Thinking Program, and the Secondary School Science Project have been well received and generally regarded as effective (Davis, 1973; Education Development Center, 1975; Gagné, 1980). This is not to say that the learning of facts, figures, names, and dates is no longer considered important—students certainly must have a base of knowledge from which to solve problems. However, the application of this knowledge to problems is the real test of any educational program. The experiences you have in this educational psychology course should help you solve teaching problems, for example. In other words, a course is likely to be of little value unless the knowledge in that course leads to a greater understanding of the world, a larger repertoire of problem solutions, and a better set of skills with which you can solve problems.

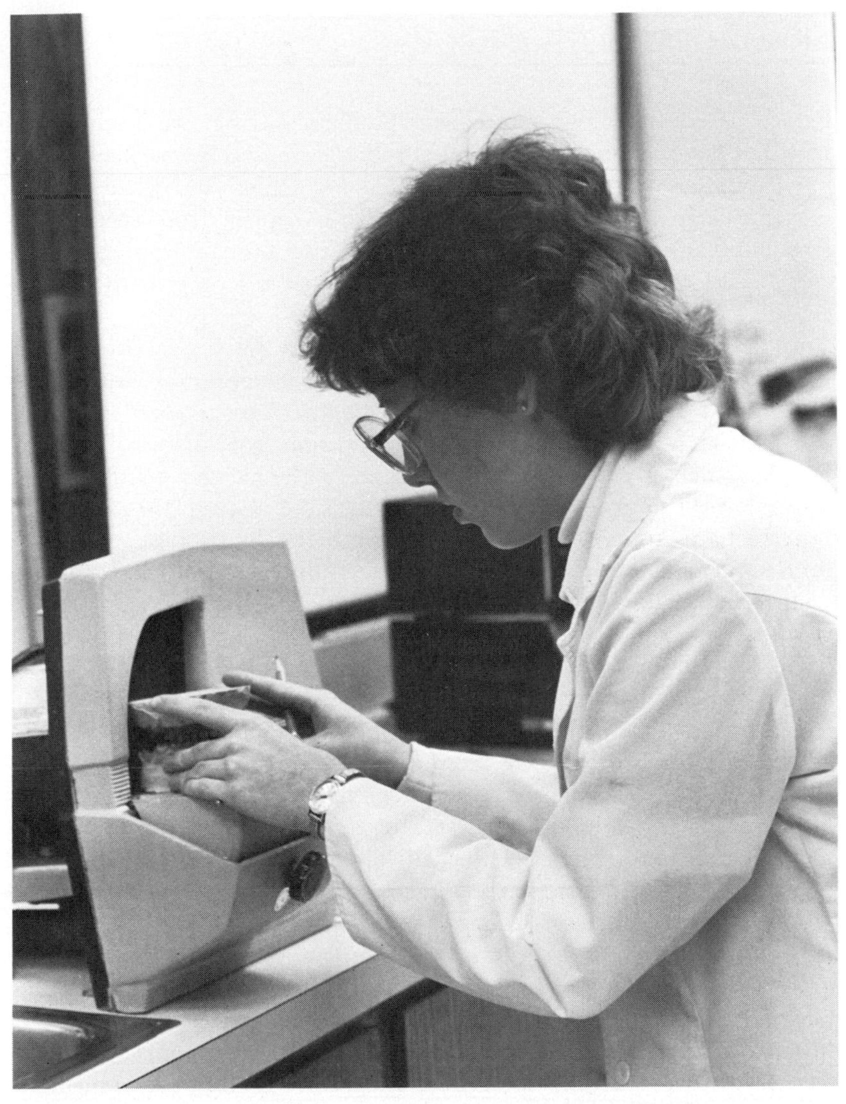

Application of knowledge to problems is the real test of education.

Many students question the relevance of courses in history, calculus, or foreign languages. "What do these courses have to do with my future career?" they ask. The answer is that by stressing the development of problem solving, some seemingly irrelevant courses can result in better problem-solving abilities, regardless of the specific content. One major goal of this chapter is to help you do a better job of structuring your teaching so that your students' problem-solving abilities will be improved.

A DEFINITION OF PROBLEM SOLVING

Before we can say much more about problem solving, we ought to establish what problems and problem solving are. Problems may be defined simply. Any time you want to be doing something else or want to be somewhere else but are unable to make it happen, you have a problem. Problems come in all sizes, shapes, and forms—from getting a date for Saturday night to determining the best teaching methods for a class.

Robert Gagné (1977) has defined problem solving more formally within a framework of cognitive skills. Gagné proposes a **hierarchy**—a set of events or phenomena ordered from simple to complex—of cognitive skills. In Gagné's learning hierarchy more sophisticated forms of learning (such as problem solving) depend on the mastery of subordinate (lower-level) cognitive skills (see Table 4–1).

The basic forms of learning in Gagné's hierarchy are best understood from a behavioral perspective. We will examine signal learning, associations, and chains of behavior in detail in Chapter Seven. The higher forms of learning in Gagné's hierarchy are helpful in tying together the cognitive functions described in Chapters Two and Three with a definition of problem solving.

Gagné defines problem solving as **rule-governed behavior**, suggesting that problem solving requires people to combine rules (or principles, as discussed in Chapter Three) to form high-order rules (or higher-order principles). When applied, these principles solve the problem. As you recall from Chapter Three, rules or principles are formed when two or more concepts are joined into a statement relating the concepts. Gagné further suggests that the learning of concepts is dependent on a lower level of learning, discrimination learning, which is a process akin to perception as described in Chapter Two. Hence, from Gagné's perspective problem solving is the most sophisticated form of learning. Discriminations, concepts, and rules or principles must be learned prior to learning the higher-order rules that allow problem solution. Clearly, Gagné would suggest that each of the components in a model such as the one we presented in Chapter Two is involved in problem solving.

An example of a simple problem should help you see what Gagné means by rule-governed behavior. Examine the drawing in Figure 4–1. As you can see, there are six squares of equal size. Now move any three lines in the drawing to make it into a drawing containing five squares. You must use the three lines you move in other places and leave no unclosed squares. The answer is pictured in Figure 4–2.

In order to solve the six squares problem you must be able to apply

TABLE 4–1
Gagné's Hierarchy of Cognitive Skills

Skills	*Description of Skill*	*Examples*
Basic Forms of Learning		
Signal learning	Making a general, diffuse response to a signal (stimulus)	A queasy feeling on seeing a hypodermic needle; mouth watering at the sight of a lemon
Associations	Connecting a stimulus with a particular response	Accelerating at a green light; becoming quiet when the school bell rings
Motor chains	Connecting a series of stimuli and responses in a physical action	Using a pay phone (entering the booth, depositing the coin, dialing the number); starting your car
Verbal chains	Verbally connecting a series of stimuli and responses	Correctly repeating the pronunciation of the phrase "et c'était comme ça"; naming the alphabet
Higher Forms of Learning		
Discrimination learning	Making distinctions among stimuli and responding appropriately to each	Correctly naming the Russian letters **Б**, **Д**, **Ф**; stopping at a red light but not at a green one
Concept learning	Organizing and identifying stimuli on the basis of abstract similarities	Learning the meaning of the words *octroi, tabard, atelier;* identifying breeds of dogs or makes of cars
Rule (principle) learning	Combining two or more concepts with a relational statement, such as "If *A*, then *B*"	Predicting changes in pitch from changes in length of a vibrating string; pouring two paint colors together to achieve a desired color
Problem solving	The combination of two or more rules into a new form which allows problems to be solved	Escaping from jail; correctly answering the question "If 60 widgets cost $51, how much do 80 of them cost?"; designing a footbridge over a creek

FIGURE 4–1
The Six Squares Problem

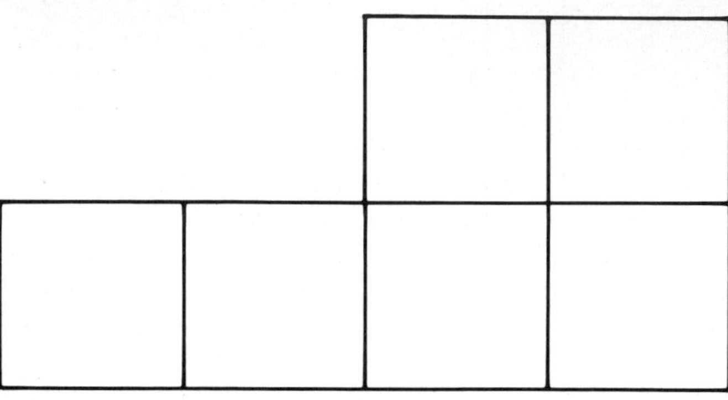

rules about squares and drawings to the situation. Specifically, you must use the higher-order rule that some lines in such figures serve only one purpose (that is, they close off one side of a square) while other lines serve two purposes (they form the sides of two different squares at once). It is also necessary to analyze the problem directions to see what is allowed. Nothing in the directions forbids the construction of a square standing alone. The original arrangement is most often a misleading cue for attempting to develop adjoining squares, which leads to difficulty in solving the problem.

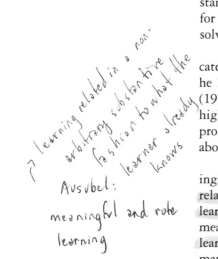

David Ausubel has also emphasized problem solving as a sophisticated form of learning (1963, 1964, 1966; Ausubel et al., 1978), but he has characterized it somewhat differently from Gagné's formulations (1977). Like Gagné, however, Ausubel considers problem solving the highest form of cognitive activity. To fully appreciate Ausubel's view of problem solving, it is necessary to examine some distinctions he makes about kinds of learning.

Ausubel distinguishes between meaningful and rote learning. Meaningful learning, he says, takes place when the "learning task can be related in a nonarbitrary, substantive (nonverbatim) fashion to what the learner already knows" (Ausubel et al., 1978, p. 27). The opposite of meaningful learning is rote learning, which is not related to what the learner already knows. As an example of rote learning, music students may memorize several lines of lyrics in French without having any understanding of what they have learned. To a student in a French class, however, the words are meaningful. They can be related to prior knowledge and their meaning can be understood.

A second distinction made by Ausubel is between receptive and discovery learning. Ausubel describes receptive learning as learning in which all new material is presented to students in its final form—the students need not discover anything. In contrast, discovery learning requires students to build their knowledge through processes of inquiry. The concept stressed in discovery learning must be "discovered by the learner before it can be meaningfully incorporated into the students' cognitive structures" (Ausubel et al., 1978, p. 24).

Receptive learning takes place in a lecture class in which students have no interaction with the teacher. Discovery learning can be seen in a guided classroom discussion in which the teacher helps students discover concepts and principles on their own. In exploring the topic of supply and demand economics, for example, a teacher can provide information that will allow students to discover for themselves that prices for commodities are tied to supply and demand. For Ausubel, problem solving is meaningful discovery learning in which prior knowledge plays an important role.

Both Gagné and Ausubel, then, view problem solving as a complex and important process. Characterizing problem solving as a highly sophisticated form of learning, however, still leaves some very important questions. How do people solve problems? What exactly is the process of problem solving? To try to answer these questions, we will first look at three historically important approaches to problem solving. We will then examine an approach that has been developed more recently, the information-processing approach.

FIGURE 4–2
Solution to the Six Squares Problem

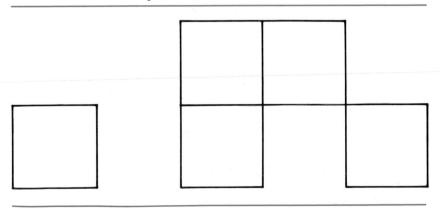

PRACTICE EXERCISE 4–1
Identifying Levels of Learning

Ten activities are described below. If students perform the activity as described, what is the highest level of learning you can be *sure of?* Make your choices from among the following three levels related to Gagné's hierarchy.

a. At least a verbal chain has been acquired.
b. At least a concept or a principle has been acquired.
c. Problem solving based on concepts and principles has occurred.

______ 1. On a test in music theory, a college student writes a correct definition of "polyphonic."

______ 2. A student teacher designs a system for classroom management that is based on principles of cognitive and behavioral psychology.

______ 3. Given a mixed list of nouns and verbs she hasn't seen before, a primary-level child identifies the nouns in the list without error.

______ 4. On a weekly test, a senior science student answers the following question: "About how many quads of energy were consumed in the United States in 1982"?

______ 5. Given the following new information, a student predicts how economic demand will be affected, other factors being equal: Kansas watermelons are succumbing to diseases induced by pollution from nearby tractors.

______ 6. Given a political cartoon he has not seen before, a student identifies the events illustrated in the cartoon.

______ 7. On a quiz, a student lists the six principles of cognitive psychology applied to teaching.

______ 8. In analyzing a poem, a student correctly points out several elements the poet has used to convey a particular mood.

______ 9. On a field trip, a sixth grader correctly labels specimens of at least five different kinds of trees.

______ 10. A senior debate student can point out two or more examples of distortion of data and logical fallacies in an excerpt of a speech delivered by a state official.

E. L. Thorndike's Trial-and-Error Approach to Problem Solving

E. L. Thorndike (1879–1949) was one of the earliest and perhaps the greatest learning theorist of all time. His interests were far ranging, spanning almost all areas of contemporary educational psychology. In his lifetime Thorndike published 507 books, journal articles, and monographs. His influence on early American psychology was so great that Edward Tolman, an eminent learning theorist in his own right, suggested that the "psychology of learning . . . has been and still is a matter of agreeing or disagreeing with Thorndike" (1938, p. 11).

In his most famous series of experiments, Thorndike (1898, 1906, 1911) placed cats (and less well remembered dogs) in wooden cages. The cages were constructed in various ways, typically with a handle sticking up from the center of the cage so that any firm touch on the handle would open a door and allow escape (see Figure 4–3). Thorndike ar-

FIGURE 4–3
Thorndike's Puzzle Box

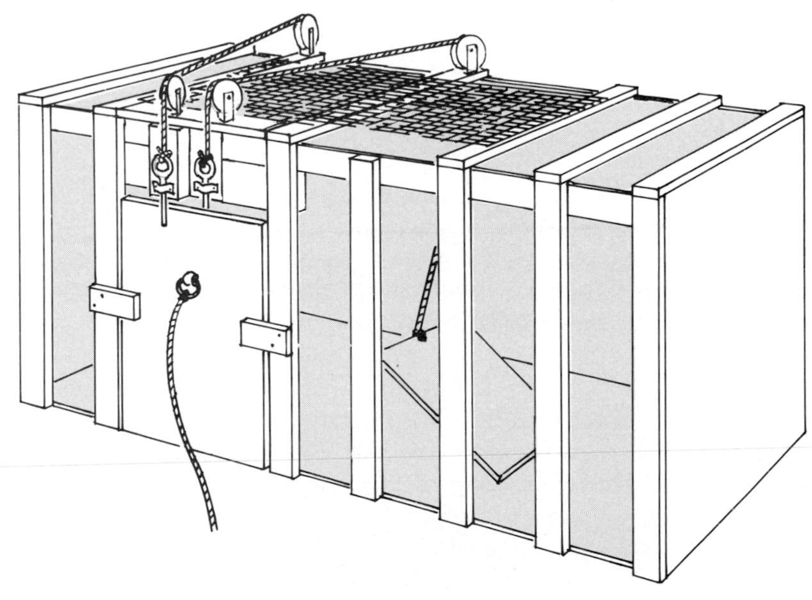

Source: E. L. Thorndike, Animal intelligence. *Psychological Review Monographs,* Supplement 2, #8, 1898. Copyright 1898 by the American Psychological Association. Adapted by permission of the American Psychological Association.

ranged events so that the cats were hungry when placed in the cage and food was available to them if they could figure out how to get out of the cage. The situation the cats found themselves in, of course, fits our definition of a problem—being in one situation, wanting (presumably) to be in another, but not knowing how to get there.

Thorndike observed the cats carefully and kept detailed records of their movements as they tried to escape. He noted that the cats would try several behaviors until they hit the handle by accident. He further noted on repeated trials that the cats made their escapes more and more quickly. Ultimately, when the cats were placed in the cage they would almost immediately perform the handle-pushing behavior that got them out of the cage during previous trials. The cats' actions led Thorndike to explain such problem solving—and all learning, for that matter—as **trial-and-error** learning.

From his experiments with cats, Thorndike concluded that their learning was incremental (that improvement was gradual, coming in small bits and pieces). He further suggested that their problem solving was not directed by thinking or reasoning:

> The cat does not look over the situation, much less think it over, and then decide what to do. It bursts out at once into the activities which instinct and experience have settled on as suitable reactions to the situation, "confinement when hungry with food outside." It does not ever in the course of its success realize that such an act brings food and therefore decide to do it and henceforth do it immediately from decision instead of impulse. *(1898, p. 45)*

Thorndike was later to argue that all mammals, including humans, learned and solved problems in much the same way (1911, 1913). For Thorndike, human problem solving was similar to that of lower organisms in that it was built on trial and error, it was incremental, and it proceeded without thinking or reasoning.

John Dewey's Pragmatic Approach to Problem Solving

While John Dewey is best known as a philosopher of education, he spent several years at the turn of the century immersed in the development of the functionalist school of psychology (Chaplin & Krawiec, 1979). As we discussed in Chapter Two, functionalists were concerned with developing techniques in psychology and education that would be applicable to real-world problems (Carr, 1925; Chaplin & Krawiec, 1979). This emphasis on the application of psychology to education was apparent in all of Dewey's work and definitely influenced his thoughts about problem solving.

From his many observations, Dewey described a sequence of steps that effective problem solvers followed (1910, 1933). These steps are still used in the development of programs to teach people various aspects of problem solving (see Clark, Gelatt, & Levine, 1965; Dixon, 1976; Dixon, Heppner, Petersen, & Ronning, 1979; D'Zurilla & Goldfried, 1971; Heppner, 1978; Urban & Ford, 1971).

Problem solving can be viewed as a set of steps.

Presentation of the Problem. Clearly, problem solutions cannot occur unless individuals are presented with problems. In this step, two kinds of directions are taken by psychologists who work with the development of problem-solving skills (Dixon et al., 1979). First, in training oriented toward solving personal problems, emphasis is placed on helping people become aware of problems they may not have previously noticed. Second, in more formal problem-solving training, emphasis is placed on the teacher's role in clearly presenting problems. The teacher must ensure that all the information necessary to solve a problem is either presented to students or has been previously mastered by them.

Problem Definition. Defining the problem is crucial to solving it. Almost any problem can be defined in several ways, and each definition is likely to lead to different attempts to solve the problem. Training in problem solving stresses students' abilities to define problems in as many ways as possible to provide the widest array of subsequent activities that will lead to problem solutions (Dixon et al., 1979). An example of such problem solving can be seen in a person who wants but cannot afford a new stereo. Is this problem one of making more money, saving more money, altering attitudes toward a new stereo, or obtaining credit? The problem can be defined in each of these ways and each definition would lead to different actions on the part of the problem solver. Certainly, helping students visualize many ways of solving problems has a greater chance of leading them to satisfactory solutions (Dixon et al., 1979).

Development of Hypotheses. Once a problem is defined, the next step is to make as many hypotheses as possible for solving the problem. The more hypotheses or alternatives a person generates, the greater the chances that a satisfactory solution will be found. Procedures for facilitating the generation of alternatives are described in Chapter Six.

Testing Hypotheses. Generating a large number of hypotheses for solving a problem places problem solvers in the position of having to choose among the hypotheses. That is, if a student develops several hypotheses for obtaining a stereo, he or she will have to settle on one of the alternatives. For this reason, psychologists who train students in problem-solving skills emphasize the testing and evaluation of hypotheses (Heppner, 1978) in terms of the potential benefits they provide and their possible drawbacks. As most of the problems students encounter (choosing a major, finding a date, purchasing a stereo, and the like) can be solved in a variety of ways, possible solutions should be carefully explored before a decision is made.

Selection of the Best Hypothesis. Once a person has evaluated the possible ways in which a problem can be solved, he or she should choose the most attractive hypothesis. Psychologists stress the use of decision-making skills in this step of the problem-solving process (see Dixon, 1976; Dixon et al., 1979; D'Zurilla & Goldfried, 1971). Typically, students are asked to weigh the advantages and disadvantages of each possible hypothesis and to select the hypothesis that promises the greatest advantages.

Insight: A Gestalt View of Problem Solving

As we saw in Chapter Two, Gestalt psychology arose in the early part of the twentieth century in reaction to structuralism and functionalism. Not surprisingly, the Gestalt view of problem solving was quite different from that of either Thorndike or Dewey. Wolfgang Köhler, the founder of Gestalt psychology most concerned with problem solving, suggested that problems bring about a cognitive imbalance in people, an imbalance that they seek to resolve. That is, problems spur people into action until the problems are solved and cognitive balance is achieved. Köhler also suggested that people ponder problems, examining all the parts of problem situations, until they suddenly see solutions in flashes of insight. Köhler disagreed strongly with Thorndike's view that problem solving was a trial-and-error process. He argued that there are no intermediate, incremental steps and that problems are either solved or unsolved with no points in between.

Köhler based his writings largely on a famous series of experiments he conducted using apes (1925).* The animals were placed in problem situations where available objects, if properly used, could be employed to achieve a solution to the problem. In one of these experiments fruit was suspended from the wire roof of the cage in such a manner that it could be reached only by stacking up several boxes scattered on the cage floor. The purpose was to see if the apes would use the materials available to them to obtain the fruit (see Figure 4–4).

In general, Köhler's apes behaved in ways that could be called insightful. When the apes found solutions, these solutions appeared to be sudden and complete. Köhler extended his hypotheses to human beings (as supported originally by Alpert, 1928, in a study with human children) and found basically the same results. We can summarize the Gestalt description of problem solving and contrast it with Thorndike's and Dewey's descriptions as follows.

*Not as well remembered is the fact that Köhler also did problem-solving research with chickens. Apparently apes were better for demonstrating insight than were chickens!

FIGURE 4–4
Insight: An Ape Solving a Problem

Source: Courtesy of the Yerkes Regional Primate Research Center of Emory University.

Identification of the Problem. Like Dewey, Köhler suggested that a problem had to be recognized before any action could take place. Thorndike's position, of course, also included the presentation or recognition of a problem as the beginning point in the search for problem solutions.

Incubation Period. Köhler's observations led him to conclude that problem solvers engaged in considerable thought during early phases of problem solving. This incubation or presolution period, Köhler felt, was characterized by the problem solver mentally trying out a number of possible solutions. Such cognitive activity, of course, was denied in Thorndike's view of problem solving. It fit well, however, with Dewey's description of the hypotheses-generation and testing steps, although Dewey was less concerned with specific cognitive functions.

Insight. When a correct hypothesis was hit upon during the incubation period, the solution occurred suddenly and completely. Köhler called this understanding of problem solutions *insight*. Here Köhler was in direct conflict with Thorndike's trial-and-error approach, but he was again not far afield from Dewey. Dewey, however, did not directly concern himself with the concept of insight in problem solving (1910, 1933).

Memorability of Insightful Solutions. Köhler believed that problem solutions achieved through insight were extremely memorable. The memorability of problem solutions was not described by Thorndike; Dewey felt that the problem solver had to work to retain the solution for possible future use.

Generalization of Insightful Solutions. For Köhler, as for Dewey, the generalization of knowledge was important. Köhler considered generalization a natural outcome of insight, while Dewey thought more effort was required on the part of the problem solver. Thorndike also discussed generalization but from a perspective that did not include cognition.

The Gestalt view of problem solving is compatible with that of Dewey, although it clearly places much more emphasis on cognitive factors such as incubation and insight. There is much less agreement between the Gestalt view and Thorndike's. For Gestalt psychologists, problem solving and all human learning were seen as insightful, all-or-none, and controlled almost totally by thinking.

Current Approaches to Problem Solving

In recent years psychologists following an information-processing approach have developed computer models of human problem solving. These models and the research they have generated have given rise to many ideas about how the human mind operates during problem solving. Information-processing psychologists believe the most important facet of problem solving is the construction of a problem representation (see Hayes, 1978).

To construct a **problem representation** a person must understand four aspects of a problem: (1) the initial state, (2) the goal state, (3) the operators, and (4) precisely how the operators are restricted or unrestricted. The initial state is the situation in which a person finds himself or herself when a problem is recognized. Suppose you are playing chess and your opponent makes a move and places your king in check. A complete understanding of your current position in the game is essential to solving your problem. Many college students have trouble deciding on their major. A successful resolution of this problem depends in large part on their ability to understand their initial state, in this case their academic strengths and weaknesses, financial position, likes and dislikes, knowledge about professions, and so on. Clearly, the more adequately students understand their initial state, the more effective they will be at solving problems.

The goal state is simply the outcome a problem solver seeks. Clearly understanding the goal you want to reach is extremely important. The chess example presents a relatively straightforward goal state—taking the king out of check. The problem of choosing a major is a different matter. Students' goals are often not clearly defined, and it is thus very difficult for them to determine what actions to take in choosing a major. When goals are clearly understood, the paths a person can take become much more explicit.

goals must be understood before potential paths can be chosen.

In addition to an understanding of the initial and goal states, a good problem representation includes an understanding of the operators, which, in information-processing terminology, are the actions a person can take in solving a problem. Consider the chess problem again. If you find yourself in check, you have very few actions open to you—you are limited to moving chess pieces or withdrawing from the game. Your

Incomplete problem representations cause difficulties in solving problems.

"I think you should be more explicit here in step two."

specific options might include moving the king or any of the other pieces you have on the board. In more ambiguous problems such as choosing a major, the number of operators available to problem solvers is far greater. Among the operators a student can choose from are sampling courses in different areas and seeking vocational counseling. Information-processing psychologists suggest that the more we understand about the actions we can perform in solving problems—that is, the more we know about our operators—the more effective we will be in solving problems.

Understanding the restrictions on operators is the last feature of problem representation. Operators often have restrictions or limits and problem solvers must understand them if they are to fully comprehend a problem. The operator of moving chess pieces is restricted in several ways. Some of the spaces on the playing board will contain other pieces and so you cannot move your pieces onto those locations, kings can only move one space at a time, knights must move in an L-shaped pattern—each piece has a set of restrictions placed on its use. A chess problem is not solvable unless the restrictions on the operators are understood. In the more personal problem of choosing a major, restrictions are defined by both the situation (a course, for example, necessarily lasts a certain number of weeks) and by the person involved ("I can't afford to just take courses until I find an area I like").

The way in which people represent problems determines the actions they consider to solve the problems. If we find ourselves at one end of a field and we want to be at the other, our operator may be walking. However, there are many paths that we could take in using our operator. Those paths that connect the initial state to the goal are known as **solution paths.** The total number of actions that the problem solver considers possible (whether correct or incorrect) is called the **problem space** (Figure 4–5). As Hayes (1978) points out, problem spaces are determined by problem solvers themselves, not by the problems. That is, possible actions are identified by the problem solver. There may be more possible actions than those allowed by the restrictions on the operators (for example, responding to the chess problem by making two moves in a row) or fewer possible actions (for example, not recognizing that one of the pieces can be moved to protect the king).

Let's take a look at some problems that will illustrate the information-processing view of problem representation.

> Ed is running for his life from a tribe of hostile cannibals. He has reached a river and must cross it to save his life. Ed has rapidly constructed a small raft from readily available materials in the forest and is now ready to paddle across the river. He has a problem, however: he has only one source of food, a bunch of bananas. He must take these with him or he will surely

FIGURE 4–5
A Representation of Problem Space

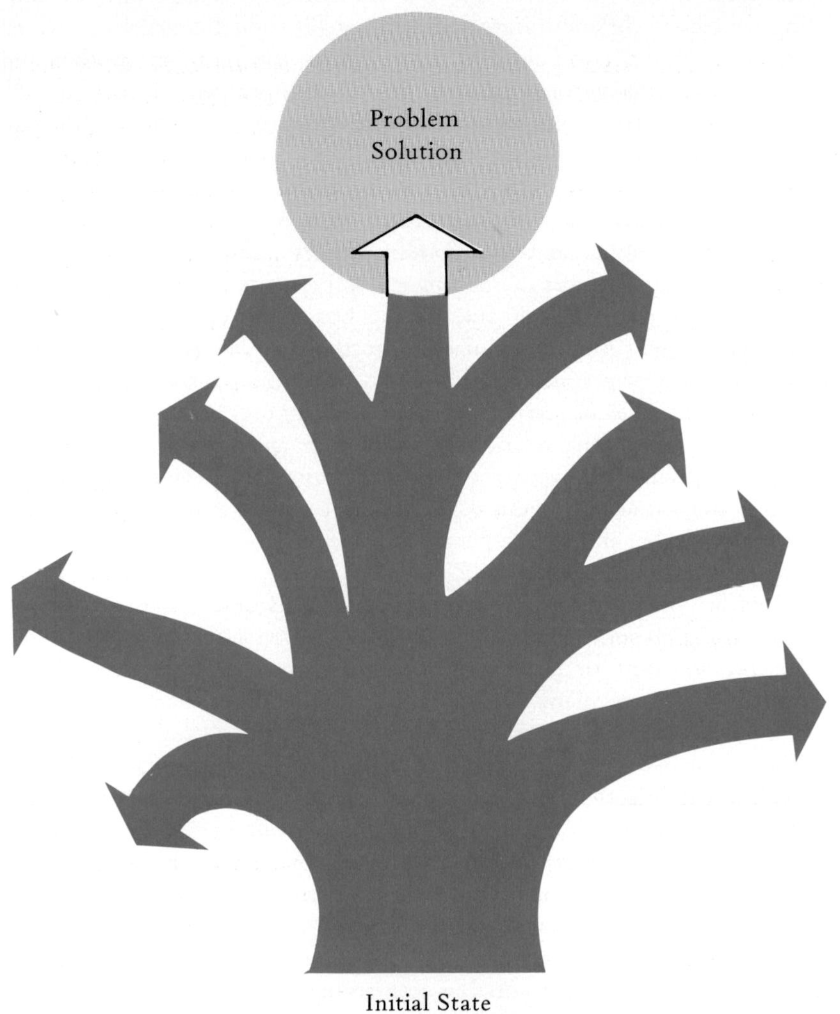

starve. Ed also has his pet chimpanzee along. Ed wants to save his chimp from certain death by taking him across the river. To further complicate matters, Ed has a leopard that he has raised since it was a cub and Ed knows he needs the leopard for protection on the other side of the river. All this is trouble enough but the situation is further compounded by the following: (1) Ed can only take one of the three things across the river with him at one time. (2) If Ed leaves the chimp with the bananas, the chimp will eat them all. (3) If Ed leaves the leopard with the chimp, the leopard will kill the chimp. How can we advise Ed in solving his problem? Remember, since there are piranha in the river, Ed and all of his belongings must cross the river on the raft; they can't swim across.

Many people have trouble with river-crossing problems. Once people are reminded that Ed can take objects across the river in *both* directions, however, they typically solve the problem easily. That is, once people understand the restrictions clearly, they can solve the problem.

Your reaction to the river-crossing problem can be used to make some points about problem representation. Ed's problem was to get himself and his belongings across the river. Luckily, many problems clearly specify actions (operators) that we can take to get from where we are (the initial state) to where we want to be (the goal state). Ed's operator was paddling across the river on a raft. Unfortunately, there were restrictions on Ed's operator (as there are in most problems), things that could happen if his belongings were left in the wrong combination. Obviously, if you want to successfully solve a problem such as Ed's, you must represent all you know about the problem in your thinking. Leaving any information out of your representation of a problem is likely to lead to an incorrect solution.*

Although many problems present all four necessary components very clearly, some do not and so problem solvers must infer them from available information.

> Joe, Schmoe, and Moe all live on the same block. They live in red, green, and blue houses. Joe doesn't live in the green or the blue house. Schmoe doesn't live in the green house. What house does each person live in?

While the initial state and the goal in this problem are clearly presented, the operators (identifying the person about which most is known) and their restrictions (we must infer that only one person lives in each house) aren't mentioned directly. You, or any other problem solver, often must infer information to develop a complete problem representation. Such problems may not necessarily be any more difficult than others; they simply require more inferences.

Problems such as the two we have presented can be clearly defined. The initial state, the operators, the restrictions on the operators, and the goals are fairly clear. Unfortunately (or fortunately, depending on your point of view) real-life problems (such as choosing a major) are

*One solution: (1) take chimp across and leave it; (2) return; (3) take bananas over and leave them; (4) take chimp back to original side and leave it; (5) take over leopard and leave it with bananas; (6) return; (7) bring chimp across.

seldom as easily defined as those we have described (Mayer, 1977). **Ill-defined problems** (Hayes, 1978; Simon, 1973) require the problem solver to contribute actively to the representation of the problem. Consider a problem involving the construction of a bridge somewhere in rural Arizona. The initial statement of the problem was presented as follows:

1. A two-lane blacktop road is to be constructed between towns *A* and *B*.
2. A river crosses the proposed path of the road at point *C*.
3. The river is dry six months of the year but reaches to within three feet of its banks at the crossing point after spring flooding two out of every five years. The other three of the five years, the river reaches within ten feet of the bank top.
4. The river has flooded over its banks once in the last seventy-five years.
5. The bridge's load will be light except for occasional farm machinery.
6. Money is definitely a factor. The cheaper you can build the bridge, the better.

A sample of engineers shown this problem statement reacted differently, but we have chosen one set of responses to demonstrate how a problem solver actively constructs the representation of the problem.

The engineer (along with all those in our sample) first started with a series of questions. He requested pictures of the location, geologists' reports, governmental specifications for bridges, and an environmental impact study. After examining the requested materials, the engineer began to redefine the problem.

"OK, it looks like we have a couple of choices at least. . . . The flooding—I don't think it's going to be a problem. We won't need to worry about that. I don't think we'll need any suspension—could do it but—no, it would be a big cost factor."

As he continued, he introduced additional concerns (such as load requirements the bridge must satisfy) and made decisions about their relative importance. Ultimately, he reconstructed the problem based on his previous experience and on his evaluation of the current situation. The problem he ended up solving was largely of his own making.*

Ill-defined problems require that we make decisions to fill in gaps in the problem definition and try out some tentative solutions before we

*Our example illustrates the role of social issues in public problem solving. Obviously, our engineer in defining the problem might adversely affect people with heavy equipment or those who wish an unimpeded stream flow. Their rights in the matter could only be preserved by their involvement in the problem-definition stage.

settle on a satisfactory answer. Obviously, the more we know about various aspects of a problem (underlying concepts, principles, and information), the better we are able to address it.

METHODS OF SOLVING PROBLEMS

In the information-processing approach, problem solving is visualized as a search for a path from where we are to where we want to be. If there are many possible paths with wrong turns or dead ends, a problem is more difficult than if there are only a few incorrect paths. As we shall see, the number of paths to choose from is not as important as how problem solvers go about their searches.

Suppose a plane is reported down somewhere in a 12-county area of western New York state. The plane must be found before nightfall because a storm is sweeping off Lake Erie. The odds of finding the plane in any one county are then 1 in 12. Easy, right? Now suppose that there are twelve 25-square-mile townships in each county. The plane could be in any one of them. So instead of 12 possibilities we must now check 12 × 12, or 144, possibilities. Assume a ground party can effectively search only 5 square miles a day—one-fifth of a township. In a ground search, we must then check 12 × 12 × 5, or 720, places. Of course, we could make the problem much larger—5 states with 200 counties and so on until the number of possibilities to check becomes enormous. Even such a problem is very small compared to the search involved in deciding the next move in a chess game, despite the fact that chess moves are well-defined problems. Newell and Simon (1972) estimate that there are about 10^{120} possible paths on a chess board, more paths than there are stars in the sky or grains of sand on the earth. So whether you are looking for a lost plane or planning a chess move, the way in which you go about solving the problem is important. You must develop systematic methods of searching problem spaces and increasing the chances of a correct choice or you will never reach the solution to many problems.

Problem-Search Techniques

There are two basic approaches to problem searches, random and heuristic. In a **random search,** chance alone determines whether the goal is reached, as in the case of Thorndike's cats. Random searches are the simplest but least efficient of all problem-solving approaches. They are conducted without any knowledge of which paths would be more favorable for reaching the goal. Simply looking for the downed plane in one of the 144 townships without any planning or strategy would be a random search. Unless the problem space is very small, random searches are inappropriate for almost all problems, although many students (and teachers) employ them from time to time.

A better form of search for a problem solution is the **heuristic* search.** Hayes (1978) defines heuristic searches as those in which problem solvers use knowledge to find promising paths to the problem solution or goal. Knowledge of the plane's probable route, last radio transmissions, and citizen reports would help change a random search into a heuristic one. There are three general kinds of heuristic approaches: proximity searches, pattern matching, and planning (Hayes, 1978; Wickelgren, 1974).

Proximity Searches. Proximity searches involve actions that allow the problem solver to get closer and closer, by approximations, to the problem solution. One form of proximity search is "hot-and-cold." For those of you who don't remember, hot-and-cold is a game that requires a hidden object, a seeker of the object, and an audience who knows where the object is. As the seeker moves closer to the object, the audience calls out "hotter," and as the seeker moves away from the object, the audience calls out "colder." Watch children play hot-and-cold sometime and you'll see a search pattern guided by information about the problem. Typically, children use cues to find hidden objects fairly effectively.

Those of us who have not actually played the game have probably still used the hot-and-cold method. Recently, one of the authors stopped his car and heard a low hissing sound. He walked around the car, moving toward the location where the hiss sounded loud and away from areas where the sound was weak until he located a leaking hose under the hood. Similarly, a faint radio transmission that either strengthened or weakened as a search party changed directions could guide rescuers to a downed plane. Such information, whether it is the response "hot" or "cold," a hissing noise, or a radio transmission, helps us reduce the number of pathways and thereby makes our problem searches more effective.

A version of a hot-and-cold search can be seen in a teacher's attempt to develop practices that best promote student learning and satisfaction. Ms. Rose understands that some people believe a class conducted in small discussion groups is best, that others argue for the use of lectures, and that still others feel simulations and games are best to promote learning. Ms. Rose knows that experts disagree, but she can't very well support her own research program to find out what will work best with her students. She can, however, use a proximity approach to solve her problem. She can take one step (perhaps using a simulation) and see

*From the Greek word *heuriskein,* which means to discover or find.

what effect this has before going further. Over several weeks she can try many things, continuing to do those that increase student learning and satisfaction while dropping those that do not seem to help her reach her goal. After a lot of trial and error, Ms. Rose is likely to reach the goal of teaching her class in an effective way. As in all proximity searches, she may not find the best possible solution but she should find one that works reasonably well.

Another form of proximity search is known as **means-ends analysis,** which is similar to hot-and-cold with an important difference. In hot-and-cold, only one way is used to get closer to the goal—walking around a car or varying instructional methods, for instance. In means-end analysis, there are choices to be made among differing methods (means) of approaching the goal. A means-end analysis involves breaking a problem down into component parts or subproblems and then using whatever means are available to solve each subproblem (called a **reduction goal** by Newell & Simon, 1972). As each subproblem is solved, the problem solver moves closer to the ends (called **apply goals**) he or she desires.

A chemistry student attempting to identify an unknown substance would apply a means-end analysis. The student can use a series of reagents, a spectrographic analysis, a light absorption test, or a flame test. Often these procedures are used in sequence with successive tests made on the basis of the findings of previous tests.

In another example of means-ends analysis, suppose you get a flat tire in a sparsely populated rural area. You have an excellent spare tire but unfortunately you have no jack with which to raise the car. Here the initial state and the final goal are both clear. You want to "move" from a flat tire that has made your car undrivable to an air-filled tire.

Typically, you would follow these steps when you have a flat tire:

1. identify the problem
2. loosen the lug nuts
3. jack up the car
4. remove the lug nuts
5. remove the flat tire — reduction goals
6. put spare tire on
7. screw on lug nuts
8. lower car
9. tighten the lug nuts
10. operate the car in a normal fashion (apply goal)

When you remove the possibility of using a jack, however, you have a problem within a problem. The new, major problem is gaining access to the tire, an apply goal located between steps 2 and 3. Everything you do to gain access to the tire is a reduction goal. Building a ramp, using a fence post and rocks to raise the car, and putting the car up on the rocks are all possible reduction goals that help you on your way to actually changing the tire.

Means-ends analysis can best be thought of as a problem search that emphasizes the various means you have to reach the ends, your goals. Anytime you make a series of secondary moves to reduce the difficulty of a problem, you have engaged in a form of means-ends analysis.

Hayes (1978) uses the analogy of a stack of plates to picture the progression of goals in a means-ends analysis. He describes goals as placed on top of one another, much like dishes in a cafeteria, so that as one is removed another pops up until you come to the final goal. Figure 4–6 allows us to picture the workings of means-ends analysis as follows. An apply goal is at the bottom of the stack, with the reduction goals pressing it down. As each reduction goal is met, the problem solver moves to the next until the apply goal is reached.

FIGURE 4–6
A Plate-Stack Representation of Reduction and Apply Goals

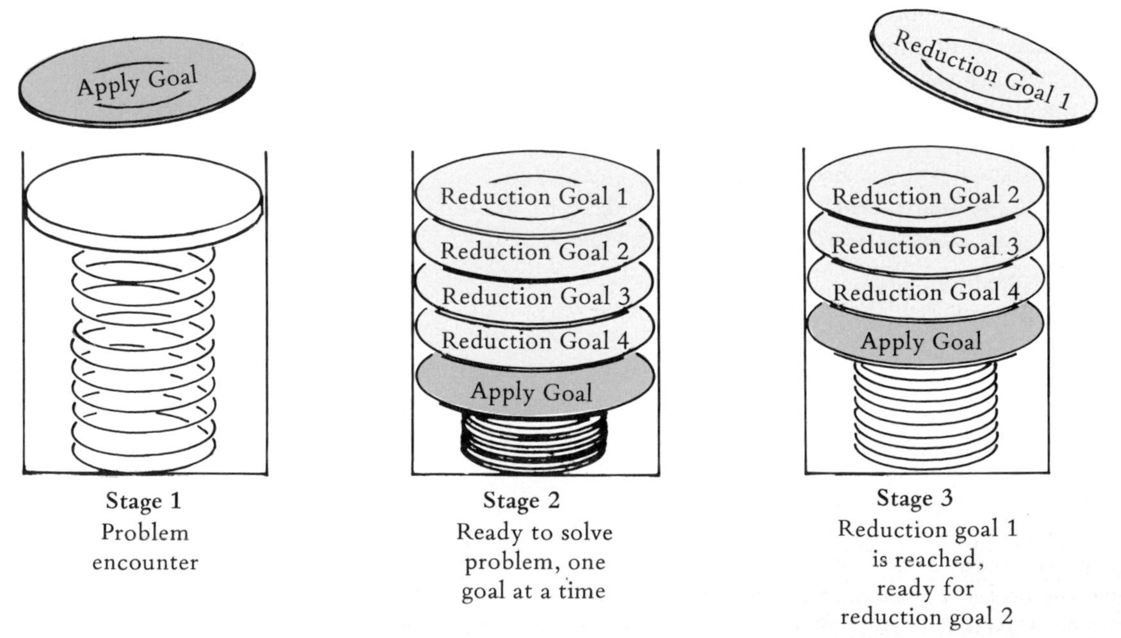

Source: J. R. Hayes, *Cognitive Psychology: Thinking and Creating.* Homewood, Illinois: Dorsey, 1978. Copyright © 1978 by Dorsey Press. Used by permission.

Planning allows us to be better problem solvers. These students anticipate problems by thinking through the next step of their experiment.

Pattern Matching. Pattern-matching searches involve an examination of a problem, identification of it, and then an attempt to locate a problem in memory that is of the same pattern. In other words, problem solvers ask themselves, "Have I been in similar situations before and can I apply the solution I learned then to the current problem?"

Clear examples of pattern-matching approaches can be seen in the game of chess (Simon & Chase, 1973; Simon & Gilmartin, 1973). Simon and his associates contrasted pattern-recognition abilities of novice and master chess players. They determined that a major difference between them was that masters had stored thousands of chessboard patterns in their memories while the novices had stored relatively few. The far greater availability of recognizable patterns in the memories of chess masters presumably results in their greater ability to play chess.

Applications of pattern-matching problem searches for classroom teachers are clear. The experiences gained in teaching as well as in reading and advanced classwork help teachers store in memory various patterns of educational problems and their solutions. When a new problem emerges—a student who does not learn or who is disruptive, for example—pattern matching can be one approach to finding possible solutions. Similarly, by recognizing a learning difficulty as a failure in, say, discrimination learning or concept learning, the teacher can apply solutions that have worked for these problems in the past.

Planning. One of the most effective approaches to problem searches occurs prior to the actual search. Planning allows us to engage in proximity and pattern-searching approaches in advance of attempting to solve the problem. Planning for problems can be seen in architects' scale models, a graphic layout of an assembly line, a sketch of a plan for a flower garden, a computer simulation of economic trends, or a term paper outline. Planning allows us to test and accept or reject problem solutions with minimal expenditure of money, effort, and risk.

PRACTICE EXERCISE 4–2

Problem Solving in Real Life

Problem solving is like any other form of learning—you get better with practice. Each of the steps we outlined earlier can be put to use in solving problems in your own life. The key to improvement, though, is simply to practice solving problems systematically.

Of course you need a problem to solve. Pick one that is important to you—choosing a major if you don't have one, for instance, or finding a good apartment at a reasonable price. Perhaps your problem is an interpersonal one. In any event, once you settle on the problem, follow the steps below in working out a solution. If you're like many people, using this guide will help you solve problems more effectively (Petersen, 1979).*

1. *Define the problem.* State the problem as clearly as you can.

   ____

   ____

2. *Identify your reasons for wanting to solve the problem.* First, what will happen if the problem stays unsolved? ______________

   ____

   ____

   What will happen if the problem is solved? ______________

   ____

   ____

3. *Assess several hypotheses for solving the problem.* Try out a number of strategies. For each, list its assets and its liabilities. As sources for ideas, think of what has worked for you in the past. Also, what do others suggest as ways to solve the problem?

Strategy	***Assets***	***Liabilities***
a. ______________	______________	______________
	______________	______________
	______________	______________

* Our thanks are expressed to Chris Petersen of American Institutes for Research whose research and problem-solving guidelines provided the major source of information for this exercise.

b. ______________ ______________ ______________

______________ ______________

______________ ______________

c. ______________ ______________ ______________

______________ ______________

______________ ______________

Write the alternative you judge to be the best

____

4. *Try out your hypothesis.* Test out your approach and see how it works.

What went right? ______________________________

What went wrong? ______________________________

5. *Is the problem solved?* ______ Yes ______ No If no, what do you need to do now in order to move toward solving the problem?

____

APPLICATIONS FOR TEACHING

Training for problem-solving skills (see D'Zurilla & Goldfried, 1971; Heppner, 1978; Dixon et al., 1979) has typically followed the sequence of steps first proposed by Dewey (1910). With these general steps as our outline, we can apply a number of the insights gained through the information-processing approach to our goal of teaching students to be effective problem solvers. Ausubel and his associates (1978) have also provided several hints that are closely related to the information-processing approach. We have incorporated many of their suggestions in the following steps for enhancing students' abilities to solve problems.

1. Give students a chance to become problem solvers. Too often, teachers feel that they must present factual information to students in the form of names, dates, and figures. Most students are far more interested in and stimulated by a well-chosen problem. Of course, effective teachers exercise care in their selection of problems for students. A problem exists only if students must work at solving it. We also must be sure that students have the necessary background to enable them to solve the particular types of problems we present. Problems must fit into previous knowledge in order to be meaningful.

2. Help students define problems. Students will define problems (create their own problem spaces) according to their perception of the information they are given (Hayes, Waterman & Robinson, 1977; Simon, 1973; Simon & Hayes, 1976). As Ausubel and his associates (1978) have stated, problem solvers must make sure they understand the problem before they try to solve it. In information-processing terms, teachers must very carefully teach students to define their problem space by exploring what their initial state is, what their goal is, what operators are permitted, and exactly what restrictions are placed on the operators. Ausubel has further suggested that problem solvers should question the reliability of information and continue to search for reliable data even after the initial problem space has been constructed. Problem solvers need to determine clearly what parts of the problem are really data and which parts are inferences.

One way to help students formulate problem spaces is to demonstrate problem representations for them. Having students orally define problems is then a good way of checking their formulations. As all scholars from Dewey (1910) to the present have indicated, a good definition of the problem greatly facilitates the next step in problem solving—the development of good hypotheses.

3. Stimulate students' development of hypotheses. The more hypotheses problem solvers can generate, the more likely it is that they will find a good solution. Ausubel (Ausubel et al., 1978) has suggested that problem solvers should avoid giving attention to only one part of the problem. In other words, the search for solution paths should not be unnecessarily restricted. On the other hand, Ausubel indicates that problem solvers should try to avoid making the same assumptions for seemingly similar problems. Pattern matching may not always be the most helpful heuristic. Students should be taught not only to look for similarities to past problems, but to search carefully for dissimilarities.

4. Have students test their hypotheses. Hypotheses can be tested in two ways: by thinking through them in the planning stage or by actually testing them in the problem situation. Either way, students should always be encouraged to be systematic and to avoid random searches.

Effective teachers expect that hypothesis testing is based on the previous stage of planning. Since your task as a teacher is to help students acquire useful processes for solving problems, you should be prepared to spend much of your time evaluating the models, diagrams, and outlines of hypotheses students make in the planning stage. Giving your students feedback on their hypotheses as they test them on the actual problem is equally vital.

Systematic heuristic methods can be taught. Specific instructions can be given, along with many broadly based examples, for students to use hot-and-cold and means-ends analysis on assigned problems. Students can be required to describe their problem searches orally or in writing.

Similarly, pattern matching should be practiced. As in mathematics or the sciences, students can be taught to relate new problems to methods and procedures they previously used with similar problems. Pattern matching can be stressed in a variety of classes, from social studies to science to literature.

Ausubel (Ausubel et al., 1978) has cautioned that problem solvers should always avoid jumping to conclusions in the hypothesis-testing stage. The first solution is not necessarily the best solution. Problem solvers should always be taught to go further than the most obvious answer, even if that answer eventually works. Proximity methods often yield solutions that are not always the best ones. Solutions should therefore be checked against outside criteria whenever possible.

Finally, if a hypothesis is unsuccessful, students should be taught to try another (Ausubel et al., 1978). Persistence in problem solving is admirable, but students should recognize a blind alley when they encounter one. Students should learn that it may be necessary to test several possible pathways before they find the solution path.

5. Help students judge the worth of their solutions. Some problems have many solutions but only one can be chosen. Factors such as cost, time, accuracy, and completeness often must be taken into account in judging the worth of a solution. In social problems, issues of ethics and morality may also enter in. Students should therefore be encouraged to practice rank-ordering of problem solutions based on several criteria. Criteria such as those above are especially important when we consider that most of the problems students will eventually face in life will be ill-defined. For most such problems, large numbers of problem definitions are possible, with an even larger number of potential solutions. Since the solutions to many problems (building highways to meet transportation needs, for example) may lead to other problems in related areas (inner-city deterioration, air pollution), testing solutions against multiple criteria becomes especially critical.

6. Be sensitive to individual differences. As we noted in Chapter Two, students have different cognitive styles. More impulsive students may need special attention in their learning processes to become systematic and thorough in solving problems. Other students may refuse to take risks in problem solving and so may need some individual help designed to develop more of a risk-taking attitude. There are, of course, other kinds of individual differences in cognition and these are considered in detail in Chapter Five. Here, however, we need to point out that each of your students will have an individual style of solving problems that you must consider in planning your instruction.

7. Help students avoid inappropriate sets. Students' abilities to solve problems are strongly influenced by their predispositions to perceive, approach, and attempt solutions in certain ways. Such predispositions are referred to as *sets* and are developed through earlier experiences with similar problems. Mostly sets are useful to problem solving. Difficulty arises, however, when old problem solutions seem to but don't quite fit new problems. Early in this chapter, for instance, you may have had difficulty in solving the six squares problem because you continually approached the problem in ways that did not allow you to see the correct answer. Clearly, you will want to help reduce set problems to the greatest extent possible among your students. One effective way is to have students work on problems that require different and varied approaches. As Gagné and Briggs (1979) have pointed out, variety and novelty in problem-solving tasks are key elements in the continued development of effective cognitive strategies. Additionally, the problem of set is greatly reduced when teachers emphasize the processes involved in solving problems rather than just the correct answers.

SUMMARY

In this chapter we briefly surveyed the importance of problem solving to society and pointed out the increasing emphasis schools are placing on the development of students' problem-solving abilities. Problem solving is one of the most crucial skills your students must acquire. Their future satisfaction with life and their effectiveness as citizens depend on their developing problem-solving skills.

Effective problem solving is considered the most sophisticated form of learning. Gagné refers to it as rule-governed behavior that results in the learning of higher-order rules, while Ausubel describes problem solving as meaningful discovery learning. Both regard problem solving as a critical goal of education.

Thorndike's early research on problem solving led him to describe it as an incremental, trial-and-error form of learning that did not involve thinking or reasoning as we usually define such terms. Köhler, a Gestalt psychologist, envisioned problem solving as an all-or-none, insightful process closely governed by reasoning, while Dewey, ever the pragmatist, concentrated on the sequence of steps that people follow in problem solving. Dewey's notions have led directly to the development of programs designed to develop problem-solving skills. Information-processing approaches to problem solving borrow from the works of Thorndike, Köhler, and Dewey, as well as from the rich tradition of memory research. The information-processing view of problem solving emphasizes what a person does with the information—constructing problem representations, building problem spaces, and testing hypotheses.

There are two basic approaches to solving problems, random and heuristic. In the long run, random methods are clearly inferior to heuristic methods. Heuristic approaches include hot-and-cold, means-ends analysis, pattern matching, and planning strategies. Ill-defined problems require problem solvers to analyze and specify the problems before experimenting with different solutions. Such problems are best solved through the heuristic strategy of systematic planning, which involves visualizing and testing alternative solutions by various analytic procedures such as diagrams, flow charts, or computer simulations.

Problem solving builds on memory and concept learning. It is an important component of human intelligence, the topic of our next chapter. Similarly, problem solving is an important feature of creativity, the topic of Chapter Six.

Suggested Readings

Dewey, J. *How we think.* New York: Heath, 1933.

Dewey's classic book is still the basis for most of the problem-solving training procedures in use today.

Gagné, R. M. Learnable aspects of problem solving. *Educational Psychologist,* 1980, *15,* 84–92.

This paper provides a good overview of Gagné's perspectives on problem solving.

Hayes, J. R. *Cognitive psychology: Thinking and creating.* Homewood, Ill.: Dorsey, 1978.

Hayes's book provides an excellent introduction to modern views of problem solving. Especially effective is his presentation of the role of computers in research on problem solving.

Köhler, W. *The mentality of apes.* New York: Harcourt, Brace, 1925.

Köhler's excellent book is not only an enjoyable description of how he studied problem solving in chimpanzees, but it also provides the foundation for contemporary cognitive views of problem solving.

Mayer, R. E. *Thinking and problem solving: An introduction to human cognition and learning.* Glenview, Ill.: Scott, Foresman, 1977.

Mayer's book presents a good introduction to modern views of problem solving.

Newell, A., & Simon, H. A. *Human problem solving.* Englewood Cliffs, N.J.: Prentice-Hall, 1972.

This advanced text is a classic in the field of problem solving.

Comments on Practice Exercise 4–1

Let's see how your choices compare to ours.

1. (a) Verbal chain. A student's ability to write the definition of a concept indicates minimally that he or she has memorized a string of words. Although students may understand the concept of polyphonic, being able to write a definition is not good evidence that they actually do understand the concept.
2. (c) Problem solving. The student has combined principles in the solution of the problem.
3. (b) Concept or principle learning. A student's ability to perform this task in a list she *hasn't seen before* indicates understanding of the concept of "noun." Had the student studied the actual list on which she were tested, we could only be sure that she had learned a verbal chain.
4. (a) Verbal chain. The student's response can be made from rote recall alone. Although the student may understand the concepts involved, no understanding is actually required in order to answer this question.
5. (b) Concept or principle learning. Prediction indicates understanding of principles of supply and demand. The "right" answer can only come from understanding, not memorization of an answer. Why not problem solving? This example is less complex than most problem solving, which involves several principles in combination.
6. (b) Concept or principle learning. The student shows understanding of concepts, the relationship between them, and their representation in the cartoon in order to derive meaning from the cartoon.
7. (a) Verbal Chain. Listing the principles can be accomplished with or without understanding. To ensure understanding, we would need to require use of the principles in analysis of a situation or in application.
8. (b) Concept or principle learning. This analytical behavior indicates

knowledge of concepts and principles of composition, unless of course the student had specifically been taught a list of techniques as they applied to this particular poem. Then we could only be sure of verbal chaining.

9. (b) Concept or principle learning. The student is identifying examples of several concepts.
10. (b) Concept or principle learning. By being able to find examples of concepts (such as "distortion of data") in a speech, the student is demonstrating that he or she knows more than simply the phrase "distortion of data." The student is making use of the concept—the best demonstration of all that the concept has been learned.

IMPORTANT EVENTS IN PROBLEM-SOLVING RESEARCH

Date(s)	*Person(s)*	*Work*	*Impact*
1898	Thorndike	"Animal intelligence: An experimental study of the associative processes in animals"	E. L. Thorndike conducted the first experimental study of problem solving. Thorndike was an associationist and his views of problem solving are still reflected in contemporary behavioral theories.
1910	Dewey	*How we think*	John Dewey published the first psychologically based guide to improving problem solving skill. His model still serves as the basis for many contemporary problem-solving workshops.
1913–1918	Köhler	*The mentality of apes* (published in 1925)	Wolfgang Köhler's problem-solving experiments with apes were the forerunners of all cognitive approaches to problem solving. Köhler stressed insight in his views of the problem-solving process.
1928	Alpert	*The solving of problem situations by preschool children*	Augusta Alpert extended Köhler's findings to problem solving in human children.
1930	Dunker	"On problem solving" (usually given as 1945)	Karl Dunker developed the concept of "functional fixedness." By this, Dunker meant the phenomenon whereby people find it hard to visualize unusual uses for common items in solving problems (employing a hammer as a pendulum weight, for example).
1933	Maier	"An aspect of human reasoning"	N. R. F. Maier demonstrated the possibility of avoiding functional fixedness by having problem solvers guard against habitual activities. He found that a brief lecture cautioning students to remain flexible in their views greatly facilitated problem solution.

Date(s)	*Person(s)*	*Work*	*Impact*
1940	Katona	*Memorizing and organizing*	G. Katona demonstrated that students benefited more from "discovery learning" in problem solving than from other teaching methods.
1942	Luchens	"Mechanization in problem solving: The effect of Einstellung"	A. S. Luchens clearly illustrated people's tendencies to approach a problem the same way each time. He called this reproductive form of behavior a set.
1946	Polya	*How to solve it*	G. Polya's book was a practical guide for problem solving that provided many extremely useful hints for students. His analysis method was one of the precursors to task analysis.
1956	Maltzman	"Thinking: From a behaviorist point of view"	Irving Maltzman's attempt to develop a behavioral theory of thought (specifically of problem solving) had the ironic effect of convincing many psychologists that behaviorism could not address thought processes. Maltzman's paper removed behavioral theories from consideration in the search for ways to explain problem solving—the opposite of what he attempted to do.
1956	Newell & Simon	"The logic theory machine: A complex information processing system"	Allen Newell and Herbert Simon developed the first computer program that employed heuristics to solve problems. This facilitated the growth of subsequent computer models of human problem solving.
1957	Cofer	"Reasoning as an associative process: III. The role of verbal responses in problem solving"	Charles Cofer investigated the use of language as a mediator in problem solving. His findings further discredited the behavioral position on problem solving.
1963	Ausubel	*The psychology of meaningful verbal learning*	David Ausubel conceived of problem solving as a form of meaningful discovery learning. His views have

Date(s)	*Person(s)*	*Work*	*Impact*
			shaped many teacher applications designed to facilitate students' problem-solving abilities.
1964	Gagné	"Problem solving"	Robert Gagné developed a hierarchy of learning tasks, the most sophisticated of which was problem solving. Gagné analyzed problem solving as rule-governed behavior and stressed the need for students to acquire background information in order to become adequate problem solvers.
1971	D'Zurilla & Goldfried	"Problem solving and behavior modification"	T. D'Zurilla and M. R. Goldfried adopted the Dewey model of problem solving and combined it with the principles of behavior modification in the development of a new model of problem solving in counseling.
1972	Newell & Simon	*Human problem solving*	Newell and Simon's book represented the state of the art in information-processing approaches to problem solving. At the time of its publication this was the most influential book on problem solving since Dewey's classic work in 1910.
1977	Hinsley, Hayes, & Simon	"From words to equations"	D. Hinsley, J. Hayes, and H. Simon's study represented a new direction in research on problem solving, employing protocol analyses to determine how people construct problem spaces.
Current	The Carnegie-Mellon group	Information-processing approaches to human problem solving	The Carnegie-Mellon group (including John Hayes, Allen Newell, and Herbert Simon) is at the forefront of scientists investigating problem solving from an information-processing perspective.

Chapter Five

INTELLIGENCE AND COGNITIVE DEVELOPMENT

Intelligence, the ability to profit from experiences, can be considered the summation of all the cognitive functions we have discussed thus far. A common theme of Chapters Two, Three, and Four was an information-processing approach to cognition. Our perspective in this chapter will change somewhat, although we shall remain in the general area of cognition. The reason for our shift in emphasis was first clearly expressed by Cronbach (1957) several years ago. He pointed out at the time that there appeared to be two disciplines in psychology that should have been interacting but were not. On the one hand was psychometry, a specialty in psychology devoted to measuring differences between people (including intellectual differences). On the other hand was experimental psychology, which, when humans were the subjects, was devoted to the investigation of psychological processes. One aspect of experimental psychology was the study of cognitive processes. While the group of psychologists interested in psychometry was engaged in measuring *differences* in the intellectual abilities of people, experimentalists were studying the *processes* that underlay these differences. Neither group (with the exception of Cronbach) paid much attention to what the other was doing. This state of affairs, however, has begun to change in the last few years (Carroll, 1981; Hunt, Lunneborg, & Lewis, 1975; Sternberg, 1981).

In our discussion of cognitive processes we have necessarily emphasized the tradition of experimental psychology. As important as this tradition has been to our understanding of human cognition, however, we must leave experimental psychology for a time and turn to psychometry in order to begin to understand the ways in which intelligence has been measured. We will trace the history of psychometric views about intelligence as psychometry and experimental psychology began to find common ground in information-processing theory (Carroll, 1981). We will also review Jean Piaget's developmental theory, which he developed in reaction to psychometric approaches (Lunzer, 1976) and which became a major influence on contemporary cognitive psychology and education.

Objectives

After reading this chapter, you should be able to meet the following objectives.

1. Describe the implications of individual differences in intelligence for your teaching practices.
2. Indicate the effect your knowledge of the nature/nurture controversy will have on your practices as a teacher.
3. Recognize the implications of developmental theories of intelligence for the decisions you will make as a teacher.

PSYCHOMETRIC APPROACHES TO INTELLIGENCE

Intelligence Tests

The idea that humans possessed intellectual abilities that could be accurately measured dates back at least to Sir Francis Galton's 1869 book *Hereditary Genius*. Galton's conception that there were different limits to each person's intellectual abilities set the tone for much of modern psychometry's views on intellectual ability (Willerman & Turner, 1979). As important as Galton's pathfinding was, it was not until after the turn of the century that the assessment of intelligence got its real start.

The Binet and Simon Scales. In 1904, the French Minister of Public Instruction called together a commission of learned people concerned with education—physicians, educators, public officials, and scientists of several persuasions—and asked them to investigate the problems of teaching so-called feeble-minded children. As it turned out, the most important work accomplished by this commission was performed by a psychologist, Alfred Binet, and a physician, Theodore Simon. Their efforts on behalf of the commission were to have a permanent impact on education and psychology.

Binet and Simon believed that before any instructional programs could be developed, it was necessary to work out some method of measuring the general cognitive functions of the children the programs were trying to help. Working from this assumption, Binet and Simon constructed a test designed to measure intelligence. Their test was based on the following definition:

> It seems to us that in intelligence there is a fundamental faculty, the alteration or the lack of which is of the utmost importance for practical life. This faculty is judgment, otherwise called good sense, practical sense, initiative, the faculty of adapting one's self to circumstances. To judge well, to comprehend well, to reason well, these are the essential activities of intelligence. *(Binet & Simon, 1905, p. 246)*

Their test consisted of a series of problems that Binet and Simon believed could be solved with little influence from children's backgrounds and required reason and judgment rather than rote memory. An indication of what the original test demanded can be seen in some of the expectations Binet had for "normal" children's performance at different ages:

> Age 3: Points to nose, eyes, and mouth when asked.
> Age 5: Can count four coins.
> Age 7: Identifies and shows left ear and right hand.
> Age 9: Can relate familiar words to other concepts.
> Age 12: When given three words, can employ them in a sentence. *(Binet & Simon, 1911, p. 91)*

As we'll see later in this chapter, a hotly debated topic is whether such items (which also appear on more recently developed intelligence tests) are truly environment- and background-free.

Between 1905, when the first version of the Binet-Simon test appeared, and 1911, when the last version was published, Binet devoted his efforts to revising and refining his test. During this time and in the

"You did very well on your I.Q. test. You're a man of 49 with the intelligence of a man of 53."

years following the appearance of the 1911 version, Binet and other psychologists observed that retarded children who were tested and then retested at a later date fell further and further behind their "normal" peers.

Typically, Binet found that the ratio of mental age (the average age of children who got a given number of items correct) to chronological age remained almost constant as children developed. For example, a child who at age five had a mental age of three would be likely to obtain a mental-age score of six at the age of ten, both mental ages being three-fifths of "normal."

This observation of a relatively constant ratio of mental and chronological age led to the expression of intelligence test results as the **intelligence quotient,** or IQ. IQ was defined as the ratio of mental age to chronological age multiplied by 100 (to create a whole number):

$$\frac{\text{mental age}}{\text{chronological age}} \times 100 = \text{IQ}$$

A five-year-old with a mental age of three would have an IQ of 60 ($3/5 \times 100 = 60$). Likewise, an eight-year-old obtaining a mental-age score of 10 would have an IQ of 125 ($10/8 \times 100 = 125$). IQs calculated in this manner have come to be known as **ratio IQs.**

The Binet-Simon test and its later revisions formed the keystone of efforts to measure intellectual abilities. It should be pointed out, however, that as a measurement device the Binet-Simon test in no way was a measure of underlying cognitive processes, such as those that are components of modern information-processing models. There was only the conjecture that responses to the test items involved "judgment," "practical sense," "initiative," and other rather loosely defined qualities thought to be important for academic success.

The Stanford-Binet. The next important event in the development of measures of intelligence took place in the United States and was guided by L. M. Terman. Terman tried out Binet's materials as well as other tests, including some of his own devising, on nearly three thousand children. He then arranged these tests into mental-age levels and published them in 1916 as the Stanford Revision of the Binet-Simon test.

For twenty years the 1916 Stanford Revision was *the* test of intelligence in the United States, the standard against which all new measures of intelligence were judged. During that time, however, it became apparent that it was unsatisfactory in some ways. Its major shortcomings were that it was not appropriate for adults; it was not appropriate for very young children; and there was only one version of the 1916 test.

Individual intelligence tests provide one estimate of intellectual ability.

Because of these problems, Terman and Maud Merrill published a revision of the Stanford-Binet in 1937. The 1937 version was developed in two forms and was extended upward so that it was appropriate for adults and downward so that it could be used for children as young as two years of age. The typical procedure for calculating mental age was not employed when the test was used to assess the intelligence of adults. That is, no one expects a fifty-year-old person to have twice the mental capacity of a twenty-five-year-old. Instead, the chronological age of adults was "corrected" to fit into the old formula (Terman & Merrill, 1937).

The Stanford-Binet was again revised in 1960 and is currently undergoing another revision. In general, the best items from previous versions of the test have been retained while poorer and outdated items have been replaced. Over the years, the Stanford-Binet has continued to be the standard of reference for all intelligence tests (Lindeman & Merenda, 1979; Thorndike & Hagen, 1977).

There have been two major changes in the later revision of the Stanford-Binet. First, while the early versions relied heavily on the language ability of the person being tested, the newer versions have included performance tests thought to be freer of language bias. That is, tests emphasizing language were noted to unfairly penalize people who did not speak English as their native language. To supplement language-oriented tasks, tests requiring nonverbal performances were developed.

An example is the form-boards task, which provides a board with holes into which test takers must fit blocks of the correct size and shape as rapidly as possible. Additionally, in the newer versions of the Stanford-Binet, IQ is no longer calculated with the mental-age/chronological-age equation. Instead IQ is expressed as a standard score (see Chapter Fifteen).

The Wechsler Scales. Another major event in the assessment of intellectual ability was the development of the Wechsler Scales. Thorndike and Hagen (1977) note that there are three major differences between the Wechsler Scales and the Stanford-Binet tests: (1) the Wechsler Scales were originally designed for adults while the Stanford-Binet was first developed for children; (2) the Wechsler Scales are organized by subtests rather than age levels; and (3) the Weschler Scales yield both a verbal and a nonverbal IQ. Thorndike and Hagen go on to suggest that there is very little difference in the utility of the Wechsler Scales and the Stanford-Binet—people will score nearly the same on both tests. The Wechsler Scales include the Wechsler Adult Intelligence Scale, Revised (WAIS-R; Wechsler, 1981), the Wechsler Intelligence Scale for Children, Revised (WISC-R; Wechsler, 1974), and the Wechsler Preschool and Primary Scale (WPPSI; Wechsler, 1967).

Group Intelligence Tests. Another important development in the assessment of intelligence was the formulation of group tests of intelligence. Group tests, as the term implies, are designed to be given to a group of people at one time and so have a very large advantage over individually administered tests such as the Stanford-Binet and the Wechsler Scales in terms of the time required to administer them. Because of the large role of reading and other language-related skills required to perform well on such tests, however, they have been severely criticized by many people and have been banned as discriminatory in some states. We will explore group tests in more detail in Chapter Fifteen, but we note here that they all were developed with either the Stanford-Binet or the Wechsler as the standard of comparison (Sattler, 1974; Thorndike & Hagen, 1977).

Psychometric Theories of Intelligence

In order to understand how psychometrists view intelligence, it is helpful to recount some of the ideas of David Hebb (1949). Hebb suggested that a distinction should be made between what he called Intelligence A and Intelligence B. He referred to Intelligence A as the innate, inborn intellectual capacity possessed by a person and Intelligence B as the average or typical level of intellectual functioning demonstrated by a person. Hebb did not claim that there were two different kinds of intelligence, but he did argue that, while neither Intelligence A nor Intelligence B was truly observable, Intelligence B was far more open to measurement. Hebb suggested that testing could allow a fairly accurate estimate of Intelligence B but that an accurate measurement of Intelligence A would be far more difficult to obtain. Most psychometrists have focused on Intelligence B in their attempts to define and measure intelligence.

Three current psychometric views of intelligence have been formulated by Freeman (1962), Kagan and Lang (1978), and Thorndike and Hagen (1977):

> Intelligence is learning ability.
>
> Intelligence is a person's ability to adapt to his or her environment.
>
> Intelligence is the ability to think abstractly.

These three definitions, of course, do not necessarily exclude one another but they do represent distinct positions about Intelligence B. The first definition emphasizes people's receptiveness to education, the second focuses on the way in which people deal with new situations, and the third definition clearly stresses people's capabilities for verbal and mathematical reasoning. When we think about the definitions, it becomes clear that learning ability must depend to some extent on adaptive skills and abstract thought. Similarly, adaptability seems to depend in part on learning ability. And while abstract thought may not necessarily overlap with adaptability, the concepts that allow abstract thought must be learned in the first place. This high degree of agreement among the three definitions indicates that psychometrists are in fairly close accord in their views. It also shows the difficulty in describing and defining intelligence apart from scores on intelligence tests (Willerman & Turner, 1979).

As it turns out, the specific types of questions on intelligence tests that best relate to overall performance on the tests are those that require numerical or verbal reasoning (Sattler, 1974). From the perspective of intelligence tests, therefore, a reasonable definition of intelligence would be ability in numerical and verbal reasoning. That certain types of test items relate well to overall test performance, however, has not put to rest the debates on the true nature of intelligence (Eysenck, 1980).

There are two general theories of intelligence that could be applied to any of the three definitions above: the general-factor theory and the multifactor theory. Both theories are based on the statistical analysis of large numbers of intelligence test scores, which allows psychologists to identify the factors that best relate to overall test performance. General-factor theories of intelligence (see Freeman, 1962; Spearman, 1927) argue that all human intellectual abilities have in common a general factor, which Spearman called the *g* factor. Spearman described the *g* factor as the mental energy that supports all mental activities and suggested that some mental operations require more *g* than do others. He also described some specific factors (*s*) in intelligence. Despite Spearman's ideas about specific factors, he believed that intelligence tests should measure *g* and that, in fact, a good, single test could do so.

Multifactor theories of intelligence (see Guilford, 1959; Thurstone, 1938) are based on the position that intelligence is best defined by separate factors or underlying abilities. Thurstone (1938) suggested that there were six factors that make up intelligence and that each is involved in several intellectual operations:

Number factor (NA): Ability to perform mathematical operations with speed and accuracy

Verbal factor (V): Ability to perform on tests of verbal (language) comprehension

Space factor (S): Ability to manipulate an object in space in one's imagination

Word fluency factor (W): Ability to think rapidly of individual words

Reasoning factor (R): Ability to determine rules through deductive or inductive thought

Rote memory factor (M): Rapid memorization ability

For Thurstone, these six factors made up the primary mental abilities. Since he thought them to be relatively independent of one another, he expected that people could score well on one or more of these factors while scoring poorly on others. As it turned out (Thorndike & Hagen, 1977), Thurstone never obtained data that fully supported the existence of six independent factors and he concluded that there must be an underlying general factor that influenced each of the six primary mental-ability factors.

The most famous of the multifactor intelligence theories was put forth by J. P. Guilford (1959), who argued that there were far more than six separate factors of intelligence. He developed a model containing 120 separate factors. As intriguing as a model containing 120 factors might be, Guilford's model has not received extensive support (Torrance, 1980) except for the distinction he developed between convergent and divergent (creative) thought. In Chapter 6 we will see the importance of Guilford's contributions to current conceptions of creativity.

The issue of whether intelligence is related to a single or multiple factor is still debated today (C. R. Reynolds, 1981), but analyzing factors in a test does not appear to take us any closer to understanding the cognitive processes underlying intelligence-test scores (Carroll, 1981; Hunt, 1978). Such research has dealt primarily with the types of test items that best predict overall test scores; generally, it has not addressed cognitive processes.

INFORMATION-PROCESSING APPROACHES TO INTELLIGENCE

As we have seen, the psychometric perspective on intelligence has been a useful yet limited way of trying to understand intelligence. Psychometricians have been most concerned with how to measure intelligence and with predicting other performance, such as classroom learning, from these scores. On the other hand, psychologists with an information-processing perspective have seldom been concerned with the measurement of overall intellectual abilities but have instead emphasized the study of thought processes (Willerman & Turner, 1979).

You will recall that the first suggestion for research integrating psychometric and cognitive psychology came from Cronbach (1957), an esteemed psychometrist and educational psychologist. It wasn't until the 1970s, however, that the research began in earnest. Hunt and his colleagues (Hunt, 1978; Hunt, Frost, & Lunneborg, 1973; Lansman & Hunt, 1982; McCleod, Hunt, & Mathews, 1978) approached their studies from a multiple-factor perspective and selected a measure of verbal ability (the Washington Pre-College Test, WPCT) as the instrument to identify groups of students with test-measured high verbal ability and low verbal ability. Working with a sample of undergraduates at the University of Washington, they determined that the WPCT reflected verbal intelligence in much the same way as did the verbal component of most intelligence tests.

High verbals rapidly convert symbols into thought. The printed symbols in reading are readily understood by the high verbal student.

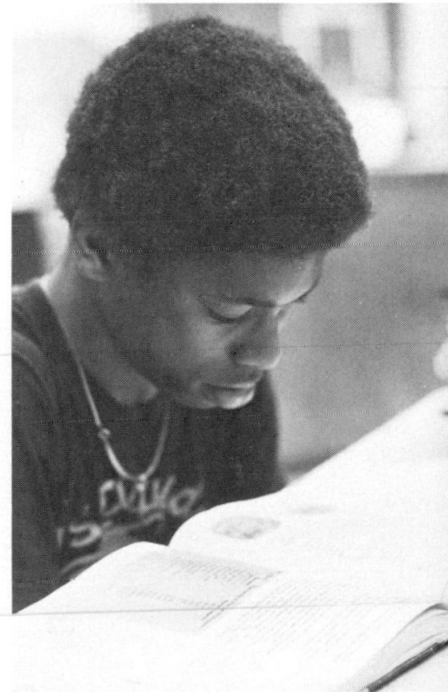

In a series of experiments Hunt and his colleagues identified students who scored in the upper quartile (the top 25 percent) and the lower quartile (bottom 25 percent) of the WPCT. Those students were required to perform a series of memory tasks. Overall, the researchers found that students in the upper quartile differed from those in the lower quartile in several interesting ways:

High-verbal subjects manipulate information in working memory more quickly than do low-verbal subjects.

High-verbals remember information in correct order more easily than do low-verbals.

High-verbals are able to retrieve greatly overlearned information (such as the letters of the alphabet) more rapidly from long-term memory than are low-verbals.

High-verbals convert symbols in written form into thought more rapidly than do low-verbals.

It appears from these studies that high-verbal individuals think more rapidly than low-verbals. These results are in general agreement with what psychometric theories of intelligence have long asserted (Binet & Simon, 1905; Spearman, 1927; Thurstone, 1938). Thus when Hunt, Lunneborg, and Lewis attempted to answer the question of what intelligence test scores mean from an information-processing perspective, they stated:

> We know that these scores [intelligence-test scores] are, for some reason, moderately successful predictors of success in a variety of situations (Herrnstein, 1973). The statistical fact is hardly in doubt, although there is great controversy concerning the reason behind it. In our terms verbal intelligence tests directly tap a person's knowledge of the language, and indirectly tap CIP (Current Information Processing) ability. Success in different tasks is probably dependent upon a host of factors, including both acquired knowledge and CIP ability. . . . It seems plausible to believe that high verbal subjects know more about the linguistic aspects of their culture because they are more rapid in CIP. *(1979, pp. 46–47)*

In general, the results of Hunt and his colleagues' research seem to indicate that tests of at least the verbal components of intelligence do measure differences in how people process information.

Recently, John Carroll, a distinguished cognitive psychologist, has begun to explore ways in which the measurement of information-processing differences might replace or at least supplement some of the traditional psychometric measures of intelligence. Carroll (1981) argues that there now is a highly sophisticated technology available, both in equipment and in statistics, to permit a thorough exploration of this possibility. Although he does not see information-processing measures as totally replacing traditional intelligence tests, his general feeling is that the study of information-processing performance can bring about improvements in the assessment of intelligence. Physiological measures of mental functioning have also begun to show promise in contributing to the ability to measure the elusive quality intelligence. In data that are quite consistent with an information-processing view, the amount of detail in tracings of brain reactions to stimuli has been shown to correspond closely with intelligence-test scores obtained by traditional testing techniques (Eysenck, 1980). The implication is that an individual's information processing, even at the simplest level, is linked to more global measures of mental ability (Sternberg, 1982).

INTELLIGENCE AND THE NATURE/NURTURE QUESTION

Regardless of whether a person views intelligence from a purely psychometric perspective or from an information-processing viewpoint, one of the facts about measured intelligence is that people's performances on intelligence tests differ widely. Many researchers and practitioners have been greatly interested in the reasons for these differences.

Why do some people have higher measured intelligence than others? One way to try to answer this question is to compare the intelligence-test scores of people with differing degrees of genetic and environmental similarity. At one extreme are identical twins reared together—persons with identical genetic makeup and with highly similar environments. At the other extreme are two unrelated persons reared separately—any two persons chosen at random. These extremes and several combinations in between give psychologists some basis for estimating the possible effects of both heredity (nature) and environment (nurture). Table 5–1 provides a summary of research on this issue based on the work of Jarvik and Erlenmeyer-Kimling (1967), Jensen (1969), Kamin (1975), and C. R. Reynolds (1981).

Identical twins are usually similar in intelligence regardless of where they are raised.

The research summarized in Table 5–1 does not provide clearcut evidence in favor of either nature or nurture. Identical twins are similar in measures of intelligence regardless of where they are reared. Kagan and Lang (1978) have pointed out, however, that differences in the

TABLE 5–1
The Relationship of Measures of Intelligence for Persons of Varying Amounts of Genetic and Environmental Similarity

Relationship	*Factors Examined in Relationship*	*Relationship between Paired Intelligence Test Scores**
Identical twins reared together	Identical genetic makeup; highly similar environments	High (+.80 to +.90)
Identical twins reared separately†	Identical genetic makeup; different environments	Moderately high (+.74)
Fraternal twins of same sex	Similar genetic makeup; similar environments	Moderate (+.50 to +.60)
Fraternal twins of different sexes	Similar genetic makeup; similar environments	Moderate (+.45 to +.55)
Non-twin siblings reared together	Similar genetic makeup; somewhat similar environments	Moderate (+.50 to +.60)
Non-twin siblings reared separately	Similar genetic makeup; different environments	Low (+.20 to +.30)
Foster parents and foster children	Different genetic makeup; somewhat similar environments	Low (+.15 to +.25)
Unrelated children raised in same home	Different genetic makeup; somewhat similar environments	Low (+.15 to +.25)
Unrelated persons raised in separate environments	Different genetic makeup; dissimilar environments	None (close to zero)

*Correlations, the figures in parentheses, describe the extent to which intelligence test scores are related. A correlation close to 1.00 indicates a high degree of relationship, while a correlation of .00 indicates no relationship at all. The values we give for correlations are the average range of those obtained in the studies we reviewed.

†A major source of data for identical twins reared apart was the research of Sir Cyril Burt, a leading figure in British psychology for nearly sixty years until his death in 1971. In 1975, Kamin drew attention to certain discrepancies in Burt's data, and in 1976 he accused Burt of systematically creating fraudulent data. As of this writing, there are very serious questions about the validity of Burt's reports. When his data for identicals reared apart are discarded, as Vernon (1979) suggests and as we have done, the average correlation is .74. Other sources may report a somewhat higher figure.

Source: L. F. Jarvik & L. Erlenmeyer-Kimling. Survey of familial correlations in measured intellectual functions. In J. Zubin and G. A. Jervis (Eds.), *Psychopathology of mental development.* New York: Grune & Stratton, 1967. Used by permission.

environments of separated identical twins are typically not great—they are rarely raised in different socioeconomic groups. Further, as you might guess, the number of separated identical twins is extremely small. On the other hand, measures of intelligence for unrelated children raised together are correlated +.23, while measures of intelligence for unrelated children raised apart have a zero relationship. Evidently both the environment and heredity play a part in the development of abilities measured by intelligence tests.

A second way in which the nature/nurture question has been examined has been through the evaluation of programs designed to help "disadvantaged" children make up preschool deficiencies. Head Start, initiated in the early 1960s, was designed with the idea that the environment of preschool children could be enriched enough to significantly increase their levels of intelligence (Hunt, 1961).

The results of the Head Start programs did not fulfill the hopes of many people. The U.S. Commission on Civil Rights (1967) concluded that "none of the compensatory education programs appear to have raised significantly the achievement of participating pupils, as a group, within the period evaluated by the Commission" (p. 138). The conclusion that compensatory education programs were not effective, however, has not been accepted by many psychologists who, like Kagan (Kagan & Lang, 1978), have argued that environmental differences do account for many observed differences in children's intellectual abilities. There also have been reports of parent training programs that have produced highly significant and long-lasting changes in children's intelligence scores (see Garber & Heber, 1977).

Other programs such as Follow Through have been designed to provide enrichment activities for "disadvantaged" children in primary grades. The effects of Follow Through (Kennedy, 1978; Stallings, 1975) have varied, depending on the ways in which it has been implemented in the schools. Both Head Start and Follow Through are still operating and may yet succeed as intended as they are adjusted through ongoing developmental research.

In psychological circles, the nature/nuture debate continued with little in the way of fiery arguments until 1969, when Arthur Jensen published an article in the *Harvard Educational Review* entitled "How much can we boost IQ and scholastic achievement?" Jensen argued that compensatory education programs failed because they were based on the assumption that the environment controlled the development of intellectual abilities. Jensen then claimed that intelligence was determined primarily by heredity and not the environment. He also stated that educational programs should not try to "create" intelligence via environmental programming but should instead take genetic differences into account.

PRACTICE EXERCISE 5–1

Intelligence and Cognitive Processes—What Do Practicing Teachers Think?

Most teachers have developed their ideas about teaching far beyond those they had in teacher training. One area where views often change is that of intelligence and its measurement. In this exercise, we want you to take advantage of teachers' experiences by interviewing one or more experienced teachers on the topic of intelligence and cognitive development. The following questions should lead you into some interesting questions about intelligence. You should also add questions of your own. If you can, get permission to tape record your interview so that you will have it available to analyze in more detail.

Questions for the Interview

1. What is your definition of intelligence?
2. Do differences in intelligence affect what you do in your classroom?
3. As a teacher, what do you think of IQ test scores as a measure of intelligence?
4. Have you ever made use of IQ test scores in your work with students?
5. Cognitive style refers to the way in which students usually approach problems—for example, impulsively or with reflection. Do you notice differences in cognitive style in your students and, if so, how does this affect your teaching?
6. What cognitive processes (examples might be memory, visualizing or problem solving) do you most hope to change in the students you teach?
7. Is there a special researcher or theorist whose views on memory, thinking, or cognitive development have had a great effect on you?

Jensen's most controversial statements, however, centered on his assertion that there were differences in the average intelligence of different ethnic groups and that certain groups, blacks in particular, would benefit most from instruction based on association-level learning as opposed to conceptual learning.

To say that Jensen's article touched off an explosive reaction is an understatement.* Other researchers accused him of misinterpreting and misusing his statistical methods. The controversy became more heated

* Jensen's more recent work (1980) is basically a greatly expanded and updated recapitulation of his earlier work, pointing out differences in measured intelligence, although he does not reassert his earlier position that the differences are genetic.

Your own questions:

8. ____

9. ____

10. ____

After you have finished your interview, judge your results (and, if possible, compare them to your classmates') on the following criteria:

1. Would you say that the teacher you interviewed is negative, neutral, or positive about the use of intelligence test scores as indicators of general mental ability?
2. Do his or her views seem valid, in your opinion? If, so, why? If not, why not?
3. Do his or her views seem consistent with those of most other teachers?
4. If this person's views were your own, would they make you a better (a more humane, effective) teacher or would they make you worse (less humane, ineffective)?

when Herrnstein (1971) and Eysenck (1971) independently performed scholarly analyses of the history of intelligence testing and the research that had examined the influence of heredity and environment on intelligence. Both concluded that approximately 80 percent of the variance in intelligence-test scores is related to genetic differences. It is important to note that both Herrnstein, of Harvard, and Eysenck, perhaps the most respected psychologist in Britain, performed their analyses with the wish to clear up the problem, not to support Jensen's position.*

* The hereditary position was taken to the point of absurdity when the physicist William Shockley (1971) asserted that "an increase of one percent in Caucasian ancestry raises Negro IQ an average of one point for low IQ populations" (p. 244).

Environmentalists (Garcia, 1972; Mercer, 1972; P. Watson, 1972) responded with well-formulated counterarguments pointing out the disadvantaged nature of environments in which many black children grow up. They argued, in general, that measures of intelligence are biased toward white middle-class children on the basis of language and experience. They also argued that the skills required to take intelligence tests were not acquired by minority-group children and that the children were not motivated to do well in test-taking situations because of a negative "self-fulfilling prophecy." Barnes (1974) has also reported that IQ scores of black children drop significantly when they are tested by white examiners rather than by blacks.

A large part of the argument for racial differences in intelligence arises from a process of reasoning by analogy. The reasoning goes like this: There are obvious physical differences between racial groups attributable to genetic differences, and there are observed differences between test scores of racial groups. Therefore, differences in scores must also be due to genetic (racial) differences. This, of course, is fallacious reasoning because the effects of nature and nurture can never be separated in human beings.*

Does the nature/nurture issue make any difference to teaching? On one hand, even the strictest proponent of the genetic viewpoint concedes that 20 to 25 percent of intelligence is environmentally determined (Jensen, 1969). On the other hand, environmentalists allow that heredity determines at least one-quarter of the variation in intelligence (Glover, 1979b). So the argument really boils down to how well teachers can nurture students' intellectual development. As teachers, we are responsible for helping *all* of our students develop to the fullest possible extent, regardless of their IQ scores. We can only take the position that through good instruction we can positively influence the intellectual development of each student.

A DEVELOPMENTAL VIEW OF INTELLIGENCE: JEAN PIAGET

So far in this chapter we have presented an overview of the psychometric approach and have seen how the limited research from an information-processing perspective appears to confirm the psychometric position. Both the psychometric and information-processing viewpoints, how-

* The nature/nurture question could be settled once and for all with a series of experiments that will never be performed. One could identify several sets of identical twins at birth, immediately take them from their parents and rear them in two separate, fully controlled environments. Observed differences would be due to environmental effects. Fortunately, no psychologist in his right mind would suggest such an experiment.

Jean Piaget: Much of what cognitive psychology is today has been influenced by his theories about the development of intellecutal processes.

ever, have some limits in scope, especially in describing how intelligence develops in human beings and what factors influence that development. The remainder of this chapter is devoted to the most comprehensive contemporary theory of intelligence, that of Jean Piaget.

Piaget (1896–1980) was a true giant in psychology, greatly affecting its development (see Flavell, 1980). In fact, it is fair to suggest that much of current cognitive psychology has been influenced by the pioneering work of Piaget (Hayes, 1978). A discussion of Piaget's theory will allow us to present a fuller, more descriptive picture of human cognition.

Piaget began his work in biology, publishing his first paper in his mid-teens. He earned his doctorate in biology at the age of twenty-two but soon became interested in psychology. His first efforts in psychology were in the study of psychoanalysis, where he developed his observational method of research (Lunzer, 1976), but his major interest in intelligence sprang from the two years he spent standardizing tests of intelligence in Theodore Simon's laboratory.

> This initiation had two effects. First, he was able to go beyond the categorization of children's answers as "right" or "wrong." Further questioning enabled him to establish how and why a reply took the form that it did. This is the line of investigation that was to be Piaget's principal preoccupation throughout his career. Second, and as a corollary to this, Piaget became disenchanted with psychometrics—and has remained so [to his death] . . . believing that other methods . . . permit the investigator to go beyond statistical recording of surface data to the analysis of process itself. *(Lunzer, 1976, p. xii)*

Piaget's ideas about intelligence were to have a profound impact on the field of education.

Why is Piaget's theory of importance to the educator and so widely applied to thinking about education? First, it is a theory that describes how thinking develops in human beings from birth to adulthood. As teachers, you will be working with students at different stages and levels, and changes occur rapidly. Second, Piaget's theory has touched on almost all aspects of human intellectual functioning, including imitation, perception, language, logic, memory, judgment, reasoning, and play. Piaget's theory, articulated in more than two hundred articles and dozens of books, is truly a comprehensive theory of the mental activity we call thinking and encompasses all aspects of human thought. Third, Piaget (and to an even greater extent his coauthor, Barbara Inhelder) has been greatly concerned with education during his career. Several of his books and articles and hundreds of publications by other authors have related Piaget's theory to the practice of teaching.

Obviously, the lifework of Jean Piaget cannot be distilled into a few pages. What we will do is set out the basic principles of his theory, relate them to other views of human cognition, and stress some educational applications.

Intelligence as Biological Adaptation

Human beings as biological organisms who adapt

Piaget viewed the development of intelligence as one way in which people adapt to the world. Humans are biological organisms who must develop means of fitting into their environment in order to survive. Intelligence is "a particular instance of biological adaptation" (Piaget, 1952, pp. 3–4) and "a biological achievement which allows the individual to interact effectively with the environment at a psychological level" (Ginsburg & Opper, 1979, p. 13).* Intelligence has its own tendencies

* Piaget does not use the term *intelligence* to refer only to the abilities usually measured by standardized tests of intelligence. Rather, he talks about intelligence as the totality of the mechanisms of thinking and adaptation available to humans. Intelligence is present in all human actions and perceptions.

toward development, organized by biological mechanisms within the individual.

This perspective is important. Piaget conceived of cognitive growth as proceeding by stages from the innate reflexes of a baby to an adult's capability for abstract, logical reasoning. According to Piaget's view, the mechanisms and states of cognitive development are universal, but each individual's cognitive development is unique. Each person's environment puts specific demands on that person. Thus the rate and content of cognitive growth are governed by universal processes of intellectual development and by the specific kinds of experiences people have. As we proceed with our discussion of Piaget's theory, this basic principle must be kept in mind.

Cognitive Organization and Adaptation

According to Piaget, cognitive growth occurs as the intelligence of the individual adapts to the demands of the environment. But how does this process of cognitive adaptation operate? Piaget does not provide a simple answer to this question. In his view, adaptation to the environment is linked to the way in which people organize the environment they encounter.

> From the biological point of view organization is inseparable from adaptation. They are two complementary processes of a single mechanism, the first being the internal aspect of the cycle of which adaptation constitutes the external aspect. *(Piaget, 1952, p. 7)*

To understand cognitive organization and adaptation, you should understand five concepts basic to Piaget's theory: schemata, schemes, assimilation, accommodation, and equilibrium. These are the concepts Piaget used to explain how and why cognitive development occurs (Ginsburg & Opper, 1979; Piaget, 1977; Piaget & Inhelder, 1973).

Schemata and Schemes. Piaget suggested that humans have two forms of knowledge about the world—operative and figurative. Operative knowledge is knowledge of how to perform actions such as tying shoes, writing a letter, or grading a paper. Figurative knowledge is knowledge of facts—that birds have wings, that mammals have a four-chambered heart, the name of the president of the United States, and so on. For Piaget, **schemes** are the cognitive structures by which people represent their knowledge for operations. That is, a scheme is a cognitive structure for performing an activity. A baby, for example, has a scheme for responding to a favorite toy that may relate to grasping it and putting it in his or her mouth. **Schemata** (singular, schema) are the inferred cognitive structures (similar to concepts as defined in Chapter Three) by which children and adults intellectually organize perceived events into categories based on common characteristics. Schemata represent figurative knowledge. A child may have a schema for "bird" that is very broad (undifferentiated). It is not until the child acquires new information and the schema changes that he or she can differentiate bats from birds. Further, some anomalous kinds of birds like penguins might not be properly classed until the information in a child's schema for "bird" has increased to the point that the child can recognize the similarities between penguins and other birds.

In infancy, many of the child's cognitive structures are reflexive and are inferred from regularities in behavior, such as sucking and grasping objects. Such cognitive structures are very closely linked to the infant's actions. Adults, in contrast, have evolved a vast array of quite complex and abstracted cognitive structures, including both schemes and schemata, that permit them to distinguish a multitude of different events, concepts, and objects.

Schemes and schemata become progressively complex with development but are derived from the early, simple cognitive structures of infancy and childhood. The processes by which schemes and schemata are modified are assimilation and accommodation (Flavell, 1977).

Assimilation and Accommodation. Assimilation and accommodation are the two complementary processes by which experiences are integrated into cognitive structures. A person experiences an event in terms of existing schemes and schemata. **Assimilation** is the process of relating new information to already existing cognitive structures. **Accommodation** is the process of modifying existing cognitive structures so that the new information may be assimilated into them. Changes in cognitive structures are necessary for the child to adjust to the impact of experiences that cannot be assimilated into existing schemes or schemata. As the situation demands, the child constructs new cognitive structures into which the information can be assimilated.

While it is possible to think about the two processes as separate functions, they always occur together. Consider the case of a child who sees a cow for the first time but already has a schema for horses (figurative knowledge). "What's that?" asks a parent. "A horsie," answers the child. The child has taken new information (seeing the cow) and assimilated it into the schema for horse. To allow this assimilation to occur, however, the horse schema was slightly modified (accommodated) so that the new information would fit. With further experience, however, the child's cognitive structures will be adapted (accommodated) so that a new schema is formed into which the child's perceptions can be assimilated. When the child sees a cow and recognizes it as such, he or she has formed a new cognitive structure for "cow" that is different from the one for "horse."

Equilibrium. Piaget refers to **equilibrium** as a balance between assimilation and accommodation. Obviously children cannot always assimilate or they would end up with a few very, very large cognitive structures and be unable to detect differences in the things they perceive. Likewise, children cannot solely accommodate because this would result in many schemes and schemata, each representing only a little of their experience, and they would not be able to detect similarities. There must be a balance between assimilation and accommodation.

Piaget contends that the child strives for equilibrium. The overriding principle is that mental growth progresses toward more and more complex and stable mental structures. When structures cannot easily assimilate new experiences, there is an imbalance between assimilation and accommodation. A sense of *disequilibrium* motivates the person to seek equilibrium. (See Chapter Nine for different views of motivation.) Equilibrium is achieved as stimuli are assimilated into modified or new cognitive structures.

Children constantly strive for equilibrium as they seek an organization that will be internally consistent for them. This organization, however, need not be and often is not the same as an adult's organization. There is no such thing as an incorrect organization from Piaget's perspective, only more complex and consistent organizations.

Factors Influencing the Development of Cognition

Piaget (1976, 1977, 1978) suggested that four general factors influence the development of thought among humans: (1) biological maturation, (2) experience with the physical environment, (3) experience with the social environment, and (4) equilibration. Biological maturation refers to the growth and change of biological structures in individuals. As children mature, their physical structures become more complete, and they are able to experience their environment in more sophisticated ways. Hence the quality of their thought changes. Piaget (1978), however, is very explicit in pointing out that intelligence is not genetically programmed and that biological maturation works in combination with other factors.

> We cannot assume there exists a hereditary program indulging the development of human intelligence, there are no innate ideas. . . . The effects of maturation consist essentially of organizing new possibilities for development; that is, giving access to structures which could not be evolved before these possibilities are offered. But between possibility and actualization, there must intervene a set of other factors such as . . . experience and social interaction. *(Piaget, 1970, pp. 719–720)*

In other words, while Piaget acknowledges the importance of biological maturation, the actual fulfillment of intellectual capabilities is very powerfully influenced by children's interactions with their environment.

One form of children's interaction with the environment is their experience with the physical world. Piaget categorized such experience into two major forms: physical and logical-mathematical. **Physical experience** "consists of acting upon objects and drawing some knowledge about the objects by abstraction from the objects" (Piaget, 1978, p. 231). A child may discover, for example, that wooden objects float by placing objects made from various materials in a bathtub. The child's interaction with the environment results in the acquisition of knowledge about some of the physical properties of objects—"wooden things float." While a considerable amount of cognitive development is guided by physical experience, logical-mathematical experience is equally important.

Logical-mathematical experience occurs when "knowledge is not drawn from the objects, but it is drawn by the action's effects upon the objects" (Piaget, 1978, p. 231). Piaget provided a classic example of logical-mathematical experience in a story he often related about the childhood experiences of one of his friends. The child (about four or five years of age at the time) was playing with some pebbles in his garden. He placed them in a row and counted them up to ten. He then recounted them from the opposite direction and still found ten. The boy found this fact fascinating. He then put the stones in a circle and counted them—still ten. Ultimately, the boy put the pebbles into several configurations, always counting them and always finding ten. The boy discovered that ten items are ten items no matter how they are arranged. He did not discover anything about the properties of pebbles themselves as would be the case in physical experience but rather discovered knowledge about an action he took (counting). The boy could have made the same discovery (configuration does not affect number) with marbles, twigs, beans, or frogs (providing they did not hop away!). The properties of the objects were not relevant to the boy's discovery.

Physical experience is an important factor influencing cognitive development. Obviously the kinds of experiences children have with their physical environment will affect the development of their thought processes to a considerable extent. Piaget, however, suggested that children's experiences with the social environment are just as important. The social environment (other people) provides opportunities for children to learn a great many things. Piaget's major focus in this area was on children's learning of language. Language, of course, plays a crucial role in permitting children to represent actions in their thoughts. However, language does not produce the development of intelligence but rather serves to facilitate its growth.

The fourth fundamental factor in cognitive development is the process of equilibration (Piaget, 1978). Piaget believes that children actively participate in their cognitive development through *equilibration* (Piaget & Inhelder, 1969), which is the child's system for regulating and integrating the changes brought about by maturation, physical experience, and social experience. Through assimilation and accommodation, equilibration moves the person from a state of disequilibrium to a state of equilibrium.

Operations and Stages of Cognitive Development

Cognitive changes are the result of developmental processes. Piaget felt that cognitive development is a coherent sequence of successive, qualitative changes in cognitive structures. The cognitive development process is logical and orderly, with each change based on prior structures and processes. Piaget (1973) categorized cognitive development into four general stages. Briefly, they are as follows:

> The *sensorimotor* stage (birth to approximately two years). During this stage children's actions become more and more intentional and integrated into patterns. Cognitive development can be observed as they display awareness of themselves and their surroundings and respond consistently to similar stimuli.
>
> The *preoperational thought* stage (approximately two to seven years). During this stage children rapidly develop language and conceptual thought.
>
> The *concrete operations* stage (approximately seven to eleven years). Children develop the ability to apply logical thought to concrete problems during this stage. Their thinking, however, is still quite closely linked to their immediate experience.
>
> The *formal operations* stage (from approximately age eleven on). Cognitive development may reach its highest level during this stage. By the age of fifteen or sixteen (approximately), many children are able to apply logic to a variety of problems, although some people never fully develop formal operational thinking.

Each of Piaget's stages is frequently given with the ages of children who possess cognitive structures characteristic of that stage. Piaget does not mean these chronological dates to be rigid. Rather, they are general approximations of where *most children* of certain ages are likely to be in their intellectual development. The stages are sequential, but children need not complete all of one stage before entering the next. A child in the preoperational stage may perform some functions characteristic of both the sensorimotor and concrete operations stages, for instance. Piaget does assert, however, that all children must pass through the same stages in the same order, although not necessarily at the same rate.

An extremely important concept for understanding Piaget's stages of development is the idea of operations (Piaget & Inhelder, 1969). An **operation** is a scheme whose major characteristic is that it can be reversed. If we took the square root of 49 to obtain 7, we know as adults that we can reverse this operation and square 7 to get back to 49. Understanding that two rows of five beads contain the same number of beads even if we lengthen or compress one of them is also an operation, as is understanding that the volume of water in a container doesn't change when we pour it into a container of another shape. Adults understand clearly that each transformation is reversible to its former state; most young children, however, do not.

While many rules and specific facts are not operations (knowing that school buses are yellow, that dogs bark, or that snow is white), operations rather than the specific facts of learning are central to intelligence as Piaget saw it. Thus you can best understand Piaget's stages of development by examining the operations that children can master during each one. Few if any operations are present during the initial two stages, sensorimotor and preoperational, but operations gradually develop during what is called the concrete operational stage.

The Sensorimotor Stage. The sensorimotor stage, like the following stages of development, is divided into substages. The first substage, immediately following birth, is dominated by reflexes such as sucking and by random body movements. During the second substage (from two weeks to four months of age), infants assimilate their cognitive structures to familiar experiences and accommodate and develop new cognitive structures for strange new objects (a bottle instead of the breast, grasping a toy). The third substage (four to eight months of age) is characterized by infants' developing sense of cause and effect, a sense that will continue to be refined. Infants learn cause and effect from their interactions with their environment—the last time the baby slapped the bottle, he got milk and so now he begins to develop a scheme for slapping the bottle. Or the last time the baby was on her back she kicked with her right knee and elbow and rolled over. The next time she is placed on the floor on her back she uses the same set of movements to roll over.

In addition to a rudimentary understanding of causation, children in the third substage of the sensorimotor period rapidly develop the ability to coordinate their vision with their touch. They can now grasp what they see and actively manipulate objects. This coordination of actions leads to experiences that in turn allow for greater cognitive development and their cognitive structures become more complex. A further general characteristic of the first three substages is that infants appear to have no conception of time—only the here and now matter.

By the fourth substage (eight to twelve months), however, infants usually develop some concept of the future. The baby crying to be picked up hushes when she hears her father walking down the hall toward her room. She understands that comfort is only a few seconds away.

Object permanence is usually understood by the age of twelve months. Objects that are removed from direct vision of infants seem to no longer exist for them. Around twelve months, however, children show by their actions an understanding that just because an object is out of their immediate sight it need not be gone. Their actions demonstrate that they can think about objects without having to see them. One-year-old children can be observed playing "peekaboo" with objects, covering and uncovering them. They will also remember that your piece of candy still exists even if you hide it.

By the beginning of the fifth substage (twelve to eighteen months), children begin to experiment with their world. They throw, bite, spit out, rearrange, and break objects just to see what will happen. At dinner a child may drop a spoon to the floor over and over as he or she experiments with the effects of dropping the spoon. Experimentation soon leads to problem solving. Where a baby might once have stood by the crib and cried until a parent came to get his blanket for him, he now grabs a corner of it and pulls it through the bars. Later he pulls a stool to the edge of the crib and reaches over the side for objects. Children in the fifth substage also increase their imitation of other people. Stick your tongue out at a baby of this age and she may stick hers back out at you!

During the sixth substage (eighteen to twenty-four months), children can better represent objects cognitively. They are beginning to abstract and to "think," and this allows them to develop new ways of solving problems. A child who remembers that the jar lids are in the box at the back of the bottom drawer in the kitchen can carry out a sequence of actions based on that knowledge. If she can think about playing with the lids, she may walk to the kitchen, open the drawer, get out the box, and play.

The ability to visualize objects and people and to predict simple outcomes of actions readies children for the next stage of development. No longer will cognition focus primarily on physical activities: in the preoperational stage the emphasis shifts to symbolic learning.

The Preoperational Stage. The preoperational stage was so named by Piaget because children do not possess operations at its outset. The story of the preoperational stage is one of acquiring cognitive operations. There are, however, many other activities of preoperational children.

Language acquisition is one of the most important. Two-year-olds have a vocabulary of about two hundred words, but by the time children start school at age five their vocabularies will likely consist of thousands of words. Prior to the age of two, it is fairly easy for parents to keep track of all the new words that a child learns. After two, however, most children accelerate their learning of words so rapidly that it is almost impossible to keep track.

Words are important in ways beyond the obvious need to communicate. Words are symbols and as such children use them to structure their worlds. Further, children assign definitions to words that suit themselves. Their meanings may be very different from those an adult would give the words.

One interesting characteristic of preoperational children is egocentricity. **Egocentricity** means, quite literally, believing that you are at the center of the universe. One of the authors recently asked his three-year-old daughter why the sun was shining. She answered, "Because it wants to." "Oh," said the author, "why does it want to?" "Because I like to play outside," she answered.

Because they organize their worlds around their own points of view, preoperational children are quite likely to be unable to see things "objectively" (Phillips, 1975). Adult reasoning will often not be effective, and an adult may despair at how self-centered a preoperational child can be. Asking a preoperational child to go downstairs and play because you must wash the dishes can be very frustrating when the child cannot see why you should bother with the dishes.

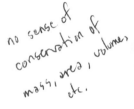

Preoperational children cannot perform the operation of conservation. **Conservation** means understanding that such features as number, mass, and area are not changed by superficial transformations of an object or set of objects. There are different forms of conservation, including conservation of number, area, length, and volume. Preoperational children, for example, do not conserve number. If a five-year-old is shown two rows of ten pennies, one longer than the other, and is told that she may have the row she wants, she will likely choose the longer one. If you ask why, you're likely to receive an answer like "Because it's the biggest." Although this answer is illogical to us as adults, it is perfectly logical within the child's own cognitive structures.

During a recent Saturday lunch at the home of one of the authors, both his two-year-old and four-year-old were given little pieces of cake for dessert. Both pieces were the same size but the author inadvertently broke the two-year-old's into pieces as it was removed from the cake pan. As both girls started to eat, the four-year-old remarked, "I'm almost full. I'm glad I didn't get as much as my sister." She had not yet acquired the operation of conservation of volume.

The major feature of operations is reversibility, and preoperational children cannot conserve because they cannot reverse processes in their minds. A broken piece of cake cannot be reconstructed mentally into a whole piece. Likewise, the conservation of number, area, and length all require reversibility, the recognition that things can be transformed back to the way they were before.

One of the characteristic things about preoperational children is the endless number of questions they ask. "Why did the puppy run across our yard?" "Why is that a tree?" "Why are airplanes loud?" Such questions require answers that are reasonable for the children within their own frame of reference. If you answer the question "Why are clouds white?" with a monologue about the reflection and absorption of different wavelengths of light, your answer will likely be lost on a preoperational child. A response stressing things that the child knows may help: "What white things do you know about?" (The child names some.) "What is the same about them?" (The child makes some guesses.) "See, clouds are kind of like a clean, fluffy ball of cotton. They look white because of how the light shines on them and because they don't have much dust or rain in them."

Preoperational children begin to develop a more accurate sense of time. They can store information for future use. Their sense of time may still be somewhat different from that of an adult, however. In telling a story, a child of one of the authors began, "Once upon a time, far, far away—in Kansas City—and long, long ago—last Tuesday. . . ." She understood the past but her ideas of "long ago" were rather different from her father's.

The Concrete Operations Stage. Piaget so named the stage of concrete operations because children during this stage can deal with concrete problems in a logical way. "Concrete" refers to the actual presence of objects and events. Concrete-operational children can master conservation problems and understand reversibility if materials are physically present. A child at this stage can cognitively restructure a broken-up piece of cake into the size and shape it once was.

In this stage children can group objects on the basis of color, size, shape, or other similarities, and they can consider more than one attribute of objects simultaneously. Given cubes and balls of two colors, children can group by all round and blue things, all square and brown things, and so on. They can also answer questions like "Are there more balls or brown objects?" Piaget referred to such reasoning abilities as **decentration;** children no longer center on only a single attribute of objects as they did in the preoperational stage.

PRACTICE EXERCISE 5–2
Conservation

One of the most fascinating things about Piaget's theory is that conservation or the lack of it is so easily observed in preoperational children. To help you get a better feel for conservation, we urge you to locate a three-to-five-year-old child and try some things. The child can be your own, a sibling, nephew or niece, or the child of a friend—it makes no difference. After you've chatted for a while and the child is comfortable in your presence, ask if he or she would like to play a brief game. If so, try some of the following conservation problems.

Conservation of Number

Make two equal rows of similar objects (marbles, chips, blocks), on a table. Be careful to make the spaces between the objects the same. Each object should have a corresponding object across from it. Ask the child, "Which row has more or do they have the same?" Most preoperational children will answer that both rows have the same amount. Now, with the child watching, increase the spaces between the objects in one of the rows. Again ask the child, "Which row has more or do they both have the same?" Children who cannot conserve number will answer that the longer row has the most. Their judgment is affected by the change in distance between the objects. You may then want to have the child count the objects and try rearranging them in several ways. The child who cannot conserve will continue to err in his or her judgment.

First Trial		Second Trial	
0	0		0
0	0	0	0
		0	
0	0	0	0
		0	
0	0	0	0
0	0		0

Conservation of Area

Make up two green cardboard sheets to use as "fields of grass." You will also need two small models or cutouts of cows and a number of barns (such as the hotels in a Monopoly game). Ask the child to pretend that the two identical cardboard sheets are fields of grass. Then place a cow in the middle of each field. Substantiate with the child the equality of the fields of grass ("Do both cows have the same amount of grass to eat or does one cow have more?"). Now place a barn in the *middle* of one field and ask, "Does this cow have the same, more, or less grass to eat than that other cow?" After the child responds (most will say the cow now has less), place a second barn in one of the corners of the other field. Ask the same question again. From this point, place two barns at a time; in one field place the barns in a scattered, random way and in the other place the barns along the edge starting in the child's left-hand corner. Each time you place a pair of barns, re-ask the question about the amount of grass available. Most young children will make errors in their judgments. To them the scattered barns mean less grass to eat, while the barns all in a row leave more for the cow!

Conservation of Volume

Conservation of volume can be tested with water and three containers, two identical and one different. Fill the two identical containers with the same amount of water. Ask the child to substantiate the equality of the water. (You may need to add a bit of water to one or the other container to satisfy the child that the amounts are "exactly the same.") Then pour the water from one of the containers into another container of a different shape. Now ask, "Do these containers have the same amount of water to drink, or does one have more water to drink?" Point to the appropriate glasses as you ask the question. Children who cannot conserve volume will inform you that the amounts of water in the two containers are not equal when water from one of the containers has been poured into another of a different shape. Their explanation of why this is so may surprise you!

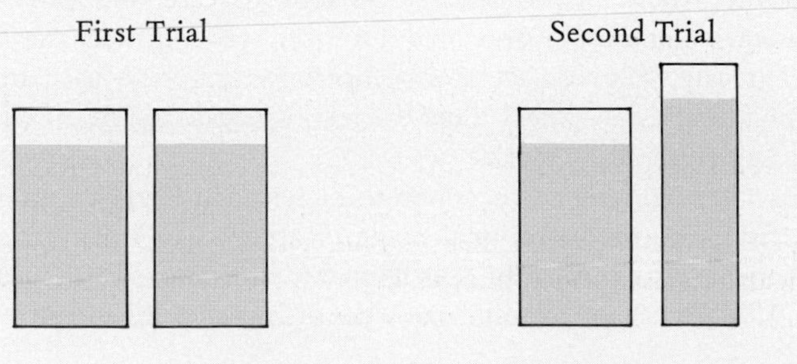

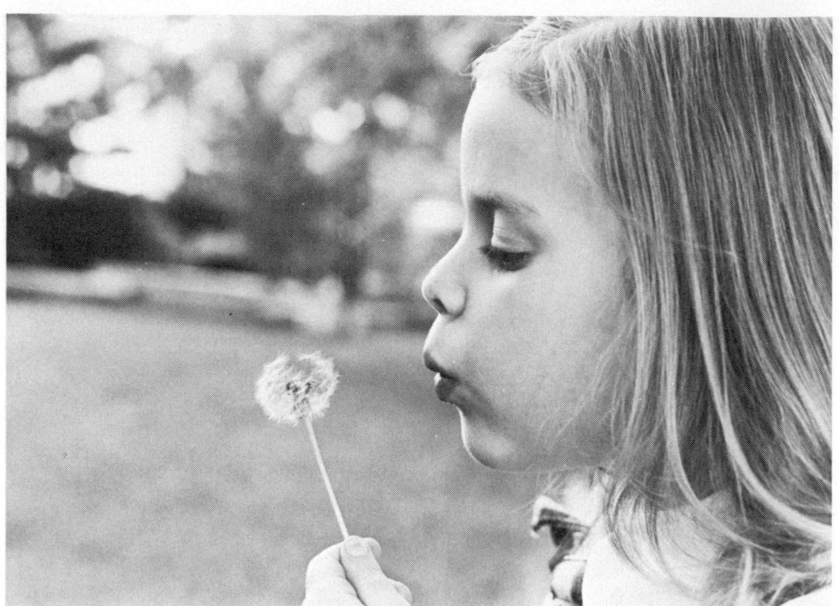

In the concrete operations stage, learning is closely linked to childrens' concrete experiences with the world.

Visual problems are solved more readily than verbal problems during the stage of concrete operations. Word problems—"There are four boys in the room. Ed is taller than Bill. Joe is shorter than Sam. Bill is taller than Sam. Who is the shortest?"—will likely only confuse concrete-operational children. But if you were to draw pictures of Ed, Bill, Sam, and Joe on the blackboard and ask, "Who is the shortest?" children at this stage would answer your question easily.

Abstract thought is not highly developed in concrete-operational children. This means that such children can accept reality more readily than hypothetical conditions. If you were chatting with a group of concrete-operational children and said something like "Suppose the sky were green," you would likely hear a chorus of "No, it isn't! The sky is blue." Or if you asked them, "What would happen if we found out the cars could run on water?" you'd likely get back, "But water won't work." Both these hypothetical assertions require manipulation of abstract ideas. Concrete-operational children are unlikely to be able to think that way. A given set of assumptions cannot be used by concrete-operational children unless they correspond exactly to how they have learned to perceive the world.

This close adherence to concrete experience leads to an interesting change from the preoperational stage. Rather than imagining all kinds of fantastic events, concrete-operational children are addicted to literal facts. "No, Papa, you can't load the dishwasher like that. That isn't how Momma does it." "No, Momma, that's not how to play dolly. You *have* to do it this way." Concrete-operational students see teachers as unfair if they test more than literal learning or rote recall. The middle elementary school years are a time of learning the facts, the dates, and the classifications of things. This sticking to the facts will soon be left behind as children enter the stage of formal operations.

The Formal Operations Stage. Piaget named this stage formal operations because children now can perform operations that require formal logic (Piaget, 1969, 1970). It is the time in which many of the characteristics of adult thought develop. Abstract thought is present, allowing children to begin to handle questions they stumbled over when they were concrete operational. If you toss out the thought "Suppose the sky were green" to formal-operational youngsters, they may think you are silly but they could deal with the notion. "I'd guess that everything would have a different color. I wonder if the sunsets would be blue or red or what?"

In the formal operations stage, the individual can construct hypotheses and test them logically. Formal-operational students are beginning to think like adults in evaluating their own reasoning. The thinking of other persons likewise is critically evaluated by formal-operational children. There is some egocentricity but it is different from that of

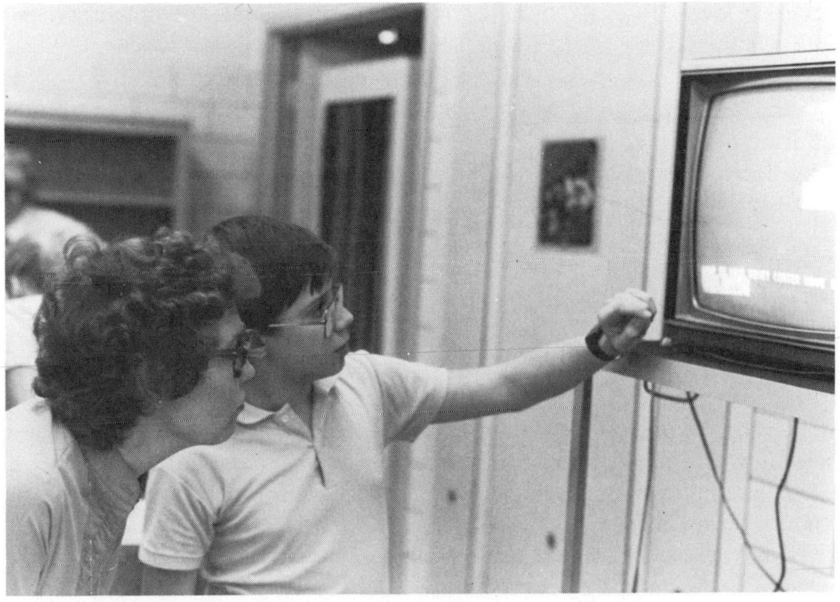

During formal operations, the individual can construct hypotheses and test them logically.

earlier years. Rather than believing that they are at the center of all things, they believe that they are in the spotlight and that others are watching and evaluating their actions. This feeling of being in the spotlight accounts for some of the acting-out behavior of adolescents.

Evaluating one's own thinking leads to introspection and to the assumption of adult roles. Formal-operational students often become concerned about society, their roles in it, and what it needs to make it better. Much of the disaffection adolescents have for society and its ground rules is a result of a newly developed ability to think critically about and evaluate the world.

As we noted earlier, not all persons ultimately develop the ability for abstract thought and formal operations. Environmental deficiencies may reduce the effects of physical experience and social interactions. Many children never have enough stimulation to take full advantage of their maturation. Even some college students and older adults remain at the level of concrete operations in many areas of their thinking.

In summary, Piaget's concept of development can be captured by the following. Development proceeds through a continuous process of generalizations and differentiations, and the continuity of development is achieved by a continuing unfolding (Maier, 1969). Each level of development finds its roots in a previous phase and continues into the following phase. Each phase entails a repetition of the previous level of cognitive development, but with different cognitive organization. Previous behavior patterns are sensed as inferior and become part of the new superior level. Piaget's view is that the natural tendency of human intelligence is to be "active and constructive" (Furth & Wachs, 1975), and cognitive processes make an active contribution to any interaction that humans have with their environments. Each person creates a unique understanding of the world through his or her own construction and organization of experience.

IMPLICATIONS FOR TEACHING

In general, psychometric approaches have not led to many direct applications for the classroom teacher. Instead, intelligence testing has been used most extensively as a part of decisions about placement in and selection of students for educational programs (see Chapter Sixteen). There are, however, some elements of the psychometric approach that are important for classroom teachers.

The measurement of intelligence has, without a doubt, led to a general understanding that there are likely to be great individual differences in cognitive abilities among the students in any given classroom (Hall & Kaye, 1980). The recognition of such differences has led a great many educators to emphasize individualized instruction in order to meet the needs of each student. In this book, we stress the need to individualize instruction, but like many others (Charles, 1976; Dick & Carey, 1978; Gagne & Briggs, 1979), our emphasis is on the analysis of what students currently know or can do and what is to be learned, rather than on measured intelligence (IQ). Processes that lead to individualization are discussed in detail in Chapters Eleven and Twelve.

A word of caution. The measurement of intelligence is a complex and controversial topic and contains many pitfalls for the unwary. We feel that, in general, intelligence-test scores should be interpreted with extreme care. IQ scores are simply scores on a test and should not be taken as measures of "potential," "capacity," or "innate ability." To do so is to risk stereotyping a student—as "gifted," "retarded," or a "slow learner." These IQ-related stereotypes are so strong that teachers (and professors) have actually been known to disregard evidence before their eyes (the achievement of a particular student, for instance) in favor of a single indicator of the student's abilities (the IQ score). It is better to disregard what the score "predicts" and to observe what students do or do not do in your classes.

As we indicated, the information-processing theory of intelligence is still in its infancy, especially as it relates to the cognitive processes of attention, perception, long-term memory, and problem solving in the working memory. Some theorists, however, have stressed a number of applications of an information-processing approach. Bruner (1966, 1971), for example, has pointed out that effective instruction should make use of all the available ways that children can represent their experiences. Younger students especially should be allowed to engage in grasping, touching, feeling, and other hands-on experiences. Later, students should still have these kinds of experiences, but instruction should begin to include pictorial and other imagery-based representations. As cognitive development continues, students should receive instruction emphasizing symbols (concepts, principles) as well as a continuation of the other, more basic forms of representation.

Like Piaget, Bruner views intellectual growth as developing from the child's interaction with the teacher, other students, and instructional materials. Student involvement is one key to meaningful learning. Another is that knowledge should be structured in such a way that it can be grasped by students. This structuring requires that the teacher analyze the knowledge and order it from simple to complex for presentation to students.

Bruner sees the processes of intellectual development as self-motivating. He de-emphasizes the use of external or "extrinsic" forms of incentives for learning. To Bruner, "the will to learn is an intrinsic motive, one that finds both its source and its reward in its own exercise." External rewards, in his view, can get learning under way and maintain it, but the bases for long-term learning are natural and spontaneous—human curiosity, playfulness, a natural motivation toward competence, and the desire to imitate others.

There are many parts of Piaget's theory of intellectual development that should affect teaching decisions. Teachers must remember that cognitive development is not automatic. The processes of assimilation and accommodation depend on both physical experience and social interactions. The kinds of schemes and schemata that students develop depend on the kinds of experiences they have. As a teacher, you influence these experiences to a great extent. The richer, more diversified experiences you provide for students, the more elaborate their cognitive structures will be.

APPLICATIONS FOR TEACHING

The preceding implications lead to some practical applications that we have adapted in part from Case (1978).

1. Relate your methods and materials to desired cognitive processes of students. Carefully observe your students so that you can predict the kinds of strategies they are likely to use when they attempt to learn new concepts and solve problems. You also need to determine what kinds of conceptual and problem-solving strategies are most appropriate for new tasks so that you may help students acquire them.

2. Make sure activities provide feedback to students on the quality of their thinking. Set up your instruction so that the limitations of students' current strategies and hypotheses will be readily apparent to them and so that they will see the need for applying other approaches to a situation.

3. Reduce the memory requirements of the task to a minimum. Implicit here is the development of new or modified cognitive structures through the processes of accommodation and assimiliation. As teachers, we want development to proceed, but always without introducing too much disequilibrium. Successful cognitive growth is most likely when the memory demands of new tasks are kept at a reasonable level.

4. Use student "errors" to gain insight into their thought processes. Any "mistakes" that students make in their reasoning are actually excellent indicators of the nature of their thought processes and the level of cognitive development they have reached. Carefully note them and use them to adjust your instruction. You may infer which operations students can perform and which ones have yet to develop. In Piaget's view, all external experiences are translated through internal mechanisms. As Furth and Wachs (1975) have said, "the educator provides, the child decides." The child's present intellectual mechanisms are the key to his or her further intellectual development.

5. Use a variety of visual aids to present new information. Different kinds of visual aids

Teachers and parents must recognize that children vary in their levels of cognitive development. In a class of fifth graders, for example, some children will be in the stage of concrete operations while others are beginning to move into the adult thinking of formal operations. Still other students may have trouble with operations, indicating that at least in part they are still developing at the preoperational stage. Our explanations, questions, and learning materials for individual children must take into account each child's level of cognitive development.

Piaget himself (1970) cautioned educators to provide experiences congruent with children's levels of development. As Furth and Wachs (1975) have stated, having experiences just beyond one's present level is the key to intellectual growth. Instructional experiences that are too advanced are likely to be ignored, not perceived, or inappropriately translated. If instruction is at too low a level, it will be seen as routine and uninteresting.

(graphics, charts, photographs, drawings, and many more) should be used to convey new information. Since almost all students think somewhat concretely about some topics, you can aid their understanding of new materials by reducing the amount of abstract information they must deal with.

6. Allow students the opportunity to manipulate objects directly. Just as visual aids provide a great help in learning new material, the chance to actually handle objects can greatly assist in the acquisition of many new concepts.

7. Expect large differences in the cognitive development of students. Keep in mind that there will be great variation in the levels of cognitive development in any group of students. In a fifth grade class, for instance, there will be some children who are primarily concrete operational, some who are well into formal operations, and some with the characteristics of both levels.

Make sure activities provide feedback to students on the quality of their thinking.

SUMMARY

Intelligence involves all of the human cognitive processes. As Binet said, "To judge well, to comprehend well, to reason well, these are the essential activities of intelligence." Although there is some agreement about the general nature of intelligence, psychologists have studied and used the concept in quite different ways over the years.

One method of studying intelligence has been through the use of tests. Psychometric (testing) approaches have concentrated on the measurement of intelligence. Individual intelligence tests such as the Wechsler and Stanford-Binet have been the major method of measuring intelligence, although group intelligence tests have also been commonly used.

A more recent approach to studying intelligence has been to apply information-processing theory. Information-processing variables such as memory and reaction times are related to scores on traditional intelligence tests.

Yet another approach is cognitive-developmental, which emphasizes changes in intellectual qualities with experience. The foremost cognitive-development theorist is Jean Piaget, whose views have greatly influenced psychologists and educators. His theory holds that intelligence is part of the biological adaptation of the human being to the world. Through the processes of assimilation and accommodation, learners acquire and modify their cognitive structures. These cognitive structures organize learners' experiences and make them meaningful.

Development of cognition, according to Piaget, occurs by stages. The sensorimotor stage reveals a shift from simple reflexive reactions in infants to the beginning of ideas of causation and future time. In the preoperational stage, language acquisition is prominent. Children are egocentric, believing themselves to be the center of the universe. They also typically do not understand that superficial changes in form and shape do not change qualities of volume, number, and mass of objects and materials.

In concrete operations, conservation is attained but thinking is closely linked to the here and now. Abstract thinking develops more fully in the last stage, formal operations.

One major application from the study of intelligence has been a recognition of the need to plan for individual differences in teaching. Cognitive-developmental theory provides us with an understanding of cognitive changes with age. The teacher needs to be aware of the cognitive level of the students and to make instruction consistent with their cognitive structures. Good teachers help their students construct and organize their experiences in increasingly more complex and adequate ways. They recognize that students' own intellectual mechanisms are the keys to further cognitive development.

Suggested Readings

Furth, H. G. *Piaget for teachers.* Englewood Cliffs, N.J.: Prentice-Hall, 1970.

Furth's brief book is an excellent overview of Piagetian theory designed specifically for teachers and future teachers.

Ginsburg, H., & Opper, S. *Piaget's theory of intellectual development* (2nd ed.). Englewood Cliffs, N.J.: Prentice-Hall, 1979.

A more in-depth overview of Piaget's theory is provided in the Ginsburg and Opper book. This text is often used as supplementary reading in classes on developmental psychology.

Hearnshaw, L. S. *Cyril Burt, psychologist.* Ithaca, N.Y.: Cornell University Press, 1979.

This book chronicles the life of Sir Cyril Burt and deals thoroughly with his alleged improper practices in research.

Hunt, E. Mechanics of verbal ability. *Psychological Review,* 1978, *85,* 109–130.

Earl Hunt's review paper provides an excellent overview of the literature on information-processing research dealing with intellectual ability.

Kamin, L. J. *The science and politics of IQ.* New York: Wiley, 1975.

Kamin's book presents an excellent review of the issues in the nature/nurture debate.

Phillips, J. L. *The origins of intellect: Piaget's theory.* San Francisco: Freeman, 1975.

Phillips's book is another summary of Piaget's theory and its applications to education. Its level of difficulty falls in between those of Furth and Ginsburg and Opper.

IMPORTANT EVENTS IN RESEARCH ON INTELLIGENCE

Date(s)	*Person(s)*	*Work*	*Impact*
1880s	Galton	Investigations of individual differences	Sir Francis Galton did not develop a true test of intelligence, but his pioneering work in examining reaction times and other performance measures was the foundation for later conceptions of intelligence.
1890	Cattell	"Mental tests and measurements"	James McKeen Cattell was the first person to use the term mental test in the psychological literature.
1904	Spearman	"General intelligence objectively determined and measured"	Charles Spearman introduced the *g* factor in intelligence, which he based on work that predated intelligence tests (measures of reaction time, rote memory, and so on). He argued that there was one underlying general intellectual ability *(g)* that was involved in all intellectual functions. He also posited that separate abilities had their own specific or *s* factors.
1905	Binet & Simon	"Application des methodes nouvelles au diagnostic du niveau intellectual chez des enfants normal et anormzux d'hospice et d'école"	Alfred Binet and Theodore Simon developed the first intelligence test for practical use. This test has had a tremendous influence on all later intelligence tests and on most theories of intelligence.
1916	Terman	The Stanford Revision of the Binet tests	L. M. Terman's revision was the first intelligence test published in the United States. It was *the* standard measure of intelligence for twenty years.
1917	Yerkes & Otis	American Psychological Association Commission on developing group measures of intelligence	A committee of psychologists headed by Robert Yerkes developed the first group intelligence test. This test was largely based on work Arthur S. Otis conducted while he was a graduate student under Terman. The test (in

Date(s)	Person(s)	Work	Impact
			two forms, the Army Alpha A and B) became the standard group measure of intelligence.
1922–1959	Terman & associates	Longitudinal research on the characteristics of gifted people	L. M. Terman's work remains the most thorough longitudinal study of the lives of gifted people. His research also provides the basis for much of what we know about the characteristics of highly intelligent people.
1925–1980	Piaget	Theory of intelligence	Jean Piaget's work outlines the most comprehensive cognitive-developmental theory of intelligence. Much of our current understanding of the development of intelligence is based on Piaget's work.
1927	Spearman	*The abilities of man*	Charles Spearman reiterated his contentions about a single general (*g*) factor on the basis of his analysis of intelligence-test results, spurring a debate between single-factor and multifactor views of intelligence.
1937	Terman & Merrill	The 1937 revision of the Stanford-Binet	L. M. Terman and M. A. Merrill's revision included several improvements on the 1916 version of the Stanford-Binet and became the standard measure of intelligence in its time. The Stanford-Binet has been revised since 1937 and is currently being revised again.
1937	Newman, Freeman, & Holzinger	*Twins: A study of heredity and environment*	While H. H. Newman, F. N. Freeman, and K. J. Holzinger's study was not the first to investigate the relative influence of environment and heredity on intelligence, it was a classic twin study, using separated identical twins to attempt to determine the relative influence of heredity and environment on intelligence.

Date(s)	*Person(s)*	*Work*	*Impact*
1938	Thurstone	"Primary mental abilities"	L. L. Thurstone's 1938 paper accounted for the correlation between fifty-six tests in terms of seven or eight primary factors in intelligence. The multiple-factor approach, which had been espoused long before Thurstone's paper was published, permeated most American views of intelligence, but Thurstone's paper is consistently cited as a keystone of the multiple-factor perspective.
1944–1974	Wechsler	Wechsler Intelligence Scales	David Wechsler's scales have been the major alternative to the Stanford-Binet for individual testing.
1949	Hebb	*The organization of behavior*	D. O. Hebb's distinction between Type A and Type B intelligence has become an accepted way of viewing the results of intelligence tests.
1950–1971	Burt	Studies on the heritability of intelligence	Hearnshaw's (1979) biography of Sir Cyril Burt leaves little doubt that Sir Cyril's data (post-1950) were fraudulent. Hence the major researcher in the area of the heritability of intelligence during this time period (and perhaps earlier also) provided data that were untrustworthy.
1956–1971	Guilford	Extension of multiple-factor theory of intelligence	J. P. Guilford extended Thurstone's factors to 120 primary mental abilities. His is the most detailed theory of multiple factors in intelligence.
1969–present	Jensen	Heritability of intelligence	Arthur Jensen's analyses of intelligence-test results sparked renewed debate over the heritability of intelligence.
1974–present	Hunt & associates	Cognitive processes underlying intelligence	The work of Earl Hunt and his colleagues has begun to link the once-separate areas of cognitive psychology and psychometrics.

Date(s)	*Person(s)*	*Work*	*Impact*
1979	Peckham	Federal district court ruling in California	Robert F. Peckham, a federal judge, ruled that IQ tests may not be used to place schoolchildren in special classes for the retarded. He based his decision on his judgment that such tests are biased against minority children, resulting in many more minority children being placed in special-education classes.
1980	Grady	*PASE* v. *Hannon*	John Grady, an Illinois judge, ruled that IQ tests are not biased and may be used to help place children in special-education classes. This decision was diametrically opposed to that of Judge Peckham. The case in question was a suit brought by a parents' group (People in Action on Special Education, PASE) against the Chicago school system after incorrect placement of two black schoolchildren in special-education classes.

Chapter Six

CREATIVITY

Creativity is obviously a cognitive function, as is memory, concept learning, and problem solving. The research in creativity, however, has been quite unlike the research in other areas of cognition and consequently this chapter has a slightly different flavor from the preceding chapters about cognition. Creativity research has emphasized three general ideas: measuring creativity, identifying people who are especially creative and determining what they are like, and developing methods designed to enhance creativity.* Very little research has been devoted to the actual cognitive processes involved in the act of creative thinking.† This difference in emphasis causes us to present a chapter that is perhaps somewhat less cognitive in orientation than the previous chapters. We believe that what is known about cognitive development, memory, and problem solving applies to creative thinking, but research has not yet bridged the gap between creativity and these other cognitive functions.

Effective teachers want their students to be creative, and they want to know how they can go about helping their students become more creative. This chapter is specifically designed for two purposes: to enhance your creativity, and to help you acquire the knowledge and skills that will assist you in developing creativity in others.

* The systematic study of creativity began rather recently. Guilford's paper in the *American Psychologist* (1950) marked the onset of serious attempts to study creativity separately from the study of intelligence. Some scholars would argue that Sir Francis Galton should be credited with initiating the study of creativity, but very little research was attempted in this area between Galton's *Hereditary Genius* in 1869 and Guilford's paper in 1950 (Glover, 1976c).

† It is fair to point out that no psychologists primarily identified with the study of memory or problem solving have investigated creativity in a systematic program of research (Glover, 1980c).

Objectives

After reading this chapter, you should be able to meet the following objectives.

1. Engage in self-management activities that will enhance your own creative abilities.
2. Develop and try out a set of activities designed to help another person become more creative.

THE DEFINITION OF CREATIVITY

The processes involved in creativity are extremely complex and, as yet, not completely understood. Research has shed light, however, on several important aspects of creativity. We cannot say that we can describe all the complex processes that make up creativity, but we can identify some of its significant elements.

Novelty and Value

When we think about creative behaviors, the most striking thing about them is their novelty. In order for any human action to be creative it must be novel—different, unusual, uncommon, surprising. Whether it is writing, painting, designing, scientific investigations, or any area of human endeavor, novelty must be present for a behavior to be considered creative. Novelty, however, is not enough. Suppose you have never disposed of chewing gum by sticking it to the ceiling. For you, such an action would be novel, but would it be creative? Of course not.

In addition to novelty, a creative behavior must also have value (Parnes & Harding, 1962). Value is not a firm, fixed concept. A behavior may have value in a utilitarian sense (if the behavior solves a problem, for instance) or it may have value in a more abstract, aesthetic sense (a poem may be pleasing or rewarding to the writer or reader). Sticking gum on the ceiling, walking to class on your hands, dyeing your hair green, eating watermelon pie for breakfast, and taking your showers at the local carwash may all be very novel behaviors for you, but if they are not judged to have value they are not creative. Novel, maybe—bizarre, maybe—but not creative.

Frame of Reference

Novelty and value can be slippery concepts. In order to define creativity adequately, we have to be able to use these two concepts in a way that allows us to reliably gauge behaviors and determine their creativity. To do so, we have to look at the three frames of reference in which behaviors (and their results—creative works) are judged (Glover, 1979a, 1980c).

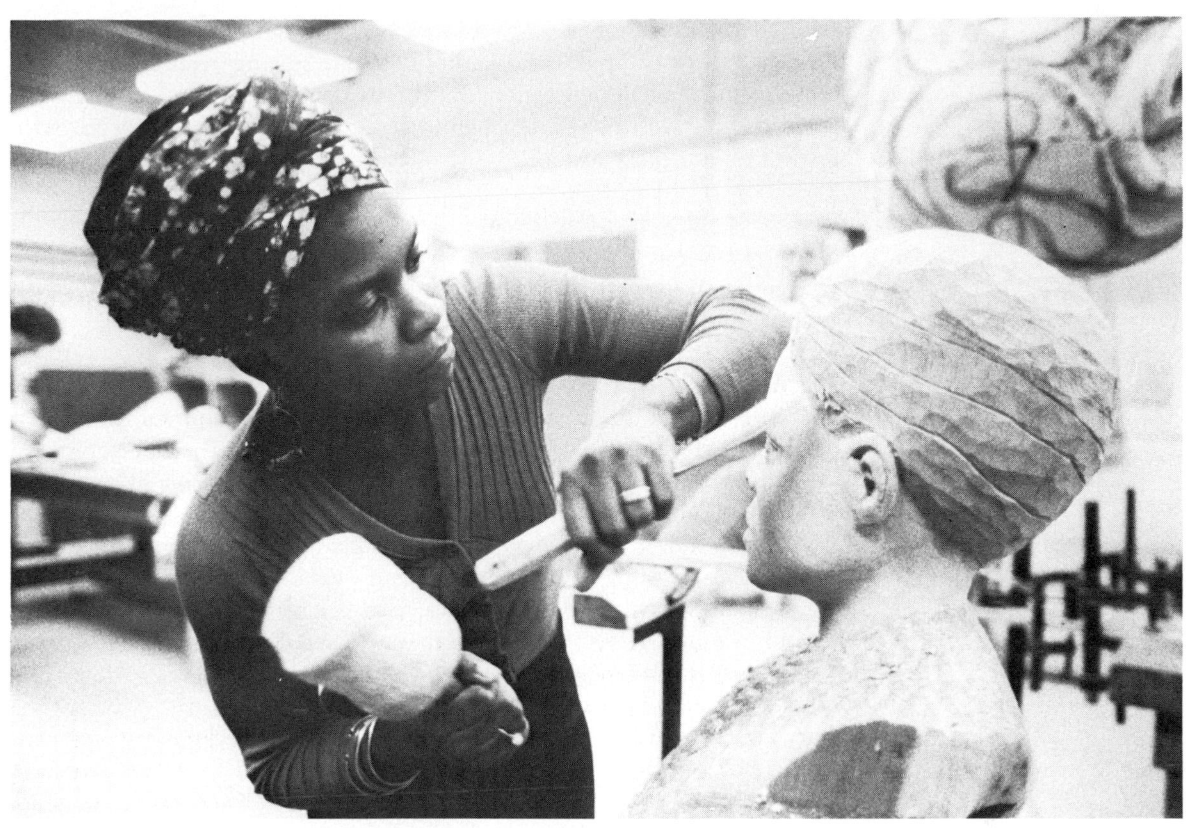

Creative acts may have abstract, aesthetic value.

Personal Reference. A personal frame of reference is unique to each person. You know what kinds of things you have done in the past, and you know whether something you do now is novel. You also know when your actions have value for you. From a personal frame of reference, then, a behavior is creative if it is novel and judged to be of personal value for that person (and perhaps no one else). If you have never painted a picture before and now do so, and you judge that your behavior was important, you have been creative.

Each of us can be creative within this frame of reference; many expressions of personal interests are creative. People can be creative when they decorate their houses or apartments, when they dress differently, engage in a hobby—any facet of life holds the potential for creative behavior.

Peer Group Reference. It is more difficult for a behavior to be judged creative from the frame of reference of one's peers. To meet the peer group's criteria of creativity, a behavior must be novel and of value for that group. Suppose you work out a new seating arrangement in an office to increase productivity. If this behavior is unique among your peers and is worthwhile to them, then you have been creative with respect to your peer group's frame of reference.

Societal Frame of Reference. The most rigorous test of whether a behavior is creative occurs within the societal frame of reference. Suppose you go home tonight and invent the steam engine. This behavior, we'll assume, might be highly creative for you—you had never before invented the steam engine, and you would judge it to be a very rewarding experience. Further, none of your peers has invented the steam engine, and they find it to be a valuable source of inspiration for their own efforts at creativity. So you have been creative at both a personal and peer group frame of reference. But have you been creative at a societal level? No. The steam engine has already been invented, so it is not particularly novel for you to invent it again. And it's not likely that your invention would be judged especially valuable for society.

Generally books, plays, movies, and scientific inventions are subject to evaluation from a societal frame of reference. Professional peers are within this frame of reference. Scientific innovations are reviewed by other scientists, for example, and novels and plays are reviewed by literary and theater critics. Movies are reviewed by moviemakers and cinema critics, while new clothing styles are evaluated by other designers and buyers. Frequently, society at large acclaims some works that are panned by professionals. The converse also occurs—works can be critically praised but fall flat with the general public. Both professional peers and society at large, however, apply yardsticks of novelty and value.*

Who is right, professional peers or the public? This question cannot be answered immediately. It requires the most rigorous test of all: time. Ultimately, we recognize creative efforts when they stand the test of the time. Works like Shakespeare's writings speak to some basic truths about humanity that transcend time; the insights of Shakespeare hundreds of years ago seem just as powerful now as they were when he conceived them. Other accomplishments such as Marie Curie's discovery

* We must take into account the common use of hyperbole to convince the public that a person, product, or process is really creative or, in the words of the ads, "new!" "different!" and "exciting!" It is very difficult to disentangle the public's reaction to any new concept from the reaction created by advertising. We should also note that disagreement about creativity is more frequent in some professional areas than others. Disagreement occurs more often in the fine arts than in some of the sciences, for instance. The reason for this is the relative lack of formal criteria for judging value in the fine arts. A piece of sculpture can be considered junk by one person and be highly admired by others.

of radium have stood the test of time because they have been shown to be major influences on the development of fields of knowledge, in this case science.

COMPONENTS OF CREATIVITY

Creativity is a complex activity, and many different approaches have been developed over the years for investigating creative behaviors. Early work in the area was done by J. P. Guilford (1950, 1959, 1962), who developed a "structure of the intellect" model based on assumed cognitive processes, forms of knowledge, and cognitive products. While he hypothesized more than 120 possible human cognitive abilities, his distinction between convergent and divergent thinking has had the greatest impact on the study of creativity. For Guilford, **convergent thinking** is the generation of ideas from given information with emphasis on problem solutions that are conventionally acceptable. **Divergent thinking,** on the other hand, is the generation of ideas from given information with emphasis on a variety and quantity of problem solutions. Divergent thinking, from Guilford's perspective, was most clearly involved in creativity.

Paul Torrance: The ideas of this prominent researcher have been used extensively in assessing and enhancing creativity.

The most important work in the area has been that of E. Paul Torrance. Torrance, building on the work of Guilford, has identified a set of components of creative behaviors that has been used extensively in assessing and enhancing creativity. We have investigated these components in our own research and believe that they are good indicators of creativity.

When we talk about components of creative behaviors we are referring to those behaviors that are a part of creativity. That is, if we ask what a behavior must be like for it to be creative (outside of what we have talked about with respect to frames of reference, novelty, and usefulness), our answer would be that creativity must be a function of fluency, flexibility, and originality.

Fluency

Fluency (Torrance, 1974) refers to the number of ideas that a person develops in response to any problem.* Generally, the greater the number of ideas a person generates, the more creative that person is on a

* As we'll see later, this concept was designed to fit tests such as Torrance's Thinking Creatively with Words test, in which people are asked to list unusual uses of a common item, ask questions about a picture, and the like. We use fluency a little more broadly to include general problem solving. The definitions of flexibility and originality that follow are also adapted from Torrance's work and are not stated exactly as he would state them. They are taken from a series of our own research articles.

specific task. Suppose you are faced with the classic problem we presented in Chapter Four of having a flat tire on a country road, miles from any help, and without a jack. You recall that the spare tire is fine, but you must think of ways to gain access to the flat tire so that you can take it off and replace it with a new tire. How many ideas can you come up with for gaining access to the flat tire? Another example is the problem of redecorating a room for the least possible expense. How many ways can you think of doing this? Still another example can be adapted from one of Torrance's subtests. How many unusual uses can you think of for some common object such as a shoe?

Fluency is important for several reasons. The more ideas a person can develop in response to a problem, the more likely he or she will find a workable solution. Additionally, when there are many ideas to choose from, the odds are much greater that novel, unusual, or uncommon solutions will be found that may have more value than some common solutions. A part of our job in helping students develop problem-solving and creativity skills is helping them learn to generate a number of solutions for problems.

Creative thought is sometimes indicated by the ability to generate unusual uses.

"It just isn't working. What shall we do?"

Flexibility

Flexibility refers to the number of different kinds of ideas a person thinks of when faced with a problem (Torrance, 1974). In our example of the flat tire, you might develop several ideas for doing things that would replace the missing jack. A post and some rocks could be used to build a lever to lift the car. A ramp constructed from a board and some rocks could be used in this situation. These ideas involve the same idea—lifting up the car. You could also develop a different set of ideas that would allow access to the tire but would not involve lifting—digging a hole under the tire or backing the car into a steep ditch so the tire is above the ground, for instance.

Generally, the more different kinds of ideas a person thinks of, the more creative that person is with respect to the problem. Another example of flexibility can be seen in some responses made by fourth graders to a task based on Torrance's Unusual Uses subtest. We did a study (Glover & Gary, 1976) in which we asked students to list as many possible uses as they could for a piece of chalk. Two lists generated in that task are presented below:

Student A

- to draw circles with
- to draw pictures with
- to mark ball fields
- to mark how tall you are on the wall
- to trace outlines

Student B

- as wheels for a small cart
- crush and put on tires in the snow to make the car go better
- draw a cartoon
- prop open a rabbit trap
- make hollow for a straw to drink milk

As you can see, each student gave five responses. Student A's responses were all in one category—drawing. Student B's responses were all in different categories—drawing, rolling, providing traction for tires, and acting as a prop and a straw. Both students would receive fluency scores of five, but Student A would receive a flexibility score of one, while Student B would receive a flexibility score of five. They each had the same number of ideas, but Student A's ideas were all of the same kind while Student B's ideas were of five different kinds.

Originality

If you think about solving problems for a moment, you will see that a workable, innovative idea is more likely if a person is highly flexible than if a person is inflexible. If you can't think of a novel way of gaining access to a flat tire, you may be out walking all night. Thus, **originality** might very well be considered the most important of the three components of creativity (Guilford, 1959; Torrance, 1962, 1967). By originality we mean the uncommon or rare; the less common ideas are, the more original they are. On one of the lists we obtained from elementary school children, a child suggested that pieces of chalk could be used "to roll the great pyramid by putting chalk under it and picking up the chalk in back and putting it back up front." This was a much more uncommon idea than that suggested by a child who wrote "draw on the blackboard."

The more uncommon, original, and infrequent ideas are, the more likely they are to be judged creative. Difficult problems may very well require solutions that may not have been thought of before. Original responses are needed at all levels—personal, peer, and societal.

These three components of creative behavior give us an indication of what people need to do to solve problems creatively. Having many original ideas about problems greatly increases the likelihood that one of the ideas will be effective and creative. We can teach ourselves and our students to respond to problems with high levels of fluency, flexibility, and originality.

Obviously, complex memory and thinking activities also must be going on during creative thinking. There is not as much known as we would like, however, about these cognitive activities. Nonetheless, there has been considerable research conducted in the general area of how creative people behave. Before we proceed to a consideration of teaching for creativity, we will discuss some characteristics of creative people.

PRACTICE EXERCISE 6–1

Developing Unusual Ideas

The following lists of unusual uses were generated by the same person over three days. Score the first list for fluency and flexibility. Score the last two for fluency, flexibility, and originality. Our responses appear at the end of the chapter and you may compare your results to ours.

Day 1

Stimulus: Stapler

1. shoulder pads
2. back scratcher
3. dental-floss holder
4. to staple cloth
5. pliers
6. a stake for a rope
7. to staple a book together
8. scratch knee with it
9. to hammer a nail
10. prop open a window with it

Day 2

Stimulus: Empty aspirin bottle

1. hold flowers in it
2. ashtray
3. scratch back with it
4. use as a hammer
5. hold marbles in it
6. prop open a window
7. hold jelly in
8. drinking glass
9. make a doll out of it

Day 3

Stimulus: Soap dish

1. hold soap in it
2. hold paper clips
3. prop open a door
4. water dish for a dog
5. scrape the frost off a windshield
6. use as a Frisbee
7. use as an ashtray
8. make a toy boat
9. make a hat out of it

THE CREATIVE PERSON

What are creative people like? Besides being fluent, flexible, and original, are creative people different from less creative people? These questions have been asked frequently by teachers and psychologists over the years but there are no firm answers. Psychologists have tried to answer these questions by assessing well-known people such as famous writers and inventors. Some of this research has been done through biographical analyses. Other research in this area has been done by identifying creative children and trying to describe the kinds of traits they possess (a trait refers to a relatively permanent pattern of behaviors).

Overall, the results are somewhat inconclusive. Imagine trying to find similarities in the traits of people like Ernest Hemingway, Emily Dickinson, Edgar Allan Poe, Marie Curie, and George Washington Carver. A compilation of the results of biographical analyses, interviews, and some testing, however, yields nine traits that are found in common in most creative people (Glover, 1980c). Keep in mind that the people analyzed are among the most creative individuals our societies have produced. All the patterns will not be present in all creative people but most people judged creative will possess some of them.

A strong sense of humor. Many creative people tend to see incongruities in situations that are not obvious to other people. They are more likely to generate many possible outcomes of a situation (fluency), more different kinds of outcomes (flexibility), and more unusual outcomes (originality). These things taken together make for people who are more likely to see humor in a given setting (Glover, 1980c; Taylor, 1961).

Self-amusement. Creative people often have a high capacity for self-amusement and are seldom as bored as less creative people. They examine even the simplest situations from many points of view. Creative people, of course, are much more likely to generate more possibilities that are original and diverse in any given setting. Sitting in a waiting room may not be particularly boring for a creative person because such a person is far more likely to think of things to do than a noncreative person.

Determination. Creative people tend to be very determined to finish the projects they start. Creative people may not be interested in doing what others want them to do, but they work very diligently in finishing off their own projects. We might call this "stick-to-itiveness" (Glover & Trammel, 1976).

Tolerance for ambiguity. Creative people are typically able to function as well at some tasks in the absence of structure as in its presence. In other words, while they may do well in situations in which there are clear guides, they tend to be more able than most people to carry on in

Picasso put a toy automobile and a cooking pot (the handle is the tail) to an unusual use in his fanciful *Baboon and Young* (1951).

the absence of specific requirements (Getzels & Jackson, 1962; Glover & Sautter, 1976, 1977b).

Fantasy life. As you might expect, given high levels of fluency, flexibility, and originality, daydreaming can be very rich and detailed among creative persons. Many highly creative scientists report daydreaming about research problems and solutions.

Unusual problem-solving strategies. This pattern of behavior should not be surprising to you after you've read about the components of creativity. Creative people often try unusual strategies for solving problems. They are fluent, flexible, and original in their thinking about problems.

Perception of complex relationships. Many times creative people perceive complex relationships that have escaped the notice of other persons (McKinnon, 1962). This too requires generating many different kinds of novel ideas.

Redefining and elaborating problems. As you would expect, given the high levels of the three components of creativity, creative people are usually able to bring more adaptable problem-solving skills to many situations. Creative people do well in tasks that require redefinition and elaboration of problems (Mednick, 1962).

Inventiveness. The most frequently mentioned pattern of behavior in describing the creative person is inventiveness. Creative people are almost always inventive, developing novel and useful ideas (Guilford, 1959; Mednick, 1962).

Keep in mind that the nine characteristics described above are general. While a person's possession of these qualities is not a guarantee of creativity, most of us can develop some, if not all, of these patterns of behavior.

CREATIVITY, INTELLIGENCE, AND TRAINING

You may have noticed that two common descriptions of inventive persons were not included in our discussion of common traits among creative people: intelligence and level of training. Many people, however, have wondered about and studied the ways in which these characteristics are related to creativity.

The research examining the relationship between intelligence and creativity has been interesting but inconclusive. In general it appears that there is only a weak relationship between creativity and intelligence (see Getzels & Jackson, 1962; R.L. Thorndike, 1963; Torrance, 1962, 1967; Wallach & Kogan, 1965). McKinnon (1962), in his studies of creative architects and mathematicians, found essentially no relationship between creativity and intelligence. Getzels and Jackson (1962) identified a group of "highly creative" adolescents who scored in the top 20 percent on measures of creativity but who were not in the top 20 percent in measures of intelligence. Similarly, they identified a group of high-IQ adolescents who scored in the top 20 percent on measures of intelligence but were not in the top 20 percent on measures of creativity. The mean IQ of Getzels and Jackson's "highly creative" group was 23 points below the mean of the high IQ group and lower than the average IQ of the entire student population in the school studied. It does appear that average intelligence is necessary for creativity, but beyond that there is no particular relationship between the two. It is also quite possible for highly intelligent people to be absolutely uncreative. What all this means is that high intelligence isn't necessary for creativity and creativity isn't necessary for intelligence. Teachers should not assume that IQ scores predict how creative a student may be or become.

The relationship between training and creativity is also interesting. We should first point out that formal training (at a university, a trade school, and so on) is not the only way in which people acquire an education. Some people can teach themselves high-level skills as well as or better than they could be taught in a formal setting. Both formal and self-guided experiences can be a part of a person's training.

What, then, is the relationship between training and creativity? In most areas, the relationship is very powerful. Without training in architecture it would seem nearly impossible for a person to become a creative architect. How could a person design structures with little or no knowledge of architecture? Without extensive musical experience it would appear to be impossible to be a creative musician. Is creative research in physics possible without a strong science education? In all professional areas, some knowledge and skills must be acquired by people before they can be creative. A person who reads and writes poorly will not write the great American novel.

A GLANCE AT ASSESSING CREATIVITY

The best-known and most widely accepted devices for assessing creativity were developed by E. Paul Torrance. Of his tests, the Thinking Creatively with Words test (1974) is the most frequently used. This test consists of a series of tasks that require people to respond to mundane stimuli in novel ways.

The Torrance tests have several subtests that all require the students to perform similar tasks. The Unusual Uses subtest, for example, presents the students with a common object and asks them to list as many possible uses for that object as they can imagine. Students are told not to worry about strange responses and are also told that they may use as many of the particular object as they wish and they may make it any size. The lists written by students are then assessed for fluency, flexibility, and originality.*

* Torrance's nonverbal tests are also scored for elaboration. We have not found success in utilizing elaboration as a means of enhancing creativity and have deleted it from our discussion.

Mednick's (1962) Remote Associates test can serve much the same purpose as Torrance's tests. A list of words is given to students and they are asked to generate words that they associate with the words in the list. For example, the word *apple* might generate the associates *pie, tree, cider, peaches,* and *pistachio.* The test is scored differently from the Torrance tests, emphasizing the remoteness (differentness) of the responses.

There are many other creativity tests but the two we mentioned are the most accessible and the most amenable to adaptation by teachers in one setting or another. There are three reasons that teachers may want to use one of these tests to determine the level of creativity among their students: (1) to provide a reference point prior to instruction in creativity so that changes in student creativity can be evaluated by retesting, (2) to permit comparison of students to national norms, and (3) to help plan ways of teaching for creativity based on the test results.

TEACHING FOR CREATIVITY

The notion of teaching for creativity in students is based on the assumption that teachers can affect creativity by the demands they make, by the expectations they have, and by their reactions. We have worked with teachers at the elementary, secondary, and college levels in structuring teaching activities that enhance the creative behaviors of students.

In one example of our research, Glover and Gary (1976) worked with a class of fourth and fifth graders attending a nonremedial summer school session. The experimenters administered Torrance's Thinking Creatively with Words test (Verbal Form B) (1974) to all the students according to standard directions. The next day they returned to the class, defined the components of creative behavior for the students, and discussed them until each student could verbally define fluency, flexibility, and originalty. When this was completed, the class was divided into two equal groups on the basis of the Torrance test results. The students were then introduced to the Unusual Uses game.

The Unusual Uses game was built on the idea of thinking of unusual uses for various objects found within the classroom. Each day, the experimenters would print the name of an object on the blackboard (pencil eraser, trash can, and so on) and ask the students to list as many possible unusual uses as they could for these objects. The two teams would gain points for fluency, flexibility, and originality on different days (some days fluency gained points, some days flexibility gained points, and so on). The lists were collected from students and scored each day while the students were engaged in a free reading period and then returned approximately thirty minutes later. Points were assigned to students for fluency, flexibility, or originality and added together for total team scores. The "winning" team received cookies and milk and a ten-minute early recess. The "losing" team could also win if it obtained 80 percent of the score of the "winning" team.

The study lasted twenty-five days, after which the Torrance tests were readministered. The students showed significantly higher levels of fluency, flexibility, and originality on the second administration of the Torrance tests. When points were given for fluency, fluency scores went up dramatically; when points were given for flexibility, flexibility scores went up greatly; and when points were given for originality, originality scores went up on the daily lists. Very similar results have been obtained by Glover and Sautter (1977a) with high-school-age students and by Glover (1979a) with elementary students given more complex forms of writing activities.

Glover (1977, 1980a) has also determined that such training procedures can be effective with college-age students. In a recent study, he conducted a twenty-one-day workshop with fourteen college students based on an unusual uses game and a problem-solving activity (Glover, 1980a). Both activities required students to list ideas that would be scored for fluency, flexibility, and originality. The students showed a significant increase in scores on standardized creativity tests, as was expected from the previous research. Remarkably, these changes were still present one year after the completion of the workshop. The results also generalized to other tasks outside the workshop, specifically to noticeably higher levels of rated creativity in essays the students wrote.

APPLICATIONS FOR TEACHING

We have summarized a number of principles taken from our research and from the general study of creativity. They should give you a good sense of how you can help your students become more creative.

1. Strange, unusual, and odd questions from students should not be discounted. **Learners who have creative questions may leave you wondering about the relevance of what they have asked. You cannot afford to react negatively to such questions. If learners see that they cannot ask their "good" questions, they just won't ask them. Far too often, we find that students who ask unusual questions are told, "be quiet," "don't get smart," or "go look it up." By accepting strange and unusual questions, of course, you run the risk of spending some time with questions that really are irrelevant. Students can enjoy asking questions designed to get the teacher off the track. This is a minor problem, however, if students learn to ask creative questions. If you can't answer the question (such as "why do pandas have six fingers?"), let learners see that you welcome such questions and try to help them find the needed answers (Glover, 1980c).**

We have found that encouraging unusual and

Strange questions should not be discounted. Try to find something positive in all ideas and follow up "bad" questions with some of your own that require the learner to think through the problem.

challenging questions can result in an increase in students' overall creative behaviors. Once students see they can really ask you what they want to know and not worry about your reaction, creative behavior tends to generalize to other areas (Glover, 1980b).

2. Try to find something positive in all ideas. Tagging some ideas and questions as "stupid," "bad," or "irrelevant" will reduce the chances of students asking better questions. The best approach is to follow up "bad" questions with some of your own that require the learner to think through the problem (Glover, 1980b, 1980c). When learners evaluate their own thinking, they are far less likely to inhibit future questioning.

3. Make it a point to systematically reward creativity from your students. Many studies have shown that rewarding creative activities increases their number (Fallon & Goetz, 1975; Goetz & Baer, 1973; Goetz & Salmonson, 1972).

4. Expect and demand creativity from your students. In those situations where you tell learners you expect them to be creative and where creativity is a part of the overall performance you will judge, you will find more creative behaviors (Glover, 1980b). You will have to define creativity for your students (we suggest using the three components of creativity we discussed earlier) so that they have a clear idea of what you mean.

5. In terms of grading, creativity ought to be an extra. Requiring creativity for a grade is somewhat unfair—after all, you will be making a subjective judgment about how creative a student's efforts are. Creativity should be rewarded, but in the form of extra credit (Glover & Sautter, 1977a).

6. Model creative behaviors. Several studies (see Gary & Glover, 1974, 1975) report that those students who are exposed to a creative model act more creatively than do students who are exposed to models that aren't particularly creative. So if you are serious about enhancing the creativity of your students, model high levels of fluency, flexibility, and originality in your own classroom behaviors. You can also invite your creative colleagues for occasional guest appearances.

Reaching one's full potential for creativity appears to be a matter of living and working in an environment that recognizes and rewards a variety of creative behaviors. It appears that the parent-child and teacher-child interactions are far more important than race, sex, or socioeconomic status (Glover, 1976b, 1976c; Knox & Glover, 1978). There will be large differences in the levels of creativity in any group of students. Some will be creative in one area, others in different areas. In large part this is the result of the extent to which their previous environments were supportive of creativity.

An Example of Teaching for Creativity: Mr. James

How can you put these ideas about teaching creativity into use? Let's use "Mr. James" as an example of a teacher who has applied the principles outlined above to increase student creativity.

Mr. James was sitting in the teacher's lounge scraping the bowl of his pipe with a small pocketknife and thinking about his students. He was particularly frustrated because he hadn't been able to get what he felt were creative solutions to a set of environmental problems he had been presenting to his seventh-grade class. He knocked the scrapings out of his pipe against his heel and started packing his pipe, trying to recall some things from a workshop in creativity training he had attended the previous summer. "Yes," he mumbled, "creativity training is what we need."

That day Mr. James was ready to begin some preliminary training activities with his fifth-period students. "What is creativity?" he asked the class. After listening carefully to several answers, he went on to define creativity in the same way in which we defined it in this chapter, being very careful to point out how the students' answers to his original question fit into his definitions. He described novelty and value. He talked about different frames of reference and then defined each of the three components of creativity. He had his students define each of the three components in their own words and stayed with the definitions until he was satisfied that each student in the class could clearly define *fluency, flexibility,* and *originality.* All this took up almost an entire period and so he passed out some ditto sheets with examples of the definitions and asked the students to read them before the next class.

Each day during their unit on ecological and environmental concerns, he decided, he would have the class take part in an ecology problem-solving game. In the first twenty minutes of the period, he would start by passing out a brief statement of an ecological problem to the class. Then each member of the class would list as many possible solutions as he or she could for the problem. The lists would be collected and scored overnight for fluency, flexibility, and originality and a total would be obtained for each student's list. Team members' scores would then be added together to find the overall point total for each team. The "winning" team would obtain a ten-minute free-time break at the end of the following class hour in which the members of the winning team could engage in any activity they wished in the classroom or library. The "losing" teams could also "win" if they achieved 80 percent of the score of the "winning" team each day.

In the first class, Mr. James also described how he would score the lists and add up the points. One point would be given for each idea (fluency). One point would be given for each different kind of idea (flexibility), and two points would be given for each original idea (originality). That is, each idea that no one else in the class came up with received two points. He told the class the game would start the next day and then went back to his lesson in ecology.

The next day he divided his class into three equal teams based on their scores on the Unusual Uses subtest that he had previously administered. (This was done so that all the teams had about the same average ability starting out.) Mr. James then passed out an ecological problem and directed the students to list as many possible ideas as they could for solving the problem. He allowed fifteen minutes for the activity and then collected the papers.

Mr. James used his training activity over the next two weeks and found (not surprisingly, since he was really redoing what we have done in our own research) that his students greatly increased their levels of fluency, flexibility, and originality. He also found that the students generalized what they had learned and were more creative in other parts of his course. Mr. James was quite pleased with himself and his students. The rest of the year was very fulfilling for him and his class.

An Analysis of Mr. James's Activity

Let's take a careful look at what Mr. James did and why it worked. First he took a measure of where his students were at the beginning of the training (the Unusual Uses subtest). He clearly defined what he meant by creativity so that his students knew what was expected from them. Then he put the students into what amounted to a "can't lose" game where practice in creativity was rewarded (we have used this general activity several times and have never had a "losing" team obtain less than 80 percent of the "winning" team's score). He expected creativity, set up a situation that demanded it, set up learning that was both meaningful and fun (the problems all pertained to his lessons but were in game format), and rewarded students' efforts.

PRACTICE EXERCISE 6–2
Developing Creative Responding

The best way to practice helping someone develop his or her creativity is to start with yourself. This activity is based on a series of research studies we have conducted over the years. To start, sit down in a quiet place with paper and pencil. Now think about buttons. You are probably wearing some buttons. Make a list of all the unusual uses you can think of for buttons. Don't worry about your ideas being odd or strange; no one will see them but you. In your unusual uses you may employ as many buttons as you wish of any size you wish. Stop reading and complete the activity now! If you dropped down to read this line, you are fudging. Complete the activity above first.

Finished? Good. Now score your list. How many ideas did you list? The number of uses you listed is your fluency score. How many *different* kinds of ideas did you list? Count only the number of really different ideas you listed; that number is your flexibility score. Originality will have to wait because it can't be scored on this list.

What you have done so far may be thought of as identifying your reference point for increasing creative responding. Below is a list containing ten objects commonly found in settings where you might be taking a course in educational psychology.

1. pencil
2. chalkboard eraser
3. book
4. paper clip
5. trash can
6. ashtray
7. bookend
8. rubber eraser
9. cellophane wrapper
10. roll of masking tape

These ten items will be the stimuli for your development of unusual uses over the next ten days.

To make the activity a little more rigorous, let's set some daily goals. Whatever your fluency score was on the first list, try to increase it by 3 every day. Try to increase your flexibility score by 2. You will want to increase your originality score by 1 each day but you won't have a reference for it until you complete the second list.

To help you work at this task, choose your favorite daily activity—watching television, reading, talking on the phone, whatever—and engage in this activity *only* if you meet the goals.* If you increase your fluency score by 3 tonight,

*After having hundreds of college students perform this activity, we found that the daily increases we gave above were reached by almost all students. The required increases may not seem very challenging, but after ten days your fluency score will have increased by 30, and the other scores will increase greatly as well. These overall increases *are* impressive.

SUMMARY

Research in creativity has helped isolate specific components of creative behavior: fluency, flexibility, and originality. These three components can be increased through the use of procedures developed by applied research in creativity. Creativity research also describes nine general patterns of behavior that seem to characterize most creative persons. These traits can serve as indicators of those students who are especially creative.

for example, give yourself the pleasure of watching television. By the way, be sure to choose an activity that you really enjoy. An activity you don't care about doesn't help motivate you to work hard on the task.

When you complete the second list based on the stimulus "pencil," score fluency and flexibility as we've already described. Then compare your list to the list you generated for "buttons." Count every idea on your "pencil" list that is in no way mentioned on your "button" list and add the total to determine your first originality score.* Suppose you write that a pencil could be used "to make a prop to hold open a window" on the second list. If on the first list, you suggested that a button could be used "to prop open a window," then you cannot consider the same response to "pencil" original. An original response must be different from all previous responses. Your goal is to increase your originality score by at least 1 every day. Stay with this activity for ten days and compare your final performance with your original score.

In order to increase the utility of your creativity training, add a second component to your tasks on about the fifth day. For ten days (the last five of the Unusual Uses activity and five more) write out a problem that occurred during the day. Such problems might include finding a parking place on the campus, replacing a button on a shirt you are wearing, figuring out how to get a date with someone, and so on. Each day, list as many possible solutions to the problem as you can think of. Once again, try to raise your fluency score by 3, your flexibility score by 2, and your originality score by 1 daily.

If you want to go one step further after your two tasks are finished, work on generalizing what you have learned. Try to generate as many possible ideas as you can for each problem that comes up during the day. It will probably be difficult for you to keep track of them, but it is the general approach to problems we are concerned with, not keeping day-to-day running lists.

It is creativity in everyday life that is important. Thinking of odd uses for buttons is pretty far removed from real-life problems, but developing your skills with such activities is a good starting place. Ultimately, you want to approach important problems with high levels of fluency, flexibility, and originality. By developing your creativity, you will do a better job of solving *all* the problems you encounter, from gardening to social interactions. Becoming more creative requires work, but you can do it.

*Originality must be scored differently here from the way we described it earlier because you are the only reference point. At first, being more original will seem simple. It will become more difficult by the time you get to lists 5 and 6.

The relationship between intelligence and creativity is not powerful. Any person of average or above-average intelligence can be creative.

What does this chapter imply for you as a teacher? You should expect to find creativity in all of your students. Every student is creative at one time or another, and some students, of course, are creative more often. You can also expect to be able to increase your own levels of creativity and apply the techniques described in this chapter to enhance the creativity of your students. Your reactions to student questions and comments can strengthen or weaken student creativity, and the creativity you exhibit will serve as a model for students.

Suggested Readings

Getzels, J. W., & Jackson, P. W. *Creativity and intelligence.* New York: Wiley, 1962.

This classic book in the field presents an overwhelming array of data on the relationship of creativity to intelligence.

Glover, J. A. *Becoming a more creative person.* Englewood Cliffs, N.J.: Prentice-Hall, 1980.

This book provides a theory-based approach to enhancing one's own creativity.

Glover, J. A., & Gary, A. L. *Behavior modification: Enhancing creativity and other good behaviors.* Pacific Grove, Calif.: Boxwood Press, 1975.

This book provides a behavioral perspective on creativity and how it can be enhanced in the classroom.

Guilford, J. P. Creativity. *American Psychologist,* 1950, *5,* 444–454.

Guilford's seminal article established the study of creativity in contemporary psychology.

Torrance, E. P. *Guiding creative talent.* Englewood Cliffs, N.J.: Prentice-Hall, 1962.

This book, one of Torrance's earliest, outlines his basic position. In general, any of Torrance's books is excellent reading for further knowledge about creavitity.

Wallach, M. A., & Kogan, N. *Modes of thinking in young children: A study of the creativity-intelligence distinction.* New York: Holt, Rinehart, & Winston, 1965.

This book is an excellent source of information about the relationship of intelligence and creativity.

Answers to Practice Exercise 6–1

Day 1
Fluency = 10 (there are 10 ideas)
Flexibility = 8 (ideas 2 and 8 are of the same kind; ideas 4 and 7 are of the same kind)

Day 2
Fluency = 9 (there are 9 ideas)
Flexibility = 5 (ideas 1, 2, 5, 7, and 8 are of the same kind, holding)
Originality = 6 (ideas 1, 2, 5, 7, 8, and 9 did not appear on the previous list)

Day 3
Fluency = 9 (there are 9 ideas)
Flexibility = 6 (ideas 1, 2, 4, and 7 are of the same kind)
Originality = 8 (ideas 1, 2, 3, 4, 5, 6, 8, and 9 did not appear on either previous list)

IMPORTANT EVENTS IN RESEARCH ON CREATIVITY

Date(s)	*Person(s)*	*Work*	*Impact*
1898	Royce	"The psychology of invention"	Josiah Royce conducted the first systematic study that attempted to enhance creativity in students.
1950	Guilford	"Creativity"	Until the appearance of J.P. Guilford's paper, psychologists did not consider creativity to be an ability separate from intelligence.
1952	Thurstone	"Creative talent"	L. L. Thurstone extracted twenty primary factors from measures of intelligence and concluded, as Guilford had done, that creativity was a distinct cognitive ability.
1953	Osborne	*Applied imagination*	Alex Osborne introduced the concept of "brainstorming" to creative problem solving. Brainstorming has served as a basis of many creative problem-solving training programs and has led to many modifications that have also been applied to creativity training.
1956–1961	Guilford	Work on the structure of intellect model	Guilford's work in the late 1950s resulted in his identification of 120 separate abilities in intelligence. The primary traits Guilford associated with creativity were fluency, flexibility, elaboration, and originality. These traits have become the most widely used indicators of creative ability.
1958–1960	Maltzman	Behavioral approaches to creativity	Irving Maltzman and his associates demonstrated that novelty could be increased in students through simple reinforcement procedures. Maltzman's work formed the basis for behavioral views of creativity in the 1960s, 1970s, and 1980s.

Date(s)	*Person(s)*	*Work*	*Impact*
1959–1972	Parnes	Development of creative problem-solving courses and classroom materials	Sidney Parnes and his associates developed classroom materials designed to facilitate creativity. These were tested in a variety of school settings and have generally proved valuable. Much of Parnes's work has formed the basis for curriculum planning for gifted children.
1960–present	Torrance	The measurement of creativity; developing means of encouraging creativity; developing programs for gifted students	E. Paul Torrance's work, more than the work of anyone else, has influenced the study of creativity. His tests are the standard measures of creativity and most programs for enhancing creativity are based on his work. Further, the recent emphasis on educational programs for gifted children has been influenced to a great degree by Torrance. The first doctoral programs for people specializing in "gifted" and "creative" students were developed by Torrance.
1961	Gordon	"Synectics"	William Gordon modified the brainstorming approach by supplying participants in problem-solving settings first with highly abstract problems and then, over the course of the time spent working with the problem, with more and more concrete cues. This model—synectics—has had widespread use, especially in industrial settings.
1962	Getzels & Jackson	*Creativity and intelligence*	J. W. Getzels and P. W. Jackson highlighted the distinction between creativity and intelligence. They found that creative students were not necessarily the most intelligent and their study is frequently cited as evidence for the distinction between creativity and intelligence.

Date(s)	*Person(s)*	*Work*	*Impact*
1962	Haefele	*Creativity and innovation*	John Haefele's book introduced the "collective notebook" method for creative problem solving, a variant of brainstorming. In this method, a notebook with the problem described on the first page is passed around. Each person adds all the possibile solutions he or she can think of.
1965	Wallach & Kogan	*Modes of thinking in young children: A study of the creativity-intelligence distinction*	Michael Wallach and Nathan Kogan generally found little relationship between levels of intelligence and creativity. Along with the Getzels and Jackson study, this book is most often cited as evidence of the distinctiveness of creative ability.
1969	Pryor, Haag, & O'Reilley	"The creative porpoise: Teaching for novel behavior"	This study was the first to demonstrate the possibility of training infrahuman subjects in novel responses.
1971–1976	Goetz	Creativity training with preschool children	Elizabeth Goetz built on the work of Maltzman and with her associates demonstrated the effects of reward in training novelty among preschool children.
1980	Glover, Zimmer, & Bruning	"Information processing approaches to creativity"	This was the first study to approach creativity from an information-processing perspective.

Part Two

GUIDING AND MOTIVATING BEHAVIOR

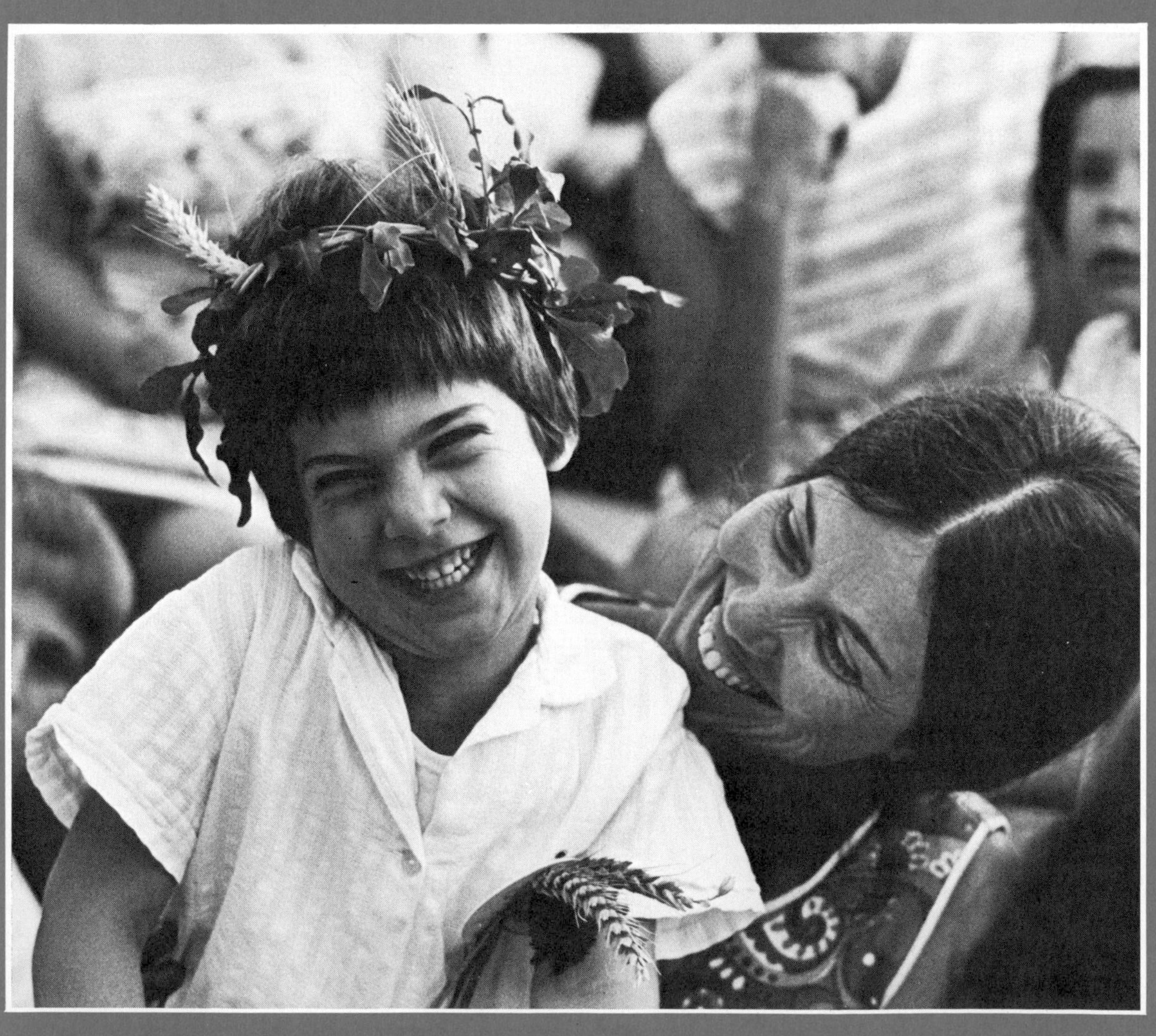

One of the most important functions of the teacher is the guidance and motivation of students. In Part One we emphasized the teacher's role in facilitating the cognitive growth of students. In this section we examine how teachers can structure classrooms so that maximum and enjoyable learning results. Chapter Seven, "An Introduction to Behavioral Psychology," presents an in-depth examination of a learning theory that, in contrast to cognitive psychology, describes the effects of external events on student behavior. Chapter Eight, "Social Learning and Modeling," stresses students' social behavior while presenting a theoretical perspective that combines important aspects of cognitive and behavioral theories. Chapter Nine, "Motivation," emphasizes the development of students' views of self as a means of enhancing achievement. Chapter Ten, "Classroom Management," is devoted to the application of the principles discussed in Chapters Seven, Eight, and Nine to the management of student behavior.

Chapter Seven

AN INTRODUCTION TO BEHAVIORAL PSYCHOLOGY

The first chapters of our text introduced you to one very important way of thinking about human learning—cognitive psychology. In this chapter we turn to a different way of thinking about learning—behavioral psychology. While cognitive psychology emphasizes the ways in which perceptions and thoughts affect behavior, behavioral psychology emphasizes how events *external* to the person affect behavior. Less attention is devoted to internal events. Clearly, to fully understand people's actions, we must be aware of the effects of both cognition and the external world. The study of behavioral psychology expands our knowledge of human learning. Moreover, principles of behavioral psychology have been successfully applied to a host of educational problems, most notably those we refer to as discipline problems. In this chapter we will examine the basic principles of behavioral psychology and in Chapter Eight we will see how those principles can be applied to achieve social learning goals in education.

Objectives

After reading this chapter, you should be able to meet the following objectives.

1. Analyze your behaviors by identifying the discriminative stimuli, the responses, and the consequences of the responses.
2. Devise a procedure whereby you can strengthen a response in a student.
3. Devise a procedure for extinguishing a student's inappropriate response.
4. Apply the principles of self-management to alter one of your behaviors.

ABOUT BEHAVIORAL PSYCHOLOGY

From its beginnings early in this century, behavioral psychology has emphasized three premises. First, behavioral psychology attempts to be "objective, ruling out all subjective data or interpretations in terms of conscious experience" (Fancher, 1979, p. 319). Objective observations of behavior are the major source of data for behavioral psychologists. Second, the goal of behavioral psychology is to "predict and control behavior" (J. B. Watson, 1913, p. 158), where **behavior** is a general term denoting any observable action of a person. Descriptions of thought processes are generally seen as outside the bounds of behavioral psychology, although recent developments in "cognitive behaviorism" have begun to recognize the utility of analyzing internal events (Meichenbaum, 1977). Third, behavioral psychologists see fundamental continuities of behavioral principles across all animal species. The principles derived from studies of animal behavior may be used to explain aspects of human behavior (Rachlin, 1976).

Behavioral psychology focuses on observable events—what people do and say. It is the study of behavior as it interacts with the environment. In order to grasp fully how the behaviorist conceives of learning, it is necessary to examine some basic concepts of the behavioral approach.

Stimuli

A person's environment—all that a person perceives external and internal to the body—is seen as being made up of stimuli. **Stimuli** are perceivable units of the environment that *may* affect behavior.* Stimuli can be of any size (a group of students, a teacher, one button on a student's shirt) and may be perceived through any one sense (a beam of light

*Behavioral psychologists typically do not consider perception to be a cognitive process as it was described in Chapter Two.

through a window can be seen but not perceived in other ways) or a number of them (a desk can be seen, tasted, smelled, felt, and even heard). In the behavioral approach stimuli are not defined by their form or size but rather by their effect on behavior. Hence we may perceive either a very faint musical tone or an entire song as a single stimulus.

The behaviorist is interested in how stimuli (sometimes referred to as *stimulus situations*) affect behavior. That is, what kinds of responses do people make to various kinds of stimuli?

Responses

Responses are reactions by organisms to stimuli; they may be complex or simple. A bright light in the eye causes the iris to contract. A tap on the knee causes leg muscles to respond with a jerk. A teacher's question results in a student saying yes in response. A dial glows on an instrument panel and the pilot responds by carefully looking at several other dials and then at his or her jet engines for smoke or other signs of trouble.

Even the simplest responses are complex in that they are made up of several component responses. The apparently simple response of saying yes is really a series of responses involving the eardrum, the aural-neural system, the brain, effector neural pathways, the jaw, tongue, throat muscles, and the muscles that control breathing.* A more complex response such as using a pay phone contains several identifiable components: inserting the coin, listening for the dial tone, dialing the number, listening for a ring or a busy signal, and so on. Any response can be divided into subcomponents. Responses are merely convenient units to use in talking about behavior. We usually speak of any reaction as a response whether it is composed of few or many component responses. So we may refer to both a slight muscle movement and a professor's long-winded answer to a question as one response.

EARLY VIEWS OF THE INTERACTION OF STIMULUS AND RESPONSE

Historians of psychology typically break the development of behavioral psychology into early and contemporary phases (Boring, 1950; Fancher, 1979; Hilgard & Bower, 1975; Schultz, 1975). Early behaviorism was characterized by an emphasis on a type of learning called classical conditioning. To understand classical conditioning, it is necessary to examine two broad classes of stimuli, neutral and unconditioned stimuli.

*From a strictly behavioral perspective, of course, thoughts are not considered to be responses because they are not observable.

Neutral Stimuli

Neutral stimuli are stimuli that have little or no effect on an organism's behavior. To understand neutral stimuli, consider how you have been reacting to your environment as you read this book. Did you occasionally hear faint sounds of traffic or people in nearby rooms? Could you hear the sound of air-conditioning or heating units? Perhaps you heard the wind outside and the sound of birds. If you were aware of these stimuli as you read, but were unaffected by them, they were neutral stimuli for you. Likewise, the smell of library stacks, the color of the walls in your study room, or the pressure of your feet as you sit probably have had no particular effect on your behavior. All of these things, until we directed your attention to them, were neutral stimuli. Unless stimuli somehow change behavior they are neutral.

The majority of stimuli we perceive are neutral. Neutral stimuli, however, can come to acquire properties that affect your behavior. We will examine these properties in greater detail as we consider other types of stimuli.

Unconditioned Stimuli

Unconditioned* or **eliciting stimuli** are stimuli that cause involuntary responses **(reflexes)** to occur. A bug flying in your eye (an unconditioned stimulus) will elicit (cause) a blink (an involuntary response). You cannot avoid blinking in the presence of such a stimulus. Likewise, an ice cube slid down your back will cause your back muscles to contract. By gritting your teeth, you may be able to inhibit screaming or waving your arms, but the cold from the ice cube will cause your muscles to contract. We're all aware of reflexive responses and might not give them much thought in terms of educational applications, but it was the discovery by Ivan Pavlov that neutral stimuli can acquire the properties of eliciting stimuli that launched behavioral psychology in the first place.

Pavlov, a physiologist, had just completed the research on digestive processes that was to win him the Nobel Prize when he became interested in some related phenomena observed during his classic research. Pavlov had fitted dogs with tubes connected to their mouths so that he could measure how much they salivated under different conditions. As part of his research into the digestive process, he had his lab assistants place meat powder in the dogs' mouths. Meat powder, of course, is an unconditioned stimulus for the reflex of salivation. There's nothing surprising about this, but Pavlov also noted that certain other stimuli present at the time of inserting the meat powder came to elicit salivation by themselves. The most striking example of this was Pavlov's observation that the dogs began to salivate when they saw lab assistants enter the laboratory—whether or not they carried food with them (Pavlov, 1928).

*Conditioning is a technical term for learning. Unconditioned stimuli, therefore, are stimuli that do not need to be learned in order to elicit (cause) a reflexive response.

"Perhaps, Dr. Pavlov, he could be taught to seal envelopes."

The dogs had learned to salivate at the sight of laboratory assistants alone.

The kind of learning Pavlov witnessed in his dogs has come to be called **classical conditioning or respondent conditioning**. We can diagram the process of classical conditioning as follows:

Stage 1: An unconditioned (eliciting) stimulus elicits a response

Unconditioned Stimulus ⟶ Unconditioned (reflexive) Response

Stage 2: A neutral stimulus is paired with the unconditioned stimulus

Neutral Stimulus + Unconditioned Stimulus ⟶ Unconditioned Response

Stage 3: After several pairings, the neutral stimulus becomes a conditioned stimulus, eliciting the response on its own

Conditioned Stimulus (formerly the neutral stimulus) ⟶ Conditioned Response

Thus, a neutral stimulus can acquire most of the properties of an unconditioned stimulus by being paired with it on several occasions. When the formerly neutral stimulus can itself bring about the reflex, it is called a **conditioned stimulus**, while the reflexive response it causes is referred to as a **conditioned response**. In Pavlov's laboratory, the sight of the laboratory assistant became a conditioned stimulus for eliciting the conditioned response of salivation. Subsequent research has shown that many emotional and physiological reactions in humans (for example, fears, increased heart rate) are learned through the process of classical conditioning.

The fact that neutral stimuli can come to elicit responses was seized upon by John Watson (e.g., Watson, 1913), who believed that classical conditioning could be used to explain much, if not all, human behavior. Watson's research and especially his books and articles designed for the general public had a tremendous impact on psychology. Not long after Watson stopped writing in psychology, about 1930, however, it became apparent that classical conditioning could explain some, but certainly not all, of the learning process. Other theorists, most notably B. F. Skinner, began to examine the relationship of stimuli and responses from a different point of view.

CONTEMPORARY VIEWS OF STIMULUS AND RESPONSE

Rather than using the reflex as the basic unit of analysis for learning, Skinner postulated that most animal and human behavior is controlled by events that precede *and* follow the behavior. Skinner referred to this form of learning as **operant conditioning**. The whole tone of modern behaviorism was set by Skinner's detailed analysis of how antecedent (preceding) events and consequent (following) events affect behavior. In general, antecedent events tell us what to do and consequent events either strengthen or weaken our behaviors (Glover & Gary, 1979). Table 7–1 presents a series of behaviors with their antecedents and consequences.

The behaviors depicted in Table 7–1 were initiated by their antecedents; the antecedent events served as cues for the behaviors. The behaviors were then either strengthened or weakened by their consequences. We can make guesses about which of the behaviors were strengthened and which were weakened, but we cannot actually determine how the behaviors were affected by their consequences without first examining some concepts basic to contemporary behaviorism. We begin with a discussion of reinforcing stimuli, consequences that strengthen behavior.

TABLE 7–1
Some Behaviors with Their Antecedents and Consequences

Antecedent	*Behavior*	*Consequence*
Teacher asks a question	Student gives the correct answer	Teacher praises student
Girl sees toy on steps	Girl picks up toy	Mother kisses girl
Phone rings	Professor picks up phone	Someone screams obscenities
Child sees shoe untied	Child ties shoe	Child feels more comfortable
Teacher says, "Any questions?"	Student asks, "Why is the sky dark at night?"	Class laughs
Radio alarm comes on very loud	Sleepy person turns it down	Person goes back to sleep
Girl says, "Hello"	Boy says, "How are you doing?"	Girl smiles
Boy feels nervous	Boy ducks behind locker out of sight of new girl	Boy feels calmer
Man enters dark room	Man flicks light switch	Man is shocked, light bulb pops

Reinforcing Stimuli

Reinforcing stimuli are stimuli that, when applied to behaviors, strengthen them. That is, they increase the probability of a behavior's occurrence in specific future situations (Skinner, 1938). The term **reinforcing stimulus,** or simply **reinforcer,** was coined by B. F. Skinner. His observations of laboratory animals' behavior indicated that some stimuli strengthened behaviors. This principle was not novel—it had been put forward by E. L. Thorndike forty years before (he called such stimuli *satisfiers*) and had been hinted at in the writings of Alexander Bain in the mid-1800s—but Skinner's rigorous research and his ability to popularize ideas firmly established the principles of reinforcement.

Reinforcers are defined by the effect they have on behavior. If a stimulus strengthens a behavior, it is by definition a reinforcer. It does not matter what the stimulus looks like, feels like, tastes like, or what someone might intend for it to do. If a stimulus strengthens behavior it is a reinforcer.

Some reinforcers follow behaviors. These are termed **positive reinforcers.** If giving a small boy a hug after he says "thank you" increases the likelihood of his saying "thank you" in similar situations in the future, the hug was a positive reinforcer. Reinforcers may also occur prior to the behaviors they strengthen. These are referred to as **negative reinforcers.** Suppose a teacher shuts a window to stop some loud construction noises from interfering with classroom activity. If she is more likely to shut the window in similar circumstances in the future, the construction noise was a negative reinforcer. We'll examine the differences between positive and negative reinforcers more carefully later in the chapter.*

The term *reinforcement* is not synonymous with the term *reward.* Rewards are given with the intent of strengthening a behavior. We know, of course, that rewards don't always work as intended. We can, for example, compliment a child in front of her friends for sharing her toys. If we then see that the child is embarrassed by our actions and *stops* her sharing behavior, we would be painfully aware that our "reward" was unsuccessful in strengthening her behavior. The compliment may have been intended as a reward but it certainly did not act as a reinforcer.

Positive reinforcers strengthen behaviors they follow. Here, a stamp and a positive comment are reinforcers for a good performance.

Any time you hear someone say, "I tried reinforcement but it didn't work," you are listening to a person who does not clearly understand reinforcement. We can determine whether stimuli are reinforcers only by observing the effect they have on behavior. If a stimulus does not strengthen a behavior, it is not a reinforcer.† Only through behavior analysis can we label a stimulus as reinforcing or not reinforcing.

Reinforcement is a complex idea. There are different ways in which reinforcers can be categorized and it is necessary for us to consider several aspects of reinforcement in order to fully understand it. One way to think about reinforcers is by categorizing them as primary and secondary reinforcers.

Primary Reinforcers. **Primary reinforcers** are stimuli that strengthen behaviors because of our biological nature. They are innately reinforcing: We need them for individual survival or survival of the human race. We need not learn about primary reinforcers in order for them to be effective. At birth certain stimuli strengthen our behaviors because they increase the probability of our survival.

Primary reinforcers include food, water, air, tactile contact, climatic comfort, rest, affection, and sexual stimulation. These reinforcers are generally thought of as physiological. Newborn infants, for example, do not encounter breast milk until birth but breast milk will serve as a reinforcer for hungry infants from the first time they consume it. Likewise, newborns do not encounter cold prior to birth but the escape from cold is reinforcing the first time it occurs. Children may learn to

*The terms *positive* and *negative* have nothing whatever to do with "positive" or "negative" behaviors, "positive" outlooks on life, or other familiar uses of the terms. They were merely used by Skinner to refer to two kinds of stimuli that strengthen behaviors in different ways.

†There are some psychologists who evidently don't understand the concept of reinforcement and fail to understand the need to wait and see what a stimulus does to behavior before labeling it a reinforcer. See Brennan and Glover (1980) for a review of this problem.

Primary reinforcers strengthen behavior because of our biological nature. Food and drink are primary reinforcers.

cry because crying results in relief from discomfort—Mama or Papa comes running at the sound of baby's cries, removes the discomfort, and thereby reinforces crying.

Secondary Reinforcers. Many of the stimuli that function as reinforcers are not primary reinforcers. **Secondary reinforcers** are formerly neutral stimuli that have acquired some of the reinforcing value of primary reinforcers by being paired with them or with other secondary reinforcers. The phenomenon is very similar to the pairing process by which neutral stimuli come to elicit a conditioned response in classical conditioning. In this case, however, the neutral stimulus is paired with a consequence of behavior. The sound of words "I love you," for example, has no biological value to anyone. But if "I love you" is spoken each time an infant is fed, cleaned, hugged, and provided with primary reinforcers, the sound of *these words alone* will acquire the ability to strengthen behavior in the absence of primary reinforcement. Similarly, money has no biological value in and of itself. You can not obtain much nourishment by eating dollar bills, and they won't directly provide you with affection, comfort, or sexual stimulation. And yet, we are all aware that money is often very powerfully reinforcing. Why? Because money is paired with so many other reinforcers: food, drink, and a host of other reinforcers can all be obtained in exchange for money.

Most of the reinforcers we encounter (praise, smiles, new clothing, record albums) are secondary reinforcers. Certainly, any observation of classroom behavior would demonstrate that students do a great many things, appropriate and inappropriate, in order to obtain praise from the teacher, good grades, free time, peer approval, laughter, and other secondary reinforcers. One important task of the teacher, as we will see in Chapter Ten, is the establishment and use of *effective* secondary reinforcers.

Potency of Reinforcement. You may wonder what we mean by "effective" reinforcers. We define the effectiveness or potency of reinforcers by examining their ability to strengthen behaviors. The greater the probability that a stimulus will strengthen a behavior, the more potent it is said to be. Money is likely to be a more potent reinforcer for maintaining ditch-digging behavior than is free dirt, for example.

The potency of a given reinforcer varies greatly among people. Books may be a highly potent secondary reinforcer for some people but have a very small behavior-strengthening effect on others. Thus some students purchase books frequently while others spend money on other things. Most stimuli will be reinforcing at different levels for the individual students in any class you teach. Praise may be a potent reinforcer for some students, but not for others; grades, attention, free time, and other stimuli may be strong reinforcers for some of your students but much weaker reinforcers for others.

The effectiveness of reinforcers also varies within the same person. While food is reinforcing when we're hungry, even the thought of food can be nauseating after we have overeaten. Similarly, a drink of water usually isn't a potent reinforcer for a person who has just finished a large iced drink. The fact that reinforcers often lose their potency as they are acquired in large amounts or in great numbers is referred to as **satiation.** Satiation can occur with both primary and secondary reinforcers. After a while, for instance, praise can lose its potency as a reinforcer if it is experienced too frequently.

The Premack Principle Some helpful ideas about reinforcement potency come from the work of David Premack. In his first studies Premack altered the probabilities of rats' running and drinking by depriving them of access to water or to a running wheel. When they were deprived of water, drinking would serve to reinforce running. When denied access to the running wheel, the rats would drink water in order to run! Premack has held (1965, pp. 143–144) that this principle makes it unnecessary to know much about an organism's past history of reinforcement. The reinforcement value of an event can be predicted from present-day levels of activity. Premack's findings were formalized into a principle that states: *Of every pair of responses or activities in which an individual engages, the more probable one will reinforce the less probable one.* In everyday terms, preferred activities will reinforce activities that are  less preferred.

Homme, DeBaca, Devine, Steinhorst, and Rickert (1963) applied the Premack Principle in a nursery school where three of the children were extremely disruptive. The children spent a great deal of time running around, screaming, pushing furniture, and playing games. These behaviors had a higher probability of occurrence than did sitting quietly and attending to classroom events. Homme instructed the children to "sit quietly" so that they could then run, scream, and play for five minutes after accomplishing the "quiet behavior." The use of high-frequency behaviors as a reinforcement for competing responses was effective. The disruptive children learned to sit quietly and attend to teachers and other learning experiences within a week or two. In general, the Premack Principle has proved to be a highly effective approach to identifying reinforcers at all age levels (Epstein, 1979).

Delay and Frequency of Reinforcement. Any delay in administration of positive reinforcement increases the probability that other responses will occur between the response you are attempting to strengthen and the reinforcer. When such delays occur, it is likely that these intervening responses rather than the desired response will be strengthened by the reinforcer. The principle is especially critical when working with young children and students who have trouble paying attention to tasks. Vargas (1977, p. 27) gives an example of a teacher deciding not to interrupt a boy who is "finally working" in order to praise him. The boy soon begins to look around and bother neighbors. The teacher *then* speaks to him and says, "You were working so well." She has, of course, delayed her praise until he was no longer "working so well" and has probably reinforced his looking around and bothering others rather than the desired, on-task behavior.

The effects of reinforcement are also correlated with the frequency of reinforcement. Generally, the more often reinforcers are experienced, the more potent they are. Increases in size or amount beyond some minimum level, however, seem to have little effect on the potency of reinforcers. A child probably won't practice the piano for three hours to obtain a single star, but if she will practice one hour for six stars, increasing the reinforcer to sixty stars per hour is unlikely to have any effect.

Effectiveness of Positive Reinforcement in the Classroom. Just how well does deliberate positive reinforcement of desired behavior work for teachers? Does it work for all teachers or only for some? Thompson and his colleagues (1974) attempted to answer these questions by training teachers in fourteen classrooms in techniques of positively reinforcing appropriate conduct while ignoring inappropriate, disruptive behavior. A control group of teachers in an adjoining school was given no training. The results were clear-cut. In the experimental classrooms the frequency of appropriate behaviors greatly increased, while in the control classes appropriate behaviors actually decreased.

More recently, McDaniel (1980) has surveyed approaches to classroom management and concluded that the most successful approaches employ positive reinforcement for appropriate behavior rather than emphasizing a decrease of inappropriate behaviors. McDaniel further recommended that courses with practical experiences in classroom management should be included in basic teacher-education programs.

Schedules of Reinforcement. Reinforcement often occurs on an intermittent basis. Sometimes our actions are reinforced and sometimes they are not. The relationship of the number of reinforcers to the number of behaviors is referred to as a **schedule of reinforcement.** Schedules of reinforcement can be naturally occurring or set by the teacher. They can be determined by the ratio of reinforcers to responses or by the time interval between reinforcers. The ratio or interval can be fixed or variable. Table 7–2 provides examples of the various types of schedules of reinforcement as they relate to instruction and classroom management.

Continuous reinforcement (CRF) is typically most useful at the beginning of a learning experience and for strengthening weak responses. A student memorizing a new set of number facts or learning how to assemble her clarinet should receive reinforcement at first for each correct response. Continuous reinforcement typically yields the fastest rates of learning and the highest rates of continued responding. It will, of course, have similar effects on inappropriate behavior such as lying, teasing, or being disruptive even though we might wish it did not.

Shifting from a continuous-reinforcement schedule to a variable schedule constitutes one step of the process known as *leaning* of reinforcement. By continuously and gradually moving to a leaner reinforcement schedule, it is possible to reduce reinforcement to practically zero but still maintain the behavior.

Fixed-ratio (FR) schedules also produce high rates of responding, but rates may be rather erratic. Performance typically slows down or

TABLE 7–2
Schedules of Reinforcement

Type and Definition	*Examples*
Continuous Reinforcement (CRF) Provision of a reinforcer for each act or response.	1. Teacher praises the student every time she contributes to a discussion. 2. Child puts a gold star on a chart each time he brushes his teeth.
Intermittent Schedules *Fixed ratio* (FR): Reinforcers given on a 1:2, 1:3, 1:4, etc., ratio to responses. An FR 50 or FR 75 means that every fiftieth or seventy-fifth response is reinforced.	1. Coach gives a "credit" for every fifth push-up or pull-up (FR 5 schedule). 2. A boy gives his dog a bite of meat for every third time the dog jumps through a hoop (FR 3). 3. A teacher gives a sticker for each ten words spelled correctly (FR 10).
Variable ratio (VR): Similar to FR, except reinforcers are given on a random basis. They average one reinforcement per *n* number of responses. VR 10 means one reinforcer is given for every ten responses, but the reinforcement may occur after the first, second, third, eleventh, or eighteenth response.	1. Mother gives one "special reward" per week after daughter has cleaned her room (VR 7). The reinforcer may be given on any day, but its use averages once per week. 2. Teacher nods and smiles at student on the average of once for each ten words the student pronounces correctly in reading an assignment (VR 10).
Fixed interval (FI): Reinforcement given for first response following an arbitrary time period. The time period is usually in minutes. FI 7 minutes means that the first response following the passage of a seven-minute interval is reinforced.	1. Shop teacher comes by student's work station every ten minutes and gives approval for the first on-task behavior noted (FI 10 minutes). 2. A girl receives a check mark from her father for every ten minutes of practicing the piano.
Variable interval (VI) Similar to FI, except time intervals are randomly chosen around an average interval length.	1. After time periods of approximately nine, fifteen, eleven, fourteen, and eleven minutes (VI 12 minutes) the teacher notifies groups in a simulation game that they have earned another point by brainstorming new ideas.

stops after a reinforcement and then resumes and picks up speed near an anticipated reinforcement. Many natural work and study situations operate on a fixed-ratio schedule. We study by reading a fixed number of pages, completing so many questions in a workbook, or solving a certain number of problems. As we near our goal, we tend to work more and more quickly.

EXAMPLES OF FIXED RATIOS

Variable-ratio (VR) schedules tend to reduce the pause that occurs right after reinforcement in the FR schedule, thus producing steady, consistent effort. Most slot machines and dice games provide reinforcement (winning) on a VR schedule. If you can imagine the so-called compulsive gambler inserting coins and pulling the lever of a slot machine hour after hour in a casino, with an overall loss of money, sleep, and meals, you understand what we mean.

Fixed-interval (FI) and **variable-interval** (VI) schedules produce steady responding but at a somewhat lower rate than ratio schedules. Variable-interval schedules are particularly useful for teaching paced responding. Classroom teachers use variable-interval schedules to increase students' abilities to work steadily and productively. Periodic checks on student seatwork, done with a smile and friendly attention to the work, can effectively reinforce good study habits.

Superstitious Learning. We are all familiar with the common superstitions of our culture: black cats crossing your path bring bad luck, breaking a mirror brings seven years bad luck, "step on a crack, break your mother's back," and so on. Most superstitions are believed only by the very young or the remarkably gullible and are probably learned by seeing older or more authoritative persons model them.

A pervasive type of superstitious learning, however, affects us all from time to time. We occasionally receive reinforcement on an accidental basis and make a connection between some act and the receipt of the reinforcer. Suppose a child shouts "abracadabra" while a torrential rain is falling outside. Coincidentally, the rain stops within seconds, as it often does in brief thundershowers. The child, having no experience with meteorological events, connects the cessation of rainfall with his "magical" word. He later discusses it with his credulous playmates and they all agree that "abracadabra" is a powerful word. Thereafter when rain interferes with his play, the child shouts his incantation. Once the shouting behavior is established, immediacy of reinforcement is not so critical. The behavior will be maintained even if the rain stops several minutes later (Reese, 1978, p. 125). The child may fervently believe in the power of the word, and this belief is strengthened by a variable-ratio schedule in which future uses of the word are occasionally followed by reinforcing events.

Teachers should recognize the frequency with which children make such spurious connections between "cause" and "effect." The resultant behavior is not stupid or silly, nor does it represent deception. It can sometimes be very difficult for a child to detect that a "consequence" has nothing to do with a behavior. This is true for superstitious learners as well as observers.

Negative Reinforcement There are times when people act to *decrease* stimuli. If you are in a small room into which a loud rasping sound (so-called white noise) is piped, you will be exceedingly uncomfortable. If there is a brightly lit switch on one wall and the noise is either stopped or reduced when you touch the switch, you will quickly learn to touch the switch when you hear the noise. Reducing a noxious stimulus is reinforcing since the responses that reduce it are strengthened.

As we mentioned before, this form of strengthening response is usually called *negative reinforcement* and the stimulus is termed a *negative reinforcer.* Most events we consider embarrassing, frightening, painful, disgusting, tasteless, or offensive can function as negative reinforcers. When we act in ways that reduce pain, embarrassment, or disgust and our actions are strengthened, the actions have been negatively reinforced.

There are three classes of behavior that are strengthened through negative reinforcement: escape, avoidance, and aggression. All are means of reducing noxious stimuli.

Escape behavior is learned by removing oneself from unpleasant situations. A young girl, for example, runs into her house when a playmate starts hitting and taunting her. Likewise, a schoolboy feigns an injured knee and leaves a rough soccer game. Escape reduces the noxious stimuli.

Escape behavior can generalize. That is, it can appear in situations other than the situation in which the original learning occurred. The girl may start running into the house when the playmate is seen approaching or when she hears other children arguing. The boy may start limping as he walks by the soccer field. The children are then acting in *anticipation* of an event, *avoiding* the aversive situation. The response patterns we refer to as "anxiety," "worry," "timidity," or "fearfulness" usually involve avoidant responses, as do lying, making alibis, and cheating. These avoidant behavior patterns are learned (through negative reinforcement) because they are successful at reducing contact with negative reinforcers.

Aggression consists of responses that act directly on negative reinforcers. Turning off a squawking radio is an "aggressive" act, as is destroying it with an hammer. One is a socially acceptable response, the other is not, especially if the radio belongs to someone else.

Punishing Stimuli

Any consequent event (a stimulus that follows a behavior) that *reduces* responding is a **punishing stimulus,** or punisher. Punishers are just the opposite of positive reinforcers, which strengthen the responses they follow. Within the definition of punisher, the characteristics of a stimulus make no difference. If candy, money, or praise lead to decreases in behavior, they are punishers. If nagging, spankings, and loss of privileges do not decrease responding, they are not punishers and so should not be termed as such, regardless of how painful or unpleasant they seem to be.

Just as there are no universal reinforcers available to teachers and parents, there are no universal punishers. For humans, context often determines whether an event is punishing or reinforcing. Prepubescent boys may react to praise from female teachers as punishing, but only when other boys are around. Similarly, a young girl may react positively to attention from a boy when they are alone but find his attention "disgusting" (punishing) when they are with her friends.

Our society frequently employs punishment and the threat of punishment in its efforts to control human behavior. Lawful behavior is at least partly motivated by threats, fines, and loss of jobs or families, which are the consequences for unlawful behavior. Likewise, schools frequently employ threats of suspension, failure in courses, and corporal punishment as motivators for cooperating and studying. Presumably, appropriate social acts are thus negatively reinforced because they enable us to avoid the threatened punishment. They also permit us to enjoy the positive reinforcers that are contingent upon acceptable behavior. Despite the prevalence of social usage, teachers are well advised to make very limited use of punishment, because it usually works against them, making it impossible to achieve their educational goals (McDaniel, 1980; Trotter, 1972). Positive reinforcement of desired behavior is usually greatly preferable.

Yet teachers and parents continue to use punishment as a primary strategy (McDaniel, 1980). Why do adults continue to make use of punishment if its results are of a deleterious nature? An analysis suggests that four separate processes are in effect: (1) ignorance of alternatives to punishment (McDaniel, 1980); (2) negative reinforcement of the person administering the punishment by the immediate decrease in problem behaviors (Staats, 1976); (3) social expectations that adults will punish children (Staats, 1976); and (4) the "visibility" of many problem behaviors.

Most teachers can verbalize the limitations of punishment but many still continue to use it. To some degree this seems a matter of negative reinforcement of the *teacher's* behavior. Punishment does, by definition, reduce responding. A teacher *can* reduce oppositional behaviors, for example, by sarcasm or threats to call in the principal. To the extent that the troublesome behavior ceases immediately, there is an increased probability that the teacher will use sarcasm or threats again. This is negative reinforcement of the teacher's behavior.

Discriminative Stimuli: Stimulus Control of Behavior

We have discussed behavior as principally under the influence of consequent stimuli—reinforcers and punishers. Behavior is obviously also influenced by antecedent stimuli. When we travel from home to work, for example, cues along the way control our turns, speed, stopping, and starting so that we arrive precisely at the right place, on time, and without traffic tickets.

The cues in the environment that "tell us what to do" are termed **discriminative stimuli.** If we wish to leave an unfamiliar building, an exit sign would be a cue for our behavior. Likewise, if we are chatting with someone as we walk through a library and see a large "no talking" sign, we use it as a cue to stop talking. Those stimuli that indicate that a behavior will be reinforced in their presence are usually referred to as S^D's ("Ess Dees," a form of technical shorthand). Those stimuli that indicate a response is inappropriate (will not be reinforced) are also

Discriminative stimuli are cues for our behavior. The conductor is providing cues for his musicians.

discriminative stimuli but are labeled S^{Δ}'s ("Ess Deltas") to differentiate them from stimuli that signal reinforcement for responding (G. S. Reynolds, 1975). A lecture, for example, is an S^{D} for listening and note taking and an S^{Δ} for speaking out. The teacher's questions, on the other hand, are S^{D}'s for speaking out and S^{Δ}'s for notetaking.

The effect that discriminative stimuli have on behavior is referred to as **stimulus control**. Discriminative stimuli do not control behavior in the sense that eliciting stimuli control reflexes in classical conditioning. When an eliciting stimulus such as a bug flying in one's eye occurs, the reflex *must* follow it—the reflex is involuntary. The behaviors that follow discriminative stimuli are voluntary—they need not occur. We answer the question "What time is it?" not because we have to but because we have typically been reinforced in the past for answering similar questions. Likewise, we follow an instructor's directions to read the next chapter not because the instructor controls our behavior but because we have learned that we are likely to gain reinforcement or at least avoid punishment by reading the assignment.

Stimulus control can be very powerful and quite automatic. Vargas (1977) reports on an actual incident in which a teenage girl driving a getaway car from a robbery was caught because of strong stimulus control. She was just about to make her getaway when a traffic light ahead of her changed to red. She slammed on her brakes and stopped! The pursuing officers apprehended her because her behavior was "controlled" by the light. How do such stimuli come to be able to "control" our behavior? That is, how are discriminative stimuli formed from neutral stimuli? We can best answer this question by looking at an example of discrimination learning.

Discrimination Learning. The process of learning to respond to just one stimulus in a whole field of stimuli is referred to as discrimination learning. Let's assume you have an antique automobile. It has a number of unfamiliar knobs and dials whose function you don't understand. You turn the key and step on the starter. The motor turns over but does not catch. You try again and again, meanwhile pulling and turning knobs and switches. After you pull a particular knob, the motor catches and roars reassuringly. The next time you try to start it, you mess with the knobs and switches again, but somewhat sooner you pull the "magic" knob and the motor catches again. Thereafter, you pull the knob labeled "choke" almost automatically as you turn the key and step on the starter.

Notice that we have refrained from saying that the choke "causes" behavior or serves to "explain" the response of pulling one knob and not the other knobs. You can look at the choke knob all day, but if you do not attempt to start the engine, you will not touch the choke. It is the *consequence* of pulling the choke that determines whether it is pulled and it is the reinforcement history of the individual that offers an explanation for the discriminated behavior.*

Generalization. Always working as a counter to discrimination learning is the process of **generalization**. Generalization is the making of one response to two or more differing stimuli. Very young children, for example, after learning to say "daddy" may call all men "daddy." Mothers usually step up discrimination training at this point, reinforcing the child for applying the label correctly and gently punishing its misapplication.

As a rule, we may say that the process of generalization is a marvelous labor saver. Since we can generalize, we do not have to undergo a new learning process each time we encounter a slight variation of a stimulus. Think of the effort required to relearn how to open a door each time we came to one if we could not generalize across all knobs, latches, pulls, and electronic aids from two or three basic types. Similarly, consider the savings in effort and time effected by learning the concepts of "animal," "plant," and "automobile" (see Chapter Three, "Memory and Concepts"). People are able to respond to these concepts rather than relearning responses for each new animal, plant, or automobile they encounter. Think especially of the convenience of a number system that applies to all objects and events regardless of size, shape, color, or context. The quantity "five" is constant regardless of its use with groups of humans, pencils, roses, or books.

To some degree, generalization is automatic. A young child will call any color "red" that is more red than orange or purple. It is only with reinforced practice that he identifies each of the large variety of red, pinks, burgundies, and maroons. The degree of generalization depends on the amount of similarity between stimuli. Colors that differ only by a few wavelengths of light are usually given the same label (burgundy and maroon, for example). The less similarity between stimuli, the less likely that they will evoke the same response. If, for example, we reinforce a little girl for saying "yellow" to light of a certain range of wavelengths, we may find that she says "yellow" to light that extends from near-orange to chartreuse. But she will make the response "yellow" more slowly and with qualifiers the farther the light is from the original reinforced stimulus.

* In infrahumans, some discriminations are made on the basis of instinct or reflex. Birds sing, for example, when light is at a certain level, not because there are special consequences of singing at dawn or sunset.

Many "inappropriate" behaviors are actually instances of incorrect generalization. Some children who learn their social behaviors in a setting that reinforces competitiveness and aggression, for example, are literally too much for the school setting. They have overgeneralized the competitiveness and aggressiveness. In such situations the teacher may need to help children through a discrimination-learning process.

Shaping

As we will see in Chapter Eight, many human behaviors are learned through observation (including reading and listening), but there is an important learning process that is governed primarily by antecedent and consequent events. **Shaping** is the learning of a response through reinforcement of successive approximations of that response. Consider how a child learns to print her name. For many reasons, mostly because the parents have systematically reinforced "reading-like" and "writing-like" behaviors, Jane likes to draw. Further, Jane's attempts to draw letters have been profusely reinforced by her parents. One day Jane works dili-

Shaping is learning through successive approximations.

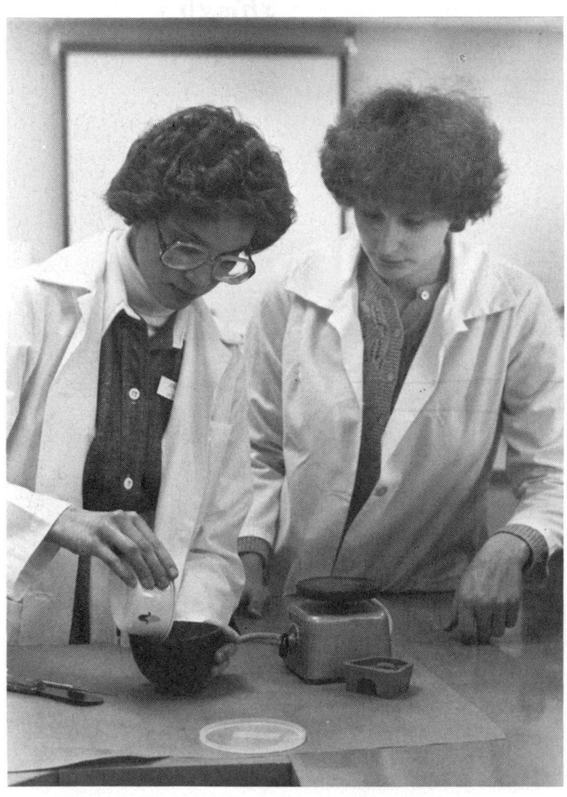

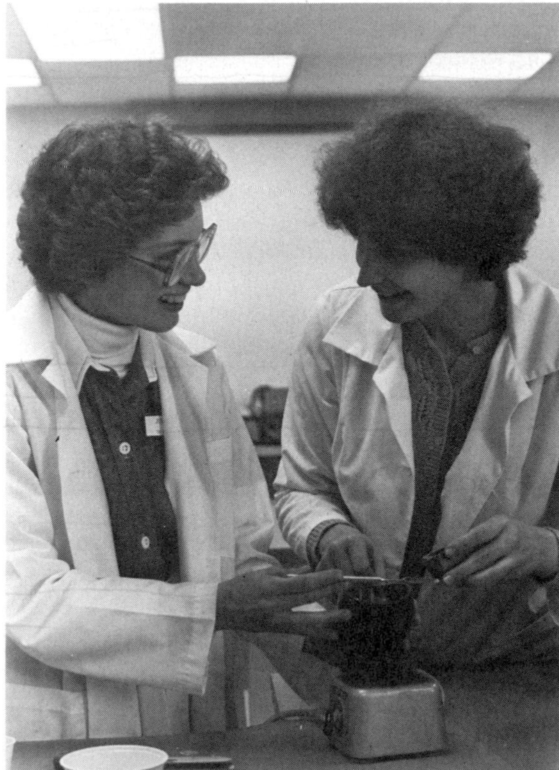

gently to draw a reasonable facsimile of her name. When she finishes the task she shows it to her parents, who are reinforced by Jane's obvious genius and hug, kiss, and greatly praise Jane for printing her name. Like most children, Jane likes to be hugged, kissed, and praised, and so she makes another attempt at printing her name. This time, though, the parents are hesitant to lavishly reinforce Jane for repeating the same level of behavior. The parents make comments about how to improve the printing as well as providing some modeling (how to make a *J* frontward instead of backward). As we follow Jane's progress over the next several weeks we see that she must make better and better approximations of printing her name correctly in order to receive reinforcement. Finally, she is able to print her name very well.

Shaping can be seen as parents teach language to their children and when children learn to use a pencil, to ride a bike, to somersault, and so on. Any time a behavior is learned primarily by reinforcement of successive approximations, shaping has occurred.

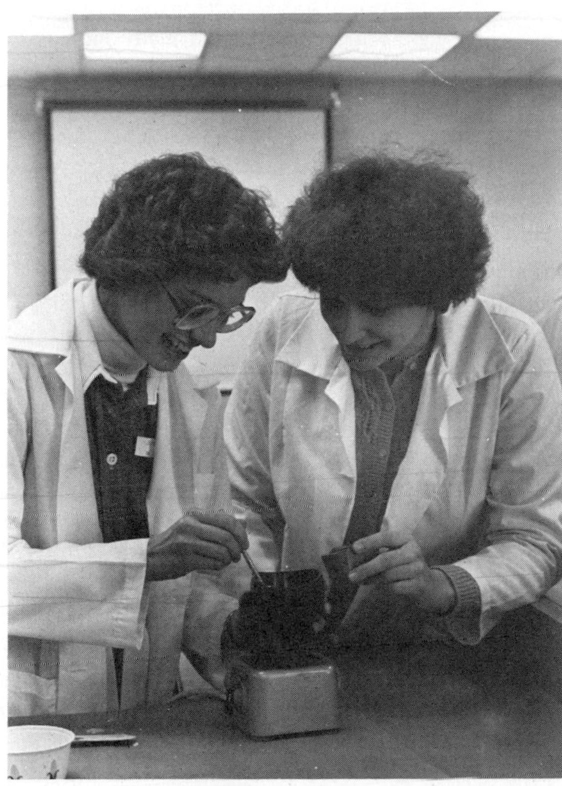

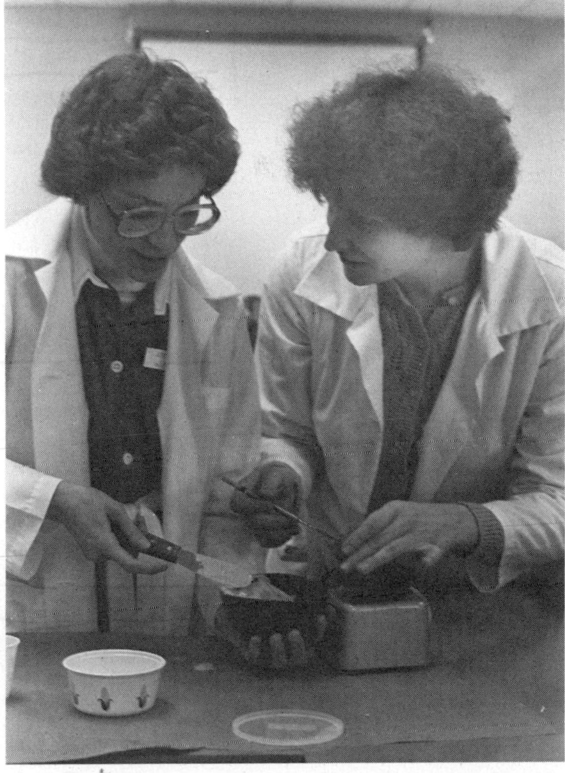

Extinction

It does sometimes happen in real life that we try, try, and try again but see no desirable effects from our efforts. Typically, unreinforced trying tapers off and eventually ceases. **Extinction** is a process in which a response occurs less and less frequently as a function of nonreinforcement. It occurs any time reinforcers for responses are discontinued. It is not the same as forgetting although, as we explained in Chapter Three, some of what we call forgetting may actually be extinction. If you learn to read but are no longer reinforced by reading, the *amount* of reading will decrease, but you will not have forgotten how to read. Extinction reduces performance, not knowledge.

The gradual nature of extinction is important. If a behavior stops abruptly, it probably has not been extinguished. It has more likely been suppressed by punishment or threat of punishment.

Recovery after Extinction.

Extinction may be followed by a spontaneous recovery. Suppose a small child's whining is ignored by his mother and it ceases. The next night, the child may start whining again. The whining response has recovered some portion of its original strength. It will not likely persist as long on successive recoveries if the mother continues to ignore it, but it is likely to start up again and again.

Consider also what can happen if a kindergarten teacher tries to extinguish a child's demanding behavior by ignoring it. After two or three days of successfully ignoring the child's demands, she decides the child has been doing well. Upon the next demand by the child, she stops and gives him a hug and tells him he has been doing "real good" for several days. Chances are that the demanding behavior will resume at full strength. The teacher has, through this process, inadvertently reinforced "demanding behavior" on a variable-ratio schedule. Many parents generate a similar problem when they attempt to ignore their children's inappropriate behaviors and fail to carry out their plan consistently. The result may actually be to strengthen the undesirable behavior.

Extinction and Response Strength.

When reinforcers are removed for certain behavior, the behavior sometimes increases in strength before gradually becoming extinct. Resistance to extinction is often taken as a measure of response strength. Responses that take five hundred unreinforced trials to extinguish are considered to be stronger than responses that extinguish after fifty trials without reinforcement. This fact has been used to test the effectiveness of differing schedules of reinforcement. By and large, responses that have been maintained on a variable-ratio or variable-interval schedule are the most resistant to extinction.

For this reason, it is advisable to use continuous reinforcement to develop a desirable response and then to shift to one of the variable schedules for maintenance of the response.

Extinction of Classically Conditioned Responses. Classically conditioned responses extinguish when the conditioned eliciting stimulus is repeatedly applied in the absence of the unconditioned eliciting stimulus. Suppose a dog has been conditioned by the use of meat powder to salivate at the sound of a buzzer. If we sound the buzzer time after time without ever again pairing it with meat powder (or some other unconditioned eliciting stimulus) the dog will eventually stop salivating at the sound of the buzzer.

Spontaneous recovery also occurs with partially extinguished classically conditioned responses. Suppose we extinguish the dog's salivation to a buzzer on Monday. If we return to the laboratory on Tuesday and again sound the buzzer, the dog will likely salivate to some extent. As in operant conditioning, however, the conditioned reflex will be far weaker than it was originally. Similar patterns have been observed in human classical conditioning, particularly of emotional behavior.

Self-Management

Is it necessary for *all* cues and consequences to come from the external environment? There are several indications that they do not need to—that individuals can prompt and reinforce themselves to bring about behavior change. This process has come to be called **self-management** or **self-control**, and it is being widely promoted as a useful procedure in counseling and education.

The term *self* as it is used here does not imply that the environment is not involved in behavior change. What it means is that one response is controlling another. A boy claps his hand over his mouth to keep from screaming. A girl jams her fist in her pocket when she is angry to keep from striking another girl. Such actions occur naturally and frequently in all our lives. Psychologists who use self-management procedures have extended the process and developed means of training individuals in making self-management responses to achieve a growing list of behavior-change objectives. Several aspects of self-management have been shown to extend students' control over what they do. These include stimulus control, self-monitoring, self-reinforcement, and cognitive self-instruction.

Stimulus Control. Stimulus control (review our previous section on discriminative stimuli) refers to a situation in which a person's frequency of response "is increased in the presence of one environment and decreased in the presence of others" (Richards, 1975, p. 431). If you set

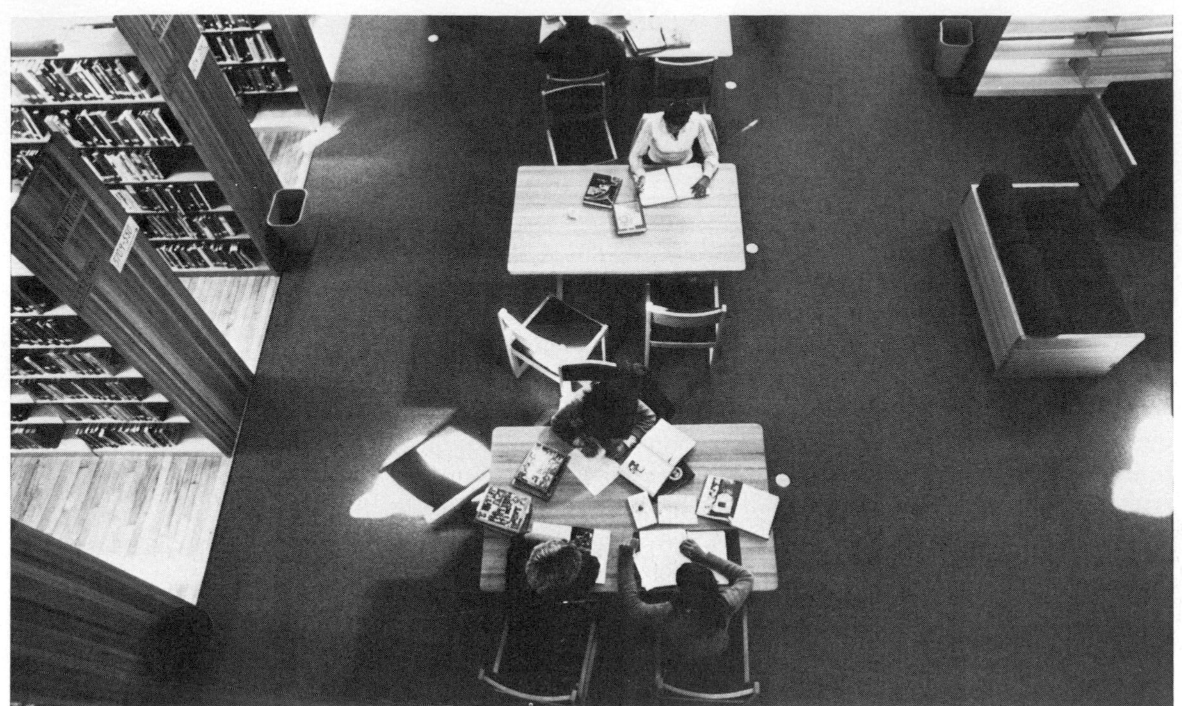

In self-management, the environment should prompt desired responses.

up an environment (a desk or an area in a room) in which study and only study takes place and is reinforced, then this setting will soon be a place in which studying will occur easily and reliably. We often are not careful about establishing stimulus control, however. Certain places and times for studying (trying to read late at night while lying on your bed or while listening to records) are not S^D's just for studying but are also S^D's for behaviors other than studying (such as falling asleep or listening to the music).

The general approach taken in establishing stimulus control as part of a self-management effort is to arrange the environment in such a way that desired responses will be prompted and reinforced. Thus a study carrel is used exclusively for studying, we employ note cards to prompt our observations for a creative-writing class, and a bedside clipboard may be used to record our impressions of the day. Distractors should be reduced to a minimum, and other activities are not to take place in the controlled environment. The more an environment becomes linked with one activity, the better the stimulus control will be.

Self-Monitoring. Self-monitoring is a technique in which students record their own activities. The responses recorded may be "good" or "bad" from the students' and others' viewpoints. Examples of self-monitored responses in schools and classrooms include participating in class discussions, meeting new people, completing homework and in-class problems, practicing an instrument, and swimming laps. Students' records of these kinds of reponses frequently have a significant effect on how often the behaviors occur. The records can also be the basis for fruitful discussion with parents, teachers, and counselors.

The effect of self-monitoring is often strong. In the area of study skills, for example, Richards and his associates (Richards, 1975; Richards, Perri, & Gortney, 1976) have shown that students who self-monitored their studying in combination with advice on study skills significantly improved their grades over students who used the knowledge of study skills alone. Monitoring alone is often sufficient to change behavior in a desired direction.

Self-Reinforcement. Another approach to self-management involves students reinforcing themselves for desired responses. Mahoney and Thoresen (1974) and Kazdin (1981) have concluded that self-reinforcement is an effective way for students to learn to control their actions. Kazdin (1981) has argued that in many cases self-reinforcement is just as effective as reinforcement administered by external sources. Teachers often first establish a reinforcement system, especially with younger students, and then move to arrangements in which self-monitoring is combined with self-reinforcement. Although there is an occasional tendency for standards to become more lenient (Kazdin, 1981), this tendency can be countered by periodic prompting and by reinforcement for maintaining high standards.

Cognitive Self-Instruction. Recently many behavioral psychologists have become more and more interested in "covert" behaviors—what people say to themselves and how these statements affect their actions. Because these psychologists' interest is in the effect of cognitive processes on behavior but their methods of analysis are derived from behaviorism, this new approach has been referred to as a **cognitive-behavioral** approach.

A simple illustration of how a self-statement might affect behavior can be seen in a common approach to dealing with provoking circumstances. People often tell themselves, "Now count to ten!" to lower their chances of doing something rash. Less obvious, but equally important, are the effects of students' statements to themselves when they are criticized, when they meet with failure or success, or when a situation might call for an extra degree of patience or restraint. In early work in this area, Meichenbaum and Goodman (1971) demonstrated that teaching impulsive children to instruct themselves as a form of self-guidance significantly improved their performance on a variety of tasks.

More recent work (see Meichenbaum, 1977; Watson & Tharp, 1977) has shown that many people who have consistent high anxiety overreact to painful stimuli, show a lack of self-control, and talk to themselves in inappropriate ways. They often label events incorrectly or have unreasonable expectations about what they do. Teaching these people to say different things to themselves often changes their reactions.

Cognitive self-instruction has been shown to be effective in a variety of studies with school-age children (O'Leary & Dubey, 1979), and its use has become more common in classroom settings (Rosenbaum & Drabman, 1979). Working with students to help them identify their statements to themselves about what happens to them is likely to become an effective way of altering overt behaviors in the classroom and school. As Rosenbaum and Drabman (1979) have pointed out, however, more research is needed to evaluate fully the worth of cognitive interventions in producing self-control.

PRACTICE EXERCISE 7–1
Modifying Your Own Behavior

Using the principles outlined in this chapter, devise a procedure to modify one of your own behaviors. You may wish to quit smoking, alter your eating so that you lose weight, change your study habits, or develop an entirely new behavior such as reading the biographies of famous psychologists (well, someone might want to do that). Follow the guidelines below.

1. Clearly define the behavior. Describe the behavior you wish to alter in observable and measurable terms.
2. What are the S^{D}'s or S^{Δ}'s for the behavior? If you wish to establish an entirely new behavior (such as keeping a diary, reading research in educational psychology, and so on) you will need to select one or more S^{D}'s.
3. What are the consequences of the behavior? Be sure to specify the immediate consequences. Increased reading may make you better equipped for solving world problems but this long-term consequence is not as important as the immediate consequence to your behavior change.
4. How will you alter the consequences of your behavior in order to strengthen or weaken it? If you want to strengthen a behavior, carefully select a reinforcing consequence you can hold contingent on the behavior's occurrence. If you want to extinguish the behavior, how will you remove reinforcing consequences?
5. Keep a daily record of your performance.

SUMMARY

In this chapter we outlined the principles of behavioral psychology. In general, five kinds of stimuli have different effects on our behavior. Neutral stimuli are perceived but have little or no effect. Unconditioned stimuli bring forth reflexive, involuntary responses. Reinforcing stimuli, both primary (those needed for biological reasons) and secondary (those that are learned), strengthen our behaviors and may take the form of positive reinforcement (following behaviors) or negative reinforcement (preceding behaviors). Punishing stimuli weaken behaviors while discriminative stimuli are cues for our behaviors.

Behavioral psychologists usually describe two forms of learning processes—classical conditioning and operant conditioning. In classical conditioning, a neutral stimulus is paired with an eliciting stimulus until the neutral stimulus can bring forth a response by itself. In operant conditioning, behaviors are strengthened or weakened by their consequences. The learning of new behavior primarily through reinforcement of successive approximations of the behavior is termed shaping, while the cessation of a behavior by withdrawing reinforcement is known as extinction. The principles of behavioral psychology may be applied by people to their own behaviors. This process, known as self-management, is becoming a more common part of what teachers may impart to their students.

Suggested Readings

Mahoney, M. J. *Cognition and behavior modification.* Cambridge, Mass.: Ballinger, 1974.

Mahoney's text is an excellent source of information about cognitive-behavioral psychology.

Pavlov, I. P. [*Lectures on conditioned reflexes.*] (W. H. Gantt, Trans.). New York: International Press, 1928.

This collection of Pavlov's original experiments gives the reader the full flavor of Pavlov's experimental work.

Reynolds, G. S. *A primer of operant conditioning* (2nd ed.). Dubuque, Iowa: Brown, 1975.

This book provides an excellent and concise exposition of operant conditioning. It is a good source book for those who want further elaboration on the concepts of behavioral psychology.

Skinner, B. F. *The technology of teaching.* New York: Appleton-Century-Crofts, 1968.

Skinner's book remains one of the best expositions of how operant psychology can be applied in educational settings.

IMPORTANT EVENTS IN BEHAVIORAL PSYCHOLOGY

Date(s)	*Person(s)*	*Work*	*Impact*
1855	Bain	*The senses and the intellect*	Alexander Bain's philosophical work was a significant precursor to Thorndike's views of behavior. Bain stressed the role of antecedents and consequences in explaining behavior. In 1859 Bain founded the first psychological journal, *Mind.* According to Keller (1965), "Bain's writings have the feel of psychology as it is taught today" (p. 37).
1863	Sechenov	*Reflexes of the brain*	Ivan Sechenov's book provided the intellectual foundation for Pavlov's work on conditioned reflexes. Sechenov stressed the role of reflexes in understanding behavior.
1894	Dewey & Angell	Formation of functionalism	The functionalist school provided the springboard for behaviorism. American behaviorism, as espoused by Watson, grew out of functionalism.
1898	Thorndike	"Animal intelligence: An experimental study of associative processes in animals"	This paper (E. L. Thorndike's dissertation) was the first of many that led to a theory of learning that stressed the consequences of behavior (satisfiers and annoyers). Thorndike's work was influenced by Bain. Later, B. F. Skinner's views were to closely parallel Thorndike's.
1899	Pavlov	Beginning of work leading to *Conditioned reflexes* (1927)	Pavlov began his research on the conditioning of reflexes in 1899 (Kaplan, 1966). He published numerous papers over the years, but his classic book *Conditioned Reflexes* did not appear in English until 1927.
1906	Sherrington	*The integrative action of the nervous system*	Charles Sherrington, a Nobel-prize-winning British physiologist, synthesized all the research available on reflexes by 1906. Pavlov (1927) based

Date(s)	*Person(s)*	*Work*	*Impact*
			many of his studies directly on Sherrington's ideas.
1913	Watson	"Psychology as the behaviorist views it"	This paper by John B. Watson set out the modern definition of behavioral psychology and led the way to the rapid growth of behavioral psychology.
1919	Watson	*Conditioning of fear responses*	In Watson's 1919 book he described the now famous "Little Albert" study. In this experiment a fear reflex was conditioned in an eleven-month-old child. No mention is made in any of Watson's writings about whether the fear was later extinguished. Watson did describe the extinction of conditioned fear responses, but with different subjects.
1932	Tolman	*Purposive behavior in animals and man*	Edward C. Tolman's book presented a theory of behavior that represented the first true cognitive-behavioral position.
1935	Guthrie	*The psychology of learning*	Edwin Ray Guthrie devised a radically associationist theory of behavior. While never obtaining a great following, his works had considerable impact on the shaping of modern behavioral theory.
1938	Skinner	*The behavior of organisms*	B. F. Skinner's book was based on research he had conducted in the early and mid-1930s. His system, operant psychology, became the major behavioral view in the 1950s and remains the most popular perspective on behaviorism today.
1943	Hull	*Principles of behavior*	Clark Hull's "logico-deductive" theory was first published in a complete form in 1943. Hull's theory was the major behavioral theory until shortly after his death in 1952.

Date(s)	*Person(s)*	*Work*	*Impact*
1944	Estes	"An experimental study of punishment"	William K. Estes, one of Skinner's students at Minnesota, for his doctoral dissertation published a comprehensive report on the effects of punishment. Many of Estes's conclusions have remained significant components of contemporary views of punishment.
1949	Skinner	*Walden two*	Skinner's novel greatly popularized behavioral psychology and also helped further establish Skinner as a first-rank propagator of behaviorism.
1950	Estes	"Toward a statistical theory of learning"	Estes's theory greatly expanded the behavioral psychology views of the antecedent-behavior-consequence paradigm.
1953	Skinner	*Science and human behavior*	With publication of his 1953 book, Skinner clearly became the dominant figure in American behavioral psychology.
1954	Skinner	"The science of learning and the art of teaching"	Skinner's article summarized behavioral applications for teaching via programmed instruction and teaching machines (based on Sidney Pressey's work in the 1920s). This seminal article provided the impetus for research in programmed instruction.
1955	Bijou	"A systematic approach to an experimental analysis of young children"	Sidney Bijou's article, based primarily on Skinner's work, provided the methodological foundation for modern behavior modification.
1958	Many individuals	*Journal of the Experimental Analysis of Behavior*	While many journals had been largely behavioral in orientation, *JEAB* (as it came to be called) was the first journal to be devoted solely to the study of behavior from the Skinnerian perspective.

Date(s)	*Person(s)*	*Work*	*Impact*
1959	Premack	"Toward empirical behavioral laws: I. Positive reinforcement	The Premack Principle made its first appearance in this article. It has been widely employed in behavioral analysis since its description.
1964	Solomon	"Punishment"	R. L. Solomon's article was the first major theoretical update of a theory of punishment since Estes's classic work. Another important paper on punishment was published in 1966 by Azrin and Holz, appearing in Honig's *Operant behavior: Areas of research and applications.* More recently, Johnston published a major theory paper in *American Psychologist* (1971).
1966	Seligman	"Chronic fear produced by unpredictable shock"	M. E. P. Seligman's paper introduced the concept of "learned helplessness," a condition arising out of frequent and unpredictable punishment.
1968	Skinner	*The technology of teaching*	Skinner's book demonstrated the clear applicability of operant theory in teaching.
1968	Many individuals	*The Journal of Applied Behavior Analysis*	*The Journal of Applied Behavior Analysis* (*JABA,* as it is called) became the major behavioral journal devoted to applications of operant theory.
1974	Mahoney	*Cognition and behavior modification*	M. J. Mahoney's book summarized the growing area of cognitive-behaviorism and pointed the way for future applications and research.
1977	Meichenbaum	*Cognitive behavior modification*	D. H. Meichenbaum's writings reflected the continued growth of cognitive-behavioral psychology, an important influence in contemporary American psychology.

Chapter Eight

SOCIAL LEARNING AND MODELING

SOCIAL BEHAVIOR

— Reciprocal Determinism
— Generality of Social Learning

SOCIAL LEARNING PROCESSES

— The Role of Reinforcement
— Modeling and Imitation

APPLICATIONS FOR TEACHING: INSTRUCTIONAL GOALS AND OBSERVATIONAL LEARNING

APPLICATIONS FOR TEACHING: SOCIAL GOALS AND OBSERVATIONAL LEARNING

THE ETHICAL-MORAL DILEMMA

SUMMARY

SUGGESTED READINGS

IMPORTANT EVENTS IN THE DEVELOPMENT OF SOCIAL LEARNING THEORY

Following on the heels of our discussion of cognitive psychology, our presentation of behavioral psychology might make it seem that there are irreconcilable differences between cognitive and behavioral theories of learning. There is, however, an important theoretical perspective that helps us bridge the apparent gaps between the two theories. **Social learning theory** tempers behaviorism by emphasizing the role of cognitive processes in the acquisition and regulation of behaviors (Hilgard & Bower, 1975).

> Social learning theory, a systematic position advanced by Bandura . . . and many others, . . . tries to provide a more balanced synthesis of cognitive psychology with the principles of [behaviorism]. It is a selective distillation of what is probably a "consensus" position of moderation on many issues of importance to any theory of learning. *(Hilgard & Bower, 1975, p. 599)*

> A valid criticism of the extreme behavioristic position is that, in a vigorous effort to [eliminate] inner causes, it neglected determinants of man's behavior arising from his cognitive functioning. Man is a thinking organism possessing capabilities that provide him with some power of self-direction. To the extent that traditional behavioral theories could be faulted, it was for providing an incomplete rather than an inaccurate account of human behavior. The social learning theory places special emphasis on the important roles played by vicarious, symbolic, and self-regulatory processes. *(Bandura, 1971, p. 2)*

This chapter is based primarily on Albert Bandura's social learning theory. Our primary emphasis is on social behaviors, which we shall first define, and we will also examine the applications of social learning theory to the classroom.

Objectives

After reading this chapter, you should be able to meet the following objectives.

1. Identify patterns of behavior that represent social learning in yourself, your acquaintances, and your future students.
2. State how a cooperative program with parents or other adults could be used to improve social behavior in your classes.
3. Describe the kinds of consultative assistance you would give to parents who are concerned about some aspect of their child's social development, such as timidity, aggressiveness, lying, or selfishness.

SOCIAL BEHAVIOR

Social behaviors are the sum total of interactions among people within a particular environment or geographic location.* Social behaviors are prompted by the actions of other people and are usually reinforced or punished by others as well. They are clear examples of the interaction of behavior and environment. To better visualize this relationship, look at the social interchanges depicted in Table 8–1. In each instance there are many alternative responses the individuals could have made. The child in Case 1, for example, could have said "None of your business" or falsified his intentions by saying "To the bathroom." The helpful boy in Case 4 could instead have laughed at the girl, pushed her down again, or looked the other way. The people in our examples made one set of responses but not others. Why? Because in their past learning, such events as a question from mother or the sight of a playmate in pain have become generalized discriminative stimuli for certain responses. The reinforcers for learning these responses are the reactions of other people, who act in reinforcing ways or stop acting in aversive ways.

The behaviors illustrated in Table 8–1 represent only a very small segment of the literally thousands of differing responses that are referred to as social behaviors. There are so many that we cannot possibly list or even think of them all. In fact, we usually speak of social behaviors in terms of *response categories* rather than as discrete acts. Many children, for example, exhibit a pattern of related responses we label "oppositional behaviors." These responses are made to requests, directions, orders, or demands from other people. They may vary from a child simply saying

* Although we will limit ourselves to social behavior among humans, other species—chimps, gorillas, and wolves, to name only three—display very complex social behaviors.

TABLE 8–1
Samples of Complex Social Interactions

Case	*Initial Cue*	*Response, Consequence, Cue*	*Response, Consequence, Cue*	*Response*
1	Mother's question, "Where are you going?"	Child stops running, smiles, says, "Outside."	Mother pats child and gives a hug, says, "Put on your coat, it's cold."	Child says, "OK." Gets coat, leaves.
2	Teacher asks discussion question.	Student makes humorous reply.	Teacher frowns, says it's a serious topic.	Student says topic is irrelevant.
3	Child sees older friend entering car.	Child smiles, waves, shouts, asks to accompany friend.	Friend hears a shout, looks, sees child, returns wave, but shakes head.	Child continues waving and shouts angrily as car drives away.
4	Boy sees girl stumble and fall.	Boy runs, helps her to her feet, asks if she's OK.	Girl shakes head, mumbles "Yes," then hurries away.	Boy turns and walks in other direction.
5	First student bumps into classmate near drinking fountain.	Second student shoves first student, who is slightly hurt. Second student remains at fountain.	First student says, "You son of a . . . ," kicks second student, and raises fists.	Second student calls a friend and they both hit first student several times.
6	Girls standing near basketball court.	Boy begins a fancy dribble. One girl points at him.	Boy dribbles faster, passes to teammate, girls yell at him.	Boy demands ball, shoots a ridiculously long shot, misses. Girls laugh.

"No" to standing behind a tree and brandishing a stick when asked by a teacher to enter a game with other children. Oppositional behavior can also consist of a child sitting rigidly in a chair and clamping her mouth tightly shut when offered a spoonful of medicine or holding on tightly when asked to relinquish a toy to another child. In all cases, the category of "oppositional behavior" includes social behaviors that serve to negate requests.

Table 8–2 presents a list of categories of social behaviors that have frequently appeared in the literature on social learning.

Reciprocal Determinism

Each of the categories in Table 8–2 is an interaction between two or more people. Bandura (1977a) views such interactions as examples of **reciprocal determinism.** In reciprocal determinism interpersonal and nonsocial environmental factors come together as interlocking determinants of each other. Reciprocal determinism holds that the behavior of individuals occurs because of prior interactions with other people *and* with the immediate environment. Diagramatically, the relationship looks like this:

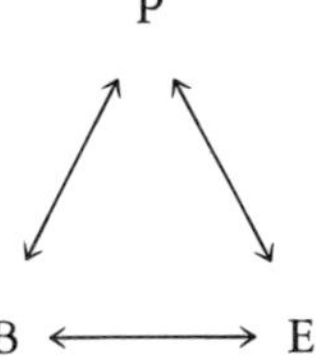

in which behavior (B) of an individual is seen as being determined by prior learning (P) and the present environment (E). The arrows indicate that the influence can be in any direction.

Reciprocal determinism, according to Bandura, predicts that the relative strength of interpersonal behavior will vary with changes in environmental factors. Sharing and competitive behaviors, for example, are usually thought to be types of interactions determined by past learning. In times of extended drought or other hardships, however, sharing and competition may be considerably modified. Prior learning interacts with the present environment to determine behavior (Bandura, 1977a, 1977b).

Generality of Social Learning

Social behaviors tend to be quite generalized (see Bandura, 1962, 1963, 1965, 1977a, 1977b). That is, they are likely to appear in a variety of settings involving many different people. Social behaviors also tend to be fairly stable, persisting over long periods of time. An individual who acts aggressively in one situation, for example, will usually

TABLE 8–2
Examples of Social Behavior Categories

Category of Social Behavior	*Component Behaviors*
Affiliative	Smiles, attends to others, speaks and greets, frequently expresses pleasure at others' company, seeks company
Assertive	Speaks often of own or others' equal rights, expresses feelings easily, refuses to be unnecessarily manipulated or "sold," speaks out against infringements of rights. Rejects unwanted attention with tact
Aggressive	Hits frequently, physically abusive, makes verbal demands, argues often, uses trickery or misleading language to control, coerces others
Dependent	Asks for help, frequently complains of inability to meet requirements, expresses fear of making mistakes, waits for others to initiate action
Sharing	Frequently offers to assist, encourages, divides materials or time
Moral-ethical	Expresses social rules for correct conduct and acts accordingly, expresses guilt or remorse at violations, predicts effects of own and others' actions on future welfare
Nonassertive	Avoids social conflict, acts to avoid evaluative situations, does not protest when rights are violated, excuses those who make errors, avoids strangers or situations where there are many strangers
Deviant	Makes violent, unprovoked attacks on others, accuses others, hallucinates, is nonresponsive to actions of others, self-stimulates, is nonresponsive to social reinforcement or punishment
Deceitful	Lies or acts to mislead others either to gain a reinforcer or to avoid a punishment
Sex role	Acts similar to own gender in own culture, states desire to be member of own or opposite gender, selects same or opposite sex as love or sex partner(s)
Cooperative	Accepts assignments to carry out joint tasks, seeks out opportunities to work with others, joins in common tasks for common benefit, expresses his preferences for doing things with others, denies own immediate gain for activities that benefit whole group
Competitive	Frequently acts to best others, expresses preferences for competition in occupation or in recreational pursuits, denies or debates about "who lost," shows evident signs of distress over losing

be aggressive in many similar situations. Likewise, the shy student in the classroom will probably be shy in many similar settings in the future.

Social learning theory explains this generalization by hypothesizing the existence of mediating responses. **Mediating responses** are considered to be symbolic events (thoughts) that usually consist of images or verbal responses that people envision when they encounter stimuli. These mediating responses help determine one's overt actions, which are then reinforced or punished by the reactions of other people.* We can picture the chain of events in social behaviors as follows:

discriminative stimuli ⟶ mediating responses ⟶ overt responses ⟶ reinforcement or punishment

Suppose that Jane is walking home from school when she encounters another little girl whom she has never seen before. Further imagine that this unknown child slips on some ice and falls down. This situation—seeing another child in distress—is a discriminative stimulus for several possible mediating responses on Jane's part. Mediating responses generally provide people with a label for an event they witness (Jane thinks, "That little girl is hurt"), a course of action to follow ("I should help her get up and see if she needs a doctor"), and an anticipation of the outcome of the course of action ("Maybe she'll be my friend if I help her"). On some occasions, mediating responses may include cautions. Consider the thoughts one may have about stopping to help a motorist in distress: "Maybe he needs help but then again maybe he's trying to lure people into a trap so that he can rob them."

Most mediating responses are easily remembered. The images and verbal responses occur so readily that they are immediately available in almost every social situation. This may account for the consistency in most people's social behaviors. Changes in social behavior *can* occur if new mediating responses are learned. Therapists, for example, have reported successful treatments based on training their patients to label events in new ways and to describe themselves more favorably (Beck, 1979; Mahoney, 1974).

SOCIAL LEARNING PROCESSES

The Role of Reinforcement

Reinforcement and the shaping of responses are major factors in social learning (Skinner, 1953). Bandura (1965, 1973, 1976, 1977a) has argued, however, that while reinforcement procedures may be used alone, they are often inefficient. There are usually much faster ways to teach complex behaviors.

*Note that this view of "thoughts" is rather different from how cognitive psychologists see things (see Chapter Two).

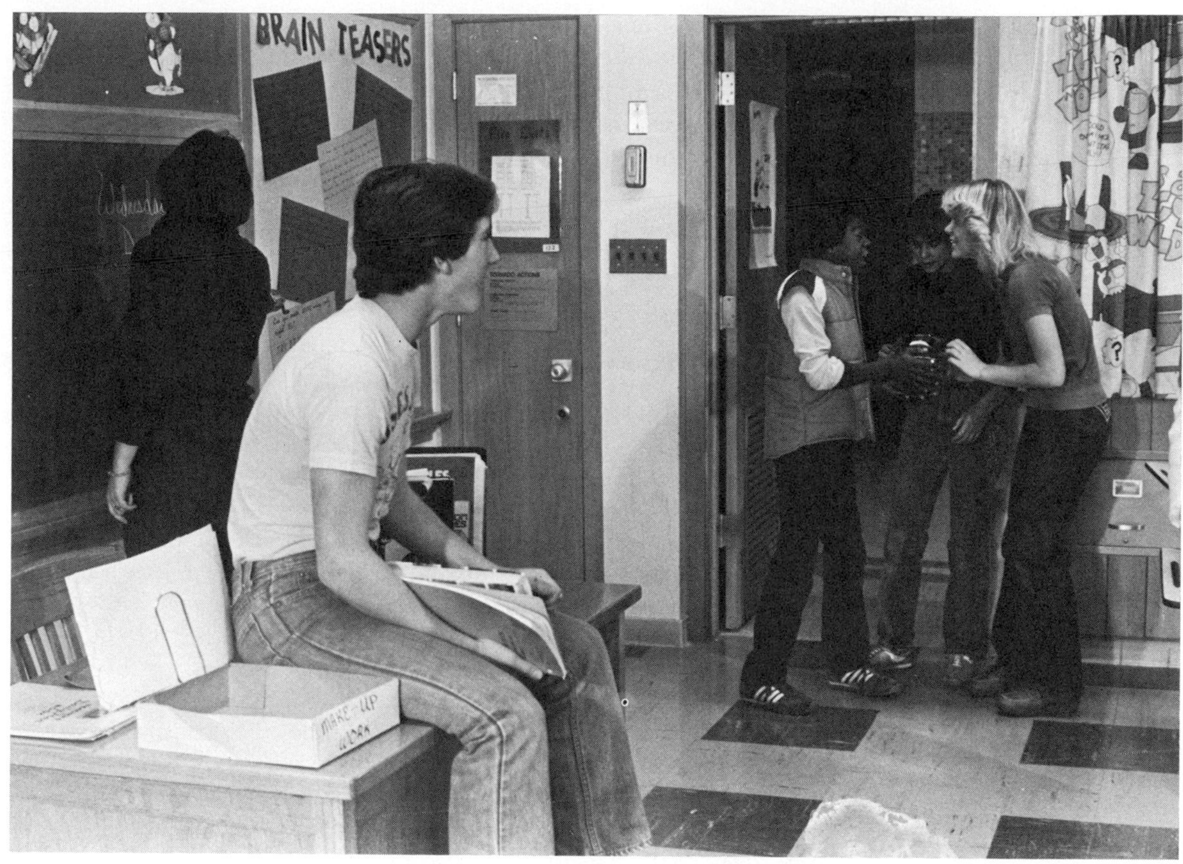

Most social behavior is learned through observation and imitation.

Consider, for example, how long it would take a teacher of the Russian language to use shaping alone to teach his or her pupils to pronounce a five-word sentence in Russian. Reinforcement by itself could get the job done, but at terrific expense in time and effort. It is much simpler to provide a model of Russian pronunciation for the students to imitate. Bandura argues that observation and imitation, not shaping, constitute the process by which almost all social learning occurs.

There is a role for reinforcement in social learning, however. Reinforcement determines two things: whether a response will be attempted again and the rate of improvement in speed and accuracy of an imitation. If a child pronounces a word he has heard his parents say, he will attempt to say it again and again if he is reinforced. Improvement will occur if reinforcers are provided.

An example of modeling and reinforcement in social learning can be seen in a study by Barton and Osborne (1978a), who reported on a procedure they employed to increase sharing behavior among a kindergarten class of five hearing-impaired children.

All the subjects in the study were reasonably bright children with severe hearing impairments and poor speech development. Unfortunately, they did not share things well and very frequently fought. Each child wanted what the other had and tried to take it. Their behavior in most aspects of their social interaction apparently resembled that of typical two-year-olds.

The teacher conducted the experimental procedure during a free-time period in which toys were distributed in the regular classroom. The nonsharing students were required by the teacher to share toys with the other students. When they failed to share, the teacher demonstrated the required sharing and had the students practice sharing. Praise and other rewards were given for sharing. Children who refused to carry out the practice were removed from the group for brief time periods.

The combination of modeling and reinforced practice led to marked increases in sharing for all the children. Verbal interchanges among the children also increased. All changed behaviors persisted for the entire fifteen-week follow-up period. The increased sharing (up to three times the level noted prior to the study) was also observed when the children were with another teacher, and sharing generalized to another classroom where there were regular, untrained students and new toys.

Social behavior is regulated by *anticipated* as well as actual consequences. A child will work for extended periods of time not only for immediate reinforcement, but also for an anticipated reward, say a weekend movie. Very likely, if the child were informed that the movie was no longer available, her chore-related behavior would cease.

Social learning research has shown that direct experience with reinforcement and punishment is not always necessary for social learning to occur. We can watch others receive rewards or punishers for engaging in an act and the likelihood of our acting in the same way will be affected. Usually, seeing others succeed increases the probability that we will attempt the same behavior. The effect of observing others receive reinforcement has been labeled **vicarious reinforcement** (see Bandura, 1977b, pp. 117–120). Observing others receive punishment for a particular act, of course, reduces the probability of our attempting it (vicarious punishment).

Bandura and others have suggested that observing reinforcement or punishment has another important effect: establishing the relative value of consequences. Suppose one student sees another receive a sticker for the completion of several workbook pages. The first child then wants one too, and so she carries out the same task in order to earn the sticker, just because she saw another child reinforced with one. Suppose the next day she observes a third child rewarded with *two* stickers for doing the same task. When the first child is again given her reward of a single sticker for her activity, she is likely to become angry or hurt (typical responses to a punisher, not to a positive reinforcer). The child's vicarious experiences have altered the reinforcement value of the sticker—reversed its value, in fact. Observation establishes rewards and punishers as relative values, not as absolute events (Buchwald, 1959, 1960).

The importance of observed consequences will be further discussed in the section on modeling. Most behaviors related to our values, self-esteem, career interests, and even our ambition are developed as a result of observation of other people achieving satisfaction from carrying out certain tasks. Observation is also a more rapid process for developing secondary reinforcers than the pairing of reinforcers described in Chapter Seven. Observing a single instance of another child experiencing satisfaction with a successful performance in spelling or math will often establish success as a reinforcer. Fears and anxieties are also quickly learned. No one is certain just why vicarious reinforcement and vicarious punishment are so effective, although Bandura (Bandura & Barab, 1971) suggests that vicarious consequences act through four related functions: information, motivation, valuation, and influence.

Information function. Observing others receive reinforcement usually permits a clear view of the connection between an act and its consequence. It also informs the observer about situations in which consequences differ, so that discriminative stimuli are quickly established.

Motivation function. Motivation to continue despite failure is improved by observing others obtain reinforcement for the same behavior (Bandura & Barab, 1971). Further, observing other people being reinforced for a behavior on a variable schedule is more likely to bring about persistence than observing others reinforced on a continuous schedule (G. M. White, 1972).

Valuation function. New reinforcers can be established through the observation of others' reactions. Students can develop new preferences (secondary reinforcers) and even come to have positive reactions to previously disliked objects (Blanchard, 1970a). Similarly, observed punishment can either lower or raise the status of engaging in various acts (Bandura, 1977b). An individual imprisoned for upholding his beliefs and principles, for example, may be praised whereas an individual imprisoned for abusing a child is reviled. In one case observation of punishment increases the likelihood of imitation. In the other, the observed consequence reduces imitation.

Influence function. Ditrichs, Simon, and Greene (1967) found that children who saw others respond favorably to rewards for completing a task tended to increase their own efforts to complete tasks. When models reject rewards, students' levels of behavior drop significantly. Similarly, Bandura (1977a) has noted that children will adopt work standards when they observe other children achieve satisfaction by setting their own standards. Interestingly, when children adopt the high performance standards they observe in others, they tend to generalize the standards to other times and places. Handwriting is a good example. A person who has a "perfect" model of script as a criterion works to achieve that model and is displeased with scrawled messages wherever and whenever he produces them.

The generalization of standards and self-reinforcement of effort constitute a form of self-management (see Chapter Seven) or, to use another label, a *value system.* In any case, we are talking about a widespread and powerful influence on the behavior of students. Teachers who seek to achieve the goal of preparing students to be self-managers will need to be skilled in the application of the principles of observational learning.

Modeling and Imitation

The components of the observational learning process include a **model** of a response, with antecedent and consequent events. The model can be live, of course, but a movie, videotape, or illustrated story may also function as one. A model can be provided by an oral discussion in which an older person asks a series of questions such as the following:

"Will the dog run toward us?"

"Will he be glad to see us or mad at us?"

"How could we show him we want to be friends?"

"How would he act when we show him we are his friends?"

"Would it be fun for him to act that way?"

A teacher demonstrating an act to a child is also providing a model. Bandura (1973) and Liebert, Neale, and Davison (1973) have shown that symbolic modeling processes are sources of many attitudes and personal styles.*

* For a more detailed description of a model procedure to allay children's fears of animals, see Bandura, Grusek, and Menlove (1967). Unafraid children modeled positive contacts with a penned dog for several days. Afterward, formerly fearful children played as enthusiastically with the dog as did their fearless peers.

The precise form of modeling makes little difference to the basic process. The effect is generally the same whether information is conveyed through examples, pictures, or words. It is probably more effective to use behavioral demonstrations when instructing learners who have language limitations, but that is a matter of adapting the process to students' needs, not a change in the basic process.

As paradoxical as it might seem, learning by imitation does not necessarily develop naturally. Matching a model's behavior (Skinner, 1953) is a skill that must be learned (Bandura, 1965). An individual who has not mastered this skill can observe modeled behavior or hear it described for hours but will make no effort to imitate it. Imitation can be taught, however. Baer, Peterson, and Sherman (1967) worked with three severely retarded children, repeatedly reinforcing them for imitating appropriate eating and self-care behaviors, and found that the children's imitative responses increased and generalized.*

Once imitation learning has been established, learners usually apply their imitation skills to the rapid acquisition of large numbers of social and academic behaviors, including grammar and other language rules, moral-ethical judgments, creativity, and sensitivity to others (see Table 8–2). Reinforcement in real life then usually leads to relatively widespread generalization. Also, once behaviors are established in one or a few individuals, modeling and imitation contribute to their diffusion to other people. The diffusion process is often helped by mass media, which explains how fads and fashions can sweep entire regions or countries almost overnight.

The effectiveness of modeling depends on a number of factors. Modeling that employs "actors" who are very similar in age, sex, and occupation to learners tends to have the greatest impact. Modeling that employs higher-status or more expert "actors" is more effective, as is modeling that portrays receipt of higher-value reinforcers. The correlates of modeling effectiveness must be interpreted cautiously, however. The status and characteristics of the models are most important if reinforcement is vague, far in the future, or rather probabilistic. If the reinforcers are abundant and potent, the status and character correlates of the models are of less significance (Bandura, 1977b, pp. 90–92).

Observational learning, of course, does not always produce desirable behaviors. Bizarre actions, strange beliefs, poor speech patterns, and

* If you have slow-learning children in your classroom, you may be interested in additional readings on the process and advantages of using reinforcement methods to train them in generalized imitation: Brigham & Sherman (1968), E. Martin (1971), Masters & Morris (1971), and Steinman & Boyce (1971).

"I love the whole thing. In fact, one day I'm going to take up either animated cartooning or violence."

high levels of competitive, aggressive, or even criminal behavior can be learned through modeling just as readily as can prosocial behaviors (see Greenberg, 1975, for a comprehensive review). One area of concern is the effect television has on behavior. Although the effects of television on social development are difficult to discriminate from other developmental influences (Kaplan & Singer, 1976), television has been clearly shown to have an impact on the social learning of both children and adults (see Eron, 1982; Jennings, Geis, & Brown, 1980). Friedrich and Stein (1973, 1975) found that even when children viewed only small amounts of "Mister Rogers' Neighborhood," increases occurred in such behaviors as cooperation, helping, sharing, and empathy. Other authors (Collins, 1974; Cosgrove & McIntyre, 1974; Shirley, 1974) have obtained similar results in the development of prosocial behaviors. These positive aspects of television as a social learning medium have resulted in some authors' prescriptions for selectively employing television to augment social learning both in the home and in the classroom (Bilowit, 1979; Comstock, Chaffe, Katzman, McCombs, & Roberts, 1978).

There are, however, many findings of negative aspects of television as a source for social learning. In general, research has consistently dem-

PRACTICE EXERCISE 8–1

The Impact of Modeling and Imitation

Modeling and imitation are important learning processes. In growing up, everyone is influenced by models. For most of us a few people have been models for behaviors that we now consider particularly important. We have imitated them consciously or unconsciously and, from our standpoint, the behaviors we have acquired may be good or bad.

We would like you to think of a person from whom you acquired one or more important behaviors through modeling and imitation. By answering the following questions you will have a chance to reflect on why you adopted the behavior.

1. The model was ______________________________.

2. Your behavior pattern that resembles that of the model is (was):

   ____

   ____

3. What reinforcers (or punishers) did you observe the model receive for his or her behavior? ______________________________

   ____

   ____

4. Did you consciously decide to adopt the behavior?

   _____ Yes _____ No

   If yes, what factors influenced your decision? ______________

   ____

   ____

5. Which of the following describe the model's relationship to you?
   a. *Age:* _____ Older _____ Same age _____ Younger
   b. *Sex:* _____ Same _____ Opposite
   c. *Relationship:* _____ Parent _____ Other older relative
   _____ Brother or sister _____ Friend _____ Other _____

6. Briefly analyze the reinforcement (or punishment) *you* subsequently received for adopting the modeled behavior: ______________

   ____

   ____

onstrated that violent television programs increase the likelihood of violence among viewers (Gross, 1980). Sex-role stereotypes are also prevalent in general programming, especially in commercials, resulting in direct effects on viewers (Jennings et al., 1980). Jennings, Geis, and Brown (1980), for example, found differences such as less self-confidence and less independent judgment among female viewers of traditional commercials than among viewers of commercials altered to avoid sex-role stereotypes. In terms of direct reactions to televised violence, children tend to become frightened when presented with even small segments of violent programming (Surbeck & Endsley, 1979), with the effects most notable among younger children and those who discriminate least well between fantasy and reality (Reeves & Lometti, 1979). In

APPLICATIONS FOR TEACHING: INSTRUCTIONAL GOALS AND OBSERVATIONAL LEARNING

Observational methods of instruction for both social and academic goals have a long history. In academic areas, teachers have traditionally included films, photographs, and demonstrations as means to improve students' mastery of the goals of instruction. Although much applied research remains to be done before all the implications of the theoretical research on observational learning for classroom instruction are understood, a number of procedures can be recommended. We have listed general teaching procedures for the use of observational learning in instruction that are based on the research on modeling and imitation.

1. Use some form of observational learning regularly. Use models or demonstrations to convey complex instruction, especially when your objectives (a) involve combinations of cognitive and motor acts (as in teaching the pronunciation of foreign words); (b) involve the use of several muscle movements (as in handling or using tools); (c) involve applying safety rules; (d) require students to make fine discriminations of dial or gauge readings; or (e) specify a rigid adherence to a standard procedure such as using laboratory equipment for making various tests and analyses. In other words, don't depend on verbal instruction alone to develop learning as complex as these examples.

2. Make use of negative models in combination with positive models. A student who uses poor grammar will benefit not only from hearing correct grammar, but also by seeing it contrasted with his or her present repertoire. Videotaped pairs of good and bad examples of grammatical usage may be very helpful in changing the student's behavior.

3. At first, direct your demonstration to one student. When personally modeling a procedure, such as making a motion in a meeting controlled by parliamentary procedure, select one student to stand or sit at the front of the group and demonstrate the correct actions to him or her. After the demonstration, ask the student to model the procedure to the class, with members prompting the student as required to give a correct demonstration.

4. Demonstrate physical activities without verbalization. Show a procedure completely without words. Then repeat the action, labeling each part verbally. It will also often be useful

fact, the overall results of research on television viewers indicate that habitual viewers have a distorted, fearful perception of the world (Gross, 1980).

Some authors view television as a relatively benign social influence with a very small likelihood of harmful effects (Comstock et al., 1978); some suggest that it is a moderately effective (but repressive) way of propagating cultural values (Gitlin, 1979); while others believe that television has the potential for doing great harm (Jennings et al., 1980). Regardless of which view is correct, it seems that the evidence supports the selective use of television (Bilowit, 1979; Gross, 1980). Ultimately, the effects of television will be determined by the responsibility that adults assume for the well-being of children.

Demonstrate physical activities without verbalization. Without talking, the instructor carefully shows students how to use a gauge.

to add two more steps: have the students "talk you through" the process, then "talk themselves through" with peers providing prompts and feedback.

5. Plan and rehearse all modeling procedures. Only by going through the process can you be sure that all needed materials are available and that they will work as expected.

6. Do not be afraid to repeat demonstrations. Learners can be easily distracted at critical points during observational learning experences. If possible, remove distractions. If this is not possible, repeat the demontrations.

7. Always talk about the knowledge that is called upon to solve problems. Carefully model rational approaches to problems, then provide reinforcement for imitation. Give plenty of opportunity for students to practice with reinforcement.

8. Model behavior in a setting similar to that in which learners will use the new skills. In other words, use field trips, simulations, and hands-on experiences where possible.

PRACTICE EXERCISE 8–2

Behavior Modeling

Many if not most physical activities are learned through modeling and imitation. The goal of this practice exercise is for you to teach someone a behavior sequence through the use of modeling. The following are examples of the kinds of behaviors you could model:

The toss and serve in tennis

Operating a ditto, mimeograph, or other office machine

Making a transparency in a media center

Putting a control card on a keypunch machine

Assembling a clarinet

The behavior you choose for your own sequence should be complex enough so that some learning is necessary, but easy enough to be completed in a few minutes. First identify your behavioral sequence and a "student" who will benefit from learning it. Then identify the steps of the sequence so that each part can be demonstrated separately if necessary. Next determine what you need to focus the learner's attention on at each step and what (if anything) you need to say at each step. An abbreviated example for the toss and serve in tennis is given below. Following it is a form for planning and evaluating your behavior modeling sequence.

Sample Plan for Modeling the Toss and Serve to a Junior High School Student

Step in Demonstration	*Draw Learner's Attention To*	*Verbal Comments*
1. Holding ball properly	How hand grips ball	"Hold the ball like this, between the thumb and first two fingers."
2. Racquet back, preparing for the serve	How elbow is lifted; position of racquet head	"Lift your elbow like this"; "Scratch your back with your racquet."
3. Toss	Lifting of the ball	"Imagine you're pushing the ball up a pipe. . . ."

Planning Form: Teaching through Modeling

Behavior to be taught ____

Student ____
(brief description)

Step in Demonstration	*Draw Learner's Attention To*	*Verbal Comments*
1. ____________	____________	____________
	____________	____________

Step in Demonstration	*Draw Learner's Attention To*	*Verbal Comments*
2. ______	______	______
	______	______
3. ______	______	______
	______	______
4. ______	______	______
	______	______
5. ______	______	______
	______	______
6. ______	______	______
	______	______

Problems that arose during your teaching session ______

______

Your overall evaluation of your teaching ______

______

______

APPLICATIONS FOR TEACHING: SOCIAL GOALS AND OBSERVATIONAL LEARNING

Classroom-based approaches for helping students meet social learning goals have received considerable attention in the last several years (Cartledge & Milburn, 1978). Effective procedures have been reported in schools for increasing sharing and altruistic behaviors (Barton & Ascione, 1979; Barton & Osborne, 1978b; Cook & Apolloni, 1976; M. B. Harris, 1970; Rogers-Warren & Baer, 1976); decreasing aggressive acts (Chiang, Iwata, & Dorsey, 1977; O'Leary & O'Leary, 1972; Sherman & Bushell, 1974); improving verbal interactions with others (Hops & Cobb, 1973; Zimmerman & Pike, 1972); and reducing racial prejudice (Aronson, Blaney, Sikes, & Snapp, 1978; Zimmerman & Brody, 1975). The features that these studies and a host of other social learning studies have in common provide several guidelines for you to help your students meet social learning goals. Here are six.

Privately praise appropriate social behavior. As they meet on the stairs, the teacher compliments the student on his behavior earlier in the day.

1. Clearly define the social behaviors to be developed. You and a student with a "temper problem," for example, may agree that angry feelings should be talked about with the person the student is angry at. The student should explain why he or she is angry. (The goal here is for the student to learn to talk out differences instead of settling them by physical means.)

2. Privately praise each time you observe a student exhibiting the desired social behavior. You might say, "Jim, I thought that was great the way you told Ann that she was not to tease you any more. She stopped and you didn't get mad."

3. Try to show both the expected behavior and its consequences. Coach students to role-play various behaviors and have them portray the consequences they would likely receive from each behavior.

4. Follow role-playing episodes with a discussion of the situation. Include appropriate alternative behaviors and their consequences. Negative consequences for inappropriate social behaviors should be discussed. You might say, "Let's see, when the guide is showing us around the museum—what could happen if we didn't follow her directions?" Several answers are appropriate and could be prompted and praised: "Other classes might not get to take a field trip to the museum" or "Other people who are touring the museum may be distracted."

5. Use small-group projects that require a division of labor. Require each person to undertake one or more assignments (Slavin, 1978, 1981). Structure small groups so that there is a rotation of several social roles among all the students. Not all instruction should be conducted in small groups, of course, but use them enough to give students several opportunities to have a unique, identifiable contribution and to receive credit.

6. Practice social skills in as many settings as possible. The emphasis on social learning should extend over the entire school day and be included in as many classes as possible in order to result in generalization.

Methods for altering student behaviors in the classroom usually raise some ethical questions, but since most such procedures usually result in changes that are useful for fostering academic learning, they are not often a source of continuing controversy. Many social behaviors, however, are linked to political philosophies, patriotism, sexual morality, religious beliefs, and even concerns about national security. What the schools do in the area of social development is everybody's business.

Consider competitiveness. This is a category including several related behaviors that some people consider to be the strength of our nation. Much of our political-social system is organized to encourage and benefit from competition. Many people therefore believe schools should systematically do what they can to develop increased levels of competi-

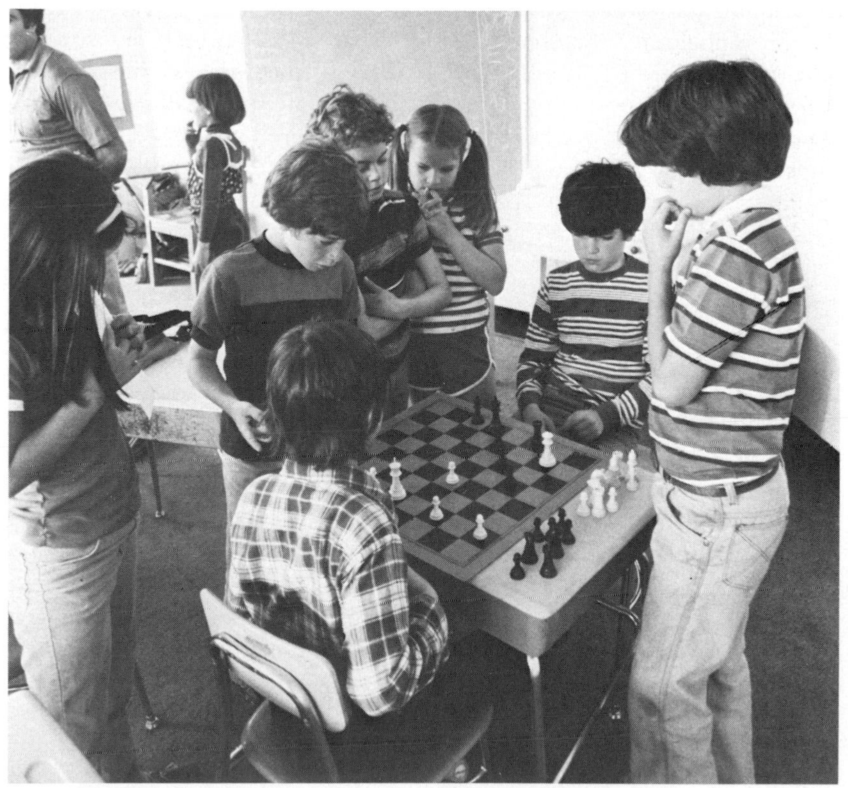

Teachers disagree about whether competition is desirable. Many believe competition helps prepare students for later life. Others point out that competitiveness can have many negative side effects.

tiveness. Others point out, however, that competitiveness is also associated with insensitivity to human needs, anti-intellectualism, and even criminal behavior and that the schools should counter competitiveness by emphasizing sharing, cooperation, and helpfulness. Likewise, concern has often been directed at matters of sexual behavior. Issues regarding the development of homosexual versus heterosexual preferences have surfaced in several communities, with referenda being held to decide if homosexual teachers have equal rights for employment.

There are no easy answers about which social learning goals should be established in the schools. There are not even fully satisfactory mechanisms to resolve the issues. There is no escape from making a decision, however. If schools or families choose to ignore such matters on the assumption that children's "natural" tendencies will determine development, they are in reality deciding to let other social influences take over. If schools and families do not employ learning processes, it is safe to assume that peer groups, television, movies, and other factors will control children's social development.

Is it preferable for the peer group or the media to influence social development? Should we intervene and counter some of the peer and media influence? Who should decide what sort of people our students should become? We have no final answers to these issues. We are quite sure that neither psychology nor any single profession shall ever have the final answers nor do we believe they should have. While many psychologists have spoken out on the consequences of extreme aggressiveness in children, for example, it is not up to psychologists alone to determine how to reduce aggressive behaviors. Such decisions, one would hope, will be forthcoming from a decision-making process involving everyone.

SUMMARY

Social behavior pervades every aspect of educational life. While reinforcement-based classroom management techniques are effective for many behaviors, social behaviors encompassing attitudes, values, and preferences are much more effectively taught through the application of social learning theory.

Central to social learning theory is observational learning. In general, many skills and behaviors are learned more effectively through observation than through reinforcement alone. Observational learning is of the utmost importance in determining reinforcers and punishers in a group setting as well as in developing group standards of conduct.

Social learning theory results in several pertinent applications for classroom instruction and student social development. Of paramount concern are the ethical issues in the use of social learning techniques. Classroom teachers must address the question of whether they have the right to emphasize values and ethics as part of their teaching responsibilities.

Suggested Readings

Bandura, A. *Social learning theory.* Englewood Cliffs, N.J.: Prentice-Hall, 1977.

Bandura's book is the most complete source of material on social learning theory.

Cartledge, G., & Milburn, J. P. The case for teaching social skills in the classroom: A review. *Review of Educational Research,* 1978, *48,* 133–156.

This thought-provoking essay provides an excellent summary of research on social skills acquisition in classroom settings.

Kaplan, R. M., & Singer, R. D. Television violence and viewer aggression: A reexamination of the evidence. *Journal of Social Issues,* 1976, *32,* 35–70.

This review paper is an excellent source of information about the effects of televised violence on viewers.

Miller, N. E., & Dollard, M. J. *Social learning and imitation.* New Haven: Yale University Press, 1941.

The basis of modern-day social learning theory is presented in this now-classic text. The content helps the reader understand the influences of early psychology on the development of modern views of social learning.

Surbeck, E., & Endsley, R. C. Children's emotional reactions to television violence: Effects of film, character, reassurance, and sex. *Journal of Social Psychology,* 1979, *109,* 269–282.

This study provides convincing evidence of the deleterious effects of televised violence on children.

IMPORTANT EVENTS IN THE DEVELOPMENT OF SOCIAL LEARNING THEORY

Date(s)	*Person(s)*	*Work*	*Impact*
1890	James	*Principles of psychology*	The ubiquitous professor William James also provided a theory of observational learning. His descriptions emphasized the "instinctive" nature of imitation.
1896	Morgan	*Habit and instinct*	C. L. Morgan's book described the first extensive theory of observational learning. He felt that observational learning was an innate ability. Later investigators have disputed whether James or Morgan had the greatest impact on early views of observational learning.
1901	Ross	*Social control*	In this book Edward Ross defined social psychology, the area that spawned social learning theory, as "the branch of knowledge that deals with the psychic interplay between man and his environing society" (p. vii).
1903	Tarde	*The laws of imitation*	G. Tarde's book represented the first attempt to document the conditions under which observational learning occurred most effectively. He believed that a proper application of the laws of imitation was sufficient for understanding the phenomenon of social change.
1908	Ross	*Social psychology*	Edward Ross's book was the first to use the term *social psychology* in its title (it preceded McDougall by a few months). His book consisted almost entirely of an expansion of Tarde's laws of imitation.

Date(s)	*Person(s)*	*Work*	*Impact*
1908	McDougall	*An introduction to social psychology*	W. McDougall's book presented a view of observational learning that diverged somewhat from Tarde's position. Imitation was de-emphasized as a social change agent. McDougall's book was the most important text in social psychology until the early 1920s.
1913	Baldwin	*Social and ethical interpretations*	J. Baldwin was a developmental psychologist who strongly emphasized the role of imitation in the formation of the self. He also was one of the first writers to use the term *social environment.*
1921	Humphrey	"Imitation and the conditioned reflex"	In response to the growing strength of behavioral psychology, it was inevitable that someone would try to explain imitation from a behavioral perspective. G. Humphrey is generally recognized as the first person to take this step, although he based his interpretation on Watson's version of classical conditioning.
1924	Allport	*Social psychology*	Floyd Allport was one of the most influential psychologists of his time. His interpretation of modeling was associationist, following the general lead of Humphrey but retaining a flavor closer to E.L. Thorndike's theories than to Watson's.
1936	Brown	*Psychology and the social order*	J. Brown was a powerful advocate of the influence of consequences on observer behavior. "Humans imitate when this type of behavior enables them to arrive at certain goals" (p. 92).

Date(s)	*Person(s)*	*Work*	*Impact*
1936	Lewin	*Principles of topological psychology*	While Kurt Lewin's book did not emphasize observational learning, he introduced (from Gestalt theory) the idea that a person's subjective interpretation of events was as important as the event itself. This complex view of stimuli was closely akin to views of stimulus situations in the 1980s.
1941	Miller & Dollard	*Social learning and imitation*	N. E. Miller and M. J. Dollard's classic book was the foundation for modern social learning theory (Bandura, 1969). It described the importance of the consequences of both the model's and the observer's behavior on imitation.
1950	Gibson	"The implications of learning theory for social psychology"	J. J. Gibson detailed many of the problems involved in attempting to apply behavioral theory to social psychology. Many of the issues raised in this article were addressed in later formulations of social learning theory.
1954	Rotter	*Social learning and clinical psychology*	Julian Rotter stressed the idea that reinforcement in social learning theory should be viewed from the perspective of both external reinforcement and internal reinforcement. Rotter expanded his research in reinforcement in several later articles including his very well known concept (1966) of locus of control.
1959–present	Bandura & associates	Modern social learning theory	Albert Bandura's work in the area of social learning theory has resulted in contemporary conceptions of the theory. When we speak of social learning theory today, we are primarily referring to Bandura's work, which has spanned all aspects of social learning.

Date(s)	*Person(s)*	*Work*	*Impact*
1962	Festinger	*Deterrents and reinforcement*	Leon Festinger's theory of "cognitive dissonance" offered an alternative view of reinforcement in social learning, suggesting that behaviors that are dissonant with beliefs are less reinforcing than behaviors congruent with beliefs.
1964	Baer & Sherman	"Reinforcement control of generalized imitation in young children"	This paper, one of Donald Baer's early efforts, demonstrated experimental control of imitation by manipulating the consequences of imitative behavior.
1967	Baer, Petersen, & Sherman	"The development of imitation by reinforcing behavioral similarity to a model"	This paper showed the possibility of teaching observational learning skills to retarded individuals. Extrapolating from this paper, we might infer that observational skills could be taught as necessary to students via simple reinforcement techniques.
1970	Creer & Miklich	"The application of self-modeling procedure to modify inappropriate behavior: A preliminary report"	T. L. Creer and D. R. Miklich's paper presented an early instance of self-observation and its use in learning. Their paper stressed role playing as the model source. Later improvements in self-modeling were developed by Dowrick and his associates in the use of videotape (see Dowrick, 1978).
1965–present	Many researchers	Use of modeling procedures in behavior therapy	Beginning with the work of Carl Thoresen, several investigators have examined the effectiveness of observational learning in behavior therapy. It is now a standard component of cognitive-behavioral approaches.
1980	Caudill & Lipscomb	"Modeling influences on alcoholics' rates of alcohol consumption"	B. D. Caudill and T. Lipscomb's paper is representative of investigations into the ways in which socially inappropriate behaviors (in this case consuming too much alcohol) can be controlled through modeling.

Chapter Nine

MOTIVATION

So far we have discussed cognition and behavioral and social learning approaches to instruction. We described many applications for teachers in aiding memory, problem solving, creativity, classroom behavior, and social learning. But we have not yet addressed the important question of why some students seem to have a much greater desire to learn than others. We have also not discussed how teachers can arouse interest in students, especially among those who lack a zest for learning. In other words, we have not dealt with the issue of motivation.

Many behavioral psychologists would suggest that our discussions in Chapters Seven and Eight have detailed what is known about the factors that arouse and direct behavior. That is, motivation—the desire to perform some act—stems directly from the consequences of behavior. People are highly motivated to perform those behaviors for which they receive potent reinforcement, and they are not motivated to perform behaviors for which there is no reinforcement. Many other psychologists, particularly those who emphasize human beings as self-directed, purposeful, and relatively independent of the environment, find the behavioral perspective inadequate for the understanding of motivation. They suggest that the immediate consequences of behaviors are not enough to account for motivation and that the process of learning itself should be innately motivating. This chapter emphasizes the latter viewpoints, particularly those of Abraham H. Maslow, who has developed the most widely known and applied theory of motivation.

Objectives

After reading this chapter, you should be able to meet the following objectives.

1. Describe the implications of Maslow's theory for your practices as a teacher.
2. Discuss the implications of attribution theory for classroom teachers.
3. Describe the effect your knowledge of achievement motivation will have on your practices as a teacher.
4. Outline the applications of motivation theory in terms of your teaching effectiveness.

A major concern of many motivational theorists is the development of human potential. In applications to education, particular emphasis has been placed on the students' feelings of worth and their personality development. A major concept is that of the self. Knowledge of one's self and a good **self-concept** (all the ways in which a person views herself or himself) are keys to motivation and to achievement.

From this theoretical viewpoint, often labeled **humanistic,** students should be largely free to choose and to seek out new learning. The teacher should not act as an authoritarian director of learning but should be responsive to student needs. The learner is all-important, the teacher much less so. Teachers should be accepting of students and their behavior. They should allow them to seek and to discover. Humanistic theorists such as Abraham Maslow and Carl Rogers believe that a supportive and nonthreatening environment reduces external threat and contributes to the possibility of genuine learning.

MASLOW'S THEORY OF MOTIVATION

Abraham Maslow, who is considered by some as the founder of humanistic psychology (Corey, 1977), developed a theory of motivation that has had significant effects on American education. His theory is based on the idea that gratification of needs is "the most important single principle underlying all development" (Maslow, 1968, p. 55). For Maslow the most important feature of motivation, "the single, holistic principle that binds together the multiplicity of human motives," is the tendency for new, higher needs to emerge as lower needs are gratified (Maslow, 1968, p. 55). As very basic (lower) needs are met—such as a need for safety—other needs replace them as motivating forces. People's motivation derives directly from their needs and human behavior is therefore oriented toward need gratification.

On the basis of his ideas about need gratification, Maslow postulated seven basic levels of needs: physiological, safety, belongingness and love, esteem, self-actualization, knowing and understanding, and aesthetics. Maslow referred to the first four as **deficiency needs** because humans are motivated to fulfill them as a result of deficits—lack of food, lack of safety, the absence of love, and lack of esteem. Maslow suggested that people were motivated to gratify the last three needs, which he called **being needs,** when their deficiency needs were met. Being needs are motivating not because of deficits but because of basic human desires for self-actualization, knowledge, and aesthetics (Maslow, 1968).

A Hierarchy of Needs

Maslow postulated that the needs in his system were steps to be completed in a progression toward self-growth. They are *hierarchical,* that is, one level of need must be met before the next becomes motivating. Maslow's hierarchy is presented in Figure 9–1. Until physiological needs are gratified, humans do not strive for safety needs. Similarly, until safety needs are gratified, humans do not seek to gratify love needs, and so on. While we can think of obvious examples of people who do not fit this hierarchical scheme (such as the painter who goes without food and comfort for extended periods of time and devotes herself fully to aesthetic pursuits), the general pattern was of greatest theoretical interest to Maslow. The motivating needs in a person's life are those that are deficient and, later, when these deficiency needs are met, those that reflect the innate human desire for self-actualization, knowledge, and aesthetics.

Implications for Teaching

Maslow's theory has often been applied to education as a framework for thinking about the motivation of students. Teachers should do everything possible to help students satisfy their deficiency needs because an inner motivation for knowledge simply will not develop until these basic needs have been met. Teachers are not always able to intervene in children's lives to the extent necessary to fulfill deficiency needs, however. They cannot replace the love a child is not receiving at home nor can they ensure the satisfaction of safety needs away from the school. Teachers, then, are in the position of providing an environment in the classroom that fulfills deficiency needs to the greatest possible extent. They also act as children's advocates in helping others, primarily parents, provide an environment in which deficit needs are met outside the

FIGURE 9–1
Maslow's Hierarchy of Needs

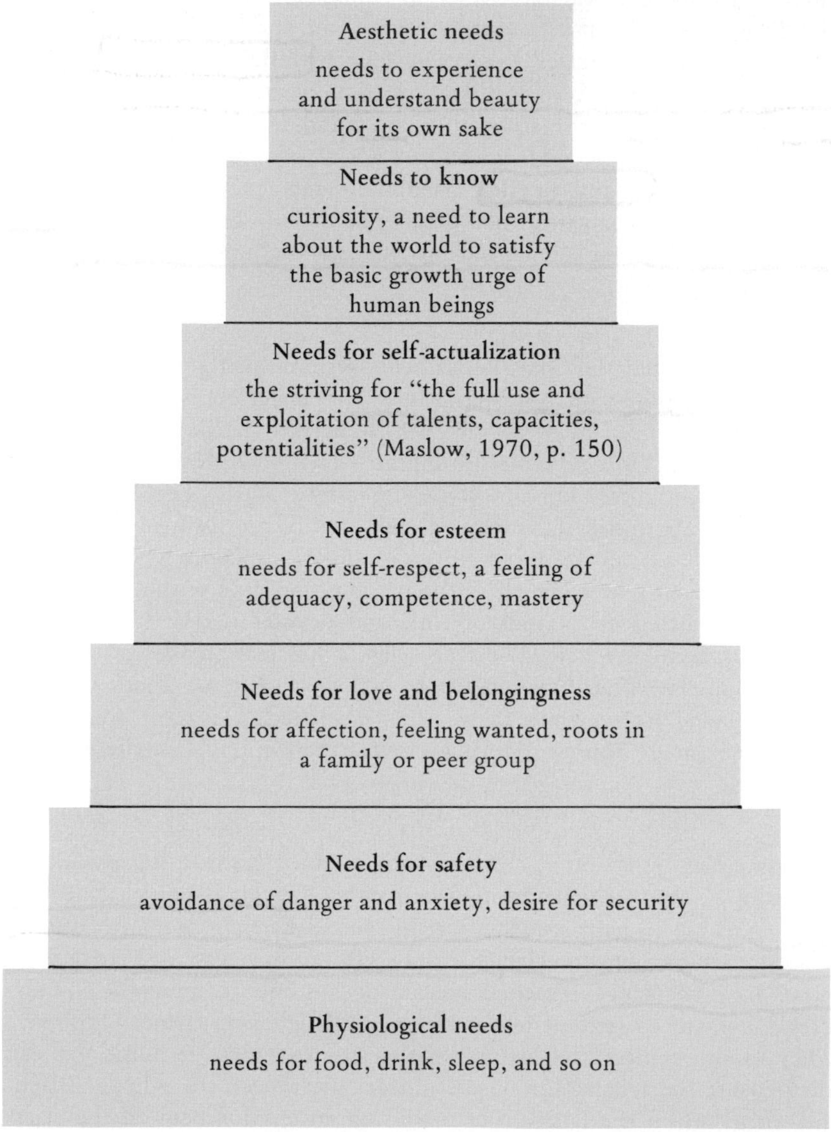

Aesthetic needs
needs to experience
and understand beauty
for its own sake

Needs to know
curiosity, a need to learn
about the world to satisfy
the basic growth urge of
human beings

Needs for self-actualization
the striving for "the full use and
exploitation of talents, capacities,
potentialities" (Maslow, 1970, p. 150)

Needs for esteem
needs for self-respect, a feeling of
adequacy, competence, mastery

Needs for love and belongingness
needs for affection, feeling wanted, roots in
a family or peer group

Needs for safety
avoidance of danger and anxiety, desire for security

Physiological needs
needs for food, drink, sleep, and so on

Source: Adapted from Maslow, 1970.

PRACTICE EXERCISE 9–1
Your Personal Hierarchy of Needs

An analysis of our motivation patterns often gives us a revealing look at ourselves. Think back over your activities in the past forty-eight hours. Associate as many of your activities as you can with the levels in Maslow's hierarchy. Then make an estimate of the proportion of your total waking time devoted to activities at each level of need. Be honest in analyzing your motivations. If you went to class because a quiz was given, you may not want to place this activity in the category "Needs for knowledge."

Percent of Time	*Needs*	*Your Actions*
______	*Aesthetic needs:* needs to experience and understand beauty for its own sake	______ ______ ______
______	*Needs for knowledge:* curiosity, a need to learn about the world to satisfy the basic growth urge	______ ______ ______
______	*Needs for self-actualization:* the striving for "the full use and exploitation of talents, capacities, potentialities" (Maslow, 1970, p. 150)	______ ______ ______
______	*Needs for esteem:* needs for self-respect, a feeling of adequacy, competence, mastery	______ ______ ______
______	*Needs for love and belongingness:* needs for affection, feeling wanted, roots in a family or peer group	______ ______ ______
______	*Needs for safety:* avoidance of danger and anxiety, desire for security	______ ______ ______
______	*Physiological needs:* needs for food, drink, sleep, and so on	______ ______ ______

Note: Are your activities generally related to the being needs or the deficiency needs? Are there any problems in seeking to fill needs primarily at one level or another? Is the pattern you indicated one that you will always be satisfied with?

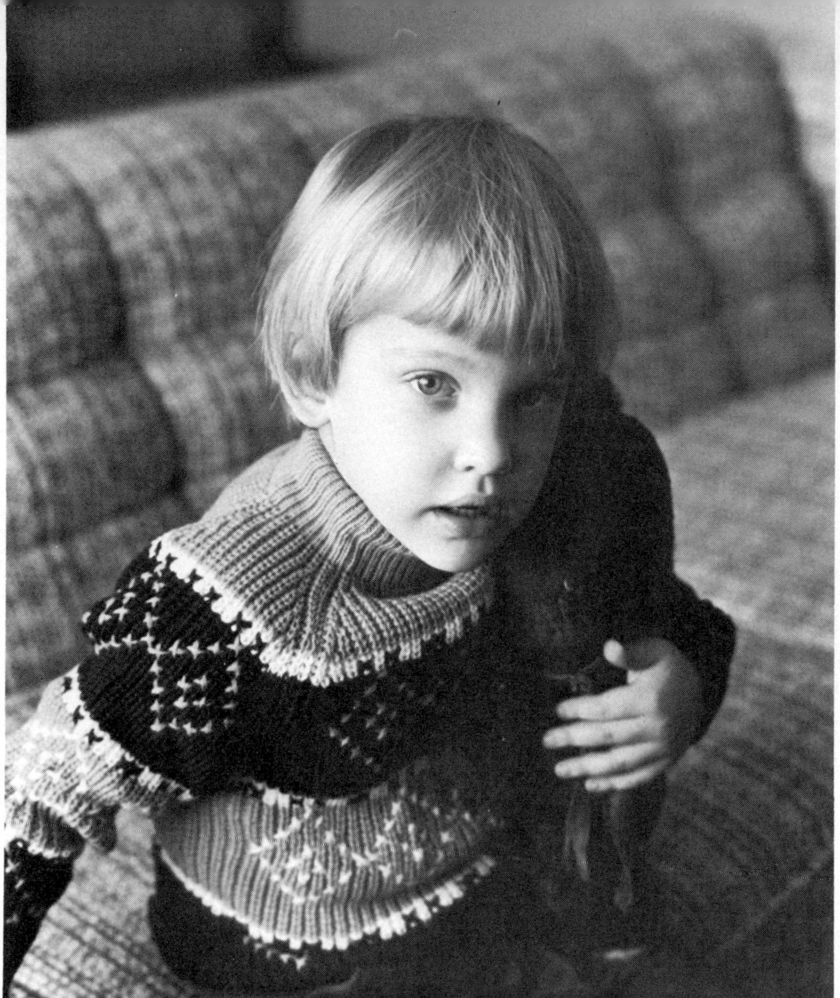

The desire for security and affection is basic to all human beings. Basic needs must be met before higher level needs can develop.

school. A common example of the advocacy role is the teacher who discerns that a child is the victim of abuse at home and who then initiates actions to remedy the problem.

When being needs are considered, teachers should do everything possible to make the acquisition of new knowledge attractive to students (Maslow, 1968). Intertwined in the development of attractive, meaningful learning experiences is the facilitation of decision making among students (Rogers, 1969). Similarly, Maslow has stressed that decisions leading to self-growth can be facilitated by "making the growth choice positively attractive and less dangerous and by making the regressive choice less attractive and more costly" (1968, p. 59). Simply stated, students need to be encouraged toward self-growth.

Of the theoretical perspectives we have examined thus far in the text, Maslow's theory is most compatible with Jean Piaget's view of motivation. The best learning, according to Maslow, is self-motivated. Like Piaget, Maslow's proponents would suggest that children, when given the opportunity, will make wise choices for their learning. Maslow's position leads naturally to the basis for "free education," an approach in which teachers arrange attractive and meaningful learning situations from which students may select those they find personally valuable. In this approach, the principles of teacher-directed classroom management are secondary to the motivating power of students' self-chosen learning activities—the learning experience itself becomes its own reward (Staw, Calder, Hess, & Sandelands, 1980).

A humanistic approach to teaching requires that teachers return to the theme we have taken up in each chapter of this book: the necessity for determining students' current abilities and needs and for deriving meaningful instruction. This theme also runs through another, closely related theory of motivation, that of Carl Rogers.

CARL ROGERS: EDUCATIONAL IMPLICATIONS OF SELF-ACTUALIZATION

While Abraham Maslow has been referred to as the founder of humanistic psychology, Carl Rogers has been the best-known proponent of humanistic *education.* Rogers's views on motivation grew out of his extensive work in counseling psychology (1942, 1951, 1965) and were presented in a form devoted to educational implications in his book *Freedom to learn* (1969).

A brief overview of Rogers's assumptions about human nature will help you better understand the implications of his theory. Rogers's view is that there is "one motivational force in man, his tendency toward self-actualization" (Meador & Rogers, 1974, p. 126). Rogers believes that self-actualization "is the inherent tendency of the . . . [person] to develop all of . . . [his or her] capacities in ways which serve to maintain or enhance the [person] . . ." (Rogers, 1969, p. 196). In other words, Rogers believes that human nature is basically good and that each person strives to meet his or her potential (Rogers, 1969).

Despite Rogers's belief that students strive for self-actualization, he points out that problems, usually related to how people view themselves, often get in the way of fully functional behavior (Rogers, 1969). The self-concept is extremely important to Rogers's theory. Four of the most important characteristics of the self are that (1) the person

"Is this it? Is this self-actualization?"

strives for a consistent self-concept, (2) behavior is consistent with self-concept, (3) experiences inconsistent with the self-concept are viewed as threatening, and (4) the self-concept changes as a result of learning and maturation. Hence a student who sees himself or herself as academically inept (as part of an overall view of self) will behave in ways consistent with this view (such as avoiding academic tasks) and may actually feel threatened by the possibility of academic success. Conversely, a student who views himself or herself as academically able behaves in ways consistent with this view (by studying, doing in-class assignments, and so on) and is threatened by experiences such as receiving a bad grade that counter this view. From this perspective, a view of self is the all-important factor in determining students' motivation. The major emphasis for educators should be to foster the development of realistic and accurate self-concepts in students. According to Rogers, an accurate and positive self-concept is necessary for full functioning (Meador & Rogers, 1974).

APPLICATIONS FOR TEACHING: THE DEVELOPMENT OF POSITIVE SELF-CONCEPTS

The following are several guidelines we have drawn from Rogers (1969) about what you can do to facilitate the development of positive self-concepts among your students.

1. Provide students with ample opportunities to participate in class. Rogers suggests that students be given opportunities to express their own opinions and to engage in give-and-take with other members of the class. Teachers must be aware that not all the students will have equal opportunities or inclinations to become involved in class discussions. They need to structure nonthreatening and supportive classroom environments so that differences of opinion are welcome and each student's opinions are valued. Small groups in particular can offer the opportunity for each student to engage in discussion. Encouraging students to participate and sincerely valuing their comments will help them develop more positive self-concepts.

2. Allow opportunities for the expression of feelings. From Rogers's perspective, schools ought to be places where students can express their emotions, not merely their thoughts. From his experience as a therapist (Meador & Rogers, 1974), Rogers has observed that many people who are alienated from themselves have learned not to express their feelings. Rogers suggests that sadness, fear, anger, happiness, and joy should be expressed by students in the classroom. Students must learn more than subject matter content in school; they should learn about themselves and how to accept their feelings. Teachers can provide a warm, accepting environment that allows for the expression of emotion. Accepting students also means accepting their feelings (Rogers, 1969).

3. Provide a classroom atmosphere of acceptance. *Acceptance* means taking students for what they are, but it doesn't mean that teachers have to accept specific student behaviors. We can reject a particular behavior (such as hitting another student) while still accepting the person. Rogers suggests that teachers be careful to separate the rejection of acts from the rejection of people. It is better to say "Susan, I cannot tolerate your being late" than it is to say "Susan, I can't tolerate *you* anymore."

A positive self-concept is necessary for full functioning.

CLEAR RULES

4. Establish clear rules for the classroom. Rogers suggests that the absence of motivation is sometimes simply the result of poor communication of expectations to students (Rogers, 1969). Communicating rules for conduct and expectations for academic tasks and enforcing them in a fair and firm manner helps students to see that we expect them to live up to certain standards. By employing and enforcing the rules and guidelines we tell students that we care about them and that they can depend on us to be fair.

5. Stress activities that are likely to lead to student success. As we will see in the next section, success and failure have powerful effects on how students think of themselves. Rogers's theory complements Maslow's and points up the need to help students form accurate and positive self-concepts. Another related theory of motivation, need achievement, also stresses how students feel about themselves, particularly in terms of academic success and failure.

ASPIRATIONS AND THE NEED FOR ACHIEVEMENT

Another theoretical perspective that considers differences in students' motivation to achieve in school has been set forth by J. W. Atkinson. Atkinson's theory of achievement motivation is based in part on the work of Hoppe (1930), Sears (1940), and McClelland (see 1961, 1971). We will first examine the contributions of Atkinson's predecessors and then survey his theory and its implications for teachers.

Hoppe's early work (1930) described the results of people's experiences with success and failure. He noted that people raised their *levels of aspiration* after successes and lowered them after failures. Hoppe felt that this shifting of aspirations protected people from experiencing continued failure or the kind of over-easy achievement that does not give a feeling of accomplishment. People choose a level of aspiration to balance two conflicting tendencies: the wish to succeed at the greatest level possible (which tends to increase aspirations) and the desire to avoid the disappointment that accompanies failure (which tends to lower aspirations). Hoppe also felt that the balancing mechanism could be thrown out of kilter. People who set unrealistically high goals will inevitably fail and, conversely, people who set goals at a very low level do not obtain any satisfaction from their accomplishments. For Hoppe, the ideal was for students to set their levels of aspiration at realistic levels—achievable but satisfying.

Sears (1940) also affected the development of Atkinson's theory through an interesting experiment she conducted on the aspirations of elementary school children (Maehr, 1978). She identified three groups of upper elementary children: a "success" group (children with a consistent history of academic success in all areas), a "failure" group (children with a consistent record of academic failure in all areas), and a "differential" group (children with consistent records of success in reading but with records of failure in mathematics). The children in these groups were given a series of twenty speed tests in reading and math. After each test, the children were asked to estimate how long it would take them to complete the next test. Further, one-half of the children, those in the "success condition," were given lavish praise for their performance after most, but not all, of the tests. Likewise, the other half of the children, the "failure condition," were given severe criticism after most but not all of the tests.

The results indicated that the children in the success condition made accurate estimates of their performances on the speed tests with their goals set at or slightly above their actual performance. This result was observed regardless of whether the children were from groups with prior success, failure, or differential records. On the other hand, children in the failure condition were noted to have much greater discrepancies between their goals and their actual performance. There was also a striking effect on how they set goals—some children set impossibly high goals while others set ridiculously low ones. Not surprisingly, the most powerful effects of the failure condition were on students with failure and differential backgrounds. Children with consistent histories of academic success (the success group) were somewhat better able to cope with repeated criticism of their performance, evidencing a more accurate and less variable pattern of goal setting.

This study seemed to provide confirmation of Hoppe's earlier ideas and pointed again to the importance of success and failure on aspirations. Success brought about fairly high but accurate aspirations, irrespective of the students' past history of success or failure. Repeated failure, in contrast, seemed to cause students—especially those with past histories of failure—to aspire to either unrealistically high or very low goals.

McClelland (1961, 1971) stated that humans acquire a need for achievement during their development and that this **achievement motivation** directly influences academic performance. McClelland and his associates (see McClelland & Winter, 1969) also developed procedures for measuring achievement motivation and conducted considerable research to demonstrate how achievement motivation differs among individuals.

Atkinson, who had worked with McClelland and was greatly influenced by his research (see McClelland, Atkinson, Clark, & Lowell, 1953), employed the overall conceptual base developed by Hoppe, Sears, and McClelland. According to Maehr (1978), he has articulated the clearest theory of achievement motivation to date. Atkinson argued (Atkinson & Raynor, 1974) that variations among peoples' need to achieve could best be explained by a contrasting need to avoid failure

Success helps students set reasonable and accurate goals. The feedback from successful performance not only encourages students but helps them judge their capabilities.

(Ceranski, Teevan, & Kalle, 1979). He further hypothesized that some people are oriented to success while others possess high levels of failure anxiety.

In a series of experiments reminiscent of those conducted by Sears, Atkinson (1965, 1966, 1967) demonstrated that success-oriented people tend to set personal goals of intermediate difficulty while people with high levels of anxiety about failure tend to set goals that are either too high or too low. Atkinson suggests that the unrealistic goal setting of anxiety-filled people allows for rationalization—"Nobody can blame me for failure because my goal was so high" or "With my goal set so low, how can I fail?" (Atkinson & Raynor, 1974). He further states that the tendency to be successful is affected by the likelihood of success and the attractiveness of its achievement. Conversely, the need to avoid failure develops when people experience repeated failure (Tachibana, 1978).

One clear implication of Atkinson's theory for teachers is that success in achievement helps students develop reasonable and accurate goals. On the other hand, repeated failure seems to result in students' developing unrealistically high *or* unrealistically low goals (Touhey & Villamez, 1980). As we noted earlier, teachers can readily adapt an existing instructional approach to ensure the greatest amount of success for each student. By identifying what students are ready to learn and providing meaningful instruction at that level, teachers can greatly facilitate students' achievement motivation.

ATTRIBUTION THEORY

A related way of thinking about achievement motivation employs the general framework of **attribution theory.** Attributions refer to people's interpretations of experience. In terms of achievement, attribution theory helps us understand how students explain their successes and failures and the implications those explanations have for achievement-oriented behavior in the future. The foundation for attribution theory was set by the work of Fritz Heider (1944, 1959) and later expanded and refined by Julian Rotter (1966), Bernard Weiner and his associates (1970, 1972), and H. M. Lefcourt (1976).

Explanations of Success and Failure

Current attribution theory suggests that people generally use one of four different forms of explanations for their successes or failures: ability, effort, difficulty of task, and luck or chance. If students fail a test, for example, they often ascribe their failure to "not studying" (lack of effort), to the "hard test" (difficulty of task), or to "studying the wrong thing" (bad luck). While one could suggest that there are other possible explanations for successes or failures ("The directions were unclear," "I was in an especially good mood"), attribution theorists generally subsume any explanation not mentioning ability, effort, or difficulty under the label of luck or chance (Kassan & Reber, 1979).

Students' explanations of their successes and failures provide information about their locus of control (Rotter, 1966). Locus of control refers to where a person feels the control of his or her successes and failures lies—internal or external to the person (Glover & Sautter, 1976). Students with an internal locus of control are likely to attribute their successes to ability and effort and their failures to lack of effort. Students with an external locus of control are likely to believe that their successes and failures are governed by task difficulty, chance, or lack of ability.

While several studies have investigated the explanations students give to success and failure (see Gilmor & Minton, 1974; Lefcourt, Hogg, Struthers, & Holmes, 1975; Luginbuhl, Crowe, & Kahan, 1975), a particularly interesting study was conducted by Gilmor and Reid (1979) with 105 university students. Their study was an extension of their earlier work on the effects of locus of control on student attributions of success and failure. Their earlier work had indicated that students with an internal locus of control attributed success to internal factors but attributed failure to external factors. Gilmor and Reid hypothesized that these results may have been due in part to the interest or value of the task the subjects in the previous study had to complete. They also suggested that "when the task is of high interest . . . to the

PRACTICE EXERCISE 9–2
Analyzing Attributions

Postmortems on athletic contests, writing or speaking competitions, music contests, and games all prompt people's explanations of why things went right or wrong. During the next week, observe at least one person who is talking about a success and another person who is describing a failure. Television interviews are a good source of such individuals, as are the newspapers. The "succeeder" or "failer" may be describing his or her own action or be serving as the spokesperson for a group (a football coach explaining a victory or a loss, for instance). Successes may include winning a race, being chosen as a representative or leader, or receiving an honor. Failure likewise may be observed in a variety of endeavors. Record below as specifically as you can what the person says about success and failure and compare your notes with those of others in your class. Does any pattern appear? Specifically answer the question of whether the attributions you observe are the kinds you hope your students will make about their own successes and failures.

Success Experience

The success was ______________________________

The person was ______________________________

To which of the following did the person attribute his or her success? (Give a quote from the person about the attribute he or she cited.)

Ability ______________________________

Effort ______________________________

Ease of task ______________________________

Good luck or other factors ______________________________

subject, the . . . attributions of internals and externals {will be} consistent with their locus of control orientation" (p. 155).

To test their hypothesis Gilmor and Reid selected college students as their sample and chose performance on in-class examinations as a task that would likely be of value and interest to all the students. After exams were returned in a course taught by one of the experimenters (three sections), students were asked to rate themselves as successful or unsuccessful and were also asked to rate the degree to which they felt ability, effort, luck or chance, and task difficulty had affected their performance. A scale developed by Reid and Ware (1974) for assessing locus of control was administered to identify "external" and "internal" students.

How realistic/accurate were the attributions, in your estimate?

____

____

____

____

Failure Experience

The failure was ____

The person was ____

To which of the following factors did the person attribute his or her failure? (Give a quote from the person about any factor he or she cited.)

Ability ____

Effort ____

Difficulty of task _________________________________

Bad luck or other factors __________________________

How realistic/accurate were the attributions, in your estimate?

____

____

____

____

The results of the study indicated that externals attributed both success and failure primarily to luck. Internals, on the other hand, were observed to be more likely to attribute both good and bad performance to ability and effort. The results, of course, are highly consistent with what would be expected from attribution theory. Even among college students (who presumably have had a fairly high rate of success in academic tasks), locus of control is related to their judgments of why they succeed or fail. The effects of internal or external loci of control, however, also depend on other variables, most notably whether students are success seekers or failure avoiders (Bar-Tal & Bar-Zohar, 1977).

Success Seekers and Failure Avoiders

Success seekers are students who have a history of successful achievement in schools. They are generally self-confident, tend to have strong achievement motivation, and an internal locus of control. Success fosters success among such students because it confirms their ideas about their abilities. Failure, for success seekers, is a signal that in the particular task in question they made a misjudgment about how much effort was required for success (Covington & Omelich, 1979b). Failure is seldom taken as an indication of lack of ability; rather it is a sign that more effort is necessary (Covington & Omelich, 1979a).

Failure avoiders, on the other hand, have very little confidence in their abilities. Many have a history of poor performance in school and are likely to have an external locus of control. Achievement motivation is seldom internal among failure avoiders and they depend heavily on external factors (approval, praise) for their motivation. Because they have a poor opinion of their own abilities, they attempt to avoid failure and thereby the loss of external support, that is, the approval of others. Failure is avoided by setting unrealistic goals, by lack of effort, or by false effort—one cannot really fail, for example, if one hasn't really tried. Each of these strategies, however, actually makes further failure almost inevitable. The repeated failures then continue to affirm the failure avoiders' beliefs in their poor ability.

Failure avoiders take failure as an indication of poor ability (Covington & Omelich, 1979a, 1979b, 1979c) but they tend to attribute success to luck, chance, or ease of task (Covington & Omelich, 1979c). It seems that *both* success and failure may damage future achievement among failure avoiders—success because it results in less future effort (Maracek & Mettee, 1972) and failure because it confirms poor self-esteem and results in greater efforts to avoid failure without increased efforts to achieve (Maracek & Mettee, 1972). However, as Weiner (1972) points out, the long-term effects of success in ability tasks (as opposed to tasks governed by chance) are generally positive. Students develop a more internal, more realistic locus of control and increase their achievement motivation.

APPLICATIONS FOR TEACHING: MOTIVATION THEORY IN THE CLASSROOM

1. Help students satisfy their deficiency needs.

Physiological needs. Teachers can help students meet their physiological needs by some fairly straightforward actions. Especially for younger children, arrange for routine snack or drink breaks. Be aware that some of your students may not have had breakfast (and possibly no supper the night before). Where there is a need, encourage student participation in breakfast and lunch programs—many are free to students from low-income families.

Allow occasional breaks in classroom instruction. It is especially important to be flexible in setting break times for small children, for whom naps or quiet times are important parts of the school day. A time to "stretch" is equally important for older children and adults.

Try to keep your room comfortable. A classroom that is too warm or too cool is not a good place to work. Remind students of the need for sweaters or the benefits of removing jackets. Be sure to ask your students about the classroom's comfort level.

Keep an eye out for students who seem to be feeling ill and make sure that you are aware of any special health problems among your students. A student who does not feel well will almost never benefit from instruction.

Safety needs. Do everything possible to make students feel comfortable and secure in your classroom. Always avoid the use of ridicule or embarrassment in dealing with children. Instead, try to provide a warm, accepting classroom environment with firm and consistent guidelines. Our discussion of classroom management in Chapter Ten should help you create such an atmosphere.

Do not allow students to bully or intimidate other students. Students need to be free from fears, including fears of physical abuse at the hands of older students. Incidents of intimidation and violent acts can and do occur in many schools. School authorities need, therefore, to work doubly hard to make the school and its grounds a safe haven for all children.

Needs for love and belongingness. While teachers cannot replace parental love, they can help students develop a sense of belonging to the classroom. Little things can be important. Learn the names of each student as soon as possible. Make your comments to students personal and specific. Let students know that you care about each one of them.

Arrange one-to-one sessions with each child

Little things can be important in satisfying needs for love and belonging. For this first grader, a special place with the teacher gives her a feeling of being cared about.

as frequently as possible. If practical, meet with the parents of each child. Encourage group activities that allow students to share personal experiences with each other. Not only do you want to show that you care about each student, you also want to develop mutual concern among the students, based on successful cooperation.

Needs for esteem. The needs each child has for esteem from others and for self-esteem can be gratified to a great extent by judicious classroom management. Avoid comparisons between students. Students are unique individuals with specific strengths and weaknesses. Build on strengths and avoid emphasizing weaknesses.

Promote cooperation and sharing to the greatest extent possible. Not only will this facilitate belongingness, it will also be an aid in replacing competitive patterns of behavior (see Skon, Johnson, & Johnson, 1981; Slavin, 1981).

In Chapters Eleven and Twelve, on objectives and task analysis, we recommend setting individual goals for students and providing praise for their mastery of the goals. These procedures are especially appropriate for building students' concepts of themselves as successful learners. Give slower-learning students individual help in attaining their goals and make sure that you sincerely praise them when they achieve their goals.

2. Help students develop the desire to meet their being needs. According to Maslow's hierarchy of needs, self-actualization, knowing and understanding, and aesthetic needs can only come into play when deficiency needs are met. Helping students develop their being needs depends on the teacher's ability to structure meaningful and attractive learning activities. As much as possible, learning should be self-guided. Students can be helped to see the potential outcomes of certain decisions. As a teacher, you can help present growth choices as more attractive and less threatening than choices that limit growth.

> Growth takes place when the next step forward is subjectively more delightful, more joyous, more intrinsically satisfying than the previous gratification. . . . The new experience validates itself rather than . . . . any outside criterion. It is self-justifying, self-validating. . . . *(Maslow, 1968, p. 45)*

Every action the teacher can take to make learning activities and growth choices more attractive is a step in the direction of facilitating internally motivated learning among students.

3. Promote feelings of success. Feelings of success will help your students develop realistic self-expectations, increase achievement motivation, and heighten positive self-regard. Several procedures teachers may use to promote feelings of success are readily available.

First, your activities and assignments should make student success likely. As we will see in Chapters Eleven and Twelve, the goals you set for instruction should represent reachable and meaningful accomplishments. Each student should work for objectives that are based on his or her needs.

Second, provide students with accurate, specific, and personal feedback on their performance. As we will point out in Chapters Thirteen and Fourteen, effective instruction requires high-quality evaluation. Good evaluation allows students to gain maximum insight into their performance. Attributions of their successes and failures are thus much less likely to be distorted.

Third, do not be afraid to use reinforcement procedures as a part of your motivation plan. Consider the use of the approaches we discuss in Chapter Ten as a way of promoting feelings of success. Reinforcers for appropriate classroom behavior can certainly be cause for feelings of satisfaction among students. Further, most behavior-management approaches can be shaped to fit the specific needs of your students.

4. Help students develop achievement motivation. Some students, regardless of how well you satisfy their deficiency needs, promote the desirability of being needs, and enhance their feelings of success, are still likely to hold back from aspiring to goals at a challenging yet reachable level. There are, fortunately, some general approaches that teachers may employ to help students acquire achievement motivation.

Model appropriate achievement motivation and arrange for other models with whom your students can identify. Recall our discussion in Chapter Eight concerning the effects of high-achieving models on students with lower levels of aspiration; consistent presentation of models who have achieved a variety of goals will help students develop achievement motivation.

In modeling achievement motivation demonstrate how you select attainable yet challenging goals. Describe how goals that are too easy and those that are unattainable can be both impractical and frustrating for you. Emphasize knowledge of self in setting goals. When you employ other persons to model achievement motivation, choose realistic models. Millionaires and professional athletes, for example, may not be particularly good models for most children's achievement, in spite of the excitement they may generate. Instead choose people who have accurately assessed their own abilities and have consistently set and met reasonable goals. It also seems especially important to choose a wide variety of models to avoid stereotypes of success and opportunity as limited by sex, ethnic group, or other characteristics.

Second, systematically encourage goal setting among students. McClelland (1965) suggests that teachers stress the benefits of achievement motivation and the ways in which achievement motivation can improve students' self-images. McClelland also proposes that teachers help students set concrete goals and keep a log of their progress toward meeting them.

Provide simulation activities on which students can practice a higher need to achieve. For instance, Kolb (1965) used a combination of descriptive information (the personal characteristics of high achievers) and practice in simulation activities (toy car races, role playing) to increase the achievement motivation of underachieving junior high school students. Throughout Kolb's training sessions, students were urged to analyze their behaviors and to consider how they could enhance their achievement motivation. Kolb's group evidently did experience an increase in need to achieve, as their grades increased after training (see also Lundgren & Loar, 1978).

5. Avoid high levels of competition. In any competition someone must lose. Continued losing, as we have seen, leads students to set unrealistic goals. Teachers should instead emphasize cooperation, students' competition with their own past achievement, and a wide range of activities that allow all students a chance to succeed. As we noted in Chapter Eight, the use of small groups can greatly facilitate the development of cooperative behaviors (see Skon et al., 1981; Slavin, 1981).

We are not suggesting that schools portray an unrealistic view of the world. Competition, of course, is an inescapable part of life outside the school. Nonetheless, students need to be nurtured in their achievement-related activities. *Preparation for competition comes from success, not from failure in competition.* Stifling someone's potential for achievement in school through ill-conceived competition cannot possibly benefit the student or society.

6. Take advantage of students' interests. Students' interests are a significant source of motivation (Maehr, 1978) and teachers often use interests in order to heighten motivation to achieve. New learning is always built on previous knowledge (see Chapter Two, "An Introduction to Cognitive Psychology") and the relationship of new topics to students' interests should be pointed out. Students who are interested in the weather, for example, are involved in a topic that is closely aligned with many other physical sciences. Effective teachers employ novelty, contrast, and humor to perk up students' curiosity about new topics. Novelty by itself is often enough to kindle students' curiosity, leading to extended interests (Glover, 1980). Not all topics are immediately interesting, however. Memorizing the multiplication tables, for example, may seem irrelevant to many elementary school children, regardless of how important it may be to the later development of skills in long division and multiplication. In

such cases, reinforcement-based methods using incentives and rewards may be required.

7. Help students develop a balanced locus of control. Students should not attribute all of the causes for success or failures to their own efforts. There obviously are mitigating circumstances from time to time. Students inclined to attribute all of their failures to a lack of effort, for example, have an unrealistic view of the world (Lefcourt, 1976). Similarly, students who attribute all their successes to external factors and refuse to attribute success to their own efforts are unlikely to become self-directed, achievement-motivated adults (Phares, 1976). A balance between the two extremes is desirable (Rotter, 1966) and recent research (see Gutkin, 1978) suggests that teachers may influence the attainment of this balance by systematically encouraging appropriate attribution statements.

To help students attain a balanced locus of control, reinforce accurate causal attributions among students. One possible reinforcer is praise of students' statements reflecting their acceptance of responsibility, when appropriate. Have students rethink and rephrase statements in which they do not appropriately accept responsibility for their own actions. Conversely, students need to become aware of self-statements indicating *too much* acceptance of responsibility. Your feedback can help students internalize reasonable standards of self-responsibility.

SUMMARY

In this chapter we examined approaches to motivation that differ considerably from the behavioral approach. Abraham Maslow's humanistic theory of a hierarchy of needs stresses the satisfaction of students' deficiency needs so that higher levels of needs (being needs) can be gratified. Self-actualization is considered to be the key motivational force by another humanistic psychologist and educator, Carl Rogers.

Atkinson's theory of achievement motivation has emphasized the role of success in the development of students' aspirations and the resultant need to achieve. Attribution theory is closely related to Atkinson's theory; it suggests that failure and success have differential effects depending on students' locus of control.

Motivation theories have direct implications for classroom teachers. The development of students' motivation can be accomplished by providing a classroom environment that both influences external behaviors and takes advantage of intrinsically motivating factors.

Suggested Readings

Gutkin, T. B. Modification of elementary students' locus of control: An operant approach. *Journal of Psychology,* 1978, *100,* 107–115.

This article presents an excellent method of employing the concepts presented in Chapter Seven to modify locus of control.

Lefcourt, H. M. *Locus of control: Current trends in theory and research.* Hillsdale, N.J.: Erlbaum, 1976.

This text provides a compendium of views on locus of control.

Maslow, A. H. *Toward a psychology of being* (2nd ed.). New York: Harper & Row, 1968.

Maslow, A. H. *Motivation and personality* (2nd ed.). New York: Harper & Row, 1970.

Maslow, A. H. *The further reaches of human nature.* New York: Viking, 1971.

These three books are Maslow's best works, and they provide an excellent exposition of his theory. The richness and subtlety of Maslow's ideas are not fully apparent without reading the original works.

Rogers, C. R. *Freedom to learn: A view of what education might become.* Columbus, Ohio: Merrill, 1969.

Of all Rogers's writings, this book is most centrally concerned with the application of his ideas to education. A good deal of humanistic education grew out of the ideas Carl Rogers outlined in this book.

Rotter, J. B. Generalized expectancies for internal versus external control of reinforcement. *Psychological Monographs,* 1966, *80*(1, Whole No. 609).

Rotter's most complete description of his original theory is presented in this monograph.

IMPORTANT EVENTS IN THE DEVELOPMENT OF CONTEMPORARY VIEWS OF MOTIVATION

The study of motivation in psychology, which is extremely difficult to separate from the study of learning, is the area in which the most has been written and the least resolved. "Motivation psychology is at once the most central and the least well-developed area in psychology" (Chaplin & Krawiec, 1979, p. 420). The number of research papers written on motivation since 1885 is staggering. If studies that deal primarily with learning but are applicable to motivation are also considered, the number of reports becomes overwhelming.

> Of all of the central issues in psychology, perhaps none has proven as recalcitrant to human understanding as those dealing with motivation. . . . In spite of the best thoughts of some of the best minds in psychology, the emergence of satisfactory explanations of [such] . . . motivational phenomena has been slow relative to those in other areas of psychology, such as learning, sensation, and perception. This fact may account for the observation that the history of motivation psychology has never been written. The absence of a consensus in the field has inhibited efforts at summing up. *(Russell, 1970, p. 1)*

Russell's statements are as accurate today as they were in 1970. Because of the diversity of the field of motivation and the vast numbers of studies published in the area, we will alter our approach to "Important Events" somewhat. Rather than highlight both significant studies and theoretical works, as we have done throughout the book, we will restrict ourselves to a brief chronology of major theories of motivation. Our chronology is not exhaustive. The reader is referred to the works of K. B. Madsen (1968, 1973, 1974), on which we have relied in the preparation of our chronology, for a more thorough analysis of theories of motivation.

Date(s)	*Person(s)*	*Work*	*Impact*
1886	Dewey	*Psychology*	John Dewey coined the term *dynamic psychology* to refer to the way people change and the factors involved in change. Dewey's conceptualization of dynamic psychology was a precursor to many studies of motivation (Schultz, 1975).
1890	James	*Principles of psychology*	William James, whose work anticipated so much of modern psychology, suggested that motivation was instinctive and generated a fairly lengthy list of instinctive motives (such as hunger and thirst). He had a profound impact on Woodworth (see below).

Date(s)	*Person(s)*	*Work*	*Impact*
1893	Külpe	*Outline of psychology*	Oswald Külpe broke with his mentor, Wilhelm Wundt, over several issues. His work on conscious experiences was the first recorded psychological experimentation in motivation.
1898	Thorndike	"Animal intelligence"	E. L. Thorndike's theory of learning, in which organisms tended to perform those behaviors that resulted in satisfying outcomes but did not perform those behaviors that resulted in annoying outcomes, was quickly integrated into an instinctual account of motivation, a line of reasoning about motivation dating back to the mid-1880s. Thorndike himself later wrote about motivation and generated a list of human instincts that motivated behavior, not unlike the list formulated by James.
1908	McDougall	*Hormic psychology*	W. McDougall's book introduced a system of psychology, Hormic psychology (from the Greek *horme,* "urge"), which explained much of human behavior on the basis of instinct. "Directly or indirectly the instincts are the prime movers of all human behaviors" (McDougall, 1908, p. 44). Basic instincts (hunger, sex, and so on), in McDougall's opinion, provided the motives for all behaviors.
1913	Watson	"Psychology as the behaviorist views it"	J. B. Watson's paper set the stage for the rapid growth of behavioral psychology. The behaviorist movement, not surprisingly, stressed environmental effects in explaining motivation. In Watson's view, stimuli brought forth or motivated behavior.

Date(s)	*Person(s)*	*Work*	*Impact*
1918	Woodworth	*Dynamic psychology*	Robert Sessions Woodworth, frequently identified with the functionalist school, developed a theory of learning that stressed *drive* as the causal agent in motivation. Woodworth's drives were similar to the instincts that McDougall talked about, but they were far less specific and could be learned. His classic example of a learned drive is a businessperson who first is motivated to work in order to satisfy the drive of hunger. The work itself, however, ultimately becomes a driving force and provides motivation in the absence of the original hunger drive.
1920	Freud	*A general introduction to psychology*	Sigmund Freud's theory has been extremely influential in modern psychology. In terms of motivation, his theory grew directly out of earlier instinct theories (Chaplin & Krawiec, 1979). He postulated a basic instinct called *libido,* which refers to both the "bodily and mental aspects of the sex instinct" (Freud, 1924, pp. 282–283). Freud stressed the importance of libido throughout his writings, with special emphasis on how it could be transformed in ways that resulted in the motivation to perform a great many actions not considered sexual in the narrow sense. This view of motivation has permeated the psychoanalytic movement since the time of Freud (Chaplin & Krawiec, 1979). Subsequent theories of motivation by Alfred Alder, Carl Jung, Karen Horney, and other analysts who broke with Freud place much more emphasis on

Date(s)	*Person(s)*	*Work*	*Impact*
			social contexts as motivating forces and de-emphasize libido.
1921	Kuo	"Giving up instincts in psychology"	Zing Yang Kuo's classic paper (and Bernard's later book; see below) provided the major impetus to discount instinct theories of motivation. For many years (until ethologists began to provide evidence of instinctive motivation in lower organisms) instinct was almost banished from experimental work in motivation. Instinct, however, remained an important concept in psychoanalytic theories.
1924	Bernard	*Instinct*	L. L. Bernard surveyed the more than four hundred instinct theories of motivation available in his time and noted that 5,759 human urges or activities had been referred to as instinctive. Bernard's book was at the center of the movement that discredited instinct theories of motivation.
1930	Hoppe	"Success and failure"	F. Hoppe's paper described an early theory of the effects of success and failure on motivation. Many of our current views of the effects of success and failure are still compatible with Hoppe's early work.
1930–1975	Cattell	Factor analysis approaches to the study of personality and motivation	Raymond B. Cattell pioneered the use of factor analysis in studying personality and motivation. His technique involved the analysis of thousands of personality tests in order to identify those factors that seemed most related to motivation.
1931	Holt	*Animal drives and the learning process*	While Woodworth first employed the term *drive*, Edwin Holt provided a focus for psychology's shift away from

Date(s)	*Person(s)*	*Work*	*Impact*
			instinctive explanations for motivation to internal physiological states. For Holt, some drives were instinctive (hunger, for instance) while others (such as work) were learned. Holt held that behaviors motivated by drives were learned (a person had to learn how to obtain the food necessary to satisfy the hunger drive).
1932	Tolman	*Purposive behavior in animals and men*	E. C. Tolman blended behavioral and Gestalt theories into his *purposive-behaviorism.* This theory suggested that there were four irreducible motivating factors in behavior: "stimuli, heredity, past training, and momentary initiating physiological states" (Tolman, 1932, p. 419). This view is very much like contemporary conceptions of motivation (Madsen, 1974).
1936	Lewin	*Principles of topological psychology*	Perhaps the best known of Kurt Lewin's ideas are his descriptions of conflict situations. In an approach-approach conflict, a person is in conflict because of two positive goals, only one of which can be attained. Avoidance-avoidance conflicts occur when a person must choose between two equally aversive outcomes. Approach-avoidance conflicts arise when an individual is both drawn toward and repelled by the same goal (as when a person wants to engage in premarital sex but believes it is a violation of his or her moral values).
1937	Allport	*Personality: A psychological interpretation*	According to Madsen (1974) Gordon W. Allport's greatest contribution to theories of motivation was his hypothesis of *functional autonomy.* That is, Allport suggested that while all mo-

Date(s)	*Person(s)*	*Work*	*Impact*
			tives have their roots in basic, biological drives, by adulthood motives are independent of the original drive.
1938	Murray	*Explorations in personality*	Henry Murray's *need-press* theory exerted considerable influence on subsequent formulations of motivation theories. Murray's theory, along with Allport's and Lewin's, clearly marked the onset of contemporary drive theories.
1938	Skinner	*Behavior of organisms*	B. F. Skinner's theory is the major behavioral view of motivation. Skinner believes motivation is externally determined by the antecedents and consequences of behavior.
1943	Hull	*Principles of behavior*	Clark Hull's theory, while imperfect, was "the most systematical and exact theory [of motivation] in psychology" (Madsen, 1974). Hull's theory is far too complex to describe in this limited space, but it was a fusion of behavioral drive theory, and Lewin's field theory. Hull's was the major theory of motivation until the early 1950s.
1943–present	Miller	Articulation of drive theory	Neal Miller's work over more than four decades clearly represents the evolution of the study of motivation. His theory has greatly influenced all subsequent accounts of motivation.
1944	Heider	"Social perception and phenomenal causality"	F. Heider's work was the basis for modern attribution theory as articulated later by Rotter (1966), Weiner (1972), and Lefcourt (1976). Attribution theory has become increasingly important, especially in the field of counseling psychology (Dixon, in press).

Date(s)	*Person(s)*	*Work*	*Impact*
1949–present	McClelland	*The achievement motive* (published 1953)	D. C. McClelland greatly popularized the phrase *achievement motivation.* His work was of great interest to educators and provided the foundation for much of the later work on academically related motivation, particularly Atkinson's. McClelland is especially noted for his work in measuring motivation.
1951	Tinbergen	*The study of instinct*	N. Tinbergen's work, based in part on the writing of Konrad Lorenz, relegitimized instinct as a source of motivation, primarily among infrahuman species. Tinbergen, a psychologist, and Lorenz, an ethologist, were the forerunners of the ethological movement in contemporary psychology.
1953–present	Atkinson	Theory of achievement motivation	Drawing on his early work with McClelland, and influenced by Lewin and Tolman, J. W. Atkinson has developed the most widely accepted contemporary theory of achievement motivation, a theory especially relevant to education.
1954–1970	Maslow	*Motivation and personality* (first edition, 1954)	Abraham Maslow, one of the major founders of the modern humanistic movement in psychology, developed a widely accepted theory of motivation. His theory has had a tremendous impact on educational thought about motivation. Madsen (1974) suggested that Maslow's theory might ultimately have the same kind of influence on all of psychology as Freud's has had.
1957	Festinger	*A theory of cognitive dissonance*	L. Festinger's theory of cognitive dissonance (briefly, that people are motivated to behave in ways that are consistent with their beliefs or to change

Date(s)	Person(s)	Work	Impact
			beliefs so that they are consistent with behavior) provided a major emphasis on the cognitive aspects of motivation. During the late 1950s and early 1960s, Festinger's theory generated more research in motivation than other theories (Madsen, 1974).
1960	Berlyne	*Conflict, arousal and curiosity*	The major thrust of D. E. Berlyne's theory was curiosity as a motivating force. He combined ideas from theorists as diverse as Piaget, Hebb, Hull, and contemporary Russian psychologists.
1961	Brown	*The motivation of behavior*	J. S. Brown's theory was a major extension of Hull's theory to include data generated by research after Hull's time. It described the formation of secondary or learned drives more clearly than previous theories.
1970–present	Maehr	Achievement motivation theory	Martin Maehr's several theoretical and review papers have related the major implications of achievement motivation theory to educational and societal contexts.
1971–present	Pribram	*Languages of the brain*	R. H. Pribram's book was the first attempt to consolidate information processing and neuropsychology into a theory of motivation.

Chapter Ten

CLASSROOM MANAGEMENT

Student behavior has been of concern to teachers for as long as there has been education. Even Socrates complained that his students "love luxury. They have bad manners and contempt for authority. They show disrespect for their elders and love chatter in the place of exercise" (Plato, *Republic*). While there have been growing concerns that today's students misbehave more frequently and more severely than their predecessors, there is little evidence to support this idea (Doyle, 1979). Nonetheless, the ability to deal with student behavior is a vital component of effective teaching. Effective instruction requires the ability to guide students' classroom behavior in ways that will result in the best possible atmosphere for learning (Gnagey, 1981; Good & Brophy, 1978).

A variety of experts have made many recommendations about classroom management. The best evidence, however, may come from the direct observation of how effective teachers structure classroom environments to contribute to learning. Kounin (1970) and Brophy and Evertson (1976) found that the most important factors in directing student behavior were teacher actions that increased the time students spent in profitable learning activities. Better organization and transitions between activities make discipline problems much less likely to occur.

These observations have been amply confirmed (see Evertson, Anderson, Anderson, & Brophy, 1980; Berliner, 1982; Good & Grouws, 1977). One important way that effective teachers differ from less effective teachers is that they *prevent* behavior problems in their classrooms by keeping students involved in meaningful learning activities. This chapter is designed to help you acquire the skills that lead to effective classroom management.

Objectives

After reading this chapter, you should be able to meet the following objectives.

1. Develop a classroom management plan that will prevent problem behaviors.
2. Devise procedures for dealing with students who present special behavioral or academic problems.
3. Implement procedures for preventing or correcting behavior problems.

APPLICATIONS FOR TEACHING: GENERAL PRINCIPLES OF CLASSROOM MANAGEMENT

In the last few years, the term *classroom management* has referred primarily to a behavioral approach for guiding classroom behaviors (Kazdin, 1981). While behavioral psychology provides some extremely important insights into the complex processes involved in guiding student activity, we cannot lose sight of the cognitive nature of human beings and the self-directed nature of learning. Successful classroom management requires a blending of cognitive, behavioral, and humanistic views of human behavior. The following six principles of effective classroom management were drawn from all three views of behavior.

1. Provide Meaningful Learning Activities. A classroom in which students have meaningful and challenging work is a key to preventing problems (Evertson et al., 1980). Classroom disruptions are much less likely to occur when students are interested in their work. As we stated in Chapter Two when we discussed cognitive processes, learning will be enhanced if the information is made meaningful to students.

How can you provide meaningful learning activities for your students? In a general educational psychology text we cannot give you specific suggestions about what materials and activities to select for your subject area and teaching level. One critical factor, however, is your knowledge of students—their interests, ways of thinking, and readiness for new learning tasks (Gnagey, 1981). By knowing your students well, you will be able to predict which materials will be most interesting to them and which activities they are likely to prefer. Chapter Twelve, "Task Analysis," will introduce you to procedures that will help you determine what new materials your students are ready for, but the choice of how to present new materials always rests with you. Wise choices lead to meaningful activities and enhanced student learning. If students are actively working on meaningful tasks, they will be less inclined to cause problems in the classroom.

2. Provide a Supportive Classroom Environment. As we saw in Chapter Nine, learning and self-growth are not likely to occur unless students' deficiency needs are met. The classroom must be a place in which children's physiological, safety, belongingness, and esteem needs are satisfied to the greatest extent possible. Clearly, a teacher cannot replace parents and provide the love and care that children must have. But teachers can certainly assure students' safety in the classroom and develop students' feelings of belonging to the class group. Esteem, in large part, is dependent on how teachers interact with students (Holt, 1970). The acceptance of each student as a unique person and sincere praise for good effort go a long way to facilitating students' attainment of esteem needs (Rogers, 1969).

Meaningful activities prevent many classroom management problems. Students who are engaged in interesting projects seldom misbehave.

3. Provide Opportunities for Successful Learning. The old saying "success breeds success" is no less true in the classroom than elsewhere. All students should have the opportunity to experience success in your classroom (Holt, 1970), from contributing something useful to a group discussion to seeing their progress in spelling. Success need not mean competing favorably with others; an improvement in one's own performance is an important source of success experiences (Rogers, 1969).

Effective teachers plan activities that are challenging but allow a great likelihood for success. Generally, tasks that are too easy become boring and uninviting to students, and tasks that are too hard result in failure. The correct choice for learning activities for students is a crucial component of effective classroom management (Evertson et al., 1980). When failure is frequent or when success is too easy, students become disenchanted with learning activities and look for other, more rewarding things to do (Gnagey, 1981). Too often, these other things disrupt the classroom atmosphere.

4. Provide Knowledge of Results. Closely related to success is the feedback teachers give students for their efforts. Feedback—knowledge of results—is an important part of motivating students to persist in learning tasks (Maehr, 1978) and in determining how much they learn (Kulhavy, 1977). Feedback not only permits students to judge their success, but it also contributes to the development of their own standards of excellence. In Chapter Fourteen, "Teacher-Made Tests," we will present specific guidelines for providing appropriate feedback. In general, appropriate feedback facilitates students' motivation to engage in learning tasks, making it less likely that misbehavior will occur.

5. Share Decisions with Students. Students need to feel a sense of control in what they do (Rogers, 1969). Unfortunately, students in poorly managed classrooms often feel that they have little or no control over their learning. When students feel that they are only giving the teacher what he or she wants, motivation to persist in learning activities is greatly reduced (Gnagey, 1981).

Effective teachers help students play an important role in determining their own learning experiences (Good & Brophy, 1978). They often allow students to make decisions about what, when, and how learning will occur. Such shared decision making helps students feel that they are in control (Rogers, 1969). When students believe that they have a significant say in the decision-making process in a classroom, motivation to persist in learning activities is enhanced and the possibilities of misbehavior are reduced (Maehr, 1978).

6. Strengthen Appropriate Behaviors. Most successful classroom management programs are based on *strengthening* appropriate behaviors (e.g., Madsen, Becker, & Thomas, 1968; McAllister, Stachowiak, Baer, & Conderman, 1969; Rincover, Cook, Peoples, & Packard, 1979), not on coping with problem behaviors. Appropriate behaviors—those that lead to the most rapid and enjoyable learning in the classroom—compete with inappropriate behaviors—those that interfere with learning. Students cannot solve math problems and talk out of turn at the same time. These behaviors compete; that is, only one of the two can happen at any one time. When appropriate behaviors are very strong and occur with regularity, misbehavior is rare. This is the basis of a problem prevention approach (Brophy & Evertson, 1976; Good & Brophy, 1978).

These six general principles were drawn from cognitive, behavioral, and humanistic psychology and emphasize that the hallmark of effective classroom management programs is *preventing* problems, not merely coping with misbehavior (see Gnagey, 1981; Madsen et al., 1968; Rincover et al., 1979; Rogers, 1969). In the next few pages, we will present two specific views of how a problem prevention approach to classroom management should proceed.

GLASSER'S APPROACH TO PROBLEM PREVENTION

William Glasser (1969, 1977, 1981) has developed a widely known model for preventing behavior problems. Glasser has reasoned that misbehavior and failure to learn from school experiences go hand in hand, a position in close accord with our discussion of motivation in Chapter Nine. Failure, he argues, leads to emotional reactions that reduce the likelihood that students will behave rationally and learn from the consequences of their behavior. Success, on the other hand, encourages rationality and learning from the behavioral consequences. To increase students' success and reduce failure, Glasser proposed the following guidelines:

Be personal. Use personal pronouns and express care for students.

Refer only to present behavior. Ask (in effect) "What are you doing now?" Avoid quizzing students about past behavior.

Stress value judgments by students. Ask if what students are now doing is helpful to them.

Plan with students for alternative behaviors. Involve students in decision making.

Be committed to the plan. Show your commitment by checking prog-

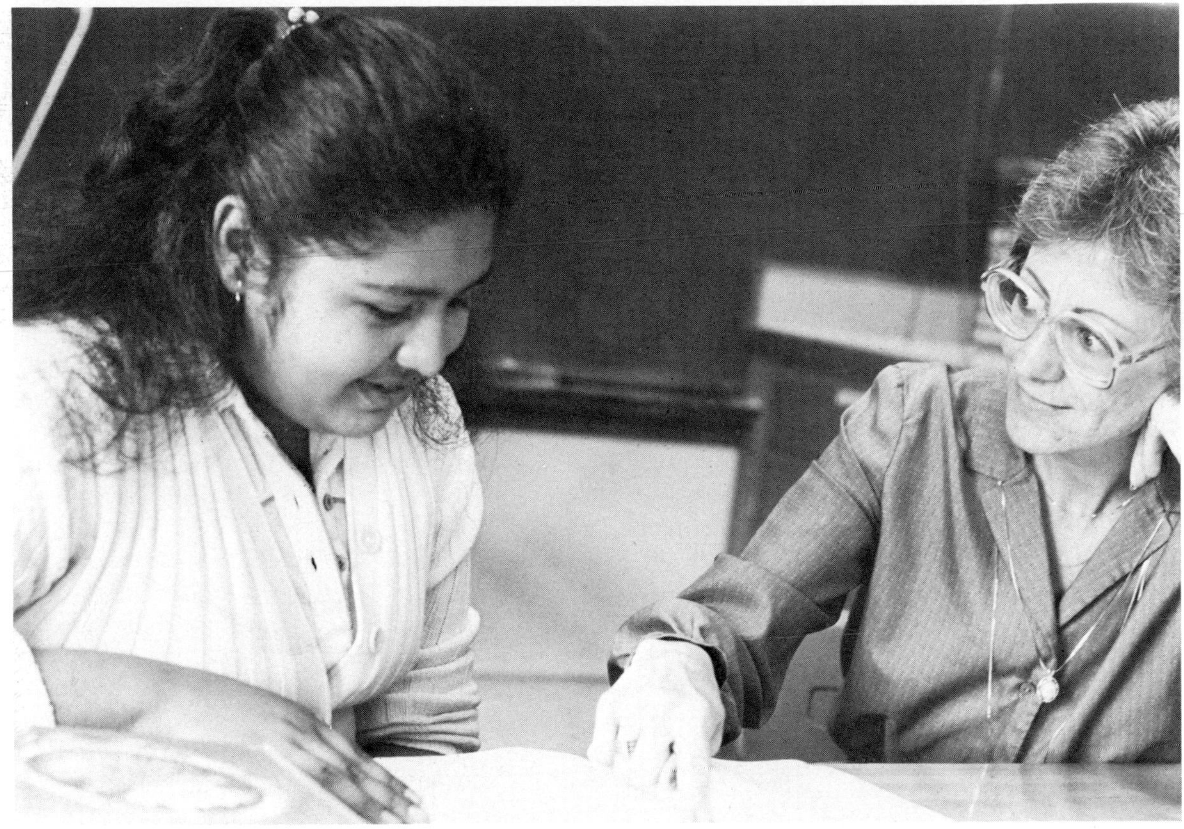

Plan with students for alternative behaviors. Planning helps both teacher and student identify desirable outcomes.

ress and providing positive reinforcement for meeting the goals of your plan.

Do not accept excuses. Don't discuss excuses and alibis with the students.

Do not punish. Punishment removes responsibility from the students.

For students needing more intensive help in becoming self-disciplined, Glasser outlined a ten-step method, briefly summarized below.

1. Set aside a time to identify and think about students who need to develop self-discipline. List your reactions to their appropriate behaviors.
2. Analyze your reactions. Are they effective? If not, discontinue them.
3. Plan alternative reactions that reinforce appropriate behavior and withdraw reinforcement for inappropriate behavior.

4. When problems recur (and they may) ask the student, "What are you doing?" Do not accept excuses as answers and insist that the student think about his or her actual behavior and its likely consequences.
5. If misbehavior continues, hold a short, private conference with the student. Repeat step 4. Then, with warmth, support, and firmness, ask, "Is what you're doing against the rules?" Then ask, "What *should* you be doing?" Have the student enter into an agreement with you (see the section on individual contracts, page 297) to perform the appropriate behavior.
6. If misbehavior persists, repeat steps 2 through 5 but eliminate the last question. Instead firmly state, "We have to work this out. What kind of plan can *you* make to follow our rules?" Insist on a positive plan, not just a plan to stop inappropriate acts.
7. If disruptions continue, use an isolation procedure or an in-class time-out procedure (see page 298) until the student develops an acceptable plan for future behavior.
8. When inappropriate acts continue despite your previous efforts, use an "in-school suspension," such as placing the student in a small room so he or she can work alone. Explain that since things are not working out in the classroom, the student must do his or her work alone. The suspension room should be comfortable and staffed by someone who continues to communicate that the student is valued as a person. The staff member should also inquire into the student's problem behavior while pressing for the student to take personal responsibility for his or her behavior.
9. If a student's behavior is totally out of control, parents must be notified and asked to take the child home. It should be pointed out that "tomorrow is a new day, and perhaps he or she can return and make a go of it then."
10. For students who remain unresponsive to these procedures, Glasser suggests that referral to a community agency or school service for treating acute behavior problems is the only answer.

Glasser's general technique has not received much research attention. Glasser (1977) reports, however, on one study in which a survey of twenty-four schools using his approach indicated that there were decreases of 5 to 80 percent in disciplinary referrals, with concomitant decreases in fighting and suspensions. Glasser's emphasis on increasing appropriate behavior, increasing success, and decreasing inappropriate behavior is an excellent complement to other classroom management techniques. Many of the specific techniques discussed later in this chapter can be blended with Glasser's approach.

PRACTICE EXERCISE 10–1
Using Glasser's Principles in Analyzing a Classroom Situation

As we have indicated, Glasser has stated seven principles in his success-based program of classroom management:

1. Be personal.
2. Refer only to present behavior.
3. Stress value judgments by students.
4. Plan alternative behaviors with students.
5. Show commitment by checking and reinforcing progress.
6. Do not accept excuses.
7. Do not punish.

Analyze the situation below in terms of these seven principles by listing the parts of the conversation in which the teacher applies Glasser's principles and the parts where her performance could have been improved by applying his principles. When you have finished go to the end of the chapter and check your analysis with ours.

Imagine the setting: Bill, a senior, has received a low grade on an examination in English that covered six weeks' study of the writings of Poe and Hawthorne. The next exam is in three weeks. Bill has come in after class to talk about his grade, and the following conversation ensues.

1. *Teacher:* Hello, Bill . . . come on in and sit down.
   Bill: (Slowly taking a seat) Well, I suppose you know why I'm here. . . . I'm pretty upset about the grade you gave me on the exam. I'm gonna end up ineligible for track for sure! Do you know what my parents are going to do when they find out that I'm not eligible for the track team? They're going to kill me. They'd planned on going up to Kirkville to see me run. Now all that's shot.
2. *Teacher:* I'm sorry, but the examination was graded fairly. You just didn't do very well, Bill. Also, I think that you can improve enough on the next test to avoid a failing grade for this quarter.
   Bill: (Upset) I thought I did pretty good. . . . I think I know this stuff. It wasn't like I didn't study or anything.
3. *Teacher:* Bill, it's always the same story with you. I get tired of hearing how you studied and all. Last semester you said the same thing whenever you got a bad grade.
   Bill: Well, it's true. . . . I study but I still get bad grades from you. I don't think you're ever fair to me when you grade my tests.
4. *Teacher:* I think I have a reputation for being fair to students. . . . *(A period of silence)* Bill, I'm not sure we're getting anywhere by

arguing about this exam. I'm sure you don't like the consequences—I know I don't—but I think we need to talk about ways to make sure the problem doesn't occur again. My goal is to have you coming out of this course as a good writer knowing about American literature. And I hope we like each other too.

Bill: You're not going to change my grade. . . .

5. *Teacher: (Firmly)* No, Bill.

   Bill: No?

6. *Teacher:* No. . . . It wouldn't be fair to the others in the class and it wouldn't really indicate what you know about Hawthorne and Poe, would it? We have another test coming up in three weeks. I think we might talk about some ways of preparing for it that will help you do better on that one.

   Bill: But I *did* prepare. . . . I studied real hard and—

7. *Teacher: (Gently interrupting)* The next test will cover several of the early twentieth-century writers. *(Checking her lesson plans)* It looks like we have six more class sessions before that exam. Let's talk about some specific things you might want to do before the next exam to make sure your performance is as good as I know it can be.

   Bill: Well, I could come to class . . . *(Smiles a little)*

8. *Teacher: (Laughing)* Well, I guess that's a start. But how about the studying? How do you generally go about getting ready for tests, Bill?

   Bill: Well, on this one I pretty much sat down and read over all the stuff you assigned the night before the test.

9. *Teacher: (A little mischievously)* And the result?

   Bill: Not too terrific, I guess.

10. *Teacher:* Could we think a bit about approaching this test a little differently? We agree that neither of us is too happy with the outcome.

    Bill: For sure!

11. *Teacher:* One thing I've found helpful is for students to work out a schedule for preparing for an exam that starts about a week before the exam takes place. That way, a person doesn't get caught at the last minute. If you'd be willing to draw up a plan for how you might prepare this time, I'd certainly be happy to meet with you after class tomorrow and have a look at it. We also could meet a couple of days before the exam and see how your preparation is coming.

    Bill: Sounds reasonable. . . . OK, I'll come in with something tomorrow.

Postive uses of Glasser's principles

Glasser's principle (by number)	*Teacher comment or question (by number)*

Failures to use Glasser's principles

Glasser's principle (by number)	*Teacher comment or question (by number)*

A BEHAVIORAL APPROACH TO PROBLEM PREVENTION

Contemporary behavioral approaches to classroom management are based primarily on behavioral psychology and social learning as discussed in Chapters Seven and Eight. Behavioral approaches draw specific attention to the antecedents and consequences of behavior that teachers manage in order to increase or decrease behaviors. From this perspective, then, the first step in a preventive approach is to select the behaviors teachers want to increase.

Desirable Student Behaviors

As a teacher, you first need to decide what goals are most important for your students. Most teachers hope that students will become better self-directed learners, that they will improve their ability to analyze and solve problems, and that they will become more creative. A prerequisite for reaching goals such as these is a smoothly operating and goal-oriented classroom. Following is a list of general student behaviors, with specific examples, that can contribute to productive activity in most classes, regardless of classroom goals. Although these student behaviors may not directly relate to every goal teachers have, their occurrence will tend to produce an atmosphere in which learning can take place. An important additional effect is that if students do these things, discipline problems become less likely.

Paying attention to class activities:
- Looking at the teacher or other students who are giving a demonstration
- Turning to pages of texts when requested
- Asking relevant questions

Working as a cooperating member of a class or group:
- Participating in discussions, planning sessions, and the like
- Volunteering for tasks
- Speaking quietly and calmly when disagreeing
- Maintaining an even temper and being friendly
- Congratulating others on their efforts
- Sharing praise with the group
- Obtaining permission before speaking out or acting in ways that might distract other students

Initiating learning activities:
- Exploring ideas
- Obtaining extra resources for learning
- Seeking additional instruction
- Practicing on one's own
- Helping other students with assignments

Observing safety rules:
- Walking in crowded places or in halls and stairs
- Checking clearances when carrying objects
- Following specific safety rules in class

Our list, of course, is not all-inclusive and will not fit every situation. You may well see some changes or additions you would make. Playground supervisors, shop teachers, music teachers, and parents at home are all in settings that differ from traditional classrooms. They must formulate their own set of problem-preventing behaviors. Nonetheless, a difference in appropriate behaviors across situations does not change the basic principle: Simply, discipline problems will be minimal if students are active and productive.

PRACTICE EXERCISE 10–2

Analyzing Student Behaviors

One very useful skill you can perfect is that of identifying productive and nonproductive student behaviors and analyzing why they occur through a behavior analysis. Set a goal for yourself of identifying at least five behaviors of each type (productive and nonproductive) in any setting in which there are individuals engaged in learning—in residence halls, in the library, in classes (lectures, discussions, lab sessions), at meals, in meetings, during tests, at social events, and on the job.

List on the following form the productive and nonproductive behaviors you observe. Also list the antecedents and consequences in order to analyze what might be maintaining each behavior. For each, briefly comment on the likely consequences of continuation of this behavior on the student's ultimate academic and social achievement. If possible, share your observations with your instructor and classmates.

Productive Behaviors

Antecedents	*Behavior*	*Consequences*	*Possible Long-Term Outcomes*

Nonproductive Behaviors

Antecedents	*Behavior*	*Consequences*	*Possible Long-Term Outcomes*

Three Keys to an Effective Behavioral Approach

In an early study of classroom management, Becker, Madsen, Arnold, and Thomas (1967) began a program of research that identified three critical principles of effective behavioral classroom management: (1) have *rules* for what is expected of students, (2) give *praise* for appropriate behaviors and indicate what the praise is for, and (3) *ignore* minor problem behaviors. These three principles should underlie all of your teaching activities. The findings that led to the three principles have been confirmed in numerous studies with children of various ages and social and ethnic backgrounds (see Cossairt, Hall, & Hopkins, 1973; Hall, Lund, & Jackson, 1968; Madsen et al., 1968). The result of consistent use of these principles is improvement in student conduct and academic performance.

There are some misbehaviors that cannot be ignored. You may want to decide in advance what behaviors cannot be allowed in your classroom.

Rules. Rules are an important part of every well-run classroom. Rules convey to students an idea of the behaviors that are expected of them. Rules may be written or oral and may be stated positively ("Put all materials away after you finish") or negatively ("Do not interrupt when another person is speaking"). Stated properly, rules can provide a clear guide to students about which behaviors will be reinforced and which

will not. To make your rules most effective, the following suggestions may be helpful.

Limit rules to the minimum necessary for effective class functioning. Ideally, you should have only as many rules as you can monitor yourself—five or six at a maximum.

Describe the appropriate behavior as clearly and positively as possible.

Always include a description of the positive effects of following a rule.

Involve students in the formulation of classroom rules. The more students are involved in determining rules, the more likely they are to follow them.

Introduce rules with an explanation of why they are necessary and discuss them thoroughly (Brophy & Evertson, 1976). Establish the precise nature of what these expectations mean for each student.

As we noted in Chapter Eight, if the behavior you are asking your students to perform is complex and can be stated only rather abstractly, demonstrations or modeling may be superior to rules. A demonstration of how to use laboratory equipment or the materials in a learning resource center is usually better than instructions or rules about those procedures. Many safety-related behaviors are best demonstrated ("Now look how I keep my hands on the wood and still guide it through the saw. You could get your hand caught if you don't hold it like this"). As with rules, always indicate the positive effects of imitating a model.

Praise and Other Positive Consequences. Rules alone will seldom keep their influence; they prompt but do not maintain appropriate behavior. In the long run, the consequences of behavior become a critical factor. A student may start out following a classroom rule by being cooperative, for example. If there are no discernible benefits or if the student finds that competitiveness rather than cooperation is actually reinforced, the new behavior will soon die out. Teachers must provide consequences consistent with rules if appropriate behaviors are to be maintained.

Effective teachers have learned to use themselves and their reactions as consequences for student behavior (Dangel & Hopkins, 1978). A smile, a word or two of sincere praise, and a careful examination of students' work are examples of teachers' actions that are likely to reinforce appropriate behavior. Another way to say this, as we stressed in Chapter Nine, is that effective teachers allow students to experience success.

For effective classroom management, positive reinforcement from teachers should be *contingent* on appropriate student behavior. **Contingent reinforcers** are closely linked to desired student actions; that is, praise and attention (indications of success) are offered on those occasions when desired behaviors occur. The teacher intentionally links his or her attention to appropriate behavior. On the other hand, if praise and attention are unconditional *(noncontingent),* students are likely to use unproductive ways to gain the teacher's attention.

In early research on classroom behavior and praise, overt praise was generally thought to be universally good—the more praise, the more positive the environment and the better the learning experience (Winett & Winkler, 1972). Two cautions are in order, however. First, praise must be sincerely offered (Cooper, 1978). Extremely frequent use of verbal praise is likely to be justifiably perceived as insincere and will probably have no effect and may even have negative effects. Second, work by Brophy and Evertson (1976) has shown that the effectiveness of praise may depend on several variables. In their work in elementary levels, they found that the most successful teachers in schools in the lower socioeconomic strata used praise and gentle encouragement as their basic approach (see Chapter Nine). Successful teachers in the higher socioeconomic levels tended at times to use more critical and demanding approaches. Also, praise that was coaxed out of teachers by students tended to have negative effects on learning. Public praise of individuals in front of the entire class as a basic teaching approach also tended to reduce achievement levels, but praise offered *privately* for achievement had very positive effects. In Brophy and Evertson's words,

> praise should be individualized and genuine; and . . . whatever it is that the teacher wishes to praise *should be specified in the process of giving praise* [emphasis added], so that the praise does in fact function as a positive incentive or motivator for the student. *(1976, p. 92)*

Ignoring Inappropriate Behavior. The natural inclination of many teachers is to very quickly correct or criticize inappropriate behaviors. In some cases, this may be acceptable, as when the teacher perceives that more severe problems are very likely to develop. There is good reason to suggest, however, that many minor misbehaviors should be ignored (Becker et al., 1967; Madsen et al., 1970) since one of the most common and most powerful reinforcers in the classroom is teacher attention and praise. When students obtain attention for inappropriate behavior it is probable that they will continue to misbehave in order to obtain additional reinforcement.

Withholding attention for inappropriate behavior will often lead to the behavior's extinction. Teachers should be careful to consider three

Small misbehaviors can often be safely ignored. Student attention is not always constant, and occasional lapses can be expected.

points in ignoring behavior, however. First, during extinction things often get worse before they get better. That is, misbehavior frequently increases when it is first ignored, presumably because the students are not obtaining expected reinforcement ("She didn't pay any attention to me. Didn't she hear me? Maybe I'd better talk louder"). Second, ignoring does not usually result in rapid decreases in behavior. As a rule, misbehavior is maintained on some form of variable schedule of reinforcement and when reinforcement is withdrawn, many unreinforced instances of the misbehavior will occur before it ceases. Third, and most important, positive reinforcement (attention and praise) for alternative behavior must be plentiful. Merely withholding reinforcement for misbehavior is not nearly so effective as coupling it with positive reinforcement for appropriate behavior. In fact, ignoring *alone* can sometimes lead to greater levels of misbehavior.

While ignoring may often be effective, there are some misbehaviors that cannot be ignored. Actions that threaten you or your students, self-injurious behaviors, severe disruptions, violations of safety rules, and similar incidents must be corrected immediately. For such problems we suggest some of the specialized techniques described in the next section.

SOME SPECIFIC INTERVENTIONS FOR MANAGING INAPPROPRIATE BEHAVIORS

When behavior problems arise in the classroom despite the teacher's best efforts to prevent them, intervention techniques may be effectively employed. It is interesting to note that most research in classroom management has investigated various techniques for correcting already existing behavior problems rather than methods of preventing problems in the first place (Kazdin, 1981). We suppose that researchers' emphases on correction rather than prevention is a direct result of the severity of some problems and the importance attached to correcting them (Glover & Gary, 1979). In this section we will briefly describe some of the more widely used (and more widely investigated) techniques for correcting behavior problems once they have started.

The Token Economy

The **token economy**, pioneered by Ayllon and Azrin (1968), is a systematic method of providing students with immediate reinforcement for appropriate behavior. Rather than relying on praise or other sources of social reinforcement, the token economy utilizes a concrete form of secondary reinforcer—tokens. The tokens (points, check marks, "smiley faces," poker chips) are presented to students contingent on their performance of appropriate behaviors specified by the classroom rules. Different behaviors in an economy will earn differing numbers of tokens: Coming to class on time might earn two tokens while turning in completed homework might earn five.

Typically, tokens can be exchanged at the end of a period of time (usually one class period; sometimes as long as one week) for backup reinforcers (Glover & Gary, 1975; Williams & Anadam, 1973). The backup reinforcers are, in a sense, purchased by students with their tokens. A student may earn enough tokens to purchase the last fifteen minutes of a period for free time or he or she may be able to purchase the opportunity to do an especially interesting activity. Attractive backup reinforcers are an important component of token economies (Kaufman & O'Leary, 1972).

Most token economies also include a *response cost* feature (Kazdin,

RESPONSE COST

"Getting an "A" or a star is all right, but I'd like some sort of profit-sharing plan around here."

1981). That is, tokens are taken away from students if they misbehave. Some token economies also place a ceiling on how many points students may lose before they are suspended from the classroom (Williams & Anadam, 1973). The point of the response cost, of course, is to weaken inappropriate behavior. The ceiling is used to place a limit on misbehavior.

Token economies have been effective at many age levels and across almost all subject areas (see Flexibrod & O'Leary, 1973; Kaufman & O'Leary, 1972; O'Leary, Becker, Evans, & Saundargas, 1969; Osborne, 1969; Wolf, Giles, & Hall, 1968). In general, it appears that the major advantages of the token economy are immediate, concrete reinforcement, high flexibility in student choice of backup reinforcement, student expectations for reinforcement that cue teacher behaviors, and ease of program revision.

Token economies should include the following components:

A set of instructions that specify the expectations held for students

Tokens that can be accumulated over time

Guidelines for awarding or taking away tokens

A procedure for identifying effective backup reinforcers

A guide for exchanging tokens for backup reinforcers

The Good Behavior Game

The Good Behavior Game developed by Barrish, Saunders, and Wolf (1969), is another effective method for managing behavior. The game requires that a class be divided into two or more teams that compete to see which team can gain the most points through appropriate behavior. The winning team typically gains an attractive reinforcer for the entire group, such as early recess, free time, or, with younger students, consumables such as an extra carton of milk.

Each team's score depends on the behavior of each team member, and so it is possible for one highly disruptive student to cause a team to lose (Barrish et al., 1969). This possibility, however, has not been encountered often (see Barrish et al., 1969; Drabman, Spitalnik, & Spitalnik, 1974; Glover, 1979; Maloney & Hopkins, 1973). Further, the game is usually set up so that any team can win if it obtains 80 percent of the score of the winning team.

The Good Behavior Game is actually a variant of the token economy. Points (or tokens) are given to teams for appropriate behavior of team members, and points are subtracted for the misbehavior of any team member. The game differs from the token economy in the use of group goals and group-contingent reinforcement. That is, the backup reinforcers are given to a group for group behavior. The Good Behavior Game has been especially effective with elementary students (see Barrish et al., 1969; Glover, 1979a; Glover & Gary, 1976; Maloney & Hopkins, 1973). The advantages of the Good Behavior Game include those of the token economy plus a high rate of student participation, peer reinforcement for earning points, and the gamelike nature of the process.

The Good Behavior Game should include the following components:

- Instructions that describe the teacher's expectations
- A set of guidelines that specify the behaviors that will gain or lose points
- A description of how the game will be administered
- A procedure for selecting group backup reinforcers

Group Contracts

Group contracts are agreements negotiated between groups of students and a teacher. They specify both student and teacher behavior (Homme, Csanyi, Gonzales, & Rechs, 1969). There are three important characteristics of group contracts. First, the teacher and students negotiate each item to be included in the contract. The teacher may wish to include certain behaviors to be reinforced while the students may wish to include others. A negotiation time of several class periods is often necessary to come to a consensus about the contents of the contract.

The second feature is that students voluntarily enter into contracts.

Any student in the class may choose *not* to sign the contract and thereby continue with whatever classroom management approach was in effect earlier. Such nonsigning students, of course, receive none of the benefits of the contract. Nonsignees may choose to enter into an agreement at any time during the contract period, however (Glover & Gary, 1975). The choice is entirely voluntary.

The third component of a group contract is that the teacher also agrees to be held accountable for certain responsibilities. If the teacher agrees to grade and return homework in twenty-four hours, for example, this is just as much a part of the contract as any behaviors the students agree to perform.

Group contracting has been found to be effective with students of all ages (Kazdin, 1981) and across many different subject areas (Glover & Gary, 1979). The advantages of group contracting include those of the token economy plus the attitudinal benefits of negotiation and voluntary participation.

The components of a group contract are:

A description of the overall rules for the classroom

A description of the behaviors of the students and the teacher

An explanation of the way in which the system will be administered

A renegotiation date

The signatures of the agreeing parties

Individual Contracts

The techniques we've discussed so far are all designed for implementation with an entire class. There are times, however, when teachers do not want to employ a comprehensive management procedure but instead want to work with only one or two students. An **individual contract,** sometimes called a *contingency contract,* is an agreement that a student will change a behavior in return for reinforcement (Walker & Shea, 1976). The use of an individual contract can be seen in the following example.

A teacher reported on a sophomore student who very defiantly placed her head down on her desk every day and kept it there during the entire class period. Other teachers reported that the girl's behavior was the same in their classes. The teacher and the student arrived at a contract whereby the student would be ready to discuss the answers to two questions that would be asked at the beginning of every class. After giving the two answers, the girl would receive a "pass" for the day and could then rest her head on her arms and go to sleep. The teacher agreed that the girl would not be called on again during the class period and that she would receive a satisfactory grade on her report card. Getting the girl to answer only two questions a day is obviously not all that was desired. This represents the starting place in a management plan. Ultimately full participation in class was expected. Contracts frequently must start with just one small step and progress gradually until the final goal is reached.

The girl responded very well to the contract. At first she answered the two questions and then put her head down as agreed on. Subsequently, she began to stay alert and to participate in discussions for longer and longer periods of time. At the end of three weeks, she was alert during the whole period and was frequently volunteering answers. She continued, however, to visit the teacher after class to get her two special questions for the next day's class. During these private contacts the teacher gave her sincere praise for participation.

Individual contracts have been used with students of all ages (Glover & Gary, 1979) and in many different settings. A major advantage is their flexibility—they can be employed for a wide range of behaviors—and the fact that they can be negotiated with individual students to meet individual needs.

In order to be most effective, individual contracts should always specify *positive* changes in behavior and contain the following components:

- The names of the agreeing parties
- A definition of the agreed-upon student behavior and an acceptable performance level
- Specification of the agreed-upon teacher behavior or other reinforcers
- The signatures of both parties

Time-Out

The techniques we have described so far have emphasized the strengthening of appropriate behaviors. There are times, however, when teachers need to suppress a misbehavior. One method, time-out, has proved to be an effective procedure for decreasing inappropriate behavior.

Time-out is the brief removal (for three to five minutes) of a child from a reinforcing setting to one that is not reinforcing. It is generally thought of as a mild punishment technique. Its basic purpose, however, is not to punish the child but rather to *interrupt* reinforced misbehavior. Generally, time-out is used when peer reinforcement maintains the inappropriate behavior or when the teacher judges that the behavior must be dealt with quickly. Time-out is not a solution; it should always lead to the use of a more positive behavior management program (Hobbs & Forehand, 1977).

Time-out is not recommended for older students, but it has been found effective with elementary school children (compare Foxx & Azrin, 1972; Hobbs & Forehand, 1977; Plummer, Baer, & LeBlanc, 1977; Solnick, Rincover, & Petersen, 1977). Generally, time-out has its greatest effect when the environment from which a child is removed is highly reinforcing (Solnick et al., 1977). Time-out also seems to be more advantageous when children are removed for brief periods of time and when children are not totally isolated (Foxx & Shapiro, 1978; Kazdin, 1979; Porterfield, Herbert-Jackson, & Risely, 1976), although total isolation may be necessary for severe behavior problems (Lahey, McNees, & McNees, 1973).

Time-out has been found to be effective in school, home, and institutional settings (Hobbs & Forehand, 1977; Kazdin, 1981). Its advantages include the rapidity with which it can be employed and the fact that teachers may employ it for a day or two while planning positively oriented behavior management programs. Time-out, however, has received some very strong criticism (see Hobbs & Forehand, 1977), mostly owing to misuses. Because of the potential for misuse, these detailed rules should be carefully adhered to in using this procedure:

Obtain the consent of parents and/or legal guardians of all students involved. Explain the procedures in detail, including: (1) the behaviors for which time-out will be invoked, (2) how it will be explained to the students, (3) the duration of the time-out and how often it will be utilized, (4) follow-up provision of reinforcers, and (5) the theory and research basis for using the system.

Prepare the student. Explain the process by pointing out that the ultimate purpose is to teach the student to better control himself or herself when angry, excited, or upset. Carefully describe the student behaviors that will lead to time-out.

Where possible, use nonisolation techniques (Kazdin, 1979, 1981). Place the child at the periphery of the group with instructions not to interact with the class for a few moments. If the child stops behaving inappropriately, allow a few minutes to pass and then have the child return to his or her original place in the group. Use isolation as a backup consequence if the behavior does not stop when the child is placed at the edge of the group (LeBlanc, Busby, & Thomson, 1974; Porterfield et al., 1976).

If isolation is used, make sure that the time-out room is comfortable, well lit, and not frightening to your students. You do not want to provide a place to go for fun but you don't want to alarm anyone either. The point is to provide a setting that gives very few opportunities for reinforcement.

When a student misbehaves, accompany him or her to the time-out area. Ask the student to sit quietly and review what led up to the misbehavior. Then ask the student to describe to himself or herself what he or she might have done differently to avoid the problem.

Notify the student when time is up (three to five minutes) and escort him or her back to the classroom.

Remind students that they can decide for themselves when it would be best to use time-out. Offer sincere praise to students who act to prevent problems. Recognize that it is difficult to walk away from trouble in order to cool off.

Home-Based Contingencies

The techniques we have described are designed for in-school administration. Many times, however, it is useful to involve parents in behavior management. Parents usually appreciate involvement in the school's efforts. One way to foster their participation is through the use of home-based contingencies.

Home-based contingencies are behavior management programs in which the backup reinforcers are administered at home by the parents (Todd, Scott, Boston, & Alexander, 1976). Home-based contingencies may be adapted for use with token economies or individual contracts, or they may evolve from an agreement that a student's achievement of specific goals during the day (as determined by the teacher or by agreement of the teacher and parents) will result in backup reinforcement from the parents.

The usefulness of home-based contingencies has been demonstrated (e.g., Budd, Leibowitz, Riner, Mindell, & Goldfarb, 1980; McKenzie, Clark, Wolf, Kothera, & Benson, 1968; Todd et al., 1976) with students of all ages and across many different settings. There are several advantages of home-based contingencies (Kazdin, 1981). First, the parents are fully involved in the program, supporting the teacher's actions. Second, with parental involvement, the behavior-change program is far more likely to be consistent and effective. Third, parents have a wider range of reinforcers (money, special snacks, weekend activities, ball gloves) available for their children's behavior than do teachers. Fourth, a load is removed from the teacher (administering backup reinforcers), freeing him or her for other duties.

In order to implement home-based contingencies, several conditions should be met:

An agreement about which behaviors will be reinforced, an acceptable level for the performance of the behavior, and a method of recording the behavior must be developed.

The parents must be willing to become fully involved in the program and *consistently* administer the backup reinforcers.

There must be an effective method of communicating with the parents. Frequently, daily 'report cards' are used in which the teacher records the student's level of goal attainment and indicates whether the student is to be reinforced.

TABLE 10–1
Representative Studies in Behavior Management*

Author(s)	*Subjects' Age Grade Level*	*Technique(s)*	*Processes and Results: Behavior Changes*
Barton & Osborne (1978)	Preschool; kindergarten (learning-impaired)	Required practice with reinforcement	Students who did not share toys were trained and required to practice sharing. Teacher praised sharing. Sharing increased threefold and increased rate continued over fifteen-week follow-up.
Hamblin et al. (1969)	Preschool; Head Start	Token economy plus praise and attention	Program reduced aggressive behaviors and increased cooperativeness, increased study time for hyperactive students, increased vocalization in a group that did not participate in discussions, developed sight reading vocabularies of 140 words in a three-year-old and of over 220 words for several others.
Salzsberg et al. (1971)	Kindergarten	Feedback of correct learning of letters	Children given rapid feedback appeared to improve their printing skills, although quality of printing was difficult to judge reliably.
O'Conner (1973)	Preschool	Modeling and reinforcement	This program first used modeling alone, then reinforcement alone, then combined the two to improve and increase social interactions. Reinforcement was effective alone, but modeling had to be included for new behaviors to persist.
Deergin et al. (1977)	Preschool	Specific instructions and models	Teachers gave specific instructions, then modeled participation in group singing and other activities. Participation rates were significantly improved in a nursery school group.
Taylor and Kratochwill (1978)	Preschool	Selective teacher praise	Kindergartners who were very messy in their bathroom behavior were selectively praised by teacher for placing paper towels in waste receptacles, flushing toilets, and turning off faucets. Target behaviors improved markedly within twelve days.
Radgoski et al. (1978)	Preschool	Cuing then using modeled response for feedback	Teachers gave a cue (picture, object, and the like) for a French term, then after student response teacher modeled correct response. Children

*The techniques and management problems described in this chapter, as well as some others of similar nature, have been studied and researched extensively. Several books have recently been published describing the research and extrapolating the findings. New research is being reported constantly in respected educational and psychological journals. There are even professional meetings devoted exclusively to behavioral management research, for instance, the annual convention of the American Association of Behavior Analysis (formerly the Midwestern Association of Behavior Analysis) each year. The number of such studies is truly staggering. Several hundred appear each year. It is impossible to cite even a portion of these in this chapter. We have, however, summarized several representative studies in this table.

Author(s)	*Subjects' Age Grade Level*	*Technique(s)*	*Processes and Results: Behavior Changes*
			developed an extensive vocabulary in a relatively short time.
Fox & Roseen (1977)	Preschool	Token system	Parent used tokens to reinforce a three-and-one-half-year-old's eating of foods on a very restrictive diet. The diet included a protein supplement the child disliked very much. The reinforcement led to a maintenance of correct eating for more than a year.
Simmons et al. (1977)	Preschool	Tangible reinforcers	Three preschoolers with learning problems were reinforced with orange juice and special toys for progressively longer periods of independent activity and for lower levels of disruption. The independent activity and low disruption periods were steadily increased to twelve minutes.
Packard (1970)	Third, fifth, and sixth graders	Instructions, attention, and tokens	Teachers recorded behavior of class as a whole after giving precise instructions on paying attention. Program led to consistent levels of attention by whole class of 70 to 85 percent with some individuals achieving 100 percent. Procedure made few demands on teacher time or energy.
Humphrey (1978)	Sixth grade	Contract with peer teacher-helper reinforcement	Peer teacher-helper was trained to reinforce a sixth grader, who had very poor attendance record, on the basis of teacher-made contract. Attendance improved to almost 100 percent.
Solomon & Wahler (1973)	Elementary	Peer reinforcement	Peers trained to deliver praise for appropriate behaviors by disruptive boys were able to reduce disruptive activities from 79 percent of the time to 42 percent.
Bologna & Brigham (1978)	Upper elementary	Instruction plus tokens and self-monitoring	Students were instructed, then reinforced for use of new vocabulary words in essays. Tokens were concerned with self-monitoring. Token reinforcement produced more use of new words and better-quality essays.
Harris (1970)	Elementary	Modeling; vicarious reinforcement	Fourth and fifth graders observed models, received reinforcers for sharing. The observers' sharing behavior increased significantly.
O'Leary & Becker (1967)	Elementary	Token system	A token system was used to reduce fighting among elementary-age boys in an adjustment class.

Author(s)	*Subjects' Age Grade Level*	*Technique(s)*	*Processes and Results: Behavior Changes*
Hops & Cobb (1973)	Elementary	Modeling plus praise	Teacher first modeled the asking of relevant questions in a second-grade class where English was the second language of students. She then praised children for asking similar questions of her. Combined techniques produced more gain than either used singly.
Bornstein et al. (1977)	Upper elementary	Assertion training; modeling-rehearsal	A group of eight-to-eleven-year-olds, who were overcooperative, excessively shy, and overconforming, were given nine sessions of assertion training in three weeks. They were given practice sessions with praise for behaving assertively. Significant increases in assertion behavior were obtained and the behavior continued.
Sanson et al. (1978)	Junior high; senior high; adolescents	Token economy plus self-recording	Girls in a delinquency program were reinforced for use of positive language and for making positive comments about other people. Program was highly effective.
Reese et al. (1977)	Junior high	Token economy plus praise and contracts	Program started across entire large urban school in low-income area. It was effective in bringing about increases in attendance, completion of assignments, and grades. Standardized test results did not change, however.
Geller et al. (1978)	Adolescents	Allowed privileges as reinforcers	Eighteen-year-old girl vomited up to seventeen times per day with no detectable organic illness. Hospital staff and family gave girl privileges for eating and taking medication without vomiting. She resumed regular eating pattern after eighteen days of selective reinforcement.
Diament & Colletti (1978)	All levels	Training of parents to use reinforcement	Children were diagnosed as "learning disabled." After eight weeks of training, parents were successful in reducing behavior problems in the home and improving relationships with their children.
Blackman et al. (1976)	All levels	Family contracting "game"	The "game" is played by members of a family with behavior problems. Game teaches family to analyze their problems and to write corrective contracts. A case study is used to illustrate how the game was used to reduce bizarre, disruptive behaviors of a disturbed fourteen-year-old, but it is applicable to other ages and problems.

Other Techniques

Researchers in education and psychology have developed a large number of specialized techniques for behavior management. Many are not suited for classroom use—particularly some developed especially for implementation in psychiatric hospitals—and others are effective only for a very limited group of behaviors ("overcorrection," for example, is an effective technique for reducing some but not all behaviors). Overall, the techniques surveyed in this chapter should be sufficient for most teachers' purposes. Certainly, given teachers' knowledge of the underlying theory, they may develop their own effective approaches to classroom management or adapt those described by others. Readers wishing to expand their knowledge of specific techniques in behavior management should consider further reading (see Gnagey, 1981).

BEHAVIORAL ASSESSMENT AND CLASSROOM MANAGEMENT

Behavioral assessment is a method of judging educational processes and outcomes by systematically recording student behaviors. Behavioral assessment can serve several useful purposes. One positive effect is to focus teacher attention on important educational activities. For example, is in-class participation at an acceptable level? Further, the *systematic* recording of behavior provides a unique data base for making sound decisions in teaching. Data that show less than expected participation or frequent disruptions, for instance, indicate a need for a change in procedures. Also, teachers are now often required to provide evidence of the effectiveness of the methods they use. Behavioral assessment is one way of documenting the results of teaching procedures.

The following are six general rules to consider in planning behavioral assessment.

Pinpoint the behavior so that it can be reliably recorded. Pinpointing means to define the behavior precisely enough so that observers can agree upon and reliably record whether a behavior has occurred.

Use a simple yes-no recording format for continuous activity. Continuous activity is ongoing behavior such as "working on assignments" or "paying attention." If it is occurring when the observation is made, "yes" is marked, and if it is not, "no" is marked. This recording method will give a reliable indication of the occurrence of those behaviors students engage in over fairly long periods of time.

Use a time-sampling procedure for most continuous activities. Time sampling involves making short observations (on the order of ten seconds) at periodic time intervals (say every ten minutes) during classes. Time samples greatly reduce the amount of effort spent in observations. If they are chosen representatively, time-sample observations will provide a reasonably accurate picture of behaviors occurring in the classroom.

Use criterion levels when observing the continuous activity of an entire group. A criterion level is a statement of how many students must be engaging in an activity in order to score it as occurring at acceptable levels. A teacher might score a group of twenty students as satisfactorily "working on assignments during free time," for example, if at least seventeen of the twenty are doing so when monitored.

Use a direct count of behaviors when observing discrete acts. Discrete acts are behaviors that have distinct starting and stopping points close to one another in time. Handing in assignments, arriving to class on time, and interrupting other students are examples of discrete actions that can be directly counted. Usually the count is reported as a rate by relating it to a period of time ("He averaged two fights per day during September").

Use a direct count for disruptive or dangerous behaviors. Following safety rules in the laboratory or shop is of crucial importance to students' well-being, for instance. You would want to record *all* occurrences of unsafe behavior (deviations from rules) to permit a quick assessment of whether changes are needed.

How much behavioral assessment data should you gather? The simplest answer is "Enough to make a decision." Your data gathering need not be an onerous task; it may be quite informal and can be done at convenient intervals or on a time-sample basis. Nonetheless, the data should be accurate, since you will be basing decisions on your findings and since others may be using your records.

Behavioral scientists, of course, use a far more stringent set of standards for behavioral recording than those we have outlined here (Hersen & Barlow, 1976). In behavioral research, there is a need to fulfill the requirements for scientific proof. Most published studies, therefore, meet high standards for reliable recording, sampling methods, and general observational plans. While teachers may wish to use these more precise methods, less formal behavioral recording approaches will generally suffice for classroom purposes.

PRACTICE EXERCISE 10–3
Planning a Behavioral Intervention

As you observe students, you no doubt will see a few students who are unmotivated, unskilled, disinterested, or just plain disruptive! If you were the teacher (or if you happen to *be* the teacher of such a student), how would you intervene to begin to solve the problem?

One good way to begin is with a plan that builds on what you already know about behavioral approaches to classroom management. The form below will help you apply what you know about behavior management to a particular situation. As you recall, it is almost always better to try to *increase* a productive behavior than to attempt to *eliminate* a problem through punishment or some other means.

Your starting point is thus to identify a *positive target behavior* that, if it increases, will begin to solve the problem. For example, a student who participates in class discussions (positive target behavior) or is working steadily (positive target behavior) is less likely to be disruptive or unmotivated. Good luck!

Behavior Change Planning Form

Student's name ____________________ Date ____________________

1. Target Behavior (What student behavior, if it increases, will help eliminate the problem? Be specific.)

____

____

____

____

____

2. Goal of the Intervention (How much of the target behavior do you expect to occur if the intervention is successful?)

____

____

____

____

______________________________________ By ______________
(date)

3. Recording Procedure (When and how will you record the behavior?)

____

____

____

____

4. Antecedents to Prompt Target Behavior (Specify what, how, and when)

____

____

____

____

____

5. Consequences for Target Behavior (Indicate also how and when they will be used)

____

____

____

____

____

6. Relate your plan to one of the behavior interventions discussed in the chapter (such as the Good Behavior Game, individual contracts). How is your intervention like the one discussed and how does it differ?

____

____

____

____

____

SUMMARY

In this chapter we saw that the principles of cognitive, behavioral, and humanistic psychology can be applied to management of classroom behavior. Six general principles of classroom management include meaningful learning activities, supportive classroom environments, the opportunity for successful learning, feedback for learning, sharing decisions with students, and strengthening appropriate behavior. Glasser's success-based approach to classroom management emphasizes the principles of humanistic psychology but is compatible with behavioral psychology. Behavioral procedures involve the teacher's analysis of the antecedents and consequences of behavior in preventing problem behaviors. The principles of rules, praise, and ignore provide the basis for effective means of increasing appropriate behavior and thereby decreasing misbehavior.

When prevention techniques fail, as they sometimes will, several specific techniques are available for teachers: token economies, the Good Behavior Game, group contracts, individual contracts, time-out, and home-based contingencies. Each of these techniques is based on the principles of behavior analysis and each will aid teachers in increasing appropriate behavior while decreasing misbehavior.

Suggested Readings

Glasser, W. *Schools without failure.* New York: Harper & Row, 1969.

This book is specifically written for teachers and parents. It provides an excellent discussion of Glasser's views on classroom management.

Good, T. L., & Brophy, J. E. *Looking in classrooms* (2nd ed.). New York: Harper & Row, 1978.

This book provides excellent coverage of Good and Brophy's research on the differences between effective and ineffective teachers.

Holt, J. *How children fail.* New York: Pitman, 1964.

Holt's book (as well as his 1970 volume What Do I Do Monday?*) provides a humanistic view of the problems of classroom management.*

Kazdin, A. E. *Behavior modification in applied settings.* Homewood, Ill.: Dorsey, 1979.

Kazdin's book is an intermediate-level text on behavior modification procedures.

Walker, J. E., & Shea, T. M. *Behavior modification: A practical approach for educators.* St. Louis, Mo.: Mosby, 1976.

Among the dozens of behavior modification primers written for teachers in the 1970s and 1980s, Walker and Shea's is one of the clearest and most comprehensive.

Comments on Practice Exercise 10–1

Here is our interpretation of the conversation between the teacher and Bill. The numbers are keyed to the teacher's comments.

1. The teacher makes a friendly, personal greeting (Principle 1, Be personal).
2. The teacher avoids being manipulated and suggests an alternative set of actions, indirectly, for improving on the next test (Principle 4, Plan alternative behaviors with students).
3. Oh, oh! The teacher slips a little here and becomes irritated and critical (Principle 7, Do not punish). Also, she refers to past behavior on Bill's part ("Last semester you said the same thing . . .") and violates Principle 2 (Refer only to present behavior).
4. Still a little defensive, the teacher comes back at Bill and violates Principle 7 (Do not punish). However, she then turns things around, pointing toward more productive behaviors (Principle 4, Plan alternative behaviors with students, and possibly Principle 3, stress value judgments by students). She also shows concern for Bill (Principle 1, Be personal).
5. The teacher remains firm.
6. The teacher calls for a value judgment by the student about the fairness of changing a grade (Principle 3, Stress value judgments) and guides the conversation toward planning for the future (Principle 4, Plan alternative behaviors with students).
7. The student is making a form of excuse by shifting the blame from himself. The teacher doesn't accept it (Principle 6, Don't accept excuses) and moves again to planning for the future (Principle 4, Plan alternative behaviors with students).
8. The teacher shows a personal interest in Bill (Principle 1, Be personal) and continues planning activity (Principle 4, Plan alternative behaviors).
9. The teacher draws the student's attention to the consequences of his previous behavior by questioning the outcomes of his method of study for the last exam (Principle 3, Stress value judgments by students).
10. The teacher continues to help the student think about the outcomes of one course of action (Principle 3, Stress value judgments by students) and about planning for the next test (Principle 4, Plan alternative behaviors with students).
11. The teacher shows her interest and commitment to Bill's welfare by offering to review his progress in advance of the test and early enough so that changes can be made in the plan if necessary (Principle 5, Show commitment by checking and reinforcing progress). Student success is the goal!

IMPORTANT EVENTS IN THE HISTORY OF CLASSROOM MANAGEMENT

The literature dealing with the management of student behavior in the classroom is so voluminous that we decided to present a thorough chronology of events in the early years of psychology, followed by only those recent works that have had the most significant impact. A more thorough listing of research articles in classroom management appears in Table 10–1.

Date(s)	*Person(s)*	*Work*	*Impact*
1881	Hall	Harvard University Saturday lectures to teachers	While the behavior of students has been of concern to educators and educational researchers since before the time of Plato, Granville Stanley Hall was the first psychologist to systematically address discipline problems in a formal setting. The success of his lectures led directly to the founding of educational psychology as a distinct discipline.
1882	Hall	"Children's lies"	Hall's paper (later reprinted in the first volume of the *Pedagogical Seminary*) was the first formal publication by a psychologist dealing with discipline problems.
1887	Hall	*American Journal of Psychology*	Hall, who took his doctorate under William James at Harvard (the first doctoral degree in psychology granted in the United States), founded the first American psychological journal. *The American Journal of Psychology* (still being published today), published many of Hall's papers dealing with student behavior.
1891	Hall	*Pedagogical Seminary*	The *Pedagogical Seminary* (now titled the *Journal of Genetic Psychology*) was founded by Hall expressly to provide an outlet for psychological studies of children, including studies of classroom behavior.

Date(s)	*Person(s)*	*Work*	*Impact*
1899	James	*Talks to teachers*	William James, who served as G. S. Hall's major advisor, published his highly popular *Talks to Teachers* in 1899. This book provided a great deal of information on psychological views of the teaching-learning process and specifically offered many ideas on the management of behavior.
1900	Dewey	Presidential address to the American Psychological Association	In John Dewey's speech, which provided great impetus to the overall movement of educational psychology, he noted practical applications of psychology to classroom behavior.
1903	Thorndike	*Educational psychology*	E. L. Thorndike published the first text to be entitled *Educational Psychology,* in which he suggested psychological applications of his theory for the management of student behavior.
1907	Witmer	*Psychological Clinic*	Lightner Witmer's journal *Psychological Clinic* was devoted almost entirely to child study. In the years Witmer published the journal (1907–1925), many articles were devoted to classroom behaviors and their management.
1910	Bagley, Bell, Seashore, & Whipple	*The Journal of Educational Psychology*	W. C. Bagley, J. Carleton Bell, Carl E. Seashore, and Guy Montrose Whipple served as the first editors of the *Journal of Educational Psychology.* While the journal is devoted to all aspects of educational psychology, it has served as one important outlet for research in classroom behavior.
1910	Thorndike	"The contribution of psychology to education"	Thorndike's paper, the opening article of the fledgling *Journal of Educational Psychology,* described the applicability of psychology to the

Date(s)	Person(s)	Work	Impact
			management of classroom behaviors as well as to many other areas.
1912	Jung	*The psychology of the unconscious*	C. G. Jung, who would later work with Sigmund Freud and then break dramatically with him, coined the term *self-actualization.* This term, with highly similar meaning, has been employed by Abraham Maslow and Carl Rogers.
1913	Watson	"Psychology as the behaviorist views it"	J. B. Watson's seminal paper set the stage for the growth of the behavioral movement in the United States. Applications of behavioral psychology to classroom management have been involved in a significant portion of the research in this area.
1913	Thorndike	*Educational psychology* (vols. 1–3)	Thorndike greatly expanded his early textbook *Educational Psychology* in 1913, including his comments about the management of classroom behavior.
1928	Watson	*Psychological care of infant and child*	J. B. Watson's "how-to" book, written for the lay public, stressed how children's behavior could be managed through the applications of behavioral principles.
1938	Skinner	*The behavior of organisms*	B. F. Skinner's book, as we have seen, marked the beginning of contemporary behaviorism and applied behavior analysis.
1942–present	Rogers	*Counseling and psychotherapy*	Carl Rogers's book presented an early view of his theory of the self. His later works further articulated his position leading to the application of humanistic psychology to education.

Date(s)	*Person(s)*	*Work*	*Impact*
1949	Fuller	"Operant conditioning of a vegetative human organism"	While studies demonstrating the applicability of classical conditioning to human behavior date back to Watson, P. R. Fuller's paper (despite its unsavory title) describes the first account of the application of operant principles to alter human behavior.
1953	Skinner	*Science and human behavior*	Skinner's book set the tone for the contemporary adaptation of behavioral psychology to education.
1956	Azrin & Lindsley	"The reinforcement of cooperation between children"	Nathan Azrin and Ogden Lindsley's paper is frequently cited as one of the first operant studies to examine behavior problems in a realistic educational setting.
1958	Page	"Teacher comments and student performance: A seventy-four classroom experiment on school motivation"	While the title of Ellis B. Page's paper is evocative of the content of our motivation chapter, his report was clearly a study of the effects of teacher behavior on student behavior. Page demonstrated, through a massive analysis of classroom behavior, how closely student behavior is linked to teacher-provided consequences.
1963	Bijou & Baer	"Some methodological contributions for a functional analysis of child development"	This review by Sidney Bijou and Donald Baer described many of the potential applications of operant psychology to student behavior.
1964	Harris, Wolf, & Baer	"Effects of adult social reinforcement on child behavior"	The research presented in this paper provided the foundation for future applications of social reinforcement in behavior-change procedures.
1964–present	Holt	Humanistic approaches to education	John Holt, through several very insightful books (*How Children Fail, What Do I Do Monday?*), became a major spokesperson for humanistic approaches to education.

Date(s)	*Person(s)*	*Work*	*Impact*
1967	Becker, Madsen, Arnold, & Thomas	"The contingent use of teacher attention and praise in reducing classroom behavior problems"	This study represents an early report of classroom contingency management. Many varieties of contingency management programs have been employed since 1967 (see Table 10–1).
1968–present	Many individuals	*Journal of Applied Behavior Analysis*	The *Journal of Applied Behavior Analysis (JABA)* has been the major outlet for classroom management research since its foundation. It was the first journal devoted solely to the experimental analysis of human behavior and led directly to the explosion of behaviorally oriented research in classroom management (see Table 10–1).
1968	Skinner	*The technology of teaching*	Skinner's book was an important popularization of the application of behavioral principles to education.
1968	Baer, Wolf, & Risely	"Some current dimensions of applied behavior analysis"	This paper was a state-of-the-art summary of the application of behavioral principles to human behavior. With the publication of this paper, Donald Baer, Montrose Wolf, and Todd Risely (all editors of *JABA* at one time or another) essentially set the tone for the next fifteen years of applied behavioral analysis research.
1969–present	Glasser	*Schools without failure*	William Glasser's book has had a continuing, significant impact through the many workshops and training institutes that Glasser and his foundation sponsor. In general, his principles are primarily humanistic, but quite compatible with behavioral approaches. Many school systems have systematically applied Glasser's techniques to equip their teachers with better classroom management skills.

Date(s)	*Person(s)*	*Work*	*Impact*
1974–present	Gordon	*Teacher effectiveness training*	Thomas Gordon's teacher effectiveness training, a derivative of his earlier parent effectiveness training, has been another popular approach to classroom management. In his 1974 book, he characterized his approach as humanistic. Like Glasser's method, Gordon's approach has also been propagated primarily through workshops and training institutes.
1977–present	Many individuals	*Education and Training of Children*	This journal, growing out of the now defunct *School Applications of Learning Theory,* is devoted solely to the application of behavioral techniques to classroom management. To the greatest extent possible, the editors have emphasized research generated by classroom teachers themselves.
1980	Gallup	"The 12th annual Gallup poll of the public's attitude toward the public schools"	In this national survey of the public's feelings about education, discipline continued to be rated as the major problem in education, despite recent advances in classroom management.

Part Three

PLANNING FOR MEANINGFUL LEARNING

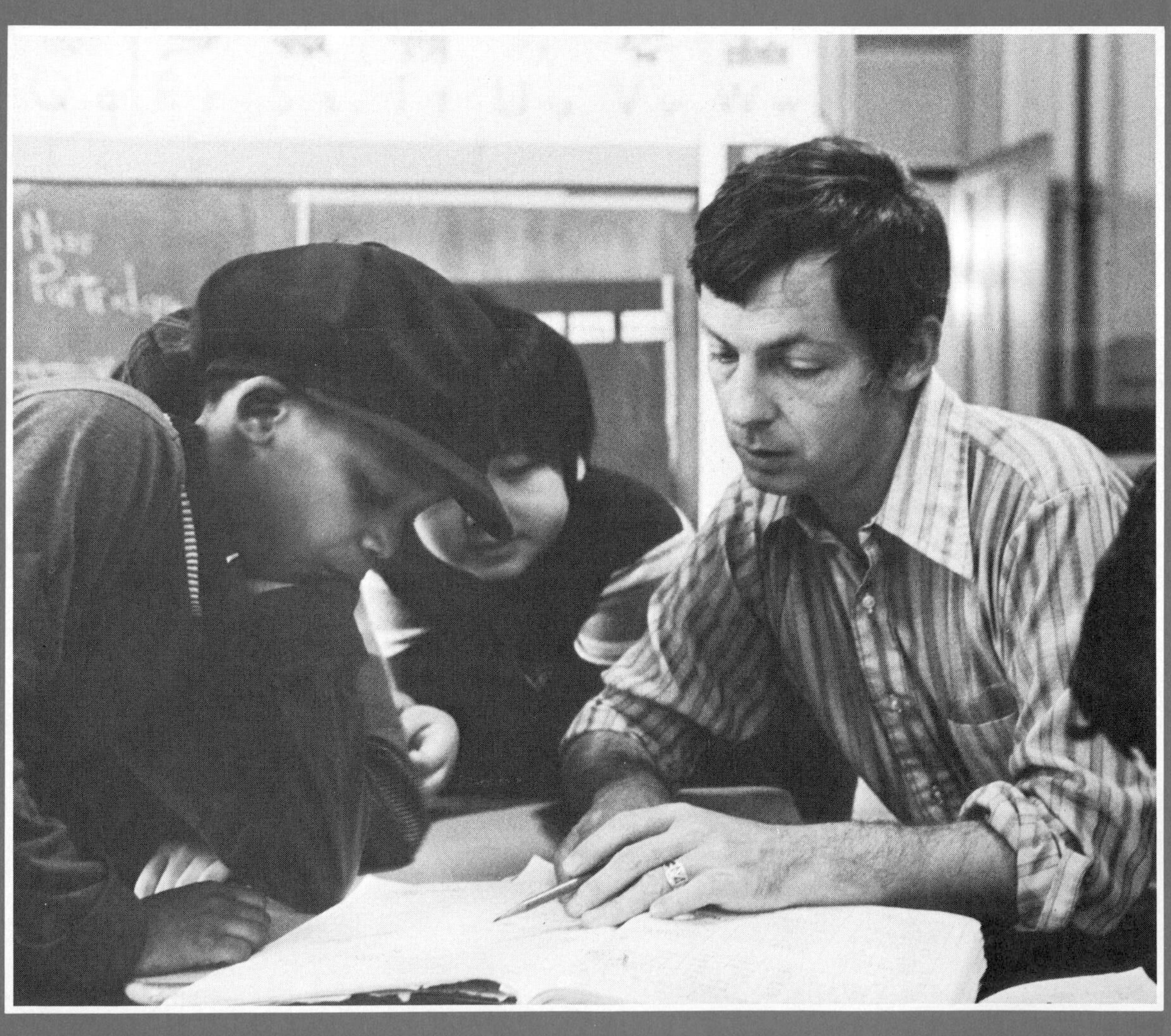

In the previous two sections of this book we examined two major views of how students learn—cognitive and behavioral. Both views are necessary to deal with the full range of a teacher's responsibilities, but by themselves they are not sufficient to ensure effective instruction. Teachers must be able to employ their own knowledge to develop meaningful learning activities. Part Three is designed to help you apply the principles of learning to your classroom instruction. Chapter Eleven, "Instructional Goals and Objectives," describes the process of formulating and communicating objectives to your students in ways that will enhance their learning. Chapter Twelve, "Task Analysis," is specifically designed to help you appropriately sequence instruction and to identify meaningful learning activities for students. Because the content in both Chapters Eleven and Twelve relates to instructional applications, separate "Teaching Applications" sections have not been included.

Chapter Eleven

INSTRUCTIONAL GOALS AND OBJECTIVES

As you begin planning for teaching, you will have to come to grips with two crucial questions: What will the goals of your instruction be and how will you clearly communicate these goals to your students? The research on effective teaching has shown that one significant difference between effective and ineffective teachers is how well they convey goals and expectations to students (Brophy & Evertson, 1976, 1981; Good & Grouws, 1979). This chapter will help you master these important skills.

Objectives

After reading this chapter, you should be able to meet the following objectives.

1. Identify correctly and incorrectly written instructional objectives.
2. Correctly write cognitive objectives at six levels of learning.
3. Correctly write psychomotor objectives.
4. Correctly write affective objectives.

EDUCATIONAL GOALS

The basic reason we provide instruction for people is to meet *educational goals*—those statements that describe "human activities which contribute to the functioning [of] society" (Gagné & Briggs, 1979, p. 20). There are obviously many things people must be able to do to help a society work smoothly. General abilities such as reading, writing, and arithmetic are recognized as important for everyone. More specific skills such as building bridges, repairing cars, and writing books are also important functions that people must perform. The goals we work toward in schools, whether for basic reading competence in the elementary grades or for sophisticated mathematics skills in the secondary grades, almost always are designed to enhance the functioning of society (Gagné & Briggs, 1979).

As you decide on the educational goals you will emphasize in your teaching, you will draw on your knowledge of how students learn, ideas about what students will need for success in subsequent courses, your concept of what students will be doing when they leave school, your own interests and values, a sense of society's needs, and tradition. Many of these goals will be explicitly stated in textbooks, curriculum guides, school regulations, and the like. Let's take a look at some representative goals taken from curriculum guides and see how they might fit into teaching.

> The students will understand our democratic government.
>
> The students will develop the abilities to solve mathematical problems encountered in day-to-day life.
>
> The students will enjoy reading.
>
> The students will protect our environment.

As you can see, these goals are very general statements describing what students should achieve after fairly extended periods of time (anytime from one semester to twelve years). They state what students will work toward, and they may guide both instruction and the student's learning.

There are some problems involved in developing instructional activities directly from such educational goals, however. Let's take the goals one at a time and see what they communicate to us.

The students will understand our democratic government. What exactly does *understand* mean? If this were one of your goals for students, you would need to determine just how to structure your lessons so that they would improve students' understanding according to your best professional estimate of what this term means.

The students will develop the abilities to solve mathematical problems encountered in day-to-day life. This seems to be somewhat less ambiguous. But what are the mathematical abilities necessary to deal with everyday life? Students ought to be able to count, add and subtract, divide and multiply, figure percentages, use decimals, use fractions, and solve for an unknown. Hmm. Do they really have to be able to do all these things? If so, *how well* must they be able to do them? Again, the answer must be determined by you, the teacher.

The students will enjoy reading. Obviously, having the students enjoy reading is a desirable goal. Again, however, the goal needs to be translated into a more specific form. Looking at it another way, what can you do to help students attain this goal and how will you know when they have done so? Once again it is you, the teacher, who must make the decisions.

The students will protect the environment. Having the students protect the environment also seems to be a very worthwhile goal but it also, no doubt, needs clarification. What will your students do to protect the environment? You must determine what this goal will mean in the daily classroom experience of your students.

The general point is that goals, while they are useful guides for teachers and students, are often not specific enough to help teachers design instruction or to give much direction to student learning. More specific statements—instructional objectives—are needed to formulate classroom experiences. The development of instructional objectives is a necessary step in translating educational goals into reality (Burns, 1977).

INSTRUCTIONAL OBJECTIVES

Instructional objectives are explicit statements of what students will be able to do as a result of instruction. They differ from goals because they are usually designed to guide instruction and learning over short periods of time (typically ranging from one class period to a few weeks). Unlike goals, they are written to be unambiguous. Educational goals

Instructional objectives help guide student efforts. Because she has a clear idea of what she is to do, this girl is able to work steadily on her own.

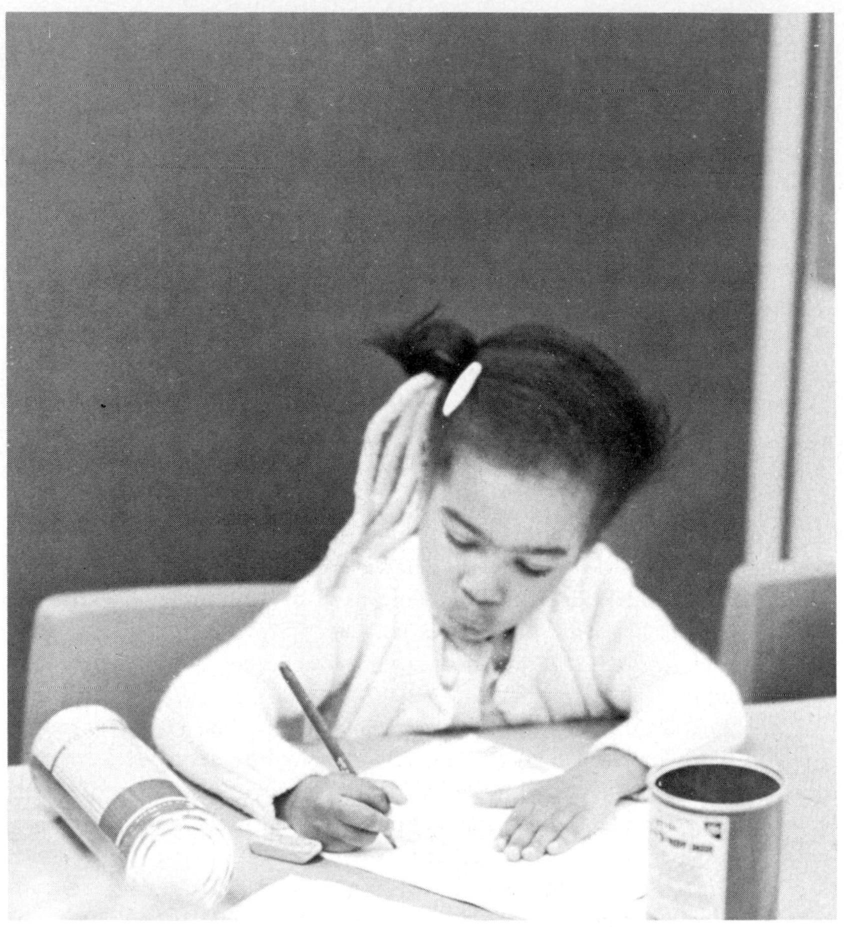

must be broadly stated because we recognize that teachers will adapt their instruction to fit their specific teaching situations. In contrast, teachers generally write instructional objectives themselves based on curriculum guides, text materials, and so on, and prepare them to fit the needs of their own students.

Instructional objectives can be used for several purposes, including (1) helping students achieve educational goals, (2) planning for daily instruction, (3) providing a basis for the assessment of student learning, and (4) providing criteria for the assessment of teaching effectiveness (Mager, 1962).

Suppose that we were working on the educational goal "The students will understand our democratic government." Obviously many, many things would be required of students to meet this goal. An example of one instructional objective that could be taken from this goal is "The students will be able to describe the three branches of the federal government." This objective directs us to teach facts about the separation of powers in the judicial, legislative, and executive branches of the federal government. The objective also gives us a criterion for determining whether such learning has occurred. Either students can describe the three branches of government or they cannot.

Suppose we were then to assess the mastery of this objective with some questions on an in-class examination, and no students could answer them correctly. Further suppose that the students all did fairly well on every other question. Evidently, something went wrong and somehow we didn't teach what we thought we were teaching. On the other hand, if every student had done well on those questions and we had known that they hadn't mastered the material prior to our instruction, then we would have reason to believe that we had done an effective job of teaching.

The objectives we derive from educational goals indicate the skills and knowledge that we want students to master as part of the attainment of each goal. When students master our objectives, we can be as certain as is possible in education that they are progressing toward the educational goals and that we and our students are succeeding.

There are many different names for statements that are generally referred to as "objectives," including "terminal behavior objectives" (Burns, 1977), "behavioral objectives" (Vargas, 1972), "performance objectives" (Gagné & Briggs, 1979), and "instructional objectives" (Mager, 1962), to name only a few. We have chosen to follow the lead of Mager (1962) and refer to our objectives as instructional objectives. As Mehrens and Lehmann (1978) have noted, "stating objectives in behavioral terms is absolutely mandatory if we are to evaluate those objectives" (p. 36). Thus our emphasis in this chapter is on instructional objectives that specify behavioral outcomes.

Components of Instructional Objectives

Instructional objectives have three necessary components (Mager, 1962): an active verb, criteria for performance, and a description of the conditions under which the learning will be assessed. We will look at each of these three components in turn and see why each is important in a good instructional objective.

Action Verbs. The verb that is chosen for an instructional objective is crucial. As we stated earlier, learning can only be inferred from behavior. So the verb we choose must describe the behavior that will tell us that the learning we specified has occurred. This means that the verb must describe a behavior that is observable and measurable. Only action verbs fall into this category (Burns, 1977; Mehrens & Lehmann, 1978).

In order to demonstrate just how important the choice of verbs is in writing objectives, we will consider some verbs taken from objectives that do not clearly specify the behaviors expected of students. Remember the teacher who wanted you to "understand" the causes of the American Revolution? Wasn't it frustrating when you then took an exam on this unit and were expected to "list five causes"? Or how about hearing that the only objective was that you "appreciate Shakespeare" at the end of a literature class? Remember how it took 190 out of 200 correct matches of quotations to characters for you to have "appreciated Shakespeare" enough to earn an A? Or how about the all-time favorite, "be aware of"? Sadly, "be aware of" almost always turned into "define" on a test.

Just what does all this mean? Your instructional objectives must be clear to *all* students. The verb you use in an instructional objective is a key component of clear communication (Vargas, 1972). If you are planning to use a multiple-choice or true-and-false test to evaluate your students' abilities to recognize new concepts, why tell them you want them to "appreciate," "understand," "be aware," or "know"? If you want them to recognize, say so. A clearly stated objective might say, "In a set of ten sentences, students will be able to recognize each instance that verb number is not in agreement with the subject of the sentence." The objective tells the students exactly what you expect. They will be able to better prepare for tests and you will be able to plan more effective instruction. Objectives that specify student behaviors using action verbs such as "construct," "compare and contrast," "define," and "describe" allow you to say exactly what you mean. If you ask students to list ten metallic elements you can see how to teach for this outcome, how to evaluate student learning (either they can list them or some part of them or they cannot), and students can see exactly how to prepare.

We do not say that words like "appreciate," "understand," and "be aware of" do not indicate good outcomes for your students. In fact, we expect you to "appreciate" the benefits of using good instructional objectives. Both the communication of expectations and the evaluation of learning, however, are enhanced through the use of more specific action verbs.

Criteria. The second major component of instructional objectives, criteria, describes the level of performance you expect from students (Burns, 1977; Mager, 1962). If students are to discuss a topic, how many points must they include? How long should their answer be? Is there some particular order in which they should present ideas? Does neatness count? What or how much will you tell students you expect to see in their behavior? In short, *how good is good enough?*

Anytime you develop an instructional objective you should also determine the quality of student responses that will be acceptable. Giving

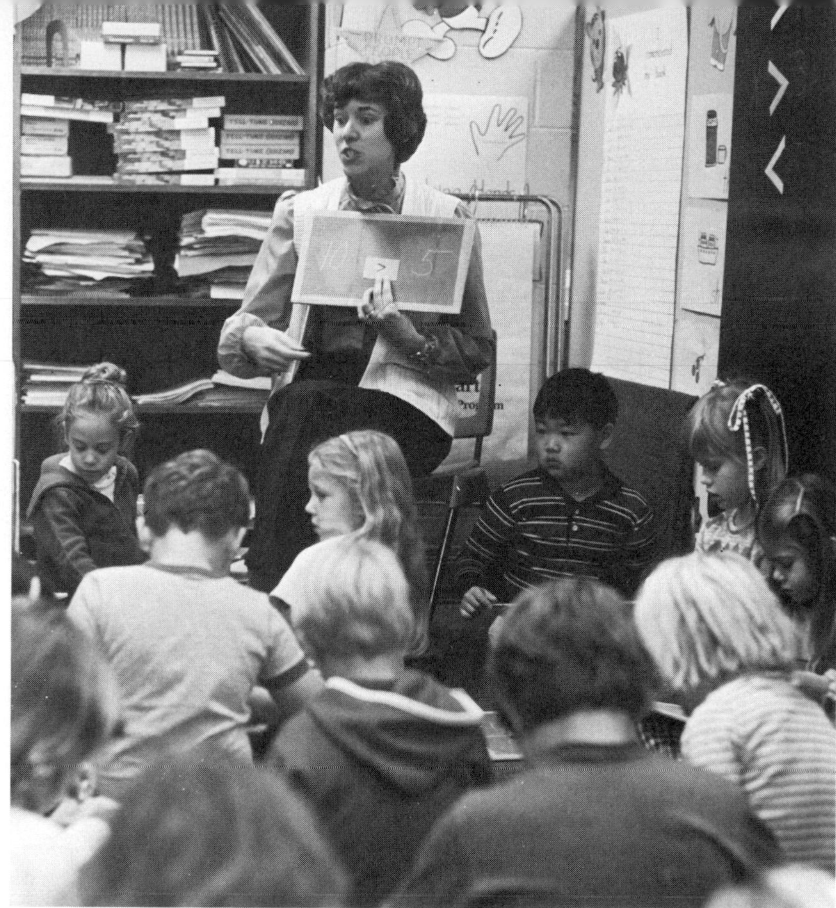

Instructional objectives must be clear to all students. Students who know the objectives for learning will progress much more rapidly than those who don't.

students the criteria on which their performance will be judged will help them prepare, it will help you plan your instruction, and it will certainly guide your evaluation.

Conditions of Assessment. The third component of good instructional objectives is an indication of the conditions under which students' performances will be evaluated (Mager, 1962; Vargas, 1972). Imagine that an objective asks you to list and describe five major causes of World War II. Would you prepare differently for this assignment if you were to be assessed on an essay exam in class, to take an oral exam in the instructor's office, to present your response as a speech to an American foreign policy seminar in which the secretary of state was a participant, or to take an at-home, open-book exam? Every person we have ever asked has said, "Yes, I would prepare quite differently." Describing the conditions of assessment also helps you plan your instructional activities, your means of assessing the students, and it certainly helps students prepare (Mehrens & Lehmann, 1978).

PRACTICE EXERCISE 11–1

Identifying Good and Poor Instructional Objectives

We have listed ten instructional objectives below. Read each one carefully and determine whether it is properly written. If it is improperly written, write on a separate sheet of paper a brief statement telling why, and rewrite it properly.

1. The students will develop an awareness of the influence of the Spanish culture on the American Southwest. An essay examination in class will be used to assess their learning.
2. On a short-answer examination, students will correctly define the concept of alliteration and write three examples they have seen in current magazines.
3. When dissecting a frog, the students will identify organs of the digestive system.
4. The students must really know the multiplication tables for an in-class oral quiz tomorrow.
5. The students will conceptualize two higher-order forms of problem solving to be brought to bear on tomorrow's laboratory experiment.

TYPES OF OBJECTIVES

Teachers help students acquire a wide range of skills and knowledge. On any given day a high school student may learn things as diverse as a new principle in mathematics, how to operate a machine, and a new attitude toward a different culture. These kinds of learning differ greatly from each other, and these differences have formed the basis for systems for classifying objectives. Such systems provide distinctions that are helpful in writing objectives as well as in devising methods of instruction and evaluation.

While many classifications of objectives have been put forward over the years, the most widely accepted has been a taxonomy of educational objectives (*taxonomy* is another way of saying "classification system") developed by Benjamin Bloom and his associates (Bloom, 1964; Bloom, Englehart, Furst, Hill, & Krathwohl, 1956). Bloom's taxonomy, as it is known, classified objectives into three major domains (categories) of learning: cognitive, psychomotor, and affective. **Cognitive objectives,** as you might guess from the first section of this text, specify processes that are primarily related to intellectual activities, such as defining,

6. The students must have a firm grasp of elementary algebra. They will have to demonstrate their knowledge on an in-class examination and score at least 70 for their performance to be acceptable.
7. When presented flash cards of words containing the letter combination *ph,* the students will correctly pronounce the words in eighteen of twenty instances.
8. The students must remember the major reasons for the downfall of the Roman Empire. They will have to know them for tomorrow's quiz.
9. Given a fifty-word speed test in class, the students will type at a rate not less than ten words per minute with fewer than two errors.
10. Given a worksheet containing twenty addition problems requiring regrouping, the students will correctly solve seventeen during class.

Now that you have responded to each of these objectives, compare your answers to ours at the end of the chapter.

evaluating, recognizing, and reasoning. A teacher helping students learn a new concept or principle is trying to assist them in meeting a cognitive objective. **Psychomotor objectives** describe skilled physical movements such as those required in typing, operating machinery, and playing a musical instrument. Students learning to operate a lathe, for example, are attempting to master several psychomotor objectives. **Affective objectives** deal with feelings, attitudes, values, and preferences. An example of an affective objective is to develop a respect for another culture's way of life.

Very few of the things we expect students to learn are contained exclusively in one of the three domains of objectives. When students learn to operate a machine, for example, they not only learn skilled physical movements but also a set of facts and rules governing the use of the machine. Likewise, when students learn to respect another culture, they learn some basic facts about that culture. Even "purely" cognitive processes have some affective components, for example, when students enjoy solving difficult math problems. Despite the fact that cognitive, psychomotor, and affective learning often occur together, it is helpful to examine each domain separately in order to formulate specific objectives.

Psychomotor objectives describe skilled physical movements. Many important objectives fall into the psychomotor domain.

Cognitive Objectives

Cognitive objectives specify behaviors that can be used to infer changes in students' cognition. Bloom's taxonomy (1956) describes six major levels into which cognitive objectives may be classified: knowledge, comprehension, application, analysis, synthesis, and evaluation (see Table 11–1). We will examine each in turn.

Knowledge. The first of the six levels of learning Bloom discusses is knowledge. Knowledge-level learning is the ability to recall or identify information (Bloom et al., 1956). We referred to this as rote learning in Chapter 3. A question such as "What is the capital of Connecticut?" requires learning at the knowledge level. Students need not understand anything about capitals in order to demonstrate knowledge-level learning about capitals. They only need to be able to recall a term ("Hartford") or other information.

An example of a knowledge-level objective is "On an in-class quiz, the students will be able to write the names of the capitals of at least ten states." As you can see, knowledge-level objectives may require only the most rudimentary learning. Some, however, can be very complex (such as memorization of the periodic table of elements). Whether they are simple or complex, it is relatively easy to assess students' mastery of such objectives. Either the students can or cannot perform the behaviors called for in the objectives.

Comprehension. Comprehension-level learning is more complex. Comprehension of information requires that a student put information into his or her own words (Bloom et al., 1956). Answering a question such as "Describe the geographical areas of the state of Tennessee in your own words" requires comprehension-level learning, as does an objective such as "On a take-home essay, the students will accurately portray the

TABLE 11–1
Acceptable Verbs for Use in Instructional Objectives at the Six Levels of Bloom's Taxonomy

Level of Learning	*Acceptable Verbs*
Knowledge	Define, distinguish, identify, recall, recognize
Comprehension	Conclude, demonstrate, differentiate, draw, explain, give in your own words, illustrate, interpret, predict, rearrange, reorder, rephrase, represent, restate, transfer, translate
Application	Apply, classify, develop, employ, generalize, organize, relate, restructure, transfer, use
Analysis	Analyze, categorize, compare, contrast, deduce, detect
Synthesis	Combine, constitute, derive, document, formulate, modify, organize, originate, produce, relate, specify, synthesize, tell, transmit, write
Evaluation	Appraise, argue, assess, decide, evaluate, judge, standardize, validate

Source: Based on a more detailed table by Metfessel, Michael, & Kirsner in "Instrumentation of Bloom's and Krathwohl's taxonomies for the writing of behavioral objectives." *Psychology in the Schools,* 1969, 6, 227–231.

plot of *The Velveteen Rabbit* in their own words." In knowledge-level learning, understanding is not necessarily required. In comprehension-level learning, students must understand concepts and principles and demonstrate this understanding by explaining the ideas in their own words.

Application. Application-level learning is still more complex. Application requires that a student use an abstraction in a concrete context (Bloom et al., 1956). A question such as "Given the following components of a chemical solution, determine its boiling point" requires application-level learning, as would the request "Given the proper equipment, take an accurate blood pressure reading from a patient." Students must be able to *use* concepts and principles (knowledge about solutions and boiling points or knowledge about taking blood pressures) in an applied problem.

Application objectives are an important aim for instruction for most teachers. An example of an application-level objective is "In the lab period, the students will perform a titration and determine the acidity of their test solution within $\pm .04$ pH." Other examples are "Given an array of circles, the students will correctly compute the area of five of them" and "Given specifications from a mechanic's manual and appropriate tools, students will set the correct gap for spark plugs on five different American engines within $\pm .001$ inch."

Analysis. Analysis-level learning requires complex cognitive activity. In analysis, students must be able to break down information into its component parts so that the relationship between all the components is clear (Bloom et al., 1956). A two-part question based on the novel *Watership Down* that would require analysis-level learning is "List and describe each of the forces acting on Hazel, the hero, that caused him to leave his original warren (a home for rabbits). What parts of Hazel's plans were based on Fiver's special skill?" (Fiver could see the future, especially to predict danger.) This question requires both comprehension (to answer the first part) and then analysis (to answer the second part). For students to analyze the situation they have to be able to comprehend it first. Thus, in Bloom's taxonomy learning is seen as *hierarchical;* higher levels of learning are built on lower levels.

Good analysis-level objectives are hard to write and this is one reason they are sometimes neglected. Additionally, analysis can sometimes be confused with knowledge or comprehension. For example, if a teacher had discussed in class the parts of Hazel's plans that were based on Fiver's skill, the students could have memorized the information and given it back word for word in their answers. You must be sure that you avoid confusion and structure situations so that the analytic thinking required in an analysis-level objective is clear. Other examples of such analysis-level objectives are "In a five-page paper, the students will identify the limits placed on the executive and legislative branches by the judicial branch of the federal government" and "Given a sample of water from the Obion River, students in the chemistry laboratory will identify at least two major pollutants deriving from industrial sources."

Synthesis. Synthesis-level learning requires that students put together old knowledge in new ways (Bloom et al., 1956). Synthesis is closely related to the processes of creativity we discussed in Chapter Six. It involves the analysis and recombination of bits of knowledge to develop

Synthesis requires originality from students.

a structure or pattern that the students did not have prior to learning. A question that requires synthesis is "Using your knowledge about the geography and climate of Peru, write an essay describing the kinds of agricultural industries likely to exist there." Such a question demands more than simply describing or analyzing what the student knows about Peru. Facts about Peru must be recombined in a way that answers a question for which students previously had no answer. If the teacher has already given students some information about Peru's agricultural industries, such a question would really sample nothing more than knowledge- or comprehension-level learning. Synthesis requires original thinking from students—they must generate the knowledge they are asked for based on facts and principles they have learned.

Generally, synthesis objectives briefly describe the information available to students and then require the students to reorganize and extend this information. An example of a synthesis-level objective is "Given a description of the conditions on the planet Venus, the students will write a short story describing the ways in which explorers on the surface of Venus would live. Students must include descriptions of at least six problems and possible solutions." Again, you should carefully note this objective would involve only comprehension if the students had previously learned how someone would live on Venus. Criteria are hard to set for synthesis objectives because subjective judgments are often required. If grades were to be assigned to the short stories about life on Venus, for example, the subjective judgment of the teacher is needed to evaluate students' attainment of the objective.

Evaluation. Evaluation-level learning is the most complex of all. Evaluation requires that students make judgments based on their knowledge about the *value* of methods and materials for some purposes (Bloom et al., 1956). An evaluation-level question is "Ed must construct a model of an island and an ocean to demonstrate tides to his science class. Ed doesn't have much money and he has only two days to build his model. Which of the following materials would be best suited for his model and why?" To answer such a question, students must be able to make judgments about each of the materials listed, determine which are the best for Ed's situation, and write a statement telling why.

Evaluation objectives ask students to make judgments based on their knowledge, and they frequently ask students to justify their decisions. Criteria tend to be qualitative and subjectively judged. An example of an evaluation-level objective is "Given the performance specifications for three automobiles and information about a hypothetical family, the students will decide which automobile would be the most appropriate for that family's use."

Objectives at Different Levels. The most important effect of the taxonomy of educational objectives has been to increase the emphasis given to higher-level cognitive activities. In spite of this, however, far too much emphasis still continues to be given to the less complex forms of learning. Trachtenburg (1974), for example, performed an analysis of *all* the test items, study questions, objectives, exercises, and suggested activities in nine recent sets of world history textbooks along with the teachers' manuals, workbooks, and test booklets that accompanied them. Of the 61,000 items he identified, more than 95 percent demanded only knowledge- or comprehension-level learning from students.

All teachers, of course, will include some knowledge- and comprehension-level objectives for their students, but they should also emphasize more complex learning. Most teachers feel that a balance of objectives across the six levels of learning enhances the effectiveness of instruction. As you will see in Chapter Fourteen, a table of specifications can help you plan for the higher levels of learning you will want your students to achieve (see pages 417–418).

Psychomotor Objectives

Psychomotor objectives are statements describing physical actions students are to perform. There is a cognitive component of most psychomotor objectives, but their basic purpose is to describe physical behavior (Kapfer & Ovard, 1971). We tend to separate cognitive and psychomotor objectives because they usually require quite different practice conditions. The outcomes of cognitive learning are ordinarily inferred from verbal behavior while in psychomotor learning changes in the speed, accuracy, integration, and coordination of body movements are directly observed.

Psychomotor objectives contain the same three components as other objectives—an action verb, criteria for performance, and conditions of assessment—as in the objective, "Given a hammer, a tenpenny nail, and a one-inch plank, students will drive the nail in five blows without bending it or marring the wood." Another psychomotor objective is "During the class period students will demonstrate the correct operation of a wood lathe." This example illustrates an important difference between many psychomotor objectives and cognitive objectives. Teachers tend to use terms like *correctly, appropriately,* or *efficiently* in writing psychomotor objectives because describing exactly what the "correct" procedure is would require so many words that the objective could end up being several paragraphs long. Imagine writing a detailed description of the "correct" way to hold a paper and pencil, place one's fingers on an oboe, or hit a baseball. "Correct" is usually specified by demonstration

PRACTICE EXERCISE 11–2
Identifying Levels of Learning

Below is a set of twelve statements taken from objectives. We have omitted conditions and criteria. Read each statement and decide which level of learning it requires. Write your answer in the blank underneath each item.

1. Using a flame test, find the unknown in a chemical solution.

   ____

2. Name the fifty states of the Union.

   ____

3. Describe in your own words the three major causes of the War of 1812.

   ____

4. Given a news editorial about compulsory military service, students can detect those statements that reflect the writer's opinion regarding the rights of individuals versus the rights of the state.

   ____

5. Write an essay in which you judge which of the three methods of distillation would be safest and most efficient for the separation of benzene from carbon tetrachloride.

   ____

6. Given the characteristics of a species of antelope and the habits of wolves in an adjoining area, write an essay describing the possible effects of wolf predation on the antelope species after three seasons.

   ____

and description. In other words, the teacher shows students the "correct" way, describes the "correct" way, and helps students make at least one "correct" response by talking or guiding them through the movement, as we saw in the sections on modeling in Chapter Eight. "Correct," therefore, is the way the task is modeled for the students. Many teachers, in fact, write psychomotor objectives that specify "as demonstrated in class" or "as illustrated in the film" to guide students in seeing what is expected of them.

When we discuss task description in the next chapter we will see how teachers may prepare materials for students so that any confusion or

7. Given a description of salt marsh ecosystems, write a statement summarizing the probable effects of an oil spill on avian life.

____

8. Given a recording of an oboe quartet, students will identify and notate the melody line and the countermelody.

____

9. Define *perspective* in your own words.

____

10. Identify the places on the street that have been designated as the right places for crossing.

____

11. Using the criteria discussed in class for a news article, categorize each of the three following news articles and write a statement telling which is the best, which is the worst, and why.

____

12. Employ the principles of nutrition and the following list of foods to plan three menus for well-balanced meals.

____

You may check your responses against the ones we present at the end of the chapter.

ambiguity about the use of "correct" can be reduced. A description of the sequence of steps in any psychomotor activity may be prepared and given to students to use as a guide in learning an activity. Teachers can also use these descriptions to guide instruction and evaluate students' learning.

Affective Objectives

Affective objectives are statements of how we want our students to *feel* about things after a period of instruction (Gagné, 1977). They are a critical dimension of learning in any class. What reading teacher would not want his students to "enjoy reading"? What science teacher would

Teachers should be concerned with affective objectives.

not want her students to be interested in "preserving the environment"? In fact, all teachers want their students to value, prefer, and be interested in the things they are taught.

Very often educational goals point directly to attitudes such as "appreciate" or "enjoy." There are some problems with this, as we saw when we tried to define such vague verbs earlier in the chapter. Another problem concerns the *use* of affective objectives. Suppose two high school students have identical averages on cognitive and psychomotor learning in one of their classes. Do teachers have the right to grade a student down because he or she "has a bad attitude" toward what was taught? It seems clear that teachers have the right and duty to evaluate cognitive and psychomotor learning for formal reports or grades. Do you have the same responsibilities for evaluating students' affective learning?

We suggest that teachers use affective objectives but that they not use them to determine grades. When we teach educational psychology, we feel that we should teach it so that students enjoy it. Our desire is that students continue to study in the area and use the techniques they've learned. What value are teachers to their students if they do not believe that students should enjoy, appreciate, or like what is taught?

Writing Affective Objectives. When writing affective objectives you should state one additional component—the affect (feelings, attitudes, and the like) that the teacher is trying to obtain. The other components—an action verb, the criteria, and the description of the conditions under which the behavior will be assessed—remain the same. Below are some examples of affective objectives that contain all four components.

> During the first semester, the students will voluntarily check out two or more books of their own choice from the school library as an indication of their enjoyment of reading.
>
> During the semester the students will make one or more unprompted comments per class period about pollution of the environment to indicate an appreciation of ecological concerns.
>
> In interactions with the teacher, the students will decrease the number of negative comments they make about themselves as an indication of a more positive self-concept.

These three objectives define affect as a set of behaviors. Each objective, however, is only one of many possible objectives for a particular affective state. The behaviors you select should be the ones you feel are most important. In other words, you want to choose behaviors such that a change in your students' behavior will indicate that your affective objective has been reached.

PRACTICE EXERCISE 11–3
Writing Instructional Objectives

Below is a list of three general educational goals. Choose one that strikes your interest and write one cognitive objective at each of Bloom's levels of learning, two psychomotor objectives, and two affective objectives relating to the goal. To check your responses, carefully examine the checklist we provide at the end of the chapter. If you have trouble, reread the chapter and try another of the three goals listed below.

Goal 1. Develop an appreciation of and a respect for the role of the fine arts in our cultural heritage.
Goal 2. Develop a positive attitude toward maintaining one's own physical, mental, and emotional health.
Goal 3. Develop a concern for measures that conserve our nation's energy reserves.

CAUTIONS IN USING OBJECTIVES

The truism that anytime you get something, you have to give something also holds for instructional objectives. We have stressed the very real advantages of using objectives, as any teacher who systematically uses them can attest. There are, however, certain costs associated with the use of objectives, and you should be familiar with them.

First, it is difficult to write good objectives. You will need to devote much time and thought to the development of objectives. Second, there is a tendency among some teachers to trivialize their courses by using too many cognitive objectives written at a knowledge or comprehension level (Eisner, 1967). Third, our experience is that students who have been given objectives tend to control teachers so that they stay "on the subject." When you use objectives you run the risk of losing a part of your flexibility. Fourth, although student mastery of objectives will increase, may studies have indicated that the learning of information not directly mentioned in the objectives may decrease (see Faw & Waller, 1976, for a review). In other words, students *will* concentrate on the learning described by your objectives but they will also pay less attention to learning material not covered by objectives.

Most closely controlled studies of objectives have examined their effects on student comprehension of reading materials. In a typical study some groups of students read passages with objectives while others read the same passages without objectives. The students' comprehension of what they read is then examined, usually by multiple-choice tests on the reading materials. The reading comprehension scores are broken into two categories, intentional learning (the learning specified by the objectives) and incidental learning (material not mentioned in the objectives).

An overwhelming number of these studies have shown that intentional learning is superior for students who are supplied with objectives (see Jenkins & Neisworth, 1973; Lawson, 1974), but incidental learning scores may be *lower* than those attained by students not receiving the objectives (see Frase & Kreitzberg, 1975; Gagné & Rothkopf, 1975). Nonetheless, Kaplan and his colleagues (Kaplan, 1974; Kaplan & Rothkopf, 1974; Kaplan & Simmons, 1974; Rothkopf & Kaplan, 1972) have collected data indicating that evenly distributed, specific, and briefly stated objectives result in heightened levels of intentional learning without adversely affecting incidental learning.

Not all the research on objectives in reading passages has shown positive effects of instructional objectives. Duell (1974), Jenkins and Deno (1971), and Petersen, Ronning, and Glover (in press), for example, found that objectives had no facilitative effect on learning from reading passages. The majority of studies, however, directly support the use of objectives to facilitate intentional learning, and apparently this can be done without sacrificing incidental learning.

Some investigators have argued that rigid adherence to objectives may cause the loss of one of the richest experiences for students—the unexpected happening. In general, however, we believe that the advantages of instructional objectives far outweigh the disadvantages. Good evaluation *requires* specification of objectives (Mehrens & Lehmann, 1978). The effort you devote to developing objectives can reduce the work and uncertainty involved in deciding what and how to teach, as we will see in the next chapter. The reduction of incidental learning is more than made up for by greater mastery of those things you include as objectives because you judge them to be important. Teachers make decisions every day about what is important and what isn't. Your objectives communicate these decisions.

Make allowances for spontaneous exploration of topics. Planning and objectives are critical to good teaching, but sometimes the best learning is unplanned.

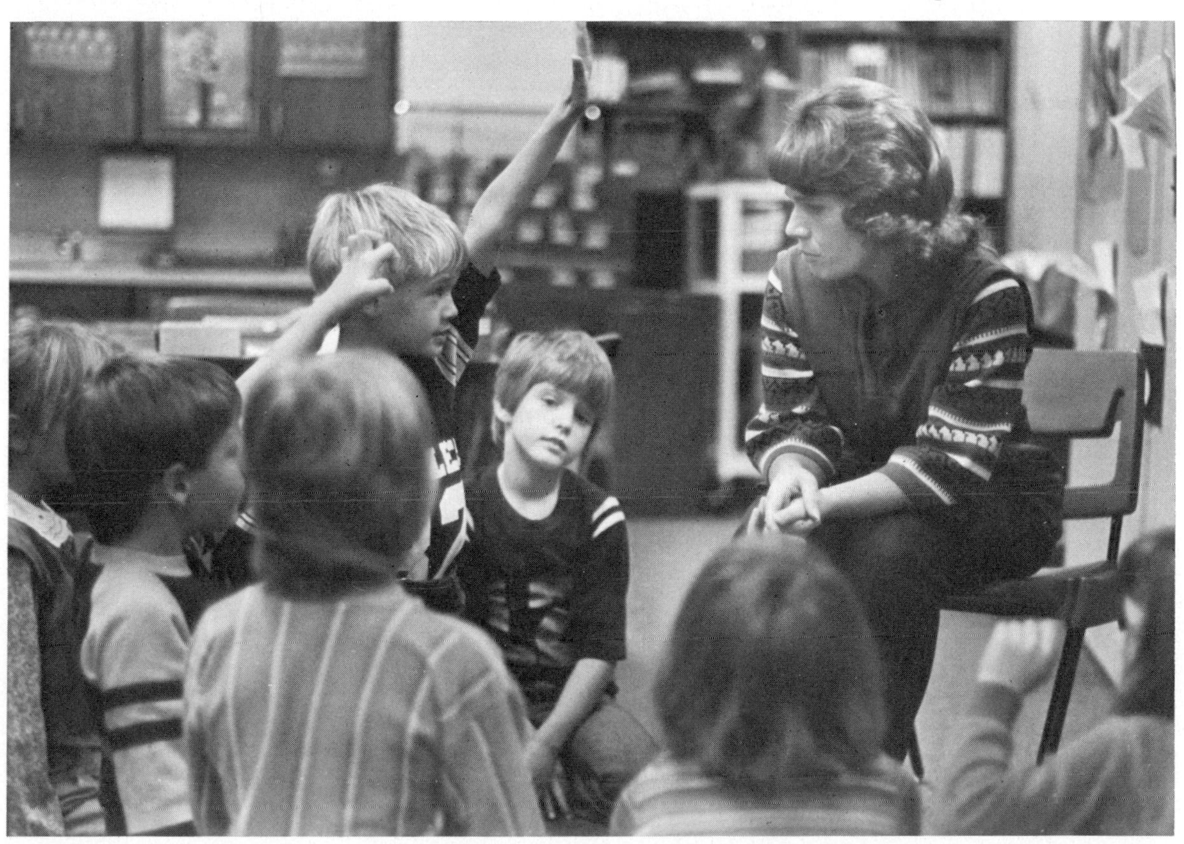

Trivialization can be avoided by working for a distribution of objectives across the six levels of learning and across the different domains. Some knowledge- and comprehension-level objectives are usually necessary, but a little planning on your part should lead to the development of application, analysis, synthesis, and evaluation objectives.

Having your students insist that you stick to the topic so they can master all the objectives is also not a bad idea. Remember, you can always add objectives to describe any learning you want students to demonstrate in addition to what you originally planned. You can also make allowances in your instructional plan so that you and your students will be free to engage in spontaneous exploration of topics that weren't incorporated in the objectives.

Tips for Writing Instructional Objectives

When you have a set of objectives such as those presented at the beginning of this chapter, you need not restate the conditions of assessment for each one.* Suppose you are teaching a one-week unit and you have developed twenty objectives for your students. If all the objectives are going to be assessed on an in-class examination, one statement prefacing your objectives should make very clear to your students the conditions under which assessment will occur. If you have one or two objectives that will be assessed under different conditions (on homework assignments or during an in-class laboratory period, for instance), you can specify the conditions for those objectives and note that all the rest will be assessed on an in-class examination. Our point is that you need not get bogged down in the petty details of writing objectives. The conditions for student performance are very important but you don't have to rewrite "on an in-class examination, without references" twenty times.

A second general point has to do with the criteria. Clearly, objectives with different criteria must have their criteria spelled out for the students. There will be occasions, however, on which several objectives have the same criteria (spelling errors and neatness, for example). If this is the case, one general statement telling students what criteria are in effect will suffice. Why write "with fewer than two misspelled words" twenty times when one general statement will do the job?

A final comment concerns the number of objectives that need to be written for any unit. Too many objectives may lead to a perception that the outcomes of learning will be trivial. On the other hand, too few objectives may result in vagueness and not direct the learner as well as

* Throughout our book we have opted to give you a shorthand form of objectives, omitting the criteria and conditions. This is because your professor will set the conditions and criteria to meet the needs of your class. Your professor is in the best position to make decisions about both conditions and criteria.

Improperly prepared objectives can lead to student behaviors that are quite different from what the teacher expects.

"This is not what we meant, Snider, when we asked for a thorough study of the laws of gravity."

more precise statements would. The "correct" number of objectives depends on many factors, of course, but perhaps it depends most on the content and the level of the learners. Generally, the more sophisticated the learners, the fewer objectives are required.

SUMMARY

Teachers use broad educational goals as a guide for their teaching. Because of the very general nature of these goals, however, teachers must translate them into teachable, short-term statements of what students are to learn—instructional objectives. Instructional objectives ordinarily have three components: an action verb, the criteria for assessing students' performances, and a description of the conditions under which the performances are to occur. Objectives fall into three domains of learning: cognitive, psychomotor, and affective.

Cognitive objectives specify behaviors used to infer intellectual changes in students. Cognitive objectives have been organized by Bloom and his associates into a taxonomy from simple to complex that encompasses six levels. Objectives may be written for learning at each of Bloom's six levels: knowledge, comprehension, application, analysis, synthesis, and evaluation. Different kinds of cognitive processes are required of students at each of these levels.

Psychomotor objectives are statements that describe physical acts students are to perform. They are relatively straightforward and typically describe behaviors that can be evaluated easily. Frequently behaviors in psychomotor objectives are described as "correct," "proper," or "efficient," which translates into performance of the behavior in the way it has been modeled for the students.

Affective objectives reflect emotional states (attitudes, values, feelings, and so on) that students are to achieve as the result of instruction. They differ from cognitive and psychomotor objectives in that the affect is named and behaviorally described within the objective. As usual, conditions and criteria must be present in affective objectives.

Suggested Readings

Bloom, B. S., Englehart, M. D., Furst, E. J., Hill, W. H., & Krathwhol, D. *Taxonomy of educational objectives. Handbook I: Cognitive domain.* New York: McKay, 1956.

Although a quarter of a century old, this book is still an excellent source for teachers. Numerous examples of questions and objectives at all six levels of learning are presented.

Burns, R. W. *New approaches to behavioral objectives* (2nd ed.). Dubuque, Iowa: Brown, 1977.

Burns's book is an excellent guide for the development of instructional objectives.

Gagné, R. M., & Briggs, L. J. *Principles of instructional design.* New York: Holt, Rinehart, & Winston, 1974.

This book is a fine source for the use of objectives in designing instruction. It places the development and use of objectives in the perspective of the overall design process.

Gronlund, N. E. *Stating objectives for classroom instruction.* New York: Macmillan, 1978.

A good, brief treatment of how to write objectives is presented in this text.

Mager, R. *Preparing instructional objectives.* Palo Alto, Calif.: Fearon, 1962.

While now more than twenty years old, Mager's book is still a valuable source for the development of instructional objectives.

Answers to Practice Exercise 11–1

1. Number 1 is a poorly written objective. The verb form "develop an awareness" is vague and unclear. Students have no way of identifying the behavior they are supposed to perform. Conditions are specified and an attempt has been made to present a criterion, although the verb makes it hard to tell what the criterion means. A better form of this objective is "On an in-class essay examination the students will describe at least four of the seven major influences of Spanish culture on the American Southwest."

2. This is a well-written objective. It contains verbs that specify observable and measurable behaviors ("define" and "write") and it clearly states the criterion for acceptance and the conditions under which the behavior is expected to occur. No statements are made about spelling or neatness so we assume that such things are not important unless the teacher has specified them elsewhere.

3. This objective illustrates a common error. It contains an appropriate verb ("identify") and it describes the conditions under which the behavior will occur ("while dissecting a frog"). Absolutely no mention is made of the criterion, however. A phrase describing the criterion, such as "at least five organs," could be inserted to improve this objective.

4. Number 4 is in really bad shape. The students won't know what they have to do—memorize, write, and so on. The conditions are explained, but absolutely no criteria for "really knowing" are provided. A better version is "Given the first part of each term in the multiplication tables, for example $9 \times 9 =$ _____, the students must be able to give the correct answer eight out of ten times on an oral quiz."

5. Objective 5 sounds very impressive, but it is also unclear. Just what is meant by "conceptualize"? What does "bring to bear" mean? Conditions are described but there is no mention of criteria. A clearer statement is "During a laboratory period students will demonstrate two methods of solving the problem, including at least five steps in the problem-solving process in each demonstration."

6. This objective definitely requires improvement. "Have a firm grasp" does not describe the students' behavior at all. A statement is made about both conditions and criteria, but the criteria are unclear. A better way to write this objective is "On the final exam, the students will correctly solve 70 percent of the equations containing one unknown."

7. Objective 7 is well written. "Correctly pronounce" is an observable and measurable behavior. Both conditions of assessment and the criterion are clearly spelled out.

8. Number 8 is, frankly, terrible. It violates practically all the

rules for writing objectives. What behavior does "remember" specify? What does "know for tomorrow's quiz" mean? Who "knows" (or, better, who can say)? Rewriting this objective depends on what outcome the teacher actually wants. This objective could specify "list," "recognize," "define," or, in fact, any action verb that would describe the behavior the teacher wants from students. Conditions and criteria also need to be included in a rewritten objective.

9. This is a well-written statement. No mistake can be made about the behavior, the conditions, or the criteria.

10. Objective 10 is generally appropriate. The behavior, the conditions, and the criteria are clear.

Answers to Practice Exercise 11–2

1. Number 1 requires *application*-level learning. Students must be able to use an abstraction about solutions in a real situation.

2. The students are not required to be able to do anything more than name—no usage of the knowledge is required. Number 2 requires *knowledge*-level learning.

3. This requires *comprehension*-level learning. Students are asked to put knowledge into their own words, but no more is required.

4. *Analysis*-level learning is called for. Students must identify component parts of a complex idea and determine their relationship to the whole.

5. *Evaluation*-level learning is necessary for number 5. Students must make judgments about procedures based on their knowledge, and then they must support these judgments.

6. Number 6 requires *synthesis*-level learning. Students must break down knowledge they already have and recombine it in a new form.

7. This also calls for *synthesis*-level learning. Students may use knowledge about salt marshes, oil spills, and birds and break this knowledge down and recombine it into a new whole—a set of predictions.

8. *Analysis* is clearly called for in number 8. Students must break a musical presentation into its component parts and identify two of them.

9. *Comprehension*-level learning is the statement of knowledge in one's own words. This is required of students in number 9.

10. Number 10 asks for *knowledge*-level learning. Children are to identify, nothing more.

11. Number 11 cannot be resolved unless students engage in *evaluation*-level learning. Students are required to make judgments based on their knowledge and to support these judgments.

12. This requires *application*-level learning. An abstraction must be applied by students in a fairly concrete setting.

Checklist for Practice Exercise 11–3

Cognitive Objectives

Check to see that each objective contains the three necessary components of a good instructional objective. Underline and label the components of each of your objectives. If you didn't use the three components, go back and start again. Remember, you must include (1) an action verb, (2) the conditions under which the students' behavior is expected to occur, and (3) the criterion for the students' behavior.

Check your knowledge-level objective to be sure that it calls for nothing more than the students' ability to recall or identify information.

Check your comprehension-level objective to be sure that it requires that students put some bit of information into their own words but nothing more.

Check your application-level objective to make sure that an abstraction is being applied to a concrete setting.

Check your analysis-level objective to be sure that it requires students to break information down into its component parts so that the relationships between the components are clear.

Check your synthesis-level objective to be sure that you are requiring the analysis and recombination of old bits of knowledge to develop something new.

Check your evaluation-level objective to be sure that you are requiring students to make judgments based on their knowledge about the *value* of methods and materials for some purposes.

Psychomotor Objectives

Your psychomotor objectives must also contain the same three components as the cognitive objectives. Carefully check to be sure that both of your psychomotor objectives contain all three components and that each actually calls for an observable physical activity.

Affective Objectives

You will remember that affective objectives must have four components: (1) the affect, (2) a behavioral specification of the affect, (3) conditions, and (4) criteria. Be sure both of your affective objectives contain all four of these components.

IMPORTANT EVENTS IN THE DEVELOPMENT OF INSTRUCTIONAL OBJECTIVES

Date(s)	*Person(s)*	*Work*	*Impact*
1880	Hall	Saturday morning lectures	G. S. Hall's famous Saturday morning lecture series included calls for the specific communication of expectations to students and the use of goals as the source of examinations.
1899	James	*Talks to teachers*	William James's text suggests in some detail the benefits of teaching from specific goals. His emphasis on the use of goals in evaluation, however, was not as strong as Hall's.
1903	Thorndike	*Educational psychology*	E. L. Thorndike's pioneering textbook emphasized the use of goals in teaching. It may be said that every educational psychology text since the time of Thorndike has included an obligatory discussion of goals.
1918	Commission on the Reorganization of Education	"The seven cardinal principles of American education"	"The Seven Cardinal Principles became the foundation for curricula throughout the nation, making an enormous and long-lasting impact on classroom teachers as well as teacher training institutions" (Bertrand & Cebula, 1980, p. 44).
1938	Educational Policies Commission	"Revision of the seven cardinal principles"	The Educational Policies Commission restated the seven cardinal principles into four general goals.
1948	American Psychological Association Special Interest Group	Informal meeting of college examiners	In an informal discussion at the American Psychological Association convention, it was agreed that work would commence on the classification of the goals of education. This meeting ultimately resulted in the Bloom et al. (1956) and Krathwohl et al. (1964) taxonomies of educational objectives.

Date(s)	*Person(s)*	*Work*	*Impact*
1951	Remers, Bloom, Krathwohl, Buros, Mowrer, & Stalnaker	"The development of a taxonomy of educational objectives"	The first formal report of work toward the cognitive domain handbook was given in this symposium at the American Psychological Assoc. convention.
1956	Bloom et al.	*Taxonomy of educational objectives. Handbook I: Cognitive domain*	The taxonomy developed by Bloom and his associates has guided the construction of educational goals, objectives, and tests since its publication.
1962	Mager	*Preparing objectives for programmed instruction*	"One of the most influential contributors in the area of objectives has been Robert F. Mager, whose 1962 book . . . instigated a revolution in the writing of objectives" (Bertrand & Cebula, 1980, p. 46).
1964	Krathwohl et al.	*Taxonomy of educational objectives. Handbook II: Affective domain*	The publication of the affective domain handbook under the leadership of David R. Krathwohl stressed the importance of affective objectives in education.
1966–present	Rothkopf & associates	Research on objectives in reading	The most intensive research on the effects of objectives has been done by E. Z. Rothkopf and his associates. Rothkopf initiated the investigation of the effects of objectives on reading comprehension.
1975	Congress	Public Law 94-142	With the passage of PL 94-142, the government of the United States in effect required teachers to employ specific instructional objectives for children identified for participation in special-education programs.
1978	Gronlund	*Stating objectives for classroom instruction*	Norman E. Gronlund's text is representative of the large number of books now available on how to write instructional objectives.

Chapter Twelve

TASK ANALYSIS

One of the major themes of this book is the importance of providing meaningful learning activities for students. Learning is far more likely to occur if we present students with new material that they can relate to information already in their memories. This chapter is designed to help you make your instruction more meaningful, specifically by developing your skills in sequencing instruction, in determining what prerequisite skills students need to start a learning experience, and in assessing students' mastery of prerequisites as a basis for deciding where to start instruction.

Objectives

After reading this chapter, you should be able to meet the following objectives.

1. Perform a task description based on instructional objectives.
2. Perform a task analysis for a cognitive, a psychomotor, and an affective objective.
3. Construct pretests based on task analyses.
4. Use pretest results to revise instructional objectives to fit the entry levels of students.

The question of how to best arrange instruction has been debated for as long as there have been instructors. It wasn't until the 1950s, however, that the issue was systematically investigated when Miller (1953a, 1953b, 1956) conducted several studies of task arrangement in the teaching of armed forces personnel (Gagné, 1974b). Miller's procedure for arranging tasks, which has been extended and improved upon by several psychologists (see Gagné, 1965, 1974; Glaser, 1965; Resnick, 1976), is known generally as *task analysis*.

Task analysis is a very broad concept referring to a process for identifying teachable components of an instructional objective (Dick & Carey, 1978). In this chapter we shall consider the use of task analysis for three purposes: (1) identifying and correctly sequencing the steps involved in performing a task (task description), (2) identifying and systematically ordering the prerequisites for a task (task analysis), and (3) using the prerequisites generated in a task analysis to identify where instruction should begin.

TASK DESCRIPTION

The success of our instruction depends on how well we and the students understand what is to be done and in what order. Consider something as "simple" as computing the area of a square.* What do you do first? What next? How do you know when you have followed a proper sequence and determined the correct area? The same kind of question can be raised about any task, from solving a long-division problem to composing an essay: What sequence of steps are students to follow?

*Complexity, as we saw in Chapter Five, is determined by learners. Adding a column of four numbers may be very complex for second graders but very simple for seventh graders.

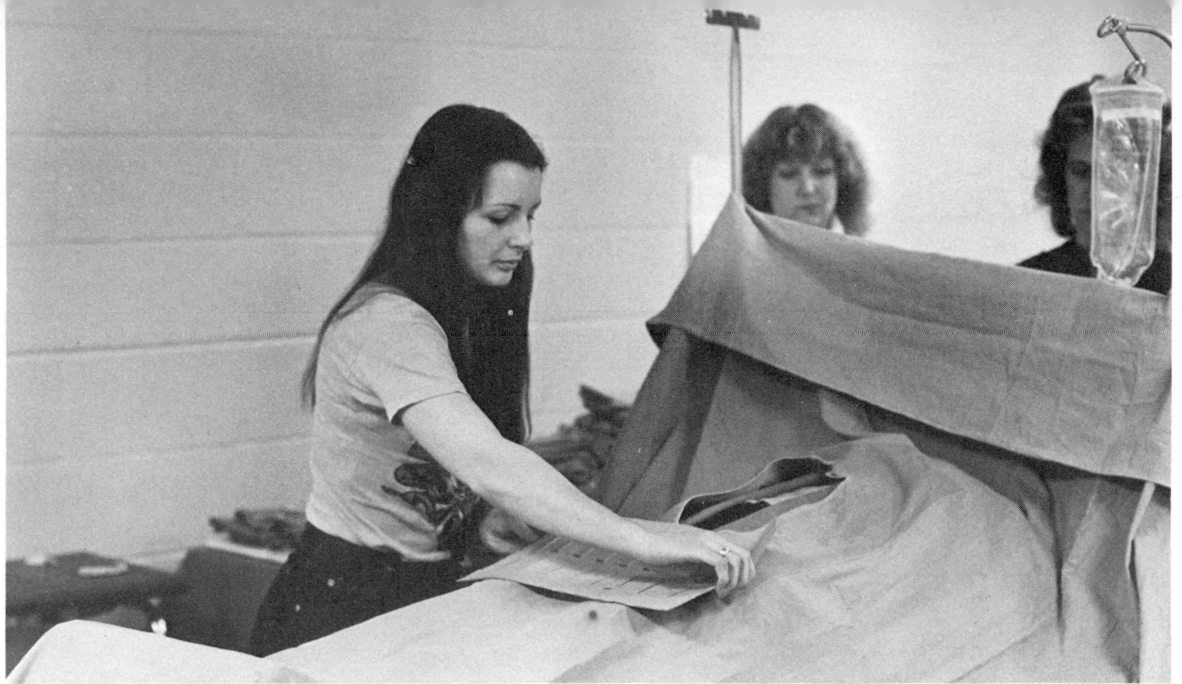

Task description outlines the sequence of steps in a task. Each step in draping a patient is specified to ensure a sterile environment for surgery.

The sequence of steps in a task is determined through the use of **task description*** (Gagné, 1977), a step-by-step description of the sequence of things to be done in a task. A task description of starting a car might look like this:†

Step 1. Fasten seat belt.

Step 2. Insert key.

Step 3. Place transmission in neutral or park.

Step 4. Depress accelerator.

Step 5. Turn key to "start" position.

In a task description all the steps in a process are listed in the order of their occurrence (Dick & Carey, 1978; Gagné, 1977; Gagné & Briggs, 1979), and substeps may also be listed (Dick & Carey, 1978). Subtracting a column of numbers, for example, can be broken into several substeps if necessary. How far you break the steps down in a task

*Task description is referred to as an "information processing approach" to task analysis in Gagné and Briggs (1979) and simply as "task description" in Gagné (1977). Dick and Carey (1978) use the term "procedural approach" to refer to task analysis. For the sake of consistency, we have chosen to refer to the process as "task description" throughout this chapter.

†Boxes with connecting arrows ("flow charts") are frequently used to denote the steps in a task. We generally prefer, however, to simply list the steps in order without the development of a flow chart.

description depends on the level of your students and your responsibilities. Task description is not designed to analyze prerequisite skills for a task; it merely lists the steps in a task performance in their correct order.

The following is an example of a task description of a psychomotor activity, bunting a ball in baseball or softball.

1. Slide the top hand to the trademark of the bat.
2. Loosen the grip on the bat with both hands.
3. Take a half step with the front foot toward the outside of the batter's box (toward the first-base side for lefties, third-base for righties).
4. Take a full step forward with the back foot so that it is aligned with or only slightly behind the front foot.
5. Bring up the elbow of the arm that holds the handle of the bat so that it is midway between the waist and shoulder while holding the forearm straight out, parallel to the ground.
6. Bring the other arm out from the body, palm up, so that it is extended far enough to hold the bat parallel to the ground at or near a 90-degree angle to a line from the pitcher's mound to home plate.
7. Crouch slightly and directly face the pitcher.
8. Decide if the pitch is a strike or a ball.
9. If the pitch is a strike, let the ball hit the bat. If the pitch is a ball, let the pitch go by.

As you can see, the task description outlines the sequence of steps for bunting a ball in order of their occurrence. As we saw in Chapter Eight, such a set of steps could be used to demonstrate the process to students, and, as we will see in Chapter Fourteen, the list can later be employed to assess students' mastery.

An example taken from basic algebra will help you see the use of task descriptions in cognitive areas. What is the sequence of steps involved in solving an equation such as $8x - 24 = 3x + 36$?

1. Add the same number to each member of the equation:
$$8x - 24 + 24 = 3x + 36 + 24$$
$$8x = 3x + 60$$
2. Subtract the same amount from each member of the equation:
$$8x - 3x = 3x - 3x + 60$$
$$5x = 60$$
3. Divide both members of the equation by the same number:
$$5x/5 = 60/5$$
$$x = 12$$

These steps could be further analyzed into substeps or, if a more complex objective were chosen, additional steps could be added.

PRACTICE EXERCISE 12–1
Writing a Task Description

Choose any of the objectives you wrote in Practice Exercise 11–3 and write a task description of the behaviors involved, arranging the components in correct order. Describe how you would demonstrate the task. Check our responses at the end of the chapter when you have finished.

Task descriptions are clearly useful for understanding what an objective calls for and properly sequencing instruction for students. They help teachers identify "individual steps which may not otherwise be obvious" (Gagné & Briggs, 1979) and form an excellent basis for writing instructions, developing rules, and giving demonstrations.

TASK ANALYSIS

Task description is a valuable tool for teachers but it does not help solve the problem of arranging instruction so that all students begin at a level appropriate to their readiness for learning. As we noted in Chapter Five, in any class of students, regardless of their age, the time of year, and subject matter, each of them will be at a different level of readiness for the new tasks to be learned (Charles, 1976). Figure 12–1 is a representation of entry levels of a class of students. The colored band in the figure represents the target objective, typically set where your texts or curricular materials assume students should be at the beginning of your instruction. Some, perhaps most, of your students will be very close to this average. Others will be above this level and are not going to benefit from instruction in content they have already mastered. Still other students will be below this level and will find instruction geared for the average too difficult. Most teachers and textbooks aim for the middle group because the majority of students will be at this level. As we have seen, however, the problems in developing materials and curricula aimed at the middle level are twofold—boredom for those students who have mastered the material and lack of meaning and frustration for those who are not ready for it.

Teaching at levels appropriate for students is a characteristic of effective teachers. As we emphasized in Chapter Ten, this practice helps prevent possible discipline problems by keeping each student involved in challenging and meaningful learning. When students are actively engaged in learning, they have little time and no reason for creating dis-

FIGURE 12–1
A Representation of Student Entry Levels in Relation to Instruction that Is Aimed at the Average Student

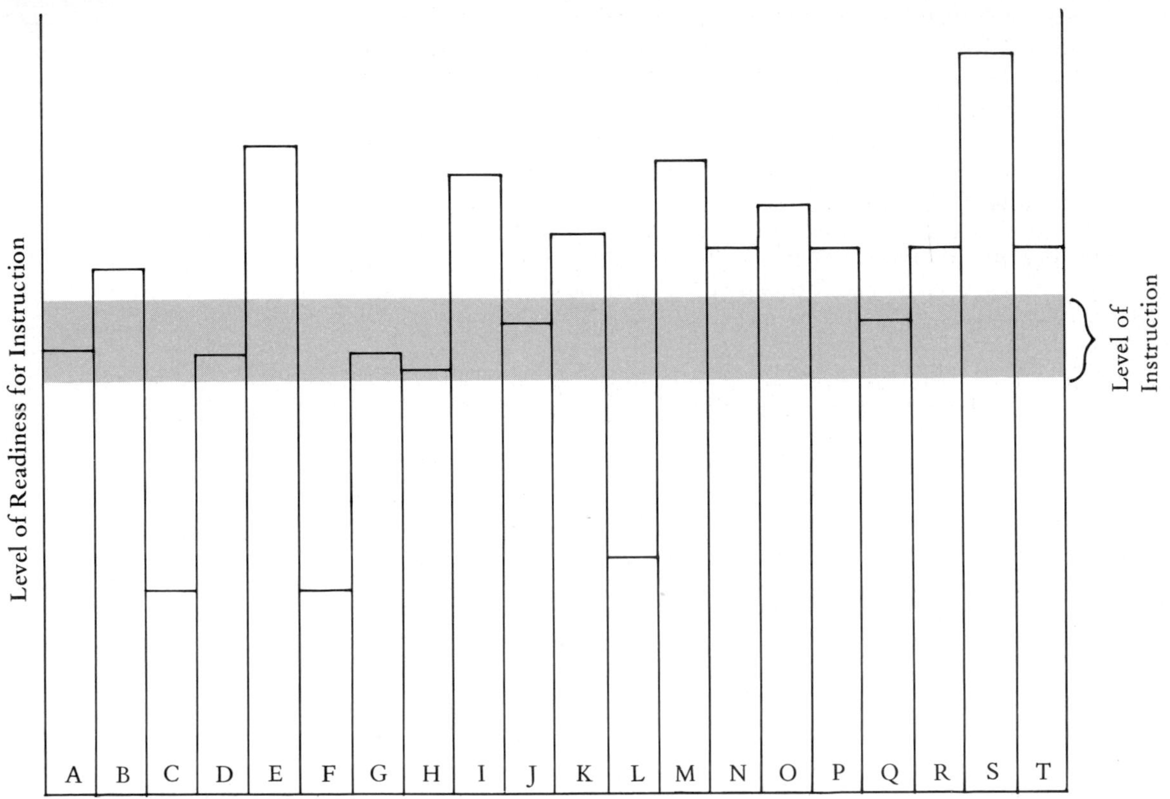

Students A through T
Some are at the level of instruction indicated by the colored band while others have not yet reached that level (they are below the band). Some other students (those above the band) have already mastered the material at the average level of instruction.

cipline problems in the classroom. There are also correspondingly fewer problems with boredom and frustration that may lead to disenchantment with school and, for some, dropping out.

How can we do a better job of identifying appropriate points to begin instruction for individual learning? This question can be answered by the use of task analysis (Gagné & Briggs, 1979). The following sections are designed to help you learn how to perform task analyses and to use them to determine the entry levels of your students.

Performing Task Analyses

A **task analysis** involves breaking down any objective you have for students (math problems, geography objectives, writing, analyzing history) into a hierarchy of *prerequisite* knowledge and skills (Gagné & Briggs, 1979; L. B. Resnick, 1976; Resnick & Wang, 1969). Usually a task analysis is performed by describing the instructional objective you have set for the students and then working backward a step at a time until you have listed all the necessary prerequisites (Gagné, 1977; Gagné & Briggs, 1979).

Gagné (1977) suggests that you start the task analysis by asking yourself the question "What must students already know so that they can learn the new task with a minimum amount of instruction?" When you ask yourself this question about any instructional objective, you should be able to identify one or more prerequisites. Once the prerequisites have been identified, you repeat the process, asking yourself the same question about the set of prerequisites you just listed. This procedure is continued until you reach a reasonable stopping place (Dick & Carey, 1978; Gagné, 1977; Gagné & Briggs, 1979).

The most effective way to show you what task analyses are is to examine some examples so that you can see what is involved. Each of the task analyses below is representative and does not contain every possible prerequisite. Rather, we have chosen to break the tasks down into components that will serve as reasonable models for you when you begin task analyses of your own.

Example 1

Cognitive Objective (Elementary Math). Given in-class worksheets of twenty problems, the students will be able to correctly divide seventeen two-digit numbers into three-digit numbers containing decimals.

Prerequisite Knowledge and Skills. What are the skills and knowledge students must have before they can benefit from instruction for this objective? Students must be able to perform the following prerequisite (enabling) tasks before the target objective is meaningful:

1. Divide a single-digit number into a two-digit number.
2. Divide a single-digit number into another single-digit number.
3. Express remainders and fractions in decimal form.
4. Use decimals in writing numbers.
5. Change fractions into decimals.
6. Define the term *decimal.*
7. Recognize a decimal.
8. Recognize the division bracket and give its definition.
9. Identify, define, and use numbers in the ones, tens, and hundreds columns.

There can be problems if we work backwards too far in any task analysis.

"Now, if we run our picture of the universe backwards several billion years, we get an object resembling Donald Duck. There is obviously a fallacy here . . ."

10. Multiply.
11. Subtract.
12. Add.
13. Count.
14. Identify number values.
15. Write numbers.
16. Say numbers.

As you can see, we have worked backward from complex to simple tasks. We could go on adding prerequisites until we filled several pages. A reasonable stopping place is the level at which you can realistically provide instruction. If you are teaching sixth graders and one student cannot add, subtract, or understand number values, for example, you should initiate a referral process to obtain special help for that student (we discuss the education of students with special needs in Chapter Sixteen).

We can use the enabling (prerequisite) tasks we generate to guide our instruction for the target objective. The example above was taken from a sixth-grade math class where the students were having difficulty mastering the objective. The task was analyzed and then broken into subtasks that were used to make up new, prerequisite objectives. Poorly learned skills were retaught, step by step, until the students arrived back at the original target objective. The division problems could not be solved until students had mastered some prerequisite skills such as the correct use of decimals.

Task analyses are similar for cognitive, psychomotor, and affective instructional objectives. In each instance, the target objective is broken down into prerequisite knowledge and skills. Each of these subtasks, in turn, can be further broken down into more basic prerequisites.

Another major use of task analysis is to locate the entry levels of your students (L. B. Resnick, 1976; White & Gagné, 1974). This may be done by putting together a set of assessment (test) items that measure the students' abilities to do those things called for in each step of the task analysis (assessment and evaluation are thoroughly discussed in Chapters Thirteen, Fourteen, and Fifteen). The following quiz is based directly on our sample task analysis of division.

1. Please complete the following addition problems:

(a) $\begin{array}{r} 126 \\ +312 \\ \hline \end{array}$ (b) $\begin{array}{r} 396 \\ +247 \\ \hline \end{array}$ (c) $\begin{array}{r} 563 \\ +682 \\ \hline \end{array}$

2. Complete the following subtraction problems:

(a) $\begin{array}{r} 919 \\ -707 \\ \hline \end{array}$ (b) $\begin{array}{r} 826 \\ -317 \\ \hline \end{array}$ (c) $\begin{array}{r} 444 \\ -312 \\ \hline \end{array}$

3. Complete the following multiplication problems:

(a) $\begin{array}{r} 12 \\ \times 14 \\ \hline \end{array}$ (b) $\begin{array}{r} 32 \\ \times 46 \\ \hline \end{array}$ (c) $\begin{array}{r} 961 \\ \times 41 \\ \hline \end{array}$

4. Place the decimal point correctly in the answer:

(a) $\begin{array}{r} 12.7 \\ +7.2 \\ \hline 199 \end{array}$ (b) $\begin{array}{r} 32.6 \\ +1.27 \\ \hline 3387 \end{array}$ (c) $\begin{array}{r} 44.9 \\ +22.2 \\ \hline 671 \end{array}$

Our example is not a complete pretest, of course, but it serves as an illustration (constructing tests is discussed fully in Chapter Fourteen). Each level in the task analysis can be the source of test questions that probe knowledge at that level. By examining the performance of your students in such a pretest, you can get a good picture of where they are with respect to your objective. Of course, there are also many other ways of determining which prerequisite skills students have attained, including observation and samples of work (see Chapters Thirteen, Fourteen, and Fifteen).

You will probably want to construct your pretests so that they test skills somewhere near the middle levels of prerequisites. Unless special circumstances exist, you can only go back so far in a typical teaching setting (Gagné & Briggs, 1979). High school teachers of second-year algebra, biology, a foreign language, or advanced business courses, for example, certainly should not go back to basic material that students should really have mastered in prerequisite courses. If some students' gaps in knowledge and skills fall far short of the average, those students should first master the prerequisite work. In settings where there are no prerequisite courses, and in cases where children have been promoted to the next grade without having learned the basic skills and knowledge in the lower grade, assistance from a resource teacher may be required (see Chapter Sixteen).

Example 2

Cognitive Objective (Elementary Science). On a take-home paper the students will describe the structure of an atom in their own words, including the terms *proton, neutron,* and *electron.*

Prerequisite Knowledge and Skills

1. Describe the complementary charges of electrons and protons.
2. Describe the charges of protons, electrons, and neutrons.
3. Define *proton.*
4. Define *electron.*
6. Define the term *charge.*
7. Define the term *nucleus.*
8. Define the term *orbit* (or *shells* or *probability clouds*).
9. Define *atoms.*
10. Define the term *matter.*
11. Define the terms *positive* and *negative.*
12. Define and use a series of relational concepts such as *bonded to, smaller than, repelled by,* and so on.

Sample Pretest Items (True/False)

_______ 1. The charge of an electron is positive.
_______ 2. The charge of a neutron is positive.
_______ 3. The charge of a proton is negative.
_______ 4. A nucleus is the outer shell of an atom.
_______ 5. Electrons pack the center of an atom.
_______ 6. Neutrons are placed in the orbits of atoms.
_______ 7. Like charges repel.

______ 8. An orbit is a path around some center point.
______ 9. Atoms are the basic building blocks of matter.
______ 10. Neutrons cause the nucleus to be held together.

Numbers 11 through 15 are short-answer items.

11. Draw the structure of an atom and label each part.
12. Write a statement telling what neutrons are.
13. Write a statement telling what electrons are.
14. Write a statement telling what a nucleus is.
15. Write a statement telling what matter is.

Example 3

Cognitive Objective (Beginning Music). On a blank staff in the treble clef, the student can write without error a simple melody heard in a recording.

Prerequisite Knowledge and Skills

1. Write on lines and spaces in the treble clef single notes that one hears.
2. Recognize that melodies can be written in various keys.
3. Recognize that each line and space on the staff represent a step (or half step) on a musical scale.
4. State how steps on a scale are represented in written musical form.
5. State how steps on a scale can be given alphabetic labels (letter names).
6. Identify higher and lower steps on a scale from a recording.
7. State the function of the treble clef.
8. Define or give an example of a step or half step on a musical scale.
9. Define or give an example of a musical scale.
10. Play, sing, or define the concept of a musical note.

Sample Pretest Items

1. Write the letter names below each of the notes of the staff.

2. Label the following lines and spaces of the staff below.

Although it isn't easy to specify what is involved in playing a musical instrument, careful analysis of how one learns to play greatly aids the music teacher. Even complex skills like this can be better taught with a task analysis.

3. In a paragraph or two, describe how notes and the staff are used to represent steps in a musical scale.
4. Play or sing a musical scale. (Response played on a piano or sung.)
5. Play or sing two notes that are one step apart on a musical scale. (Response played on a piano or sung.)
6. (Several different notes played on the piano or sung by instructor.) Which note is higher, the first or the second one played (sung)?

Depending on your musical literacy, this task can be extremely easy or very complex. As you can see, underlying the ability to write music at this simplest of levels are a number of more basic skills and understandings, including the concepts of musical scales, steps in a scale, notes, and the like. Each of these concepts itself is actually very complex and represents a general area for instruction. The task analysis and the pretesting in these areas help the teacher to see where students are now and to focus his or her instruction where knowledge or skill is lacking.

Cognitive Objective (High School Science). Given a variety of materials in class, the students will construct an apparatus that generates alternating electrical current.

Example 4

Prerequisite Knowledge and Skills

1. Describe the generation of alternating current.
2. Describe the effect of a magnetic field on electrons in a conductor passing through that field.
3. Give an example of, describe, and pictorially represent magnetic fields.
4. Describe and pictorially represent the formation of dipoles in a magnetized conductor.
5. Describe and give examples of methods that may be used to generate a magnetic field.
6. Define and pictorially represent *electron flow.*
7. Describe and pictorially represent the generation of direct current.
8. Define *dipole.*
9. Describe and define *electron.*
10. Locate, define, and describe conductors and nonconductors.

Sample Pretest Items

1. Write a statement describing the generation of alternating current.
2. Describe the effect of a magnetic field on electrons in a conductor passing through that field.
3. Alternating current is generated by:
   (a) cyclically passing a conductor through a magnetic field.
   (b) setting up dipole differences across an electron bond.
   (c) passing direct current through a magnetic field.
   (d) any source of electrons.
4. (True/false) When a conductor passes through a magnetic field, the electrons in the conductor are pushed to the center of the conductor.
5. Which of the following generate magnetic fields?

(a) power lines	(f) batteries
(b) radio antennas	(g) dipolar molecules
(c) nonconductors	(h) static charges
(d) any flow of electric current	(i) lightning
(e) power switches	

This example is definitely complex. It is, however, concrete in the sense that alternating electrical current can be easily generated and measured given a magnet, some wire, and a voltmeter. The task analysis stops at a relatively advanced level.* If none of the things outlined in the task analysis have been mastered, the students must have instruction in other areas before instruction for the objective can possibly be of any benefit.† We have greatly abbreviated the pretest because by now you should be getting the feel of putting together pretest items based on the learning suggested by a task analysis.

Example 5

Cognitive Objective (Elementary English). In a paragraph written in class, the students will use three pairs of antonyms.

Prerequisite Knowledge and Skills

1. List at least ten words and their antonyms.
2. Define *antonym.*
3. Identify antonyms.
4. Define and give examples of "opposite of."
5. Write a paragraph.
6. Write a topic sentence.
7. Write a summary sentence.
8. Write sentences.

Sample Pretest Items

1. (True/false) An antonym is a word that is opposite in meaning to another word.
2. Circle the following pairs of words that are antonyms.
   (a) boy-girl (e) heavy-durable
   (b) cat-bird (f) wash-dirty
   (c) dark-light (g) tall-short
   (d) big-small (h) smart-silly
3. Write ten pairs of words that are antonyms.

We'll cut the pretest short for this one because you no doubt see by now how to move from task analysis directly into a pretest.

Example 6

Psychomotor Objective (High School Business). In twenty seconds or less, the students will type the sentence "The quick red fox jumps over the lazy brown dog" without error.

*Note that we assumed that the high school students exposed to Example 4 had mastered certain elementary objectives, among them the structure of atoms.

† Students can construct such a device without understanding any of the principles involved! Prerequisite understanding is necessary in order to make the exercise worthwhile, however.

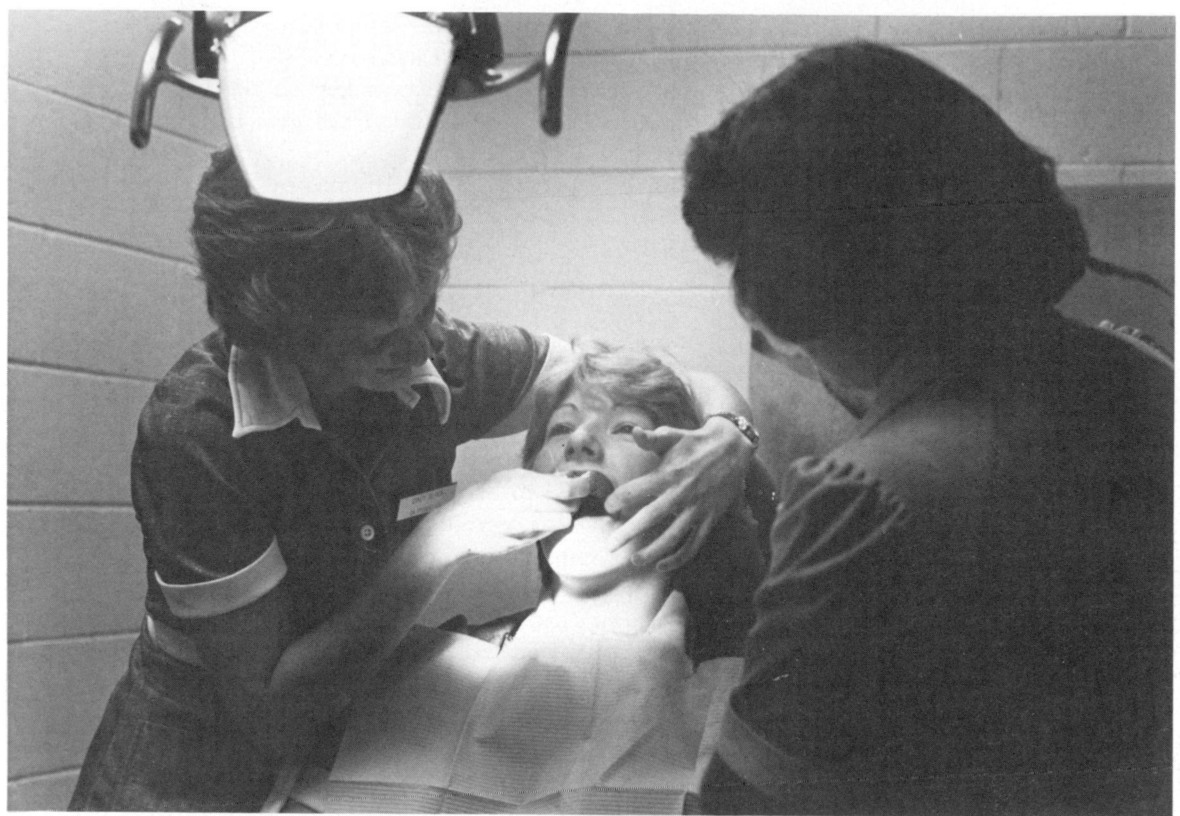

Complex psychomotor abilities, such as those required of these dental technicians, need to be analyzed into their prerequisite knowledge and skills.

Prerequisite Knowledge and Skills

1. Correctly strike each key used in typing the entire sentence without looking at the keyboard.
2. Type from copy.
3. Place fingers on the home keys without looking at the keyboard.
4. Identify all the home keys.
5. Identify all keys on the keyboard.
6. Correctly load a sheet of paper in the typewriter.

Sample Pretest Items. A checklist for basic typing skills could be used for the pretest. The instructor observes the students typing and makes the following judgments, noting if students demonstrate the skills.

______ 1. The student quickly and accurately loads the paper into the carriage.

______ 2. Fingers are placed on the home keys without looking at the keyboard nine of ten times.

______ 3. The student can strike each key on the keyboard without looking at the keyboard and can give the name of the key struck.

______ 4. The student is able to type from copy at 90 percent accuracy without looking at the keyboard.

______ 5. The student can type the practice sentence at 100 percent accuracy in less than twenty seconds without looking at the keyboard.

This objective is obviously a mixture of both cognitive and psychomotor abilities. The cognitive functions such as reading the words and identifying letters must have been previously learned to allow mastery of most of the physical actions. In this case, these cognitive skills would probably not need to be pretested. For the psychomotor components, the best method of pretesting is to list them on a checklist and have the students attempt to perform the tasks as you observe.

The use of direct observation and checklists is an important part of psychomotor pretesting. (Chapter Fourteen provides examples of teacher-constructed checklists). You will remember that we used the terms *correct, efficient,* and *appropriate* when we discussed psychomotor objectives in the last chapter. Your checklists may serve both as guides for teaching (having the students practice each step you develop) and as guides for student preparation (each student can have a copy of the checklist to see directly what a "correct" performance is).

Example 7

Psychomotor Objective (Early Elementary or Preschool). Given ten words containing the letters *M* and *N,* the students will print the letters correctly within at least nine of ten words.

Prerequisite Knowledge and Skills

1. Recognize the letters *M* and *N* as they occur in words.
2. Print within the lines on a piece of paper.
3. Reproduce copies of symbols.
4. Draw vertical and slanted lines.
5. Correctly hold a pencil and make marks with it.
6. Correctly hold writing paper.
7. Identify the letters *M* and *N.*
8. Follow directions.

As you can see, a pretest of these prerequisites would require observation of the students' performance. Placing the students at their entry levels may follow from the observation.

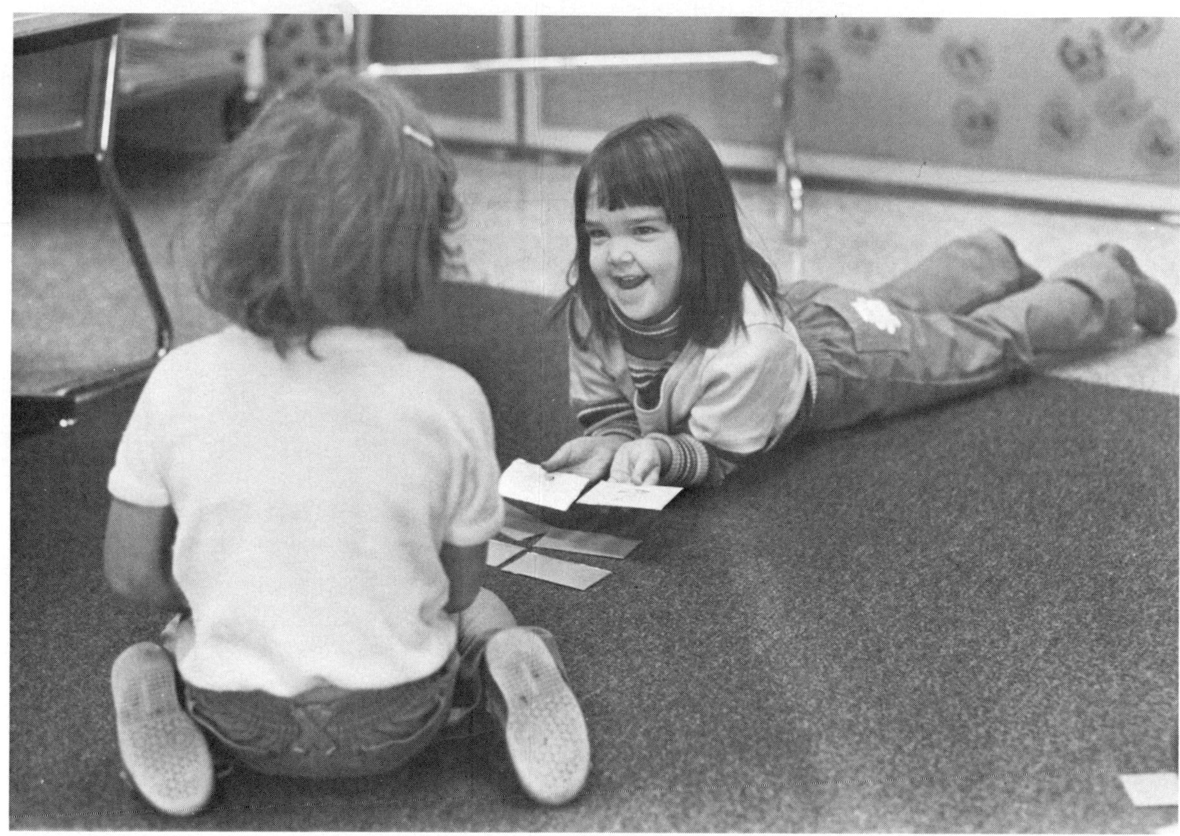

Even affective objectives as complex as enjoying one's classmates can be task analyzed.

Sample Pretest Items. The teacher prints words containing the letters *M* and *N* on the chalkboard in large print. He or she then watches each child pick up a pencil, checks how it is held and how each child holds the paper, and then watches each child's attempts to print. The teacher uses the eight items above as an observation guide.

Example 8

Affective Objective (Junior High Science). The students will demonstrate their respect and concern for classmates by correctly maintaining and using the laboratory equipment.

Prerequisite Knowledge and Skills. As you recall from Chapter Eleven, affective objectives describe the behaviors that we feel are important indicators of the mood, feeling, or attitude we are interested in. Here we have defined *respect and concern* as a set of student behaviors we could easily observe. Our task analysis is thus a listing of the prerequisites necessary for the behaviors our objective describes.

PRACTICE EXERCISE 12–2
Performing Task Analyses

1. Choose one of the following abbreviated cognitive objectives and perform a task analysis of at least ten prerequisite steps.
   a. The students must be able to use at least three adverbs in a written paragraph.
   b. The students must be able to determine any angle of a triangle given two sides and one other angle.
   c. The students will be able to define and describe the process of mitosis.
   d. The students must be able to write a statement summarizing the nature of initiatives and referenda. They must then determine which would be the most effective in changing the law for the legal driving age in this state.
2. Choose one of the following abbreviated psychomotor objectives and perform a task analysis of at least ten prerequisite steps.
   a. The students will be able to correctly hold a pair of scissors and cut along lines.
   b. The students will correctly use a centrifuge in the laboratory to test an unknown chemical.
   c. The students will be able to use a file to make a correct bevel on a cutting edge.
   d. The students will correctly make a buttonhole by hand.
3. Choose one of the following abbreviated affective objectives and perform a task analysis of at least five prerequisite steps. Remember that you will be listing the prerequisites for behaviors you choose to represent the affect.
   a. The students will describe the waste recycling program and its benefits and participate in the program as an indication of concern for our environment.
   b. The students will make more self-accepting statements in class and volunteer for participation in advanced learning activities as a means of showing their development of more positive self-concepts.
   c. The students will voluntarily complete a review of the literature (citing at least ten sources) in an area of their choice in educational psychology as an indication of their enjoyment of the course.
   d. When given the opportunity to conduct a meeting in a variety of formats, the students will choose the parliamentary procedure described in *Robert's Rules of Order* as a demonstration of their respect for democratic processes.

1. Properly maintain the equipment when given prompts and instructions.
2. Describe the correct use of the equipment when given prompts and hints.
3. Describe the consequences of not maintaining the equipment.
4. Follow general laboratory rules.
5. Demonstrate skills in the basic procedures for using laboratory equipment.

Sample Pretest Items. The students are asked to describe briefly in writing the maintenance of each piece of equipment and to state the general laboratory rules. If the laboratory has been set up for each student's use, the teacher could pass from work area to work area asking the students to demonstrate the use and maintenance of the various pieces of equipment in the laboratory.

Throughout this text we have stressed meaningful learning activities: Teaching must begin where students are. The best-prepared objectives in the world are worthless if students are not ready for them. Task analysis, in addition to outlining steps in instruction, may be used to develop pretests to locate where students are when instruction begins. The results of pretests can tell both student and teacher which of the prerequisite skills (if any) have been mastered and which have not. The first step in the outline that has not been mastered is the point where instruction must begin.

SUMMARY

Writing good instructional objectives is only one part of developing effective instruction. Task descriptions help teachers appropriately sequence the steps in tasks that students are to master. Identifying and ordering the steps involved in a task help teachers give demonstrations, write instructions, and give feedback.

Task analysis is the process of deriving the prerequisites for a learning task in hierarchical order. This hierarchy—a list of prerequisites—may then be used to construct a pretest that will determine those tasks in the hierarchy that students must master before they are ready for the original objectives. Once the prerequisite tasks that students have not yet mastered are identified, they become the new instructional objectives.

Suggested Readings

Dick, W., & Carey, L. *The systematic design of instruction.* Glenview, Ill.: Scott, Foresman, 1978.

This book provides excellent reading with lucid descriptions of the process of instructional design.

Gagné, R. M. Task analysis: Its relation to content analysis. *Educational Psychologist,* 1974, *11,* 11–18.

Gagné summarizes his views on task analysis and its relationship to content analysis in this cogent article.

Gagné, R. M., & Briggs, L. J. *Principles of instructional design* (2nd ed.). New York: Holt, Rinehart, & Winston, 1979.

This book is the most thorough text available on the topic of instructional design.

Comments on Practice Exercise 12–1

The sure-fire test to see whether you wrote a good task description is to try to perform the activity using only the steps you listed. If it works, you have done well. If it doesn't work, you have left out a step or added one too many. If you're still unsure, have one of your classmates try out the task according to your steps. Keep revising your task description until you or your classmate can perform the task flawlessly from your description.

Answers to Practice Exercise 12–2

Compare your answers to ours. Your task analyses need not be identical to ours but they should follow our form.

1a. Task analysis for using adverbs in a paragraph.

1. Properly use adverbs in a sentence.
2. List at least ten adverbs.
3. Define *adverb.*
4. Identify adverbs.
5. Write paragraphs.
6. Write topic sentences.
7. Write summary sentences.
8. Define *sentence object* and identify some.
9. Define *sentence subject* and identify some.
10. Define *sentence verb* and identify some.

There are obviously a whole series of tasks that could be added to this analysis. You may have taken any one of our prerequisites and broken it down further into additional steps. Check only to see that you followed our general pattern.

1b. Geometry.

1. Use the formula for computing the angle of a triangle given two sides and one angle.
2. Give the total number of degrees in the three angles in a triangle and describe their relationship.

3. Give the number of sides in a triangle and their relationship.
4. Be able to use, define, and identify sines (perhaps cosines, tangents, cotangents, and so on).
5. Define and identify triangles.
6. Divide.
7. Multiply.
8. Add.
9. Subtract.
10. Count.

As you can see, several of the prerequisites listed here can easily be broken down into many others. You need only refer back to our task analysis of long division to see how complex the step "division" is.

1c. Mitosis.

1. Define and describe *prophase.*
2. Define and describe *metaphase.*
3. Define and describe *anaphase.*
4. Define and describe *teleophase.*
5. Outline the function of RNA and DNA.
6. Indicate the role of genes in cell division.
7. Describe the function of chromosomes.
8. Define *diploid.*
9. Characterize cell nuclei.
10. Give the properties of cell membranes.

Some of you may have lumped together the various phases of mitosis and so you may have a very different-looking analysis. Then, too, there are many ways of approaching knowledge about genes, DNA, RNA, dipoles, and chromosomes. Does your pattern fit a reasonable hierarchy?

1d. Politics.

1. Define and describe *initiative.*
2. Define and describe *referendum.*
3. Outline the processes for changing laws.
4. Explain in your own words the pertinent portions of the state constitution.
5. Distinguish between majorities and pluralities.
6. Indicate the function of petitions.
7. Describe your particular state legislature's powers.
8. Describe the executive powers in your state.
9. Outline your state's driving laws with respect to age.
10. Define and describe votes, ballots, and the like.

Again, each of the prerequisites we listed could be broken down further.

2a. Scissors.

1. Move paper and scissors to continue to cut along lines.
2. "Feed in" paper.

3. Guide scissors along lines.
4. Move thumb and forefinger in unison.
5. Hold scissors.
6. Hold paper.
7. Describe the use of scissors.
8. Right-left hand coordination to move scissors and paper together.
9. Eye-hand coordination to move scissors.
10. Follow directions.

As you can see, many of the prerequisites in this example are developmental. The students may not have developed enough physically to perform some of the activities.

2b. Centrifuge.

1. Pour off (decant) separated layers properly (several prerequisites).
2. Properly remove a test tube from the centrifuge.
3. Use the control switches on the centrifuge.
4. Calculate the time necessary for the sample.
5. Properly insert test tube in centrifuge with a counterbalance.
6. Properly prepare sample for centrifuge (several prerequisites).
7. Properly prepare the test solution (several prerequisites).
8. Describe the results of centrifugal force on a liquid contained in a closed container.
9. Determine the density of different substances (several prerequisites).
10. Define *centrifugal force.*

Many, if not all, of these prerequisites contain a series of subtasks.

2c. Sharpening.

1. File an edge properly.
2. Estimate bevels while working.
3. Make a proper cut with a file.
4. Properly join the file and the cutting surface to be sharpened.
5. Define the term *bevel.*
6. Discriminate between tools that are sharpened by a file and those that must be sharpened in other ways.
7. Determine the proper bevel for various tools (several prerequisites).
8. Hold a file properly.
9. Describe the use of a file.
10. Hand-eye coordination.

2d. Making a buttonhole.

1. Cut open the center of the buttonhole (requires the use of scissors or a razor blade, several more possible prerequisites).

2. Stitch the buttonhole.
3. Mark the appropriate area on the fabric.
4. Make basic stitches in fabric (several possible prerequisites).
5. Tie off thread.
6. Measure the size of the buttonhole (many prerequisites).
7. Thread the needle.
8. Appropriately hold the needle and thread.
9. Describe and identify buttonholes.
10. Describe and identify needles.

3a. Concern for the environment.
1. Describe wastes that can be recycled.
2. Identify the location of recycling deposit areas.
3. Describe the purpose of recycling.
4. State the benefits of waste recycling programs.
5. State the relationship between natural resources and waste matter.
6. Identify and describe waste matter.

3b. More positive self-concepts.
1. Identify self-accepting statements.
2. Make self-descriptive statements.
3. Refer to self in discussion.
4. Identify new learning experiences.
5. Distinguish between voluntary and compulsory behaviors.

3c. Enjoying educational psychology.
1. Be able to say why an in-depth study of educational psychology is worthwhile.
2. Synthesize several sources into a coherent discussion (many prerequisites).
3. Analyze the contents of reading materials (many prerequisites).
4. Identify readings as appropriate to specific subareas in educational psychology.
5. A host of library skills.
6. A host of writing and reading skills.

3d. Respecting democratic processes.
1. Be able to say why each rule in *Roberts' Rules of Order* contributes to conducting a democratic meeting.
2. Describe *Roberts' Rules of Order* (many prerequisites).
3. Refer to *Roberts' Rules of Order* for information about specific points of order.
4. Give the meanings of a series of terms necessary to operate parliamentary meetings, such as *amendment, motion, order.*
5. Describe the term *parliamentary procedure.*

IMPORTANT EVENTS IN THE DEVELOPMENT OF TASK ANALYSIS

Date(s)	*Person(s)*	*Work*	*Impact*
1953	Miller	"A method for man-machine task analysis"	R. B. Miller is credited with the development of the first formal system for performing task analyses (Gagné, 1974) for the U.S. Air Force.
1965	Gagné	"The analysis of instructional objectives for the design of instruction"	Robert Gagné, a major figure in contemporary educational psychology, greatly expanded on the work of Miller and popularized task analysis.
1965	Glaser	*Teaching machines and programmed learning II: Data and directions*	R. Glaser's book, which contained Gagné's chapter (above), contributed to the expanded use of task analysis in education.
1969	Resnick & Wang	"Approaches to the validation of learning hierarchies"	This paper provided significant insights into validation of hierarchies of prerequisites developed in task analysis.
1974	Gagné	"Task analysis: Its relation to content analysis"	Gagné's paper represented the major theoretical contribution to task analysis, and it strongly influenced the views of educational psychologists on the use of task analysis.
1974	Gagné & Briggs	*Principles of instructional design*	This text was the first major book in the area of educational psychology to include significant elements of the theory and practice of task analysis.
1975	U.S. Congress	Public Law 94-142	With the passage of PL 94-142, Congress required the development of individualized educational programs (IEPs) for each student assigned to special programs. Part and parcel of IEP design is task analysis.
1976–present	Many individuals	*Journal of Personalized Instruction*	Even though the emphasis of the *Journal of Personalized Instruction* is behavioral, it has been the major outlet for

Date(s)	*Person(s)*	*Work*	*Impact*
			research in the use of task analysis. The journal was not published in 1980 because of financial difficulties, but it has been reorganized and is again a source of information in task analysis techniques.
1979	Gagné & Briggs	*Principles of instructional design* (2nd ed.)	The success of the first edition of Gagné and Briggs's text led to a revised edition. It is a major source in the area of instructional design.

Part Four

EDUCATIONAL MEASUREMENT AND EVALUATION

In the previous section we saw how you can structure learning activities by applying your knowledge of learning. Regardless of how well learning activities are planned, however, teachers cannot be sure about the efficacy of their instruction or the level of student learning without some means of measurement. Measuring student learning, of course, is important for all educational decisions. Part Four is designed to help you understand the purposes and principles of measurement and the applications of measurement techniques. Chapter Thirteen, "An Introduction to Measurement," will acquaint you with the basic principles of measurement. Chapter Fourteen, "Teacher-Made Tests," will help you employ a wide variety of measurement techniques. Chapter Fifteen, "Standardized Tests," provides you with information necessary to use and interpret standardized tests.

Chapter Thirteen

AN INTRODUCTION TO MEASUREMENT

Decisions about how to measure student learning are as important as decisions about what to teach. In fact, the most fundamental decisions you must make as a teacher may be those about measurement. Measurement is at the heart of all education. We test, we rate, we check, and we grade in order to evaluate the student, ourselves, and the educational process. How to ensure the meaningfulness of learning activities, how to grade students, how to motivate them, how to give them feedback, how to pace instruction, how to evaluate our own performance as teachers—each decision relies on measurement of student learning. The better your measurement, the more confident you can be that the decisions you make are sound ones.

Good teaching demands excellent measurement. This chapter will help you understand the decisions you must make in developing and selecting the best possible measures of student performance. It describes the purposes of measurement and introduces you to the general categories of measurement used in education. The principles that underlie good educational measurement are also outlined and they are further elaborated in Chapters Fourteen and Fifteen. We hope they will become a basic part of your teaching.

Objectives

After reading this chapter, you should be able to meet the following objectives.

1. Identify steps for improving the reliability of measures with low reliability.
2. Suggest procedures for improving the validity of measures that have unsatisfactory validity.
3. Select the appropriate form of measurement for a variety of decisions in which measurement and evaluation are required.

USES OF MEASUREMENT IN EDUCATIONAL SETTINGS

Measurement is the process of assigning numbers to persons or objects based on the degree to which they possess a characteristic (Ebel, 1979). Some measurement is simple, such as determining the height of a chair. We simply stretch a tape measure or ruler from the ground to the top of the chair and read off the number of meters and centimeters indicated on the tape. Such measurement is easy, accurate, and repeatable. Unfortunately, many of the things educators must measure are far more complex and elusive than the height of a chair. We are often unsure about our ability to measure some things accurately, and sometimes don't even know quite what to measure! If you want to measure the attitudes of your students toward your last instructional unit, you must decide first exactly what an attitude is and then how to measure it. You will be faced with similar definition problems in many of the units you teach that are concerned with hard-to-measure abilities like "inquiry skills." Other units may require the measurement of subtle aesthetic qualities like "expressiveness" or "visual literacy."

There are many forms of measurement teachers use to assess student progress. Tests, observations, work samples, self-reports, projects, and oral reports are all forms of educational measurement. When teachers seek to evaluate learning they must examine changes in student behavior. But no matter how you choose to assess behavior, there is a set of principles that will help you select the best possible measures. One of our major goals in this chapter is to help you understand and apply these general principles so that your measurement practices as a teacher will be as useful and accurate as possible.

Measurement is a key to almost every aspect of the educational process. Formal education begins with measurement of children's abilities and aptitudes, and measurement continues to play an important role in elementary school, high school, and college. Even at the level of professional and graduate education, measurement is a critical tool. Measure-

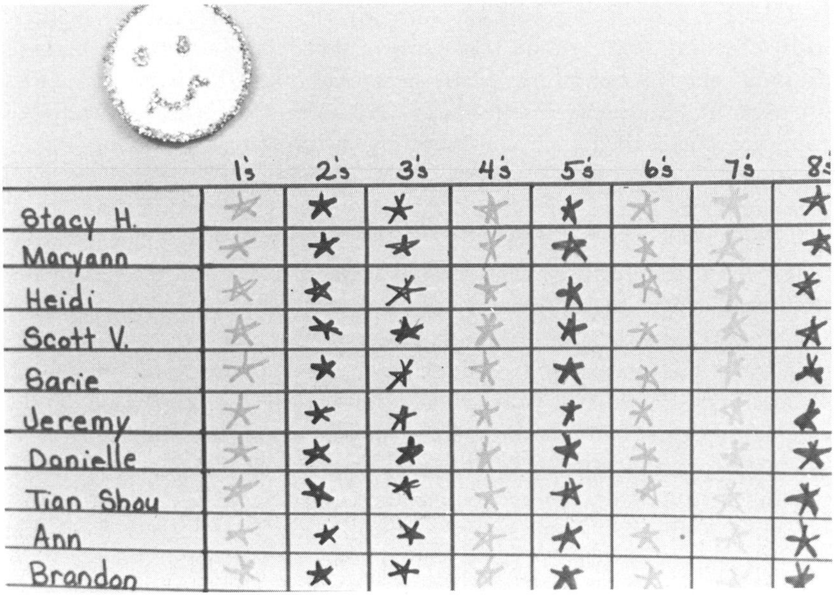

Teachers use many forms of measurement to assess student progress.

ment, of course, is also critically important to business and industry. The same principles we stress in education apply directly to other settings where human performance is evaluated. We need to determine which persons are qualified to be doctors, lawyers, and architects. These decisions, like the countless others that preceded them in the educational process, need to be based on the measurement of human qualities. We must know how skillful a person is, how comprehensive a person's knowledge is, how frequently an activity occurs, and how strong feelings are in order to make good decisions in education.

Measurement is useful for many purposes besides evaluation of student achievement by teachers. Students themselves benefit from the measurement of their skills and knowledge. Parents need to know about their children's progress. School administrators and the general public require information about education programs in order to make critical decisions on funding and program changes. Measurement can provide the necessary data on which to base these and many other decisions.

A look at some of the uses of measurement will point out that measurement has a key role in every part of education.

Selecting participants for programs. Measurement of the skills and aptitudes of candidates is a part of most selection processes and is employed to select the most qualified people. The military, for example, does extensive measurement to determine eligibility for general entrance and specialized training in the armed forces. Candidates to graduate or professional schools are selected through the use of tests. In sports, many coaching staffs "grade" the films of prospective recruits in making decisions about scholarships. Many personnel offices for large companies use tests to assess the intellectual, mechanical, or other aptitudes of applicants, and then they consider this information in making hiring decisions. Good selection processes, for any purpose, are based on good measurement.*

Establishing the meaningfulness of instruction. Measurement prior to instruction or training (see Chapter Twelve) can assist the teacher in determining where to begin instruction so that new information will be meaningful for students. Although students may prefer to be tested *after* they have had instruction, pretesting can be a useful tool for both teacher and students. If your students already have a command of the geography of the United States, for example, beginning your geography instruction at a more basic level would be wasteful. On the other hand, starting instruction at a level too advanced for your students can be just as serious a mistake, resulting in nonmeaningful material and confusion and frustration for the students. Pretesting will usually show a wide range of individual differences, with some students well advanced over others, implying that individualized programming may be the most useful strategy for instructing everyone.

Determining mastery of objectives. One of the most important functions of educational measurement is determining if students have mastered instructional objectives. If students are expected to be able to "solve for one unknown in an equation," for example, measurement is required to see if the students can perform this task at the criterion level specified by the teacher. Instructional objectives are of little value if teachers do not measure students' mastery of them. Decisions about reviewing material, providing remedial instruction, and going on to the next set of instructional objectives all need to be based on the measurement of students' mastery of objectives.

Providing feedback to students. When we think of measurement in education, we usually think of providing feedback to students. Feedback refers to any information that students can use to judge the quality of their performance (Kulhavy, 1977). Some form of feedback is necessary if learning is to occur. Providing learners with knowledge of how well they are doing (answering questions correctly or incorrectly, performing a skill adequately, and so on) increases the likelihood of their respond-

* Civil rights legislation has strongly influenced the selection procedures for employment and admission to educational programs. All measures used must be shown to be fair to all applicants and relevant to the position sought. Possible sources of test bias are discussed in Chapter 15.

ing correctly in the future. Kulhavy noted that feedback is most effective when (1) the learners are at appropriate entry levels for the learning task, (2) the learners cannot obtain feedback until after they have studied and made a response, (3) it is given as frequently as possible during a lesson, and (4) incorrect responses are corrected rather than correct responses simply being confirmed.

In many schools feedback to students has traditionally meant grading, a process linked closely to testing. Recently, however, measurement results are provided more often as competency statements ("You've successfully completed the paragraph-interpretation section of the Regular Reading Series" or "You've mastered the addition and subtraction of two-digit numbers"). Results of ratings, such as teacher or peer judgments of speech, are also frequently provided to students. Other feedback to learners may be the time of a performance ("Your time in the shuttle run was 9.8 seconds"), a frequency count ("You did eleven pull-ups"), or a rate measure ("You did seventeen in one minute").

No matter what form the feedback takes—how well, how often, how quick, or how many—its purpose is to inform the student. A student cannot learn without feedback, and measurement provides us with a very important form of feedback. The better and more frequent the measurement, the better the feedback we can give to our students.

Providing feedback to the instructor. Let's not forget the benefits teachers obtain from good measurement. As teachers, you will constantly use the results of measurement in your instruction. Just as the results of measurement are useful in determining where to *begin* instruction, continuous measurement of student performance is a part of many other decisions you need to make *during* instruction. Good measures will reveal who is learning what, the depth of their learning, and how they are feeling about the material you are presenting. You can use this information to ensure meaningful instruction by matching your instruction to the needs of your students. The end of the semester is not too late for measurement. Student evaluations of your performance and theirs tell you a great deal about your effectiveness as an instructor. Teaching is a cyclic process: Good planning for future instruction begins with the measurement of current instruction.

Providing feedback to other interested persons. More and more parents are asserting their rights to be significantly involved in their children's education. As part of this involvement, parents are receiving feedback on their children's performance or potential for performance. This information comes from measures such as classroom tests, standardized tests, or ratings.

The decisions that parents make, like teacher's decisions, are only as good as the information on which they are based. Suppose that several

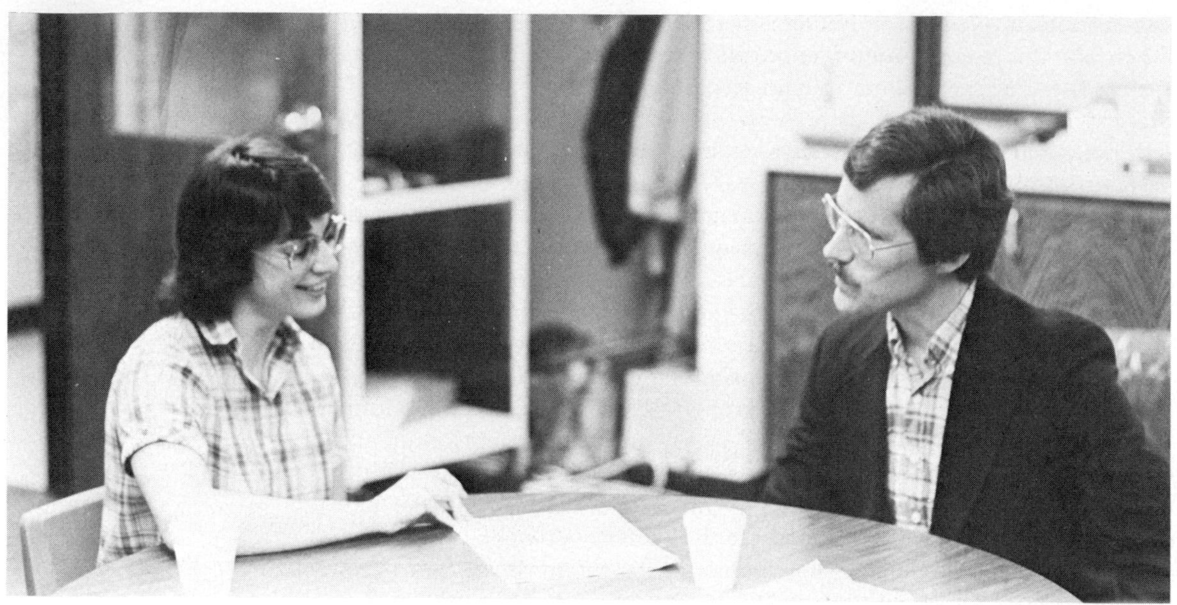

Parents need accurate knowledge about their children's performance in school.

measures all point to a significant educational problem for a child, such as mental retardation. If the parents of such a child can gain accurate information about the measurement results, they will be in a good position to make intelligent decisions about potential educational programs for their child. Not having this knowledge would surely reduce their chances of making a good decision.

Students expect their schools to communicate measures of their performance to future employers and to advanced education programs. People looking at this information may learn a great deal about students' abilities, work habits, interests, and even developmental patterns. Colleges and universities use grade transcripts as a basis for advisement and awarding scholarships. The measures provide information that can be readily applied by the interested agencies.*

Diagnosing problem areas. Measurement helps us identify problems in student learning and student development. While our informal observations may reveal a student's difficulty with certain kinds of learning, measurement can help us identify the source of the problem. A slow learner can be handicapped by any of a large number of factors—impaired hearing, low reading ability, poor general knowledge, or lack of interest. If we can measure these factors, we can make a diagnosis about

* This is not to say that measurements cannot be misused or misinterpreted. Without proper instructions and guidance in interpreting scores, people can come to incorrect conclusions about an individual or group.

which factor or factors are problem areas. While accurate diagnosis does not always lead to a solution (determining that a student has low general ability does not tell us what to do next), it helps us avoid bad decisions. Measurement can help us identify the poor reader who may gain from remedial instruction, the hearing-impaired student who will benefit from a hearing aid, or the gifted student whose talent may have gone unnoticed. It requires no great imagination to visualize the harm that can be done to such students by misdiagnosis based on poor measurement or none at all.

Motivating and stimulating study and preparation. "What are you doing?" "Oh, I'm studying for a test." How many times have we heard that exchange between two people? Measurement, particularly testing, is used so frequently in education as a motivator for learning that we recognize and accept this use as legitimate. The prospect of having their performance graded is a powerful stimulus for most people.

Other measures besides tests can be used to motivate students. Teachers routinely exhort students to prepare for upcoming measures. A band director points to an upcoming music contest's rating system, a speech teacher emphasizes the scoring system for a public-speaking contest, and a physical education instructor publicizes standards for physical fitness awards—all are ways of motivating students. Because measurement offers the prospect of both positive and negative results, we seek the rewards of doing well and try to avoid doing poorly. For most learners the prospect of being evaluated is an incentive for attempting to improve performance.

Providing an occasion for learning. Measurement in education samples behaviors that indicate what the learner can do, knows about, or feels. Whenever these behaviors are measured, some learning occurs. The test taker may learn how much he or she knows and what the instructor considers to be important. Even reading the questions on a test may provide new information to the learner.

The greatest amount of learning from measurement occurs when feedback is given (see Kulhavy, 1977). General feedback may involve giving students an indication of how their performance compares to others' performances or to a standard. For maximum learning, however, *specific* feedback is required. If the students know the exact causes of missed questions or low ratings, they are more likely to improve subsequent performances because areas needing improvement are obvious to them.

Certifying skills and abilities. Measurement provides educators with a basis for certifying that a person is competent to do something. In the course of most education and training programs, students are rated and tested for performance and knowledge. These measurements during and at the completion of a program form the basis for the most critical of decisions: Are we willing to certify that this person is competent? Physicians, nurses, lawyers, architects, and others must pass state board examinations testing the range and depth of their knowledge and skills. Graduate schools give comprehensive examinations, while schools at all levels ordinarily require minimum standards of scholarship or performance for receipt of a diploma. In each case, good measurement is the key to our having confidence in our judgment to certify or not to certify.

Advisement and guidance. One of the traditional roles of the teacher is as an advisor to students. Measurement often provides a quantitative basis for advising, and it also assists students in their decision making. Data from general aptitude tests, performance tests, or interest inventories can help students immensely. Some measures, such as aptitude tests, provide students with a basis for estimating their chances for success in eduation programs. Other measures help students understand how they are like or unlike various vocational groups. Still others may give students an insight into their personal qualities. Measurement can help students learn about themselves and help us assist them in making sensible decisions.

Evaluating programs. In education, we need to know what is working and what is not. We need to know why good programs are good and where bad programs went wrong. Measures provide us with information that helps us make these judgments.

Schoolwide achievement testing helps teachers determine how their school's performance in reading, mathematics, spelling, or writing compares to that of earlier years or to that of a city, state, or national norm. Attitude measures can help determine the success of an adult education program. Judgments about programs are only as good as the measures on which the judgments are based. Even good measures can be misinterpreted, but without them evaluation is sure to be faulty and misleading.

THE RELATIONSHIP OF MEASUREMENT TO EVALUATION

We have stressed the many uses of measurement in education, particularly those involving decision making. The process of using measurements in making decisions is commonly referred to as **evaluation.** Worthen and Sanders (1973) define *evaluation* in a way that stresses the decision-making process:

> Evaluation is the determination of the worth of a thing. It includes obtaining information for use in judging the worth of a program, product, procedure or objective, or the potential utility of alternative approaches designed to attain specified objectives. *(p. 19)*

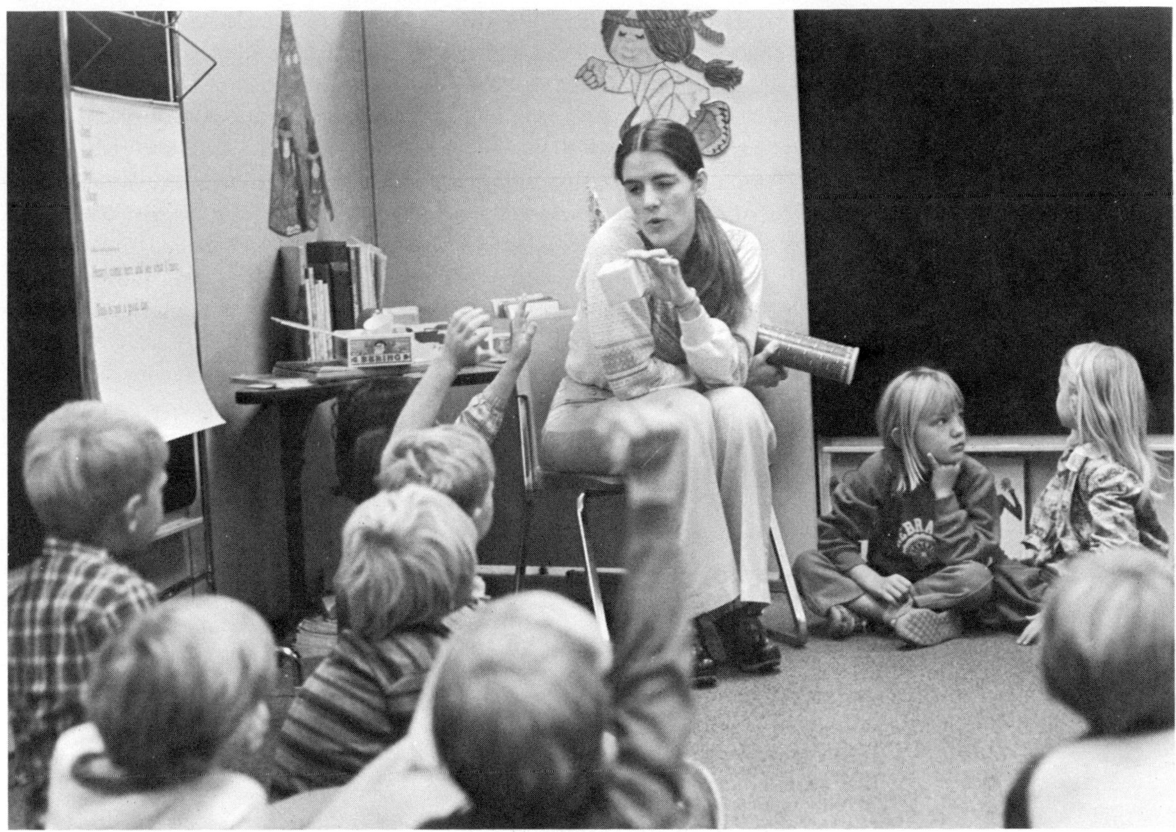

Formative evaluation can take many forms and should occur as often as possible. Here the teacher assesses how well the students understand the concept of "cube."

Evaluation in education involves judging the quality of learning, teaching, and programs. There are four general categories of evaluation (Bloom, Hastings, & Madeus, 1971; Cronbach, 1975; Dick, 1977; Skager, 1978): formative, summative, placement, and diagnostic. In the following sections we examine how the uses of measurement can be related to each category.

Formative Evaluation

Formative evaluation takes place *during* instruction and is designed to help you adjust your instruction to help students meet their objectives. You may use homework as a source of formative evaluation. By scoring the homework you should be able to determine how well your students are progressing toward mastery of your objectives.

Because formative evaluation is designed to give the teacher information about how student learning is progressing, it can and should take many forms, including quizzes, homework, oral responses to teacher questions, or observations. Many teachers have students solve math problems on the chalkboard and, by watching their performance, the teachers can determine how well the students are learning. Other teachers initiate class discussions and use their students' comments as a guide for their own actions.

Formative evaluation should occur as frequently as possible during instruction because it has several important functions: It provides feedback to students and to the instructor; it helps provide pacing (Bloom et al., 1971) and motivation for student learning; and, most important, it allows teachers to adjust their instructional activities to achieve meaningful learning.

The decision of whether to use the results of formative evaluation as a source of grades rests with each individual teacher. Many teachers believe that unless some sort of grade is attached to homework and quizzes (perhaps a check for completed homework or a number grade for quiz results), students will not be motivated to do their best. Other teachers, however, feel that the results of formative evaluation should not be used to determine grades. They reason that the students have not completed their learning and that the results of formative evaluation should be used primarily to help students correct errors (Bertrand & Cebula, 1980). We are inclined to agree with this second line of thought. While some sort of acknowledgment may need to be made for completing assignments, formative evaluation, by its nature, is not suited for formal grading. (A thorough discussion of grading is presented in the next chapter.)

Formative evaluation is often neglected: testing, homework, and other measurements are infrequently used. To neglect formative evaluation, however, is to squander a considerable resource for your teaching and for student learning.

Summative Evaluation

Summative evaluation typically occurs at the end of instruction and is designed to determine the extent to which the goals of instruction have been met. According to Bloom, Hastings, and Madeus, "Summative evaluation has as its primary goals grading or certifying students, judging the effectiveness of the teacher, and comparing curricula" (1971, p. 20). There are many ways in which summative evaluation can take place. Final examinations on a unit of instruction, term papers, work samples (such as a painting, a sculpture, or a specific type of weld), performances, and ratings of attitudes are all possible forms of summative evaluation. Summative evaluation must be congruent with instructional objectives. It is administered not so much to direct learning as to determine if learning has taken place.

Placement Evaluation

Placement evaluation is made *before* the start of instruction. The goal of placement evaluation is to match students with beneficial instruction based on their entry characteristics. Determining whether a child should enter kindergarten early is an example of a placement evaluation, as is deciding which instructional group a student should join.

As Bloom and his associates (1971) point out, summative evaluations from prior learning can be used in making placement decisions. Grades, for example, can be used as a criterion for student participation in a program. Standardized tests are also frequently used for placement. Seldom, however, do standardized tests or other summative measures provide enough information for making decisions about instruction. The best placement decisions take both the learner and the setting into account. Instructional decisions require specific knowledge of how well the student's preparation and abilities are matched to what is to be learned, as we saw in Chapter Twelve. Such knowledge can best be gained by specific, teacher-designed measures that diagnose students' prior learning in relation to instructional objectives.

Diagnostic Evaluation

Diagnostic evaluation, which is used to determine why students are having problems in learning, is usually conducted *during* instruction. Teachers need to know if students' learning problems stem from their general background, perceptual abilities, motivational deficiencies, or the ineffectiveness of educational programs. Ideally, diagnosis will lead to an effective remedial program. We know that this often does not happen, however. A behavioral disorder may be labeled and defined (as when a child is determined to be "emotionally disturbed"), but only a few diagnoses lead directly to a prescription of steps that will solve the problem. A diagnosis can be very useful when we try to experiment with ways of dealing with a child's problem. The more we know about the nature of a child's difficulty, the greater the likelihood of finding an effective program. A thorough diagnosis may also reveal that the problem is not within the child himself or herself but that the child's current program is ineffective. Proper motivational conditions may be lacking, for example, or the content may be poorly sequenced. When such factors are corrected, the child's "problem" may disappear.

Teacher-made tests can be effective diagnostic devices because of their close relationship to the curriculum, although traditionally most diagnostic tests have been standardized. Teacher-made tests may reveal specific areas of instruction in which a student needs remedial help. Standardized tests (discussed in detail in Chapter Fifteen) may be superior in a number of technical ways, but they may lack validity for the specific curriculum in which the student is involved (Popham, 1978).

Diagnostic evaluation sometimes resembles formative evaluation in that it is an ongoing process carried out during instruction. Formative assessment can identify failures in learning and imply alternative approaches to instruction, but if failure continues, diagnostic evaluation may be necessary to more completely identify the causes of failure. Formative evaluation is usually more specific and keyed to particular units of instruction, while diagnostic evaluation is more general and organized around psychological characteristics of the student.

Research on the Forms of Evaluation

What have researchers found out about the use of formative, summative, placement, and diagnostic evaluation in instruction? Daniel Hursh (1976) reviewed the research on individualized instruction and concluded that all four types were necessary. Programs that omitted one or more of the four were not as effective as programs that included them all. Omitting any of the forms of evaluation reduced student learning and feedback to students and teachers and generally impeded the way in which instruction could be adjusted to fit the needs of individuals.

Semb and his colleagues (Conrad, Spencer, & Semb, 1978; Semb, 1974) studied forms of individualized instruction that included variations in evaluation. Overall, there was a great deal of flexibility in how programs implemented evaluation, but evaluation was always an essential part of effective instruction. Conrad and colleagues (1978), for example, compared proctor grading* to self-grading, two types of formative evaluation. They determined that both types had positive effects on student learning. The most accurate evaluations were from self-grading but the biggest impact on the final examination came from proctor grading.

The effects of evaluation have been examined in many settings and in a wide range of courses. The results are almost uniformly positive. Even the production of creative ideas, a skill long thought to be best nurtured in nonevaluative settings, has been shown to benefit from evaluation. Glover (1979b), for example, demonstrated that groups working on creative problem-solving tasks (as discussed in Chapter 6) generated more ideas, more different kinds of ideas, and more original ideas if they expected and received evaluation than if they did not. In general, it appears that properly used evaluation helps student learning in all areas of the educational process (Buros, 1977).

* A proctor is a person who is trained to grade papers, monitor tests, and provide feedback—usually a person who has already completed the course, sometimes a graduate student, but not the instructor.

PRACTICE EXERCISE 13–1
Types of Evaluation

For each of the following situations, classify the evaluation as (a) formative, (b) summative, (c) placement, or (d) diagnostic.

1. Each Friday, teachers in an experimental team-taught class collect "reaction cards" (on which students write whatever thoughts they have about the week's teaching), talk about the reaction cards as a team, and adjust their plans for the upcoming week.
2. The professor in Zoology 478 gives a comprehensive final examination of 100 multiple-choice questions and 6 short essay questions that cover the entire course.
3. An architect takes the examination of the state board of examiners in order to become fully certified as a practicing architect in the state of California.
4. For each forty units of instruction, the fourth-grade reading teachers devise their own brief skills test that is keyed to the objectives and that permits analysis of how well the objectives have been obtained.
5. A second grader who has been referred to a school psychologist because of lack of success in the classroom is tested with a variety of measures, including the Wechsler Intelligence Scale for Children-Revised (WISC-R) and the McCarthy Scales of Children's Abilities.
6. Applicants for graduate study in a department of educational psychology (to which about 10 percent of applicants are admitted) are required to take the Graduate Record Examination as part of the admission process.
7. At a biweekly meeting, directors of a federal project intended to identify handicapped children who have been served by special education services evaluate their success and failures and set their goals for the next two weeks.
8. End-of-semester grades are used to "track" students into three levels of second-semester English.
9. Students in doctoral programs are required by the graduate college and their supervisory committees to take comprehensive written and oral examinations covering the general area of graduate training and their particular research specialty.
10. A university student who is troubled with who she is and what she is going to be takes several personality and interest inventories as a part of her visits with a counselor at the university counseling center.

Properly used evaluation greatly aids student learning. The teacher's judgment of a student's negatives in a photography class helps the student see how well she has applied several new concepts.

Summary of Formative, Summative, Placement, and Diagnostic Evaluation

Measurement is used in many different forms of evaluation. Formative evaluation is usually specific, frequent, and keyed to instructional units. It attempts to improve the learning process as it occurs. Summative evaluation takes place at the culmination of learning for the purpose of grading or certifying student performance. It is usually more general than formative evaluation and occurs less frequently.

Placement evaluation occurs prior to instruction and is used to determine what kind of instruction students will benefit from. Diagnosis during instruction is usually problem oriented, that is, it is used to locate problems impeding learning. Failures in instruction and in subsequent attempts at remediation often lead to diagnostic evaluation.

NORM-REFERENCED AND CRITERION-REFERENCED MEASURES

An important distinction is commonly made between norm-referenced and criterion-referenced measures. **Norm-referenced** measures are constructed with the intent of ranking students on a numerical (0–100) or letter (A–F) scale. Simply, the major purpose of norm-referenced measures is to compare one person's performance *with the performance of others*. In standardized testing, an individual's score is compared to the performance of a carefully selected group of individuals (the "norm group"). In the classroom, other students make up the reference group to which an individual's score is compared.

Criterion-referenced measures compare an individual's score *to a standard of performance,* not to other students. A level of achievement is ordinarily fixed in advance; the learner is then judged as either having achieved or not having achieved the objectives satisfactorily. While criterion-referenced measures were developed at the turn of the century (Payne, 1974), they were never widely used and it wasn't until Glaser (1963) and Popham and Husek (1969) reintroduced them that they gained general use, especially in individualized instruction.

Determining the standard of performance is often the most difficult part of a criterion-referenced evaluation. If we are trying to set a standard for the quality of essays written by tenth-grade students, for example, we would surely have to spend a great deal of time thinking about such things as punctuation (How well do the students have to punctuate?), organization (What kinds of organization are acceptable? How many errors can students make in organization?), and many other important elements in producing an essay (spelling, grammar, style, consistency of tense, and so on). Finally, we would have to set a minimum standard for acceptable student performance in essay writing.

How does one decide whether to use a norm-referenced or a criterion-referenced form of measurement? Ebel (1978) argues that it is not an either/or decision but rather one of which/when. The starting point for each type of measure is much the same, as Ebel points out:

> Looked at individually, the items used in the two tests are indistinguishable. Both are intended to assess achievement in learning. The kinds of tasks to be included in each can be specified precisely. The territory and boundaries of the domain of achievements from which particular tasks are to be selected can be defined with all the precision that is necessary for either type of test. *(1978, p. 4)*

Ebel (1978) argues, however, that there are several advantages to norm-referenced forms of measurement, among them the following:

> They assess pupils' broad general level of knowledge and understanding of a subject, not their mastery of a few particulars.
>
> They assess achievement at all levels of excellence and mediocrity. They do not focus primarily on minimum essentials.
>
> They are consistent with the view that achievement in learning is a

> matter of more or less, not of everything (master) or nothing (didn't master). *(p. 5)*

Because they provide a single score that summarizes a pupil's general level of achievement, and not "an extended inventory of things learned or not learned," norm-referenced measures are most useful for summative, not formative, evaluation. They show how successful students' learning has been in comparison to others' learning and how successful teachers' efforts were in bringing about that learning.

Criterion-referenced measures appear to be particularly useful in judging the mastery of instructional objectives (see Bloom et al., 1971). Mehrens and Lehmann (1975) offer the following viewpoint:

> Traditionally, the principal use of criterion-referenced measurement has been in "mastery tests." A mastery test is a particular type of criterion-referenced test. Mastery, as the word is typically used, connotes an either/or situation. The person has either achieved (mastered) the objective(s) satisfactorily or has not. Mastery tests are used in programs of individualized instruction. . . . Such instructional programs are composed of units or modules, usually considered hierarchical, each based on one or more instructional objectives. Each individual is required to work on the unit until he has achieved or "mastered" the unit. In such programs the instructional decision of what to do with a student is not dependent on how his performance compares to others. If he has performed adequately on the objectives, then the decision is to move on to the next units of study. . . . If instructional procedures are organized so that time is the dimension that varies and degree of mastery is held constant, then mastery tests should be used in greater proportion than they are now. *(p. 52)*

Other uses of criterion-referenced measures are to provide information for decision making about instructional programs (have the instructional objectives been reached?). Similarly, criterion-referenced measures may be useful in diagnosing learning difficulties (on which objectives did a particular student do poorly?).

Generally speaking, criterion-referenced measurement is used when there is less concern about comparing students but more concern about ensuring competence. For an ambulance attendant, "fairly good" performance in applying an air splint to a fracture is obviously not good enough. A demonstration of full mastery of the skill is needed. Criterion-referenced measurement requires clear statements of objectives and a fixed level of judging satisfactory achievement (on each of five simulated victims, without leaving out any of the six steps in the procedure, the ambulance attendance can apply . . .). Typically, the form of evaluation best suited to individualized instruction is criterion-referenced.

Traditionally, however, the majority of educational measures have been of the norm-referenced type. Norm-referenced measures lend themselves well to grading (the person who earns 91 on a test can be compared with a person who scores 78 or 64). If norm-referenced tests are carefully constructed, they can provide the teacher and others with accurate and valid information on how students compare to one another. They also can provide invaluable feedback to learners on their achievement relative to others in the group.

In sum, then, the major distinction in the designation of measurement as norm- or criterion-referenced is made on the basis of the form of the test or observation (for example, the choice between a rating scale and a checklist) and the use of the measure (comparing students versus assessing competence). If your purpose in measurement is to rank students and to be able to compare them to one another, your measurement

In norm referenced measures, our students' performances are compared with the performances of others.

should be of the norm-referenced type, If you want to determine whether your students meet a particular standard, then your choice should be criterion-referenced.

RELIABILITY AND VALIDITY OF MEASURES

We have seen that there are a large number of uses for measurement in education and that the type of measurement chosen should relate closely to the purpose of that measurement. Regardless of the form of measurement chosen, however, the measurement must be consistent (it must be reliable) and it must measure what it claims to measure (it must be valid).

Reliability

A measure is reliable if it is consistent and accurate. If a student took the same test twice in a row, scoring 91 on the first administration and only 64 on the second, we would say that the test was unreliable. Unreliable measures are of little, if any, value in education. What good is it to know that a student scored 91 on a test when this student scored quite differently on a retest? If we were to retest students using the same test (assuming no learning or changes on their part) and find that their scores were almost identical, however, then we could have much greater confidence in our measurement. If our measurements are not reliable, we can never be sure whether the results mean anything. Our decisions concerning the future of students are far too important to trust to unreliable measurements. But how can we improve the reliability of our tests and observations? A good place to begin is with the cause of unreliability—measurement error.

Measurement error is the part of a person's score unrelated to the quality you are trying to measure. Suppose that you have constructed a test to measure your students' knowledge of American history in the period 1900–1910. If anything else besides their knowledge of American history affects their score, you are faced with a measurement error. A score on an essay examination may result from any of a variety of factors; how much the person knows about that period of history (which is what you are trying to measure), scoring mistakes, misreading of the questions by the student, a broken pencil at a crucial moment, critical lapses in memory at just the wrong times, or a poorly constructed test. All of these factors except knowledge of history are sources of error and will make the test unreliable. Practically speaking, this means that we cannot completely trust such a score since retesting may result in a very different score, even if the student's knowledge remains relatively constant.

APPLICATIONS FOR TEACHING

How can measurement error be reduced? Listed below are some general principles of measurement that can be incorporated into the design of any measurement device—quizzes, tests, observations, ratings, and checklists. Use of these principles will result in reliable measurement.

1. Directions to the student should be clear and unambiguous. If students are faced with ambiguous directions and unclear descriptions of what you expect, error will be introduced into the measurement process. Unclear directions are likely to cause students to do things you don't want them to do. Instructions that are too wordy can turn a mathematics quiz into a reading quiz, as students struggle to decipher the instructions. You don't want to have a measure of student learning ruined because your directions weren't clear.

Likewise, students need to understand the criteria for evaluation in performance areas such as music, speech, and athletics. If students know the factors on which their performance will be rated, they are more likely to give a performance that is representative of their capabilities. A student who does not perform well because he or she has not understood exactly what to do has not been rated on performance, but instead on ability to understand the directions.

2. Make your scoring or rating as objective as possible. One of the greatest sources of error in measurement is the changeability of graders and observers. Without clear guidelines, graders are likely to rate some answers or papers higher and some lower for the wrong reasons—their mood when grading, the neatness of the paper, their own misunderstanding of what criteria students are being evaluated on, or just plain fatigue. Graders of student work and raters of student performance need to have objective criteria to help them make their judgments. These criteria are statements or models that tell clearly what levels of student performance are inadequate, adequate, or superior. Model answers, for example, provide a standard of comparison on which graders can base their judgments.

Sometimes different formats are called for. Compared to essay examinations, objective tests reduce the chances of error in scoring and increase reliability. Similarly, a checklist may serve to guide observers and reduce subjectivity in the observations they make. Any method that reduces subjectivity will help increase the reliability of measures.

3. Sample as much of the students' behavior as possible. You may not think of a test as a sample of behavior, but it most surely is: Each item or question requires students to make a response and samples some aspect of the students' abilities. In general, the longer tests are, the more likely they are to be reliable. Similarly, several samples of work (such as several short papers) are more likely to result in accurate measurement of the students' abilities than only one sample. In the performance areas, the more observations you make of students, the greater the likelihood that the composite of your observations will be a reliable assessment of the actual level of student performance. If you ask a student only one question about an entire chapter, for example, chances are that luck will play an important part in whether the student will answer that question correctly. The student may not know much about the chapter but just happen to know the one thing you asked. Conversely, it is possible for a student to know a great deal about the chapter but the single thing you asked turns out to be the one thing the student doesn't know.

If reliable measurement is your goal, it needs to be comprehensive enough to avoid errors in sampling. As the amount of student work you assess increases, so does the probable reliability. For reliability, the more the better! Of course, you need to balance the goal of reliability against what you can reasonably ask of your students (a four-hour test?) and of yourself.

Methods of Estimating Reliability

Reliability can be estimated by a variety of quantitative methods, most of which involve the computation of a correlation coefficient. The **correlation coefficient** is a numerical index of the degree of relationship between two sets of measures. The values of the correlation coefficient can range from +1.00 to −1.00. High relationships are shown by values near +1.00 or −1.00, while little or no relationship is shown by values near zero. Positive correlation coefficients indicate *direct* relationships. If we gave a group of students the same test on two different days, for example, a direct relationship would exist if the high scorers on one day were also the high scorers the next day and the low scorers were the same on both days. That is, a positive correlation coefficient is obtained if a test for a group of students shows the same pattern of individual scores on two different administrations of the test.

A correlation coefficient of +1.00 indicates a perfect agreement in the pattern of scores across two administrations of a test. Generally, a correlation coefficient that is high and positive (+.75 through +1.00) indicates that a test is reliable.

Negative correlation coefficients indicate *inverse* relationships. If a group of students was given the same test on two occasions and the results were inverted on the second administration (high scorers on the first day got low scores on the second administration while low scorers on the first day tended to make high scores on the second administration), a negative correlation coefficient would be obtained. A negative coefficient results when scores on two administrations of a test show an opposite (or inverse) pattern. A correlation coefficient of −1.00 indicates complete reversal of the order of scores across two administrations of a test.

Test-Retest Reliability.

Test-retest reliability measures the stability of scores from one administration of a test to a second administration of the same test. Are the scores stable? If they are—that is, the high scorers on the first test are also the high scorers on the second test, the middle scorers are the middle scorers, and the low scorers are still the low scorers—then the correlation and reliability will be high and positive.

The most common means of computing the correlation coefficient is the Pearson *r*. This method is computationally complex, however, and hand calculation can be somewhat difficult. A less complex set of calculations is required for the Spearman ρ (rho).* The following is a com-

*The Pearson *r* is the preferred correlation coefficient for most educational data, since it makes use of the actual scores rather than simply the ranks of the scores. Because of this, the Spearman rho is a somewhat less sensitive measure of correlation and will sometimes miss detecting relationships that actually exist.

putation of the Spearman rho for a sample set of scores from two tests. The formula is as follows:

$$\text{rho} = 1 - \frac{6\Sigma D^2}{N\,(N^2 - 1)}$$

where Σ refers to the sum of a set of numbers, D is the difference in ranks of two scores, and N is the number of pairs of scores available. Assume that scores on the two tests were those in the first two columns of the table below:*

First Test	*Second Test*	*Rank on First Test*	*Rank on Second Test*	D	D^2
94	92	1	1	0	0
89	80	2	3	−1	1
82	88	3	2	1	1
74	64	4	5	−1	1
56	66	5	4	1	1
38	44	6	6	0	0
					$\Sigma D^2 = 4$

$$\text{rho} = 1 - \frac{6\Sigma D^2}{N(N^2 - 1)} = 1 - \frac{6(4)}{6(36 - 1)} = 1 - \frac{24}{6(35)}$$

$$= 1 - \frac{24}{210} = 1 - .11 = +.89$$

Since the index (+.89) is relatively close to +1.00 (which would indicate a perfect correspondence between the ranks on the two tests), we can conclude that the scores were quite stable on the two tests and, hence, quite reliable. A low correlation (+.20 or +.30) or a negative correlation (−.15) would be evidence of unsatisfactory reliability.

Measures of Internal Consistency. It is usually not feasible to give the same test a second time to obtain test-retest reliability. Recall of items from the first test may affect scoring on the second, particularly if the interval between tests is short. If the interval is long, forgetting may occur in some students and not in others. For these reasons, estimates of reliability based on a single administration of a test are used somewhat more frequently.

Measures of *internal consistency* allow us to estimate reliability from one test administration. **Split-half reliability** compares students' performance on one half of a test to their performance on the second half of

*When scores tie, their ranks are averaged. For example, if two people had scored 94 on the first test, their ranks would be (1 + 2) ÷ 2, or 1.5.

"What with the primary mental ability test and the differential aptitude test and the reading readiness test and the basic skills test and the IQ test and the sequential tests of educational progress and the mental maturity test, we haven't been learning *anything* at school."

the test (their scores on the odd items might be compared to their scores on the even items, for example). Ordinarily, the Pearson r correlation is used in these computations. If the test were a reliable one, higher scorers on one part of the test will also be the higher scorers on the other part. Conversely, the lower scorers will be the lower scorers on both halves of the test. A simple formula, the **Spearman-Brown Prophecy Formula,*** is then used to estimate the reliability of the total test, which will be higher than the correlation between the two halves.

Other measures of internal consistency used to estimate reliability are the **Kuder-Richardson 20** and **Kuder-Richardson 21** estimates. Both give us reliability coefficients based on students' performance on a single test. The Kuder-Richardson 20 requires that one look at students' performance on individual items; the Kuder-Richardson 21 can be more easily used by teachers since the only data required are the number of items, the mean of the test, and the variance.†

In all cases, the higher the reliability coefficient, the more confidence we can have in the test. Techniques such as item analysis (discussed in the next chapter) can help us improve test reliability by help-

*Do you recall the effect of the length of the test on reliability? The Spearman-Brown formula is an estimate of what the reliability will be if the length of the test is doubled.

† The concept of variance and its derivative, the standard deviation, are measures of "spread" of test scores. These concepts are important to your in-depth understanding of tests and measurements, and they are discussed, with their computation, in Chapter Fifteen.

ing us eliminate faulty, ambiguous, and confusing items. Our earlier suggestions for improving reliability are also appropriate, including enough test items, giving clear directions, and sampling the content adequately. Also, higher reliability can be attained by making most items moderately difficult, rather than too easy or too hard. Items in an intermediate category best distinguish between good and poor students and thus contribute to accurate measurement.

The field of educational measurement is a highly technical and sophisticated area of inquiry. At the introductory level, most institutions of higher education offer courses in tests and measurements in which detailed analyses of the characteristics of tests and test statistics are carried out. Advanced courses dealing with many specialized measurement topics are also offered in graduate schools of most major institutions. For excellent general descriptions of the areas of tests and measurements, the reader is referred to texts by F. G. Brown (1976), Ebel (1979), Hopkins and Stanley (1981), and Mehrens and Lehmann (1975).

Validity

Reliability is one essential characteristic of good measurement; **validity** is the other. A measurement is said to be valid if it measures what it is intended to measure. Validity requires reliability, but reliability does not assure validity. A test of aptitude for electronics is valid only if it truly measures this aptitude consistently, that is, if it correlates closely with other known measures of this aptitude or it predicts future performance in the area of electronics.

There are several subcategories of validity. **Content validity** is the extent to which a measure samples and represents the content areas to be measured. A biology unit test, for example, would have content validity if and only if it accurately sampled the various areas covered in instruction. For a measure to be valid it must give the same emphasis to content and level of learning as given in instruction. On the other hand, almost everyone has had the depressing experience of a teacher presenting one set of materials and then testing something entirely different. This type of testing (besides being unfair) has very low content validity.

A second category of validity, **construct validity,** is mostly applied to psychological tests. A construct refers to an unobservable concept that is used by investigators to account for regularities in a person's behavior (Thorndike & Hagen, 1978). "Intelligence" and "motivation" are both constructs. Neither is directly observable. They are constructs used to explain why people behave in certain ways. A test is said to have construct validity if we can be reasonably confident that it measures the quality in question (that is, an "intelligence test" is a measure of the construct of intelligence and not some other quality such as motivation or creativity). Tests intended to measure a construct should correlate highly with other measures of the same construct. An example of construct validity would be taking scores from a test of sociability (which presumably measures the construct of sociability) and showing that students possessing more of this construct will have more friends than students possessing less of this construct. "By comparing the number of people who report to be friends of high test scorers with the number

---

PRACTICE EXERCISE 13–2
Improving Reliability and Validity

For each of the following measurement situations, a problem exists that will lead to lowered reliability and validity. Identify the primary problem as related to: (a) unclear directions given to the person being measured, (b) lack of objectivity in scoring, or (c) poor sampling of the person's behavior. Suggest a change in procedures to remedy the problem.

1. Professor Shaetz, in a class in music theory, gives a midterm essay examination that counts for 40 percent of the grade and a final examination (also an essay examination) that counts for 60 percent of the grade.
2. On a multiple-choice test, questions 6 through 10 all pertain to the situation described in question 5. Most students realize this and answer the questions correctly. Several students, however, didn't use the information from item 5. Most of those students miss three or four of the items.
3. The promotion and tenure committee is examining the file for Professor Bailey, who is being considered for promotion. Included in his file are student ratings of his teaching. For most classes he has taught, Professor Bailey has been able to get back ratings from about half of his students. Most are mildly positive.
4. As several professors look over the responses of Helen Dinsmore, a doctoral student, to her comprehensive examination, it is obvious that Helen has misread question 3 and given it an interpretation different from that intended by the writer of the question. Her response is excellent, but it doesn't answer the question. The professors are faced with a serious decision about what to do because her exam hangs in balance.
5. Ms. Brenegan gives a single question on an examination that reads, "Discuss the theory of comprehensive musicianship."
6. Six members of the residence hall staff are interviewing a large number of applicants for several student-assistant positions. With some they talk about the weather, with others their studies, and with others their views of campus issues. They rate the applicants on a scale after spending about five to ten minutes with each per-

reporting friendship for lower scorers, the construct validity of the test can be determined" (Tuckman, 1975, pp. 235–236).

If people don't perform on a test in the way that would be predicted from the nature of the construct, the test has low construct validity. At that point, the test maker or user can doubt either the test *or* the theory, depending on which of the two he or she has least confidence in.

---

son. The five highest scorers are selected. Some people have a real doubt that the best people have been selected and that the process has been fair.

7. Halfway through a stack of term papers, Mr. Webb is interrupted by his two children, who are fighting. After separating them and sending both to their rooms, he resumes his reading of the papers and finishes them. As he is recording the grades the next morning, he discovers that the scores on the thirteen papers he graded after the interruption average nearly 5 points lower than those graded before.
8. Teachers at Belman Elementary School have been justifiably concerned about the noise level in the cafeteria, which ranges between a din and cacophony. Two psychologists monitor the noise level by means of a noise meter, preparing to set up a system in which the students are rewarded for lower noise levels. They find it interesting to note that teachers' judgments of the noise level bear little relation to the actual level. That is, the teachers often complain about the noise at times when it is actually lower than usual, and high-noise days are occasionally judged as "less noisy than usual."
9. The committee for the arts and crafts festival of Lakewood School must judge the entries in each of several categories, such as painting, woodworking, and lithography. Each person on the five-member committee is told to independently select a top-ranking entry in each of the categories. Four of the people are in general agreement on most of the categories but the judgments of the fifth person are "way out." His top choices in each category don't even appear on other people's lists.
10. In a group project in an adult education class, the groups turn in reports that vary widely in quality. Even though most groups appear to have worked hard, several projects are failed or are rated low. A talk with members of the groups reveals that many were unsure about what qualified as an acceptable project, how each member was to contribute, how long the report was to be, and how it was to be organized.

A test with construct validity will perform as expected if it is a measure of the trait in question and if the theory that is related to the trait is a sound one.

The degree to which a measure can accurately predict a future performance is called **predictive validity.** It is of great interest in the use of tests for selection and advisement purposes. If we used an interest inventory (a scale on which individuals indicate their likes and dislikes in interest, vocational, and scholastic areas) to guide students into vocational or career choices, we would need to feel confident that the inventory is meaningfully related to future job performance or satisfaction. What value would there be in giving students advice based on tests that have no predictive validity?

The most critical form of validity for the classroom teacher is content validity. Teachers need to know whether classroom tests accurately and fairly sample the content and the levels of learning they expect of students. The single best way that you can ensure that your tests and measures have content validity is to carefully match them to your instructional objectives by means of a blueprint (or, more formally, a table of specifications). The table of specifications ensures that any measure you construct fits the objectives and levels of learning you require of your students. The process of constructing and using tables of specifications is described in detail in the next chapter (see pages 417–418).

Summary of Reliability and Validity

The principles of reliability and validity enter into every measurement of human performance. They apply in any setting in which performance is judged: courtrooms, classrooms, homes, and the workplace. The question of reliability will always be something like the following: "Can we be sure that we have made an accurate observation; is our observation repeatable?"

Beyond accurate measurement is the question of *what* is being measured. Trivial outcomes can be measured accurately. In fact, many trivial outcomes are much easier to measure than more significant ones. Recall of facts is more readily measured than the ability to apply ideas, solve problems, or be creative, for instance. But is measurement of knowledge of facts valid for our instructional objectives? Usually not. Measures must measure what they are intended to measure. If the objectives of a course in Russian literature include knowledge of characters, recognition of recurring themes, and proper identification of metaphorical references, then a valid evaluation will assess all of these areas. In the same way, ratings of attitudes, interests, or psychomotor skills should measure what they are intended to measure, not attractiveness, personality, or some other dimension.

CHOOSING A METHOD OF MEASUREMENT

A great many elements enter into the decisions you make in choosing a method of measurement. The most basic judgment, of course, is determining whether measurement is needed and what the purpose of the measurement is. Is the measurement to be done in the cognitive, affective, or psychomotor domain? Is the measurement to be used for diagnostic, formative, summative, or placement purposes? Will norm-referenced or criterion-referenced measurement be best for your purposes? Also, does the measurement meet the necessary technical requirements for good measurement, that is, does it sample a representative part of what the student knows or can do, does it sample enough student behavior, and do the students understand clearly enough what is expected of them in order for you to obtain a reliable and valid measure?

The basic questions that arise in the choices you make about measurement are summarized in Table 13–1. These will help you think about the choices you will constantly be making as an evaluator of student performance, of your own teaching, and of the worth of programs in which you are involved.

All of the judgments you make relate to the central concern in measurement—is the method of measurement that you use the best one for measuring the critical outcomes of learning and teaching? For affective outcomes, rating scales or behavioral observations may represent a better choice than other methods, particularly testing. In psychomotor skill areas, checklists or rating scales are likely to match up most validly with the behaviors being measured. In the cognitive areas, a wide range of measurement methods is available. Your choice among types of test, work samples, or other forms of assessment will be determined in large part by your instructional objectives (Bloom et al., 1956).

TABLE 13–1
Key Questions in Decisions about Methods of Measurement

1. Is there a purpose for the measurement?
2. Are the objectives being measured in the cognitive, affective, or psychomotor domain?
3. Is the measurement used for placement, diagnostic, formative, or summative evaluation?
4. Does the measure meet the requirements for reliability?
5. Does the measure meet the requirements for validity?
6. Is the measure feasible from the standpoint of administration, student time required, and scoring?

SUMMARY

Measurement pervades all of education and provides us with the data necessary for making educational decisions. The use of educational measurement in decision making is referred to as evaluation. Formative evaluation is designed to improve the learning process while it occurs. Summative evaluation occurs at the culmination of learning and is used to grade or certify students. Placement evaluation is designed to determine what kinds of instruction students will benefit from, and diagnostic evaluation is used to locate problems that may be impeding learning.

Criterion-referenced evaluation is based on the determination of whether learners have achieved a standard of performance. It is well suited for certifying competency and determining progress in individualized instruction. Norm-referenced evaluation, which compares a student's performance to that of others, is best suited for providing feedback on achievement relative to that of others in a group.

Since educational decisions can only be as good as the data on which they are based, measures must be carefully chosen so that they are both reliable and valid. A reliable measure makes consistent measurements over multiple administrations, and a valid measure measures what it is intended to measure. As you continue through Chapters Fourteen and Fifteen you will obtain the knowledge and skills necessary to make good decisions about educational measurement. Chapter Fourteen presents a detailed discussion of the major forms of testing, observational methods, and product assessments available to the classroom teacher. Chapter Fifteen presents the major categories of standardized testing.

Suggested Readings

Buros, O. K. Fifty years in testing: Some reminiscences, criticisms, and suggestions. *Educational Researcher,* 1977, *6,* 9–15.

This brief article, written by Oscar Buros late in his life, provides some interesting insights into the development of the field of testing.

Ebel, R. L. The case for norm-referenced measurements. *Educational Researcher,* 1978, *7,* 3–5.

Ebel's article is an excellent exposition of the positive features of norm-referenced evaluation.

Hopkins, K. D., & Stanley, J. C. *Educational and psychological measurement and evaluation* (6th ed.). Englewood Cliffs, N.J.: Prentice-Hall, 1981.

This text has long been recognized as an excellent introduction to educational measurement.

Kulhavy, R. W. Feedback in written instruction. *Review of Educational Research,* 1977, *47,* 211–232.

This article is an excellent in-depth source for information about feedback.

Popham, W. J. The case for criterion-referenced measurements. *Educational Researcher,* 1978, *7,* 6–10.

A companion to Ebel's article on norm-referenced measurement, Popham's article provides an excellent summary of the advantages of criterion-referenced evaluation.

Answers to Practice Exercise 13–1

1. *Formative.* Information is collected during the educational experiences and is used to change or modify ongoing instruction.
2. *Summative.* The examination is at the conclusion of instruction and is intended as a general measure of achievement in the course.
3. *Placement.* In conjunction with other evidence, the examination results are used either to accept or reject the architect's application for full certification.
4. *Formative.* This example contains most of the characteristics of formative evaluation: It is keyed to specific objectives, occurs frequently during learning, and is used analytically.
5. *Diagnostic.* The purpose here is to identify more precisely the nature of the second grader's problems in terms of such variables as intelligence and developmental level.
6. *Placement.* The examination is a part of the screening process by which applicants are selected for graduate study.
7. *Formative.* This evaluation is used to guide the project. It takes place frequently within the project and is keyed to the project objectives.
8. *Placement.* Summative evaluations from earlier experiences are sometimes used for subsequent placement. The particular use described in the example is not a good one, in the authors' opinion. A better approach would be to pretest students on the basis of their attainment of the objectives of the second course and modify instruction in light of the results.
9. *Summative.* This is an end-of-learning evaluation intended to determine and certify the competence of the individual.
10. *Diagnostic.* The evaluations occur as a result of problems the student encountered. They are intended to further her and the counselor's understanding of why she is experiencing these difficulties and to help them work out solutions to the problem.

Answers to Practice Exercise 13–2

1. *Poor sampling.* Only two examinations, particularly two essay examinations, do not constitute an adequate sample of what students may know and can do. More tests, shorter tests, shorter assign-

ments, and other work samples would give the teacher a more reliable sample of student learning.

2. *Unclear directions.* Confusion on an exam often results from lack of explanation of expected performance. Material relevant to answering questions should be clearly indicated and highlighted if necessary.
3. *Poor sampling.* We don't know what the ratings would have been had all of them been received. Are the missing ratings positive or negative? We don't know, but might suspect that students who didn't like the course might not bother to turn in a student rating form. The best solution is to make sure ratings are obtained from all or nearly all of the students.
4. *Unclear directions.* Although misreading may be deliberate, the fault is usually in an unclear or poorly worded question. Essay questions on any exam should direct the learner to the type of response that will be acceptable. The solution, although it is too late for this situation, is to write unambiguous questions and to try them out on other people, such as another faculty member, in advance.
5. *Unclear directions.* This is only a little better than "Discuss the Civil War." Rewrite the question, focusing the student response on specific issues and areas.
6. *Poor sampling.* Each person is "tested" under different conditions and then only a brief sample of behavior is obtained. At the very least, interview conditions should be made standard. An even better approach would be to interview each person for a longer time (a larger sample) and to obtain other persons' judgments of their skills (more samples of behavior). Problems are also likely to exist in the areas of unclear directions (does the applicant know what is expected of him or her?) and subjective scoring (what criteria form the basis for the rating?), but the sampling problem is especially severe.
7. *Lack of objectivity in scoring.* The lower scores seem to have resulted from a change in the scorer, rather than from any real difference in the papers. Having "model" answers, specifying criteria for scoring the questions, and scoring each question on all papers before scoring a second question are all ways to reduce this kind of error.
8. *Lack of objectivity in scoring.* Teachers' judgments form a kind of scale—terribly noisy, noisy, less noisy than usual. The point is that teacher judgments are highly subjective. Whereas the meter readings represent a more precise and objective measure, the teacher ratings obviously contain some sources of bias, such as whether the teacher feels good or bad, what the teacher is paying attention to, and to whom the teacher is talking. We need to confirm our judgments with others whenever possible. Better yet, we need to rely

more on objective data—perhaps not noise meters, but information that is less subject to distortion.

9. *Lack of objectivity in scoring.* Here is an obvious example of different people having different ideas about excellence. To make this judgment fairer, criteria for making the judgment should be outlined. Each entry might be ranked by each judge for originality and technical execution, for example, with these characteristics defined as clearly as possible. In that case everyone would be rating approximately the same qualities.
10. *Unclear directions.* It is unlikely that people will reach a goal if they don't know what the goal is. What's more, the task of comparing one project to another becomes very difficult because there may be few criteria that cut across diverse projects. Most damaging, however, is that students are not judged on how well they can do the project but on how lucky they are in interpreting the assignment. The solution is simple. The professor should be clear in explaining what he or she expects the groups to do.

IMPORTANT EVENTS IN THE DEVELOPMENT OF EDUCATIONAL MEASUREMENT

The topic of educational measurement includes important contributions from the fields of astronomy, mathematics, physics, economics, agriculture, and sociology. In the beginning of our chronology we emphasize events pertinent to the topics discussed in this chapter. We do not list developments in probability theory and the application of this theory to statistical techniques. Similary, important events more closely associated with Chapters Fourteen and Fifteen are not listed here. The work of Charles Spearman, for example, is listed in the chronology following Chapter Fifteen. An excellent source book for early events in the formation of statistical methods in psychology is Miller's *Mathematics and Psychology* (1964).

Date(s)	***Person(s)***	***Work***	***Impact***
1845	Boston schoools	Comparative testing	The Boston schools first employed a comparative-testing approach by administering the same examination to students in seventeen Boston schools (as well as one in Roxbury) (Englehart & Thomas, 1972).
1845	Mann	"Boston grammar and writing schools"	In 1845 Horace Mann, reacting to the testing procedures of the Boston schools, strongly urged that educators stop their heavy reliance on oral testing and turn more to written evaluations.
1846	Bravais	Basic theoretical work on correlation	Auguste Bravais's theoretical work set the stage for contemporary methods of computing reliability, validity, and tests of statistical significance (Boring, 1950).
1869	Galton	*Hereditary genius*	Sir Francis Galton's efforts in assigning degrees of genius mark the first attempts to assess human intellectual abilities from the perspective of the normal curve.
1877	Galton	Basic work on correlation	"It was Galton who first worked out the methods of statistical correlation"

Date(s)	*Person(s)*	*Work*	*Impact*
			(Boring, 1950, p. 479). Correlation, of course, is widely employed in modern psychological and educational research.
1890	Cattell	"Mental tests and measurements"	In this report, J. M. Cattell used the term *mental test* for the first time. He described a variety of verbal, physical, and sensory measures and how they were constructed.
1892	Edgeworth	Description of basic statistical methods	F. Y. Edgeworth coined the term *coefficient of correlation (r),* which has been in use since his time.
1895–1905	Rice	Comparative testing	J. M. Rice is typically credited as the major developer of comparative testing in the United States (Englehart & Thomas, 1972; C. C. Ross, 1947).
1896	Pearson	Contemporary methods of computing correlation	While many people contributed to the development of the correlation technique, Karl Pearson was the person who first worked out correlation problems in modern form (Boring, 1950). In fact, the most-used correlation coefficient is called the Pearson *r*.
1901	Galton, Pearson, & Weldon	*Biometrika*	Galton, Pearson, and W. F. R. Weldon established the journal *Biometrika,* the first journal devoted primarily to mathematical research in psychology and biology.
1904	Thorndike	*An introduction to the theory of mental and social measurement*	E. L. Thorndike's text was the first major book written for educators and psychologists on measurement. He was the first person to demonstrate the applicability of statistical methods to problems of psychological and educational measurement.

Date(s)	*Person(s)*	*Work*	*Impact*
1910	Whipple	*Manual of mental and physical tests*	G. M. Whipple's manual for teachers was one of the first books designed to facilitate teachers' use of tests. His book included fifty-four examples of measures and gave precise instructions for administering and scoring them.
1916	Starch	*Educational measurement*	Daniel Starch's textbook was the major text employed to instruct educators in measurement techniques from 1916 to the early 1920s.
1918	Ayres	"History and present status of educational measurements"	Leonard Ayres wrote the first history of educational measurement in the United States. His work defined the area in 1918.
1918	Thorndike	"The nature, purposes, and general methods of measurements of educational products"	"In February 1918, Thorndike published what has proved to be probably the most influential paper that has ever appeared on educational measurements" (Ross, 1947, p. 49). His emphasis on "whatever exists at all exists in some amount" (E. L. Thorndike, 1918, p. 16) has guided educational measurement ever since.
1922	McCall	*How to measure in education*	W. A. McCall's text was the first popularized book aimed at classroom measurement. McCall advocated the use of standard scores (see Chapter Fifteen) to permit comparability of performance in different subject areas.
1925–1977	Lindquist	Basic work in educational measurement	E. F. Lindquist, a professor at the University of Iowa, was perhaps the dominant figure in educational measurement from 1925 until his death in 1977. His efforts and accomplishments in the area are too numerous to recount and have become accepted in all areas of educational measurement.

Date(s)	*Person(s)*	*Work*	*Impact*
1936	Guilford	*Psychometric methods*	J. P. Guilford's text was an early and comprehensive guide for constructing tests and scales for measuring psychological and educational outcomes. Guilford had a broad influence on test construction and usage.
1936	Thompson	Factor analysis	Godfrey H. Thompson was the major figure in the development and use of factor analysis procedures in educational measurement (Boring, 1950).
1936	Hawkes, Lindquist, & Mann	*The construction and use of achievement examinations*	This text, sponsored by the American Council on Education, provided the first comprehensive and teachable coverage of educational measurement for teachers (Lindquist, 1951).
1936	Many individuals	*Psychometrika*	*Psychometrika* was the first journal devoted solely to issues in psychological measurement.
1940	Kuder	*Psychological and Educational Measurement*	G. Frederic Kuder, widely known for his work in developing interest inventories, founded the journal *Psychological and Educational Measurement,* which was a major outlet for measurement research in psychology and education.
1942	Tyler	"General statement on evaluation"	Ralph W. Tyler, a major figure in educational measurement for more than forty years, provided an excellent overview of educational measurement in this article in the *Journal of Educational Research.*
1945	National Society for the Study of Education	*Forty-fifth yearbook, part I: Measurement of understanding*	This report reviewed the state of the art of educational testing circa 1945 and outlined several critical issues that became important research areas in subsequent years.

Date(s)	*Person(s)*	*Work*	*Impact*
1950–present	Thorndike	Primary work in educational and psychological measurement	Robert L. Thorndike, the son of E. L. Thorndike, is one of the major figures in educational measurement during the last thirty years. Especially well known are his general texts on educational and psychological measurement.
1951	Lindquist	*Educational measurement*	This text, edited by E. F. Lindquist, became the classic measurement text against which others were judged for many years.
1956	Bloom et al.	*Taxonomy of education objectives: The classification of educational goals. Handbook I: Cognitive domain*	The taxonomy developed by Bloom and his associates provided an impetus for the development of teacher-made tests that could assess higher-order levels of student learning.
1963	Many individuals	*Journal of Educational Measurement*	The *Journal of Educational Measurement* has been the major journal in educational measurement since its inception.
1969	Popham & Husek	"Implications of criterion-referenced measurement"	James Popham and T. F. Husek outlined characteristics of criterion-referenced measurement in this article, which ushered in the era of criterion-referenced tests keyed to instructional objectives.
1971	Bloom, Hastings, & Madeus	*Handbook on formative and summative evaluation of student learning*	This text represented a state-of-the-art description of the evaluation of student learning at the beginning of the 1970s.
1979	Many individuals	*Behavior Assessment*	The journal *Behavior Assessment* was founded to provide an outlet for behaviorally oriented research in measurement.
1980	Plake	"A comparison of a statistical and subjective procedure to ascertain item validity"	This article by Barbara Plake showed that subjective methods of identifying biased items on achievement tests are

Date(s)	*Person(s)*	*Work*	*Impact*
			not always reliable. Because of research of this type, statistical methods are now typically used to help identify items that may unfairly discriminate by age, sex, or ethnic group membership.

Chapter Fourteen

TEACHER-MADE TESTS

TESTING

— **Planning Tests**
— **Essay Questions** / Form of Essay Questions / Scoring Essay Examinations
— **Objective Questions** / Completion Items / True-False Items / Multiple-Choice Items / Matching Items

APPLICATIONS FOR TEACHING: ITEM ANALYSIS

OBSERVATIONAL METHODS

— **Performances and Work Samples**
— **Rating Scales**
— **Checklists**
— **Behavioral Observation**

OTHER EVALUATION METHODS

— **Anecdotal Records**
— **Sociometric Methods**
— **Self-Report Methods**

GRADING

— **Norm-Referenced Grading**
— **Criterion-Referenced Grading**
— **Grading on Improvement**
— **Grading on Expectations**
— **Grading by Contract**

APPLICATIONS FOR TEACHING: MISTAKES TO AVOID WHEN GRADING

SUMMARY

SUGGESTED READINGS

ANSWERS TO PRACTICE EXERCISES

IMPORTANT EVENTS IN THE DEVELOPMENT OF TEACHER-MADE TESTS

An old saying in education is that the single best way to evaluate teachers is to look at the tests they give. Good tests and measures are the foundation of good teaching. The more adaptable and competent you are in measuring student knowledge and performance, the better your teaching will be.

For most people, the idea of measurement in education has always been synonymous with testing, that is, giving students a set of questions to which they must respond. Indeed, the title of this chapter recognizes their importance. Educational measurement, however, includes much more than testing.

In this chapter you will learn about a variety of methods for measuring the outcomes of learning. We hope that the acquaintance becomes more than a passing one. Skill in constructing and using a variety of measurement methods will greatly increase your overall effectiveness as a teacher.

Objectives

After reading this chapter, you should be able to meet the following objectives.

1. Develop tables of specifications for measures of student learning.
2. Construct appropriate essay questions and scoring guides.
3. Construct high-quality true-false, completion, matching, and multiple-choice items.
4. Perform an item analysis on a test.
5. Construct rating scales and checklists.
6. Use and interpret two forms of sociometric evaluations.
7. Make accurate decisions about the form of assessment to use in different educational settings.

TESTING

As F. G. Brown (1976) has pointed out, *test* is a common word that is seldom precisely defined. At the most general level of meaning, all of the measures we discuss in this chapter could be classified as tests; that is, they represent a systematic procedure for measuring a sample of behavior (F. G. Brown, 1976, pp. 7–8). In this chapter, however, we will use a more specific and familiar definition. A **test** is a sample of questions that requires students to select or supply written or oral responses. These responses are then judged and evaluated for accuracy and completeness. Testing defined in this way is the most frequently used and most important measure of achievement at every level of education (Ebel, 1979). By the time most people are adults they have taken literally hundreds of tests ranging from classroom quizzes to standardized achievement tests. Testing is the cornerstone of measuring the cognitive goals of education: acquisition of knowledge, ability to analyze and synthesize, and capabilities for problem solving (Bertrand & Cebula, 1980).

While the assessment of cognitive objectives is a major purpose of testing, tests are also frequently used to assist in the validation of complex psychomotor performances (Thorndike & Hagen, 1978). Examinations for drivers' licenses almost always include a test that assesses knowledge of driving laws and safe driving practices. The assumption, of course, is that this knowledge is related to the desired psychomotor performances, namely, safe driving habits. Coupled with appropriate psychomotor assessment, testing helps us make better judgments.

Testing may also be used as part of an overall assessment of students' attainment of affective objectives (Hopkins & Stanley, 1981). In many people's estimation, an affective objective such as "cultural appreciation" requires prior knowledge of historical information and current cultural practices (Anderson & Sclove, 1980). Tests may be used to assess such basic knowledge. Of course, we need to realize that the testing of knowledge is not enough to assess whether affective goals have been attained, just as it is not enough to assure us that psychomotor objectives have been reached (Hopkins & Stanley, 1981). Other, additional measures are needed.

Planning Tests

High-quality testing begins with careful planning (Ebel, 1979). What is the purpose of the test? What should the test cover? What should the test be like—should it be essay, oral, or objective? Is a test really the best way of measuring the attainment of the objectives or should observation or some other method be employed? These questions can best be answered if one begins at the right place—with your instructional objectives (Hopkins & Stanley, 1981). A test is developed from instructional objectives by means of a blueprint or, as it is more formally called, a table of specifications.

A **table of specifications** contains a minimum of two parts: the areas (groupings of objectives) to be covered in the test and an indication of how much of the test will be assigned to each area (Hopkins & Stanley, 1981). Many teachers also like to include some indication of the level of learning being assessed. Table 14–1 shows a sample table of

TABLE 14–1
An Instructor's Table of Specifications for a Hypothetical 40-Item Test On Chapter Thirteen, An Introduction to Measurement

				Number of Test Items for Each Level of Learning	
Content Area	*Time Spent Instructing (in minutes)*	*Emphasis (as percentage of total time)*	*Number of Test Items*	*Knowledge/ Comprehension*	*Application/ Analysis/ Evaluation*
Uses of measurement	30	15	6	2	4
Measurement & evaluation	40	20	8	2	6
Norm- and criterion-referenced evaluation	50	25	10	3	7
Reliability	50	25	10	2	8
Validity	30	15	6	1	5
Total	**200**	**100**	**40**	**10**	**30**

specifications for a test on Chapter Thirteen, "'An Introduction to Measurement." The general idea is that the test accurately represent the emphasis given in instruction and in the instructional objectives. Table 14–1 shows that the teacher has given most of the instructional emphasis to the topics of norm- and criterion-referenced measurement (25%) and to reliability (25%). The test reflects that emphasis by containing ten items from each of these two areas.

You can follow a similar plan for any test you construct. Place the content areas down the left-hand column. Then record how much time you spent on each content area (our example assumes four 50-minute periods, or 200 minutes). Calculate the percentage of emphasis placed on each instructional area and record this in the next column. Then derive directly from this percentage the number of test items for each area.

A second dimension of Table 14–1 is the use of Bloom's taxonomy to divide items into those measuring lower-level (knowledge and comprehension) and higher-level learning (application, analysis, and evaluation). This division is particularly helpful as you make up the test. It ensures that higher levels of thinking are tested, along with rote recall. If your test items match well-written instructional objectives, you will avoid the cardinal sin of using trite, lower-order items to try to measure significant, higher-order learning.

The table of specifications helps ensure the content validity of the test, but it may have another use. Some test experts recommend sharing the table of specifications with students to help them prepare for the test (see Bloom et al., 1971). In our experience, the table is quite useful to students and is certainly worth sharing with them.

The next part of planning any test is the choice of items. Classroom tests may be made up of two major categories of items: essay questions and objective questions. Types of essay questions include short-answer, discussion, and oral questions (Mehrens & Lehmann, 1975), and objective questions include completion, true-false, multiple-choice, and matching items. Each type of item has its strengths and weaknesses. Your approach should be to select those items that best measure the attainment of your instructional objectives. The following discussion should help you make that choice.

Essay Questions

Essay questions ask students to construct an answer in their own words and to respond either in writing or orally (Ebel, 1979; Thorndike & Hagen, 1977). Essay questions can take many different forms and require a variety of mental processes including recall, organization of information, comparison, analysis, and evaluation. Essay questions may ask students to compare things, to make decisions for or against a controversial issue, to identify causes and effects, or to reorganize information (Hopkins & Stanley, 1981; Mehrens & Lehmann, 1975).

Form of Essay Questions. A common form of essay question is the **restricted-response** or **short-answer** form. In this type of question, the students are asked to respond briefly, usually in a half page or less, to a question that is fairly narrow in scope (Gronlund, 1981). An example of such a question is the following: "In three or four sentences, describe the general effect of shortening a test upon its reliability."

In an **extended-response** essay question, few restrictions are placed upon the person answering the question. The response may run from one to several pages, depending on the scope of question and the abilities and intent of the student (Gronlund, 1981). An example of such a question is "Take a position regarding your use of norm-referenced or criterion-referenced assessment in your first year of teaching. Defend your position by relating it to the nature of the subject matter you will teach, the level of the students you will have, and grading policies in your school district."

Both types of written essay questions require that students recall information, choose appropriate responses, and organize an answer in a logical and coherent fashion. Restricted-response questions permit a better sampling of content areas because more topics can be touched on in the same period of time (Gronlund, 1981). The extended-response essay suffers on the sampling dimension. No matter how well it is constructed, it will not be able to sample content as well as several short, carefully selected restricted-response questions can (Bertrand & Cebula, 1980). The extended-response question is useful, however, in determining whether a student is able to organize large amounts of information into a coherent form and to construct logical arguments based on a wide range of information (Gronlund, 1981).

Oral essay questions differ from written essay questions in that the questions and responses are spoken (Mehrens & Lehmann, 1975). They require recall of information and construction of logical and organized answers. Oral questions allow for clarification of responses by the person answering the question and for detailed probing by the examiner. On the minus side, this method is extremely time-consuming since only one person can be examined at a time. There is a potential for unreliability in scoring because there usually is not a "product" to review after the interview has been completed. Also, reliability and validity may suffer if evaluation is made on factors that are unrelated to the objectives being assessed (social and expressive skills or appearance, for example). Further, as with all essay exams, sampling of content often is poor.

Oral questions are usually a part of the evaluation process for advanced degrees. Typically, however, the intent of such examinations is not to sample broadly across content areas but rather to probe the depth of a student's knowledge in a restricted area of inquiry such as the topic addressed in a thesis or dissertation.

Scoring Essay Examinations. Gronlund (1981) describes two general approaches for grading essay questions—the point method and the rating method. In the **point method** (sometimes called the *analytical method*) an "ideal" answer is envisioned by the teacher, and points are assigned to desired features of the ideal answer. The student's response is then compared to the ideal answer and scored on each of the desired dimensions. The student's score is the total number of points received.

Consider the 20-point question "Identify causes of low morale among the labor force at Consolidated Steel, Inc., and suggest steps for improving morale." The teacher might construct the following "ideal" answer and assign point values to parts of the answer.

1. Identifies three causes of low morale from the descriptions given (2 points for each cause, 6 points possible)
2. Suggests three or more workable steps to improve morale (2 points for each step, 6 points possible)
3. Places situation in general economic perspective (2 points possible)
4. Shows evidence of knowledge of prevailing working conditions in the industry (3 points possible)
5. Expresses self in an organized way (3 points possible)

A student may write an answer in which he or she identifies four causes (6 points) and suggests two steps to improve morale (4 points). Assuming the student shows some evidence of economic perspective (1 point), excellent knowledge of prevailing working conditions (3 points), and skill in organization and expression (3 points), he or she would receive a total of 17 points for this question.

In the **rating method** (sometimes called the *global* method), the ideal answer still serves as an overall standard for comparison, but it is not broken down into parts or features (Gronlund, 1981). There are several commonly used rating methods. One method involves establishing a series of categories (for example, a five-category scale ranging from "very poor quality" to "very superior quality"). The grader sorts the papers into the categories based upon how they compare to the "ideal" answer. A variation of this method is to select several papers at each rating level to serve as standards of comparison.

Generally the rating method is quicker than the point method and is appropriate if a large number of essay questions are to be read (Gronlund, 1981). If you use the rating method you should read each essay a second time to be sure that it has been categorized properly. The point method focuses the grader's attention more closely on details of the answer and assists the grader in giving feedback to learners. The point method is used somewhat more frequently and is generally recommended for restricted-response essay questions where answers tend to be fairly specific (Gronlund, 1981).

A major problem of essay testing is that scoring, whether by the point or rating method, has been shown to be notoriously unreliable. Over the years, research has shown a low correspondence between scores given to the same answer by different graders, and even the same grader is likely to score an answer very differently on two different occasions (Myers, McConville, & Coffman, 1966; Starch & Elliott, 1912, 1913a, 1913b; Traxler & Anderson, 1935).

Chase (1979) performed a simple but intriguing study in which he examined one variable known to affect scores given to essay responses, namely, handwriting, along with the variable of grader expectations for student achievement (see Chase, 1968; A. W. James, 1927; Marshall & Powers, 1969; Sheppard, 1929). Chase prepared two sets of identical essays, one with very clear handwriting and one with very poor handwriting. The two sets of essays contained the same content, word for word. The essays were prefaced with a cover sheet purporting to describe the "student's" achievement during the previous semester by listing course grades. The same courses were listed on all of the cover sheets but the grades were altered so that one half of the cover sheets reported a D+ average while the other half reported an A− average. Chase used these cover sheets to develop an expectancy of performance among the graders.

This procedure resulted in the four groups of essays listed below:

High expectation + poor handwriting
High expectation + clear handwriting
Low expectation + poor handwriting
Low expectation + clear handwriting

Chase then distributed one set of essays to each of sixty-two graders. All the graders had taught or were teaching and all had studied the topic of grading essay examinations in their recent graduate work. Chase made sure that the graders would pay attention to the achievement results by having them briefly rate the "student's" achievement as "a very good record," "satisfactory," or "clearly weak" (Chase, 1979, p. 40). Chase also furnished graders with a general scoring format for marking the papers.

Both handwriting and expectancy had a strong effect on the supposedly "objective" scores. Although the essays were identical in content, the scores assigned to the essays differed significantly on the basis of both expectations and handwriting. Higher scores were assigned to both groups of "high-expectation" essays than to the "low-expectation" essays. There was, however, an interesting effect observed for handwriting. The highest scores were given to the poor-handwriting plus high-expectation essays, while the lowest scores were given to the low-expectation plus poor-handwriting essays.

Chase concluded that while grader expectations obviously influenced scores, poor handwriting inflated the scores of high-expectation papers while deflating the scores of low-expectation essays. Obviously, teachers need to take special precautions to ensure fair grading. Generally the procedures outlined below will help you avoid many of the problems of unreliability associated with grading responses to essay questions. We have adapted the guidelines from the work of Gronlund (1981) and Mehrens and Lehmann (1975) for you to follow as you score essay exams.

Prepare a scoring key for each question. Nothing will reduce reliability more quickly than a changing standard. A scoring guide or ideal answer is essential.

Grade only one question at a time across all papers. This reduces the possibility that your judgment of one question may carry over to affect how you grade another question, a "halo" effect.

Shuffle the papers after each question. A random order helps reduce the possibility of systematic bias. Any bias that is present will be evened out over the grading of several questions.

If possible, grade the responses anonymously. While this is not always possible, it is desirable. The answers should speak for themselves, and your knowledge of other facts about students can unconsciously affect your grading.

Judge the mechanics of writing separately from the content. Often content and expression are not separated and students are graded on factors such as handwriting or grammar that are irrelevant to the objectives. If expression is one of your objectives for the exam, it should still be evaluated separately from content.

Avoid the use of optional questions. Optional questions remove the possibility of comparing everyone on the same standard, causing both reliability and validity to suffer.

In addition to the six guidelines for scoring essay questions, two other steps may be taken to improve reliability. First, better sampling of content can be accomplished by using more and shorter questions. Second, questions should direct the students to the nature of the response required. Ambiguous or completely open-ended questions ("Discuss the concept of validity") only cause students to become confused or to answer the "wrong" question. A good essay question should limit the area under consideration and should point to the expected nature and length of the answer. (See Table 14–2.)

Objective Questions

Objective questions require students to make very brief responses that are compared to predetermined answers (Hopkins & Stanley, 1981). Such items are called "objective" because they require little, if any, judgment for correct scoring. There are several formats that objective test items may take:

Completion: The students must supply a word or phrase to complete an incomplete sentence or answer a question.

True-False: The students must judge statements as either correct or incorrect.

TABLE 14–2
Constructing Good Essay Items

Advantages of the Essay Item

1. Measures higher-level abilities to organize, think logically, and to express oneself effectively.
2. May stimulate desirable study habits, such as relating information, organizing, summarizing.
3. Usually relatively easy for the teacher to prepare.

Disadvantages of the Essay Items

1. Poorer sampling of content than that obtained by objective forms of testing.
2. Reliability is relatively low.
3. Difficult and subjective scoring.
4. Irrelevant factors such as spelling and handwriting may affect scoring of questions.

Suggestions for Constructing Essay Items

1. Make sure the question spells out the nature of the expected response to the student.
2. Use more restricted-response questions rather than fewer extended-response questions if better sampling is desired.
3. Use essay questions only where they are clearly the most suitable for measuring the learning outcomes.
4. Avoid giving optional questions.

Note: The suggestions for writing these and other measurement forms are drawn from Brown (1976), Douglas (1967), Ebel (1975, 1979), Gronlund (1981), Mehrens and Lehmann (1975), and Tuckman (1975).

Multiple-Choice: The students must choose a correct answer from a set of alternative responses to a question.

Matching: The students must match items from one list to corresponding items in another list.

A great deal of controversy surrounds the use of objective test items. Among the more frequently voiced criticisms are (1) that some teachers tend to use objective items to measure trivial outcomes, (2) that objective items do not assess students' abilities to organize and express themselves, and (3) that the possibility of guessing correct answers may lead to poor student preparation. Advocates of objective testing usually counter these arguments by stressing the potential for increased reliability and validity (see Ebel, 1979; Mehrens & Lehmann, 1975).

Multiple-item objective tests have a much better chance of adequately sampling course content than do essay tests that are limited to a few items. While the preparation of objective items is usually difficult, scoring is quick, accurate, and easy, thus facilitating rapid feedback. Additionally, objective items can be constructed that measure very complex abilities such as reasoning, problem solving, and data interpretation (F. G. Brown, 1976; Ebel, 1975; Gronlund, 1981).

We believe that the problems or limitations of objective tests are often overestimated and their potential benefits often overlooked. With proper care in the construction of objective items, very complex levels of learning can be assessed. Test authorities maintain that the testing of trivial outcomes by objective items is not an inherent problem of this form (see Ebel, 1979; Gronlund, 1981). Important gains in the reliability and content validity of a test can often be made through the use of objective items. A set of carefully constructed multiple-choice questions, for example, can systematically assess the comprehension, analysis, and evaluation capabilities of students while sampling a wide variety of content.

Objective testing is certainly not the answer to every assessment problem (there is a great deal that you do *not* learn about a student if you use objective testing alone). However, the potential of this method can be realized only if you acquire the skills necessary to construct excellent objective items.

Completion Items.

Completion items require a short answer—a word or a phrase—as the response. The item may be in the form of a question:

In what form of item is either a word or phrase supplied as the correct answer? ___(completion)___

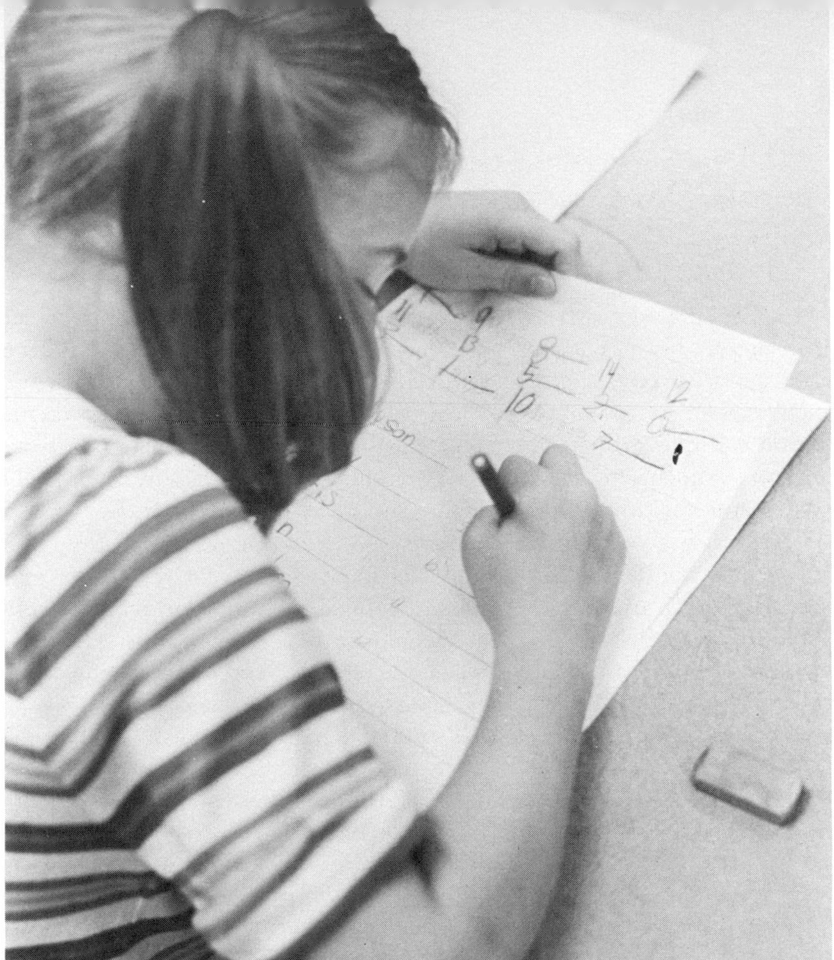

Completion items permit a wide sampling of content.

or it may take a sentence-completion form:

A word or phrase is supplied as the correct answer in
__(completion)__ items.

A similar format that can be used with proper instructions is the presentation of a list of items (for example, a set of dates) with blanks next to them. The students must give a response to each item on the list. For example:

Below is a list of dates. Fill in the blank next to each date with the name of a major historical event that affected westward expansion.

1. 1845 __(Texas admitted to Union)__
2. 1848 __(Gold discovered at Sutter's Mill)__

3. 1853 (Gadsden Purchase)

4. 1865 (Civil War ends)

5. 1907 (Oklahoma admitted to Union)

Completion items can sometimes encourage the learning of trivial information because of the nature of the required responses, but the ability to correctly label and recall is important in many subject areas, such as biology, foreign language, and medicine. Completion items permit a wide sampling of content with minimal response requirements, allowing students to answer a large number of questions in a relatively short period of time. (See Table 14–3.)

To write good completion items, avoid quoting directly from the text. Quotations often provide poor prompts for the correct answer and may lose much of their meaning by being lifted out of context. These verbatim items also tend to encourage rote recall. The items should be written as clearly as possible so that the sense of the item is understood prior to the point where the response is required. For this reason, blanks should usually appear later rather than earlier in the items.

True-False Items. **True-false items** are statements that students must judge to be correct or incorrect (Ebel, 1979). Students may re-

TABLE 14–3
Constructing Good Completion Items

Advantages of the Completion Item

1. Ease of construction.
2. Can sample a wide range of subject matter.
3. Requires that a student supply the response from memory.

Disadvantages of the Completion Item

1. Not well suited to measuring complex learning outcomes.
2. Scoring can be quite subjective.

Suggestions for Constructing Completion Items

1. Write each item so that it has one and only one correct response.
2. Avoid verbatim quotations from the text.
3. Blanks should appear near the end of the sentence rather than toward the beginning.
4. Avoid excessive blanks in a single sentence.
5. All blanks for answers should be of the same length; avoid giving clues by the length of the line.

TABLE 14–4
Constructing Good True-False Items

Advantages of the True-False Item

1. Provides a simple and direct means of assessing educational outcomes.
2. May be used to sample a wide range of subject matter.
3. Ease and objectivity of scoring.

Disadvantages of the True-False Item

1. Susceptibility to guessing is high.
2. Constructing statements that are neither obvious nor ambiguous is difficult.
3. May encourage poor preparation in students.

Suggestions for Constructing True-False Items

1. Absolute terms like *always* and *never* should be avoided since absolutely true or false statements are rare.
2. Avoid the use of negative statements and especially double negatives (such as "lengthening a test will *not* cause it to become *un*reliable").
3. Avoid complex statements containing two or more ideas.
4. True statements should not be longer than false statements.*
5. Avoid terms such as *usually* or *in general* that tend to indicate true items.

*A natural tendency is to insert extra qualifying words in true statements to ensure their correctness. Length of the statement then becomes a clue to the student.

spond to them by marking true or false, yes or no, or correct or incorrect. Some examples are presented below.

(F) Completion items are statements that students judge to be correct or incorrect.

(T) The highest level in Bloom's taxonomy is the evaluation level.

(F) Working memory has an unlimited capacity.

(F) Essay questions are usually more reliable than objective items.

True-false items are very widely used. They can be generated relatively quickly, scored rapidly and objectively, and, *if constructed properly,* test higher levels of learning. A large number can be answered in a relatively short period of time. Douglas (1967) indicates, for example, that average secondary school students can complete about three to five true-false items per minute. True-false items are generally considered useful for younger students and for poorer readers, provided they are written in simple, direct language. (See Table 14–4.)

There are serious concerns about the true-false format, however. Good true-false items, which are not completely obvious on the one hand or ambiguous on the other, are sometimes difficult to construct. Other major criticisms as recounted by Ebel (1975) are triviality, ambiguity, guessing, and encouragement of rote learning. Although Ebel presents a rather convincing argument* that the major defects of true-false questions can be removed by careful construction, most other measurement specialists have strong reservations about the use of true-false items. Many items can be answered correctly regardless of the level of preparation of the student. Further, the diagnostic value of any particular item is very low since chance plays such a strong part in the potential for getting a specific item correct. Gronlund (1976, 1981) feels that the problems of true-false items are so serious that such a format should be used only when no other format is appropriate, such as situations in which there are only two possible alternatives (a valid or an invalid conclusion for an argument, for instance).

Multiple-Choice Items. Like true-false items, **multiple-choice items** present a limited number of possible responses to the student, who must choose the correct or best response. Typically, a multiple-choice item will consist of a *stem,* which may be either a question or an incomplete statement, and a set of *alternatives* (usually four or five) from which to choose the best or correct answer (Gronlund, 1981; Hopkins & Stanley, 1981). The multiple-choice item is adaptable to testing a variety of learning outcomes—from knowledge of specific facts to understanding and application of concepts and principles. The following item is an example:

The average span of immediate memory is about how many units?

a. 7
b. 10
c. 13
d. 16

*Ebel (1975, 1979) has argued that all verbal knowledge, which in his opinion is the central aspect of educational achievement, can be expressed in propositions, a proposition being any sentence that can be said to be true or false. Thus, the extent of a student's knowledge can be measured by his or her success in judging the truth or falsity of propositions related to the area of knowledge. In Ebel's opinion, the writing of worthwhile true-false items is more a task of creative writing than of copying statements from the text. Copying statements not only can encourage trivial learning, but it may render statements meaningless as they are removed from context. Good true-false items, Ebel maintains, encourage understanding and application of principles. Poor items emphasize memory for isolated details.

This item illustrates a common use for multiple-choice questions—testing for retention of specific facts (the correct answer is *a,* 7 units). Overuse of the multiple-choice item to measure knowledge of facts and terminology has led to a great deal of criticism of multiple-choice testing as unsuited for measuring many instructional outcomes. With careful construction, however, multiple-choice items can quite effectively measure higher-order levels of learning (see Gronlund, 1981; Miller, Williams, & Haladyna, 1978). Consider the following item:

> You've all taken classes in which the teacher lectured profoundly and tested trivia. The testing concept that is lacking in this unfortunate state of affairs is
>
> a. item analysis of the test
> b. validity of the test
> c. reliability of the test
> d. norm-referenced testing

In order to answer the item correctly (unless you have studied this specific item or made a lucky guess), you need to understand certain concepts and make a decision about which best applies to the situation (alternative *b* is the correct choice). Simply memorizing the definition of validity isn't enough. If you want students to understand and apply information, tests should be aimed, at least in part, at this higher level of learning.

One excellent multiple-choice method for measuring higher levels of understanding is the interpretive exercise. An **interpretive exercise** consists of a descriptive statement or paragraph, pictorial materials, or both, followed by a series of multiple-choice questions that require the student to interpret the material (Gronlund, 1981). The following exercise is of this type:

> A first-grade teacher, concerned about the inability of her students to follow directions, devises an instruction-following game to develop this skill. In a beginning phase, students are provided with boxes filled with a large variety of small objects. Working with small groups, the teacher gives instructions to do certain things with the objects and to interact with other group members. Each time an instruction is carried out, students are reinforced by means of approval and a check on a record form. Students can trade their checks for time in an area where they can play with toys from home, read, or engage in any activity that they like. Following instructions on actual classroom tasks becomes the focus in later stages of training.

1. The category of learning that is the better explanatory model for the above is
   (a.) operant/instrumental conditioning
   b. respondent/classical conditioning
2. Within a reinforcement framework, the instructions given by the teacher are most appropriately conceptualized as
   a. reinforcers
   (b.) discriminative stimuli
   c. variable-ratio schedules
   d. respondent conditioning
3. Assume the teacher felt the children were having difficulty telling the difference between instructions and other kinds of things she said. She introduced a hand signal (such as an upraised hand) that meant, in effect, "Please pay attention. This is something to be acted on." She would have introduced an additional ___?___ for the children's instruction following.
   a. reinforcer
   b. extinction procedure
   c. reinforcement schedule
   (d.) discriminative stimulus
4. If the children learn that instruction following is rewarded when the hand signal is given, but that other verbalizations of the teacher don't require their attention they can be said to have acquired a
   a. shaping procedure
   b. behavioral chain
   (c.) discrimination
   d. generalization

Such exercises have been used extensively in standardized testing and are increasingly used by classroom teachers because of their ability to test higher levels of achievement (Gronlund, 1981). While they are fairly difficult to prepare, interpretive exercises are well matched to objectives such as application of principles and evaluation of complex situations. The ability to make predictions about the effects of certain changes in a fragile environment or to make interpretations of poetry or prose passages might be tested by a series of interpretive questions.

A number of useful guides for constructing items to test higher levels of learning are available. The oldest and still the most complete guide is the *Taxonomy of Educational Objectives* (Bloom et al., 1956). Items are presented in the taxonomy that illustrate the assessment of learning outcomes at each level of learning. Another useful guide for the construction of achievement test items is a review article by R. C. Anderson (1972), in which he gives rules for avoiding the testing of lower levels of learning by the use of paraphrase in test items and by requirements for interpretation of situations. Miller et al. (1978) also give practical suggestions for measuring higher levels of learning by objective items.

Multiple-choice items are perhaps the most versatile form of testing. They can sample widely across content areas and, if well written, can measure the attainment of higher levels of learning (Gronlund, 1981; Hopkins & Stanley, 1981). Moreover, the technique of item analysis (see page 435) can also be used on multiple-choice tests to detect and revise faulty items. (See Table 14–5.)

Matching Items. **Matching items** consist of two parallel lists, one containing a series of words or phrases (stems) and the other made up of a series of responses (F. G. Brown, 1976). The student must match up the items in the response list with the items in the stimulus list.

Matching items have the advantage of being compact and easy to

TABLE 14–5
Constructing Good Multiple-Choice Items

Advantages of the Multiple-Choice Item

1. Better sampling of content than essay forms of testing.
2. Reliability can be relatively high.
3. Ease and objectivity of scoring.
4. Analysis of item performance and revision are possible.

Disadvantages of the Multiple-Choice Item

1. Under some circumstances, may encourage less than adequate preparation.
2. Sometimes misused to test only verbatim recall.
3. May encourage guessing.
4. Difficulty in preparation.

Suggestions for Constructing Multiple-Choice Items

1. Attempt to test for higher-order learning, not just verbatim recall of facts.
2. The stem of the item should present a meaningful problem.
3. Watch that the length of alternatives and the grammer don't give away the answers.
4. Make sure all alternatives are plausible, but that there is only one "best" or correct answer.
5. Where possible, eliminate negatively stated items (such as "which of the following is *not* . . .") and alternatives such as "none of the above," "all of the above," and "*a* and *b* above."

construct. Gronlund (1981) points out that there are a large number of relationships between two things that are important educational outcomes. People and achievements, dates and historical events, symbols and concepts, foreign words and English equivalents, plants and clas-

---

PRACTICE EXERCISE 14–1

Judging and Writing Multiple-Choice Items

Correct each of the following objective items, using the suggestions in Table 14–5 as a guide. The first few items are keyed to particular suggestions. After that you're on your own. Our "better" versions are on page 456.

1. Reliability
   a. is that portion of any score caused by error
   b. refers to the consistency of measurement
   c. declines as the length of the test increases
   d. is the extent to which a measure represents the content it is supposed to measure

   (See suggestion number 2, Table 14–5.)

2. In norm-referenced testing, you are comparing an individual's performance to
   a. others
   b. the self
   c. "normal work"
   d. a preestablished standard of acceptable performance

   (See suggestion number 3, Table 14–5.)

3. A test that measures achievement against a standard (for example, many drivers' license examinations) is called a
   a. norm-referenced test
   b. reliable test
   c. criterion-referenced test
   d. *a* and *c* above
   e. all of the above

   (See suggestion number 5, Table 14–5.)

4. The reliablity of a test
   a. can best be improved by shortening the test
   b. will be strengthened by including a greater number of difficult items
   c. will increase upon the addition of additional items to the test
   d. will go down if the test is changed from criterion-referenced to norm-referenced

   (See suggestion number 2, Table 14–5.)

sifications, and authors and books are but a few of many important pairings.

Learning measured by matching items can be at a relatively low level—the association between two bits of factual information—but with

5. The most justifiable criticism of teacher-made objective tests is that they
   a. often emphasize rote learning
   b. discrimination against the poorer students
   c. broader sampling than is actually necessary
   d. less reliable than other forms of evaluation

6. If your goal was to sample students' recall of information from a wide variety of content areas, you would not be justified in using
   a. multiple-choice questions
   b. true-false questions
   c. short-answer questions
   d. all of the above
   e. none of the above

7. Grading essay items by counting the number of lines would be
   a. somewhat reliable but not very valid
   b. somewhat valid but not very reliable
   c. neither somewhat valid nor partly reliable
   d. more often valid than somewhat reliable

8. Teacher-made tests typically are not
   a. checked for internal consistency
   b. standardized against norm groups
   c. highly reliable measures of learning
   d. not invalid measures of classroom learning

9. Rating scales
   a. are most commonly used for rote-level learning
   b. are occasionally used for knowledge-level learning
   c. can be used for application-level learning
   d. are very commonly used to assess psychomotor learning

10. Sociograms do not have which of the following uses:
    a. not establishing content validity nor internal consistency
    b. not identifying isolates nor group interactions
    c. assessing affective and psychomotor learning
    d. assessing cognitive and psychomotor learning

some thought given to the construction of matching exercises, levels of learning well above rote recall can be measured. Consider the following example:

Directions: Write the letter of the concept in column B next to the situation in column A with which it best fits. Letters from Column B may be used once, more than once, or not at all.

	Column A	*Column B*
(E)	1. High school grades are correlated with college grades.	A. Internal consistency reliability
(D)	2. For a new test of "locus of control," experts agree that the test measures what it is intended to measure	B. Test-retest reliability
(B)	3. Students receive approximately the same score on an aptitude test the second time they take it.	C. Content validity
(C)	4. The teacher uses a table of specifications to match a test to instruction.	D. Construct validity
(A)	5. In general, performance on individual items is correlated with performance on the total test.	E. Predictive validity
(E)	6. Scholastic Aptitude Test scores correlate +.40 with grade point average in freshman year of college.	F. Equivalent forms reliability
(C)	7. The test over the geometry unit contains the same proportions of items per topic as did the geometry unit itself.	

Variations of matching items include having students match names with points on a map or parts of a diagram. Music teachers may require matching of keyboard locations to notes, while shop teachers may ask

TABLE 14–6
Constructing Good Matching Items

Advantages of the Matching Item

1. Suited to measuring associations between concepts.
2. Requires little reading time.
3. Can be constructed with relative ease.

Disadvantages of the Matching Item

1. If used improperly, may encourage rote memorization of facts and figures.
2. Limited application to some higher levels of learning.

Suggestions for Constructing Matching Items

1. All parts of any one item should deal with a single topic.
2. Each list should contain no more than five to seven items.
3. The longer phrases should serve as stems and the shorter responses should be placed in the second column.
4. Unequal numbers of stems and responses should be used to diminish successful guessing.
5. Instruct learners that responses may be used once, more than once, or not at all in a given item.

for correct labeling of tools used in projects. A football player may be asked to correctly associate blocking or tackling assignments with a given play. The variety of applications, plus the relative ease of preparation, makes matching items popular with many teachers. Like all item forms, however, they must actually measure the goals of learning for the classroom. (See Table 14–6.)

APPLICATIONS FOR TEACHING: ITEM ANALYSIS

One of the best arguments for using objective items, particularly multiple-choice items, is that they can be analyzed and improved. The techniques for doing this are called, collectively, *item analysis.* Item analysis provides two important kinds of information for each item on a norm-referenced test: how hard it is (item difficulty) and whether "good students" get the item right more often than "poor students" (item discrimination) (Ebel, 1979; Gronlund, 1981; Hopkins & Stanley, 1981).

Items that are too difficult or too easy tend to make a test unreliable and so the test maker is usually looking for items of medium difficulty (Thorndike & Hagen, 1977). If item analysis shows that almost everyone in the group got the item wrong, then perhaps some revision is in order.

An item should also distinguish between students who know more about the subject being tested and those who know less about it (Gronlund, 1981). For example, if most of the students in the lower half of the class got the item right and most of the students in the upper half

Many teachers develop pools of excellent items from which they can select items for their tests.

of the class got it wrong, we would certainly question whether that item belonged on the test in its present form. That is exactly what happens in some cases, however: Poorly written items mislead the better students, while poorly prepared students answer correctly.

Professional test authors employ computers to analyze the quality of their test items. Correlation techniques are used to determine if items are discriminating properly and to estimate the overall reliability of the test. If you're like most teachers, though, you may not have ready access to this kind of analysis. Nonetheless, some simple procedures are available that allow you to make substantial improvements in your items and greatly increase the overall quality of your tests. Many teachers develop pools of excellent items for their instructional objectives from which they can select items for their tests. Each time an item appears on a test, student performance is used to analyze whether the item is of appropriate difficulty and whether it discriminates (distinguishes) between the better and the poorer students.*

*While many textbooks provide sets of objective items in their teachers' manuals, such items vary greatly in quality and many need substantial improvement. Item analysis will provide objective information to help you identify and improve defective items.

The following steps represent some agreed-upon procedures for item analysis. Although the example employs multiple-choice items, the procedures can easily be generalized to true-false items and to other item forms (Ebel, 1979).

1. Type or write each item on a separate 5-by-7-inch card. Below is an item at the comprehension level for a cognitive development objective taken from an educational psychology course.

Course: 882 *Objective:* Cognitive Development
Level: Comprehension
Difficulty: ________ *Discrimination:* ________

Which of the following best distinguishes the period of formal operations from the period of concrete operations?

a. an increase in reflexive behavior
b. a tendency toward centrism
(c.) presence of propositional thinking
d. increasing belief in animistic concepts

Alternatives	*A*	*B*	*(C)*	*D*	*Omits*
Lower Group					
Upper Group					

By putting items on cards, you easily develop a file of items matched to your objectives. To construct a test, a sample of items matching your objectives can be pulled from the file and arranged in any order you desire.

2. After a test has been administered, rank the papers from top to bottom in terms of total score.

3. Divide the papers into two groups, upper and lower,* and count the number of students in each group who selected each alternative for each item. Enter these numbers on your card for the item. For the sample item, the result might be as follows for a 30-member class. "Omits" refer to people who did not answer the question at all.

Alternatives	*A*	*B*	*(C)*	*D*	*Omits*
Upper Group	1	1	12	1	0
Lower Group	2	6	5	2	0

4. Next, compute the *item difficulty* as follows:

$$\text{Difficulty} = \frac{\text{Number who got the item right}}{\text{Total number of students}} \times 100$$

For this item, (12 + 5), or 17, out of 30 students chose *C,* the correct answer. Thus the difficulty is (17 ÷ 30) × 100, or 57 percent, which indicates a relatively difficult item.*

5. The second computation is an estimate of item reliability or discriminating power. If the item is "working" properly, students who did well on the total test should also do well on this item, while those who scored less well on the test should do less well as a group on this item. This happened in our example—twelve out of fifteen people in the upper group got the item correct, compared to only five out of the fifteen in the lower group. The computation of *item discrimination* is as follows:

$$\text{Discrimination} = \frac{\left(\begin{array}{c}\text{Number}\\ \text{correct}\\ \text{in upper}\end{array}\right) - \left(\begin{array}{c}\text{Number}\\ \text{correct}\\ \text{in lower}\end{array}\right)}{1/2\ (\text{Total number of students})}$$

In this case we have (12 − 5) ÷ [(½)(30)], or 7/15, or .47.

The item discrimination index is a form of

* Theoretically, the best result is obtained by selecting the upper 27 percent and the lower 27 percent as the upper and lower groups. For most classroom settings, however, groups may be too small to give reliable results, and simply dividing the class in half is a better procedure.

* The average score on the total test is related to the difficulty of the individual items. Thus, if items were to average around 50 percent, the average total test score would also be quite low.

correlation coefficient. It can either be positive (up to +1.00) or negative (to −1.00). A clear problem exists with an item in which you get a very low positive (around zero) or negative discrimination index. A negative figure results when more students in the *lower* scoring group get an item right than do students in the *upper* group. Such items should be revised if possible or discarded if necessary. Something in the item—wording, ambiguity, or misinformation—is usually misleading the better students. Looking at the pattern of choices will help you determine what the problem is (Mehrens & Lehmann, 1975).

In general, *the higher the discrimination index,* the better your item. Certainly, low or negative discriminating items should be examined carefully. They either add little to or actually lower the reliability of your test.

For difficulty, a moderate range—neither too easy nor too hard—is recommended. In four-alternative multiple-choice tests, an average difficulty level of about 75 percent will result in the highest reliability (Mehrens & Lehmann, 1975). For motivational purposes, however, the test writer will often wish to include items easier than this, with difficulty levels of 85, 90 or even 100 percent. Although these items won't contribute to the reliability of your test, they will help students feel better about their overall performance.

OBSERVATIONAL METHODS

Teachers not only measure the achievement of cognitive goals, but they are also concerned with assessing skills and attitudes (Hopkins & Stanley, 1981). Physical education teachers, for example, need to determine student improvement in a variety of physical activities, such as tumbling, diving, and handball. In each performance area, teachers observe what students do, evaluate their performances, and provide feedback to encourage improvement. Music teachers evaluate their students on dimensions such as expression and accuracy. In home economics classes, teachers are likely to judge several different performances and products, such as diet selection, food preparation, and clothing construction. Other teachers must determine whether a drill press is properly operated or whether trainees can close a sale in a retail establishment. Is testing the best approach for assessing all these competencies? Probably not. A better way is a direct evaluation of actual task performance or an examination of a sample of completed work (Hopkins & Stanley, 1981). Such methods of direct evaluation are known as **observational methods.**

Performances and Work Samples

The methods described in this section may be applied to activities that are in progress (performances) or to the products of those activities (work samples). Examples of performances are playing a song, drilling a hole, giving a speech, shooting a basket, administering cardiopulmonary resuscitation (CPR), and dismounting from parallel bars. Work samples may be as diverse as a plan for a solar heater, a papier-mâché model of a landscape, a birdhouse, a bookcase, a letter to the editor, or a report of activities. Most criteria applied in rating performances can also be applied in judging work samples (Bertrand & Cebula, 1980). The job of the rater is much the same in both cases.

There are times when observing performances is of greater benefit to the teacher than observing work samples. Naturally, the converse is also sometimes the case. Direct observation of tool handling, for instance, is much more valuable from a teaching standpoint than observing that a student's work sample is poorly constructed. On the other hand, direct observation sometimes isn't feasible or desirable. Students may complete projects in settings or at times when observation would be impossible, or the activity may be largely a mental one and there may not be anything to observe. Ideally, we want to provide as much relevant feedback to learners as possible and this includes feedback on both performance and product. In practice, teachers can observe only that which is possible within the limitations of class size, time, location, and the nature of the task.

Rating Scales

A rating scale typically indicates a trait or characteristic to be judged and a scale on which the rating can be made (Gronlund, 1981). Rating scales are frequently used to evaluate performance in the psychomotor and the affective domains (Hopkins & Stanley, 1981). Panels of judges, for example, give ratings to divers and gymnasts. Another common use of rating scales is in student evaluations of courses and instructors.

The simplest form of rating scale is the *numerical scale,* in which numbers indicate the degree to which a particular characteristic is present (Anderson & Sclove, 1980; Gronlund, 1981). The following is an example of a numerical scale:

> *Instructions:* Please indicate your degree of confidence in using each of the following instructional methods. 1 = Little or no confidence; 2 = Some confidence; 3 = Great confidence.

1. Inquiry teaching	1	2	3
2. Instructional modules	1	2	3
3. Simulations	1	2	3

Another form of rating scale is the *graphic scale* (Gronlund, 1981), which requires that the rating be made by checking along a line. The purpose is identical to that of the numerical rating scale; only the method for indicating responses is different. The following sample of a graphic scale has been used to obtain the reaction of participants toward instructional sessions in adult education courses.

Instructions: Please indicate your reaction to the session by checking the point on the horizontal line that best represents your feelings.

1. Topical importance to you

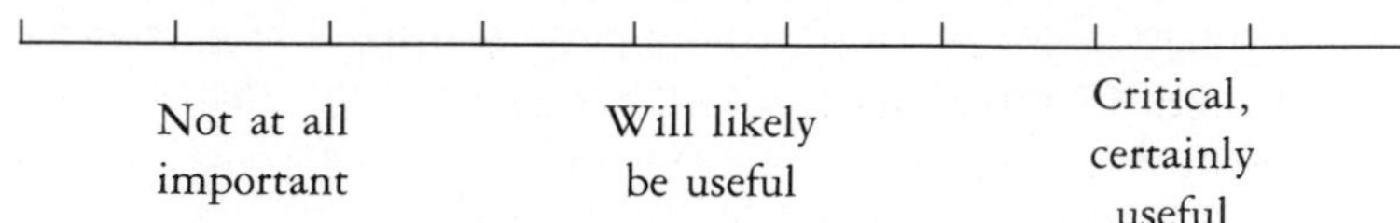

2. Would you recommend this session to future participants?

Strongly suggest avoiding	Would generally recommend	Very highly recommend

A *comparative scale** provides samples of a product to be evaluated, usually at five to seven levels of quality. Examples of descriptive paragraphs, for instance, might be arranged into a scale of increasing quality for use by an elementary school language arts teacher. The teacher can then rate the paragraphs that students write by matching them against the samples that represent the levels of quality. The following samples of children's writing define points of a comparative scale. As you can see, general writing skills (spelling, grammar, use of complex sentences, and so on) increase from level 1 to level 5.

Level 1 His a smartolk mean dumb and not ril nice.

Level 2 Scott is nice. I like him a lot. He's good in socker.

Level 3 Melissa is 10 years old and will be 11 in April. She's going to move at the end of the month.

Level 4 DeVone makes a good friend. She likes to have me come over and play and when we do, we have fun.

Level 5 Joette is a very pretty and intelligent girl. Sometimes she is very loud, but I really admire her. She is smart (I think) and very original.

Handwriting progress can also be measured by using a comparative scale to examine samples of students' writing on several occasions. Music teachers can use taped performances of songs to rate how well current students are performing. Recordings of students' speeches of varying

* Gronlund (1981) has referred to this scale as a "product scale." Since other forms of rating can also be applied to products, however, we have used the terminology of Mehrens and Lehmann (1975) here.

proficiency can help speech teachers judge how effective current student speeches are. Such standards greatly assist both teachers and students in attaining the highest possible level of performance.

For ratings to be most successful, the principles of test construction that produce high reliability and validity must be followed. The behavior observed should be matched to instructional objectives and should be a representative sample of the students' actual performances. Only observable characteristics should be rated, and points on each scale should be clearly defined. Steps should be taken to reduce rater biases: Some raters are too lenient, others are too strict, and others rate everyone about average. Another possible bias to be avoided is the halo effect, in which the raters' knowledge of other traits of the persons being rated may affect their judgments. A popular teacher, for example, may be judged as more organized than he or she actually is or the "class clown" may be rated as low in motivation by a teacher even though he or she generally turns in work as punctually as other members of the class.

Clear instructions to raters can help reduce rater biases. To counter the halo effect, raters should be told to rate each item independently and to judge the traits objectively. To cope with tendencies to be too

TABLE 14–7

Constructing Good Rating Scales

Advantages of the Rating Scale

1. Useful for evaluating important learning objectives in the affective and psychomotor domain.
2. Can convey information on quality, frequency, and level of performance.
3. Useful for judging either performances or products.

Disadvantages of the Rating Scale

1. Subject to a variety of rater biases, including leniency, strictness, and the halo effect.
2. Subject to social expectations and, hence, susceptible to faking.

Suggestions for Constructing Rating Scales

1. Begin with a blueprint of the behaviors or traits in order to ensure valid sampling of the area.
2. Clearly define the traits to be rated in the most behavioral way possible.
3. Divide the rating continuum into as many points as are needed for clarity, usually from three to seven.
4. Clearly define the points on the continuum so that there is no question as to what each rating means.
5. Train and motivate the raters to be as accurate and objective as possible.

strict, too lenient, or too cautious, raters should be instructed to use all points on the scale. Drawing attention to a comparison group ("compared to all instructors you have had, this instructor . . ."; "compared to other persons who have completed this minicourse, this student's performance . . .") can provide a more objective basis for making ratings and reducing biases. (See Table 14–7.)

Checklists

A checklist is "a listing of steps, activities, or behaviors which the observer records" during an observation (Mehrens & Lehmann, 1975, p. 351). Checklists are used to determine whether particular elements are present or absent in either a process or a product. They call for simple yes-no judgments (Gronlund, 1981). A chemistry instructor might use a checklist to see if students include all the necessary safety precautions in setting up an experiment. A vocational teacher can use a checklist to determine whether students can properly maintain a piece of machinery. In institutional settings, checklists are often used to assess the performance of retarded individuals in self-care skills. An example of a checklist used in determining whether students have acquired emergency cardiac care skills is given below.

______ Establishes unresponsiveness

______ Calls out for help

______ Properly tilts head with one hand on forehead, neck lift or chin lift with other

______ Checks carotid pulse correctly on near side

______ Stimulates activation of EMS system

______ Produces proper body position for compression/ventilation cycles

______ Does vertical compression

______ Ventilates properly

______ Checks pulse and breathing

Checklists are particularly helpful to teachers in diagnosing missing elements in performances, such as in the emergency cardiac care procedure above (see Table 14–8). By entering numbers rather than checks into the blanks (1 for first action, 2 for second, and so on) the sequence of actions can be analyzed, a factor that is very important in many performances.

Behavioral Observation

Behavioral observations are made of the occurrence or nonoccurrence of specified categories of behavior, such as talking, writing, reading, fighting, and the like. Typically, one or two categories of behavior are

TABLE 14–8
Preparing Good Checklists

Advantages of the Checklist Format

1. Useful in analysis of learning of psychomotor performances and for determining growth in personal/social areas.
2. May be used for either processes or products.
3. May be used to analyze sequences and correct order of actions.
4. Simple and easy to use.

Disadvantages of the Checklist Format

1. Does not permit an estimate of the degree to which a behavior or trait is present.
2. Since only presence or absence of trait or behavior is noted, it is not useful in summarizing general impressions.

Suggestions for Constructing Checklists

1. Perform a task analysis on complex psychomotor performances to determine the component behaviors.
2. Clearly specify behaviors or traits to be observed, including any actions that represent common errors.
3. Arrange the behaviors or traits to be observed, including expected errors, in roughly the order they will occur.
4. Keep separate checklists for each person observed. For comparison, transfer information later to a master list.
5. Reduce invalid judgments by giving clear directions and training observers.

selected for observation and observations are repeated on several occasions to assess possible changes. The behaviors are carefully defined and specified (reading, for instance, may be defined by number of pages read) and then a count is made of the behavior over a period of days or weeks (Craighead, Kazdin, & Mahoney, 1981).

Informal behavioral observations can be very useful to you as a teacher. In monitoring group activity, for example, charting student participation can give some extremely useful information on the functioning of the group. By recording participation you can see how much interaction is taking place, who is doing most of the talking, and who is being left out. As we saw in Chapter Ten, behavioral observations may sensitize us to events we might not otherwise notice.*

* For additional reading on this topic an excellent and detailed discussion of the methods of specifying behaviors and of the various formal recording methods can be found in Sulzer-Azaroff and Mayer (1977).

OTHER EVALUATION METHODS

Anecdotal Records

Anecdotal records are written reports of specific incidents. They usually relate to areas of social adjustment, but they may pertain to any area of interest. Many supervisors of student teachers, for example, make extensive use of anecdotal records in which they write comments related to the students' teaching effectiveness.

Anecdotal records can provide information that more formal methods of observation often miss. They are most useful for noting unplanned but significant events that cannot be categorized easily (Gronlund, 1981). Although anecdotal records are not as systematic as many other recording methods, they can be rich sources of information to help make decisions concerning students. (See Table 14–9.)

Sociometric Methods

Sociometric methods are used "for evaluating the social acceptance of individual pupils and the social structure of a group" (Gronlund, 1981, p. 460). One sociometric method is the *nominating technique* (Mehrens & Lehmann, 1975), in which students are asked to list a person or persons whom they would choose as companions for various work and play situations. Children are told that their responses will be held in confidence. They may be asked whom they would like to sit next to in the classroom

TABLE 14–9
Constructing Good Anecdotal Records

Advantages of Anecdotal Records

1. Record spontaneous events that cannot be measured systematically.
2. Provide in-depth information about events.
3. Increase awareness of unique behaviors of students.

Disadvantages of Anecdotal Records

1. Time-consuming to write.
2. May become subjective and gossipy unless writer is well trained.
3. Tend to sample negative or problem behavior.

Suggestions for Constructing Anecdotal Records

1. The anecdotal records should be part of a general system for recording student behavior.
2. Each anecdote should be limited to a brief description of a single incident.
3. Record both positive and negative events.
4. Records should be as factual and objective as possible.
5. The record should reveal enough of the context of the behavior so that it is not subject to misinterpretation.

Some children have few friends in their classes. Sociometric methods can help teachers identify such socially isolated students so that they can be helped to interact more with others.

or accompany on a trip. This device can help teachers identify isolated children (those no one chooses) and understand the general social structure of the classroom. Teachers may then use this information to incorporate isolated children into the activities of the group or to structure groups in the classroom so that wider ranges of acquaintances are developed. Closely related to the nominating method is the *"Guess Who" technique.* Students are given a list of descriptions of persons (such as "this boy makes our class more fun") and are asked to name one or more persons who fit these descriptions (Gronlund, 1981).

The information from sociometric techniques can be reported in a variety of ways; for instance, the number of nominations can simply be tallied for each student. Often, however, we are also interested in who made the nominations. For this purpose, a matrix constructed by listing group members along both the top and side of a grid can be used to tally who made the nominations *and* who received the nominations. Mutual choices can be circled. Students who are most popular (stars) and those who receive no choices at all (isolates) can be identified from this kind of graphical representation. A more complex method, the *sociogram* (Gronlund, 1981) can give us an even clearer picture of the social structure of a group. Isolates, stars, mutual choices, and rejections can be clearly identified by the use of a sociogram, such as the one pictured in Figure 14–1.

Self-Report Methods

Knowledge of student activities and feelings is desired by many teachers. The more teachers know about students, the better they will be able to provide for their educational and social needs. In **self-reports** students furnish information by talking or writing about themselves; they provide a good way of obtaining in-depth information.

Personal interviews are an important form of self-report. Teachers with well-developed interviewing skills can learn a great deal about students, both cognitively and affectively. The key drawback to interviews, however, is the amount of time they require. With the number of students in most classrooms, an interview with each student is a luxury that many teachers simply cannot afford. Other self-report methods are necessary. One such method is the activity checklist (Gronlund, 1981). A typical activity checklist asks students to check educational or cultural activities in which they participate outside of school. Activities students perform on their own are of interest to many teachers as they attempt to assess carry-over from classroom experiences.

Attitude scales are frequently used to allow students to report on

TABLE 14–10
Using Sociometric Methods

Advantages of Sociometric Methods

1. Reveal judgments of peers about individuals in class or group.
2. Relatively simple to design and employ.

Disadvantages of Sociometric Methods

1. Relationships obtained may vary depending on the question asked.
2. Relationships may be quite unstable, especially in younger children.
3. Methods are susceptible to faking.

Suggestions for Using Sociometric Methods

1. Write questions that fit the level of the students and that will elicit honest reactions.
2. Match the number of choices that students must make to the level of the student.
3. Avoid asking negative questions (such as "whom would you *not* like to go with on a field trip?").

FIGURE 14–1
A Simple Sociogram

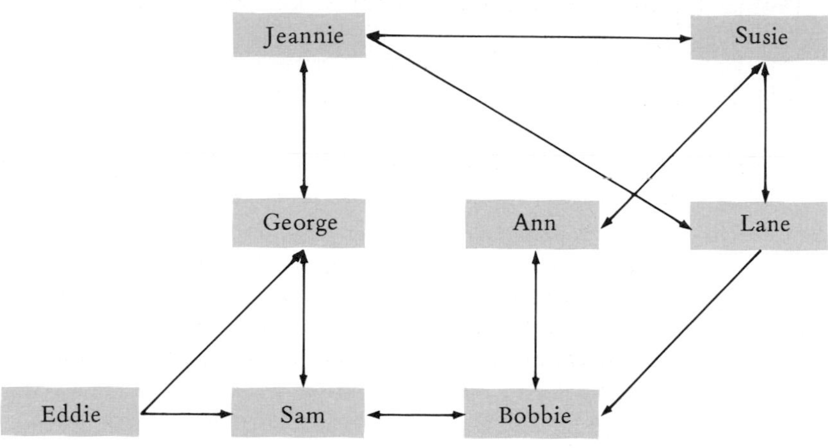

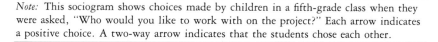

Note: This sociogram shows choices made by children in a fifth-grade class when they were asked, "Who would you like to work with on the project?" Each arrow indicates a positive choice. A two-way arrow indicates that the students chose each other.

feelings and opinions (Bertrand & Cebula, 1980). In an *attitude scale* a person can rate the extent of favorable or unfavorable feelings about a person, group, or topic. Although there are a number of highly sophisticated methods for formal construction of attitude scales, teachers can use attitude scales informally to help determine students' feelings about a variety of topics. The following items related to attitudes toward teaching handicapped students are intended for teacher trainees:

> *Instructions:* Rate each of the following items in this set by circling your choice. SA = strongly agree, A = agree, U = undecided, D = disagree, and SD = strongly disagree.
>
> 1. I'm not temperamentally suited to work with handicapped students. SA A U D SD
> 2. I'm looking forward to the challenge of working with handicapped students. SA A U D SD

This type of scale uses statements that are either positive or negative about the topic in question. Students then rate the degree of their agreement or disagreement with each statement. Of course, such scales are

TABLE 14–11
Constructing Good Attitude Scales

Advantages of Attitude Scales

1. Can be used to obtain a measure of feelings toward a variety of topics.
2. May be effectively used in self-appraisal.

Disadvantages of Attitude Scales

1. Highly susceptible to responses that are socially desirable and to faking.
2. Measures verbal behavior that may not relate to other forms of behavior.

Suggestions for Constructing Attitude Scales

1. Clearly identify the topic (focus) of the attitude measurement.
2. Write clear, direct, and simple statements about the topic.
3. Include both positive and negative statements on your scale.
4. Make sure each statement contains only a single idea.
5. Avoid factual statements.
6. Use the scale under conditions in which persons are likely to give honest and accurate responses.

susceptible to "faking" and the possibility of a student's simply giving a socially desirable response should be recognized.

Simple attitude scales designed for children can be quite illuminating, however, since children are less likely to give socially desirable responses or to anticipate how the attitude data will be used. Even with adults, attitude scales can be useful and effective. Respondents must have trust in the person gathering the information, however, and be carefully instructed to respond openly and honestly (see Table 14–11). As you can see, attitude scales greatly resemble the rating scales discussed earlier. The major difference is that attitude scales are more likely to focus on the feelings of respondents than on the objective judgments of raters.

GRADING

Grading, or, as it is sometimes called, marking, is an evaluative activity that involves some subjectivity and calls for making comparisons. Your ability to use a grading method that actually reflects student achievement is a big step toward becoming an effective teacher. There are many ways of making comparisons but none is flawless—all have strong and weak points. We will examine five of the most common ways of grading and making comparisons.

PRACTICE EXERCISE 14–2

Making Decisions About Methods of Assessment

For each setting use the list below to specify the assessment method that would be your *first* (not necessarily your only) choice in attempting to answer the question. Our responses are presented on page 458.

Assessment Methods

a. Essay testing—restricted response, extended response, or oral questioning
b. Objective testing—completion, true-false, multiple-choice, or matching items
c. Ratings—process or product
d. Checklists—process or product
e. Self-report—activity, problem checklists, attitude scales

1. *Setting:* You ask, "I wonder if my students understand the organization of Congress?"
   Method:

2. *Setting:* You wonder if your biology students can properly prepare a specimen for microscopic study.
   Method:

3. *Setting:* "How successful has my unit in music appreciation been?"
   Method:

4. *Setting:* Is little Al, who plays the tuba, ready to move into the senior band?
   Method:

5. *Setting:* You wonder if your students read current events on their own.
   Method:

6. *Setting:* You need to know if your students can relate the principles of civil liberties contained in the Constitution to today's news stories.
   Method:

7. *Setting:* What knowledge do your students have of important accounting terminology?
   Method:

8. *Setting:* Could your students tell the difference between a logical and an illogical argument?
   Method:

TABLE 14–12
A Grade Distribution Based on the Normal Curve

Letter Grade	*Percentage of Students to Receive Grade*
A	7
B	24
C	38
D	24
F	7

Norm-Referenced Grading

Many teachers apply the concept of norm-referenced measurement (discussed in Chapter Thirteen) to their grading. Norm-referenced grading (sometimes called "grading on the curve") involves evaluating students by comparing them to their classmates. Most teachers do not make arbitrary decisions about what percentage of students will obtain each grade, but this method can be tied to the normal curve by giving fixed percentages of each grade. An unfortunate result of this procedure is that some teachers become more concerned with the statistical distribution of grades than with what their students have actually learned. (See Table 14–12).

The norm-referenced approach has some good features. It is based on the often correct assumption that ability and achievement are normally distributed.* When the norm-referenced approach is used, teachers don't have to develop standards of performance—a savings in time and effort. Additionally, no explanation of the norm-referenced approach is needed for students, parents, or administrators—everybody has had experience with it. The method also has some severe deficits. When only a limited number of A's are allowed, the difference between the lowest A and the highest B is often trivial. The possibility also exists that an entire class could work hard, learn a great deal, and the majority still obtain mediocre grades. There is also no way to differentiate between the "easy A" obtained in one class and the A in another class

* At least this is so under ordinary instructional conditions. In criterion-referenced instruction that requires mastery learning (see Chapter Thirteen) and in individual tutoring, the normal curve for achievement essentially disappears (Bloom, 1981). The majority of students can successfully achieve most classroom goals under ideal instructional conditions.

that required much more effort. Another shortcoming is the highly competitive atmosphere that can be generated in a classroom in which norm-referenced grading is used. In some classes students have actually sabotaged the work of their classmates in order to win the competition for higher grades.

Criterion-Referenced Grading

Criterion-referenced grading is based on the criterion-referenced measurement approach discussed in Chapter Thirteen. In this method, teachers determine a standard of performance and grade students based on *how well they attain the standards* rather than comparing students to each other. A welding instructor, for example, may set a standard of five consecutive correct welds for students. For a class in chemistry, the teacher might require that students correctly identify the unknown element in two of three solutions.

One of the strongest points of the criterion-referenced approach is that students are not in competition with each other for a limited number of good grades. Instead, students compete with themselves to meet

The injudicious use of feedback can have a harmful effect on students.

"That's *it?* That's peer review?"

a well-defined standard of performance. A second advantage is that a students' relative standings in a class are not as important as the mastery of objectives. This eliminates the possibility of a student learning a great deal and still not obtaining a good grade. Criterion-referenced grading is especially well suited to all forms of individualized instruction.

The criterion-referenced approach also has disadvantages. The teacher, often without any firm guidelines from curricula or standardized measures, must set the standards of performance. If the standards are set too high it can result in an excessive number of failures. On the other hand, if the standards are set too low, students may obtain grades that they really don't deserve (an A for little or no work, for instance). Criterion-referenced grading requires well-written objectives. While we certainly do not believe that this is a major shortcoming, teachers who do not use objectives will have great difficulty in implementing a criterion-referenced approach. Well-written objectives that contain clearly specified criteria can easily be used, however, to set standards of performance.

A recurring problem with criterion-referenced grading is how to turn the results of comparisons with standards into number or letter grades. When students master objectives, their performance certainly deserves an A. But should students who just miss the standard of performance obtain F's? In a different vein, suppose that you ask students to write a report about a field trip. One student turns in a report that meets all of your standards and, in fact, goes much further. Obviously, this paper deserves an A. But what about another student who turns in a report that just barely meets your standards with nothing extra at all? Does this student also obtain an A? Supporters of the criterion-referenced approach might say yes, but a lot of teachers might wish to give this second report a B or C.

One way to deal with these problems is to award grades on the basis of a percentage of objectives mastered. Students who master 90 percent or more of the objectives receive an A. Students who master between 80 and 90 percent obtain a B, and so on. This approach allows teachers to grade on the basis of standards of performance and further allows any number of students to make A's or B's and so on. Of course, some critics suggest that introducing percentages violates the criterion-referenced approach and is a form of norm-referenced evaluation.

Grading on Improvement

Some teachers feel that grades should be based on the amount of improvement or growth that students demonstrate during a grading period. Those students who show the greatest improvement obtain A's; those with less improvement receive lower grades. This method is actually a norm-referenced approach using comparisons of improvement rather than absolute levels of achievement. With the addition of two disadvantages, the advantages and disadvantages of the norm-referenced approach apply here. First, the students who know the most about new material at the beginning of a unit are penalized, and, second, students might be encouraged to fake ignorance at the beginning of a unit so that their "growth" will seem greater than it is.

Grading on Expectations

There are teachers who believe that they should assign grades to students on the basis of what the students are *capable* of doing, rather than by comparing their achievement to a standard of performance or norms. In this method, a student could achieve the highest score on a test and still be told, "Eddie, you're able to do a lot better than this. I'm not going to give you an A until you work up to your potential."

We don't recommend this form of grading. The problems associated with it include the extreme difficulty of determining students' abilities, the difficulty of deciding if a student has actually worked up to his or her potential, and the punishment, on occasion, of high achievement. A teacher's grading decisions with this method are largely subjective and subject to errors.

APPLICATIONS FOR TEACHING: MISTAKES TO AVOID WHEN GRADING

Several authors have provided excellent lists of commonly made mistakes in grading (see Hills, 1976; Palmer, 1962; Payne, 1974). We have prepared a composite list of seven errors in grading that you should *avoid.*

1. *Abdicating responsibility.* Don't adjust your courses so that you can use tests developed by other teachers or textbook writers, regardless of how overworked you are.
2. *Employing grades to alter attitudes.* Don't give bonus points for good behavior or subtract points for misbehavior.
3. *Becoming lazy.* No matter how much you might dislike grading, don't base students' semester or course grades on a single test.
4. *Going overboard.* Don't make your courses an exercise in endurance in which students are assessed for everything short of the number of times they shift in their seat.
5. *Using "special insight."* Don't come to the conclusion that you have special insights that allow you to "see" how much students have learned without using any measurements.
6. *Increasing difficulty levels.* Don't change the difficulty level of your tests as the course progresses in an attempt to increase the standards of the course.
7. *Demanding perfection.* Students are human too.

Grading is a complex issue without clear-cut answers. Each grading method has strong and weak points. As you develop your own grading approach you may choose one of those we summarize or work out your own. No matter what the method, however, the most important factor is that grades should be a fair, objective reflection of student achievement.

Grading by Contract

There are several different methods whereby the teacher and student can contract for grades in a course. In grading by contract the teacher and individual students jointly choose objectives to be met and the methods of demonstrating mastery of objectives. A student and teacher might agree that the student's completion of a book report meeting certain criteria, four summaries of short stories meeting specific standards, and one eight-stanza poem composed by the student will constitute a grade of A for a three-week grading period. In general, methods that involve grading by contract are best suited to programs where instruction is individualized. Contract grading allows the teacher to utilize standards of performance for the mastery of objectives while at the same time taking each student's entry level into account.

In contract grading, the teacher and student jointly determine objectives, how they will be used, and how each grade can be obtained.

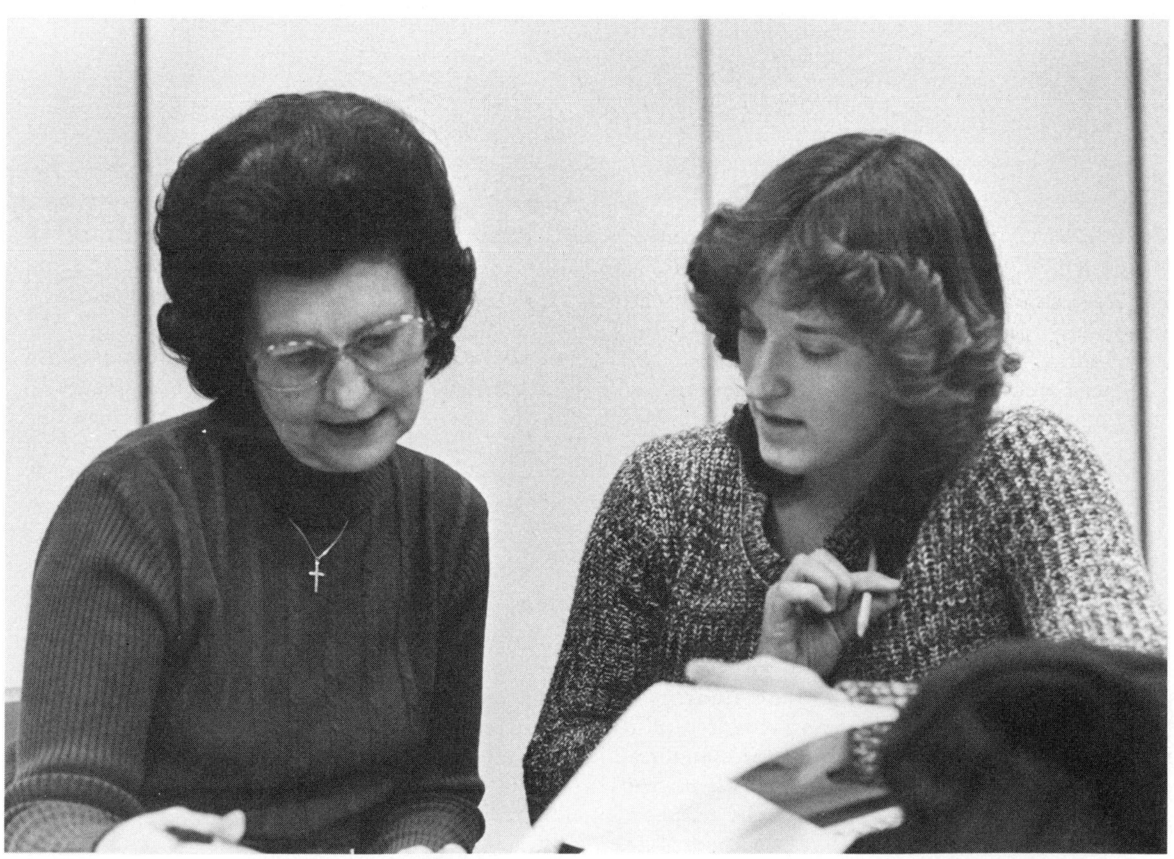

SUMMARY

This chapter was concerned with teacher-constructed forms of evaluation. The most widely used method of evaluating the mastery of cognitive objectives is testing, but testing is also used to evaluate components of psychomotor and affective learning. Teachers should always start the planning of a test from their objectives and the emphasis given to those objectives in their lessons. The best tests are constructed from tables of specifications, which help ensure that the levels of learning required in the objectives are reflected on the tests.

Test questions can be grouped into two major categories, essay and objective. Essay questions, whether open-ended, restricted-response, or oral, have the advantage of causing students to organize their thoughts and to present them in cogent oral or written form. Because of sampling and logistic problems, restricted-response essay questions are probably best for most purposes.

Objective questions generally require far less subjectivity in scoring than do essay questions. Well-written objective items can sample higher levels of student learning and need not be restricted to assessing knowledge of facts. The most flexible form of objective question is the multiple-choice item, but true-false, matching, and completion items are also widely used.

Observation methods of evaluation are typically better suited to psychomotor and affective learning than are tests. Additionally, observation methods can frequently be used in conjunction with tests to evaluate the mastery of cognitive objectives.

Observations can be made of either process or products. Most observational evaluation methods are appropriate for either. Descriptions were provided for rating scales, checklists, behavioral observations, anecdotal records, sociometric methods, and self-report methods. Guides for the development and use of each form as well as the advantages and disadvantages of each were presented. Five methods of grading were discussed as well as several mistakes in grading that should be avoided.

Suggested Readings

Bertrand, A., & Cebula, J. P. *Tests, measurements, and evaluation.* Reading, Mass.: Addison-Wesley, 1980.

This text provides a good introduction to teacher-made tests and is useful to most beginning students.

Chase, C. I. The impact of achievement expectation and handwriting quality on scoring essay tests. *Journal of Educational Measurement,* 1979, *16,* 39–42.

This article is useful reading for exploring the disadvantages of essay items.

Ebel, R. L. Can teachers write good true-false items? *Journal of Educational Measurement,* 1975, *12,* 31–35.

This article surveys the advantages of true-false items.

Ebel, R. L. *Essentials of educational measurement* (3rd ed.). Englewood Cliffs, N.J.: Prentice-Hall, 1979.

This book provides a good, intermediate-level introduction to teacher-made tests.

Gronlund, N. E. *Measurement and evaluation in teaching* (4th ed.). New York: Macmillan, 1981.

Gronlund's book has been acknowledged as one of the better texts on measurement through all four of its editions.

Answers to Practice Exercise 14–1

1. The flaw in the original item was the brevity of the stem. It did not communicate a meaningful problem to readers. A better version is:

Reliability refers to the extent to which a test
- a. measures the content it is supposed to measure
- (b.) consistently measures what it is supposed to measure
- c. contains components of measurement error
- d. loses value as its length decreases

2. The major flaw in the original item was the inordinate length of alternative *d.* The following item is much better:

In norm-referenced testing you are comparing an individual's performance to
- (a.) the performance of others
- b. a person's own performance
- c. a standard of "normal work"
- d. a standard of excellence

3. Alternatives *d* ("*a* and *c* above") and *e* ("all of the above") in the original item were poor. They are likely to confuse students. Avoid such alternatives. Here is our improved item:

A test that measures achievement against a standard of performance (for example, many drivers' license examinations) is called a
- a. norm-referenced test
- b. reliable test
- (c.) criterion-referenced test
- d. psychomotor test

4. The original item contained a stem that was too short to present a meaningful problem. The following is better:

The reliability of a test can best be improved by

a. shortening the test
b. including more difficult items
(c.) lengthening the test
d. making it criterion-referenced

5. The correct answer was the only alternative *(a)* that agreed grammatically with the stem. An alternative could be:

The most justifiable criticism of teacher-made tests is that they
(a.) often emphasize rote learning
b. discriminate against poorer students
c. sample more broadly than is actually necessary
d. are less reliable than other forms of evaluation

6. The original item was stated negatively ("not be justified in . . .") and alternatives *d* and *e* were inappropriate. Better phrasing would be:

If your goal were to sample students' recall of information from a wide variety of content areas, you would be justified in using
(a.) multiple-choice questions
b. oral essay questions
c. restricted essay questions
d. open-ended essay questions

7. The original item contained alternatives that did not offer readers any clear distinctions. This version does:

Grading essay items by counting the number of lines would likely be
a. unreliable and invalid
(b.) reliable and invalid
c. reliable and valid
d. valid and unreliable

8. The original item contained a stem that was negatively worded ("typically are not"). The new item avoids the problem:

Teacher-made tests usually have reasonably high
(a.) content validity
b. internal consistency
c. test-retest reliability
d. construct validity

9. The original item had a stem that was so brief it could not communicate a meaningful problem to readers. The version below is better:

Rating scales are most commonly used for which forms of learning?
a. rote and knowledge
b. social and behavioral

c. application and analysis
(d.) psychomotor and affective

10. The original item was negatively worded, as were two of the alternatives. This item is much easier to understand:

Sociograms have two basic classroom uses. They are
a. assessing cognitive and psychomotor learning
b. assessing affective and psychomotor learning
(c.) identifying isolates and group interactions
d. establishing content validity and internal consistency

Answers to Practice Exercise 14–2

1. *(b) Objective testing.* Some form of objective testing is probably best for determining knowledge of a complex organization such as the Congress. In order to adequately sample all of these areas, multiple questions would be required.
2. *(d) Checklist.* A checklist would be our first choice. The steps involved in preparing a specimen could be outlined in detail and students could be assessed on their completion of these steps.
3. *(e) Self-report.* In order to assess the affective component, our choice would be self-report—either activity checklists (number of music pieces listened to, any records purchased, and so on) or simple attitude scales ("compared to six months ago, my enjoyment of music of the baroque period is (a) greater than it was then, (b) about the same, (c) less than it was then"). As mentioned in the chapter, basic knowledge in an area may be necessary in order for higher-level affective objectives to be reached. Some form of testing, either essay or objective, may also be appropriate. One caution, however, is that the cognitive assessment should not be used in such a way that it generates negative attitudes toward the subject area.
4. *(c) Ratings.* A rating scale is probably most appropriate. A comparative scale, in which standard performances form the basis for judgment, may be useful.
5. *(e) Self-report.* The problem is basically one of determining motivation. Assessment of reading habits, however, can form an important basis for determining the appropriate levels of instruction for the students. An activity checklist would reveal a great deal to the teacher about students' reading habits.
6. *(a) Essay test.* This type of knowledge is typically assessed by essay examinations, often the extended-response type. In essay tests the student has the opportunity to organize his or her thoughts and to explain relationships between principles and events. An oral question is also well suited for this type of situation. The objective test, particularly multiple-choice questions, should not be eliminated

from consideration, however. With proper construction, multiple-choice items could measure students' abilities to apply principles.

7. *(b) Objective questions.* Knowledge of terminology is best assessed by means of objective questions. The multiple-choice format is quite versatile for most levels of learning.
8. *(a) Essay test.* The students could be instructed to judge each argument as logical or illogical in a restricted-response essay and to briefly outline the reasons for their judgment. If the argument is a complex one (for example, a court opinion), the extended-response essay would be required. Objective items such as multiple-choice questions should not automatically be eliminated. A series of well-constructed items in an interpretive exercise can effectively assess students' abilities to judge the logic in an argument.

IMPORTANT EVENTS IN THE DEVELOPMENT OF TEACHER-MADE TESTS

The research on teacher-made tests is voluminous, with large literatures in each area of specialization (testing in social studies, testing in mathematics, and so on). For this reason, our chronology will not deal with specific subject areas. Additionally, the number of measurement texts designed for teachers since 1935 is simply too great to detail. Hence our post-1935 history touches only on important commentary and on the most significant texts.

Date(s)	*Person(s)*	*Work*	*Impact*
1845	Mann	"Boston grammar and writing schools"	Until the time of Horace Mann, the majority of teacher-administered tests were oral. His paper pointed out the shortcomings of oral exams and called for more frequent use of written examinations.
1880	Hall	Saturday morning lectures	In G. Stanley Hall's Saturday morning lectures, he emphasized the value of employing written rather than oral exams.
1881	Hall	Introduction of the questionnaire method to the United States	Using Sir Francis Galton's work, Hall introduced the idea of questionnaire and survey methods to American education (Boring, 1950).
1886	White	*The elements of pedagogy*	By 1886, despite the efforts of Mann and Hall, most teacher-made tests were still oral. Emerson E. White's book included a strong call for the use of written examinations. He based his arguments primarily on the greater validity and reliability of written exams.
1896	Binet & Henri	"La psychologie individuelle"	The publication of H. Binet and V. Henri's paper, preceding Binet and Simon's intelligence scale by nine years, provided considerable insight into the testing of higher-order abilities (Boring, 1950).

Date(s)	*Person(s)*	*Work*	*Impact*
1897	Ebbinghaus	Introduction of the completion item	Hermann Ebbinghaus, a German psychologist, invented the completion item for use by local schools.
1903	Thorndike	*Educational psychology*	E. L. Thorndike's classic text suggested the kinds of tests best suited for measuring and predicting academic success. He emphasized the new forms of objective items.
1904	Thorndike	*Introduction to the theory of mental and social measurements*	E. L. Thorndike's measurement text strongly influenced the training of teachers and prompted the use of objective test items by classroom teachers.
1908	Meyer	"The grading of students"	Max Meyer's paper brought the unreliability of teachers' grading practices to public attention. This paper started the movement toward more reliable and valid grading practices for essay examinations and gave further impetus to the new objective items.
1908	Stone	*Stone arithmetic test*	C. W. Stone, a student of Thorndike, published the first standardized achievement test in 1908. This test influenced the construction of teacher-made math tests for several years.
1910	Thorndike	*Thorndike handwriting scale*	Thorndike, whose work forms the basis of so much of educational psychology, published the first scale for educational use in 1910.
1911	Hamilton & Yerkes	Formal development of the multiple-choice item	While the exact circumstances surrounding the invention of the multiple-choice method remain obscure, by 1911 G. V. Hamilton and Robert M. Yerkes had developed its use for standardized testing (Boring, 1950). Surprisingly, their technique was originally devised for the testing of

Date(s)	*Person(s)*	*Work*	*Impact*
			laboratory animals—multiple choices were available for, say, rats running a maze.
1918	Thorndike	"The nature, purposes, and general methods of measurements of educational products"	This paper has been called "the most important paper in the history of measurement" (Ross, 1947). It gave a great boost to the use of objective test items by teachers.
1920	McCall	"A new kind of school examination"	William A. McCall seems to be the first person to suggest the use of multiple-choice testing procedures for the classroom teacher.
1924	Ruch	*The improvement of the written examination*	G. M. Ruch's book was the first devoted solely to the development of objective test items.
1927	Ruch & Stoddard	*Tests and measurements in high school instruction*	G. M. Ruch and G. D. Stoddard's text, along with P. M. Symond's *Measurement in Secondary Education,* was the first text devoted solely to high school teachers' testing practices.
1936	Monroe	"Hazards in the measurement of achievement"	Walter Monroe's review paper reported on the rapid growth of objective testing in American schools and pointed out the problems associated with objective tests. He called for a balanced measurement approach including objective and essay items.
1945	Monroe	"Educational measurement in 1920 and 1945"	Monroe's paper described the explosive growth of the objective testing movement in the United States from 1920 to 1945. Despite problems with objective items (see Monroe's "Hazards" paper), objective tests had become the dominant form of classroom test by 1945. Bloom's taxonomy greatly facilitated the development of

Date(s)	*Person(s)*	*Work*	*Impact*
			objective tests that measured higher-order levels of learning.
1971	Bloom, Hastings, & Madeus	*Handbook on formative and summative evaluation of student learning*	By 1971, there were literally dozens of measurement texts available for educators. This Bloom text, however, offered coverage of specific subject areas and was designed with particular emphasis on helping teachers develop tests.
1981	Gronlund	*Measurement and education in teaching*	This text, in its fourth edition, is typical of the wide variety of measurement texts now available for classroom teachers. Like those by Hopkins and Stanley, Ebel, and others, it advocates careful attention to measurement that is soundly based in measurement theory.

Chapter Fifteen

STANDARDIZED TESTS

CHARACTERISTICS OF STANDARDIZED TESTS

— Achievement Tests
— Diagnostic Achievement Tests
— Single-Subject-Area Achievement Tests
— Survey Batteries
— Uses of Standardized Achievement Tests / Uses in Classroom Instruction / Uses for Guidance / Uses for Evaluation of Instruction
— Summary of Achievement Tests

ABILITY TESTS

— Intelligence Tests and Scholastic Aptitude Tests
— Uses of Ability Test Results / Uses for Placement / Uses for Guidance / Uses for Classroom Instruction
— Summary of Ability Tests

MEASURES OF INTERESTS

INTERPRETING SCORES ON A STANDARDIZED TEST

— How Scores Are Described
— The Normal Curve
— Reporting Standardized Test Scores
— Imprecision of Scores: Standard Error of Measurement

APPLICATIONS FOR TEACHING

PROFESSIONAL ETHICS AND STANDARDIZED TESTS

SUMMARY

SUGGESTED READINGS

ANSWERS FOR PRACTICE EXERCISE

IMPORTANT EVENTS IN THE DEVELOPMENT OF STANDARDIZED TESTS

Few educational issues have caused as much controversy as the use of standardized tests (L. B. Resnick, 1981). On the one hand, some persons have demanded that standardized tests not be used at all, declaring their use to be unethical, contrary to the aims of education, and against the best interests of children, especially minority group children (Jackson, 1975; Nairn & Associates, 1980). On the other hand, proponents of standardized tests argue that they are excellent educational tools, among the most accurate and least biased measures of students' achievements, abilities, and interests (see Educational Testing Service, 1980; C. R. Reynolds, 1981).

Obviously, with such a marked divergence of opinion, they can't all be right: Somebody has to be wrong—or everybody has to be at least partly wrong. In spite of this, it seems that standardized tests will be part of the educational scene for many years to come (D. P. Resnick, 1981). No doubt their form will change from time to time, and the extent of their use will wax and wane, but they will continue to be used in education and it will be necessary for teachers to be knowledgeable about them (Salmon-Cox, 1981; Sproull & Zubrow, 1981).

As a teacher, you will frequently come into contact with standardized tests. You are likely to be asked to administer them and to interpret their results. The proper understanding and use of standardized tests can enhance your performance as a teacher. The misuse of standardized tests can lead to poor decisions that may harm students' educational careers.

This chapter will provide you with basic information about standardized tests so that you will be able to weigh the issues with accuracy and to communicate with your future students and their parents about such tests. The chapter will survey the concepts and principles underlying all standardized tests and will deal specifically with the kinds of standardized tests used most often in education: achievement tests, ability tests, and interest inventories.

Objectives

After reading this chapter, you should be able to meet the following objectives.

1. Select the appropriate type(s) of standardized test(s) for given purposes.
2. Properly interpret test scores to students, parents, and others, correctly conveying meanings of such concepts as mean, median, mode, standard deviation, z-score, T score, percentile rank, standard error of measurement, age and grade equivalents, and IQ scores.
3. Explain to students and parents their rights to privacy and the confidentiality of standardized tests scores and other personal school records.

CHARACTERISTICS OF STANDARDIZED TESTS

In Chapters Thirteen and Fourteen we outlined the uses of measurement and the basic principles of measurement, and we discussed how you can create classroom tests based on sound measurement principles. This chapter shifts from teacher-made tests to commercially published standardized tests that schools purchase.

Standardized tests have three factors that set them apart from other forms of tests: (1) They have been carefully prepared, tried out, analyzed, and reviewed; (2) the instructions and conditions for administering and scoring them are uniform; and (3) the test results may be interpreted by comparison with tables of norms (Ebel, 1979; Gronlund, 1981; Lindeman & Merenda, 1979; Thorndike and Hagen, 1977).

Development of a typical standardized test begins with a table of specifications or plan that describes either curriculum content or specific mental abilities to be measured. Items are then carefully developed, reviewed, and revised. They are pretested, and the best items are chosen for the final form of the test.

Uniform directions make it possible to accurately interpret standardized test results over the wide range of users (Gronlund, 1981). If one test administrator were to allow thirty minutes for a part of a test and another only fifteen, the results of the two testing sessions would not be comparable. Uniform directions and administration are absolutely mandatory for valid standardized testing.

Tables of norms are developed by administration of the test to a standardization group. The **standardization sample** (norm group) is a carefully selected sample of persons representative of the individuals for whom the test is targeted. Their scores, called *norms,* serve as the frame

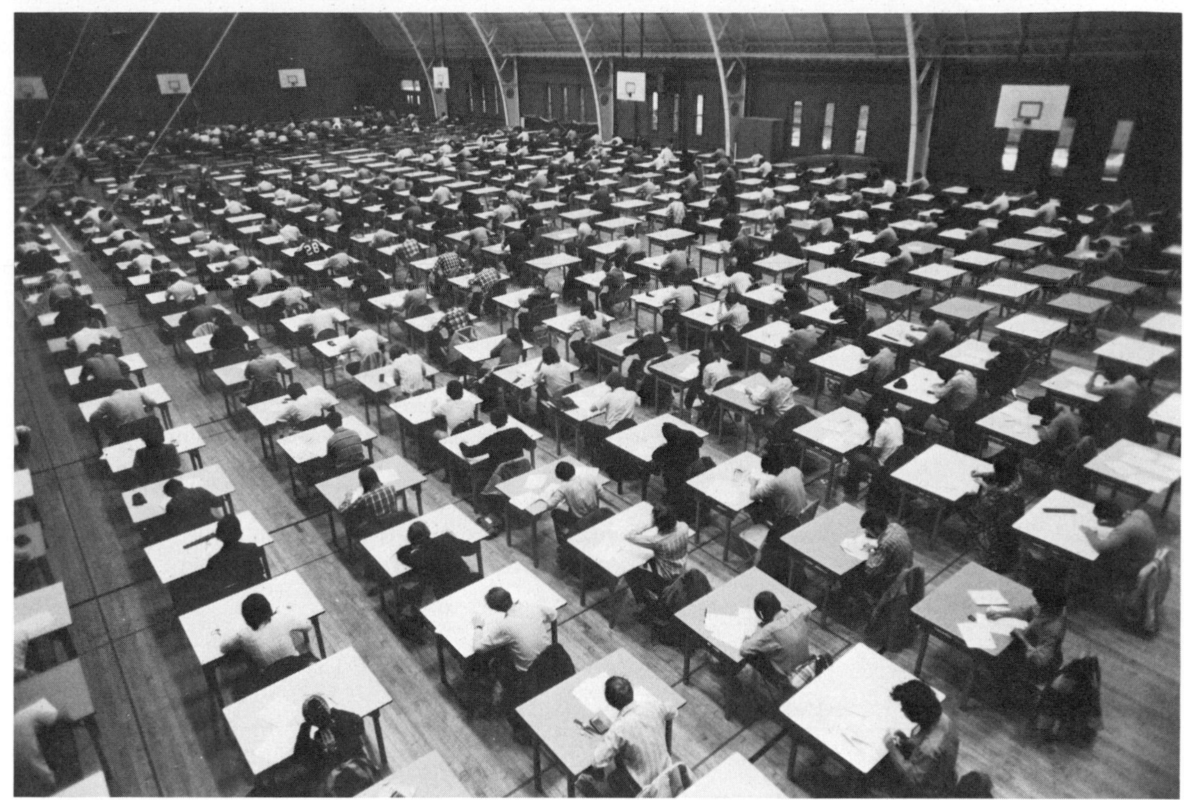

For today's students, veterans of a barrage of standardized tests, scenes like this one are familiar.

of reference by which the scores of your students are evaluated. A 100-item test designed to measure reading comprehension among junior high school and high school students might first be given to several thousand representative junior high and high school students across the country. Care would be taken to represent all racial and ethnic groups, socioeconomic levels, and areas of the country in the norm group. After the test is given, the test maker would have test scores that might show, for example, that beginning seventh graders in the norm group averaged 52 questions right, beginning eighth graders averaged 59 questions right, and so on. Future takers of the test will then have their performances compared to these scores.

How does one know whether a particular standardized test is valid for a given purpose? The starting point, of course, should be a specific definition of the kind of information sought through testing. To select the proper test, we first need to identify our reasons for testing. Are we interested in assessing attainment of instructional objectives, in grouping students, or in advising students about their vocational goals? Each different use, of course, implies a very different type of standardized test.

Although there are many ways in which standardized tests can be categorized, one of the most common is to group them according to their purposes into three broad classes: (1) achievement tests, (2) ability tests, and (3) interest inventories. Most schools have a standardized testing program that includes all three kinds of tests (Sproull & Zubrow, 1981).

Achievement Tests

Achievement tests are designed to measure the knowledge and abilities of students in subject matter areas (Gronlund, 1981; Lindeman & Merenda, 1979). Table 15–1 contrasts standardized achievement tests to those constructed by classroom teachers. The amount of effort and expertise brought to bear on the development of a test and the goals of testing differ for these two types of tests. Commercial achievement tests are usually prepared by a team of measurement, research, and curriculum experts who work full-time on the development of a test, while a classroom teacher has to develop dozens of tests on top of all the other

TABLE 15–1
A Comparison of Teacher-Made and Standardized Tests

Teacher-Made Achievement Tests	*Standardized Achievement Tests*
1. Directions are usually flexible, not uniform.	1. Directions for administering and scoring are uniform.
2. Test content is based on the teacher's own objectives. Content is specific to what has been taught.	2. Test content is determined by experts who survey texts and curricula to attempt to determine national trends.
3. Test construction is specific to the teacher's needs and time constraints. Less trying out or revision.	3. Test construction is meticulous. Tests are tried out and revised until they are at an excellent technical level.
4. Students' scores are compared only to the scores of students in the same classroom or to a criterion level established as a "passing" score.	4. Students' scores may be compared to national norms that usually include ages and grade equivalents.
5. Best suited for determining whether classroom objectives have been met. Useful as a basis for grading and marking.	5. Most appropriate for assessing broad curriculum goals, comparing students to national norms, and evaluating the performance of a teaching program.
6. Most useful for assessing specific weaknesses of individual students.	6. Most useful for identifying gaps in general ability or knowledge.
7. Prediction usually not advisable.	7. Prediction of future performance can often be made.

duties of teaching. Typically, standardized achievement tests are superior for estimation of overall student performance because of the care in their construction and the *availability of norms.* Teacher-made tests, in contrast, are usually superior for assessing the mastery of classroom objectives.

In general, there are three types of standardized achievement tests: (1) diagnostic tests, designed to identify patterns of students' strengths and weaknesses in specific areas; (2) single-subject-area tests, which assess students' general knowledge and abilities in a particular subject area; and (3) survey batteries (or, as they are sometimes called, multitest batteries), which are really a set of single-subject-area tests standardized on the same norm group. All three forms of achievement tests are important to teachers. Because they have different purposes, cover different content, and are constructed differently (Hopkins & Stanley, 1981; Thorndike & Hagen, 1977), we shall examine each in more detail.

Diagnostic Achievement Tests

Diagnostic achievement tests are designed to identify weaknesses in students' knowledge or abilities in specific subject areas. They are usually employed when other information indicates the possibility of deficiencies in skills or knowledge. A diagnostic arithmetic test, for example, may help us determine if students have trouble with fractions, addition, or long division, while a diagnostic reading test may help us determine if students are poorly prepared in phonics, word-attack skills, vocabulary, or comprehension.

Diagnostic tests are very valuable for locating weaknesses, but they do not give us information about *why* weaknesses exist. As Thorndike and Hagen (1977) point out, teachers must follow up diagnostic tests with direct observation of student performance to find out why difficulties exist.

Single-Subject-Area Achievement Tests

Single-subject-area achievement tests provide in-depth coverage of one subject area. In elementary school, the most common single-subject tests are those for reading and arithmetic. Reading-readiness tests, for example, are often administered near the end of the kindergarten year to identify students who are not yet ready for reading and to group students for instruction.

A wide range of single-subject-area tests is also available at the upper elementary and high school levels. Single-subject tests can be particularly appropriate in subjects, such as music and foreign languages, that are unlikely to be covered in a survey battery. Some schools rely on particular single-subject tests because their content coincides closely with the objectives of the schools' programs.

Survey Batteries

Wide-range achievement tests with several subtests that assess knowledge and abilities across many subject areas are referred to as **survey batteries.** Such broad-spectrum tests allow us to assess students' strengths and weaknesses in several subject areas. Survey batteries are most commonly used in the elementary grades, although there are several designed for use in secondary schools. The principal advantage of survey batteries is that each subtest has been standardized on the same norm group. This allows norm-based comparisons of students' relative performance across each of the subtests. The basic skills and subtests listed in Table 15–2 are typical of those appearing in such survey batteries as the California Achievement Tests, the Iowa Tests of Basic Skills, the Metropolitan Achievement Tests, and the Stanford Achievement Tests.

Uses of Standardized Achievement Tests

Some schools purchase, administer, and score achievement tests and then simply file the scores. This practice is both ethically and economically questionable. Achievement tests have many potentially valuable uses for classroom teachers, counselors, administrators, and students themselves. Information that can be gleaned from achievement tests can be used in a variety of ways to help develop better educational programs.

Uses in Classroom Instruction. Throughout this text we emphasize that instruction should begin at the point where students need it. Diagnostic tests and readiness tests help us determine where students are having difficulty and give us some basis for determing why the difficulties exist. Once teachers have identified the problem, they may begin to devise remedial instruction. This use alone makes standardized achievement tests potentially valuable. Single-subject tests and survey batteries may also be used to determine the strong and weak points of a class, allowing teachers to adjust their instructional techniques. Standardized test results can help identify objectives that have not been met and need to be reviewed.

Another classroom use of standardized achievement tests is to monitor grading procedures (Mehrens & Lehmann, 1978). We have all heard stories to the effect that Ms. Snell is a "hard grader" in math and Ms. Simms is an "easy grader." While standardized tests should not be used to assign grades (Gronlund, 1981; Thorndike & Hagen, 1977), someone like Ms. Simms can compare the performance of her students to that of Ms. Snell's pupils on the same test. If Ms. Simms's students do not perform as well as Ms. Snell's on standardized measures of achievement, then perhaps Ms. Simms should consider adjusting her grading or teaching practices.

A more general use of standardized achievement test results is the

TABLE 15–2
Basic Skills and Subtests in a Typical Survey Battery

Basic Skill	*Subtests*
Reading	Decoding skills (discrimination, analysis) Vocabulary (meaning of words) Comprehension (meaning of written materials)
Language	Mechanics (capitalization, punctuation) Expression (correctness, effectiveness) Spelling (from dictation or identifying misspelled words)
Mathematics	Computation (fundamental operations) Concepts (meaning of mathematical concepts) Problem solving (solving story problems)
Study skills	Library and reference skills Reading maps, graphs, and tables

Source: Adapted with permission of Macmillan Publishing Co., Inc., from Gronlund, N., *Measurement and evaluation in teaching* (4th ed.) (New York: Macmillan, 1981), p. 308. Copyright © 1981 by Norman E. Gronlund.

overall determination of strengths and weaknesses of all students. As we noted in Chapter Thirteen, tests can be used to help place students in educational programs. Achievement test results allow us to make more accurate decisions in placing new or transfer students into appropriate educational experiences. The results of achievement tests can also be used to help determine who might benefit from enrichment activities and who needs remedial work. If it is instructionally sound to group students to provide more individualized instruction, standardized achievement test results can supply some of the information for that decision-making process.

It is important to remember that achievement tests should never be used as the sole source of information for instructional decisions (Mehrens & Lehmann, 1978). These tests can provide teachers with another perspective on the achievement of their classes that will complement their own observations and evaluations (Madeus, 1981). They can add information about individuals and groups that teachers should consider before making decisions.

Uses for Guidance. Achievement test results can be used to help students make decisions about their educational and vocational goals. A student who professes a desire to become a research scientist, for example, might be asked some pointed questions by a counselor who notes that the student's achievement test scores in math and science are well below average. The counselor may further point out that the chances of success in the field, given such scores, have not been promising for similar students. The counselor would want the student to realize his or her strengths, weaknesses, and interests and to use these in making a decision. Given the information, the student may make a more realistic choice.

Uses for Evaluation of Instruction. Standardized achievement tests may be used as a part of the process of evaluating instruction. The performance of students in one class may be compared to other local classes and to norm groups as a reference point in order to check progress. Caution must be urged, however, in the use of achievement tests for this purpose. First, no two classes of students are identical. Second, like any test, achievement tests measure previous learning. A third-grade teacher may be very effective but not be able to make up everything that was badly taught in previous years. Third, no two teachers teach alike. Different skills are emphasized at different times by different teachers. Fourth, some teachers "teach for the test" (Mehrens & Lehmann, 1978) when they know their teaching will be evaluated by a standardized test. Learning of test content occurs at the expense of concepts not specific to the test, and high scores on the test may not indicate a generally high level of knowledge.

Summary of Achievement Tests

Standardized achievement tests measure the knowledge and abilities of students in subject matter areas. Diagnostic and readiness achievement tests can help us identify student weaknesses and help provide the basis from which we develop remedial instruction. Single-subject achievement tests and survey batteries allow us to compare students' performances to one another and to national norms. Typically, the results of standardized achievement tests are used to help guide teaching practices, to provide guidance for students, and to help evaluate instruction.

ABILITY TESTS

Intelligence Tests and Scholastic Aptitude Tests

As we discussed in Chapter Five, intelligence tests are designed to measure students' general mental abilities. Like any other form of ability test, intelligence tests measure what the individual has learned (Wesman, 1970). They provide a general estimate of how much people have profited from past experience and how well they will adapt to new situations.

The most prominent of the individual intelligence tests, the Stanford-Binet and the Wechsler Intelligence Scales, are discussed in detail in Chapter Five. They are designed for administration to one person at a time. For most individual tests, a trained examiner is required to give directions, present problems, interpret answers, and score the overall test results.

While the term **intelligence test** is commonly used to refer to individual mental-ability tests such as the Stanford-Binet and the Wechsler Scales, its use is much less common in describing group tests of mental ability. Instead, these group tests are often referred to as **scholastic aptitude tests** (Gronlund, 1981). There are several reasons for this difference in labeling: (1) many people wrongly associate the term *intelligence* with inherited ability, (2) there is a great deal of controversy over the concept of intelligence (what it means and what it includes), and (3) group tests are usually employed to predict later scholastic performance (Gronlund, 1981, p. 334).

This girl's performance on a reading test will help her teacher design the best possible reading program for her.

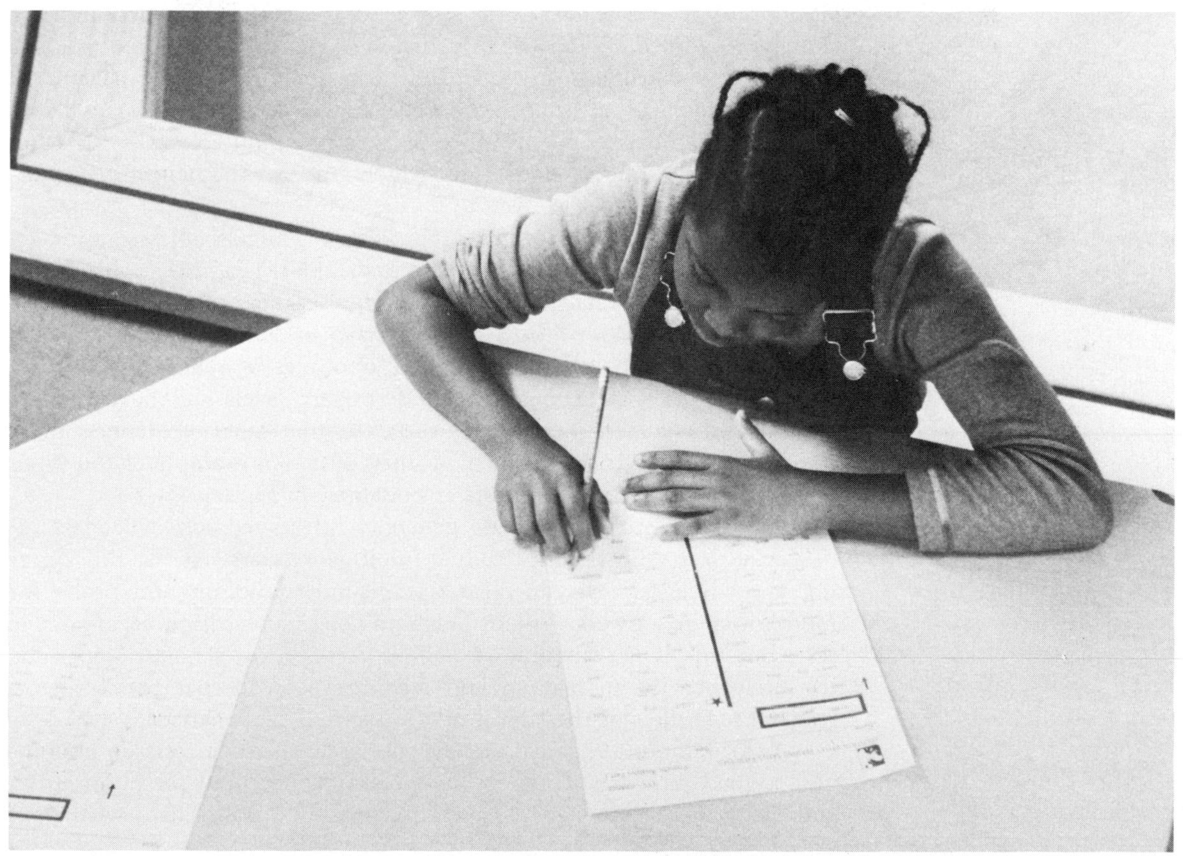

Unlike individual intelligence tests, scholastic aptitude tests are given in groups. They require the examinee to read questions and to mark responses on an answer sheet. There is little one-to-one contact with the examiner, whose role is usually restricted to reading test directions, timing the test, and distributing and gathering up the answer sheets. Most scholastic aptitude tests consist of multiple-choice items presented in a booklet.

Compared to individual intelligence tests, these features might be considered disadvantages (Sattler, 1974), but they are compensated for in part by the ease with which large numbers of people can be tested. Little time is spent in administering and scoring the tests. Additionally, if the test manual is carefully followed, the administrators need not have the level of skill required for administering individual measures of intelligence.

Scholastic aptitude tests sometimes yield a single score as a global measure of scholastic aptitude, but more often they provide a separate verbal (V) and quantitative (Q) score. The assumption behind separate verbal and quantitative scores is that the verbal scores best predict achievement in courses in which verbal concepts are emphasized (such as English, social studies) and quantitative scores best predict success in mathematics-based areas (algebra, chemistry, physics, and the like). The separate scores generally provide a basis for differential prediction and may alert a teacher to areas in which students may encounter difficulties (Gronlund, 1981).

Many schools have testing programs in which scholastic aptitude tests are administered (Sproull & Zubrow, 1981). Each year, for example, over two and a half million high school seniors take the Scholastic Aptitude Tests, which have a major impact on admissions decisions in many colleges and universities. Other examples of scholastic aptitude tests widely used at elementary and secondary levels are the Henmon-Nelson Tests of Mental Abilities, the California Tests of Mental Maturity, and the Otis-Lennon School Ability Test. An example of the types of items appearing on these tests is presented in Figure 15–1.

Scholastic aptitude tests are generally considered somewhat less reliable and less valid than individual intelligence tests. An examiner giving an individual test can clear up misunderstandings and probe for more complete answers without damaging the standardized nature of the test, but this is not possible in a group test. Also, scholastic aptitude tests rely heavily on reading and reading speed so that poor or slow readers, regardless of their level of ability, may be penalized.

As Gronlund (1981) has stated, scholastic aptitude tests do *not* provide a good estimate of undeveloped learning potential for pupils from cultural minorities or disadvantaged homes or for students with poor

FIGURE 15–1
Sample Items from the Otis-Lennon School Ability Test

Practice Problems

V. △ is to ▲ as □ is to — a. □ b. △ c. ■ d. ▲ e. ■

W. The numbers in the box go together in a certain way. Find the number that goes where you see the question mark (?) in the box.

6	7	8
5	6	7
4	5	?

f. 9 g. 8 h. 7 j. 6 k. 5

X. What letter comes next in this series?
A B D E G H J K ?

a. N b. M c. L d. K e. I

Y. Hat is to head as shoe is to—

f. sock g. toe h. buckle j. leg k. foot

Z. The drawings in the first part of the row go together to form a series. In the next part of the row, find the drawing that goes where you see the question mark (?) in the series.

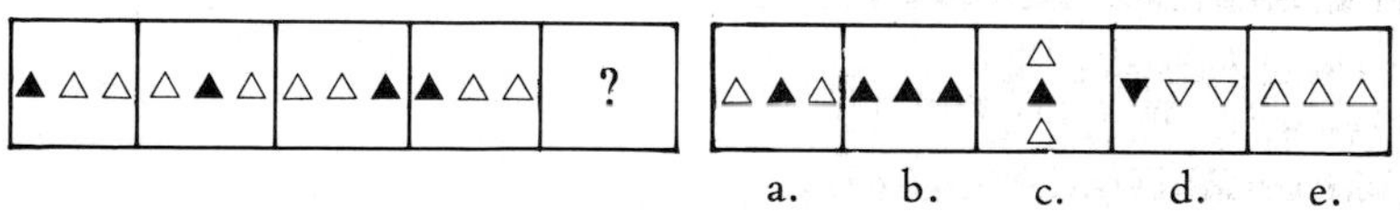

Source: Reproduced by permission from the Otis-Lennon School Ability Test.

reading skills. Neither scholastic aptitude tests nor intelligence tests measure native capacity or learning potential *directly*. According to Gronlund (1981), such tests are valid measures of learning potential only if all pupils have had an equal opportunity to learn the types of tasks presented on the test, are equally motivated, and have no hindrances (such as reading difficulties or emotional problems). Consequently, it is never proper to interpret scholastic aptitude scores as direct and unmodifiable measures of academic learning potential (Gronlund, 1981).

Uses of Ability Test Results

Before discussing the uses of ability tests, we must point out that the results of any such test should be viewed very cautiously. An IQ or other mental-ability score is only one bit of evidence to be added to other information about a person. It is quite possible for a student to have a "bad day" when a test is given. Illness, hunger, fatigue, and just "feeling rotten" can lower a person's performance on standardized tests. Additionally, we should be alert to possible cultural biases in intelligence and scholastic aptitude tests. It is clear that environment (experience) directly influences the learned skills that are measured on ability tests. Obviously, for example, a student's vocabulary knowledge will be determined by the kind of vocabulary used in his or her immediate environment. The importance of one or two test scores should not be overemphasized in making decisions about students' futures.

PRACTICE EXERCISE 15–1

Reviewing Standardized Tests

There is no better way to become acquainted with standardized tests than by reading them and their accompanying manuals. Utilizing your school's library, the counseling center, or a public school materials center, summarize on the following form an achievement test, a scholastic aptitude test, or an interest inventory. You may wish to consult with the Buros *Mental Measurement Yearbooks** for aid in reviewing the test you choose.

1. Test name ______________________________
2. Publisher ______________________________
3. Purpose of the test ______________________________
   ____
   ____
4. Statements of validity and reliability (drawn from Buros or the test manuals) ______________________________
   ____

* O.K. Buros's *Mental Measurement Yearbooks* contain expert critical reviews of all existing tests in print. The latest *Mental Measurement Yearbook* is the eighth (Highland Park, N.J.: Gryphon Press, 1978). Future editions will be developed by the Buros Institute of Mental Measurements at the University of Nebraska and published by the University of Nebraska Press.

Uses for Placement. Intelligence and scholastic aptitude tests, along with other information about students, may help us identify those children who would benefit from special programs. Additionally, if instructional grouping is used in a school, a measure of general academic ability can help teachers place children of approximately equal ability in the same group. The use of such tests in placement, particularly in the placement of mentally retarded students in special education, has recently been seriously challenged, however (see Chapter Seventeen).

Uses for Guidance. A well-trained counselor's careful use of ability test results can be helpful in providing guidance for students and their parents who are making educational and vocational plans. Combined with achievement test results, grades, and indications of interests, a

---

5. Desirable features (if any) ______________________________

____

6. Undesirable features (if any) ______________________________

____

____

7. Competitors (drawn from Buros) ______________________________

____

____

8. General comments and recommendations on the use of the test ______

____

____

____

9. Personal, affective reaction to the test ______________________

____

____

A second activity that you may find helpful is to visit a counseling center and complete your own interest inventory. This is especially useful if you are still not quite sure what vocational and educational directions you wish to take.

measure of general learning ability can help us give students a more complete picture of themselves.

Uses for Classroom Instruction. There are few uses of ability tests in classroom instruction. It is possible to use ability test results to alter the form and pacing of your instruction to more closely meet your students' needs, but other information will likely be more valuable for instructional decisions than will knowledge of students' intelligence and aptitude test scores.

Summary of Ability Tests

Ability tests are designed to measure individuals' abilities to profit from experience and to adapt to new situations. They fall into two major categories. Individual intelligence tests have the advantage of the interaction of a trained examiner and a subject, a process that usually results in a reliable and valid measure. Group tests, usually referred to as scholastic aptitude tests, are more efficient to administer to large numbers of people and do not require highly skilled testers. Intelligence and scholastic aptitude test results can be used in conjunction with other information in placement and guidance decisions, but they have limited application for classroom instruction. Teachers must recognize the role of cultural background and academic preparation in each student's score and should refrain from making any inferences about innate or native potential from a student's score.

MEASURES OF INTERESTS

The discussion so far has revolved around measures of achievement and ability, but we have continually emphasized that the results of achievement and ability measures must be used in conjunction with other information, particularly information about academic performance and interests. In this section, we shall briefly survey interest inventories.*

Interests are usually defined as feelings toward activities (Mehrens & Lehmann, 1978; Thorndike & Hagen, 1977). **Interest inventories,** then, are designed to assess how people feel about various kinds of ac-

* There are other types of noncognitive measures besides interest inventories. You have probably heard of tests like the Rorschach "inkblot" test, the Minnesota Multiphasic Personality Inventory, and similar instruments. Such personality tests "are not yet ready for general use in our schools and should not be . . . normally and routinely administered in school testing programs" (Mehrens & Lehmann, 1978, p. 581). They reveal little to the teacher that cannot be gained from a careful observation of a student's behavior.

Early measures of personality were not always highly valid.

"The forward thrust of the antlers shows a determined personality, yet the small sun indicates a lack of self-confidence . . ."

tivities. The first interest inventory was developed by G. Stanley Hall in 1907 to assess children's interests in various types of recreation. It was not until 1919, however, during a summer institute at the Carnegie Institute of Technology, that an interest inventory was created based on formal scientific approaches. The Strong Vocational Interest Blank was developed from the work at that institute and remained the only standardized interest inventory available for twenty years. The Strong inventory has since been revised several times and now appears as the Strong-Campbell Interest Inventory (SCII).

Other measures of interest include the Kuder Preference Record, the Lee-Thorpe Occupational Interest Inventory, and Guilford's Interest Survey. In general, interest inventories are based on five assumptions:

1. Interests are learned, not innate.
2. Children's interests are unstable but become relatively permanent by early adulthood.

3. People in specific occupations or educational programs have common likes and dislikes for activities.
4. There are differences in how intensely people feel about participating in certain activities.
5. Interests motivate people to select activities and to continue in them.

Typically, interest inventories contain several scales that have been standardized on specific vocational groups (artists, mechanics, photographers, psychologists) or specific educational groups (pre-med students, engineering students). People's responses on the inventory are compared to the norm group's responses. A counselor might say, "The results of your interest inventory indicate that you have many interests in common with musicians and not so many in common with physicians or dentists. Perhaps it would clarify matters if we looked at what it is about medicine and dentistry that seemed to attract you at first."

One very important factor to keep in mind about interest inventories is that they are not really tests because no item has a "right" answer (Mehrens & Lehmann, 1978). There is nothing "right" or "wrong" about a young woman preferring the sciences to business, for example.

Faking is a problem with interest inventories. Suppose you were asked to respond to the following item:

Choose the one statement that you agree with the most.

a. I very much enjoy gardening.
b. I really enjoy playing cards.
c. I like to contemplate my navel.

If for some reason you wanted to convey to the test administrator that you were industrious, you might mark *a,* even though you really didn't like gardening all that much.

Then, too, items such as this cannot possibly deal with people who like activities *a, b,* and *c* equally well. There is also no way for such items to reflect the intensity of a person's feelings. In general, the validity and reliability of interest inventories are lower than those of cognitive tests (Mehrens & Lehmann, 1978), and predictions based on interest inventories are much less precise.

These problems, as well as sex biases that still crop up in some noncognitive tests, give us good reason to be cautious in the use of interest inventories. They may be helpful, however, in generating thoughtful discussions about vocational choices, especially in the hands of a well-trained counselor. Nonetheless, for the typical classroom teacher, we believe that they probably provide less useful information than interviews and observational data for determining students' significant interests.

INTERPRETING SCORES ON A STANDARDIZED TEST

In order to interpret standardized test results, you need to understand how norms are reported and how the scores of students taking the tests are compared to the norms. The following sections present important information for understanding and interpreting standardized test results.

How Scores Are Described

When a measurement is taken of any human characteristic—height, weight, reading test scores, or how far a ball is thrown—we do not expect each person to obtain the same score. If we examined the scores of twenty tenth-grade students on a reading comprehension test, the results might look like those pictured in Table 15–3. This tally of how many students obtained each score is called a **frequency distribution.** The scores being tallied are called **raw scores**—they are simply the number of items correct on the test.

Several concepts important to interpreting standardized test scores can be seen in a frequency distribution such as the one presented in Table 15–3. As you can see, the scores range widely, from a low of 53 to a high of 82, and they seem to bunch between 65 and 75.

TABLE 15–3
A Frequency Distribution for a Class of Twenty Tenth-Grade Students on a 100-Item Reading Comprehension Test

Scores
82
80
78
77
75
74, 74
73
71, 71
70, 70, 70
69
67
66
65, 65
58
53

The scores are spread out, but one score (70) was obtained more frequently than any other (three times). This most frequently occurring score is known as the **mode** (sometimes called the *modal score*).* The mode is one measure of **central tendency,** which refers to an average score or scores that best represent the performance of a group of students taking a test.

A second measure of central tendency is the **mean** *(M).* The mean is computed for a distribution by adding up the scores (82 + 80 + 78 + 77 + . . . + 53 = 1408) and dividing by the number of scores (20). The formula for mean *(M)* is as follows:

$$M = \frac{\Sigma X}{N}$$

where Σ = sum of; X = individual scores; N = number of scores. In our example,

$$M = \frac{\Sigma X}{N} = \frac{1408}{20} = 70.4.$$

A third measure of central tendency is the median. The **median** is the midpoint of a set of scores—half the scores fall above it and half the scores fall below it. In our example, since there are 20 scores, we are looking for the point above which there are 10 scores and below which there are 10 scores.

If we count up from the bottom, we see that the tenth score from the bottom is 70 and the eleventh is 71. With an *even* number of scores, as in this example, the median is usually considered to be halfway between the two middle scores. Thus the median in this case is 70.5.

Things are even simpler if there is an *odd* number of scores in the distribution. In that case the middle score itself is usually considered to be the median since there are equal numbers of scores above and below it.†

* Some distributions have more than one mode. In a different group, three students each might have scored at 71 and 73, with fewer students receiving other scores.

† There are more complex ways of determining the median. If we gave a 100-item test to 300 people, many would obtain the same scores. So by grouping scores into intervals (everyone who made between 51 and 55, and so on) and remembering some basic mathematical concepts (numbers and intervals have theoretical limits; the lower theoretical limit of 49 is 48.5), we would calculate the median with the following formula:

$$\text{Median} = L + \frac{(N/2) - F}{f_m}(i)$$

where L = the lower theoretical limit of the interval in which the median score is found; N = the number of scores; F = the total frequency below the interval in which

You will find that measures of central tendency affect your interpretation of test results in two ways:

1. The central tendency for a group is the best single indicator of that group's standing or performance. You can compare two sections of, say, freshman English by comparing their average scores on spelling or reading speed.
2. Each individual in a group can be compared to others in the class. You can evaluate individuals by noting if they are higher or lower than the class average or if they achieve objectives more or less speedily than the class average.

It is a rather limited interpretation, however, to know only that one group is higher on the average than another or that an individual exceeds or is exceeded by the class average. It is often necessary to know how much the performances differ. To do this we must know how to measure the **variability** of test scores, that is, the way scores are spread around the measure of central tendency. Two sets of scores can be quite different in this respect.

Table 15–4 presents the results of the reading test we considered in Table 15–3 from a second class that has the same mean score as the first but with a quite different spread of scores. The second group clusters more closely around the mean. Its scores are much less *variable* than the scores in the first class.

The most common method for measuring the degree of variability of scores is the **standard deviation,** an index of how spread out scores are from the mean. It is an extremely important factor in interpreting test results. Tests in which scores are widely spread have large standard deviations, while tests with closely bunched distributions of scores have smaller standard deviations. The standard deviation (SD) is found with the following formula.

$$\text{SD} = \sqrt{\frac{\Sigma(X - M)^2}{N}}$$

where Σ = the sum of; X = the individual scores; M = the mean of the distribution; and N = the number of scores.

Essentially, to find the standard deviation of a set of scores, (1) find each score's distance from the mean $(X - M)$, (2) square the result

---

the median score is found; f_m = the number of scores or the frequency within the median interval; and i = the size of the interval (the interval 51–55 spans five numbers and so its size is 5). For most classroom purposes, however, the simpler computation will suffice.

TABLE 15–4
Frequency Distributions for Two Classes of Twenty Tenth-Graders on a 100-Item Reading Comprehension Test

Scores	
First Class	***Second Class***
82	
80	
78	
77	
	76
75	
74, 74	74, 74, 74
73	73, 73
71, 71	71, 71, 71
70, 70, 70	70, 70, 70, 70, 70
69	69, 69, 69
67	67
66	
65, 65	65
	62
58	
53	

(which will eliminate negative numbers), (3) total the squared numbers, and (4) divide the total by the number of scores *(N).* The result is called the *variance.* The square root of the variance is the standard deviation.

In both classes of 20 students, the mean was 70.4. Thus, for the first class, we would subtract 70.4 from 82, from 80, from 78, and so on, square each difference—$(11.8)^2$, $(9.6)^2$, and so on—and total the squared numbers. The total is then divided by the number of scores, in this case 20. The square root of this number is the standard deviation. Computation is as follows for the scores from the first class:

$$\text{SD} = \sqrt{\frac{\Sigma(X - M)^2}{N}} = \sqrt{\frac{930.8}{20}} = \sqrt{46.54} = 6.82.$$

For the second class:

$$SD = \sqrt{\frac{\Sigma(X - M)^2}{N}} = \sqrt{\frac{202.8}{20}} = \sqrt{10.14} = 3.18.$$

As you can see, the standard deviation for the second class is much smaller than for the first class. In a sense, the standard deviation is a kind of average—an average of how much the scores in a distribution deviate from the mean score. In standardized tests, the standard deviation is the measuring stick for describing how far above or below the mean a given student scores.

Test makers routinely compute the mean, median, mode, standard deviation, and other statistics for the standardization sample in order to develop norms for their tests. Norms might be available for each grade level of the norm group for the 100-item reading comprehension test mentioned earlier. Norms then become the point of comparison for your students' scores. Are your seventh graders above or below the mean as compared to the norm group? How far above or below the mean is a particular student? How do your students rank in reading achievement compared to other students? Standardized test results help provide teachers with answers to such questions.

The Normal Curve

As we noted earlier, tests are standardized on large groups rather than on the small classes of twenty we used to demonstrate the computation of the mode, mean, median, and standard deviation. When a test is

PRACTICE EXERCISE 15–2

Calculating Mode, Mean, Median, and Standard Deviation

Examine the data in the chart below:

94	86	75	68
93	86	73	67
90	86	72	66
88	86	71	65
87	80	70	64

These figures represent the scores on a 100-point math test. Using the information on the chart, answer the following questions:

1. What is the mode?
2. What is the mean?
3. What is the median?
4. What is the standard deviation?

Our answers appear at the end of the chapter.

given to a large group, there is the possibility of some students marking all items correctly and others marking none correctly. Most students would fall somewhere in between these extremes. Even in the two small classes we used as illustrations, scores tended to bunch toward the middle. Such a distribution is typical of most human characteristics. This phenomenon was first noted by the Belgian mathematician, Lambert Quetelet (1776–1874) when he was measuring soldiers' height and weight. He graphed his results and determined they very nearly coincided with a mathematical distribution known as the Gaussian distribution, a bell-shaped curve.

Quetelet's work came to the attention of many people (most notably Sir Francis Galton) and resulted in some misleading ideas. Since so many human (and animal) characteristics approximated the Gaussian distribution, with most measures falling close to the mean, deviations from the

PRACTICE EXERCISE 15–3

Plotting a Normal Curve

One way to better understand how normal curves are constructed is to construct a graph yourself. Consider the frequency distribution below:

Score	*Number of Persons Making the Score*	*Score*	*Number of Persons Making the Score*
100	1	83	25
99	5	82	23
98	7	81	20
96	6	80	20
95	10	79	19
94	12	78	18
93	15	77	16
92	17	76	15
91	17	75	14
90	20	74	12
89	26	73	10
88	24	72	9
87	26	71	8
86	28	70	5
85	30	69	6
84	28	68	1

Using the graph framework we have constructed (opposite), plot the frequencies as dots and then connect the dots. We have plotted the first two points to give you the general idea (i.e., one person scored 68, six scored 69).

mean were thought of as "errors" because "nature's ideal" was obviously the mean (Kolstoe, 1973). Hence, this kind of distribution of scores came to be called the **normal curve.** The term normal curve has stayed in use although we no longer view deviations from the mean as errors.

Figure 15–2 presents a normal distribution of scores. Notice that the bottom line, the abscissa, represents scores, in this case the scores of several thousand randomly selected persons on the Wechsler Scales. It could be any human characteristic that is being considered, of course—height, weight, or a measure of strength. The vertical line (ordinate) represents the number of times each score occurs (this vertical line is usually not present in most depictions of normal curves; we use it here to help you understand the meaning of the curve). The higher the point along the curve, the greater the number of scores at that point along the abscissa. In our example, 100 individuals have IQ scores of exactly 100.

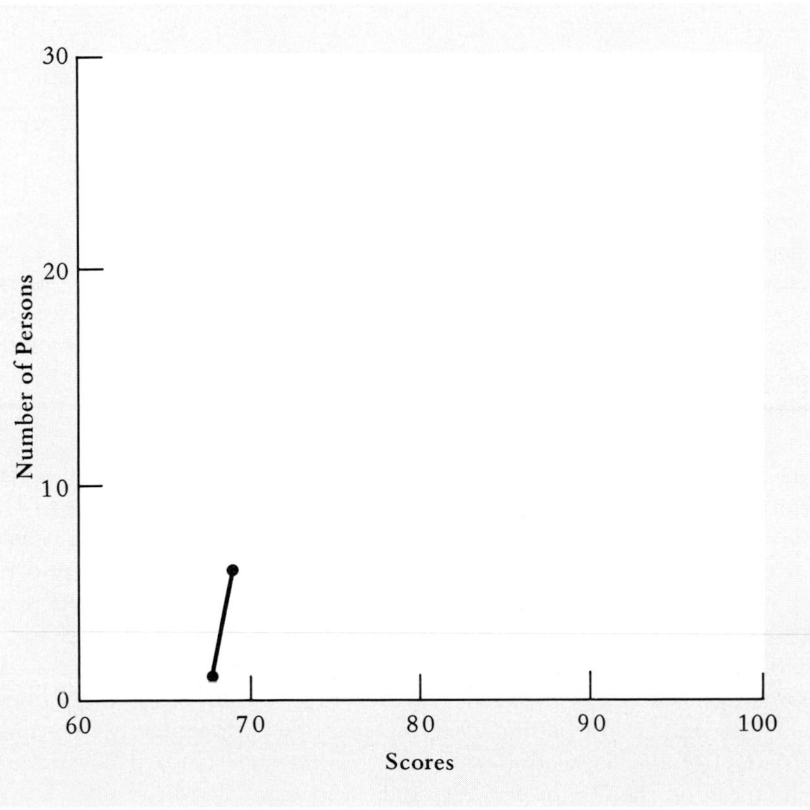

FIGURE 15–2
The Normal Distribution of Intelligence Test Scores

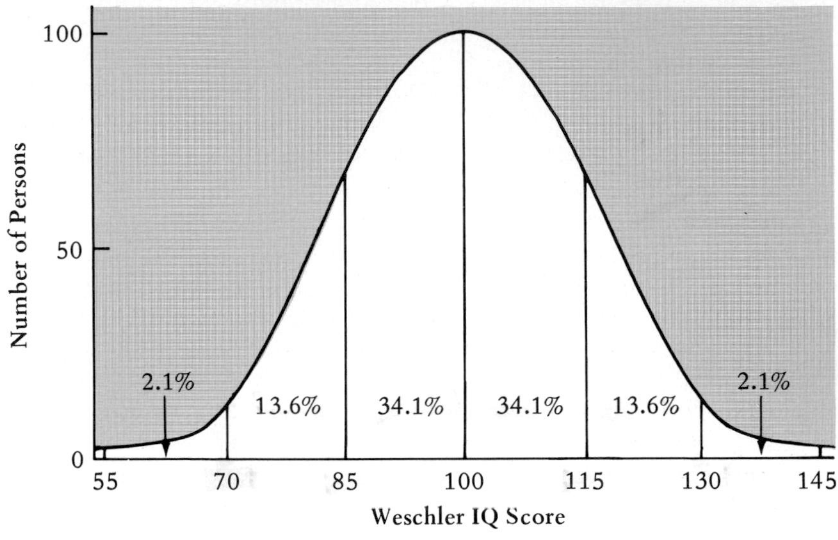

In a normal curve, the mean, the median, and the mode will be identical; they will all fall at the same place on the curve, the center. The curve is symmetrical around this point, with the number of scores decreasing as we move in either direction from the midpoint. On the curve in Figure 15–2, we can see that 100 is the most common (modal) score, the mean score, and the midpoint (median) of IQ scores of the people in the sample. Fewer persons obtained scores of 85 or 115 and very few individuals scored either below 70 or above 130.

Reporting Standardized Test Scores

In most standardized tests, the scores will approximate a normal distribution such as that in Figure 15–2. Test makers take advantage of this fact since predictable proportions of scores occur in each part of a normal distribution. The area between 100 and 115, for example, represents the range from the mean (100) to one standard deviation above the mean (in this case 115, since the standard deviation of the Wechsler Scales is 15). Approximately one-third of the scores (34.1%) fall in this area, the same number as fall between 100 and 85, that is, between the mean and one standard deviation *below* the mean. So approximately two-thirds (68.2%) of the population will score within one standard deviation of the mean on the Wechsler Scales and on most standardized tests.

Between +1 standard deviation and +2 standard deviations (between 115 and 130 in our IQ test example in Figure 15–2) we find another 13.6% of the scores. The same percentage falls between −1 and −2 standard deviations. Thus, a total of about 95% of the scores will fall between −2 standard deviations and +2 standard deviations. Almost all scores, 99.8%, fall between −3 standard deviations and +3 standard deviations. On the Wechsler Scale, this would mean that fewer than one out of a thousand persons would obtain IQ scores either below 55 or above 145. Extreme scores are very rare on standardized tests!

On standardized tests the raw scores (the actual scores received on the test, that is, the number of items correct) are almost always converted into standard scores. **Standard scores** are scores based on standard deviations and on the assumption that the distribution of scores is a normal one. By looking at a standard score, one can tell immediately how far above or below the mean a person's score is.

The simplest form of standard score is the *z*-score. The ***z*-score** simply gives a person's performance on a test in standard deviation units above or below the mean. For example, a *z*-score of +1.0 is equal to one standard deviation above the mean, a *z*-score of −2.0 is equal to two standard deviations below the mean, and so forth. Raw scores are turned into *z*-scores by the following formula:

$$z = \frac{X - M}{SD}$$

where X = the student's raw score; M = the mean of all scores; and SD = the standard deviation of the distribution.

As an example, suppose a student gets 79 items correct on our reading achievement test. Let's also say that the mean for her grade level in the norm group was 70 and the standard deviation was 5. The student's *z*-score would be:

$$z = \frac{X - M}{SD} = \frac{79 - 70}{5} = \frac{9}{5} = +1.8.$$

The student scored just less than two standard deviations *above* the mean, well above the average of the norm group.

Other kinds of standard scores include the T score (in which the mean is set at 50 with a standard deviation of 10), IQ scores (in which the mean is 100 with a standard deviation of 15),* and scores used by the College Entrance Examination Board and many upper-level scholastic aptitude tests such as the Scholastic Aptitude Test (in which the mean is 500 and the standard deviation 100). Suppose you are looking

* The Stanford-Binet has a standard deviation of 16.

over a high school senior's results on the Scholastic Aptitude Test. You notice that the student received a standard score of 600. This tells you immediately that the student scored one standard deviation above the mean on that test compared to the norm group.

Other ways of comparing a student's performance to the norms are by grade-equivalent and age-equivalent scores. **Grade-equivalent scores** are best described with examples. If a child obtains a score on a test that is the same as the *median* score for all beginning fifth graders in the standardization group (Grade 5.0), that child is given a grade-equivalent score of 5.0. Likewise, another child who makes a score identical to the median of beginning third graders is given a grade equivalent of 3.0. If the score were at the median of end-of-year third graders (Grade 3.9), the grade equivalent would be 3.9. By examining the grade equivalents of students' test scores, we can compare them with the performance of norm-group students at various grade levels.

Age-equivalent scores are determined in the same way as grade equivalents except that chronological age rather than grade level is used (Ebel, 1979). An age-equivalent score of 10.0 means that a particular student has scored at the median for individuals exactly ten years old. Age norms allow us to compare our students to the median performance of norm-group students at various ages. Like grade equivalents, they are often used to measure student growth over a period of time.

Another frequent way in which standardized test scores are reported is through **percentile rankings** or, simply, *percentiles*. A student's percentile on a standardized test tells us what proportion of students in the norm group obtained scores that were the same or lower than our target student. A student with a percentile of 89 did as well as or better than 89 percent of the norm group for that test. In contrast, a score at the 5th percentile is quite low, equaling or exceeding only five percent of the scores in the norm group. The relationship among the various kinds of standard scores is shown in Figure 15–3.

The information we obtain from tests with standardized scoring enables us to compare a student's performance with other students' performances across subtests and across tests. Standard scores are used to "make standard" the test scores by putting them on a common scale. Comparing the raw scores on thirty-item, forty-five-item, and twenty-four-item subtests would be nearly impossible, but in standardized tests the raw scores have been converted to standard scores with known means and standard deviations. Thus, rather than reporting that a student received scores of, say, 24, 31, and 21 on the subtests, the subtest scores might be reported as *T* scores or as percentiles—for instance, the 80th percentile in spelling, 50th percentile in mathematics, and 98th percentile in language comprehension. From the standard score—the percentile—we can see immediately that the student scored above four-fifths of the students in spelling, was at the median in math, but was higher than all but 2 percent of the students in language comprehension. Standard scores make such comparisons possible.

Imprecision of Scores: Standard Error of Measurement

Imagine for a moment that, of all things, you're standing at the free-throw line of your local basketball court, basketball in hand. How many free throws can you make out of ten? Well, you say, "I'll just shoot ten free throws and find out!" So you shoot ten and five go in. But is five what you will always score with ten tries? What if you were to be selected as a team member on the basis of this single score—would you have confidence that this score represents your true ability? Probably not. So you shoot another ten and make six, another ten and you sink four, yet another ten and you make five. As you shoot more and more

FIGURE 15–3
The Relationship of Standard Scores in a Normal Distribution

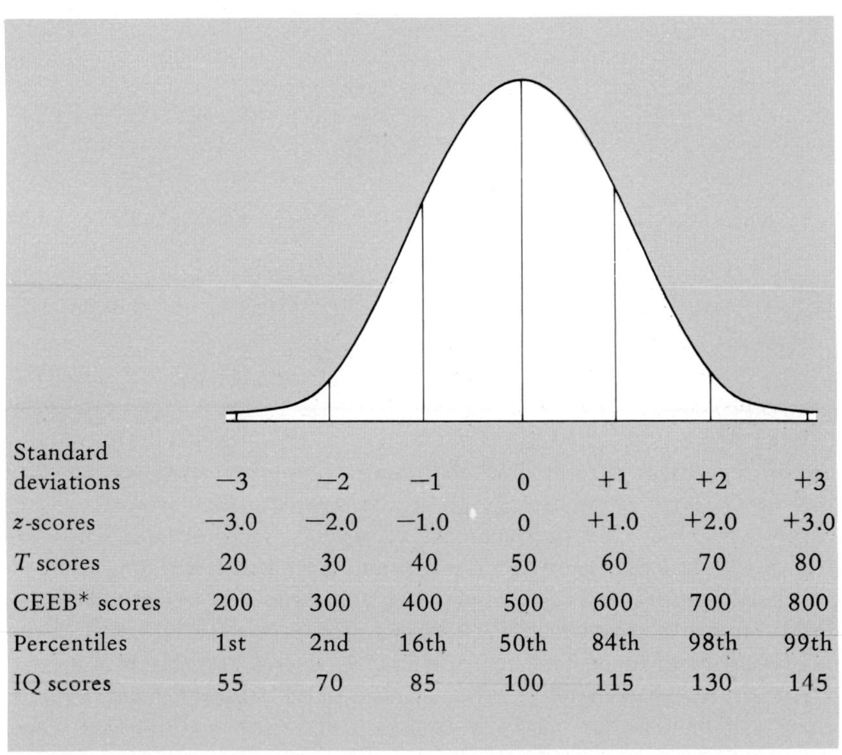

Standard deviations	−3	−2	−1	0	+1	+2	+3
z-scores	−3.0	−2.0	−1.0	0	+1.0	+2.0	+3.0
T scores	20	30	40	50	60	70	80
CEEB* scores	200	300	400	500	600	700	800
Percentiles	1st	2nd	16th	50th	84th	98th	99th
IQ scores	55	70	85	100	115	130	145

*CEEB = College Entrance Examination Board

Comparing his class's scores with the norms for a standardized test helps this teacher better understand his student's classroom performance.

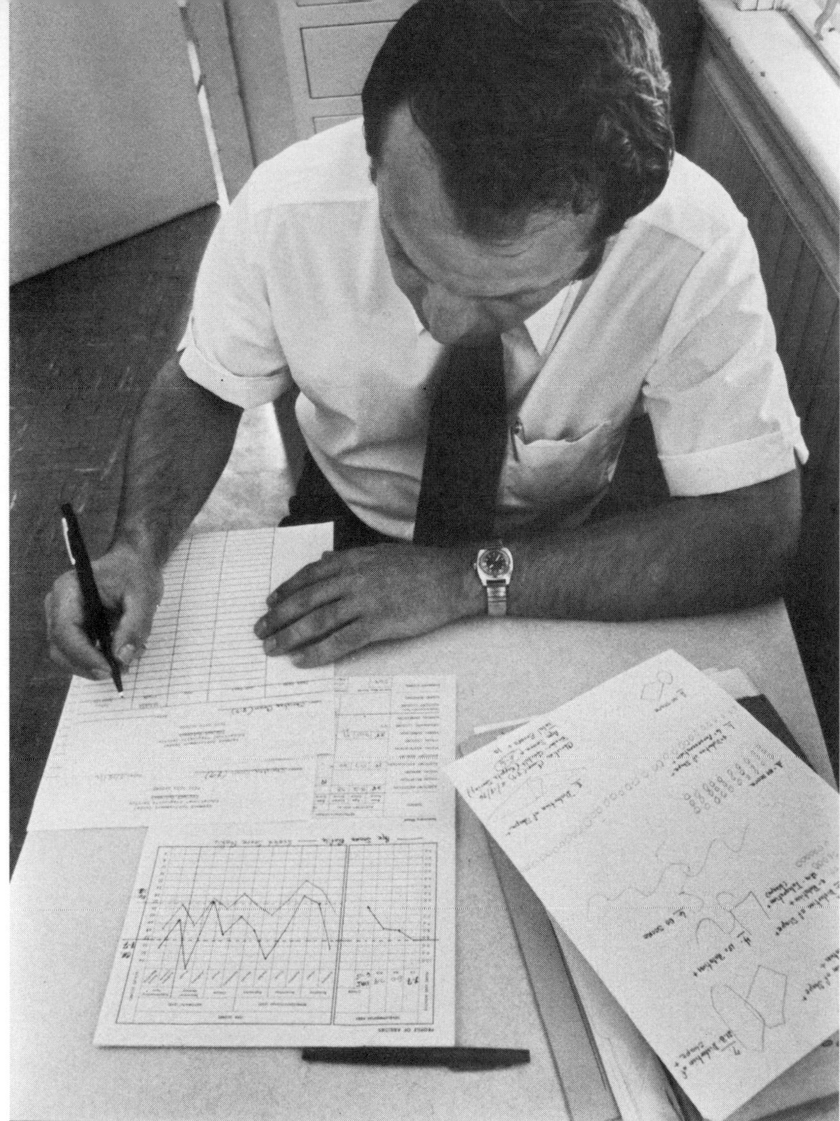

sets of ten, it becomes obvious that your scores are not always the same but vary around some average point. By shooting fifty sets of ten free throws, you may find that your average is 5.5, most of your scores are five or six, and that your best is eight and your worst is three.

To determine the typical spread of your scores in free-throw shooting, you could compute their standard deviation. The standard deviation of a set of an *individual's own scores* is referred to as the **standard error of measurement** (SEM). The standard error of measurement, then, can be thought of as the deviation of a person's observed scores around an average, "true" score.

The uses of the standard error of measurement are twofold. First, it conveys to us that any one score is imprecise. It is just one indicator of a person's actual ability and may be somewhat in error. Second, because of some statistical properties of the standard error of measurement, test users can estimate the probability that a person's "true" score lies within a certain interval. What are the chances, for example, that five of ten is a reasonable estimate of your free-throw shooting ability?

Let's see what this concept means for interpreting standardized tests. Because errors in measurement are assumed to be normally distributed, we can estimate that the chances are about two in three (68 percent), for instance, that a person's "true" score lies in an interval between one standard error below and one standard error above the actual score the person obtained on a test. Again, using what we know about the normal curve and the proportions of cases in each part of it, we can guess that the chances are about 95 percent that the person's true score is in an interval from two standard errors below to two standard errors above his or her observed score. The true score can be thought of as a best estimate of what the person's score would be if there were no measurement error.

Educational measurements, of course, are seldom if ever repeated as they were in our basketball example. A test taken over and over, for instance, is soon invalid. Even a second administration of a test is often impossible or at least impractical. How, then, is the standard error of measurement computed? Luckily, there is a simple method of estimating standard error based on (1) the reliability of the test (as described in Chapter Thirteen) and (2) the standard deviation of the group taking the test. The formula for computing the standard error of measurement of a test is as follows:

$$\text{SEM} = \text{SD}\sqrt{1 - r}$$

where SEM = standard error of measurement; SD = standard deviation of the test; and r = the reliability coefficient of the test.

Suppose a test has a standard deviation of 8 and a reliability coefficient of .84. The standard error of measurement of this test would be $8\sqrt{1 - .84}$ or $8\sqrt{.16} = 8(.4) = 3.2$. You can see from the formula that as the reliability of the test decreases, the SEM increases. Also note that as the standard deviation of the test increases so does the SEM. You will seldom have to calculate the standard error of measurement of standardized tests, however. Test makers routinely report the standard error of measurement for tests and subtests. They do so to indicate that the score obtained is *only one estimate* of the person's true score. In other words, it is likely that a person retaking the test might receive a somewhat different score. As we have seen, the possibility of obtaining a different score depends to a great extent on the test's reliability and the standard deviation of the test.

Because there is always error in standardized test scores, percentile scores are often presented as *percentile bands.* This practice, used by such achievement tests as the California Achievement Tests, is based on the concept of standard error of measurement. Rather than report that a student scored at the 60th percentile, the test represents the student's score by a percentile band that ranges from, say the 52nd percentile to the 65th percentile. The best estimate of the student's true score is somewhere in this interval.

Percentile bands show that there is a chance of error in the score obtained on any test. Shorter, less reliable tests, for example, will have wider percentile bands, while longer and more reliable tests will have narrower bands. In other words, the more reliable the test or subtest, the more confidence we have that the score a student obtains is reasonably accurate. Error is never completely removed, however, no matter how reliable a test may be. Teachers should always keep in mind that error is a part of any testing process, including standardized testing. A score is only an *estimate* of the trait or ability being measured.

APPLICATIONS FOR TEACHING

The results of standardized tests can significantly aid a teacher's efforts if they are wisely employed. We have drawn the following set of guidelines for the use of standardized tests from the literature.

1. Be familiar with any test you use. **Before using any standardized test, you should thoroughly acquaint yourself with the test itself and the manuals that accompany it. Specifically, you should know such information as the norm group used in the test, the means and standard deviations of the test and its subtests, the form of standard scores used, and the standard error of measurement for the test and its subtests. Such information will greatly affect your ability to administer the test competently and interpret the results accurately.**

2. Follow all instructions for test administration exactly. **Remember that any comparisons to the norm group are only valid if the test's instructions have been followed exactly. If you are involved in giving a standardized test, give it in a professional manner.**

3. Treat all standardized test results as confidential. **Do not discuss the results of standardized tests unless a student's parents or guardians have given you express permission to do so.**

4. Keep test results in proper perspective. **The results of a standardized test provide only one small sample of a student's abilities. While the score on a standardized test can help you make better educational decisions, it must be used in conjunction with other evidence, particularly your judgment of the student's in-class performance.**

5. Interpret test results to parents and guardians accurately. **Parents need to have valid feed-**

PROFESSIONAL ETHICS AND STANDARDIZED TESTS

The codes of ethics for the National Education Association and the American Psychological Association both assume that test results are the property of the test taker (or his or her guardian). Therefore, teachers, psychologists, and schools are prohibited from releasing test results without the written consent of the test taker or his or her guardian.

This means that idle conversation about an individual's performance or any public release of test information gained by schools is unethical. There have been numerous cases in which individuals' rights to privacy have been violated by careless talk or improper dissemination of school records. To guard against unauthorized distribution of test results, most schools now have (or should have) forms on which students must specifically indicate that they wish test scores to be released to potential employers or to other schools. In any event, the wise teacher will refrain from discussing performance on any standardized test.

back on their child's performance on measures of achievement, ability, and interest. Because they typically do not have the technical expertise to interpret test results, you must be prepared to explain the tests, what they measure, and what the results indicate. In particular, you need to stress the concept of measurement error—that the results of any one test represent a single measure subject to possible change. Often the best forum for sharing these results is a parent-teacher conference where you can answer parents' questions.

6. Prepare students for taking standardized tests. While "teaching to the test" is not recommended, your students should be aware of the general purpose of tests and how they will be administered. For results to be valid, the students also need to be motivated to try to perform well on the tests. Try to reduce any anxiety but stress the fact that they are to work as hard as possible on the test.

7. Use tests for their intended purposes. Each standardized test has been developed for a specific purpose. Other uses of the test are probably unwise and may be unethical. Also, if a test requires a trained or licensed examiner and you do not have that credential, you have no business using that particular test.

8. Be aware of potential cultural biases in standardized test results. As we noted before, standardized tests provide only one bit of information about students. This information may merely reveal how discrepant a student's background is from the cultural framework represented by the test. Although test makers generally work hard at eliminating cultural biases, the possibility of biases still exists in most standardized measures.

SUMMARY

Standardized tests have a carefully prepared and fixed set of test items, uniform procedures for administration and scoring, and norms based on a clearly defined standardization sample. Standardized achievement tests—diagnostic, single-subject-area, and survey achievement batteries—are designed to assess the knowledge and skills of students in specific subject areas. Diagnostic achievement tests are used when there is reason to believe that a student has deficiencies in skills or knowledge. They are intended to furnish information that will help pinpoint the areas of deficiency. Single-subject-area tests survey the knowledge and skills of students in one content area. Survey batteries assess several content areas, allowing for comparisons of performance across areas. Intelligence tests are designed to measure the ability students have to profit from experience and to adapt to new situations. Individual intelligence tests are somewhat more reliable and valid, while group measures of scholastic aptitude are more convenient. Like any other test, intelligence tests and tests of scholastic aptitude are sensitive to prior learning. They should never be regarded as measures of innate ability or potential.

Interest inventories are designed to assess how students feel about certain activities. They are based on the assumptions that interests are learned, that interests are relatively stable by adulthood, that members of vocational groups share common interests, that there are differences in how intensely people feel about activities, and that interests are motivating factors in behavior. While there are problems with reliability and validity, interest inventories can help students develop an additional perspective on their own interests.

A number of statistical concepts underlie standardized testing—namely, the mean, median, mode, standard deviation, and the standard error of measurement. The concept of the normal distribution is also important to the reporting and interpretation of scores for most standardized tests. These concepts are used by test makers to convert raw scores—the actual number of items right—to standard scores. Standard scores are then used to report a student's scores across subtests and to compare students with the norms.

Measurement error is always a part of any test, and standardized tests are no exception. Standardized tests should never be used as the sole source of evidence for decision making, but they can help both teachers and students get a better picture of student achievement, ability, and interests. Standardized test scores should always be regarded with great caution and care. They are the property of the student and can be released only with consent.

Suggested Readings

Aiken, L. R. *Psychological testing and assessment* (3rd ed.). Boston: Allyn & Bacon, 1979.

This is a good source of additional readings on standardized tests.

Anderson, T. W., & Sclove, S. L. *Introductory statistical analysis.* Boston: Houghton-Mifflin, 1980.

This test provides an excellent introduction to statistics.

Fallows, J. The tests and the "brightest": How fair are the College Boards? *Atlantic Monthly,* 1980, *245,* 37–48.

This interesting article argues that what ability tests measure is largely the degree of exposure to upper-middle-class culture.

Salmon-Cox, L. Teachers and standardized achievement tests: What's really happening? *Phi Delta Kappan,* 1981, *62,* 631–634.

This brief article provides an interesting commentary on the use and lack of use of achievement test results by teachers.

Tuckman, B. W. *Measuring educational outcomes: Fundamentals of testing.* New York: Harcourt, Brace, Jovanovich, 1975.

Tuckman's book contains excellent, intermediate-level content on standardized tests.

Wesman, A. G. Intelligent testing. In B. L. Kintz & J. L. Bruning (Eds.)., *Research in psychology.* Glenview, Ill.: Scott, Foresman, 1970.

This review article provides an excellent perspective on the proper use of standardized tests, particularly intelligence tests.

Answers for Practice Exercise 15–2

1. 86
2. 78.35
3. 77.5
4. 9.95

IMPORTANT EVENTS IN THE DEVELOPMENT OF STANDARDIZED TESTS

There are so many standardized instruments now available that a thorough listing of them would constitute a major text in testing. In this chronology we have listed only the major developments in standardized testing and the historical antecedents of those events.

Date(s)	*Person(s)*	*Work*	*Impact*
1786	Laplace	Development of the normal curve	Using the work of deMoiure (1733), Laplace first worked out the normal law of error that produces the bell-shaped or "normal" curve (Boring, 1950). (Incidentally, Laplace was also the first person to work out the principles of black holes, superdense suns that do not allow light to escape their gravity fields.)
1809	Gauss	Application of the normal law of error	Gauss did not, as many people believe, develop the normal curve, but he did work out many applications of the curve to then-contemporary problems. Thus, the normal curve is often referred to as the Gaussian curve despite its having been developed by Laplace. C. C. Ross (1947), however, points out that the curve is called the Laplace curve in France.
1835	Quetelet	Application of the normal law of error to the distribution of measures of human characteristics	Quetelet, the founder of modern statistics (Boring, 1950), applied the work of Laplace and Gauss to measurements of human characteristics. His work was the first application of the normal curve to humans.
1880s	Galton	Investigations of individual differences	Sir Francis Galton, as we noted in Chapter Five, did not actually develop standardized tests, but his work in investigating individual differences laid the foundation for their development.

Date(s)	*Person(s)*	*Work*	*Impact*
1890	Cattell	"Mental tests and measurements"	Cattell was the first to employ the term *mental tests* in the psychological literature.
1895	Rice	First comparative tests	As we have noted, J. M. Rice employed the first true comparative tests, although the Boston schools had used common tests as early as 1845.
1896	Binet & Henri	"La psychologie individuelle"	This crucial paper proposed the development of standardized tests "of memory, imagery, imagination, attention, comprehension, suggestability, esthetic appreciation, moral sentiments, strength of will, and motor skill" (Boring, 1950, p. 572).
1897	Ebbinghaus	Development of the completion item	The development of the completion item by Herman Ebbinghaus provided an excellent format for standardized tests.
1904	Thorndike	*An introduction to the theory of mental and social measurements*	E. L. Thorndike's book was an immediate precursor to the first standardized tests in the United States. The conceptual basis for standardized testing was essentially provided in this text.
1905	Binet & Simon	First standardized test of intelligence	The Binet-Simon test, an individual test of intelligence, was the first true standardized test.
1908	Stone	*Stone Arithmetic Test*	C. P. Stone, one of Thorndike's students, published the first standardized achievement test.
1910	Thorndike	*Thorndike Handwriting Scale*	E. L. Thorndike published the first standardized performance scale.
1916	Terman	The Stanford revision of the Binet tests	L. M. Terman's revision of the Binet-Simon test, although not the first En-

Date(s)	*Person(s)*	*Work*	*Impact*
			glish translation, was the first intelligence test published in the United States.
1917	Yerkes & Otis	American Psychological Association Commission on Developing Group Measures of Intelligence	The committee, chaired by Robert Yerkes (who also did the initial work on multiple-choice items), developed the first group intelligence test, the Army Alpha A and B. Most of the items on this test were developed by Arthur Otis when he was a graduate student under Terman.
1923	Kelley, Ruch, & Terman	Stanford Achievement Test	Truman L. Kelley, Giles M. Ruch, and Lewis M. Terman published the Stanford Achievement Test. While it was not the first multitest battery (two were published in 1920), it became the most influential standardized achievement test of its time.
1920s	Many individuals	Development of diagnostic tests	The middle 1920s saw publication of a whole series of standardized diagnostic tests. Most of these tests dealt with reading or mathematics.
1926	Many individuals	College Board Scholastic Aptitude Test	The Scholastic Aptitude Test (SAT) has been the major college entrance examination since its publication in 1926.
1927	Strong	Strong Vocational Interest Blank	Edward K. Strong published one of the first, and perhaps the most influential, interest inventories.
1934	Tiegs & Clark	California Achievement Tests	The California Achievement Tests, prepared by Ernest W. Tiegs and Willis W. Clark, became a major competitor of the Stanford Achievement Test.

Date(s)	*Person(s)*	*Work*	*Impact*
1934	Kuder	Kuder Preference Scale	In 1934 G. Frederic Kuder published his preference scale, and, with the Strong interest test, it was the major preference scale for many years. Kuder, the founder of the *Journal of Psychological and Educational Measurement,* was a major contributor to the development of educational measurement.
1937	Terman & Merrill	The 1937 revision of the Stanford-Binet	L. M. Terman and Maud Merrill's revision of the Stanford-Binet greatly improved the 1916 version. The Stanford-Binet has been revised several times since 1937 and is currently being revised again by R. L. Thorndike, the son of E. L. Thorndike.
1938	Buros	*Mental measurement yearbooks*	Oscar Buros's *Mental Measurement Yearbooks* have been the standard reference on tests for over forty years. Since Buros's death in 1978, the Buros Institute of Mental Measurements at the University of Nebraska has continued the publication of the yearbooks as well as of *Tests in Print.* Currently, James Mitchell is director of the Buros Institute.
1944	Wechsler	Wechsler Intelligence Scales	David Wechsler's scales have been the primary alternative to the Stanford-Binet for individual testing, and they are preferred for adult testing.
1949	Educational Testing Service	Graduate Record Examination	The Graduate Record Examination, developed by the Educational Testing Service, is the major standardized test of achievement for college graduates seeking to enter graduate school. Many of you will be taking the GRE in a few months.

Date(s)	*Person(s)*	*Work*	*Impact*
1959	American College Testing Program	ACT	The American College Testing Program's college entrance examination, ACT, is one of two major college entrance examinations. It is the major competitor of the SAT.
1964	Educational Testing Service	College Level Examination Program (CLEP)	The CLEP tests are the major standardized tests of achievement used to determine the awarding of credit to students for nontraditional experiences. They are often used to "test-out" of courses.
1974	Bardis	Sexometer	Panos P. Bardis's test is an example of one of the more unusual uses to which standardized instruments have been put. This test purports to measure sexual knowledge.
1977	Mercer	System of Multicultural Pluralistic Assessment (SOMPA)	Jane Mercer's approach to intelligence testing uses an adjustment of individuals' IQ scores based on environmental and cultural factors. The result is presumed to be a fairer measure of scholastic aptitude than traditional tests. Over the years, however, most attempts at building "cultural fairness" into mental-ability tests have been notably unsuccessful.
1979	CTB/McGraw-Hill	California Achievement Tests (Forms C & D)	The CAT C & D are examples of modern achievement testing sophistication. They were standardized on a huge standardization sample (over 200,000 students) from all parts of the United States and can provide both norm-referenced information and criterion-referenced feedback on specific objectives to the classroom teacher. Used with a companion test, it can give an estimate of under- or overachievement.

Date(s)	*Person(s)*	*Work*	*Impact*
Mid 1980s	Buros Institute	*Mental measurements yearbook* (9th ed.)	The latest edition of the *Mental Measurement Yearbook* contains independent critical test reviews and other data on standardized tests published in the United States.

Part Five

ADAPTING TO CHANGING REQUIREMENTS

To this point we have discussed how human beings learn from both a cognitive and behavioral perspective, how this knowledge may be applied in planning for instruction, and how learning can be evaluated. In this section of the text we are primarily concerned with several issues that have become increasingly important in contemporary education. Chapter Sixteen, "The Exceptional Student," deals with the role of the regular classroom teacher in working with students who have special needs. Chapter Seventeen, "Reading," presents basic information about the processes involved in reading. It describes how you may best provide instruction for students across a wide range of abilities and ages in the most critical of all educational skills.

Chapter Sixteen

THE EXCEPTIONAL STUDENT

In any group of students you will see a wide range of individual differences. Physical differences are the most obvious—some students are tall, some are short, some are overweight, and others are thin. But after only a short time, teachers note other kinds of differences among students that are critical to instruction. Students vary greatly in their approaches to learning, in their abilities to remember, and in their capabilities to think logically.

Students also approach challenges and problems in very different ways. Some plunge right into a task, while others are cautious and hold back. Some students enjoy new activities, while others prefer the tried and true. Some are decisive and others cannot make up their minds.

Individual differences such as these require that teachers adapt their teaching methods. Education should reach every individual. As we have stressed throughout this book, effective teaching always starts with an analysis of the particular abilities of *each* student.

The students whose abilities and characteristics are furthest from the norm are the so-called exceptional students. Kirk (1972) defines the exceptional student as one who "deviates from the average or normal child (1) in mental characteristics, (2) in sensory abilities, (3) in neuromuscular or physical characteristics, (4) in social or emotional behavior, (5) in communication abilities, or (6) in multiple handicaps to such an extent that he (she) requires a modification of school practices, or special educational services, in order to develop to his (her) maximum capacity" (p. 4).

The term *exceptional student* thus includes both handicapped and academically talented students. It also emphasizes the need to modify education to fit individual differences. Academically talented students, for example, may become bored with instruction that isn't challenging, while mentally retarded children may find it difficult or impossible to learn when teaching methods designed for the average student are used.

Exceptional students—both handicapped and gifted—are now most often taught in the regular classroom. In order to maximize the learning of *all* of your students, you need to be aware of the special needs of exceptional learners. This awareness and the special techniques outlined in this chapter should help you teach all of your students more effectively.

Objectives

After reading this chapter, you should be able to meet the following objectives.

1. Recognize individual differences of exceptional students and the implications of individual differences for teaching.
2. Describe current practices in the education of handicapped students, based on an interview with a classroom teacher.
3. Assess your confidence in working with handicapped students and examine the basis for your assessment.
4. Make decisions about the best educational environment for several students, given brief descriptions of each student's capabilities and characteristics.

INDIVIDUAL DIFFERENCES AND EXCEPTIONALITY

Modern psychology's beginnings can be traced back to the pioneering psychological laboratories that were devoted to the study of individual differences. Early researchers such as Wundt, Galton, and Cattell attempted to measure mental abilities by a variety of sensory and perceptual measures—by having people judge the passage of time, repeat letters, bisect a line, and discriminate colors, for example. While early investigators found that people vary greatly in their abilities to perform such tasks, none of these measures seemed related to anything important.

The first really significant step in the measurement of important individual differences in mental ability came with the work of Alfred Binet and Theodore Simon in France (see Chapter 5). They devised an "intelligence scale" that could distinguish normal children from mentally retarded children. This early scale led the way to the standardized testing of intelligence and other mental abilities.

Testing, as it was developed in the 1930s, 1940s, and 1950s, provided a method for reliably* assessing individual differences in cog-

* The concepts of reliability (measuring consistently) and validity (measuring what you say you are measuring) are both critical to mental-ability testing, particularly intelligence testing (see Chapters Thirteen and Fifteen). There is little controversy about the reliability of most standardized mental-ability tests. Many persons, however, question the *validity* of what these tests measure, particularly across different cultural groups.

nitive ability. Because test scores are at least partly related to children's performance in school and other settings, the scores began to be used in educational decisions. On the basis of test scores, children were classified as "trainable," "educable," "borderline retarded," or "gifted," for example, and soon classes were formed for various categories of students.*

The practice of grouping exceptional students for instruction, however, was not limited to mentally retarded and academically talented students. Special classes and schools were also developed for other categories of exceptional students, such as orthopedically handicapped, visually impaired, deaf and hard-of-hearing, and learning-disabled students.

Categorization of Exceptional Students

By the 1960s, separate instruction for specifically categorized groups of exceptional students had become accepted practice. Such categories are still in use today, although they are somewhat less closely linked to separate instruction. Eligibility for accelerated programs, special education placement, and state and federal funding for the handicapped, however, are all still tied to categorization. Schools can be reimbursed by state governments for part of the expenses of educating a student if that student is classified as "mentally retarded," that is, if the student meets the state's criteria for mental retardation.

The practice of categorization has had both good and bad effects. On one hand, categorization has brought increased awareness that exceptional students have special needs. As a result, adapted materials, specially-trained teachers, and structured classroom methods were developed to meet the problems of students with particular handicapping conditions.

On the other hand, categorization of handicapped students (and some say of gifted students) undeniably has led to negative stereotyped views and segregation (Scriven, 1976). Special schools, special classrooms, and labels based on categories ("emotionally disturbed" or "mentally retarded," for example) often unnecessarily separated children with special needs from their peers. Separate programs tend to magnify differences and reduce perceptions of similarity to other children.

To call some students "normal" and others "retarded," for example, can reinforce the idea that all persons with a particular label are somehow alike and will act in the same way. Categorization and labeling can

* At one time, many decisions about students were based almost exclusively on intelligence test scores. One student whose IQ was 73 would be placed in a special education class, for example, while another with an IQ of 75 would not. Now intelligence tests are usually viewed as providing important information, but many other factors (such as social behavior, attention span) are taken into account in deciding what program is best for each student.

also bring about a self-fulfilling prophecy in which handicapped students begin to view themselves as incapable of learning. Once they act on this view and reduce their efforts at learning, the prophecy is fulfilled—they do indeed fall further behind their peers (Dunn, 1968; Reynolds & Balow, 1972).

CATEGORIES OF EXCEPTIONAL STUDENTS

For good or bad, exceptional students continue to be grouped because of legislative requirements, tradition, or planning and administration. Federal legislation administered through the U.S. Office of Education, for instance, puts handicapped children into nine categories. In the following sections we will discuss several of these categories (see Table 16–1 for a summary of these categories). Our goal is to make you more aware of the special needs of each student. As you look at each category, remember that every student is unique. There are often more differences

TABLE 16–1
Characteristics of Selected Categories of Exceptionality

Category of Exceptionality	*Characteristics*	*Critical Elements of Teaching*
Mental retardation	Has difficulty remembering Lags significantly behind peers in academic achievement Is behind in language development Has trouble making discriminations Has difficulty forming verbal and numerical concepts	Commence teaching at entry levels Carefully sequence instruction Give reinforcement for small steps of achievement Emphasize generalization of knowledge Present only defining attributes of new concepts
Learning disability: general	Normal or above average intelligence Uneven pattern of intellectual development Typically does not progress well in reading or language-related skills	Pay careful attention to entry levels Adapt instruction to the student's abilities in different areas Carefully sequence instruction in difficult areas Reinforce language use and reading-related behaviors Attempt to develop intrinsic motivation

Category of Exceptionality	*Characteristics*	*Critical Elements of Teaching*
Learning disability: hyperactivity	Excessive activity, far beyond normal levels Extremely short attention spans Frequent impulsive behavior High susceptibility to distraction Disruptive behaviors	Know about student's medical treatment and medications, if any Pay careful attention to classroom management techniques Arrange for school-home cooperation in behavior management programs Assist other students in developing tolerance for the hyperactive student's behavior
Hearing impairment	Lack of attention Frequently needs oral directions repeated Turning or cocking of head Watches speakers' lips rather than making eye contact Poor speech production Disruptive, stubborn, or shy Difficulty in auditory tasks Cannot locate direction of sounds	Speak clearly and face student when speaking Arrange preferential seating Employ written or mimed instructions Rephrase when repeating information Use joint programming designed by resource teacher and parents Employ interpreter as needed
Visual impairment	Rubs eyes frequently Complains of poor vision or of pains in eyes Sensitivity to light Holds books or other materials too close or far away Eyes water frequently Holds head at odd angles when looking at things	Arrange preferential seating Place emphasis on tactile and auditory learning Obtain special materials (such as audiotapes of books) as needed from libraries for the visually impaired and blind For partially sighted, provide large-type materials
Speech and language disorders	Delayed language development Exhibits nasal or tremorous sound production Lisps or stutters Reverses sounds or words; "emeny" for "enemy" for example Has vocabulary and speech of a much younger child	Model acceptable speech patterns Give systematic reinforcement for speech production in your class Become aware of goals of speech therapy and reinforce achievement toward these goals Do not show disapproval of student speech efforts Work toward developing the student's self-acceptance and self-concept

Category of Exceptionality	*Characteristics*	*Critical Elements of Teaching*
Behavioral and emotional disturbances	Hostile aggressiveness Impulsive and disruptive Withdrawn into a fantasy world Socially isolated Depressed Extremely self-deprecating Has unrealistic fears and phobias Seeks attention despite negative consequences Engages in self-injurious actions	Use systematic behavioral management approaches to provide a consistent environment Stay abreast of any psychological or medical treatment Identify target behaviors to reinforce Seek understanding of other class members both before and after problem behaviors occur Plan your actions before crises occur Work jointly on programs devised by you, the resource teacher, psychologists, and others
Physical disability and health impairment	Usually previously identified by medical personnel	Thoroughly familiarize yourself with the medical condition Attend to the comfort of the student Acquire appropriate skills for possible emergencies Provide or arrange for assistance in fulfilling basic needs (movement into inaccessible areas, and so on) Carefully nuture development of a positive self-concept
Gifted	Well above average in measured intelligence High levels of performance in academic tasks May be exceptional in one area but not in other areas Generally reasonably healthy, active, and emotionally stable in relation to peers	Provide materials and activities that challenge the learner Allow student to assume responsibility for structuring his or her own approaches to learning Avoid unnecessary separation of the student from his or her peers

Note: Obviously we are suggesting that all students receive instruction at their entry levels, and that all students receive reinforcement for their achievements. In general, keep in mind that the most effective teaching procedures for exceptional students are adaptations of methods that are effective for all students. This table highlights the particular needs that some exceptional students have for particular components of instruction.

among students within a category than there are differences between categories. Just because students fall in a given category does not mean grouping them for instruction is appropriate.

Handicapped Students

Overall, the number of children categorized as having recognizable and significant handicaps—mental, emotional, and physical—is quite large. There is a strong likelihood that you will be teaching some handicapped students, and the need to be well prepared is obvious. Hayden (1979) estimates that as many as 17 percent of the preschool population may be handicapped in some way. The estimates are about 14 percent at the elementary level (perhaps three or four students in a typical class) and about 6 percent at the secondary level. (See Table 16–2.) To some extent, the drop in percentage reflects maturation and remedial teaching, but it also results from the disproportionately high dropout rates of these students (Halpern, 1979, p. 518).

Mentally Retarded Students. All mental retardation involves below-average mental functioning. In IQ test performance, mental retardation is usually indicated by a score below 70 or 75, with the definition

TABLE 16–2
Prevalence of Handicapped Children in the United States

Category	*Percent of Population*	*Estimated Number of Children Aged 5–18* (in thousands)*
Mentally retarded	2.0–3.0	1,110–1,650
Learning disabled	2.0–3.0	1,110–1,650
Hearing impaired and deaf	0.5–0.7	275–385
Visually impaired and blind	0.1	55
Speech handicapped	3.0–4.0	1,650–2,200
Behaviorally and emotionally disordered	2.0–3.0	1,110–1,650
Physically handicapped and health impaired	0.5	275

*Based on 1982 population estimates.
Source: Adapted from Gearheart, B. R., & Weishahn, M. W., *The handicapped student in the regular classroom* (2nd ed.) (St. Louis: Mosby, 1980). Used by permission.

varying from state to state. As we saw in Chapter Fifteen, such scores would be in the lowest 2 to 5 percent of all IQ scores. A second criterion is that the mental retardation must have its onset sometime before late adolescence. Although some individuals who suffer brain damage from accidents or illness as adults have greatly reduced mental ability, they are not usually considered retarded. Third, there is an impairment in adaptive behavior in mental retardation. Adaptive behavior refers to sensorimotor development (walking, sitting up, talking) during the preschool years and, later, to a person's academic and social adjustment. Most mentally retarded students lag significantly behind their peers in reading, mathematics, and social development.

Retarded individuals have sometimes been divided into the following subgroups: (1) mildly or educably mentally retarded (approximate IQ range from 55 to 69), (2) moderately or trainably mentally retarded (approximate IQ range from 40 to 54), and (3) severely or profoundly retarded (IQs below 40).* By far the greatest number of mentally retarded children fall in the first category, mild retardation. Most mildly retarded individuals have significant difficulties with the challenges of the regular classroom if no special support is available. With appropriate planning and support, however, most mildly retarded children can benefit from instruction provided in the regular classroom. Certain special services, such as extra drill on particular skills, are often provided in part-time placement in special classes. Some mildly retarded students may also require assistance in social or economic adjustment, particularly under times of unusual stress. The majority of mildly retarded children can go on to become self-supporting and socially adjusted adults (Hewett & Forness, 1974).

Kirk (1972) has estimated that, in an average community, about two and one-half percent of school-age children are mildly retarded, while perhaps five out of a thousand have more severe mental handicaps. The incidence of mental retardation, however, varies with the social and economic conditions of the communities. Some areas have higher proportions of children with mental retardation, while other more advantaged areas have lower proportions. These differences across communities seem to relate to a number of factors—quality of prenatal care, nutrition, levels of stress, children's preschool experiences, language experience, social background, and parental education, to name only a few of many possible influencing effects.

* Terms such as *imbecile, idiot,* and *moron,* which we now find repugnant, were once used to describe different levels of retardation. These words were invented to replace earlier terms that had developed negative connotations. Over time, however, these words themselves came to have dehumanizing meanings.

"Dyslexia? What's Lysdexia?"

Learning-Disabled Students. There are some students with very specific learning deficits, as opposed to the more general learning difficulties of mentally retarded students.* The term *learning disabled* was suggested some time ago by Samuel Kirk (Kirk & Bateman, 1962) to describe this group of students. Learning-disabled students are a very diverse group of children who have normal or near-normal intelligence levels but who have quite severe difficulties in understanding or using spoken or written language (Knott, 1980). Gearheart and Weishahn (1980) offer the following definition of learning-disabled students:

> Students with learning disabilities exhibit a disorder in learning, which may be manifested as a problem in reading, writing, spelling, arithmetic, talking, thinking, or listening. Usually this involves processes relating to language usage (either spoken or written). To be considered a learning disability, there must be a *significant discrepancy* [emphasis ours] between the individual's actual achievement or performance and his apparent ability to achieve or perform. (*p. 159*)

Some learning-disabled students have unusual problems in reading,† writing, spelling, or arithmetic—unusual because adequate per-

* Great caution must be used in labeling mental retardation as a general deficit, however. Many children in special education programs can and do function normally in all aspects of their lives *except* in the classroom.

† See Chapter Seventeen for a discussion of reading disabilities, one type of learning disability.

formance in these areas is ordinarily not difficult for children of near-normal or above-normal intelligence. Some learning disabled students with normal mental ability may only be able to read at a third or fourth grade level upon entering high school, for example. Although the label "learning disabilities" has been greatly misused (for instance, calling every student who fails for unknown reasons "learning disabled"), there is a relatively small number of children for whom learning certain skills is extraordinarily difficult.

Some learning-disabled students are also hyperactive. Hyperactivity has been defined in a number of ways, but the following criteria are now common to most definitions (Weiss & Hechtman, 1979):

> *Excessive activity.* Hyperactive students are likely to talk, walk, fidget, and move about incessantly. In general, there is a marked inability to sit still.
>
> *Inattentiveness.* Hyperactive students have great difficulty in paying attention. Often they are disorganized, even chaotic, in their approaches to tasks. Their work is often incomplete and they do not follow instructions well.
>
> *Impulsiveness.* Hyperactive students often react quickly, resulting in sloppy work and low tolerance for frustration. They may interrupt often or make strange sounds.

Many such children have been extremely active since early infancy. As Weiss and Hechtman (1979) write:

> Hyperactive toddlers are described as children who never walked, but ran, jumped up and down holding onto the crib bars wearing a hole in the mattress, or climbed over the crib bars even when extra bars were inserted. The hyperactive two-year-old is into everything, but does not play more than seconds with one object. . . . A combination of impulsivity and an unusual lack of fear results in children who dart into busy streets or climb into medicine chests, getting into dangerous situations unless closely supervised. (*pp. 1348–1349*)

The elementary school's demands for children to be reasonably attentive and restrained by the time they are five or six years old often clash with the characteristics of learning-disabled children, particularly those who are hyperactive. In addition, relationships with peers do not always go well. Impulsivity and low frustration tolerance make it hard for peers to enjoy interacting with them. Problems may also arise during adolescence. Learning-disabled students have a higher than normal incidence of antisocial and destructive behavior, along with increased school failure and dropout rate. For students who are hyperactive, impulsiveness continues to be a severe problem in adolescence (Weiss & Hechtman, 1979).

How extensive are learning disabilities? Estimates vary widely because of problems in definition and identification, but most researchers suggest about 2 to 3 percent (Gearheart & Weishahn, 1980; Hewett & Forness, 1974). Boys are affected far more often than girls, as many as six to ten times as frequently in some samples (Benton, 1975).

No one teaching method is likely to be effective for all learning-disabled students because their problems are so varied. Some authorities (see Gearheart & Weishahn, 1980) advocate using tactile and kinesthetic senses, for example, to assist the learning-disabled student who has problems in reading. Many teachers have used behavioral programs for attempting to control hyperactivity. Often such behavioral programs are coupled with medical treatment, particularly with the use of stimulant drugs that, paradoxically, seem to improve attention span, reduce anxiety levels, and decrease impulsivity in some hyperactive children.

A broad perspective needs to be maintained on the entire area of learning disabilities. The teacher must take many factors into account, and no one approach—instructional, medical, or behavioral—is likely to be totally successful. Weiss and Hechtman (1979) conclude that medications *can* be helpful but that long-term studies of stimulant drugs in treating hyperactivity "make clear that drugs alone are not enough to produce a favorable outcome" (p. 1352). Teachers need to adapt instructional approaches to each learning-disabled student and use all the instructional techniques at their disposal.

Hearing-Impaired and Deaf Students. These two categories, although quite similar, are usually considered separately. **Hearing-impaired** students have partial hearing while **deaf** students have no functional hearing at all. Hearing impairment may range from mild to severe. Mild hearing impairment may affect perception of only distant or faint sounds. Mildly impaired students may perceive nearby sounds or normal conversation, although they may need hearing aids. In severe hearing loss and deafness, even the loudest sounds are not heard.

About five children per thousand have hearing problems that require special attention in school, and of these a significant proportion may require special classes in speech reading (which involves deciphering the lip, face, and throat movements of speakers) or the use of sign language. The typical teacher might expect to have one or two hearing-impaired or deaf students over a three- or four-year span.

Teachers should be alert to identify hearing problems that may have slipped through health examinations or have recently developed. Signs of hearing impairment include instances in which students:

Are repeatedly inattentive

Mispronounce many words

Give "off-beat" answers to questions

Speak in a monotone or with inappropriately modulated words or sentences

Always turn one ear toward a speaker

Of course, some of these actions may be simple inattentiveness or incorrect learning. If the classroom management techniques described in Chapter Ten are not effective, however, the possiblity of hearing loss should be taken seriously and the child's hearing should be tested.

Teachers should expect to devote extra attention to the needs of hearing-impaired students. Children with impaired hearing will often miss information, explanations, descriptions, and directions. Always permit them to be seated where they can hear and see optimally. You will need to state instructions, directions, and important points slowly and clearly and to arrange for the students to signal when they have not understood.

Conceptual and language development will often be affected by more severe hearing loss. Deaf children, for instance, are often unable to develop verbal concepts and associated vocabulary. If hearing loss occurs early in life, deaf children may find some types of learning virtually impossible. Since their early experiences are largely visual and tactile, their first communication is usually through a gestural, or sign, language (Benderly, 1980; Morariu & Bruning, 1982). Learning to read and to use an auditory-based language such as English is difficult at best.

Children with severe hearing losses from birth will learn to speak only with the greatest difficulty. Correct speech and language use depend on hearing oneself and models speak. Without hearing, correct speech cannot be identified and mistakes cannot be corrected. Infants born deaf initially make the full range of sounds made by all children; however, vocalizations soon rapidly decrease, and they often cease well before the child is one year old. Without feedback, the making of sounds is extinguished.

Most students with more than mild hearing impairment require significant amounts of time in special classrooms or schools in which skills in signing and speech reading are learned. In signing (signed communication), the language is gestural. American Sign Language, for example, is used by about a half-million deaf persons in the United States alone (Benderly, 1980), although many schools concentrate on signed English, a gestural language that relates signs to English-language equivalents. Speech reading is often useful if there is some functional hearing. To enable the more severely hearing-impaired students to take part in regular classroom activities, a teacher-interpreter fluent in signed communication is usually needed. Regular classroom teachers who have learned some sign language have found that their ability to use signs has opened up a whole range of communication with hearing-impaired students in their classes. Additionally, many schools now teach some signing to their normal-hearing students to make possible more meaningful relationships with deaf and hard-of-hearing students.

Visually Impaired and Blind Students. Students are classified as **visually impaired** if special adaptations of educational programs and materials are required because of their vision. Even after correction, the visually impaired child will have substantial impairment. While many children have imperfect vision, simply wearing glasses or contact lenses is not considered an indication of visual impairment.

Blindness is usually defined in terms of visual acuity (sharpness of

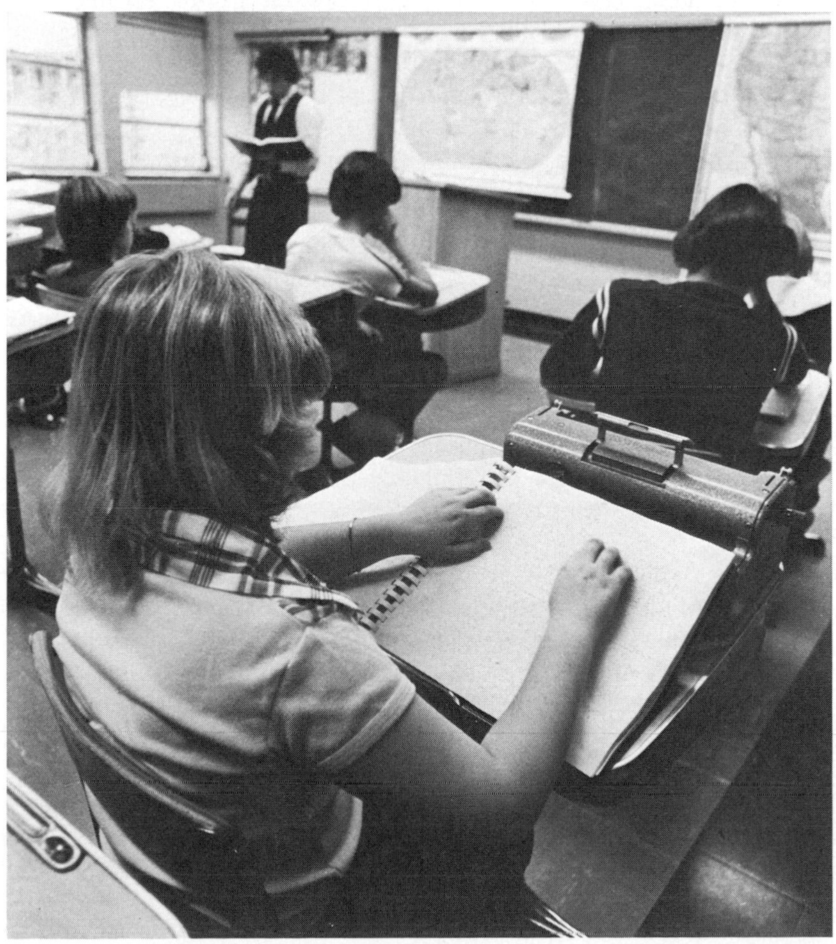

Braille books and a Braille typewriter help this child learn along with her classmates, but such devices can't do all the work. The teacher must be alert to the child's needs and tailor instruction, as much as possible, to those needs.

vision), which is often measured by a wall chart containing letters or figures. On an eye chart the legally blind person (tested with corrective lenses on the person's better eye) can read letters from 20 feet away that a person with normal vision can read at 200 feet (20/200 vision). Other blind individuals, of course, have no vision at all. The degree of visual loss obviously dictates the types of adjustments that need to be made in instruction. Some visually impaired or legally blind students can read ordinary print with corrective devices, while others require Braille materials or audiotaped versions of reading materials and texts.

Visually impaired and blind students constitute a relatively small but significant group of handicapped school-age children. Perhaps one in three thousand children is legally blind and about one in five hundred is visually handicapped (Hewett & Forness, 1974). Despite the low incidence, visual impairment and blindness are severe problems. Telford and Sawrey (1977) suggest that blindness prevents normal reading, limits the student's mobility in all but familiar surroundings, limits perception of the distant environment, and limits detection of social cues.

While some blind children still attend special schools, most receive instruction in classrooms and schools in their own communities. Visually impaired and blind students were among the first handicapped students to be systematically placed in regular classrooms (Gearheart & Weishahn, 1980).

Although visually impaired and blind students are few in number, the nature of their handicap requires teachers to respond intelligently for meaningful learning to take place. Teachers should be aware that each state has one or more special libraries for the blind, with Braille, audiotape, and large-print materials available for instructional purposes. Instruction emphasizing kinesthetic and auditory learning will be of particular benefit to visually handicapped pupils. These students need to receive instruction in the perceptual modes from which they can gain the most.

Speech-Handicapped Students. Speech is a critical component of human communication. Language and conceptual development are both affected by the ability to pronounce words and sounds as meaningful units. Problems in the area of speech can cause several learning deficits. Gardner (1977) classified speech handicaps as generally involving (1) *articulation problems,* such as substituting or omitting sounds, (2) *voice problems,* in which the voice is pitched too high or there is poor-quality sound, and (3) *stuttering,* in which speech production is halting and erratic. Additional speech problems include delayed speech, cleft palate, and speech difficulties associated with hearing impairment, cerebral palsy, or mental retardation (Hewett & Forness, 1974). Van Riper (1978) has suggested that "speech is defective when it deviates so far from the speech of other people that it calls attention to itself, interferes with communication, or causes the speaker or his listeners to be distressed" (p. 43). Speech disorders can occur alone or they may accompany other handicapping conditions.

About 3 to 4 percent of school-age students have speech handicaps (Fallen & McGovern, 1978; Gardner, 1977; Hewett & Forness, 1974). This means that, on the average, one child in most classrooms may have a speech problem severe enough to warrant special attention.

Speech problems often result in other problems. Many students with speech impairments have difficulties with social adjustment. Special care must be taken to help them develop positive self-concepts and to help them meet their deficit needs to the greatest extent possible (see Chapter Nine). Future vocational limitations (there are professions in which speech impairments are a tremendous obstacle to success) can largely be avoided through programs jointly developed by speech therapists, parents, and teachers. Nonetheless, vocational guidance may be needed to help some speech-impaired students form realistic life goals.

Behaviorally and Emotionally Disturbed Students. A major factor in classifying children as behaviorally or emotionally disturbed is that the difficulty is severe and lasts over a long period of time. Behaviors such as impulsive, aggressive, and antisocial acts, as well as extreme withdrawal and depression, may lead to a student's classification as emotionally disturbed. Some emotionally disturbed children show extreme immaturity compared to their peers, others are involved in delinquent behavior, and still others are "troubled personalities"—chronically unhappy, anxious, fearful, or physically distressed.

Unfortunately, people often cannot agree about whether a behavior or behaviors should be called "disturbed." An action that is considered extremely serious by one person or group of people (hostility to authority figures, for instance) may be of little or no consequence to others. The severity of many problem behaviors is at least partly in the eyes of the beholder.

How many children have serious behavioral and emotional disorders? Because of the problems in definition, no one knows for certain, but a reasonable estimate is 2 to 3 percent (Gardner, 1977). In some settings, however (such as in disadvantaged neighborhoods), there is a much higher proportion of emotional disorders. Less stressful settings produce significantly fewer problems.

Physically Handicapped and Health-Impaired Students. Many children have medically related problems that interfere with their success in school. Not counting students with visual or auditory handicaps, about one in two hundred children has a significant orthopedic or health

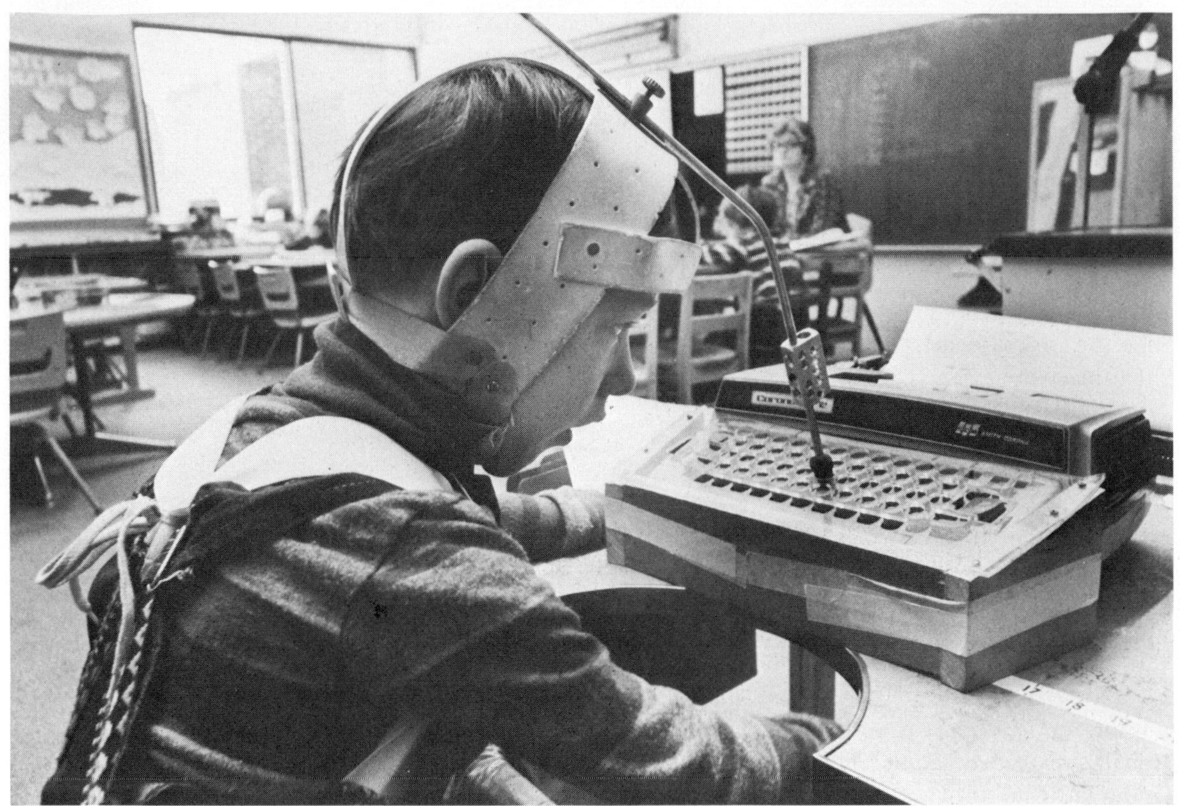

A specially designed typewriter helps this child function in the classroom despite the weakness of his arms. Equipment like this gives the child greater flexibility to adjust to the classroom.

impairment. Some of these students have nervous system diseases such as cerebral palsy or epilepsy, while others may be crippled. Still other children have congenital heart problems, diabetes, severe asthma, or arthritis.

The instructional needs of students with such handicaps vary greatly depending on the nature of the handicap. Teachers first of all must know the appropriate responses to certain emergency conditions. If a teacher has a student with diabetes, he or she should be aware of the signs of an insulin reaction so that medically sound steps can be quickly taken if necessary. Teachers should also be thoroughly familiar with the workings and care of any prosthetic devices (such as wheelchairs or braces) used by their students. Because such devices often require periodic checking and adjustment, the teacher needs to monitor the posture and comfort of students using these aids. Other health-related handicaps require some teacher attention to activity levels or diet in accord with a physician's orders. Teachers may also need to provide assistance to physically handicapped students in toileting, dressing, or negotiating stairs.

Gifted Students

Definitions of the "gifted student" vary. Some definitions include only those students who have superior intellectual ability as measured by intelligence tests, while other definitions include students with superior talent in areas that are not strictly academic, such as art, writing, and music. Estimates of the number of gifted students, using intellectual ability as the definition, cluster around 3 percent (Mitchell & Erickson, 1978). In terms of measured intelligence, this figure would identify students with IQ scores above approximately 130. Some schools provide additional programs for "highly" gifted students, who are a much smaller group, with IQs of 145 or above.

Despite some negative stereotypes, gifted students actually tend to be larger, healthier, more active, more emotionally stable, and happier than the general school population (Albert, 1973, 1979; Cox, 1926; Terman et al., 1925). The image of scrawny, myopic bookworms without any social skills is simply not accurate in describing most gifted children. They seem to be favored in many aspects of their lives.

Differences between gifted and average students are typically described in terms of IQ or performance on achievement tests. Recently, however, psychologists have begun to address differences in the cognitive processes of gifted students and average students. Gifted students are able to manipulate information more rapidly in short-term memory, access long-term memory more quickly, and sequence unordered information more accurately (Hunt, Lunneborg, & Lewis, 1979). These differences in information-processing ability become greater as tasks become more difficult (Eysenck, 1980; Hunt et al., 1979).

For many handicapped students, adaptations in instruction must be made or learning will not occur at all. Changes in instruction for gifted students, however, are made to provide advanced programs and to increase flexibility beyond a basic program. Educators are sharply divided in their views of how education of the gifted should be conducted. Some (e.g., Bailey, 1980) argue that with proper organization and support, individualized programs for the gifted can and should be based in the regular classroom. These experts argue that gifted students should not be set apart from other students. Other educators, however, argue that there should be special programs or even special schools for gifted students, particularly for the highly academically gifted and otherwise talented students. In a special setting, they say, the gifted can develop their abilities to the fullest by interacting with other gifted students and receiving special instruction (Crabbe, 1980).

The choice of educational programs for gifted students relates to people's values. While special programs may advance gifted students' abilities in one or more areas, those same programs may hinder their social development. Similarly, regular classroom-based programs may enhance social development but not maximize cognitive development.

Musical talent often appears early in young children. Several things must be present, however, to develop this talent to its fullest: excellent models, steady adult encouragement, time to practice, and feedback on performance.

Some parents and teachers will choose to emphasize high intellectual or artistic achievement. Others see these goals as secondary to social adjustment goals that they believe will be better for the students in the long run. Our view is that neither of these goals should take total precedence. Both society and gifted students are likely to be best served by programs that develop the special abilities of this group but that also do not neglect social development goals.

BILINGUAL STUDENTS

Bilingualism, the speaking of two languages, has always been a part of our culture in the United States. One hundred years ago, many people in this country spoke Italian, German, Polish, or Russian as a first language and then became bilingual as they acquired English as a second language. In many areas of the United States today, there are large numbers of schoolchildren who speak Spanish, Vietnamese, or French as their first language. In some urban areas, schoolchildren may represent as many as twenty or more distinct language backgrounds. Many of these children know no English until they enter school.

Are bilingual students exceptional students? Strictly speaking, they are not. Language and cultural background cannot really be considered an exceptionality of any kind, at least not in the same way as giftedness or a learning disability is. Bilingualism, however, may have important implications for children's educational programs, and bilingual students form a distinct group.

PRACTICE EXERCISE 16–1

Rating Your Confidence in Teaching Special Needs Students

1. On a five-point scale, rate your confidence in teaching students with the following special needs.

	No Confidence		Some Confidence		Highly Confident
a. Mentally retarded students	1	2	3	4	5
b Learning-disabled students	1	2	3	4	5
c. Hearing-impaired and deaf students	1	2	3	4	5
d Visually impaired and blind students	1	2	3	4	5
e. Speech-handicapped students	1	2	3	4	5
f. Behaviorally and emotionally disturbed students	1	2	3	4	5
g. Physically handicapped students	1	2	3	4	5
h. Academically talented students	1	2	3	4	5

2. In which category were you *least* confident of your skills?

3. List one or more reasons for your lack of confidence below. For each reason, list a step you can take to help remove the reason.

Reason for lack of confidence	***Action to eliminate this reason***
______________________	______________________
______________________	______________________
______________________	______________________

Most favored are those children who have the language of the schools as their native tongue and who learn a second or even a third language. Many English-speaking students in the United States, for instance, study Spanish, French, or German and become bilingual. Similarly, children in Switzerland often study German, French, and Italian so that they are able to be effective citizens in their multilingual country. In these kinds of situations, bilingualism can be associated with real educational advantages. Perl and Lambert (1962) demonstrated that children in Montreal who spoke both French and English outperformed monolingual children of the same socioeconomic status on measures of intelligence and achievement. Bilingual children in this study also had more positive attitudes toward members of the culture whose language they learned as a second language. Such results have been supported on several occasions (see Anderson & Boyer, 1970; Lambert & Tucker, 1972).

A very different situation arises, however, when the child's first language is *not* the language of instruction. The problems most children face in learning and social adjustment are greatly magnified when classroom instruction, assignments, and reading materials are difficult or incomprehensible because of language differences (Pope, 1982). Not only must these children learn to understand instruction and communicate with teachers and peers in an unfamiliar language, they must also cope with major differences in cultural habits, patterns, and values. Adequate self-expression can be nearly impossible.

Problems with comprehension can be solved to some extent by providing children with instruction in mathematics, science, history, health, or other subjects in their first language while they are at the same time learning the "mainstream" second language. Then, as the children progress in the second language, more and more of their instruction in other subjects can be shifted to it. Providing instruction in the first language for students who are not yet fully bilingual should also help reduce problems of separation. When children can question, talk, and react to the school experience in the framework of their own language and culture, adjustment is more likely. Resource persons with background in students' cultures can also aid the transition.

Problems of cultural differences seem harder to resolve. Certainly teachers need to be knowledgeable about the cultures their students represent and should adapt instruction as much as possible to fit the cultural norms of their students and thereby make instruction meaningful. Teachers need to take great care not to devalue the language and culture of bilingual students. This is plainly undesirable and can take a severe toll on students' feelings of self-worth and pride.

A question raised in recent years is how far bilingual education

Children need a solid background in the language of instruction before they can function comfortably, both academically and socially, in the classroom.

should go. That is, should the emphasis in bilingual education be on readying children to interact primarily in the language of the majority or should basic competence in the second language be all that is required, with education in the first language continuing throughout the children's education? The issue has been hotly debated in recent years, and we suspect that arguments will continue in the United States until they are settled in the courts. At this point, however, we must reiterate what has been the major theme of our text: Learning is possible only when the information students are to learn is meaningful. Either instruction must be in the first language of the child or the child must be given all possible assistance to master the second language and become completely bilingual. Regardless of what the ultimate goal of bilingual education is determined to be, meaningful instruction, whether in English or another language, remains the primary purpose of education.

PROGRAMS FOR HANDICAPPED STUDENTS

Public school programs for handicapped students are a relatively recent phenomenon. By the late nineteenth century, states had begun to accept responsibility for the care and better treatment of handicapped individuals. Hewett and Forness (1974) observe that the nineteenth century marked the real beginning of special education in facilities or institutions set aside for the care of the handicapped.

Residential Care

By the late nineteenth century, a number of private, city, or state-run institutions or "homes" had been established to provide residential care for handicapped individuals. In most instances, this care was more custodial than educational. Institutionalization often meant hope had been lost and custodial care was "all that could be done" for a handicapped person. A positive feature of this period, nonetheless, was a dawning recognition of the special needs of handicapped persons.

Residential care is still a major part of services to the handicapped, particularly those with severe disabilities. This care has been regulated more and more carefully, programs have been initiated to meet the individual needs of residents, and there is now the potential of leaving institutions for settings that integrate the handicapped into a community. Although there are some exceptions, residential facilities are no longer viewed as places where residents are permanently housed, but rather they are seen as places where people can develop skills that allow them to function outside the institutions.

Special Classes

At the turn of the twentieth century, public schools began to establish special classes for handicapped students, particularly mildly retarded and physically handicapped children. By the 1960s there were tens of thousands of special classes in the United States. Placement in these classes was based on the identification and labeling of children, with intelligence testing playing a key role in this process. Schools attempted to tailor classes to the needs of handicapped students by having separate classes for groups such as "trainable mentally retarded," "educable mentally retarded," and "learning-disabled" students.

As services to handicapped students increased, however, so did expectations for improvement. The solutions of the 1950s and 1960s, especially segregated classrooms, were increasingly questioned. In an influential article appearing in 1968, Lloyd Dunn argued that special class placement was a poor solution to the needs of mildly retarded students. He argued that special classes almost always included an overrepresentation of minority and lower-socioeconomic-status children, and he cited research results that demonstrated that mentally retarded stu-

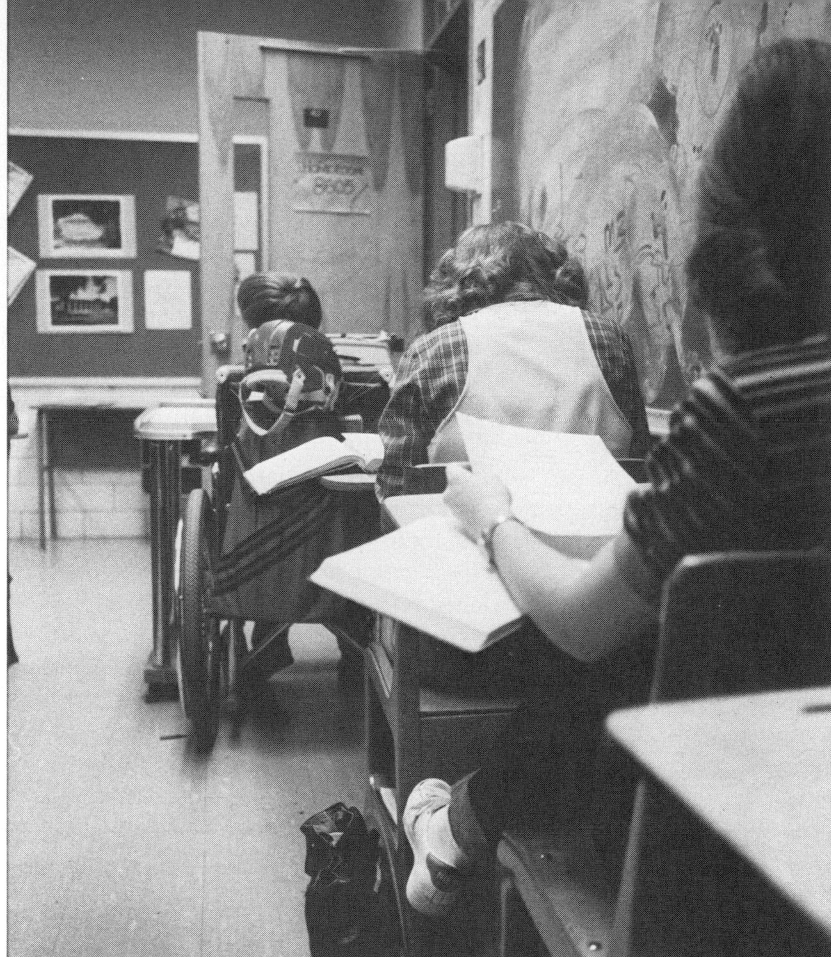

At its best, mainstreaming benefits both handicapped students, who are not isolated or stereotyped, and nonhandicapped students, who learn that diversity can be the source of many new and rewarding experiences.

dents' academic achievement was no higher in special classes than it would have been in regular classrooms. Dunn also felt that improvements in regular education made it possible to provide better services to handicapped children than ever before. His most important point, however, was that labeling and stereotyping are an almost inevitable consequence of placement in special classes (Scriven, 1976). As people considered these arguments, they soon began to search for new ways to educate handicapped students.

The Least Restrictive Environment and Mainstreaming

Rather than automatically teaching handicapped students in special classes, educators reasoned, why not try to find a **least restrictive environment** for each handicapped student.* The least restrictive environment is defined as the program or setting that provides the greatest

* Some educators have found the term *least restrictive environment* to be more negative and legalistic than they would like. This term is a part of most legislation for the handicapped, however, and will likely remain in general use.

opportunity for the individual development of a handicapped student—emotionally, socially, or intellectually. What is least restrictive for a particular student depends on the nature and severity of his or her handicap and on what is available in a school system.

The *regular classroom* is currently believed to be the least restrictive school environment for the majority of handicapped students. Most authorities now agree that most handicapped students will learn best, experience the greatest social benefits, and be labeled and segregated the least when most, if not all, of their school time is spent with their peers in regular classes. Special help is almost always needed, however, in providing handicapped students with meaningful instruction. A person with special-education expertise (a resource teacher) often will provide assistance to the regular classroom teacher in planning, evaluating, and, in some cases, delivering instruction to handicapped students.

Having handicapped students remain in the regular classroom is popularly referred to as **mainstreaming.** Mainstreamed handicapped children are usually those with mild to moderate handicaps. Many schools also have a resource room staffed by special-education teachers. Children with a handicap can spend varying amounts of time in the resource room depending on their need for specialized instruction. The major goal of the resource room, however, is to maximize the time students spend in the regular classroom. Typically, resource teachers help handicapped students develop the skills that are most likely to make their regular classroom experiences successful.

Children with severe handicaps are mainstreamed somewhat less often. Students who are deaf or blind or who have severe orthopedic handicaps often attend special classes or schools. More and more often the judgment is being made by many people that the regular classroom may be the best setting for learning, even for children with quite severe handicaps.

A Related Concept: Aptitude-Treatment Interaction. You will recall that throughout this text we have stressed the need to assess each learner's capabilities and to modify instruction accordingly. An underlying assumption of this approach, and of the least restrictive environment concept, is that the teaching methods that are best for one learner are not necessarily best for another. Stated more technically, there is often an interaction of student capabilities (aptitudes) with the teaching method used (treatment). This interaction is called an **aptitude-treatment interaction** (Cronbach & Snow, 1977; Messick, 1976). Figure 16–1 shows an aptitude-treatment interaction between (1) ability level of learners and (2) degree of structure of teaching methods. For students with low general ability, highly structured teaching activities work

FIGURE 16–1
Success in Learning: An Interaction of Ability Level and Structure of Teaching Methods

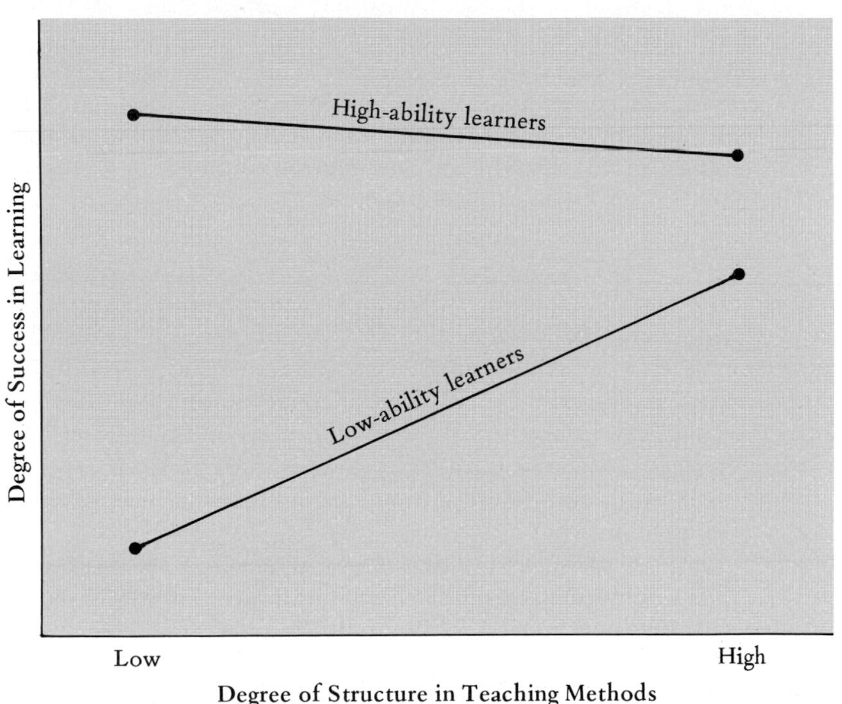

best. Examples of highly structured teaching include programmed instruction or instructional modules that very clearly specify objectives and activities. In contrast, less structured approaches, such as individual projects and discovery learning techniques, generally produce good results for higher-ability learners. For many students, standard conditions are not the best conditions for learning (Cronbach & Snow, 1977). In other words, good instruction for some students may be poor instruction for others. A single approach to teaching is unlikely to be effective for all students.

Education for the Handicapped: Public Law 94-142. The concepts of least restrictive environment and, by inference, mainstreaming are also key themes of a federal law, passed in 1975—Public Law 94-142, the Education for All Handicapped Children Act. This law brought together a large number of influences in education of the handicapped and gave them the force of law (Harvey, 1978). In the foreseeable future, the education of handicapped students will be strongly affected by the provisions of this law:

A free public education should be available to all handicapped children. Previously, many handicapped students were denied access to public schools if school personnel felt that they could not adjust to school requirements. Now the schools must provide education to all handi-

TABLE 16–3
Elements of a Typical Individual Educational Plan (IEP)

Element	Description
1. Personal data and general information	General descriptive data—name, address, age, grade, parents' names, and so on.
2. Period of time covered by the IEP	IEPs are required by law to be prepared annually for handicapped students. Often an IEP will cover a shorter period of time, such as six months.
3. Present performance levels in academic, social, self-help, language, vocational, and psychomotor areas	What can the student do now? Which performances are adequate and which need improvement? Performance levels are usually stated behaviorally.
4. Program placement and justification	In what program/setting is the student now receiving education (regular classroom with resource teacher assistance, special classroom, part-time in resource room, homebound, and so on). A statement is included justifying the placement.
5. Annual or semiannual goals	What are the most important educational and social goals for this student in the time period covered by the IEP?
6. Short-term, specific instructional objectives	Specific objectives with target dates for completion, locations of the experiences, times required per week, and responsible persons indicated for each objective.
7. Methods for measuring attainment of the objectives (evaluation methods)	The methods of documenting progress are indicated for each objective. These may be in the form of behavior frequencies or rates, tests scores, or ratings by observers.
8. Signatures of the regular classroom teacher, the resource teachers, other school officials (as appropriate), and the parents	The signatures indicate that everyone, including the parents, has agreed that this is the best plan for this student at this time. Often, approval of this plan is obtained at a meeting in which all concerned persons are present.

PRACTICE EXERCISE 16–2
Choosing a Least Restrictive Environment

For each of the following, make a judgment about the type of services that would provide the *least restrictive environment* for the student. Which of the following settings are likely to be the best setting for the child to receive educational services the majority of the time? The choices are (a) regular (mainstreamed) classroom; (b) special classroom (resource room); (c) nonschool setting. Check your answers with ours at the end of the chapter.

1. Bill is a bright nine-year-old, but he is easily distracted and "hyper." He walks around the classroom frequently, constantly moves his hands or feet, and rocks in his chair. His classroom achievement is well below expected levels, and he does distract some other students, although most pay little attention to him.
2. Harriet has trouble keeping up. She is at or near the bottom of her sixth-grade class in most areas. She is very slow paced, mentally and physically. She is a large girl, "a little lazy," in her father's words, and not terribly well coordinated. Her measured intelligence (IQ) is around 80.
3. Natalie is thirteen years old. She has no verbal communication, bowel or bladder control, or self-care skills such as feeding or dressing. She does not sit up, crawl, or move about without someone's assistance. She has no measurable IQ level and has been classified as "profoundly retarded."
4. Jane has a severe hearing impairment that has been related to her mother's contracting rubella (German measles) during pregnancy. She actually has no functional hearing. At age eight, Jane does not have intelligible speech but does communicate some needs by short cries and vocalizations. She has a small vocabulary in American Sign Language. She cannot read speech (that is, she cannot lip-read) or print.
5. Jim, a fifth grader, has repeatedly attacked other students when he is angered, which occurs unpredictably and frequently. In the latest incident, another pupil required minor surgery after Jim bit his arm. Supervision is almost constant, but incidents have still occurred often, and other children and their parents are fearful of the children's safety.
6. Milton is a "slow learner." Classmates frequently ridicule him because he is uncoordinated and socially inept. He is below average in most school subjects but usually does not score the lowest in the class. Nonetheless, he is taunted with jeers of "Milton the Moron" by his classmates.

capped pupils or contract with someone else to provide it if no programs are available in the district.

An individualized educational plan (IEP) must be written for each handicapped student. The IEP is a precisely written set of statements outlining the program of education for a handicapped student. It relates closely to several concepts outlined in this book. The IEP must include clearly stated instructional objectives (see Chapter Eleven) derived from a task analysis (see Chapter Twelve). The teaching methods and the measurement instruments to be used must be specified (see Chapters Thirteen, Fourteen, and Fifteen). The time period to attain the objectives must also be indicated. Table 16–3 outlines the major components of an IEP.

Handicapped and nonhandicapped students should be educated together whenever possible. Special classes and schools for handicapped students are chosen only if there clearly is no alternative. The law doesn't require that everyone receive the same instruction but that handicapped and nonhandicapped children be separated only when it is absolutely necessary.

Parental approval is required for special-education placement and programming. Previously, parents did not always have much influence on decisions made about their children. The law now specifies that parents must be consulted in placement decisions. Their permission or "informed consent" is required in all such decisions.

PRACTICE EXERCISE 16–3

Teachers' Views of Education of the Handicapped

Interview an experienced teacher and ask how education of the handicapped has changed in the past five years. You will want to probe the following points:

1. How have school policies and procedures changed in the past five years, if at all?
2. Has the teacher's own role in the education of handicapped students changed in the past five years?
3. In the teacher's judgment, has education of the handicapped improved? If it has, what are some areas that need additional improvement? If it hasn't, what specifically needs to be accomplished?

APPLICATIONS FOR TEACHING

As recently as five to ten years ago, many handicapped students were taught primarily by special-education teachers. Others received no special help at all. Because of mainstreaming, the regular classroom teacher now has a much greater role in the education of handicapped students. Teaching handicapped students requires a new and more adaptive set of instructional skills. The following are some guidelines for the regular classroom teacher who hopes to effectively teach handicapped students. The teacher should:

1. Expect to use resource personnel and services. The *resource teacher* is a trained special educator who has the role of helping regular classroom teachers work with handicapped students. He or she is trained not only in special education skills but also as a consultant to other teachers. The IEP is almost always developed jointly by the resource teacher and the regular classroom teacher.

Other people in the school who provide assistance to classroom teachers are the school psychologist, the counselor, and the school nurse. Each has a role in planning education for handicapped students. Paid or volunteer aides can often be used effectively to help teachers individualize instruction for handicapped learners. Teachers should also be aware of the many services available for handicapped students in the community, state, and region. Local and state chapters of the Council for Exceptional Children, the Epilepsy Foundation, the Easter Seal Society, the United Cerebral Palsy Association, and other advocate groups can provide information about particular handicapping conditions. They can also help teachers locate needed instructional materials.

2. Expect to adapt the goals, methods, and evaluation of your teaching. Modifications often need to be made in the instructional materials used by handicapped students. Sometimes existing materials are unsuitable. The resource teacher can usually help in adapting materials or obtaining new materials. Goals may also need to be changed. It is rather silly to expect a student to learn American history by reading, for example, if that student's reading skills are extremely poor. The American history goals may need to be postponed or at least modified until the more basic goal of adequate reading is reached.

One controversial but often-needed modification is in the area of grading. Comparing mentally retarded students to other students on a norm-referenced grading system (see Chapter Thirteen) will be punishing to the retarded students, because even a high degree of accomplishment and effort will not result in a high grade when their performance is compared to that of their classmates. It is better to compare the retarded student's performance to objectives in a criterion-referenced system than to "reward" what may be exceptional effort with a D or F on a norm-referenced scale.

3. Avoid labeling and categorization. The problems with labeling are many. Labels often adversely affect teacher expectations (see Algozzine, Mercer, & Countermine, 1977). The use of labels may also produce isolation, stigmatization, and difficulty in gaining status (Reynolds & Balow, 1972). Not only may handicapped students suffer from separation that stems from labeling, but the nonhandicapped students are likely to develop erroneous concepts and stereotypes about what a handicap means. As Scriven (1976) has pointed out, there is difficulty in "adequately relating to people with whom one has no social exchange" (p. 61).

4. Work toward social as well as cognitive development. Subject area knowledge is only one

part of the educational picture. The school is a social setting in which students learn many things about themselves and others (Johnson, Rynders, Johnson, Schmidt, & Harder, 1979). If social learning is neglected, students may come to dislike and avoid people who are different. They may become prejudiced and belittle individuals with less ability. On the other hand, if social learning goals are fostered, students learn to interact as friends and companions and to treat their classmates with respect regardless of their abilities.

We now have more knowledge about how desired social interaction goals can be reached (see Gresham, 1981, for a review of research in this area). From the standpoint of developing positive social interactions and attitudes in both handicapped and nonhandicapped students, the following principles should be considered:

Verbal prompting and rehearsal. Preparation of both handicapped and nonhandicapped students can greatly improve the chances for good relationships. Often some discussion of the handicapping condition, the feelings of the students, and ways of interacting can be extremely useful.

Beyond this positive start, the teacher may want to describe situations that are likely to occur and perhaps rehearse some possible reactions. Rather than leaving reactions to chance, the teacher can make all the students much more at ease and eliminate potentially harmful situations.

Modeling desired interaction patterns. Teachers' actions will have a great effect on how their classes act. By drawing attention to some of their own behaviors, teachers can increase the chances that students will imitate them (for example, by making nonhandicapped students aware that working with a particular handicapped student is interesting and enjoyable). Teachers can also subtly draw attention to students who are interacting positively. Other students will observe this activity and be likely to imitate it.

Reinforcing appropriate social interactions. Teachers need to pay attention to exchanges between handicapped and nonhandicapped students and to use their attention to strengthen positive interactions. When you see handicapped and nonhandicapped students together, for example, you can move toward them, visit with them, put your hand on their shoulders, smile, and so on, in confirmation of their exchange. Your attention will help increase the chances that their interactions will continue.

Teachers can also reinforce nonhandicapped students for including handicapped students in social groups and making positive comments about them. In the same way, the positive social behaviors of handicapped students (initiating conversations, helping others) can also be prompted and reinforced.

Designing mutually rewarding situations. Many group activities are set up in such a way that the failure or slow work of one student leads to the failure of the entire group. If the group finishes last because of a handicapped student's performance, for example, other students may become angry and resentful. The fault, however, is with the person who designed the group activity, not the students. It is better to use only those group activities in which the roles of both handicapped and nonhandicapped students are linked to group success. It takes some thinking on the part of the teacher to do this, but by careful planning the teacher can find useful, productive roles for all children in group activities (D. W. Johnson & R. Johnson, 1978; R. T. Johnson and D. W. Johnson, 1981). This may mean, however, that teachers must largely eliminate competitive group arrangements, particularly where one child's less than adequate performance can keep a group from being rewarded.

A team of researchers at the University of Minnesota led by Roger and David Johnson has been concerned with what happens socially to handicapped students in the regular classroom.

They have noted that, by itself, close contact between handicapped and nonhandicapped students is not enough to reduce the rejection and stereotyping that sometimes occur. In their view, neither individualized instruction nor competitive group arrangements are likely to bring about successful mainstreaming.

Individualized instruction, they say, tends to separate handicapped from nonhandicapped students. Competitive groups also lead away from desired positive interactions; competition leads to winning and losing and if groups fail because of a handicapped member, the handicapped student may be rejected by others. Their solution is the *cooperative group,* in which students can contribute to the success of their group by their performance but not subtract from the group's success.

In a study published in the *American Educational Research Journal* (Johnson, Rynders, Johnson, Schmidt, & Harder, 1979), mentally retarded and nonhandicapped students participated together in a bowling activity in a physical education class. Students participated in teams, each containing three nonhandicapped and two handicapped students. In a *laissez faire* condition, students were given only instructions on how to bowl. In an *individualistic* condition, students were asked to improve their scores by a set amount (10 pins) each week. In the *cooperative* condition, team members were asked to help each other and offer assistance as needed to try to reach a team improvement goal of 50 pins. Two outcomes were recorded: (1) the number of positive, neutral, and negative interactions, and (2) the number of spontaneous cheers by a group for one of its bowlers.

The results were quite striking. On the average, each handicapped student participated in seventeen positive interactions per hour in the cooperative condition, versus only five in the individualistic condition and only seven in the laissez faire condition. There were fifty-five team cheers in the cooperative condition compared to only six and three in the individualistic and control conditions.

The results of this and later studies of classroom interactions seem to indicate that mainstreaming by itself only sets the stage for the inclusion of handicapped students in the social and intellectual life of the school. Mainstreaming permits interaction to take place, but the teacher needs to set up conditions that make positive interaction likely.

Developing independence and assertion in the handicapped student. Some handicapped students, particularly those with physical and health-related handicaps, may develop a very passive approach to the world. For many reasons, some handicapped children may come to learn to depend on others to initiate activity, take care of their needs, and select their goals. Many of the methods of classroom management—selecting target activities that need to be increased, prompting assertive responses, and providing reinforcement for independence—can help such children work toward independence.

In some cases, a handicapped student (or any student) may not have the social skills that will encourage others to be friendly. Behaviors such as failure to listen, distractibility, clumsiness, loud yelling, bullying, or being withdrawn may make it very hard for the student to gain acceptance. If appropriate social skills are developed (see Chapter Eight) the way is opened for handicapped and nonhandicapped students to experience each other in the most positive way possible.

5. Learn emergency procedures. With some handicaps, emergencies may occur that require prompt, skilled actions to prevent mental or physical harm. Teachers should become familiar with the possible signs of emergencies in the handicapped students in their classrooms and should work out emergency procedures in advance. They should be alert for unusual signs in handicapped children, particularly those on medication or with chronic health problems.

SUMMARY

Effective instruction must be based on the recognition of individual differences. Individual differences are most pronounced in exceptional students, who vary the most from the majority of students in one or more traits, abilities, or characteristics. Exceptional students include handicapped students, who may have a physical disability, a behavior disorder, or intellectual limitations. Exceptional students also include gifted students, who may have outstanding aptitude for academic work. Effective instruction for both handicapped and gifted students depends on matching instruction to the special needs of the learner.

Exceptional students have traditionally been categorized into groups, including the mentally retarded, learning disabled, hearing impaired or deaf, visually impaired or blind, speech handicapped, behaviorally or emotionally disordered, physically handicapped, and exceptionally academically talented. Many educators, however, have had strong reservations about labeling and grouping exceptional students and believe that it is harmful to base educational decisions on such categories.

An alternative approach grows out of the concepts of least restrictive environment, mainstreaming, and aptitude-treatment interaction. Least restrictive environment implies that there is a "best" environment for each student, regardless of the category of handicap. Mainstreaming refers to teaching exceptional students together with their nonhandicapped peers in the regular classroom. The aptitude-treatment interaction concept implies that some methods of instruction are relatively more effective than others for students with different traits or levels of ability. For most handicapped students, it is believed that the regular classroom, with appropriate resources, will be the least restrictive environment and provide the best opportunity for matching instruction to the needs of students.

Regular classroom teachers require a number of skills in order to make mainstreaming an effective approach. These skills include using resource personnel; adapting objectives, methods, and evaluation; and facilitating social as well as academic growth.

Suggested Readings

Fallen, N. H., & McGovern, J. E. *Young children with special needs.* Columbus, Ohio: Merrill, 1978.

This book is a fine introduction to the psychology of exceptional children.

Gardner, W. I. *Learning and behavior characteristics of exceptional children and youth.* Boston: Allyn & Bacon, 1977.

This book is an excellent introduction to the psychology of exceptional children. In many ways it is more thorough than similar introductory texts.

Gearheart, B. R., & Weishahn, M. W. *The handicapped student in the regular classroom* (2nd ed.). St. Louis: Mosby, 1980.

This book contains information on how to teach exceptional children in the regular classroom.

Johnson, R. T., & Johnson, D. W. Building friendships between handicapped and nonhandicapped students: Effects of cooperative and individualistic instruction. *American Educational Research Journal,* 1981, *18,* 415–423.

This article demonstrates the positive aspects of cooperative approaches to group work in the classroom.

Willerman, L. *The psychology of individual and group differences.* San Francisco: Freeman, 1979.

This book is a good introduction to the psychology of individual differences.

Answers to Practice Exercise 16–2

1. *Mainstreamed regular classroom.* Although Bill's behaviors are somewhat disruptive to others and often unproductive, he will do best in the regular classroom. A resource teacher or school psychologist may be of considerable assistance in helping the teacher devise a behavioral program to moderate Bill's excessive activity and to build more attention to classroom tasks.

2. *Mainstreamed regular classroom.* Formerly, many such children were placed in a special-education classroom. Most are now mainstreamed. The teacher will require special help from the school psychologist and resource teacher; with no help, the regular classroom would not be a good place for Harriet. With resources, however, Harriet's achievement can be improved.

3. *Nonschool setting.* By careful programming, useful behaviors can be taught in many instances to profoundly retarded children such as Natalie. Because of the extensive nature of her disabilities, however, general care is required that ordinarily is now best provided in an institutional setting. This care includes programs to shape and teach basic skills whenever possible, nursing and other medical services, and round-the-clock supervision. A child like Natalie will often live in an institution for the mentally retarded. Individuals who have more skills than Natalie (such as mobility and self-care) may be placed in community-based programs, which often combine training with group-home living arrangements. In some cases, the public schools are part of such programming.

4. *Nonschool setting.* Perhaps more than any other handicapped

group, the deaf and hearing impaired have advocated a residential school approach. Many deaf and hearing-impaired individuals strongly believe that the auditorily impaired student can be adequately educated *only* in a residential school. Specific skills such as signing and speech reading are often needed. The public schools are not often viewed as potential direct providers of much of this instruction. For hearing-impaired students with less severe disabilities, however, mainstreaming has been attempted with many positive (but some negative) outcomes.

5. *Special classroom.* A temporary placement in a special class setting may be appropriate in this instance. Jim needs to learn self-control, which is often best taught by systematic programs in a *controlled* environment. The regular classroom might involve too many unpredictable factors and too large a student/teacher ratio to expect that self-control could be learned there. Jim eventually needs to learn to live in the regular classroom and the "real world," however. An effective program would be to establish self-control skills in the special class and then to gradually reintegrate Jim into the regular classroom.

6. *Mainstreamed regular classroom.* No other placement should even be considered, but conditions in the regular classroom certainly could use some improvement. Specifically, the teacher needs to plan for individualized instruction, work with the rest of the class on their social behavior, and help Milton improve his interactive skills.

IMPORTANT EVENTS IN WORKING WITH EXCEPTIONAL CHILDREN

Date	*Person(s)*	*Event*	*Impact*
1620	Bonet	Publication of a system of instruction for the deaf	Juan Bonet devised and published a manual on finger spelling that was a precursor to later manual alphabets. Several educators for the deaf appeared in the sixteenth and seventeenth centuries, including Ponce de Leon, who taught several deaf children from noble families.
1780	Pinel	Beginnings of change in treatment of mentally ill individuals	Philippe Pinel was the superintendent of two major French hospitals for the mentally ill. He led a reform movement toward enlightened methods of working with mentally deranged individuals. Pinel had the conviction that the "mentally ill, far from deserving punishment, as sick people . . . deserve consideration" (Hewett & Forness, 1974).
1798	Itard	*The wild boy of Aveyron*	Itard undertook a program to educate a boy of eleven or twelve who was found roaming wild near Aveyron in southern France. The boy, taken to Paris for study, was animallike in appearance and actions, but Itard was convinced that proper training could lead the child to become normal. Although Itard finally despaired of teaching the boy, the attempt foreshadowed modern educational programs for retarded students.
1829	Braille	Invention of the Braille code	Louis Braille, a young student at the Paris School for the Blind, adapted a military code (used for night communication) to the needs of the blind. First called *sonography,* the code soon

Date	Person(s)	Event	Impact
			became known simply by its inventor's name, Braille.
1837	Seguin	Establishment of the first successful school for training mentally retarded individuals	Edouard Seguin was "perhaps the greatest teacher ever to address his attention to the mentally deficient" (Doll, 1962). His accomplishments inspired many efforts in teaching retarded individuals. After emigration to the United States, he assisted in setting up the first educationally oriented facilities for the mentally retarded in the United States.
1848	Dix	Presentation to the U.S. Congress	Dorothea Dix made an eloquent plea on behalf of mentally retarded, epileptic, and insane individuals. Between 1841 and 1881, this amazingly dedicated reformer established or helped establish thirty-two modern mental hospitals.
1897	Sullivan & Keller	Efforts to teach a deaf and blind individual were successful	Anne Sullivan, a gifted teacher who was visually handicapped, and Helen Keller, who was deaf and blind, combined to produce one of the most amazing success stories in American special education. In a well-known sequence, Sullivan achieved a breakthrough with her young pupil as she pumped water over Helen's hands and finger-spelled the word *water.* At that moment, Helen revealed her first understanding of the relation between experiences and symbols. Keller, highly gifted herself, went on to graduate *cum laude* from Radcliffe and to write several books.
1905	Binet & Simon	Development of a workable measure of intelligence	Alfred Binet and Theodore Simon together created the first reliable measure of mental ability, the so-called

Date	*Person(s)*	*Event*	*Impact*
			intelligence test. Intelligence testing led to classification of mentally retarded individuals. Binet himself was not as optimistic as some of his peers were about the possibility of educating all retarded children; in fact, he stated that some attempts were useless (Hewett & Forness, 1974).
1936	Doll	"Preliminary standardization of the Vineland social maturity scale"	E. A. Doll devised a scale, worked out on much the same plan as the Binet test, for measuring a student's social age rather than mental age. The Vineland Scale was made up of items that have significance for a student's adjustment in society.
1939	Skeels & Dye	"A study of the effects of differential stimulation on mentally retarded children"	H. M. Skeels, a psychologist, and H. B. Dye, a physician, placed thirteen infants diagnosed as "feebleminded" on a ward with older female residents. A few months later, Skeels was surprised to find large gains in intellectual growth that he attributed to the stimulation and attention from the older residents. Those who believed in fixed intelligence objected strongly, but this experiment and follow-up studies helped establish the belief in the modifiability of intelligence and the importance of infant stimulation.
1943	Kanner	"Autistic disturbances of affective contact"	Leo Kanner was the first to identify and name the condition of *autism* (sometimes called Kanner's syndrome). Autistic children show unusual, bizarre behaviors and actions that are often stereotypic and ritualistic. Autistic children seem unable to establish social relationships and have little if any oral communication skills.

Date	*Person(s)*	*Event*	*Impact*
1955	Pressey	"Toward more and better American geniuses"	In a *Scientific Monthly* article, Sidney Pressey put into capsule form the tenets of a sound educational program for gifted students: "A . . . genius is provided by giving a precocious able youngster early encouragement, intensive instruction, a congruent stimulating social life, and cumulative success experiences" (Pressey, 1955).
1961	Kennedy	President's Committee on Mental Retardation	President John F. Kennedy commited a significant amount of federal resources to the cause of handicapped individuals and to the mentally retarded in particular. The President's Committee was made up of leading experts in problems of the retarded.
1967	Many workers	Bureau of Education for the Handicapped (BEH)	The Bureau of Education for the Handicapped was established in the U.S. Office of Education to administer research, education, and training programs related to the handicapped and the teaching of handicapped individuals. Many programs for handicapped students were supported in part or in full by BEH funds.
1968	Dunn	"Special education for the mildly retarded: Is much of it justifiable?"	In this article in *Exceptional Children,* Lloyd Dunn questioned whether special-education classes were the best approach for mentally retarded students.
1971–1972	Many workers	*PARC* v. *Pennsylvania*	The result of this class action suit brought on behalf of fourteen retarded children by the Pennsylvania Association for Retarded Children was that the state of Pennsylvania was obligated to search for and find all retarded children in the state and to begin immediately to provide each child

Date	Person(s)	Event	Impact
			with an appropriate education. Previous practices of excluding many retarded children from public schools were prohibited. This case helped establish the right of the handicapped to public education.
1972	Heber et al.	"Rehabilitation of familes at risk for mental retardation"	R. Heber and his associates conducted an intervention program designed to teach low-IQ mothers methods for teaching their children. The results of this intensive early intervention showed that the superior gains in intellectual growth of children from trained mothers were maintained many years later. Other, less intensive interventions have shown effects, but they have usually disappeared in a relatively short time.
1975	Many workers	Public Law 94-142	This comprehensive law, called the Education for All Handicapped Children Act, culminated a long fight by parents, advocates, and reformers to ensure the rights of handicapped children to education in the United States.
1977	McCall	"Childhood IQs as predictors of adult educational and occupational status"	This *Science* article by Robert B. McCall showed that childhood (by age eight) IQ predicts later adult educational level and occupational level moderately well (r = approximately +.50). Correlations of child IQ with adult IQ are much higher (approximately +.75). Combined parent educations predict the child's educational and occupational level much better, however. Obviously, factors other than intelligence are involved in educational and occupational attainment.

Date	*Person(s)*	*Event*	*Impact*
1978	National Education Association	NEA Resolution 78-37: Education for All Handicapped Children	The National Education Association cautiously endorsed the provisions of Public Law 94-142 and the concept of mainstreaming handicapped students, but it pointed out that regular classroom teachers need support services for mainstreaming to be effective.
1981	Gresham	Review of status of social skills training with the handicapped	Frank Gresham's *Review of Educational Research* article on social skills training illustrates the current view that the success of mainstreaming will depend on the quality of social interactions between handicapped and non-handicapped students. Fostering positive social interactions among all students is seen as a major challenge to teachers in the 1980s (Stephens, 1981).

Chapter Seventeen

READING AND READING DISABILITIES

It is hard to imagine life without reading. We read the morning paper and news magazines, quickly scanning over less interesting stories and reading in detail those that capture our attention. Most of us read advertisements on billboards, and a few of us read the backs of cereal boxes. We read road signs, tax forms, operating instructions, and job applications. Although it may be true that a picture is worth a thousand words, the written word is of paramount importance in our lives. Even television ads—the epitome of influence through images and associations—clarify their messages by an overlay of printed words lest we miss the point.

Obviously, reading is of critical importance for success in school; it is one of the primary ways of learning. History, science, and even mathematics require reading skills. Achievement of basic reading skills opens the way to all areas of learning.

Not all students are successful readers, however, and failures in reading are much more common than we would like to admit. In some cities, as many as one-fifth of high school seniors are not able to read at the fourth-grade level! Why do such a sizable number of students, many of whom are average or above average in intelligence, read poorly? To understand both successes and failures in reading, we need to understand more about what reading is.

Objectives

After reading this chapter, you should be able to meet the following objectives.

1. Analyze a basal reading series by describing the types of reading activities appearing at each level in the series.
2. Develop increased flexibility in your own reading.
3. Identify several potential problems that arise in schools for students who are poor readers.
4. Outline elements of a program that would assist poor readers in developing their reading skills.

ABOUT READING

Just exactly what is this process called reading? Perhaps a good starting point is the definition offered by A. J. Harris (1970): "Reading is a meaningful interpretation of written or printed verbal symbols" (p. 3). Gibson and Levin (1975) describe reading as "extracting information from text" (p. 5). While the term *reading* is sometimes used to refer to a wide range of activities that revolve around gaining information, such as "reading" defenses in football or "reading" public opinion on a particular issue, we don't think of such processes as falling within the usual definition of reading. Reading is almost always a *meaningful* activity (as we defined it in Chapter Two). It involves more than matching up sounds with symbols on a printed page. It is a cognitive process in which readers' perspectives and reading processes have much to do with what they learn. Reading is a skill that we all take for granted, but it is a complex, sophisticated process that includes many different components, which we will examine in the following sections.

Components of the Reading Process

For a long period of time reading research concentrated rather unproductively on comparisons of one general teaching method with another (Pflaum, Walberg, Karegianes, & Rasher, 1980). Recently, however, there has been an increasingly sophisticated analysis of reading (see Just, 1981; Just & Carpenter, 1980). Let's look at some of the components of reading and see what is involved.

A Writing System. The starting point of all reading is some sort of writing—the letter, the word, or the printed page. Gibson and Levin (1975) point out that writing has a number of distinguishing characteristics: It is patterned, it has gaps between units, it is composed of parallel lines of print, and it has various forms (such as printed and cursive) that are not usually mixed (pp. 165–167). Most languages are written from left to right. Some languages, however, are written from right to left (Hebrew) or from top to bottom (Japanese). As Gibson and Levin (1975) indicate, there seems to be no particular advantage of writing in one direction or another. We simply adapt to the particular writing system of our native language.

The earliest writing appeared in Egypt about 4000 B.C. and was a form called **logography** (Gleitman & Rozin, 1977). In logographic languages, each word or concept is represented by a symbol for that word, called a *logogram.* Some logograms (more precisely, pictograms) represent an action or object by a picture, while other logograms are arbitrary symbols (diagrams) intended to represent words that are not associated

The starting point of all reading is some sort of writing system. The marks that we call letters, words, and paragraphs are given meaning through the process of reading.

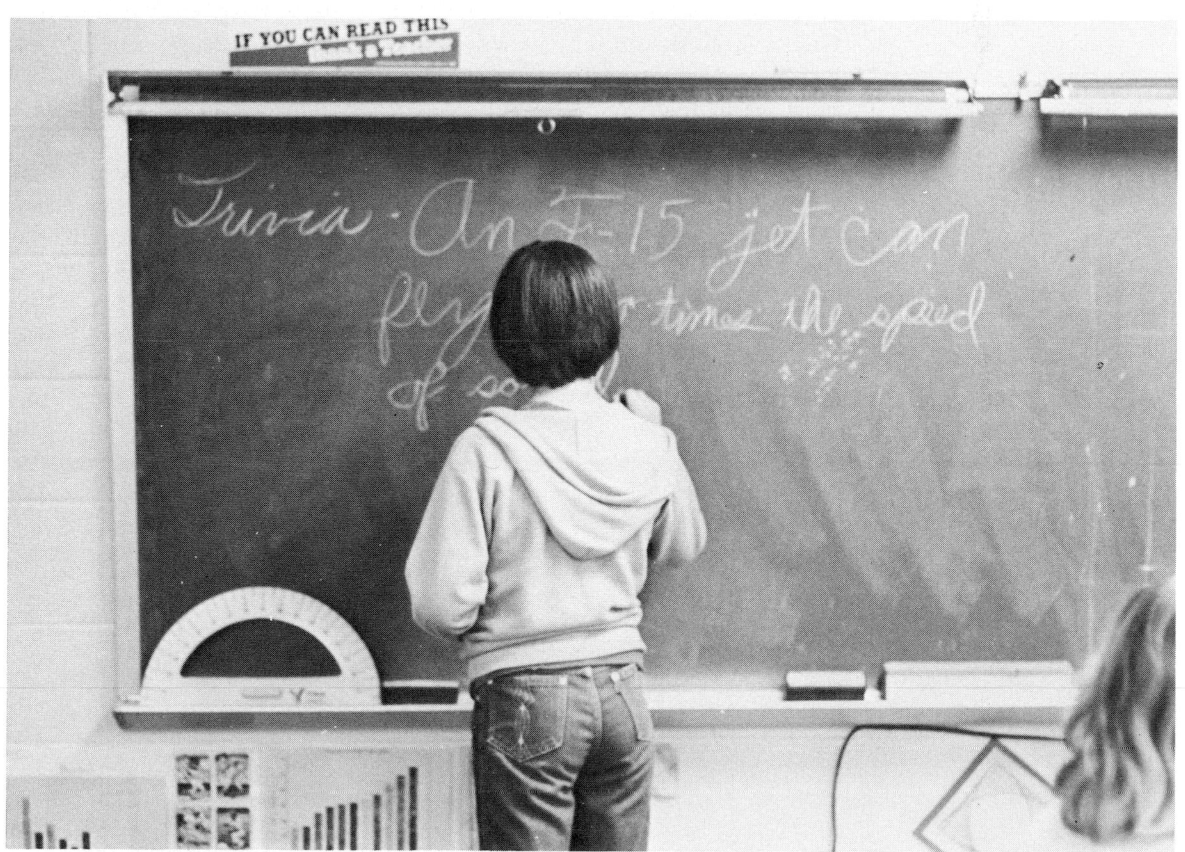

with pictures. Some modern languages such as Chinese are written in logographic form.

A second type of written language describes the *sounds* of the spoken language. Such languages are called **phonographic** languages. A primitive form of phonographic language is the *rebus,* in which pictures or symbols are used to represent sounds. A simple rebus is presented in Figure 17–1. Each of the items in the rebus represents a sound or sounds in the English language.

A more complex type of phonographic language is the **syllabary.** A syllabary contains written symbols for consonants and consonant-vowel combinations (syllables). The Japanese language, for instance, has two distinct syllabary forms—Hiragana and Katakana. A third form of Japanese writing, the Kanji, is logographic.

The majority of linguists agree that the most versatile form of written symbol system is alphabetic. **Alphabetic** writing includes symbols for *both* consonant and vowel sounds and is used in many phonographic languages. Alphabetic writing was first fully developed in ancient Greece; English and most other European languages are alphabetic.

An alphabet greatly reduces the number of symbols that readers must learn. English, for example, uses a system of only twenty-six letters to represent all of its sounds. In contrast, a logography such as that of the Chinese language may require as many as fifty thousand visual symbols. Some alphabetic languages, such as Finnish, possess a strict (regular) relationship between the writing system (orthography) and the sound of the spoken language. In other words, spelling and pronunciation are almost always related. Other alphabetic languages, such as English, have many more irregularities, and pronunciations may vary tremendously for similar spellings (consider *rough, plough, though*). This makes beginning reading more difficult in such languages.

FIGURE 17–1
A Simple Rebus

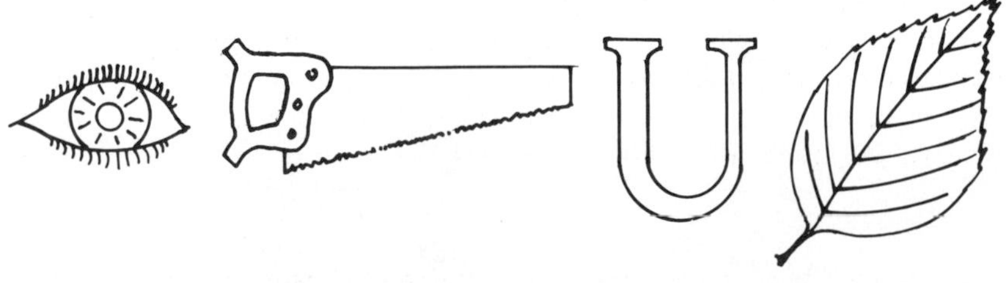

The predictability of languages has much to do with the acquisition of reading skills (Just & Carpenter, 1980). Certain letters often "go together" in English *(ch)* while others usually do not *(hp)*. Regularly occurring letter combinations allow the reader to predict with some accuracy what letters will come next in a sequence or to reduce the possibilities to a few *(hel_, mu_)*. In the same way, the grammar patterns of English permit some word orders but not others.* A relatively large number of words can be deleted from many texts without loss of comprehensibility because our language is rich and in many ways predictable (Goodman, 1970).

Eye movements and fixations. One of the few observable aspects of reading is the movement of the eyes across the printed page. Eye movements in reading are not smooth like those we make when looking at slowly moving objects, but they are a series of start-stop jumps across a line of print. The jumps are called **saccades,** while the period of time in which the eyes come to rest are called **fixations.** The eye movements in reading are much like those involved in looking at various objects in a room: The eyes jump from point to point (Smith, 1978).

Each saccade is very rapid, taking only a few thousandths of a second (somewhat longer for larger shifts in angle), and usually covers about seven to nine characters on a line (Rayner & Bertera, 1979). The eye is essentially blind during the saccade. Most information is processed during the fixations, which take up more than 90 percent of total reading time (Tinker, 1965).

Almost every content word (noun, verb, adjective, and so on) is fixated at least once during ordinary reading. When readers are given text materials that are matched to their age level, they average about 1.2 words per fixation. Words not fixated are usually short words such as *the, of,* and *a* (Just, 1981).

When good readers encounter simple materials, such as a child's story, they skip more words, however. In difficult materials, there are many more *regressions,* in which the eyes return to an earlier position. Unfamiliar words, for instance, are fixated repeatedly as readers attempt to comprehend their meaning (Just, 1981).

The eye fixations (given in seconds) of a college student reading a passage about weightarms are shown in Figure 17–2. As you can see, this reader spent the most time on words important to understanding the passage, such as "weightarms." He also spent somewhat longer

* We would understand the sentence "Him write I yesterday a letter," but would recognize it as unusual English, to say the least.

FIGURE 17–2
Eye Fixations of a College Student Reading a Passage (in seconds)

.267 .283 .200 .350 .283 .283 .733 .333
The Egyptian engineer of 5,000 years ago may have used a

.266 .183 .467 .200 1.201 .333
simple wooden device called a weightarm for handling the

.367 1.151 .583 .568 .417 .267 .183 .217
2-½ to 7 ton pyramid blocks. The weightarm is like a lever

.600 .167 .200 .617 .267 .367
or beam pivoting on a fulcrum . . . Weightarms may have

.256 .283 .234 .384 .216 .356 .267
been used to lift the blocks off the barges which came

.250 .433 .899
from the upriver quarries.

Source: Adapted by permission from Carpenter, P., and Just, M. A., What your eyes do while your mind is reading. In K. Rayner (Ed.), *Eye movements in reading: Perceptual and language processes.* New York: Academic Press, 1982. Used by permission.

times on the last words in sentences, presumably because he was attempting to integrate the information in the sentence he had just completed (Carpenter & Just, 1982).

The information we have just presented comes from studies of eye movements in reading that date back to the first part of this century. That early work, in particular, is a tribute to scientific resourcefulness and, perhaps, to the perseverance of the subjects. One successful early method was that of Heuy (1908), in which he attached a suction cup to the surface of the eye and, by mechanical and electrical means, recorded eye movements by markings on a smoked drum. Modern methods involve the reflection of regular or infrared light off the cornea of the eye and then recording the light on a film or videotape of what the person is looking at.

The most advanced research techniques for the study of eye movements in reading now link computers to eye-movement recording devices (Just, 1981; Just & Carpenter, 1980; Rayner & Bertera, 1979; Rayner & McConkie, 1977) to enable investigators to perform sophisticated research on the perceptual and cognitive processes involved in reading. McConkie and Rayner, for example, demonstrated that readers generally cannot process information from their peripheral vision (Mc-

Conkie & Rayner, 1976; Rayner, 1978). Typically, only seven or eight letters can be processed meaningfully in a single fixation. Thus, some of the more extravagant claims for speed-reading have been shown to be physically impossible.

Eye-movement research has also shown that eye-movement patterns tend to change as people acquire increased skills in reading, with fixations becoming somewhat shorter and regressions fewer. Figure 17–3 shows the contrast between the fixation times of a skilled and an unskilled reader.

Such data, however, have sometimes been misinterpreted by clinicians and classroom teachers. They reason that since good readers' fixations are short and their regressions few, training poor readers to make "better" eye movements should help them become better readers. This thinking unfortunately confuses cause with effect. Do eye movements determine the success of reading or are they caused by the student's reading skills? Most serious scholars in the area of reading research conclude that the *brain,* rather than the eye, is the key to reading (see Just, 1981; Smith, 1978). Information processing controls the physical activities of reading rather than the physical activities controlling the processing. As Gibson and Levin (1975) point out:

> The truth of the matter turns out to be that good readers move their eyes efficiently, but drilling in "shaping" eye movements does not improve reading. The cause of efficient eye movement is *knowing how to read well.* (p. 54)

FIGURE 17–3
Sequence and Location of Fixations for a Good Reader (A) and a Poor Reader (B)

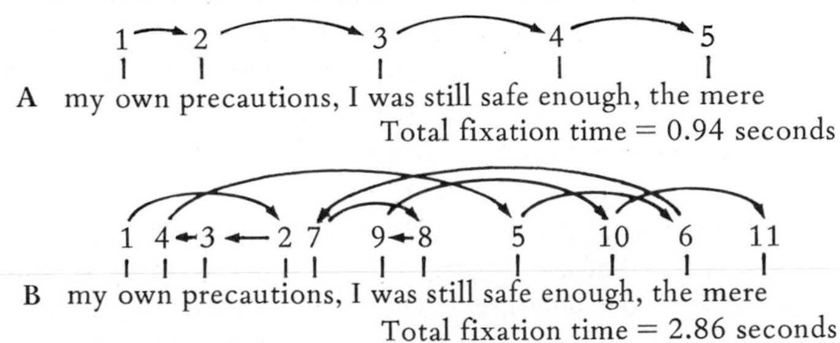

Source: Adapted from Tinker, M. S., *Bases for effective reading* (Minneapolis: University of Minnesota Press, 1965). Copyright © 1965 by the University of Minnesota.

An Information-Processing Model of Reading. Marcel Just and Patricia Carpenter (1980) have developed a useful model of the major cognitive processes involved in reading, which we present in modified form in Figure 17–4. As you can see, it has a great deal in common with the information-processing model of cognition we presented in Chapter Two. Reading, of course, is a cognitive activity. In Just and Carpenter's model of reading, the activities and processes by which information is gleaned from the text are depicted on the left. The reader encounters new information through reading and assigns it preliminary meanings. Long-term memory, pictured on the right, likewise contributes to the reading process. Memory for alphabet characteristics, for concepts, word order, the structure of passages, and prior information all influence the process.

The main activities of reading, like all other cognitive processes, occur in working memory. In Just and Carpenter's view, incoming information and prior knowledge interact in working memory, each influencing the other. On one hand, prior knowledge and knowledge structures affect the information we can take in and the way in which we take it in (that is, the way in which we read). Conversely, existing knowledge is modified and transformed by the new content. As with all cognitive activities, reading is a dynamic, interactive process. The meaning that students obtain while reading is influenced both by the content of what they read and by their prior knowledge, their goals for reading, and the context of the reading event. An expert in reading who is reviewing this chapter, for example, will learn different things (style, level of sophistication, breadth of coverage) than will a student taking his or her first course in educational psychology.

Attention. Not pictured in our adaptation of Just and Carpenter's model, but of importance in reading as well as in all other cognitive processes, is how the reader's attention is allocated to the reading process. In order to read effectively, readers must devote their attention to the task (Samuels, 1977). We are all aware of the effects that distractions can have upon our reading. As our attention wavers when someone speaks to us or when we become sleepy, we find it difficult to understand what we are reading.

Another aspect of attention is more subtle, but equally important. As we read, our attention can be directed to an infinite variety of things—the words themselves, concepts associated with the content we are reading, emotions, and so on. These cognitive processes play an extremely critical role in what we learn. Out of numerous stimuli that we can pay attention to, we select only a few. The page you are looking at now has a great many features to which you *could* pay attention: the

FIGURE 17–4
A Model of Cognitive Processes in Reading

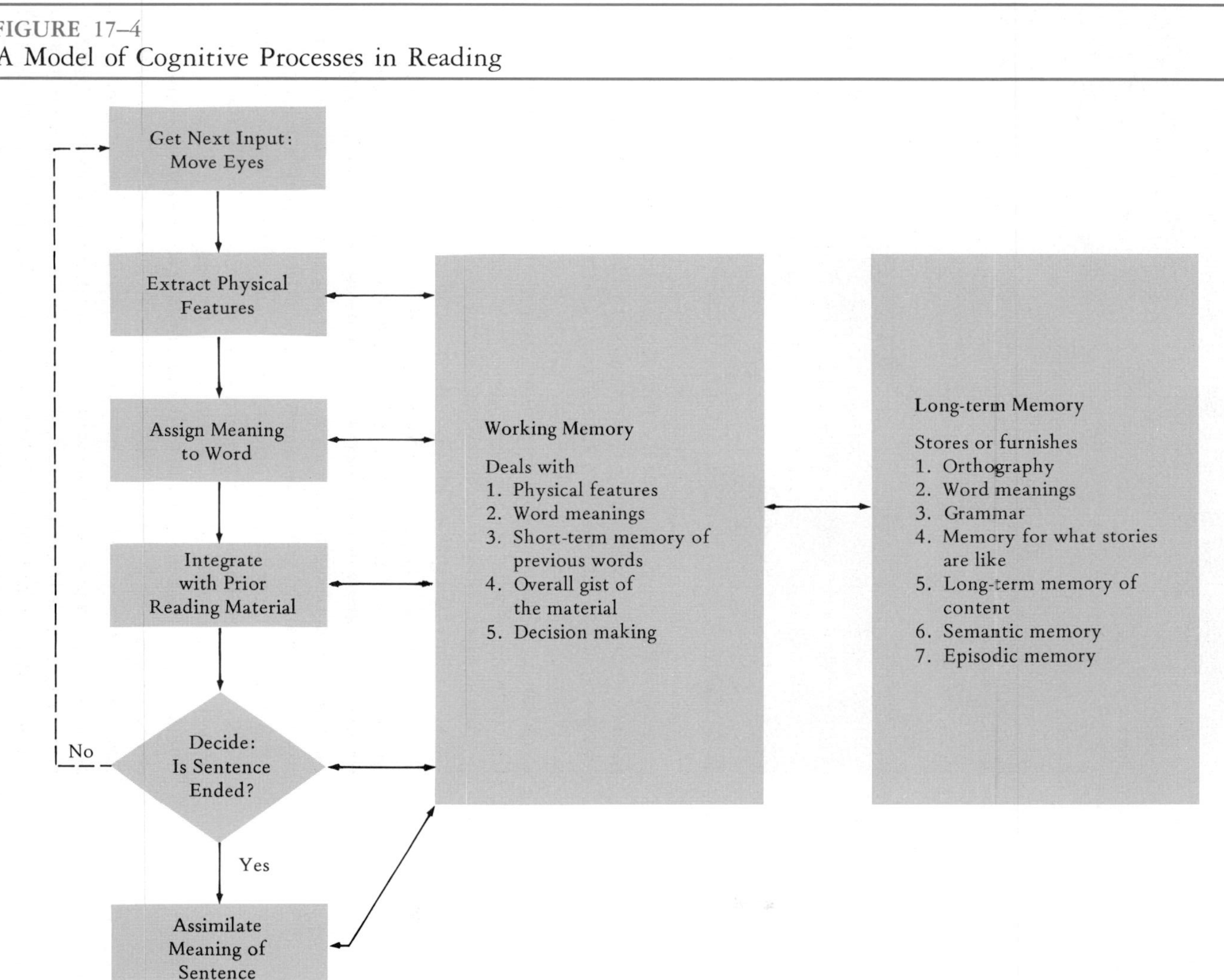

Source: From Just, M., and Carpenter, P., A theory of reading: From eye fixations to comprehension. *Psychological Review,* 1980, 87, 329–354. Copyright 1980 by the American Psychological Association. Adapted by permission of the authors.

In order to read effectively, readers must devote their full attention to the reading process. Reading must be a meaningful activity.

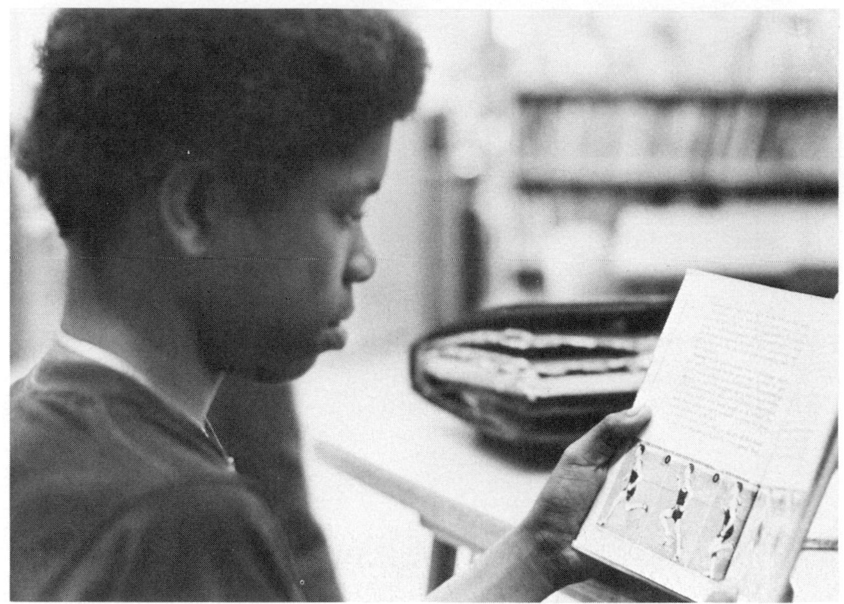

page number, the type of print used, the texture of the paper. As adult readers, however, we usually concentrate mainly on the meaning or *gist* of a passage. In fact, we often are not particularly aware of the surrounding features or even the individual letters or the words we read. Our attention is usually focused on those features that help us comprehend the meaning of what we are reading.

One reason our attention is so selective, as we noted in Chapter Two, is that our capacity for processing incoming information in working memory is very limited (Smith, 1978). Attention can be shifted quickly from one feature of a text to another, but large amounts of information cannot be processed simultaneously. The limited capacity of working memory often creates a bottleneck for incoming information.

Many reading problems involve faulty attention, as when students simply do not spend time reading or when they try to study under distracting conditions. Such problems can often be very effectively dealt with by using some of the behavioral self-management procedures we discussed in Chapter Seven. Another attention problem occurs when students are reading but their reading processes are misdirected or inefficient. Their reading strategies may not be appropriate for their purposes. Reading to prepare for a speech or for a discussion with a professor requires quite different patterns of attention than does reading one's favorite novel on the bus going home. We discuss a number of approaches for improving reading strategies later in this chapter.

Decoding and Comprehension. The cognitive processes involved in reading may be divided into two stages (LaBerge, 1980; LaBerge & Samuels, 1974). Obtaining the meaning of individual words (identifying the physical features and assigning meaning in Just and Carpenter's model) is referred to as **decoding.** The second stage of reading, **comprehending,** refers to the processes whereby the reader gains an overall understanding of the content. Determining the meaning of the word *logography* is an example of decoding, while gaining an understanding of the gist of this paragraph is an example of comprehension.

Decoding occurs when readers consciously direct their attention to individual words, or it may occur automatically after much practice (LaBerge & Samuels, 1974). For example, you probably did not stop to decode the word *practice* in the previous sentence—your decoding was automatic. According to LaBerge and Samuels, skilled reading of reasonably familiar materials involves *automatic* decoding of word meanings while the reader's attention is directed to the comprehension of what is being read. In their view, this process is somewhat analogous to a skilled musician's being able to concentrate on the expressive aspects of music rather than on the individual notes. If a reader encounters an unfamiliar word or if the materials become difficult, however, decoding is no longer automatic. In such instances, decoding itself occupies the reader's attention (Just, 1981). We may say a difficult word to ourselves (for example, "ex-i-gu-ous") and use a sounding-out process in an attempt to decode it.

An important part of learning to read with comprehension is the development of fluent decoding skills. Beginning readers need to be able to recognize automatically the distinguishing features of letters, syllables, and words (McConkie & Rayner, 1976; Williams, 1977). When the processing of letters or words is automatic, readers can begin to concentrate their attention on comprehension. When poor or immature readers need to devote most of their attention to decoding letters and words, comprehension is more difficult and less likely to occur (Bruning, Burton, & Ballering, 1978; Montgomery & Bruning, 1978).

STAGES IN LEARNING TO READ

Learning to read is often considered to occur in stages, beginning with reading readiness and culminating in the refinement of reading skills in high school and adulthood (see A. J. Harris, 1970; Harris & Sipay, 1979). Each stage has its own unique tasks that readers master in order to progress.

Reading Readiness

There is a great deal of variation in definitions of reading readiness. Some experts (see Spache, 1972; Spache & Spache, 1977) take a very broad perspective and define reading readiness by a large group of characteristics, including visual skills (such as eye-hand coordination), auditory factors (such as the ability to distinguish pitch and rhythms), sex, age, and socioeconomic status. This broad definition leads to the advocacy of programs that stress the development of general skills. A sample of these programs includes many of the activities of the typical kindergarten and playground—skipping rope, cutting, pasting, tracing, stringing beads, using the balance beam, marching, reproducing tapping patterns, and listening to and telling stories (Spache, 1972). The underlying assumption is that training in general coordination and visual skills will ultimately benefit reading ability.

Other researchers such as Venezky (1975) have defined reading readiness much more narrowly, using the methods of task analysis we discussed in Chapter Twelve. Instead of a broad concept of reading readiness, Venezky prefers to identify specific prerequisites for reading. He defines prereading skills as "those skills which relate most closely either to the reading process or to the procedures which are employed in teaching reading . . ." (p. 120). Venezky attempted to identify those skills by working backward with the two most important tasks of initial read-

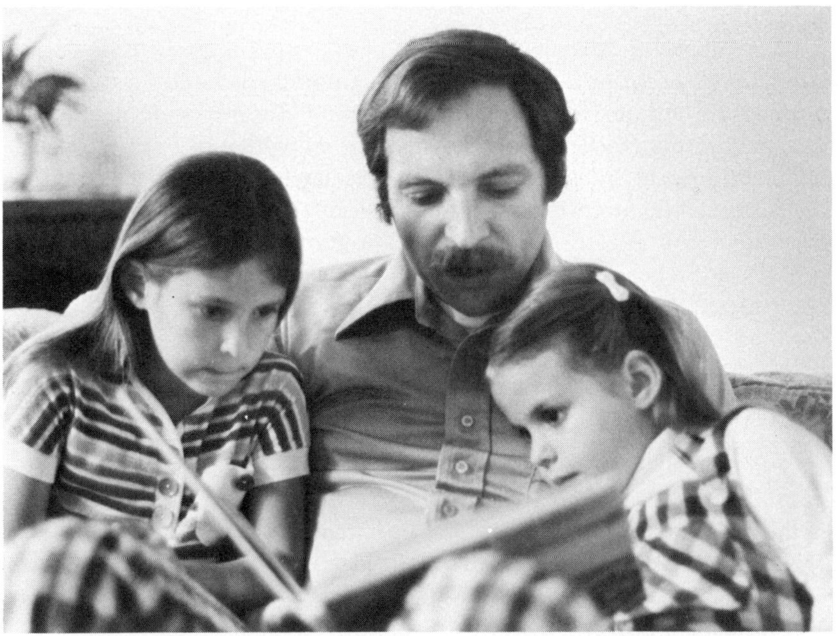

Children should be read to frequently. Research has shown that experiences with reading in early childhood relate to later skill in reading.

APPLICATIONS FOR TEACHING: GUIDELINES FOR ENHANCING PREREADING SKILLS

For parents and teachers of prereaders who would like to work with children on developing prereading skills, we suggest the following principles. They emphasize development of reading and reading-related skills in a positive atmosphere that is likely to stimulate a child's interest in reading.

1. Reading and reading enjoyment should be modeled (see Chapter Eight). **Children can learn about the importance and fun of reading from what they see adults do.**

2. All children should be examined for any possible perceptual problems that might interfere with reading. **Problems in visual and auditory perception should be identified early and treated if possible. Reading is difficult enough for many children without their having to cope with additional problems.**

3. Children should be taught how to pay attention prior to any formal reading instruction. **Paying attention, following directions, and staying on task are requirements for any kind of learning, especially learning to read. Behavioral approaches (see Chapters Seven and Ten) can often be used effectively to teach general attentional skills.**

4. Children should be read to frequently. **Reading to children not only provides a model of reading but helps them discover that reading is enjoyable and that printed symbols have meaning. Of course, reading to children also helps develop their vocabularies as they encounter new words.**

5. Games and exercises can be used to develop the general motor and perceptual skills necessary for reading. **Simple discrimination tasks, eye-hand coordination activities, scribbling, and drawing should all be encouraged.**

6. Do not pressure a prereader to master reading-related tasks. **If a child sees reading as enjoyable, he or she will usually develop the appropriate prereading skills. When reading activities become pressured, children may stop seeing reading as fun and seek to avoid the activities (Torrey, 1979).**

---

ing, sight word recognition and decoding. By this process he identified the following critical prereading skills.

> *Attending to letter order* (a child can notice the difference between *was* and *saw*)
>
> *Attending to letter orientation* (a child differentiates between *d* and *b* or between *m* and *w*)
>
> *Attending to word detail* (a child sees that *bite* is different from *bit* or *bike*)
>
> *Matching sounds* (a child can sort pictures by their initial sounds, for example, grouping pictures of a *b*ird, *b*at, and *b*all together)
>
> *Blending sounds* (*i* and *g* are pronounced together correctly in the words *dig* and *big*)

According to Venezky, these skills should be the object of prereading instruction. Readiness to read is best fostered by training in those skills that are most directly a part of the reading process, as shown by the task analysis, rather than by training in activities that are less directly involved.

Over the years, there have been many studies of the optimum age at which reading instruction should begin. Morphett and Washburne (1931), two early researchers, concluded that it is best to postpone reading instruction until children reach a mental age of six years and six months (see Chapter Five). By so doing, they argued, the chances for failure in reading instruction would be greatly reduced, since they had noticed a sharp increase in the number of children making "satisfactory progress" at this mental age. Although this study had serious defects as scientific research, it became, as Coltheart (1979) has pointed out, an important part of a general belief among reading teachers that reading instruction should not begin until age six or later. Thus, in the United States most reading instruction begins in the first grade, when the majority of children reach the mental age of six years and six months.*

Some authorities (see Durkin, 1974) have shown that precocious (early) readers benefit from their early start, but of course it is recognized that most such readers learned to read on their own without benefit of formal instruction. While there are a fairly large number of early readers and there have been some studies showing positive effects of early reading instruction, the question of when formal reading instruction should begin is still open (Torrey, 1979). Obviously, there is a very wide range of individual differences in reading and no one age standard is appropriate for everyone. More important is the question of how well the abilities of a given child match those required by beginning reading instruction. A well-rounded approach to ready a child for reading requires attention to individual abilities and to the specific components of beginning reading.

Beginning Reading

A variety of methods for teaching beginning reading have come and gone over the years. Methods of teaching reading, perhaps more than in any other instructional area, have been promoted with great zeal and attacked with equal vigor. Today, hundreds of commercial programs are available that draw from a variety of theoretical approaches.

One common approach to beginning reading is the phonics method. **Phonics** emphasizes decoding of sounds from letters and words, particularly the learning of letter-sound relationships and using these relation-

* This belief is not universally held. Reading instruction begins at age five in such countries as Great Britain and Israel (Downing, 1973) and not until age seven in Denmark, Sweden, and the Soviet Union (Bronfenbrenner, 1970).

ships to decode word meanings. Some phonics approaches teach the letter-sound patterns in relative isolation (how to pronounce *sp, st,* and *br*), while others employ phonics within words and stories.

One instructional method with a strong phonics emphasis is the Initial Teaching Alphabet, or ITA. The ITA is an alphabet with forty-four characters (see Figures 17–5 and 17–6). Each character has a *single* meaningful sound associated with it. In contrast, English letters may have any number of sounds associated with them (consider the *u* in *quick, cut, put,* and *cute*) and, as a consequence, there are a very large number of letter-sound associations that must be learned. Because ITA

FIGURE 17–5
The Initial Teaching Alphabet

Number	*Character*	*Name*	*Example*	*Traditional spelling*	*Number*	*Character*	*Name*	*Example*	*Traditional spelling*
1	æ	ae	ræt	rate	23	y	i-ae	yell	yell
2	b	bee	big	big	24	z	zed or zee	fizz	fizz
3	c	kee	cat	cat	25	ʓ	zess	houʓeʓ	houses
4	d	dee	dog	dog	26	wh	whae	when	when
5	ee	ee	meet	meet	27	ch	chae	chick	chick
6	f	ef	fill	fill	28	th	ith	thaut	thought
7	g	gae	gun	gun	29	th	thee	the	the
8	h	hae	hat	hat	30	ʃh	ish	ʃhip	ship
9	ie	ie	tie	tie	31	ʒ	zhee	meʒuer	measure
10	j	jae	jelly	jelly	32	ŋ	ing	siŋ	sing
11	k	kae	kit	kit	33	ɑ	ah	fɑr	far
12	l	el	lamp	lamp	34	au	au	ɑutum	autumn
13	m	em	man	man	35	a	at	appl	apple
14	n	en	net	net	36	e	et	egg	egg
15	œ	oe	tœ	toe	37	i	it	dip	dip
16	p	pee	pig	pig	38	o	ot	hot	hot
17	r	rae	run	run	39	u	ut	ugly	ugly
18	s	ess	sad	sad	40	ω	oot	bωk	book
19	t	tee	tap	tap	41	ωω	oo	mωωn	moon
20	ue	ue	due	due	42	ou	ow	bou	bough
21	v	vee	van	van	43	oi	oi	toi	toy
22	w	wae	will	will					

Source: From Downing (1965), p. 71. Used by permission of the author.

FIGURE 17–6
A Sample of Writing Using the Initial Teaching Alphabet

Wuns upon a tiem

livd a jient.

Hee had a big casul

and a majic goos.

is phonetically regular, its proponents argue that it can minimize many decoding problems. As we noted earlier, there is evidence that regular spelling-sound correspondence can help beginning readers. In languages that have this characteristic, such as Finnish, for example, early reading is more frequent and illiteracy much less common than in other languages (Rozin & Gleitman, 1977).

There are, however, several major difficulties with the ITA method. First, appropriate materials written in ITA are often not available. Second, reading outside of schools does not employ the ITA. Third, and perhaps most important, students must make the transition back to regular English.

The *language experience* approach emphasizes the relationship of reading to children's general language experiences. Reading is viewed as the process of relating written to oral language. Children's own oral stories about themselves, their families, or their neighborhoods may be written down to become the basis for reading. The language experience approach is especially useful for children whose spoken language is different from standard English.

Most current instructional methods now draw from both the phonics and language experience approaches. Methods that combine these and other approaches are called *eclectic.* Basal readers are the most prominent examples of eclectic reading instruction. Basal readers are coordinated sets of texts, workbooks, and activities used in most American schools. Diverse aspects of reading such as learning letter sounds and sound blends and using context to extract meanings may be included in the same basal series. While basal readers have been criticized for many reasons (unrealistic content, cultural and ethnic biases, sexism, among others) the majority have been adjusted and they continue to form the core of most children's beginning reading experiences.

PRACTICE EXERCISE 17–1
Reviewing a Reading Series

There are hundreds of commercially available programs for teaching beginning reading. Committees of teachers and others usually choose a reading program series for a school after careful examination of several series.

Analyze the program series used in your local school system (sample sets are available at your school or from your college elementary teacher education program) on one or more of the following dimensions.

1. *What is to be learned at each level of the series?* What are some of the key elements being taught at each level of the basal reading series? How are new concepts introduced? Does the program emphasize phonics or reading for meaning?
2. *Are the skills of reading taught effectively?* Are all important reading skills covered? Is enough time devoted to critical topics and is the method of teaching concepts usually clear?
3. *What roles are portrayed in the reading materials?* Are male and female roles stereotyped? Are families always depicted as "typical" familes? Are there any ethnic or racial biases that you can detect in your analyses?
4. *How are illustrations used?* How are pictures used in relation to the content? Do they provide context or do they distract? Are they clear and attractive?
5. *What are the usual outcomes of stories?* Are they unrealistically positive and pollyannish or do they depict real-life outcomes for children?
6. *What are the settings for the stories?* Are settings rural or urban, are they imaginary or real? Would they be interesting to a child?

APPLICATIONS FOR TEACHING: GUIDELINES FOR TEACHING BEGINNING READING

Many reading experts view beginning reading as a set of skills that can be separated into parts—such as the ability to discriminate between letters, to blend sounds, and so on. In contrast, Frank Smith (1982) takes the position that reading is more a process of bringing meaning to print than of decoding. For Smith, reading is a process of testing hypotheses and making guesses about what is on the page. The major objectives in learning to read are understanding that print is meaningful and that words are language and getting the chance to learn to read through frequent practice.

We generally agree with Smith's position. Such practices as insisting on perfection in reading, teaching letters and words in isolation, and discouraging guessing can interfere with children's experience of reading as meaningful and enjoyable (Smith, 1982). A certain way to ensure that some beginning readers will fail is to demand conformity and to force children to work toward the impossible criterion of perfection in reading. The following guidelines stress meaningfulness in learning to read and the individual nature of this process. Following them should benefit all beginning readers.

1. Make reading and activities associated with reading enjoyable. To become good readers, children must devote time and effort to reading activities. These activities should be enjoyable so that children will want to read rather than avoid reading. For many children, beginning reading is hard work and hard work is more palatable when it's fun.

2. Stress experiences that will lead to success. It is important to carefully plan beginning reading activities for students so that they experience feelings of success in reading. Not only must the activities allow for success, but each child should feel a sense of genuine accomplishment.

3. Emphasize meaningful reading experiences. As we have stressed throughout this book, learning is most likely to occur when learning experiences can be related to what students already know, when new experiences are meaningful. From this perspective, the teacher should carefully choose or construct reading materials that employ the vocabulary and concepts that are a part of students' prior knowledge.

4. Be prepared to employ several different methods in reading instruction. While some students may benefit from a phonetic approach, other students may not. Instruction in reading at this crucial time should be geared as much as possible to individual needs.

5. Have students reread materials with which they are already familiar. Students need to gain confidence in reading and experience the sense of "I can really do it!" Having students reread materials they have already mastered is one way to foster feelings of confidence in reading (Montgomery & Bruning, 1978).

6. Stress accomplishment rather than errors. Beginning readers will make mistakes. The emphasis should be on recognizing improvement rather than on harping on mistakes.

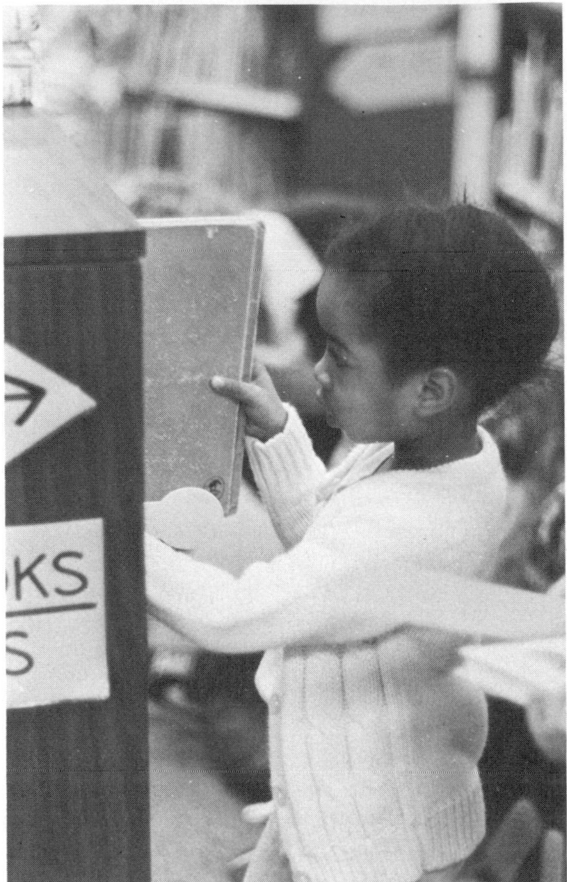

Time should be set aside for children to use the library.

7. Allow guessing. Beginning readers, through the use of pictures or the verbal context of stories, are often able to guess words as they read. This is not a bad approach. As adults we often guess the meanings of unfamiliar words on the basis of context. Fluency in reading is more important in beginning reading than is perfection.

8. Practice, practice, practice. The more students read, the better they will read. As in any other skill, reading improves with practice.

9. Identify possible perceptual problems (see Chapter Sixteen) and have them treated as rapidly as possible. Despite the fact that most schools require a check on children's visual and auditory abilities prior to kindergarten, some problems are not identified. If you suspect a perceptual problem, notify the parents and appropriate school authorities as soon as you can. Beginning reading is difficult enough without the presence of uncorrected perceptual problems.

10. Include self-directed reading activities. Set aside some time at least once a week when the students may use the school library to choose books (within their overall ability levels) to read on their own.

11. Encourage reading at home. The development of pride in a new skill can be enhanced by encouraging children to read to parents and siblings. Besides, children need all the practice in reading they can get.

The Middle Years: Developing Comprehension

After students have acquired basic decoding skills, more and more emphasis can be placed on the development of comprehension. Reading comprehension goals include recognizing the main thought in a passage, placing ideas in their proper sequence, predicting outcomes, and following written directions (Tierney & Pearson, 1981). By the upper elementary grades, the emphasis has thus shifted from learning *to* read to learning *through* reading. Reading is now more and more functional as students read to learn, to obtain instructions, and to enjoy themselves.

APPLICATIONS FOR TEACHING: GUIDELINES FOR DEVELOPING COMPREHENSION

Several possible applications for developing reading comprehension can be drawn from the research on reading.

1. Use instructional objectives when there is specific information you want students to extract from the text. (See Chapter Eleven.) The use of objectives as well as study questions typically increases student comprehension of what was required in the objectives or questions (Petersen, Glover, & Ronning, in press).

2. Use advance organizers to help students better comprehend new reading materials. Advance organizers are brief prefaces to reading materials that help students relate the new information in the text to their existing knowledge structures. (Advance organizers are discussed in more detail later in this chapter.)

3. Give clear instructions stressing the purpose of reading. Knowing the purpose for reading usually helps students' comprehension. Also, the point of view that students take in reading affects which content they will learn and which they will not (Pichert & Anderson, 1977).

4. Give students feedback on their reading performance. Practice with feedback on different comprehension tasks (such as requiring students to orally summarize a short passage, asking them to judge the validity of inferences from a passage) is necessary to continue to sharpen reading skills. Students must be given frequent practice in reading for comprehension and must receive feedback for their efforts (Tierney & Pearson, 1981).

The Adult Reader

As students proceed through junior and senior high school into adulthood, the demands on their reading abilities become more complex. One particularly important demand is the need to develop flexible reading rates (A. J. Harris, 1970). That is, readers should learn to vary their rates in accord with the demands of different reading tasks (Sherman & Kulhavy, 1980). Based on early work by Yoakam (1955), Harris suggests the following rates appropriate to different purposes:

Skimming rate:	appropriate to finding references, getting the general point or gist of an article
Rapid rate:	used to reread familiar material, to get information for temporary use
Normal rate:	used in finding answers to questions, noting details, and relating details to main ideas
Careful rate:	employed to master content, to read poetry, to learn details in sequence

"You have a choice of three courses. You could increase speed somewhat and retain your comprehension, you could increase speed considerably and reduce comprehension, or you could increase speed tremendously and eliminate comprehension completely."

PRACTICE EXERCISE 17–2
Developing Reading Flexibility

One way to become a better reader is to develop flexible reading rates. Obtain some reading materials that require varying rates: careful, normal, rapid, and skimming. A textbook, for example, would be read carefully. A novel or short story would be read normally. Any review materials—perhaps the rereading of a textbook chapter—can be read rapidly, while a news magazine can serve as an excellent source for material to skim.

When you have obtained the appropriate reading materials, estimate the number of words (a per-line count multiplied by lines on a page or in a column will do) so that you can have approximately 2500 words from each source. When you have done this, read each item as you customarily would read it and time yourself. Then divide 2500 words by the number of minutes and seconds you spent reading, to get words per minute. Your words per minute rate should be different for the different styles of reading. If this is the case, fine. If not, decide whether you need to slow down or speed up some of your reading.

Practice reading at different rates for different purposes. To do this, use your careful reading rate and a normal rate you just measured as your starting point. Was your normal rate comfortable? Could you easily recall the material you read? If your careful rate was not slower than your normal rate, ask yourself if you learned more while reading carefully than while reading normally. If so, speed up your normal rate. If not, slow down your careful rate. A general rule of thumb is that rapid reading ought to be between 25 and 50 percent faster than normal reading, and skimming should be between 50 and 100 percent faster than normal. If you didn't obtain differences close to this, practice rapid reading and skimming by reading standard lengths of materials with a timer set to go off at a time that indicates a certain rate of reading. Your goal, of course, is to try to read the passage before the timer goes off while retaining as much comprehension as possible.

Harris maintains that flexibility can be taught but that most persons are not flexible readers (Harris, 1970, p. 483).

The majority of readers with about a twelfth-grade education have a silent reading rate of about 200 words per minute (Just, 1981), but there is a wide range of individual differences. Interestingly, silent reading rates tend to be about the same rate at which persons can listen and comprehend speech. As we have previously noted, the controlling factor in reading comprehension seems to be how the information is processed rather than the physical activities of reading.

Adjunct Aids for Comprehension. Techniques designed to facilitate students' comprehension of reading materials are called adjunct aids. How they affect reading comprehension has been the topic of a great deal of research, and there are several applications that should be especially helpful for teachers. Most of the research on adjunct aids has grown out of the work of Ausubel (1960, 1980) and Rothkopf (1970). In general, adjunct aids can be classed into one of four categories: objectives, questions, advance organizers, and active response modes (T. N. Anderson, 1981). We will examine each of the adjunct aids more closely below.

Objectives are statements of the learning that should occur from reading a set of materials. Objectives used this way are identical to those discussed in Chapter Eleven, but conditions and criteria are not usually described. Researchers commonly investigate the effects of objectives by examining intentional learning (the learning of information specified in the objectives) and incidental learning (the learning of information not specified in the objectives). In general, when time spent reading is not a concern, the research findings support the following statements: (1) objectives increase intentional learning at the expense of incidental learning (Jenkins & Neisworth, 1973; Lawson, 1974); (2) incidental learning is greatest *without* objectives (Frase & Kreitzburg, 1975; Gagné & Rothkopf, 1975); and (3) specific, terse, and distributed objectives result in superior intentional learning with smaller negative effects on incidental learning (R. Kaplan, 1974; Kaplan & Rothkopf, 1974; Kaplan & Simmons, 1974; Rothkopf & Kaplan, 1972).

All the results of research in the use of objectives as adjunct aids to reading have not been positive (see Faw & Waller, 1976, for a good review of the area). When time for reading is the same for groups of students given objectives and groups not given objectives, there is no positive effect of objectives on overall comprehension (Jenkins & Deno, 1971; Petersen et al., in press; Zimmer, Petersen, Ronning, & Glover, 1978). Nonetheless, objectives have been observed to increase intentional learning in almost all studies.

The procedure of using **questions** inserted in reading materials requires students to answer questions as they read. In general, when time spent reading does not matter, the following conclusions can be drawn from the research: (1) questions presented prior to reading material facilitate intentional learning but have no particular effect on incidental learning, and (2) questions that follow reading increase intentional learning significantly and also produce smaller but reliable increases in incidental learning (Boyd, 1973; Frase, 1967, 1968; Frase, Patrick, & Shumer, 1970; McGraw & Grotelueschen, 1972; Rothkopf, 1966, 1972; Rothkopf & Bisbicos, 1967; Rothkopf & Bloom, 1970; Snowman & Cunningham, 1975). When time is held constant for readers

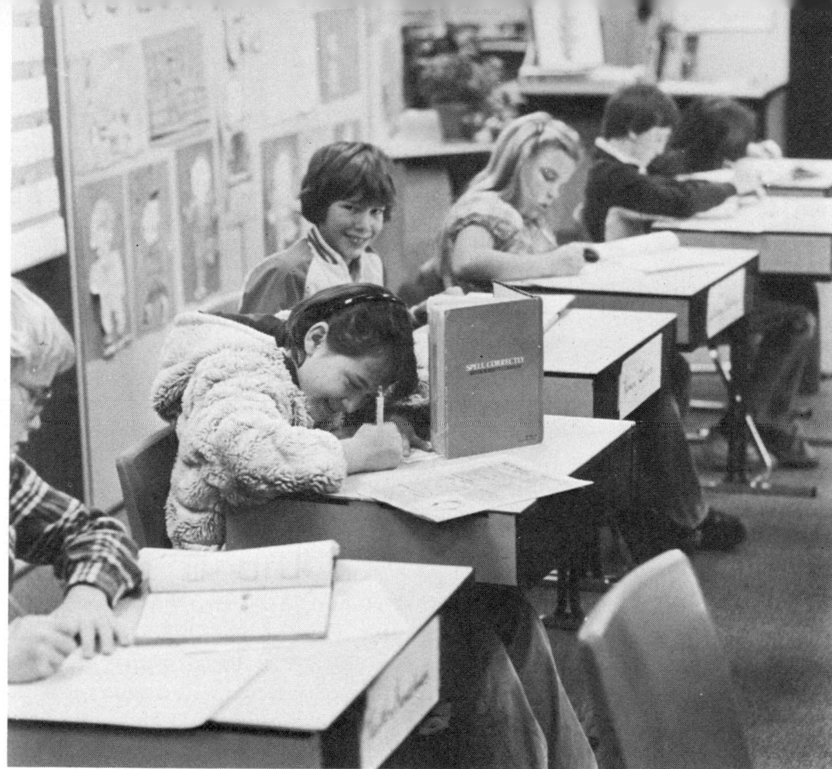

Taking notes requires active processing that helps make information meaningful and benefits comprehension.

with and without questions, however, questions do not seem to have a significant effect on comprehension (Hiller, 1974; Hunkins, 1969; Winne, 1981).

Advance organizers are overviews of major ideas in reading materials. They are written at a high level of abstraction and do not provide specific information that will be included in any posttest over the material (Ausubel, 1960, 1980). The research on advance organizers, not employing time controls, generally indicates that advance organizers are most useful for facilitating recall among students of low ability or poor educational backgrounds (Ausubel & Fitzgerald, 1961; Ausubel & Youssef, 1963). When time is controlled, and students are of roughly equal reading ability, advance organizers seem to have no significant effect on recall. However, they do have a positive effect on transfer (Mayer, 1979).

Active response modes are activities such as underlining, highlighting, and note taking that students engage in while reading. Almost all of the recent research results suggest that causing students to use such active response modes has no effect on comprehension (see Barnes & Clawson, 1975; Mayer, 1979; Mayer & Bromage, 1980). Some research has indicated, however, that note taking and summarizing may be valuable means of helping students integrate new information from reading passages into their memories (Brown, Campione, & Day, 1981; Peper & Mayer, 1978).

APPLICATIONS FOR TEACHING: GUIDELINES FOR USING ADJUNCT AIDS

An overall view of the research on adjunct aids (see Anderson, 1981; Faw & Waller, 1976; Reder, 1980) seems to most strongly support the following uses of adjunct aids by classroom teachers.

1. Write objectives at higher levels of learning. Objectives and questions are most effective in increasing intentional learning when they are written at the higher levels of Bloom's taxonomy (Andre, 1979).

2. Allow time for using adjunct aids. Readers utilizing adjunct aids should be allowed more time for reading than when adjunct aids are not used. To quote Reynolds, Standiford, & Anderson (1979), "time is cheap and achievement is dear."

3. Use advance organizers when introducing unfamiliar topics. Advance organizers seem especially helpful for novel material. They are particularly effective for students with poor backgrounds and students who learn somewhat slowly (Mayer, 1979).

4. Encourage note taking. Note-taking skills should be taught as a means of helping students integrate new knowledge into existing memory structures (Peper & Mayer, 1978).

5. Avoid trivial objectives and knowledge-level questions. Objectives and questions should deal with meaningful aspects of the reading materials. A few meaningful objectives can effectively guide student learning.

6. Use objectives and questions when you wish to target learning. Do not use objectives or questions unless you are willing to give up some incidental learning. Students will invest most of their learning time on topics you single out in your questions or objectives (Reynolds & Anderson, 1980).

7. Distribute the adjunct aids throughout the materials. Objectives and questions should be distributed such that one or two are presented every so often along with a relatively short segment of the reading materials.

READING DISABILITIES

The success of most children and adults with reading has to be balanced against the reading problems that often occur. Over 10 percent of the population of the United States is functionally illiterate; that is, they read below the fourth-grade level (Rozin & Gleitman, 1977). Fifteen percent of all schoolchildren—over eight million—have severe reading disabilities (Satz, 1977). Because reading is so important, reading failure often leads directly to other problems such as poor academic achievement, frustration and anger with school, and high dropout rates.

Many terms have been used to describe reading failure—dyslexia, minimal brain dysfunction, specific reading disability, reading retardation, and psychoneurological learning disability. In a representative definition of one such term (reading retardation) Spache (1976) offered the following:

> The retarded reader is one who . . . is retarded in a number of major reading skills . . . is retarded by one year or more if in the primary grades, or by two years or more if older . . . is retarded below that level necessary for full participation in the reading tasks of his age or grade or socioeconomic group . . . is an individual who has had normal opportunities for schooling . . . [and] has continued to show this degree of retardation below his sociocultural peers despite corrective efforts. *(pp. 4–7)*

Some persons are very poor readers because of their low general intellectual ability. Simply, their intellectual capacity limits decoding and comprehension. For many others, however, the causes of poor reading are more complex and puzzling. Some students of normal or above-normal intelligence may lag far behind their expected reading level. There is a large discrepancy between their expected and actual achievement in reading, and reading instruction has failed. Such students are usually said to possess a *reading disability* (see Chapter Sixteen).

Causes of Reading Disabilities

Many factors seem to be involved in reading disabilities. No one factor completely explains the existence of a reading disability, but several seem to be strongly associated with unexpected reading failures. These factors are genetic, environmental, health-related, and motivational.

Genetic Factors. A number of studies (see Foch, DeFries, McClearn, & Singer, 1977; Owen, 1968) show that there is a definite tendency for reading disabilities to run in families, a fact long noted by teachers. Genetic factors, however, are hard to identify with certainty. This is due in part to the lack of accurate classifications of reading-disabled students (Satz, 1977). Without a clear definition of who is reading disabled and who is not, genetic factors cannot be pinpointed with accuracy. Families with reading problems are not necessarily evidence for genetic factors since family similarity can as easily result from environmental influences. It appears, however, that heredity does play some role in the occurrence of reading disabilities—what is unclear is how strong a role it plays.

Environmental Factors. The environment seems to have an important effect on whether children are likely to encounter severe reading difficulties. In one study reported by Owen (1974), 27 percent of inner-city children read two or more grade levels below their expected level, while in middle-class suburbs the proportion was 15 percent. In upper-class neighborhoods, the incidence was 3 percent, and in private preparatory schools, the percent of reading disabled students was zero. Other research (see Satz, 1977) also shows that social class is strongly related to reading disability: children from lower socioeconomic backgrounds encounter more reading problems. A common finding is that the incidence of reading disabilities among black students is two or three times higher than among white students.

How might the environment be involved in differences in the number of students having severe difficulty with reading? In many homes, language stimulation is lacking (Satz, 1977). Verbal communication is sparse and printed materials absent. Some children may never have been read to or have seen others read. Still other homes are bilingual, and children from these homes may be unfamiliar with the language of instruction. Of course, inferior schools in some depressed areas may make deficits even worse.

Children from all social classes begin school with high expectations for their performance in reading (Entwisle, 1977). Obviously, however, these expectations do not come true for many lower-class and minority children. The combination of increasing failures in reading and unmet expectations can set children up for frustration and negative attitudes toward reading.

Health-Related Factors. Many experts have stressed the role of medical factors in reading disabilities, and many of the terms used to describe reading problems sound like medical terms. Minimal brain dysfunction, psychoneurological learning disability, visual-motor irregularity, central processing dysfunctions, dyslexia, specific reading disability, and strephosymbolia have all appeared in the reading disability literature. Frequently, though, such terms have not provided any help in understanding reading problems, which are often educational rather than medical. Also, "diagnosis" cannot usually be made with any accuracy (Satz, 1977). Furthermore, diagnoses often do not lead directly to any treatment of the problem.

A number of legitimate medical factors, however, are involved in some cases of reading disability. Prenatal complications, brain injuries, and infections can result in learning disabilities (see Chapter Sixteen). Sensory defects may strongly affect reading performance, and problems that stem from injuries, chemical imbalances, and biological factors can and do affect reading. Behavior-regulation programs, careful control of diets, and medication have been shown to be beneficial in some cases.

Motivational Factors. Reading difficulties are often related to motivational problems. Some children not only grow up in homes where nobody reads but may have parents who regard reading as a waste of time. It is easy for children from such homes to adopt the attitudes of their parents. Other children may approach reading with initial enthusiasm but lose motivation because of poor instruction or failures that result from their lack of necessary background.

In many settings, children can function very well without reading. Problems begin to arise, however, when children must learn to read. Because of many factors over which children have no control, learning to read may be a frustrating rather than a rewarding experience. Understanding what we are reading is satisfying to us; failure to understand can be quite punishing. As poor readers struggle to decode syllables and single words, meaning is often lost.

Oral reading errors by poor readers can also contribute to lowered motivation. Required segments of oral reading contain a large number of events that are almost certainly punishing for most poor readers. Even though teachers are well meaning, their corrections and the class's reactions can be quite upsetting. One consequence that we have observed is that poor readers will read very hesitantly and will "fish" for every possible clue from teachers and classmates. In this way, poor readers are able to avoid reading as much as possible.

Theories of Reading Disabilities

A number of experts in reading have attempted to integrate what is known about reading disabilities into a theory. There are several general viewpoints, some stressing health-related factors, others placing more emphasis on the environment and experiences of the individual.

The most commonly held theory is the perceptual deficit theory, which can be traced back to the early work of Orton (1937). One tendency of poor readers is to reverse letters and words. Many children with reading problems have difficulty recognizing and pronouncing certain letters and words, such as pronouncing *b* as *d* or writing *saw* as *was*. There are also research findings showing slower development of motor-perceptual skills, such as throwing, balancing, and jumping, in poor readers. This evidence has led people such as Orton to hypothesize a general perceptual deficit or, in clinical terminology, a minimal brain dysfunction (MBD) as the cause of reading problems. The perceptual-deficit approach pictures problems of the disabled readers as stemming from poor neurological organization, particularly in the left hemisphere of the brain.

Vellutino (1977), however, has argued that the evidence for the perceptual-deficit hypothesis is weak. If perception were the primary cause of reading disability, poor readers should also give evidence of perceptual problems in many other areas, but for the most part they do not. Relationships of reading confusions to other perceptual measures are quite weak overall (Benton, 1975).

Another possible explanation of reading disabilities is that poor readers cannot *integrate* information from different modes of input—from sight and sound, for example. This means that disabled readers are somehow handicapped in transferring information from one mode to another (such as in matching written materials to what they have heard).

APPLICATIONS FOR TEACHING: REMEDIAL APPROACHES TO READING DISABILITIES

Because there have been many different points of view on the sources of reading disabilities, and even greater disagreement on definitions, remedial programs have been developed to match almost every theory. Some have stressed the development of coordination to facilitate neurological organization in the hope that reading will be improved. Others have stressed training in auditory perception to enhance perceptual skills, or psychotherapy to deal with emotional problems that presumably have caused reading failures. Programs have been devised to teach specific letter and word discrimination skills, to speed the reading process, and to overcome general language deficits through enrichment activities. Some multisensory approaches have been developed to teach the integration of sensory inputs of diverse types.

None of these programs has been a total waste of time—in fact, many have been quite effective—but no one approach has seemed to be the entire solution to a particular child's reading problems, and certainly no single approach has been proven successful with the range of problems that exist under the label of reading disabilities. Complex problems with many causes require large-scale and sophisticated efforts to solve them. A number of principles of effective remedial reading instruction that cut across all programs are listed below.

1. Reading should be made as rewarding as possible. With the history of failure that many students have, it is important that rewards for reading be carefully planned. At first, rewards should be quite frequent. "Natural" rewards should also be planned, so that reading leads to the desired goals of the student.

2. Students should read as much as possible. Like any skill, reading can improve only with practice. No improvement in reading can take place unless students have the opportunity to read frequently.

3. Rereading should be encouraged. Rereading materials allows students to gain confidence in their ability to extract information from a text. How well would the musician read music, for example, if he or she read each score once and only once? Fluent reading will develop most quickly when the reading material is familiar.

4. As much as possible, the language of reading should be the language that the student has experienced. A principle of cognitive processing is that what we already know determines to a great extent what we can learn. Reading, particularly for the reading-disabled student, should focus on the familiar. When familiar materials are used, the student doesn't have to struggle with comprehension but can concentrate on decoding while reading at a reasonable speed.

5. Skill training should take place in the most meaningful context possible. There is sometimes a tendency to study the subskills of reading in isolation. But as Smith (1978) and others point out, this may make a difficult task impossible for the disabled reader. Many clues to meaning are removed when words are taken out of context; the disabled reader may need these very clues.

6. Consider medical problems as possible causes of reading disability. A number of reading problems have relationships to medical factors. Hearing losses, brain injuries, hormone imbalances, and some forms of hyperactivity contribute to reading difficulty and failure. Just as there is little sense in treating medical problems as educational ones, it doesn't make sense to ignore possible medical reasons for reading failure. If you suspect a medically related problem, arrange for the proper testing or referral.

However, research support has not been clear-cut for this theory (Bruning et al., 1978) and other hypotheses are equally plausible.

Another possible explanation sees reading disability as stemming from problems in temporal order recall, such as the recall sequences of sounds or rhythms. A failure to perceive which sounds come first or which letters precede others would obviously be a critical problem for would-be readers. As with the other theories, there is no clear-cut research support.

The most supportable theory seems to be that most reading difficulties are related to overall *verbal deficit* (Vellutino, 1977). In general, a lack of awareness of the many facets of language—phonetics, syntax and vocabulary—greatly handicaps students in reading. Skilled reading requires the ability to use information in *both* the spoken and the written language.

If a child has a severely limited vocabulary, the task of word recognition can become extremely difficult (Smith, 1978). Further, insufficient knowledge of language structures, such as grammatical principles, can make fluent reading impossible. Poor readers show significantly less retention of structural information (Waller, 1976) than do good readers, an indication that general verbal deficits are related to reading difficulties.

The verbal-deficit hypothesis also fits well with the variety of possible causes of reading disability: genetic, environmental, health-related, and motivational. Each of these areas can contribute to the existence of a verbal deficit, which in turn makes it difficult for children to have successful experiences with reading.

SUMMARY

Reading, one of the most important of all educational skills, is a complex cognitive process involving several components. The starting point for reading is a writing system. There are several forms of writing systems. In English, the writing system is alphabetic. The major observable aspect of reading is the movements made by the eyes. Eye movements across the printed page are referred to as saccades while the stops are called fixations. Information is gathered during the fixations. Patterns of saccades and fixations are very different between good and poor readers. The idea of training eye movements in order to improve reading must be rejected, however, because these movements are controlled by the student's cognitive processes.

An information-processing model pictures reading as a dynamic, interactional process with both the content and the reader contributing to what is learned. Attention, as in all cognitive processes, is a key component of reading. The cognitive processes in reading can be viewed in two stages—decoding (understanding the meaning of individual words) and comprehending (obtaining the gist of what is read). Good readers decode automatically and concentrate on comprehension while poor readers struggle with decoding and comprehend far less.

Learning to read occurs in stages: reading readiness, beginning reading, and the development of comprehension skills. Reading instruction has many similar goals across these stages but there are important differences. Activities in reading instruction differ in important ways, depending on the goals.

Disabilities in reading are a major problem in education. The potential causes of reading disabilities include genetic, environmental, motivational, and health-related factors. Several explanations have been put forth to account for reading disabilities. The most reasonable view suggests that information-processing deficits are at the root of the problem. While there have been several different approaches to the treatment of reading disabilities, a set of principles seems to cut across all effective treatment programs. These principles stress the need to develop reading as a high-frequency, rewarding, and meaningful activity.

CLOSING COMMENTS

We're pleased to have been a part of your introduction to educational psychology. We believe that the concepts, principles, and skills we have written about are important for effective teaching. Learning about teaching, though, is a lifelong process. Children change, educational systems change, the world changes, we change, and new techniques are developed.

If teaching is to be your profession you will spend the rest of your life learning it. You are now completing a course in educational psychology. As you complete it, we hope that this experience becomes a stepping-stone for your continued growth as a teacher.

Suggested Readings

Chall, J. *Learning to read: The great debate.* New York: McGraw-Hill, 1967.

This text is a must for all serious scholars beginning to study the area of reading. It is out of date, but it presents a state-of-the-art view of reading instruction in the mid-1960s.

Gibson, E. J., & Rozin, P. *The psychology of reading.* Cambridge, Mass.: MIT Press, 1975.

A thorough introduction to the psychology of reading is presented in a clear and cogent style in this intermediate-level text.

Just, M. A., & Carpenter, P. A. A theory of reading: From eye fixations to comprehension. *Psychological Review,* 1980, *87,* 329–354.

This is an important review paper for those concerned with the direction of the psychology of reading.

Otto, W., Peters, C. W., & Peters, N. (Eds.). *Reading problems: A multidisciplinary perspective.* Reading, Mass.: Addison-Wesley, 1977.

An overview of reading problems is presented in this well-organized book of readings.

Reber, A. S., & Scarborough, D. L. (Eds.). *Toward a psychology of reading.* Hillsdale, N.J.: Erlbaum, 1977.

This book of readings provides in-depth materials for further exploration of the psychology of reading.

IMPORTANT EVENTS IN READING AND READING DISABILITIES

Instruction in reading dates to the invention of writing. In the United States, it dates to the founding of the colonies and the publication of the old *New England Primer.* Rather than attempt to provide a history of instruction in reading (which requires a major text of its own) we begin with the involvement of psychologists in reading research and trace what we have identified as significant developments in the psychology of reading.

Date	*Person(s)*	*Work*	*Impact*
1880	Hall	Saturday morning lectures	G. S. Hall's Saturday morning lectures on education mark the first discussion by a psychologist of problems associated with reading.
1890	James	*Principles of psychology*	William James, who so profoundly affected all of American psychology, was the first psychologist to describe reading as a dynamic, interactive cognitive process.
1896	Morgan	First formal report of a reading disability	W. Pringle Morgan was the first person to report a case of reading disability (he called it congenital word blindness), a boy of apparently normal intelligence who could not learn to read.
1898	Dewey	New York Teachers' Monographs, November 1898	John Dewey's monograph was a rambling discussion that included several important statements about reading. Perhaps most important were his thoughts about when students were ready to learn to read and why teachers should be sensitive to individual differences in reading readiness.
1908	Huey	*The psychology and pedagogy of reading*	Edmund Burke Huey published the first psychology text on reading. Huey's influence on the psychology of reading was dramatic, retaining an impact well into the 1930s. This book was republished in the late 1960s.

Date	*Person(s)*	*Work*	*Impact*
1915	Gray	*The Gray Standardized Oral Reading Paragraphs*	William S. Gray developed the first standardized test of reading.
1917	Thorndike	"Reading as reasoning: A study of mistakes in paragraph reading"	E. L. Thorndike was one of the first researchers to attempt to study the relationship between reading and mental processes. His emphasis on learning about reading from the mistakes children make has remained an important component of research on reading.
1922	Gates	*Psychology of reading and spelling with special reference to disability*	Arthur I. Gates's text, a major influence on the psychology of reading, was influential in the movement away from a phonics-only approach to the teaching of reading. This book, as well as the volume by William S. Gray, was the first to extensively examine reading disabilities.
1922	Gray	"Remedial cases in reading: Their diagnosis and treatment"	William S. Gray's report was the first comprehensive study of reading devoted solely to the treatment of reading disabilities.
1925	National Committee on Reading	First popularization of the term *reading readiness*	The twenty-fourth yearbook on the Study of Education was devoted to an analysis of the state of the art in reading instruction. This report was the first to strongly support the concept of reading readiness.
1931	Morphett & Washburne	"When should children begin to read?"	Mable Morphett and C. Washburne determined that children should begin to read when they attain the mental age of six years and six months. Despite several methodological errors in their study, it has been accepted in large part as the evidence for beginning reading instruction at age six.

Date	*Person(s)*	*Work*	*Impact*
1942	Bloomfield	"Linguistics and reading"	Leonard Bloomfield's paper (and earlier work published in 1933) emphasized the need to incorporate linguistics into the teaching of beginning reading. Bloomfield was the forerunner of contemporary linguistic approaches to the teaching of reading (Chall, 1965).
1947	International Council for the Improvement of Reading Instruction	*The Reading Teacher*	*The Reading Teacher* was the first journal established solely for the dissemination of research and methods in the teaching of reading.
1955	Many workers	International Reading Association	The International Reading Association was formed in 1955 when the National Association for Remedial Teaching and the International Council for the Improvement of Reading Instruction merged. The IRA is now the largest organization devoted to the study of reading. It publishes *The Reading Teacher,* the *Journal of Reading,* and *Reading Research Quarterly.*
1955	Flesch	*Why Johnny can't read and what you can do about it*	Rudolph Flesch's book was the most controversial book on reading ever published (Chall, 1967). He ridiculed contemporary practices and offered phonics as the only way to teach reading. This book led to the reemphasis of phonics and spawned a great deal of research comparing various methods of teaching reading.
1960	Ausubel	"The use of advanced organizers in the learning and retention of meaningful verbal material"	David Ausubel's paper provided the foundation for much research over the last twenty years on aids to reading comprehension. His concept of advance organizers received wide acceptance but is still hotly debated in the research literature.

Date(s)	*Person(s)*	*Work*	*Impact*
1965	Rothkopf	"Some theoretical and experimental approaches to problems in written instruction"	E. Z. Rothkopf's development of the concept of mathemagenic behavior (behaviors that result in learning) gave rise to research on the effects of questions and instructional objectives inserted in reading material.
1967	Chall	*Learning to read: The great debate*	Jeanne Chall's classic book represented a significant effort to summarize the field of reading and to evaluate the research on teaching of reading.
1969	National Reading Conference	*Journal of Reading Behavior*	By 1969, there were many journals devoted to one aspect or another of reading. The *Journal of Reading Behavior* is one of the newer publications, heavily emphasizing a psychological approach to research in reading.
1975	Meyer	*The organization of prose and its effects on research*	Bonnie Meyer's book represented the approaches cognitive psychologists were to take in the study of reading in the late 1970s and early 1980s. She emphasized the need to analyze how reading materials were structured and how the reader-material interaction results in learning.
1981	Brown, Campione, & Day	*"Learning to learn: On training students to learn from texts"*	Ann Brown's work is representative of the renewed emphasis on the applied aspects of cognitive research. Her training program is theoretically based and has demonstrated effective ways of enhancing reading comprehension.
1981	Just	"What your mind does while your eyes are reading: Old myths and new facts"	Marcel Just's paper describes his attempts to tie together data from eye-movement studies as well as information-processing approaches to the study of cognition. His work represents a holistic approach to the development of theories of reading.

(continued from page iv)

Page 9: Elizabeth Crews/Stock, Boston.
Page 18: B. A. King.
Page 32, left: The Bettman Archive, Inc.
Page 32, middle: Brown Brothers.
Page 32, right: Historical Pictures Service, Inc., Chicago.
Page 111: Peter Vandermark.
Page 133: © 1980 Dwight Cendrowski from Black Star.
Page 139: © 1980 Yves de Braine from Black Star.
Page 167: Owen Franken/Stock, Boston.
Page 169: Courtesy of Paul Torrance.
Page 174: PICASSO, Pablo. *Baboon and Young.* 1951. Bronze (cast 1955), after found objects, 21″ high, base 13¼″ × 6 ⅞″. Collection, The Museum of Modern Art, New York. Mrs. Simon Guggenheim Fund.
Page 188: Owen Franken/Stock, Boston.
Page 199: Peter Vandermark.
Page 214: Peter Vandermark.
Page 241: Peter Vandermark.
Page 257: Peter Vandermark.
Page 260: B.A. King.
Page 290: Peter Vandermark.
Page 316: Elizabeth Hamlin/Stock, Boston.
Page 336: Bohdan Hrynewych.
Page 374: B.A. King.
Page 467: Arthur Grace/Stock, Boston.
Page 473: Bohdan Hrynewych/Stock, Boston.
Page 492: George Bellerose/Stock, Boston.
Page 504: Freda Leinwand/Monkmeyer Press Photo Service.
Page 519: Jean-Claude LeJeune/Stock, Boston.
Page 522: George Bellerose/Stock, Boston.
Page 524: Ralph Granger/University of Maine at Farmington, from *Teaching Exceptional Students in the Regular Classroom,* © 1982 by Ramond M. Glass, Jeanne Christiansen, and James L. Christiansen (Boston: Little, Brown and Company, 1982).
Page 527: Elizabeth Crews/Stock, Boston.
Page 529: Meri Houtchens-Kitchens/THE PICTURE CUBE.

GLOSSARY

Accommodation: Accommodation, according to Piaget, is the process of modifying existing cognitive structures so that new information can be assimilated. (*See* Assimilation.)

Achievement motivation: Achievement motivation refers to acquired needs to perform successfully.

Achievement test: An achievement test is designed to measure the knowledge and abilities of students in subject matter areas.

Advance organizer: An advancc organizer is an overview of major ideas in reading materials designed to facilitate comprehension. Students read it prior to reading the materials.

Affective objective: An affective objective is an instructional objective that specifies learning outcomes related to students' values, preferences, and feelings.

Alphabetic writing: Alphabetic writing includes symbols for both consonant and vowel sounds. English and other Western languages use alphabetic writing.

Anecdotal record: An anecdotal record is a written report of specific incidents occurring in the classroom or elsewhere.

Applied research: Applied research in educational psychology is conducted to find solutions to actual educational problems.

Apply goal: The term apply goal refers to the final goal to be reached in a means-end analysis of problem solving.

Aptitude test: An aptitude test is used to predict future cognitive or psychomotor performance.

Assimilation: Assimilation, in Piaget's theory, is the process of relating new information to already existing cognitive structures.

Attention: Attention refers to the focus of cognitive functions on particular aspects of tasks engaged in by an individual.

Attribute: *See* Concept attribute.

Attribution theory: Attribution theory seeks to explain behavior in terms of the kinds of interpretations people make about their experiences.

Basic research: Basic research in educational psychology is conducted to answer fundamental questions about the nature of learning or teaching without concern for any direct applications of the results.

Behavioral assessment: Behavioral assessment is a method of judging educational processes and outcomes by systematically recording student behaviors.

Behavioral psychology: Behavioral psychology is the study of the behavior of organisms. It focuses on observable events and has as its goal the prediction and control of behavior.

Being needs: In Maslow's hierarchy, being needs are based on the basic human desires for self-actualization, knowledge, and aesthetics.

Biculturalism: Biculturalism refers to a situation in which individuals experience and assimilate the language and customs of two cultures. One possible goal of bilingual education is that students become bicultural.
Bilingualism: Bilingualism is, strictly speaking, the ability to function fluently and interchangeably in two languages. Bilingualism may exist in degrees, however, ranging from complete competence in two languages to partial competence in either or both.

Central tendency: Central tendency refers to an average score or scores that best represent the performance of a group of students who have taken a test. The mean, median, and mode are measures of central tendency.
Checklist: A checklist is a listing of steps, actions, or activities that an observer can mark as present or absent during an observation of student performance.
Classical conditioning: Classical conditioning is a form of learning in which a neutral stimulus, after being paired with an eliciting (unconditioned) stimulus, acquires the ability to bring forth the original reflex.
Cognitive objective: A cognitive objective is an instructional objective that specifies cognitive learning outcomes, such as concept learning or problem solving.
Cognitive processes: The general term cognitive processes refers to all the functions of the mind, including attention, memory, concept learning, problem solving, and creative thinking.
Cognitive psychology: The systematic study of cognitive processes is referred to as cognitive psychology.
Cognitive style: Cognitive style refers to variations in how students typically approach, process, and remember information.
Completion question: A completion question, one type of objective test item, requires students to supply a word or phrase to complete an incomplete sentence or to answer a question.
Comprehension: Comprehension is the second stage of reading, in which the reader gains an overall understanding of the content.
Concept: A concept is a class of stimuli (information) that people group together on the basis of perceived commonalities.
Concept attribute: A concept attribute is a similarity occurring across examples of a concept. Some attributes (defining attributes) are essential to defining the concept while others (characteristic attributes) may pertain to only some examples.
Concrete operations: During the concrete operations stage (approximately seven to eleven years of age) of Piaget's stages of cognitive development, children develop the ability to apply logical thought to concrete problems.
Conditioned response: In classical conditioning, a response that is elicited by a formerly neutral stimulus (conditioned stimulus) is called a conditioned response.
Conditioned stimulus: A conditioned stimulus is a formerly neutral stimulus that, through being paired with an eliciting (unconditioned) stimulus, comes to be able to elicit a conditioned response.

Conjunctive concept: A conjunctive concept is defined by common (shared) attributes. "Shoe" is a conjunctive concept because all shoes have in common the attributes of a sole and some means of being attached to the foot.
Conservation: Conservation, in Piaget's theory, means understanding that such features of objects as number, mass, and area are not changed by superficial transformations of the objects or set of objects.
Construct validity: Construct validity refers to how well a test or other instrument measures a psychological construct, which is an inferred state within a person such as creativity, intelligence, or personality that cannot be directly observed but must be inferred from visible evidence.
Content validity: Content validity is the extent to which a test fairly samples and represents the content areas to be measured.
Contingency contract: *See* Individual contract.
Convergent thinking: Convergent thinking is the generation of ideas from given information with the emphasis on problem solutions that are conventionally acceptable.
Correlation coefficient: The correlation coefficient is a numerical index of the degree of relationship between two sets of measures. The values of the correlation coefficient can range from $+1.00$ to -1.00.
Creative behavior: A creative behavior is one that is both novel and of value.
Criterion-referenced measure: A criterion-referenced measure (test) compares an individual's performance to a standard of performance, not to the performance of other persons.

Deafness: Deafness is the absence of functional hearing.
Decay theory: Decay theory states that memories fade with the passage of time.
Decentration: In Piagetian theory, decentration occurs when children no longer focus on a single attribute of objects but begin to consider more than one feature at a time.
Decoding: Decoding is the initial stage of reading, in which the reader obtains the meaning of individual words.
Deficiency needs: In Maslow's hierarchy, deficiency needs are needs that humans are motivated to fulfill as a result of their lacking them (physiological needs, safety needs, needs for love, needs for esteem).
Diagnostic evaluation: Diagnostic evaluation is conducted to determine the reasons why a student is having problems in learning.
Discriminative stimulus: A discriminative stimulus is a cue for operant behavior. (*See* S^D and $S^{\triangle}$.)
Disjunctive concept: A disjunctive concept is defined by attributes of either one type or another type. An object is a member of a particular concept category if it possesses either one set of attributes *or* a second set of attributes.
Divergent thinking: Divergent thinking is the generation of ideas from given information with the emphasis on variety and quantity of problem solutions.

Educational psychology: Educational psychology is the branch of psychology devoted to the study of how humans learn and how to help them learn.

Egocentrism: In Piaget's theory, egocentrism refers to the self-centered perspective of preoperational children, who cannot assume the viewpoints of others.
Eliciting stimuli: Eliciting or unconditioned stimuli cause involuntary responses. A bright light shining in the eye is an eliciting stimulus for contraction of the pupil.
Encoding: Encoding refers to the taking in of new information and the representation of it symbolically in thought.
Episodic memory: Episodic memory is a memory system that holds information about people's personal experiences.
Equilibration: Piaget referred to equilibration as the process that motivates humans to attempt to balance accommodation and assimilation.
Essay question: An essay question asks people to construct an answer in their own words in either written or oral form.
Evaluation: The process of using measurements to make a judgment of the value of something is commonly referred to as evaluation.
Extinction: In operant conditioning, extinction is a process in which a response occurs less and less frequently as a function of nonreinforcement. In classical conditioning, extinction of a conditioned response occurs when the conditioned stimulus is no longer paired with the eliciting (unconditioned) stimulus.

Fixation: In reading, fixation refers to the brief period of time in which the eyes come to rest on the text. (*See* Saccades.)
Flexibility: In measures of creativity, flexibility refers to the number of *different* kinds of ideas a persons thinks of when faced with a problem.
Fluency: In measures of creativity, fluency refers to the number of ideas a person develops in response to a problem.
Formal operations: Formal operations is the last of the stages of cognitive development described by Piaget (eleven years through adulthood). During this stage many children are able to apply logic to a host of problems, both concrete and abstract. Some individuals apparently never attain formal operations.
Formative evaluation: Formative evaluation takes place during instruction and is designed to help teachers adjust their instruction to better help students meet their objectives.
Frequency distribution: A frequency distribution is a tally of how many students obtain each score on a test or other measure.
Functionalism: Functionalism was the first truly American school of thought in psychology. Its objectives were to determine how mental activity occurs, what it accomplishes, and why it happens.

Generalization: Generalization is the making of the same response to two or more differing stimuli.
Gestalt psychology: Gestalt psychology, a German school of thought, rejected atomism and reductionism and argued that humans perceive experiences as an organized field of events that interact and mutually affect one another. Gestalt psychology was the forerunner of much of contemporary cognitive psychology.

Gifted student: A gifted student is one who possesses superior intellectual or other abilities. The specific definitions vary from state to state but usually consist of criteria based on intelligence-test results, achievement test results, or creativity test results.
Goal state: In a problem representation, the goal state refers to the situation a person wants to be in when the problem is solved.
Good Behavior Game: The Good Behavior Game is a variant of the token economy in which group competition is coupled with token reinforcement procedures.
Group contract: A group contract is an agreement negotiated between a teacher and a group of students that specifies both student and teacher behavior.

Hearing impaired: Hearing-impaired people have partial hearing. (*See* Deafness.)
Heuristic searches: In problem solving, a heuristic search is one that is guided by some plan or body of knowledge.
Home-based contingencies: Home-based contingencies are behavior management programs in which the backup reinforcers are administered at home by the parents.
Hyperactivity: Hyperactivity (hyperkinesis) is a learning disorder characterized by excessive activity, inattentiveness, and impulsiveness.

Ill-defined problem: An ill-defined problem requires that the problem solver furnish the information necessary to solve the problem. Typically, there is not necessarily one right answer for ill-defined problems.
Imitation: Imitation refers to the copying of the actions of one individual by another. (*See* Modeling.)
Individual contract: An individual contract is an agreement negotiated between one student and a teacher. The student generally agrees to change a behavior in return for reinforcement.
Information-processing model: A model of human cognition based on computers is referred to as an information-processing model.
Initial state: In a problem representation, the initial state refers to conditions existing at the onset of a problem.
Instructional objectives: An instructional objective is an explicit statement of what students will be able to do as a result of instruction.
Intelligence quotient: The intelligence quotient (IQ) was originally defined as the ratio of mental age to chronological age, multiplied by 100. Newer tests of intelligence use an IQ measure derived from standard scores. (*See* Standard scores.)
Intelligence test: An intelligence test is designed to measure students' general mental abilities. It provides an estimate of how much a person has profited from past experience and how well he or she adapts to new situations.
Interest inventory: An interest inventory assesses how people feel about various kinds of activities and how closely their interests parallel those of individuals already holding certain jobs.

Interference: *See* Proactive interference and Retroactive interference.
Interpretive exercise: An interpretive exercise consists of a descriptive statement or paragraph, pictorial materials, or both, followed by a series of multiple-choice questions that require the student to interpret the material.
Introspection: Introspection was the major data-gathering method used by the structuralists. Introspection involves having experimental subjects report their mental events.
Item analysis: Item analysis is a set of techniques for judging the worth of questions. It provides two kinds of information: item difficulty and item discrimination (whether "good" students got the item right more often than "poor" students).

Learning disability: Students with learning disabilities have normal or near-normal intelligence but have severe difficulties in understanding or using spoken or written language.
Least restrictive environment: Least restrictive environment refers to an important part of the Education for All Handicapped Children Act (P.L. 94-142). The least restrictive environment for a special-needs student is the program or setting that provides the most normal but also the most effective environment for learning.
Levels-of-processing: Levels-of-processing is a model for memory research developed by Fergus Craik and his associates that suggests that what a person remembers about an event is determined by the depth of the analysis of the material.
Locus of control: Locus of control, a term coined by Julian Rotter, refers to whether people feel the control of their successes and failures lies internally or externally to themselves.
Logography: A logography is a written language in which each word or concept is represented by a symbol for that word (a logogram).
Long-term memory: The permanent repository of information acquired from the world around us is referred to as long-term memory.

Mainstreaming: Mainstreaming refers to the education of handicapped students in the regular classroom for all or parts of the school day.
Matching questions: A matching question is a form of objective question in which students match items from one list to corresponding items in another list.
Mean: The mean is the arithmetic average of a set of scores.
Meaningful learning: Learning is meaningful when it can be related to what is already known. Meaningful learning requires comprehension and understanding of the material to be learned.
Means-end analysis: A means-end analysis is a method of problem solving in which a problem is broken down into its component parts or subproblems and then solved using different means to resolve each subproblem.
Measurement error: Measurement error is the part of a person's score unrelated to the quality that was being measured. Measurement error is present in all test scores and ratings of performance.

Median: The median of a set of scores is that point above which half the scores fall and below which half the scores fall, that is, the midpoint of all scores.
Mediating responses: In Bandura's social learning theory, mediating responses are symbolic events (thoughts) that people envision when they encounter stimuli.
Mental age: Mental age refers to the average raw score of children in the norm group of a specific age on measures of intelligence. If the median number of items correct for children in the norm group who were exactly ten years old was fifty items, then children later taking the test who get fifty items right would receive a mental-age score of 10.0.
Mentally retarded students: All mentally retarded students have below-average mental functioning and ordinarily some delay in social or other areas of development.
Mnemonic: A mnemonic is a familiar word or image that is paired with new information to make the new information more meaningful.
Mode: Mode refers to the most frequently occurring score on a test.
Modeling: Modeling is a demonstration of a behavior to be imitated by others.
Multiple-choice question: A multiple-choice question is a form of objective question that requires students to choose a correct answer from a set of alternative responses.

Nature/nurture question: The nature/nurture question concerns the relative influence of heredity (nature) and the environment (nurture) on individual abilities.
Negative reinforcer: A negative reinforcer is a form of reinforcer that precedes the behaviors it strengthens. Negative reinforcers strengthen escape or avoidance behavior.
Network model: A network model is a model of semantic memory that pictures memories as hierarchical. Memories in such a hierarchy are thought to be connected to one another, with specific bits of knowledge placed at separate locations.
Neutral stimulus: A neutral stimulus is perceived by learners but has little or no effect on behavior.
Normal curve: In a normal curve (or normal distribution), the mean, the median, and the mode are identical, and they all fall at the same place on the curve, the center. The curve is symmetrical around this point with the number of scores decreasing away from the midpoint.
Norm-referenced measure: A norm-referenced measure is constructed to compare one person's performance with the performance of others.

Objective question: An objective question requires students to make very brief responses that are compared to predetermined answers.
Operant conditioning: Operant or instrumental conditioning refers to learning that is strengthened or modified by the consequences it produces.
Operation: An operation is a scheme whose major characteristic is that it can be reversed.

Operator: In a problem of representation, an operator is an action a person may take to reach the goal state.
Originality: In measures of creativity, originality refers to the development of rare or uncommon ideas.

Pattern matching: In problem solving, pattern matching is a form of heuristic search in which the problem solver attempts to recall previous actions that solved similar problems.
Percentile rank: A percentile rank (percentile) describes a particular student's test performance by giving the proportion of students in the norm group who obtained scores at or lower than the student's score.
Perception: In cognitive psychology, perception is the process of determining the meaning of what is sensed.
Phonics: Phonics refers to the decoding of sounds from letters and words and is the basis for a common approach to the teaching of reading.
Phonographic language: A phonographic language is a form of written language in which the symbols represent the sounds of the spoken language.
Placement evaluation: Placement evaluation is made prior to the start of instruction to match students with instruction based on their entry characteristics.
Positive reinforcer: A positive reinforcer is a reinforcing stimulus that occurs subsequent to behavior and strengthens the behavior that it follows. Positive reinforcers play a major role in operant conditioning.
Predictive validity: The degree to which a measure can accurately predict future performance is called predictive validity.
Premack Principle: The Premack Principle states that for every pair of responses or activities in which an individual engages, the more probable one will reinforce the less probable one.
Preoperational stage: During the preoperational stage of cognitive development, as posited by Piaget, children rapidly develop language and conceptual thought. The stage is thought to begin at about age two and continue until approximately age seven.
Primary reinforcer: A primary reinforcer is a stimulus that strengthens behaviors because of our biological nature. Food and water are primary reinforcers.
Principle: A principle is a statement or rule that describes the relationship between two or more concepts.
Proactive interference: Proactive interference occurs when a learner is given a first set of information to learn followed by a second set of information to learn. Then, when the learner is tested on the second set of information, the first set inhibits the recall of the second set of information.
Problem: A problem exists when a person is in one situation, wants to be in another, but doesn't know how to get there.
Problem representation: Problem representation refers to how people understand problems. A complete problem representation involves understanding of the initial state, the goal state, the operators, and restrictions on the operators.
Problem space: The problem space is the total number of actions a problem solver considers possible in solving a problem.

Proximity search: In problem solving, proximity searches are heuristics that employ environmental feedback to determine whether the problem solver is moving closer to or further from the goal.
Psychometry: Psychometry is the measurement of psychological variables.
Psychomotor objectives: A psychomotor objective is an instructional objective that specifies learning outcomes related primarily to skilled physical movements.
Punishing stimulus: A stimulus that occurs subsequent to behaviors and decreases the occurrence of the behaviors it follows is referred to as a punishing stimulus or, simply, as a punisher.

Random search: In problem solving, a random search is one that is not guided by a plan or a body of knowledge.
Rating scale: A rating scale usually indicates a trait or characteristic to be judged and a scale on which the rating can be made.
Raw score: A raw score is usually the number of items a student answers correctly on a test prior to any type of transformation of the score. (*See* Standard scores.)
Reciprocal determinism: Bandura's concept of reciprocal determinism holds that the social behavior of individuals occurs because of prior interactions with other people and with the immediate environment.
Reduction goal: In problem solving, reduction goals are subgoals met on the way to reaching the final goal.
Reinforcement potency: The effectiveness or potency of reinforcers is determined by their ability to strengthen behaviors. The greater the probability that a reinforcer will strengthen a behavior, the more potent it is said to be.
Reinforcing stimulus: A reinforcing stimulus (reinforcer) is a stimulus that, when applied to a behavior, strengthens it.
Relational concept: A relational concept is defined by a relationship between two or more of the concept's attributes (for example, north, above).
Reliability: A measure is reliable (has reliability) if it is a consistent and accurate measure.
Respondent conditioning: *See* Classical conditioning.
Response: A response is a reaction by an organism to a stimulus.
Retrieval: Retrieval refers to the recall or recognition of information stored in memory.
Retroactive interference: Retroactive interference occurs when a person learns one set of information, followed by a second set of information, and the second set then inhibits recall of the first set of information.
Rote learning: Rote learning is learning that has little or no meaning to the learner. In rote learning, the person recalls the information exactly as he or she learned it.

S^D: An S^D is a discriminative stimulus that signals that certain behaviors will be reinforced in its presence. For example, a green traffic light is an S^D for accelerating a car.
$S^\triangle$: An $S^\triangle$ (Ess-Delta) is a discriminative stimulus that signals that certain

behaviors will not be reinforced in its presence. For instance, a red traffic light is an $S^{\triangle}$ for accelerating your car.

Saccade: A saccade is the jump the eyes make from one fixation to the next during reading. (*See* Fixations.)

Satiation: The fact that reinforcers often lose their potency as they are acquired in large amounts or in great numbers is referred to as satiation.

Schedule of reinforcement: The relationship of the number of reinforcers to the number of behaviors necessary to acquire the reinforcers is referred to as a schedule of reinforcement. Common schedules include continuous, fixed-interval, variable-interval, fixed-ratio, and variable-ratio reinforcement.

Schema: A schema, in Piaget's terms, is a cognitive structure similar to a concept, by which people organize events and objects on the basis of common characteristics.

Scheme: In Piaget's terms, a scheme is a cognitive structure by which people represent their operative knowledge.

Scholastic aptitude test: Scholastic aptitude test usually refers to group tests of general mental ability. They are used often to predict future academic performance.

Secondary reinforcer: A secondary reinforcer is a formerly neutral stimulus that has acquired some of the reinforcing value of primary reinforcers by being paired with them or other secondary reinforcers.

Self-concept: The self-concept refers to a person's view of himself or herself. People with a positive self-concept consider themselves worthwhile; people with a negative self-concept generally devalue their own worth.

Self-report: A self-report is a record of information students have furnished by talking or writing about themselves.

Semantic memory: Semantic memory refers to a memory system that stores memory for knowledge. The central feature of most models of semantic memory is the concept.

Sense receptors: The organs that allow us to contact the world and the information in it are referred to as sense receptors (eyes, ears, nose, mouth, and so on).

Sensing: In cognitive psychology, sensing refers to an awareness of an element of the environment prior to perception.

Sensorimotor stage: During the sensorimotor stage of cognitive development (birth to approximately two years of age), children's cognitive processes are closely linked to motor activity. Sensorimotor children do not yet think abstractly, although cognitive development can be observed as they display awareness of themselves and their surroundings.

Sensory registers: Sensory registers are holding systems that briefly maintain stimuli so they can be analyzed. It is thought that each of the senses has its own sensory register.

Set: Set refers to a person's tendency to approach different problems in the same way.

Set-theoretic model: A set-theoretic model of semantic memory suggests that memory is stored as sets of elements such that each set includes all instances of that set as well as its attributes.

Shaping: Shaping is a technique for modifying a response through reinforcement of successive approximations of that response.

Short-term memory: Short-term memory is the part of the working memory in which incoming information is briefly stored.

Social behavior: Social behavior includes all of the many kinds of interactions among people within a particular environment or geographic location.

Sociometric assessment: Sociometric assessment refers to the evaluation of the level of social acceptance of students and the social structures of groups.

Solution path: In problem solving, a solution path refers to a way of employing operators that will take the problem solver from the initial state to the goal state.

Spontaneous recovery: Spontaneous recovery is the term used to denote the recurrence of an apparently extinguished response.

Standard deviation: The standard deviation is an index of how spread out a set of test scores is from the mean of those scores.

Standard error of measurement: The standard error of measurement can be thought of as the standard deviation of a set of an individual's own scores. It is usually determined on the basis of a test's reliability and standard deviation and indicates the likelihood that an individual's obtained score is a good estimate of his or her true score.

Standard score: A standard score is a test score based on standard deviations and the assumption that the distribution of scores is normal.

Standardized test: A standardized test is identified by three criteria: (1) it has been carefully prepared, tried out, analyzed, and reviewed; (2) the instructions and conditions for administering and scoring it are uniform; and (3) the results of the test may be interpreted by comparing them to tables of norms.

Standardization sample: The standardization sample (norm group) is a carefully selected sample of persons representative of the individuals for whom a standardized test is targeted. Their scores, called norms, serve as the frame of reference for evaluating the scores of future takers of the test.

Stimulus: A stimulus is a perceivable unit of the environment that may affect behavior.

Storage: In models of memory, storage refers to the holding of memories across time.

Structuralism: Structuralism was the first school of thought in psychology. Founded by Wilhelm Wundt, it sought to identify basic cognitive processes, the ways in which the elements of thought combined, and the relationship of cognitive to physiological processes.

Summative evaluation: Summative evaluation occurs at the end of instruction and is designed to determine the extent to which the goals of instruction have been met.

Superstitious behavior: Superstitious behavior (superstition) is seen when reinforcement occurs on an accidental basis but a person nonetheless makes a connection between an action not associated with reinforcement and the occurrence of the reinforcement. Behavior is strengthened accidentally.

Syllabary: A syllabary is a form of written language in which there are written symbols for consonants and consonant-vowel combinations.

T score: A T score is a standard score with a mean of 50 and a standard deviation of 10.
Table of specifications: A table of specifications is a blueprint for a test that relates the course objectives to the construction of the test.
Task analysis: A task analysis is the breaking down of an objective into a hierarchy of prerequisite knowledge and skills.
Task description: A task description is a step-by-step description of the sequence of things to be done in a task.
Test: A test is a sample of questions that require students to select or supply written or oral responses.
Test-retest reliability: Test-retest reliability measures the stability of scores from one administration of a test to a second administration of the same test.
Time-out: Time-out is the brief removal of a child from a reinforcing setting to one that is not reinforcing.
Token economy: A token economy is a systematic method of providing students with immediate reinforcement for behavior using some form of tokens (checks, points, and the like).
True-false question: A true-false question is a form of objective question that requires students to judge statements as either correct or incorrect.

Unconditioned response: In classical conditioning, an unconditioned response is an unlearned, involuntary reaction to an eliciting (unconditioned) stimulus. The reflex linking the unconditioned stimulus and the unconditioned response is unlearned.
Unconditioned stimulus: An unconditioned or eliciting stimulus brings forth an unlearned, involuntary response. Unconditioned stimuli do not require learning to elicit a response (a puff of air on the eye brings forth a blink).

Validity: A measurement is said to possess validity (be valid) if it measures what it is supposed to measure.
Variability: Variability refers to the extent to which scores on a test are spread out around the measure of central tendency.
Vicarious reinforcement: The reinforcing effect of a person's observing models who receive reinforcement is termed vicarious reinforcement.
Visually impaired: Students are classified as visually impaired if special adaptations of educational programs and materials are required because of their vision. Blind people have no functional vision.

Well-defined problem: A well-defined problem presents a problem situation that contains all the necessary information for a solution. Usually there is only one (or a few) right answers to a well-defined problem.
Working memory: Working memory is the component of cognitive models in which thinking occurs. It is the executive component of models of cognition.

z-score: A z-score is a standard score that gives a person's performance on a test in standard deviation units above or below the mean. z-scores have a mean of 0 and a standard deviation of 1.

REFERENCES

Aiken, L. R. *Psychological testing and assessment* (3rd ed.). Boston: Allyn & Bacon, 1979.

Albert, R. S. *Genius, eminence, and creative behavior.* Fort Lee, N.J.: Behavioral Science Tape Library, 1973.

Albert, R. S. Toward a behavioral definition of genius. In L. Willerman & R. G. Turner (Eds.), *Readings about individual and group differences.* San Francisco: Freeman, 1979.

Algozzine, B., Mercer, C. D., & Countermine, T. The effects of labels and behavior on teacher expectations. *Exceptional Children,* 1977, *44,* 121–132.

Allen, D. I. Some effects of advance organizers and level of questions on the learning and retention of written social studies material. *Journal of Educational Psychology,* 1970, *61,* 333–339.

Allport, F. H. *Social psychology.* Cambridge, Mass.: Riverside Press, 1924.

Allport, G. W. *Personality: A psychological interpretation.* New York: Holt, Rinehart, & Winston, 1937.

Alpert, A. *The solving of problem situations by preschool children.* New York: Columbia University Press, 1928.

Anderson, J. R. *Cognitive psychology and its implications.* San Francisco: Freeman, 1980.

Anderson, J. R., & Bower, G. H. *Human associative memory.* Washington, D.C.: Winston, 1973.

Anderson, J. R., Kline, P. J., & Lewis, C. H. A production system model of language processing. In M. A. Just & P. A. Carpenter (Eds.), *Cognitive processes in comprehension.* Hillsdale, N.J.: Erlbaum, 1977.

Anderson, J. R., & Ross, B. H. Evidence against a semantic-episodic distinction. *Journal of Experimental Psychology: Human Learning and Memory,* 1980, *6,* 441–465.

Anderson, R. C. How to construct achievement tests to assess comprehension. *Review of Educational Research,* 1972, *42,* 145–170.

Anderson, R. C., Spiro, R. J., & Anderson, M. C. Schemata as scaffolding for the representation of information in connected discourse. *American Educational Research Journal,* 1978, *15,* 433–439.

Anderson, T., & Boyer, M. *Bilingual schooling in the United States* (Vols. 1 & 2). Washington, D.C.: U.S. Government Printing Office, 1970.

Anderson, T. N. Active response modes: Comprehension "aids" in need of a theory. *Journal of Reading Behavior,* 1981.

Anderson, T. W., & Sclove, S. L. *Introductory statistical analysis.* Boston: Houghton Mifflin, 1980.

Andre, T. Does answering higher-level questions while reading facilitate productive learning? *Review of Educational Research,* 1979, *49,* 280–318.

Aronson, E., Blaney, N., Sikes, J., & Snapp, M. *The jigsaw classroom.* Beverly Hills, Calif.: Sage Press, 1978.

Atkinson, J. W. Some general implications of conceptual developments in the study of achievement-oriented behavior. In M. R. Jones (Ed.), *Human motivation: A symposium.* Lincoln: University of Nebraska Press, 1965.

Atkinson, J. W. Mainsprings of achievement oriented activity. In J. D. Krumboltz (Ed.), *Learning and the Educational Process.* Chicago: Rand McNally, 1966.

Atkinson, J. W. *Implications of curvilinearity in the relationship of efficiency of performance to strength of motivation for studies of individual differences in achievement-related motives.* Paper presented at the meeting of the National Academy of Sciences, University of Michigan, October 24, 1967.

Atkinson, J. W., & Raynor, J. O. (Eds.). *Motivation and achievement.* Washington, D.C.: Winston, 1974.

Atkinson, R. C., & Shiffrin, R. M. Human memory: A proposed system and its control processes. In K. W. Spence & J. T. Spence (Eds.), *The psychology of learning and motivation: Advances in research and theory* (Vol. 2). New York: Academic Press, 1968.

Ausubel, D. P. The use of advance organizers in the learning and retention of meaningful verbal material. *Journal of Educational Psychology,* 1960, *51,* 267–272.

Ausubel, D. P. In defense of verbal learning. *Education Theory,* 1961, *11,* 15–25.

Ausubel, D. P. A subsumption theory of meaningful verbal learning and retention. *Journal of General Psychology,* 1962, *66,* 213–224.

Ausubel, D. P. *The psychology of meaningful verbal material.* New York: Grune & Stratton, 1963.

Ausubel, D. P. Some psychological aspects of the structure of knowledge. In S. Elam (Ed.), *Education and the structure of knowledge.* Skokie, Ill.: Rand McNally, 1964.

Ausubel, D. P. Early versus delayed review of meaningful learning. *Psychology in Schools,* 1966, *3,* 195–198.

Ausubel, D. P. Schemata, cognitive structure, and advance organizers: A reply to Anderson, Spiro, and Anderson. *American Educational Research Journal,* 1980, *17,* 400–404.

Ausubel, D. P., & Fitzgerald, D. The role of discriminability in meaningful verbal learning and retention. *Journal of Educational Psychology,* 1961, *52,* 266–274.

Ausubel, D. P., & Fitzgerald, D. Organizer, general background, and antecedent learning variables in sequential verbal learning. *Journal of Educational Psychology,* 1962, *53,* 243–249.

Ausubel, D. P., Novak, J. D., & Hanesian, H. *Educational psychology: A cognitive view.* New York: Holt, Rinehart, & Winston, 1978.

Ausubel, D. P., & Youssef, M. Role of discriminability in meaningful parallel learning. *Journal of Educational Psychology,* 1963, *54,* 331–336.

Ayers, L. P. History and present status of educational measurements. In *Seventeenth yearbook of the National Society for the Study of Education* (Part II). Bloomington, Ill.: Public School Publishing Company, 1918.

Ayllon, T., & Azrin, N. H. *The token economy: A motivation system for therapy and rehabilitation.* New York: Appleton-Century-Crofts, 1968.

Azrin, N. H., & Lindsley, O. R. The reinforcement of cooperation between children. *Journal of Abnormal Social Psychology,* 1956, *52,* 100–102.

Baer, D., Peterson, R. F., & Sherman, J. A. The development of imitation by reinforcing behavioral similarity to a model. *Journal of Experimental Analysis of Behavior,* 1967, *10,* 405–416.

Baer, D. M., & Sherman, J. A. Reinforcement control of generalized imitation in young children. *Journal of Experimental Child Psychology,* 1964, *1,* 37–49.

Bagley, W. C., Bell, J. C., Seashore, C. E., & Whipple, G. M. Editorial. *Journal of Educational Psychology,* 1910, *1,* 1–3.

Bailey, G. *Administering programs for gifted students.* Address to the Nebraska Symposium on the Education of Gifted Children, University of Nebraska, Lincoln, 1980.

Baldwin, J. *Social and ethical interpretation.* New York: Macmillan, 1913.

Bandura, A. Social learning through imitation. In M. R. Jones (Ed.), *Nebraska Symposium on Motivation: 1962.* Lincoln: University of Nebraska Press, 1962.

Bandura, A. The influence of social reinforcement on the behavior of models in shaping children's moral judgment. *Journal of Personality and Social Psychology,* 1963, *67,*274–281.

Bandura, A. Influence of models' reinforcement contingencies on the acquisition of imitation responses. *Journal of Personality and Social Psychology,* 1965, *1,* 589–595.

Bandura, A. *Principles of behavior modification.* New York: Holt, Rinehart, & Winston, 1969.

Bandura, A. *Psychological modeling: Conflicting theories.* New York: Aldine-Atherton, 1971.

Bandura, A. *Aggression: A social learning analysis.* Englewood Cliffs, N.J.: Prentice-Hall, 1973.

Bandura, A. Effecting change through participant modeling. In J. D. Krumboltz & C. E. Thoresen (Eds.), *Counseling methods.* New York: Holt, Rinehart, & Winston, 1976.

Bandura, A. Self-efficiency: Toward a unifying theory of behavior change. *Psychological Review,* 1977, *84,*191–215. (a)

Bandura, A. *Social learning theory.* Englewood Cliffs, N.J.: Prentice-Hall, 1977. (b)

Bandura, A., & Barab, P. G. Conditions governing nonreinforced imitation. *Developmental Psychology,*1971, *5,* 244–255.

Bandura, A., Grusek, J. E., & Manlove, F. L. Vicarious extinction of avoidance behaviors. *Journal of Personality and Social Psychology,* 1967, *5,* 16–23.

Barnes, B. R., & Clawson, E. V. Do advance organizers facilitate learning? Recommendations for further research based on an analysis of 32 studies. *Review of Educational Research,* 1975, *45,* 637–660.

Barnes, E. J. Cultural retardation or shortcomings of assessment techniques? In R. J. Jones & D. L. MacMillan (Eds.), *Special education in transition.* Boston: Allyn & Bacon, 1974

Barnes, J. M., & Underwood, B. J. "Fate" of first-list associations in transfer theory. *Journal of Experimental Psychology,* 1959, *58,* 97–105.

Barrish, H. H., Saunders, M., & Wolf, M. M. Good Behavior Game: Effects of individual contingencies for group consequences on disruptive behavior in a classroom. *Journal of Applied Behavior Analysis,* 1969, *2,* 119–124.

Bar-Tal, D., & Bar-Zohar, Y. The relationship between perception of locus of control and academic achievement. *Contemporary Educational Psychology,* 1977, *2,* 181-199.

Barton, E. J., & Ascione, F. R. Sharing in pre-school children: Facilitation, stimulus generalization and maintenance. *Journal of Applied Behavior Analysis,* 1979, *3,* 417–430.

Barton, E. J., & Osborne, J. G. The development of classroom sharing by a teacher using positive practice. *Behavior Modification,* 1978, *2,* 231–250. (a)

Barton, E. J., & Osborne, J. G. *The development of physical sharing by a classroom teacher through the use of positive practice.* Paper presented at the Annual Convention of Midwest Association of Behavior Analysis, Chicago, 1978. (b)

Beck, T. C. Cognitive therapy: Nature and relation to behavior therapy. *Behavior Therapy,* 1979, *1,* 184–200.

Becker, W. C., Madsen, C. A., Arnold, C. R., & Thomas, D. R. The contingent use of teacher attention and praise in reducing classroom behavior problems. *Journal of Special Education,* 1967, *1,* 287–307.

Benderly, B. L. Dialogue of the deaf. *Psychology Today,* 1980, 66–77.

Benton, A. L. Developmental dyslexia: Neurological aspects. In W. J. Friedlander (Ed.), *Advances in neurology* (Vol. 7). New York: Raven Press, 1975.

Berlyne, D. E. *Conflict, arousal, and curiosity.* New York: McGraw-Hill, 1960.

Bernard, L. L. *Instinct.* New York: Holt, Rinehart, & Winston, 1924.

Bernoulli, D. Exposition of a new theory on the measurement of risk (L. Sommer, trans.). *Econometrica,* 1954, *22,* 23–26.

Bertrand, A., & Cebula, J. P. *Tests, measurement and evaluation.* Reading, Mass.: Addison-Wesley, 1980.

Bijou, S. W. A systematic approach to an experimental analysis of young children. *Child Development,* 1955, *26,* 161–168.

Bijou, S. W., & Baer, D. M. Some methodological contributions from a functional analysis of child development. In L. P. Lipsitt & C. S. Spiker (Eds.), *Advances in child development and behavior.* New York: Academic Press, 1963.

Bilowit, D. W. Teaching children to "use" TV. *Television Quarterly,* 1979, *15*(4), 27–29.

Bindra, A. *Motivation: A systematic reinterpretation.* New York: Ronald Press, 1969.

Binet, A., & Henri, V. La psychologie individuelle. *Année Psychologie,* 1896, *2,* 411–465.

Binet, A., & Simon, T. Methodes nouvelles pour le diagnostic du niveau intellectuel des arnomaux. *Année Psychologie,* 1905, *11,* 191–244.

Binet, A., & Simon, T. La mesure du développement de l'intelligence chex les jeunes enfants. *Bulletin de la Société Libra Pour L'étude Psychologique de l'enfant,* 1911, *12,* 187–248.

Binet, A., & Simon, T. The development of intelligence in children. In L. Willerman & R. G. Turner (Eds.), *Readings about individual and group differences.* San Francisco: Freeman, 1979.

Blackman, E. A., Olson, D. H. L., Shornagel, C. Y., Halsdorf, M., & Turner, A. J. The Family Contract Game: Techniques and case study. *Journal of Consulting Psychology,* 1976, *44,* 449–455.

Blanchard, E. G. The generalization of vicarious extinction effects. *Behavior Research and Therapy,* 1970, *8,* 323–330. (a)

Blanchard, E. G. The relative contributions of modeling, informational influences and physical contact in the extinction of phobic behavior. *Journal of Abnormal Psychology,* 1970, *76,* 231–239. (b)

Bloom, B. S. *Stability and change in human characteristics.* New York: Wiley, 1964.

Bloom, B. S. *The new direction in educational research and measurement: Alterable variables.* Invited address presented to the Annual Meeting of the American Educational Research Association, Los Angeles, 1981.

Bloom, B. S., Englehart, M. D., Furst, E. J., Hill, W. H., & Krathwohl, D. R. *Taxonomy of educational objectives. Handbook I: Cognitive domain.* New York: McKay, 1956.

Bloom, B. S., Hastings, J. T., & Madeus, G. F. *Handbook on formative and summative evaluation of student learning.* New York: McGraw-Hill, 1971.

Bloomfield, L. Linguistics and reading. *Elementary English Review,* 1942, *19,* 125–130, 183–186.

Bologna, N., & Brigham, T. *Analysis of procedures designed to increase the use of newly-acquired vocabulary words in essays.* Paper presented at the Annual Convention of the Midwest Association for Behavior Analysis, Chicago, 1978.

Boltwood, C. E., & Blick, K. A. The delineation and application of three mnemonic techniques. *Psychonomic Science,* 1970, *20,* 339–341.

Boren, A. R., & Foree, S. B. Personalized instruction applied to food and nutrition in higher education. *Journal of Personalized Instruction,* 1977, *2,* 39–42.

Boring, E. *A history of experimental psychology.* New York: Appleton-Century-Crofts, 1950.

Bornstein, M. R., Bellack, A. S., & Hersen, M. Social-skills training for unassertive children: A multiple baseline analysis. *Journal of Applied Behavior Analysis,* 1977,*10,* 183–185.

Bourne, L. E., Dominowski, R. L., & Loftus, E. F. *Cognitive processes.* Englewood Cliffs, N.J., Prentice-Hall, 1979.

Bousfield, W. A. The occurrence of clustering and the recall of randomly arranged associates. *Journal of General Psychology,* 1953, *49,* 229–240.

Bower, G. H. Analysis of a mnemonic device. *American Scientist,* 1970, *58,* 496–510.

Bower, G. H., & Clark, M. C. Narrative stories as mediators for serial learning. *Psychonomic Science,* 1969, *14,* 181–182.

Boyd, W. M. Repeating questions in prose learning. *Journal of Educational Psychology,* 1973, *64,*31–38.

Brennan, T., & Glover, J. A. A re-examination of the intrinsic-extrinsic reinforcement debate. *Social Behavior and Personality,* 1980, *8,* 27–32.

Brigham, T. A., & Sherman, J. A. An experimental analysis of verbal imitation in pre-school children. *Journal of Applied Behavior Analysis.* 1968, *1,* 151–158.

Broadbent, D. E. *Perception and communication.* London: Pergamon, 1958.

Bronfenbrenner, U. *Two worlds of childhood, U.S. and U.S.S.R.* New York: Russell Sage Foundation, 1970.

Brophy, J. Successful teaching strategies for the inner-city child. *Phi Delta Kappan,* 1982, *63,* 527–530.

Brophy, J. E., & Evertson, C. M. *Learning from teaching: A developmental perspective.* Boston: Allyn & Bacon, 1976.

Brophy, J. E., & Everston, C. M. *Student characteristics and teaching.* New York: Longman, 1981.

Brown, A., Campione, J. C., & Day, J. D. Learning to learn: On teaching students to learn from texts. *Educational Researcher,* 1981, *10,* 14–21.

Brown, J. F. *Psychology and the social order.* New York: McGraw-Hill, 1936.

Brown, J. S. *The motivation of behavior.* New York: McGraw-Hill, 1961.

Brown, F. G. *Principles of educational and psychological testing* (2nd ed.). New York: Holt, Rinehart, & Winston, 1976.

Bruner, J. *Toward a theory of instruction.* Cambridge, Mass.: Belknap Press, 1966.

Bruner, J. S. *The relevance of education.* New York: Norton, 1971.

Bruner, J. S., Goodnow, J. J., & Austin, G. A. *A study of thinking.* New York: Wiley, 1956.

Bruning, R. H., Burton, J. K., & Ballering, M. Visual and auditory memory: Relationship to reading achievement. *Contemporary Educational Psychology,* 1978, *3,* 340–351.

Buchwald, A. M. Experimental alterations in the effectiveness of verbal reinforcement combinations. *Journal of Experimental Psychology,* 1959, *57,* 351–361.

Buchwald, A. M. Effects of "right" and "wrong" on subsequent behavior: A new interpretation. *Psychological Review,* 1960, *76,* 132–145.

Budd, K. S., Leibowitz, J. M., Riner, L. S., Mindell, C., & Goldfarb, A. L. Home-based treatment of severe disruptive behaviors in preschool and kindergarten children. *Behavior Modification,* 1980 (in press).

Burns, R. W. *New approaches to behavioral objectives* (2nd ed.). Dubuque, Iowa: Brown, 1977.

Buros, O. K. Fifty years in testing: Some reminiscences, criticisms and suggestions. *Educational Research,* 1977, 6,(7), 9–15.

Carpenter, P. A., & Just, M. A. What your eyes do while your mind is reading. In K. Rayner (Ed.), *Eye movements in reading: Perceptual and language processes.* New York: Academic Press, 1982.

Carr, H. A. *Psychology: A study of mental activity.* New York: Longmans, Green, 1925.

Carroll, J. B. Ability and task difficulty in cognitive psychology. *Educational Researcher,* 1981, *10,* 11–21.

Cartledge, G., & Milburn, J. F. The case for teaching social skills in the classroom: A review. *Review of Educational Research.* 1978, *48,* 133–156.

Carver, R. P. Speed readers don't read; they skim. *Psychology Today,* 1972, *6,* 22–30.

Case, R. A developmentally based theory and technology for instruction. *Review of Educational Research,* 1978, *48,* 439–463.

Cattell, J. McK. Mental tests and measurements. *Mind,* 1890, *15,* 373–380.

Caudill, B. D., & Lipscomb, T. Modeling influences on alcoholics' rates of alcohol consumption. *Journal of Applied Behavior Analysis,* 1980, *13,* 355–365.

Ceranski, D. S., Teevan, R., & Kalle, R. J. A comparison of three measures of the motive to avoid failure: Hostile press, test anxiety, and resultant achievement motivation. *Motivation and Emotion,* 1979, *3,*(4), 395–404.

Ceraso, J. The interference theory of forgetting. *Scientific American, 1967, 217*(4), 117–124.

Ceraso, J., & Henderson, A. Unavailability and associative loss in RI and PI. *Journal of Experimental Psychology,* 1966, *72,*(2), 314–316.

Chall, J. *Learning to read: The great debate.* New York: McGraw-Hill, 1967.

Chaplin, J. P., & Krawiec, T. S. *Systems and theories of psychology* (3rd ed.). New York: Holt, Rinehart, & Winston, 1974.

Chaplin, J. P., & Krawiec, T. S. *Systems and theories of psychology* (4th ed.). New York: Holt, Rinehart, & Winston, 1979.

Charles, C. M. *Individualizing instruction.* St. Louis, Mo.: Mosby, 1976.

Chase, C. I. The impact of some obvious variables on essay-tests. *Journal of Educational Measurement,* 1968, *5,* 315–318.

Chase, C. I. The impact of achievement expectations and handwriting quality on scoring essay tests. *Journal of Educational Measurement,* 1979, *16*, 39–42.

Chiang, S. F., Iwata, B. A., & Dorsey, M. *Elimination of disruptive bus riding behavior via token reinforcement.* Paper presented at the Annual Meeting of the Midwestern Association for Behavior Analysis, Chicago, May 1978.

Chomsky, A. N. Three models for the description of language. *IRE Transactions on Information Theory,* 1956, *2,* 113–124.

Clark, R., Gelatt, H. B., & Levine, L. A decision-making paradigm for local guidance research. *Personnel and Guidance Journal,* 1965, *44,* 40–51.

Clawson, E. U., & Barnes, B. R. The effects of organizers on the learning of structured anthropology materials in the elementary grades. *Journal of Experimental Education,* 1973, *42,* 11–15.

Cofer, C.N. Reason as an associative process. III: The role

of verbal responses in problem solving. *Journal of General Psychology,* 1957, *57,* 55–68.

Collins, A. M., & Loftus, E. F. A spreading activation theory of semantic processing. *Psychological Review,* 1975, *82,* 407–428.

Collins, A. M., & Quillian, M. R. Retrieval time from semantic memory. *Journal of Verbal Learning and Verbal Behavior,* 1969, *8,* 240–247.

Collins, H. F. *The influence of prosocial television programs emphasizing the positive value of differences on children's attitudes toward differences and children's behavior in choice situations.* Unpublished doctoral dissertation, Pennsylvania State University, 1974.

Coltheart, M. When can children learn to read—and when should they be taught? In T. G. Waller & G. E. MacKinnon (Eds.), *Reading research: Advances in theory and practice* (Vol. 1). New York: Academic Press, 1979.

Comstock, G., Chaffe, S., Katzman, N., McCombs, M., & Roberts, D. Television and human behavior. *Television Quarterly,* 1978, *15*(2),5–16.

Conrad, C. Cognitive economy in semantic memory. *Journal of Experimental Psychology,* 1972, *92,* 149-154.

Conrad, C. J., Spencer, R. E., & Semb, B. An analysis of student self-grading versus proctor grading in a personalized university course. *Journal of Personalized Instruction,* 1978, *3,*(1), 23–28.

Cook, T. P., & Apolloni, T. Developing positive social-emotional behaviors: A study of training and generalization effects. *Journal of Applied Behavior Analysis,* 1976, *9,* 65–78.

Cooper, D. *Behavior specific effects of teacher praise.* Paper presented at the Annual Convention of the Midwest Association for Behavior Analysis, Chicago, 1978.

Corey, G. *Theory and practice of counseling and psychotherapy.* Monterey, Calif.: Brooks/Cole, 1977.

Cosgrove, M., & McIntyre, C. W. *The influence of "Mister Rogers' Neighborhood" on nursery school children's prosocial behavior.* Paper presented at the meeting of the Southeastern Regional Society for Research in Child Development, Chapel Hill, N.C., March 1974.

Cossairt, A., Hall, R. V., & Hopkins, B. L. The effects of experimenter instructions, feedback and praise on teacher praise and student attending behavior. *Journal of Applied Behavioral Analysis,* 1973, *6,* 89–100.

Covington, M. V., & Omelich, C. L. Are causal attributions causal? An evaluation of the cognitive model of achievement behavior. *Journal of Personality and Social Psychology,* 1979, *37,* 169–182. (a)

Covington, M. V., & Omelich, C. L. Effort: The double-edged sword in school achievement. *Journal of Educational Psychology,* 1979, *71,* 169–182. (b)

Covington, M. V., & Omelich, C. L. It's best to be able and virtuous too: Student and teacher evaluative reactions to successful effort. *Journal of Educational Psychology,* 1979, *71,* 193–204. (c)

Cox, D. *The early mental traits of three hundred genuises: Genetic studies of genius* (Vol. 2). Stanford: Stanford University Press, 1926.

Crabbe, A. *Guidelines for implementation of "pull-out" programs for the gifted.* Address to the Nebraska Symposium on the Education of Gifted Children, University of Nebraska, Lincoln, 1980.

Craighead, W. E., Kazdin, A. E., & Mahoney, M. J. *Behavior modification: Principles, issues, and applications.* Boston: Houghton Mifflin, 1981.

Craik, F. I. M., & Lockhart, R. S. Levels of processing: A framework for memory research. *Journal of Verbal Learning and Verbal Behavior,* 1972, *11,* 671–684.

Craik, F. I. M., & Lockhart, R. S. Levels of processing: A reply to Eysenck. *British Journal of Psychology,* 1978, *69,* 171–175.

Creer, T. L., & Miklich, D. R. The application of a self-modeling procedure to modify inappropriate behavior: A preliminary report. *Behavior, Research and Therapy,* 1979, *8,* 91–92.

Cronbach, L. J. The two disciplines of scientific psychology. *American Psychologist,* 1957, *12,* 671–684.

Cronbach, L. J. The role of the university in improving education. *Phi Delta Kappan,* 1966, *47,* 539–545.

Cronbach, L. J. Course improvement through evaluation. In D. A. Payne & R. F. McMorris (Eds.), *Educational and psychological measurement.* Morristown, N.J.: General Learning Press, 1975.

Cronbach, L. J. *Toward reform of program evaluation.* San Francisco: Jossey-Bass, 1980.

Cronbach, L. J., & Snow, R. E. *Aptitudes and instructional methods.* New York: Irvington, 1977.

Crutchfield, R. W. Nurturing the cognitive skills of productive thinking. In *Life skills in school and society.* Washington, D.C.: Association for Supervision and Curriculum Development, 1969.

Dangel, R. F., & Hopkins, B. L. Be still, be quiet, be docile: What do the data say? *Journal of Applied Behavior Analysis,* 1978, *10,* 127–133.

Davie, R., Butler, N., & Goldstein, L. *From birth to seven.* London: Longman, 1972.

Davis, G. A. Current status of research and theory in human problem solving. *Psychological Bulletin,* 1966, *66,* 36–54.

Davis, G. A. *Psychology of problem solving: Theory and practice.* New York: Basic Books, 1973.

DeGroot, A. D. *Thought and choice in chess.* The Hague: Mouton, 1965.

Dewey, J. *Psychology.* New York: Harper, 1886.

Dewey, J. The reflex arc concept in psychology. *Psychological Review,* 1896, *3,* 357–370.

Dewey, J. *New York teachers' monographs.* New York: Teachers College Press, November 1898.

Dewey, J. *How we think.* Boston: Heath, 1910.

Dewey, J. *How we think.* New York: Heath, 1933.

Dick, W. Summative evaluation. In L. J. Briggs (Ed.), *Instructional design.* Englewood Cliffs, N.J.: Educational Technology Publications, 1977.

Dick, W., & Carey, L. *The systematic design of instruction.* Glenview, Ill.: Scott, Foresman, 1978.

Ditrichs, R., Simon, S., & Greene, B. Effect of vicarious scheduling on the verbal conditioning of hostility in children. *Journal of Personality and Social Psychology,* 1967, *6,* 71–78.

Dixon, D. N. *A problem solving/relationship model for counseling.* Paper presented at the Annual Meeting of the American Educational Research Association, San Francisco, April 1976.

Dixon, D. N., Heppner, P. P., Petersen, C. H., & Ronning, R. R. Problem solving workshop training. *Journal of Counseling Psychology,* 1979, *26*(2), 133–139.

Doll, E. A. A historical survey of research and management of mental retardation in the United States. In E. P. Trapp & P. Himmelstein (Eds.), *Readings on the exceptional child: Research and theory.* New York: Appleton-Century-Crofts, 1962.

Doll, E. A. *Vineland Social Maturity Scale.* Minneapolis: American Guidance Service, 1965.

Douglas, L. M. *The secondary teacher at work.* Lexington, Mass.: Heath, 1967.

Downing, J. The initial teaching alphabet: Reading experiment. Glenview, Ill.: Scott, Foresman, 1965.

Downing, J. *Comparative reading.* New York: Macmillan, 1973.

Dowrick, P. W. Suggestions for the use of edited video replay in training behavioral skills. *Journal of Practical Approaches to Developmental Handicaps,* 1978, *2,* 21–24.

Doyle, W. Making managerial decisions in classrooms. In D. Duke (Ed.), *Seventy-eighth Yearbook of the National Society for the Study of Education.* New York: National Society for the Study of Education, 1979.

Drabman, R., Spitalnik, R., & Spitalnik, K. Sociometric and disruptive behavior as a function of four types of token reinforcement programs. *Journal of Applied Behavior Analysis,* 1974, *7,* 93–101.

Drumheller, S. J. *Handbook of curriculum design for individualized instruction: A systems approach.* Englewood Cliffs, N.J.: Educational Technology Publications, 1971.

Duchastel, P. C., & Merrill, P. F. The effects of behavioral objectives on learning: A review of empirical studies. *Review of Educational Research,* 1973, *43,* 53–69.

Duell, O. K. Effect and types of objectives, level of test questions, and judged importance of tested materials upon posttest performance. *Journal of Educational Psychology,* 1974, *66,* 225–232.

Duffey, E. *Activation and behavior.* New York: Wiley, 1962.

Duncan, C. P. Recent research on human problem solving. *Psychological Bulletin,* 1959, *56*(6), 397–429.

Dunker, K. On problem solving (L. S. Lees, trans.). *Psychological Monographs,* 1945, *58,* 407–416, 478.

Dunn, L. M. Special education for the mildly retarded: Is much of it justifiable? *Exceptional Children,* 1968, *35,* 5-22.

Durkin, D. A six year study of children who learned to read in school at the age of four. *Reading Research Quarterly,* 1974, *10,* 9–16.

D'Zurilla, T. J., & Goldfried, M. R. Problem solving and behavior modification. *Journal of Abnormal Psychology,* 1971, *78,* 107–126.

Ebbinghaus, H. Uber das gedachtnis (1885). In H. A. Roger & C. Bossinger (Trans.), *On memory.* New York: Teachers College, 1913.

Ebel, R. L. Can teachers write good true-false items? *Journal of Educational Measurement,* 1975, *12,* 31–35.

Ebel, R. L. The case for norm-referenced measurements. *Educational Researcher,* 1978, *7,* 3–5.

Ebel, R. L. *Essentials of educational measurement* (3rd ed.). Englewood Cliffs, N.J.: Prentice-Hall, 1979.

Education Development Center, Inc. *Comprehension problem solving in secondary schools: A conference report.* Boston: Houghton Mifflin, 1975.

Educational Testing Service. *Test use and validity: A response to changes in the Nader/Nairn report on ETS.* Princeton: Educational Testing Service, 1980.

Ehri, L. Beginning reading from a psycholinguistic perspective: Amalgamation of word identities. In F. B. Murray (Ed.), *The recognition of words.* Newark, Del.: International Reading Association, 1978.

Eich, J. E. The cue-dependent nature of state-dependent retrieval. *Memory and Cognition,* 1980, *8,* 157–173.

Eisner, E. W. Educational objectives, help or hindrance? *The School Review,* 1967, *75,* 250–260.

Elardo, R. Behavior modification in an elementary school: Problems and issues. *Phi Delta Kappan,* 1978, *59,* 334–338.

Elkind, D. Educational psychology. In P. Mussen & M. R. Rosenzweig (Eds.), *Psychology: An introduction.* Lexington, Mass.: Heath, 1973.

Englehart, M. D., & Thomas, M. Rice as the inventor of the comparative test. In V. H. Noll, D. P. Scannell, & R. P. Noll (Eds.), *Indroductory readings in educational measurements.* Boston: Houghton Mifflin, 1972.

Entwisle, D. R. A sociologist looks at reading. In W. Otto, C. W. Peters, & N. Peters (Eds.), *Reading problems, a multidisciplinary perspective.* Reading, Mass.: Addison-Wesley, 1977.

Epstein, C. *Classroom management and teaching.* Reston, Va.: Reston, 1979.

Eron, L. D. Parent-child interaction, television violence, and aggression of children. *American Psychologist,* 1982, *37,* 197–211.

Estes, W. K. An experimental study of punishment. *Psychological Monographs,* 1944, *57,* 1–40.

Estes, W. K. Toward a statistical theory of learning. *Psychological Review,* 1950, *57,* 94–107.

Evertson, C. M., Anderson, C. W., Anderson, L. M., & Brophy, J. E. Relationships between classroom behaviors and student outcomes in junior high mathematics and English classes. *American Education Research Journal,* 1980, *17,* 43–60.

Eysenck, H J. *The I.Q. argument.* New York: Library Press, 1971.

Eysenck, H. J. *Biological basis of intelligence.* Paper read at the American Psychological Association Convention, Montreal, September 1980.

Fallen, N. H., & McGovern, J. E. *Young children with special needs.* Columbus, Ohio: Merrill, 1978.

Fallon, M. P., & Goetz, E. M. The creative teacher: Effects of descriptive social reinforcement upon the drawing behavior of three preschool children. *School Applications of Learning Theory,* 1975, *7,* 27–42.

Fancher, R. E. *Pioneers of psychology.* New York: Norton, 1979.

Faw, H., & Waller, T. G. Mathemagenic behaviors and efficiency in learning from prose. *Review of Educational Research,* 1976, *46,* 691–720.

Feingold, B. F. *Why your child is hyperactive.* New York: Random House, 1974.

Festinger, L. *A theory of cognitive dissonance.* Evanston, Ill.: Row, Petersen, 1957.

Festinger, L. *A theory of cognitive dissonance.* Stanford: Stanford University Press, 1959.

Flavell, J. H. *Cognitive development.* Englewood Cliffs, N.J.: Prentice-Hall, 1977.

Flavell, J. H. On Jean Piaget. *Newsletter, Society for Research in Child Development, Inc.,* 1980, p. 1.

Flesch, R. *Why Johnny can't read and what you can do about it.* New York: Harper & Brothers, 1955.

Flexibrod, J. J., & O'Leary, K. D. Effects of reinforcement on children's academic behavior as a function of self-determined and externally imposed contingencies. *Journal of Applied Behavior Analysis,* 1973, *6,* 241–250.

Foch, T. T., DeFries, J. C., McClearn, G. E., & Singer, S. M. Familial patterns of impairment in reading disability. *Journal of Educational Psychology,* 1977, *69,* 316–329.

Fox, R. A., & Roseen, D. L. A parent administered token program for dietary regulation of phenylketonuria. *Journal of Behavior Therapy and Experimental Psychiatry,* 1977, *8,* 441–443.

Foxx, R. M., & Azrin, N. H. Restitution: A method of eliminating aggressive-disruptive behavior of retarded and brain-damaged patients. *Behavior, Research and Therapy,* 1972, *10,* 15–27.

Foxx, R. M., & Shapiro, S. T. The time-out ribbon: A nonexclusionary time-out procedure. *Journal of Applied Behavior Analysis,* 1978, *11,* 125–136.

Franks, J. J., Plybon, C. J., & Auble, P. M. Units of episodic memory in perceptual recognition. *Memory & Cognition,* 1982, *10,* 62–68.

Frase, L. T. Learning from prose material: Length of passage, knowledge of results and position of questions. *Journal of Educational Psychology,* 1967, *58,* 266–272.

Frase, L. T. Effect of question location, pacing, and mode upon retention of prose material. *Journal of Educational Psychology,* 1968, *59*(4), 244–249.

Frase, L. T., & Kreitzberg, V. S. Effects of topical and indirect learning directions on prose recall. *Journal of Educational Psychology,* 1975, *67,* 320–324.

Frase, L. T., Patrick, E., & Schumer, H. Effect of question position and frequency upon learning from text under different levels of incentive. *Journal of Educational Psychology,* 1970, *61,* 52–56.

Freeman, F. S. *Theory and practice of psychological testing* (3rd ed.). New York: Holt, Rinehart, & Winston, 1962.

Freud, S. *A general introduction to psychoanalysis.* New York: Liveright, 1920.

Freud, S. *Collected papers* (Vol. 1). London: Hogarth, 1924.

Friedman, F., & Richards, J. P. Effect of level, review, and sequence of inserted questions on text processing. *Journal of Educational Psychology,* 1981, *73,*, 427–436.

Friedrich, L. K., & Stein, A. H. Aggression and prosocial television programs and the natural behavior of pre-school children. *Monographs of the Society for Research in Child Development,* 1973, *38*(51).

Friedrich, L. K., & Stein, A. H. Prosocial television and young children: The effects of verbal labeling and role playing on learning and behavior. *Child Development,* 1975, *46,* 27–38.

Fries, C. C. *Linguistics and reading.* New York: Holt, Rinehart, & Winston, 1962.

Fuller, P. R. Operant conditioning of a vegetative human organism. *American Journal of Psychology,* 1949, *62,* 587–590.

Funderbunk, F. R. Reinforcement control of classroom creativity. In T. Brigham, R. Hawkins, J. Scott, & T. F.

McLaughlin (Eds.), *Behavior analysis in education: Self-control and reading*. Dubuque, Iowa: Kendall/Hunt, 1976.

Furth, H. G., & Wachs, H. *Thinking goes to school: Piaget's theory in practice.* New York: Oxford University Press, 1975.

Gagné, E. D., & Rothkopf, E. Z. Text organization and learning goals. *Journal of Educational Psychology,* 1975, *67,* 445–450.

Gagné, R. M. Problem solving. In A. W. Melton (Ed.), *Categories of human learning.* New York: Academic Press, 1964.

Gagné, R. M. The analysis of instructional objectives for the design of instruction. In R. Glaser (Ed.), *Teaching machines and programmed learning, II: Data and direction.* Washington, D.C.: National Education Association, 1965.

Gagné, R. M. Domains of learning. *Interchange,* 1972, *3,* 1–8.

Gagné, R. M. *Essentials of learning for instruction.* New York: Holt, Rinehart, & Winston, 1974. (a)

Gagné, R. M. Task analysis—its relation to content analysis. *Educational Psychologist,* 1974, *11,* 11–18. (b)

Gagné, R. M. *The conditions of learning* (2nd ed.). New York: Holt, Rinehart, & Winston, 1977.

Gagné, R. M. *The conditions of learning* (3rd ed.). New York: Holt, Rinehart, & Winston, 1979.

Gagné, R. M. Learnable aspects of problem solving. *Educational Psychologist,* 1980, *15,* 84–92.

Gagné, R. M., & Briggs, L. J. *Principles of instructional design.* New York: Holt, Rinehart, & Winston, 1974.

Gagné, R. M., & Briggs, L. J. *Principles of instructional design* (2nd ed.). New York: Holt, Rinehart, & Winston, 1979.

Gallup, G. H. The 12th annual Gallup poll of the public's attitudes toward the public schools. *Phi Delta Kappan,* 1980, *61,* 34.

Galton, F. *Hereditary genius.* London: Macmillan, 1869.

Galton, F. *Hereditary genius* (reprint). Gloucester, Mass.: Peter Smith, 1972.

Garber, H., & Heber, F. R. The Milwaukee Project. Indications of the effectiveness of early intervention in preventing mental retardation. In P. Mittler (Ed.), *Research to practice in mental retardation: Care and intervention* (Vol. 1). Baltimore: University Park Press, 1977.

Garcia, J. I.Q. The conspiracy. *Psychology Today,* 1972, 6(4), 40–94.

Gardner, W. I. *Learning and behavior characteristics of exceptional children and youth.* Boston: Allyn & Bacon, 1977.

Gary, A. L., & Glover, J. A. *Modeling effects on creative responding.* Paper read at the Southeastern Psychological Association Convention, Hollywood, Fla., 1974.

Gary, A. L., & Glover, J. A. Eye color and sex: Their relationship to modeled learning. *Psychotherapy: Theory, Research and Practice,* 1975, *12*(4), 425–428.

Gates, A. I. *Psychology of reading and spelling with special reference to disability.* New York: Teachers College, 1922.

Gearheart, B. R., & Weishahn, M. W. *The handicapped child in the regular classroom.* St. Louis, Mo.: Mosby, 1976.

Gearheart, B. R., & Weishahn, M. W. *The handicapped student in the regular classroom* (2nd ed.). St. Louis, Mo.: Mosby, 1980.

Geller, M. I., Kelly, J. A., Traxler, W. T., & Marone, F. J. Behavioral treatment of an adolescent female's Bulemic Anorexia: Modification of immediate consequences and antecedent conditions. *Journal of Clinical Child Psychology,* 1978, *3,* 138–142.

Getzels, J. W., & Jackson, P. W. *Creativity and intelligence.* New York: Wiley, 1962.

Gibson, E. J., & Levin, H. *The psychology of reading.* Cambridge, Mass.: MIT Press, 1975.

Gibson, J. J. The implications of learning theory for social psychology. In J. G. Miller (Ed.), *Experiments in social process.* New York: McGraw-Hill, 1950.

Gilmore, T. M., & Minton, H. L. Internal versus external attribution of task performance as a function of locus of control, initial confidence, and success-failure outcome. *Journal of Personality,* 1974, *42,* 159–174.

Gilmore, T. M., & Reid, D. W. Locus of control and causal attribution for positive and negative outcomes on university examinations. *Journal of Research in Personality,* 1979, *13,* 154–160.

Ginsburg, H., & Opper, S. *Piaget's theory of intellectual development* (2nd ed.). Englewood Cliffs, N.J.: Prentice-Hall, 1979.

Gitlin, T. Prime time ideology: The hegemonic process in television entertainment. *Social Problems,* 1979, *26*(3), 251–266.

Glaser, R. Instructional technology and the measurement of learning outcomes. *American Psychologist,* 1963, *18,* 519–521.

Glaser, R. *Teaching machines and programmed learning, II: Data and directions.* Washington, D.C.: National Education Association, 1965.

Glaser, R. Educational psychology and education. *American Psychologist,* 1973, *28,* 557–566.

Glass, A. L., & Holyoak, K. J. Alternative conceptions of semantic memory. *Cognition,* 1975, *3*(4), 313–339.

Glasser, W. *Schools without failure.* New York: Harper & Row, 1969.

Glasser, W. 10 steps to good discipline. *Today's Schools,* 1977, *66,* 61–63.

Glasser, W. *Stations of the mind: New directions for reality therapy.* New York: Harper & Row, 1981.

Gleitman, L. R., & Rozin, P. The structure and acquisition of reading, I: Relations between orthographies and the structure of language. In A. S. Reber & D. L. Scarborough (Eds.), *Toward a psychology of reading.* Hillsdale, N.J.: Erlbaum, 1977.

Glover, J. A. Comparative levels of creative ability among elementary school children. *Journal of Genetic Psychology,* 1976, *129,* 131–135. (a)

Glover, J. A. A comparison of the levels of creative ability between black and white college students. *Journal of Genetic Psychology,* 1976, *128,* 95–99. (b)

Glover, J. A. *Predicting the unpredictable: Enhancing creative behavior.* Paper read at the Division 25 Symposium on Applied Behavior Analysis and Creativity at the American Psychological Association Convention, Washington, D.C., 1976. (c)

Glover, J. A. Risky shift and creativity. *Social Behavior and Personality,* 1977, *5,* 317–320.

Glover, J. A. Creative writing in elementary school students. *The Journal of Applied Behavior Analysis,* 1979, *12,* 483. (a)

Glover, J. A. *A parent's guide to intelligence testing.* Chicago: Nelson-Hall, 1979. (b)

Glover, J. A. *Becoming a more creative person.* Englewood Cliffs, N.J.: Prentice-Hall, 1980.

Glover, J. A. The effects of three forms of contingencies on the creative production of the group. *Small Group Behavior* (in press). (a)

Glover, J. A. Levels of questions asked in interview and reading sessions by creative and relatively non-creative college students. *The Journal of Genetic Psychology* (in press). (b)

Glover, J. A. A workshop for creativity training: Long term and transfer effects. *The Journal of Genetic Psychology* (in press). (c)

Glover, J. A., & Chambers, T. The creative production of the group: Effects of small group structure. *Small Group Behavior,* 1978, *9,* 387–392.

Glover, J. A., & Gary, A. L. *Behavior modification: Enhancing creativity and other good behaviors.* Pacific Grove, Calif.: Boxwood, 1975.

Glover, J. A., & Gary, A. L. Procedures to increase some aspects of creativity. *The Journal of Applied Behavior Analysis,* 1976, *9,* 79–84.

Glover, J. A., & Gary, A. L. *Behavior modification: An empirical approach to self-control.* Chicago: Nelson-Hall, 1979.

Glover, J. A., Ronning, R. R., & Filbeck, R. W. *Teaching: Why not try psychology?* Des Moines, Iowa: Kendall/Hunt, 1977.

Glover, J. A., Ronning, R. R., Zimmer, J. W., & Petersen, C. H. A topographical analysis of prose processing activities. *The Journal of Genetic Psychology* (in press).

Glover, J. A., & Sautter, F. J. The effects of locus of control on four components of creative behavior. *Social Behavior and Personality,* 1976, *4,* 257–260.

Glover, J. A., & Sautter, F. J. Procedures for increasing four behaviorally defined components of creativity within formal written assignments among high school students. *School Applications of Learning Theory,* 1977, *9*(4), 3–22. (a)

Glover, J. A., & Sautter, F. J. The relationship of risk taking to creative behavior. *Psychological Reports,* 1977, *41,* 227–230. (b)

Glover, J. A., & Trammel, S. Comparative levels of creative ability among behavioral problem and non-behavioral problem students. *Psychological Reports,* 1976, *38,* 1171–1174.

Gnagey, W. J. *Motivating classroom discipline.* New York: Macmillan, 1981.

Goetz, E. M., & Baer, D. M. Descriptive social reinforcement of "creative " blockbuilding by young children. In E. Ramp & B. L. Hopkins (Eds.), *A new direction for education: Behavior analysis.* Lawrence, Kans.: Support and Development Center for Follow-Through, 1971.

Goetz, E. M., & Baer, D. M. Social control of form diversity and the emergence of new forms in children's blockbuilding. *The Journal of Applied Behavior Analysis,* 1973, *6,* 209–218.

Goetz, E. M., & Salmonson, M. The effects of general and descriptive reinforcement on "creativity" in easel painting. In G. Semb (Ed.), *Behavior analyses and education.* Lawrence, Kans.: Support and Development Center for Follow-Through, 1972.

Good, T., Biddle, B. J., & Brophy, J. E. *Teachers make a difference.* New York: Holt, Rinehart, & Winston, 1975.

Good, T., & Brophy, J. *Looking in classrooms.* New York: Holt, Rinehart, & Winston, 1978.

Good, T., & Grouws, D. Teaching effects: A process-product study in fourth grade mathematics classes. *Journal of Teacher Education,* 1977, *28,* 49–54.

Good, T., & Grouws, D. A. The Missouri Mathematics Effectiveness Project: An experimental study in fourth grade classrooms. *Journal of Educational Psychology,* 1979, *71,* 355–362.

Goodman, K. S. Reading: A psycholinguistic guessing game. In H. Singer & R. B. Ruddell (Eds.), *Theoretical models and processes of reading.* Newark, Del.: International Reading Association, 1970.

Gordon, T. *Teacher effectiveness training.* New York: McKay, 1974.

Gordon, W. J. J. *Synectics: The development of creative capacity.* New York: Harper & Row, 1961.

Gottlieb, J. Improving attitudes toward retarded children by using group discussion. *Exceptional Children,* 1980, *47,* 106–111.

Gray, W. S. Remedial cases in reading: Their diagnosis and treatment. *Supplementary Educational Monographs* (No. 22). Chicago: University of Chicago Press, 1922.

Greenberg, B. S. British children and televised violence. *Public Opinion Quarterly,* 1975, *38,* 531–547.

Greeno, J. C. Hobbits and Orcs: Acquisition of a sequential concept. *Cognitive Psychology,* 1974, *6,* 270–292.

Greeno, J. G., James, C. T., & DaPolito, F. J. A cognitive interpretation of negative transfer and forgetting of paired associates. *Journal of Verbal Learning and Verbal Behavior,* 1971, *10,* 331–345.

Gresham, F. M. Social skills training with handicapped children: A review. *Review of Educational Research,* 1981, *51,* 139–176.

Gronlund, N. E. *Measurement and evaluation in teaching* (3rd ed.). New York: Macmillan, 1976.

Gronlund, N. E. *Stating objectives for classroom instruction.* New York: Macmillan, 1978.

Gronlund, N. E. *Measurement and evaluation in teaching* (4th ed.). New York: Macmillan, 1981.

Gross, H. The audience as a pressure group—"The heat is on!" *Television Quarterly,* 1980, *16*(4), 47–50.

Grueneberg, M. The role of memorization techniques in final examination preparation. *Educational Research,* 1973, *15,* 134–139.

Guilford, J. P. *Psychometric methods.* New York: McGraw-Hill, 1936.

Guilford, J. P. Creativity. *American Psychologist,* 1950, *5,* 444–454.

Guilford, J. P. Three faces of intellect. *American Psychologist,* 1959, *14,* 469–479.

Guilford, J. P. Factors that aid and hinder creativity. *Teacher's College Record,* 1962, *63,* 380–392.

Guthrie, E. R. *The psychology of learning.* New York: Harper & Row, 1935.

Gutkin, T. B. Modification of elementary students' locus of control: An operant approach. *Journal of Psychology,* 1978, *100,* 107–115.

Haefele, J. W. *Creativity and innovation.* New York: Reinhold, 1962.

Hall, G. S. Editorial. *American Journal of Psychology,* 1887, *1,* iii–vi.

Hall, G. S. Children's lies. *Pedagogical Seminary,* 1891, *1,* 211–218.

Hall, G. S. Editorial. *Pedagogical Seminary,* 1891, *1,* iii–viii.

Hall, R. V., Lund, D., & Jackson, D. Effects of teacher attention on study behavior. *Journal of Applied Behavior Analysis,* 1968, *1,* 1–12.

Hall, V. C., & Kaye, D. B. Early patterns of cognitive development. *Monographs of the Society for Research in Child Development,* 1980, *45*(Whole No. 184).

Halpern, A. S. Adolescents and young adults. *Exceptional Children,* 1979, *45,* 518–523.

Hamblin, R. L., Buckholdt, D., Bushell, D., Ellis, D., & Ferritor, D. Changing the game from "get the teacher" to "learn." *Trans-action,* 1969, *1,* 1–15.

Harris, A. J. *How to increase reading ability* (5th ed.). New York: McKay, 1970.

Harris, A. J., & Sipay, E. R. *How to teach reading.* New York: Longman, 1979.

Harris, F. R., Wolf, M. M., & Baer, D. M. Effects of adult social reinforcement on child behavior. *Young Children,* 1964, *20,* 8–17.

Harris, M. B. Reciprocity and generosity: Some determinants of sharing in children. *Child Development,* 1970, *41,* 222–245.

Harvey, J. Legislative intent and progress. *Exceptional Children,* 1978, *44,* 234–237.

Hayden, A. H. Handicapped children, birth to age three. *Exceptional Children,* 1979, *45,* 510–516.

Hayes, J. R. *Cognitive psychology: Thinking and creating.* Homewood, Ill.: Dorsey, 1978.

Hayes, J. R., & Simon, H. A. Understanding written problem instructions. In L. W. Gregg (Ed.), *Knowledge and cognition.* Potomac, Md.: Erlbaum, 1974.

Hayes, J. R., & Simon, H. A. Psychological differences among problem isomorphs. In N. Castellon, Jr., D. Pisoni, & G. Potts (Eds.), *Cognitive theory* (Vol. II). Potomac, Md.: Erlbaum, 1976.

Hayes, J. R., Waterman, D. A., & Robinson, C. S. Identifying relevant aspects of a problem text. *Cognitive Science,* 1977, *5,* 297–313.

Hearnshaw, L. S. *Cyril Burt, psychologist.* Ithaca, N.Y.: Cornell University Press, 1979.

Hebb, D. O. *The organization of behavior.* New York: Wiley, 1949.

Heber, R., Garber, H., Harrington, S., Hoffman, C., & Falender, C. *Rehabilitation of families at risk for mental retardation.* Progress report of the Rehabilitation Research and Training Center in Mental Retardation, University of Wisconsin, Madison, February 1972.

Heider, F. Social perception and phenomenal causality. *Psychological Review,* 1944, *51,* 358–374.

Heider, F. Social perception and phenomenal causality. *Psychological Issues,* 1959, *1,* 35–52.

Heppner, P. P. A review of the problem-solving literature and its relationship to the counseling process. *Journal of Counseling Psychology,* 1978, *25,* 366–375.

Hergenhahn, B. R. *An introduction to theories of learning.* Englewood Cliffs, N.J.: Prentice-Hall, 1976.

Herrnstein, R. IQ. *The Atlantic,* 1973, *228,* 43–64.
Hersen, M., & Barlow, D. H. *Single case experimental designs.* New York: Pergamon, 1976.
Hershberger, W. Self-evaluational responding and typographical cueing: Techniques for programming self-instructional reading materials. *Journal of Educational Psychology,* 1974, *55,* 288–296.
Hewett, F. M., & Forness, S. R. *Education of exceptional learners.* Boston: Allyn & Bacon, 1974.
Highet, G. *The art of teaching.* New York: Vintage, 1957.
Hilgard, E. R., & Bower, G. H. *Theories of learning* (4th ed.). Englewood Cliffs, N.J.: Prentice-Hall, 1975.
Hiller, J. H. Learning from prose text: Effects of readability level, inserted question difficulty, and individual differences. *Journal of Educational Psychology,* 1974, *66,* 202–211.
Hillinger, M. L. Priming effects with phonetically similar words: The encoding-bias hypothesis reconsidered. *Memory and Cognition,* 1980, *8,* 115–123.
Hills, J. R. *Measurement and evaluation in the classroom.* Columbus, Ohio: Merrill, 1976.
Hinsely, D., Hayes, J. R., & Simon, H. A. From words to equations. In P. Carpenter & M. Just (Eds.), *Cognitive processes in comprehension.* Hillsdale, N.J.: Erlbaum, 1977.
Hobbs, S. A., & Forehand, R. Important parameters in the use of time-out with children: A re-examination. *Journal of Behavior Therapy and Experimental Psychiatry,* 1977, *8,* 365–370.
Holt, E. B. *Animal drive and the learning process.* New York: Holt, Rinehart, & Winston, 1931.
Holt, J. *How children fail.* New York: Pitman, 1964.
Holt, J. *What do I do Monday?* New York: Dutton, 1970.
Homme, L., Csanyi, A. P., Gonzales, M. A., & Rechs, J. R. *How to use contingency contracting in the classroom.* Champaign, Ill.: Research Press, 1969.
Homme, L. E., DeBaca, P. C., Devine, J., Steinhorst, R., & Rickert, E. J. Use of the Premack Principle in controlling the behavior of nursery school children. *Journal of Experimental Analysis of Behavior,* 1963, *6,* 43–54.
Hopkins, K. D., & Stanley, J. C. *Educational and psychological measurement and evaluation* (6th ed.). Englewood Cliffs, N.J.: Prentice-Hall, 1981.
Hoppe, F. Erfolg and misserfolg. *Psychologische Forschung,* 1930, *14,* 1–62.
Hops, H., & Cobb, J. Survival behaviors in the educational setting: Their implications for research and intervention. In L. A. Hammerlynk, L. C. Handy, & E. S. Mash (Eds.), *Behavior change.* Champaign, Ill.: Research Press, 1973.
Houston, J. P. Stimulus recall and experimental paradigm. *Journal of Experimental Psychology,* 1966, *72,* 619–621.
Huey, E. B. *The psychology and pedagogy of reading.* New York: Macmillan, 1908.
Huey, E. B. *The psychology and pedagogy of reading* (1908). Cambridge, Mass.: MIT Press, 1968.
Hull, C. L. *Principles of behavior.* Englewood Cliffs, N.J.: Prentice-Hall, 1943.
Humphrey, G. Imitation and the conditioned reflex. *Pedagogical Seminary,* 1921, *28,* 1–21.
Humphrey, J. E. *Increasing school attendance with the aid of peer helpers and rewards: A case study.* Paper presented at the Annual Convention of the Midwest Association of Behavior Analysis, Chicago, 1978.
Hunkins, F. P. Effects of analysis and evaluation questions on various levels of achievement. *Journal of Experimental Education,* 1969, *38,* 45–58.
Hunt, E. Mechanics of verbal ability. *Psychological Review,* 1978, *85,* 109–130.
Hunt, E., Frost, N., & Lunneborg, C. Individual differences in cognition: A new approach to intelligence. In G. Bower (Ed.), *The psychology of learning and motivation* (Vol. 7). New York: Academic Press, 1973.
Hunt, E., Lunneborg, C., & Lewis, J. What does it mean to be high verbal? *Cognitive Psychology,* 1975, *7,* 194–227.
Hunt, E., Lunneborg, C., & Lewis, J. What does it mean to be high verbal? In L. Willerman & R. G. Turner (Eds.), *Readings about individual and group differences.* San Francisco: Freeman, 1979.
Hunt, J. McV. *Intelligence and experience.* New York: Ronald Press, 1961.
Hursh, D. E. Personalized systems of instruction: What do the data indicate? *Journal of Personalized Instruction,* 1976, *1,* 91–105.
Itard, J. M. G. *The wild boy of Aveyron.* New York: Appleton-Century-Crofts, 1962.
Jackson, C. D. On the report of the Ad Hoc Committee on Educational Uses of Tests with Disadvantaged Students: Another psychological view from the Association of Black Psychologists. *American Psychologist,* 1975, *30,* 86–90.
Jacobs, J. F., & Degraaf, C. A.. *Expectancy and race: The influences upon the scoring of individual intelligence tests.* Paper presented at the Annual Meeting of the American Educational Research Association, New Orleans, 1973.
Jacoby, L. L., & Craik, F. I. M. Effects of elaboration of processing at encoding and retrieval. Trace distinctiveness and recovery of initial content. In L. S. Cermak & F. I. M. Craik (Eds.), *Levels of processing and human memory.* Hillsdale, N.J.: Erlbaum, 1979.
Jacoby, L. L., Craik, F. I. M., & Begg, I. Effects of decision difficulty on recognition and recall. *Journal of Verbal Learning and Verbal Behavior,* 1979, *18,* 585–600.

James, A. W. The effect of handwriting on grading. *English Journal,* 1927, *16,* 180–205.

James, W. *The principles of psychology* (Vols. 1 & 2). New York: Holt, 1890.

James, W. *Talks to teachers on psychology and to students on some of life's ideals.* New York: Holt, 1899.

James, W. *Pragmatism: A new name for old ways of thinking.* New York: Longmans, Green, 1909.

Jarvik, L. F., & Erlenmeyer-Kimling, L. Survey of familial correlations in measured intellectual functions. In J. Zubin & G. A. Jervis (Eds.), *Psychopathology of mental development.* New York: Grune & Stratton, 1967.

Jenkins, J. G., & Dallenbach, K. M. Oblivescence during sleep and waking. *American Journal of Psychology,* 1924, *35,* 605–612.

Jenkins, J. J. Remember that old theory of memory? Well, forget it! *American Psychologist,* 1974, *29,* 785–795.

Jenkins, J. R., & Deno, S. L. Influence of knowledge and type of objectives on subject-matter learning. *Journal of Educational Psychology,* 1971, *62,* 67–70.

Jenkins, J. R., & Neisworth, J. T. The facilitative influence of instructional objectives. *Journal of Educational Research,* 1973, *66,* 254–256.

Jennings, J., Geis, F. L., & Brown, V. Influence of television commercials on women's self-confidence and independent judgment. *Journal of Personality and Social Psychology,* 1980, *38*(2), 203–210.

Jensen, A. R. How much can we boost I.Q. and scholastic achievement? *Harvard Educational Review,* 1969, *39,* 32–112.

Jensen, A. R. *Bias in mental testing.* New York: Free Press, 1980.

Johnson, D. W., & Johnson, R. (Eds.). Social interdependence in the classroom: Cooperation, competition, and individualism. *Journal of Research and Development in Education,* 1978, *12,* 1–152.

Johnson, D. W., & Johnson, R. Effects of cooperative and individualistic learning experiences on interethnic interaction. *Journal of Educational Psychology,* 1981, *73,* 444–449.

Johnson, D. W., Johnson, R. T., Nelson, D., & Read, S. *Mainstreaming: Development of positive interdependence between handicapped and nonhandicapped students.* Minneapolis: National Support Systems Project, 1978.

Johnson, D. W., Skon, L., & Johnson, R. Effects of cooperative, competitive, and individualistic conditions on children's problem-solving performance. *American Educational Research Journal,* 1980, *17,* 83–93.

Johnson, E. S. Validation of concept-learning strategies. *Journal of Experimental Psychology: General,* 1978, *107,* 237–266.

Johnson, R., Rynders, J., Johnson, D. W., Schmidt, B., & Harder, I. Interaction between handicapped and nonhandicapped teenagers as a function of situational goal structuring: Implications for mainstreaming. *American Educational Research Journal,* 1979, *16,* 161–167.

Johnson, R. T., & Johnson, D. W. Building friendships between handicapped and nonhandicapped students: Effects of cooperative and individualistic instruction. *American Educational Research Journal,* 1981, *18,* 415–423.

Jung, C. *The psychology of the unconscious.* Leipzig: Franz Deuticke, 1912.

Just, M. A. *What your mind does while your eyes are reading: Old myths and new facts.* Address presented at the American Educational Research Association Convention, Los Angeles, April 1981.

Just, M. A., & Carpenter, P. A. A theory of reading: From eye fixations to comprehension. *Psychological Review,* 1980, *87,* 329–354.

Kagan, J., & Lang, C. *Psychology and education: An introduction.* New York: Harcourt, Brace, Jovanovich, 1978.

Kagen, J., & Kogan, N. Individual variations in cognitive processes. In P. Mussen (Ed.), *Carmichael's manual in child psychology* (Vol. 1). New York: Wiley, 1970.

Kamin, L. J. *The science and politics of I.Q.* New York: Wiley, 1975.

Kanner, L. Autistic disturbances of affective contact. *Nervous Child,* 1943, *2,* 217–250.

Kapfer, P. G., & Ovard, G. F. *Preparing and using individualized learning packages.* Englewood Cliffs, N.J.: Educational Technology Publications, 1971.

Kaplan, M. *The essential works of Pavlov.* New York: Bantam, 1966.

Kaplan, R. Effects of learning with part vs. whole presentations of instructional objectives. *Journal of Educational Psychology,* 1974, *66,* 787–792.

Kaplan, R., & Rothkopf, E. Z. Instructional objectives as directions to learners: Effect of passage length and amount of objective-relevant content. *Journal of Educational Psychology,* 1974, *66,* 449–456.

Kaplan, R., & Simmons, F. G. Effects of instructional objectives used as orienting stimuli or as summary/review upon prose learning. *Journal of Educational Psychology,* 1974, *66,* 614–622.

Kaplan, R. M., & Singer, R. D. Television violence and viewer aggression: A reexamination of the evidence. *Journal of Social Issues,* 1976, *32,* 35–70.

Kassan, S. M., & Reber, A. S. Locus of control and the learning of an artificial language. *Journal of Research in Personality,* 1979, *13,* 112–118.

Katona, G. *Organizing and memorizing.* New York: Columbia University Press, 1940.

Kaufman, K. F., & O'Leary, K. D. Reward, cost, and

self-evaluation procedures for disruptive adolescents in a psychiatric hospital school. *Journal of Applied Behavior Analysis,* 1972, *5,* 293–309.

Kaufman, R. A. *Identifying and solving problems: A systems approach.* LaJolla, Calif.: University Associates, 1976.

Kazdin, A. E. *Behavior modification in applied settings* (2nd ed.). Homewood, Ill.: Dorsey, 1979.

Kazdin, A. E. Applied behavioral principles in the schools. In C. R. Reynolds & T. E. Gutkin (Eds.), *A handbook for school psychology.* New York: Wiley, 1981.

Keller, F. S. *The definition of psychology.* New York: Appleton-Century-Crofts, 1937.

Keller, F. S. *The definition of psychology* (2nd ed.). New York: Appleton-Century-Crofts, 1965.

Keller, M. F., & Carlson, P.M. The use of symbolic modeling to promote social skills in pre-school children with low levels of social responsiveness. *Child Development,* 1974, *45,* 912–919.

Kennedy, M. M. Findings from the Follow Through planned variation study. *Educational Researcher,* 1978, 7(6), 3–11.

Kintsch, W. Notes on the structure of semantic memory. In E. Tulving & W. Donaldson (Eds.), *Organization of memory.* New York: Academic Press, 1972.

Kintsch, W. *The representation of meaning in memory.* Hillsdale, N.J.: Erlbaum, 1974.

Kirk, S. A. *Educating exceptional children* (2nd ed.). Boston: Houghton Mifflin, 1972.

Kirk, S. A., & Bateman, B. Diagnosis and remediation of learning disabilities. *Exceptional Children,* 1962, *29,* 72.

Klatzky, R. L. *Human memory: Structures and processes* (2nd ed.). San Francisco: Freeman, 1980.

Kline, C. L. The adolescents with learning problems: How long must they wait? *Journal of Learning Disabilities,* 1972, *5,* 262–271.

Knott, G. P. Communicative competence and secondary learning disabled students. *The Directive Teacher,* 1980, *2,* 22–24.

Knox, B. J., & Glover, J. A. The effects of pre-school experience on I.Q., creativity and readiness to learn among black and white first graders. *The Journal of Genetic Psychology,* 1978, *132*(1), 151.

Köhler, A. *The mentality of apes.* New York: Harcourt, Brace, 1925.

Kolb, D. A. Achievement motivation training for underachieving boys. *Journal of Personality and Social Psychology,* 1965, *21,* 783–792.

Kolstoc, R. H. *Introduction to statistics for the behavioral sciences.* Homewood, Ill.: Dorsey, 1973.

Koppenall, R. J. Time changes in the strength of A-B, A-C lists; spontaneous recovery? *Journal of Verbal Learning and Verbal Behavior,* 1963, *2,* 310–319.

Kounin, J. *Discipline and group management in classrooms.* New York: Holt, Rinehart, & Winston, 1970.

Krathwohl, D. R., Bloom, B. S., & Masia, B. B. *Taxonomy of educational objectives. The classification of educational goals. Handbook II: Affective domain.* New York: McKay, 1964.

Krumboltz, J. D., & Thoresen, C. E. (Eds.). *Counseling methods.* New York: Holt, Rinehart, & Winston, 1976.

Kulhavy, R. W. Feedback in written instruction. *Review of Educational Research,* 1977, *47,* 211–232.

Külpe, O. *Outline of psychology.* Leipzig: Engleman, 1893.

Kuo, L. Z. Giving up instincts in psychology. *Journal of Philosophy,* 1921, *17,* 645–664.

LaBerge, D. Unitization and automaticity in perception. In J. Flowers (Ed.), *Nebraska symposium on motivation.* Lincoln: University of Nebraska Press, 1980.

LaBerge, D., & Samuels, S. J. Toward a theory of automatic information processing in reading. *Cognitive Psychology,* 1974, *6,* 283–323.

Lahey, B. B., McNees, P. M., & McNees, M. C. Control of an obscene "verbal tick" through time-out in an elementary classroom. *Journal of Applied Behavior Analysis,* 1973, *6,* 101–104.

Lakoff, G. *Hedges: A study in meaning criteria and the logic of funny concepts.* Paper presented at the Eighth Regional Meeting, Chicago Linguistic Society, University of Chicago Linguistic Department, Chicago, 1972.

Lambert, W. E., & Tucker, G. R. *Bilingual education of children.* Rowley, Mass.: Newburg House, 1972.

Lansman, M., & Hunt, E. Individual differences in secondary task performance. *Memory & Cognition,* 1982, *10,* 10–24.

Lawson, T. E. Effects of instruction objectives on learning and retention. *Instructional Science,* 1974, *3,* 1–21.

Lawton, J. T., & Wanska, S. K. Advance organizers as a teaching strategy: A reply to Clawson and Barnes. *Review of Educational Research,* 1977, *47,* 233–244.

LeBlanc, J. M., Busby, K. H., & Thomson, C. L. The functions of time-out for changing the aggressive behaviors of a preschool child: A multiple-baseline analysis. In R. Ulrich, T. Stachnik, & J. Mabry (Eds.), *Control of human behavior* (Vol. 4). Glenview, Ill.: Scott, Foresman, 1974.

Lefcourt, H. M. *Locus of control: Current trends in theory and research.* Hillsdale, N.J.: Erlbaum, 1976.

Lefcourt, H. M., Hogg, E., Struthers, S., & Holmes, C. Causal attributions as a function of locus of control, initial confidence, and performance outcomes. *Journal of Personality and Social Psychology,* 1975, *32,* 391–397.

Lewin, K. *Principles of topological psychology.* New York: McGraw-Hill, 1936.

Li, Y., & Reames, F. M. Physics education needs PSE: A

report on its use at Tuskegee Institute. *American Journal of Physics,* 1977, *45,* 208–209.

Liebert, R. M., Neale, J. M., & Davidson, T. *The early window: Effects of television on children and youth.* New York: Pergamon, 1973.

Lindeman, R. J., & Merenda, P. F. *Educational measurement* (2nd ed.). Glenview, Ill.: Scott, Foresman, 1979.

Lindsay, P. H., & Norman, D. A. *Human information processing: An introduction to psychology* (2nd ed.). New York: Academic Press, 1977.

Lindsley, O. R. Precision teaching in perspective: An interview with Ogden R. Lindsley. *Teaching Exceptional Children,* 1971, *3*(3), 114–119.

Linquist, E. F. (Ed.). *Educational measurement.* Menasha, Wis.: Banta, 1951.

Loftus, E. F. Activation of semantic memory. *American Journal of Psychology,* 1973, *86,* 331–337.

Loftus, G. R., & Loftus, E. F. *Human memory: The processing of information.* New York: Wiley, 1977.

Loney, J. Hyperkinesis comes of age: What do we know and where should we go? *American Journal of Orthopsychiatry,* 1980, *50,* 28–42.

Luchens, A. S. Mechanization in problem solving. *Psychological Monographs,* 1942, *54*(Whole No. 6).

Luginbuhl, J. E., Crowe, D. H., & Kahan, J. P. Causal attributions for success and failure. *Journal of Personality and Social Psychology,* 1975, *31,* 86–93.

Lundgren, T. D., & Loar, R. M. CLUG: The spirit of capitalism and the success of a simulation. *Simulation and Games,* 1978, *9*(2), 201–207.

Lundin, R. W. *Theories and systems of psychology.* Lexington, Mass.: Heath, 1972.

Lunzer, E. A. Jean Piaget: A biographical sketch. In N. P. Varma & P. Williams (Eds.), *Piaget, psychology and education.* Itasca, Ill.: Peacock, 1976.

Lyon, D. O. The relation of length of material to time taken for learning and the optimum distribution of time. *Journal of Educational Psychology,* 1914, *5,* 1–9, 85–91, 155–163.

MacLeod, C. M., Hunt, E. B., & Mathews, N. N. Individual differences in the verification of sentence-picture relationships. *Journal of Verbal Learning and Verbal Behavior,* 1978, *17,* 345–357.

Madeus, G. F. Reactions to the "Pittsburgh Papers." *Phi Delta Kappan,* 1981, *62,* 634–636.

Madsen, C. H., Madsen, C. K., Sandargas, R. A., Hammond, W. R., & Edgar, D. E. *Classroom RAID (rules, approval, ignore, disapproval): A cooperative approach for professionals and volunteers.* Unpublished manuscript, University of Florida, 1970.

Madsen, C. H., Jr., Becker, W. C., & Thomas, D. R. Rules, praise and ignoring: Elements of elementary classroom control. *Journal of Applied Behavior Analysis,* 1968, *1,* 139–151.

Madsen, K. B. *Theories of motivation* (4th ed.). Copenhagen: Munksgaard, 1968.

Madsen, K. B. Theories of motivation. In B. Wolman (Ed.), *Handbook of general psychology.* Englewood Cliffs, N.J.: Prentice-Hall, 1973.

Madsen, K. B. *Modern theories of motivation.* New York: Wiley, 1974.

Maehr, M. L. *Sociocultural origins of achievement motivation.* Unpublished manuscript, 1978.

Maehr, M. L., & Sjorgren, D. D. Atkinson's theory of achievement motivation: First step toward a theory of academic motivation? *Review of Educational Research,* 1971, *41*(2), 143–159.

Mager, R. *Preparing instructional objectives.* Palo Alto, Calif.: Fearon, 1962.

Mahoney, M. J., & Thoresen, C. E. *Behavioral self-control.* New York: Holt, Rinehart, & Winston, 1974.

Mahoney, M. J. *Cognition and behavior modification.* Cambridge, Mass.: Ballinger, 1974.

Maier, H. W. *Three theories of child redevelopment* (Rev. ed.). New York: Harper & Row, 1969.

Maier, N. R. F. An aspect of human reasoning. *British Journal of Psychology,* 1933, *24,* 144–155.

Maloney, K. B., & Hopkins, B. L. The modification of sentence structure and its relationship to subjective judgments of creativity in writing. *The Journal of Applied Behavior Analysis,* 1973, *6,* 425–433.

Maltzman, I. Thinking. From a behavioristic point of view. *Psychological Review,* 1955, *62,* 275–286.

Maltzman, I., Bogartz, W., & Bregar, L. A procedure for increasing word association originality and its transfer effects. *Journal of Experimental Psychology,* 1958, *56,* 392–398.

Maltzman, I., Simon, S., Raskin, D., & Licht, L. Experimental studies in the training of originality. *Psychological Monographs: General and Applied,* 1960, *74*(6), 1–17.

Mandler, G. *Mind and emotion.* New York: Wiley, 1975.

Mann, H. Boston grammar and writing schools. *Common School Journal,* 1845, *7,* 289–368.

Maracek, J., & Mettee, D. R. Avoidance of continued success as a function of self-esteem, level of esteem certainty, and responsibility for success. *Journal of Personality and Social Psychology,* 1972, *22,* 98–107.

Marshall, A. M., & Sherman, J. A. *Token economies: An incomplete technology?* Paper presented at the Annual Convention of the Midwest Association for Behavior Analysis, Chicago, 1978.

Marshall, J. C., & Powers, J. M. Writing neatness, composition errors, and essay grades. *Journal of Educational*

Measurement, 1969, *6,* 97–101.

Marshall, K. You can turn around the failing student. *Learning,* 1977, *6,* 50.

Martin, E. Verbal learning theory and independent retrieval phenomena. *Psychological Review,* 1971, *78,* 314–332.

Martin, J. A. The control of imitative and non-imitative behavior in severely retarded children through "generalized instruction following." *Journal of Experimental Child Psychology,* 1971, *11,* 390–400.

Maslow, A. H. *Toward a psychology of being* (2nd ed.). Princeton: Van Nostrand, 1968.

Maslow, A. H. *Motivation and personality* (2nd ed.). New York: Harper & Row, 1970.

Maslow, A. H. *The further reaches of human nature.* New York: Viking, 1971.

Masters, T. C., & Morris, R. S. Effects of contingent and non-contingent reinforcement upon generalized imitation. *Child Development,* 1971, *42,* 285–397.

May, Y. Personalized self-instruction at the Cambridge School. *The Science Teacher,* 1977, *44,* 22–23.

Mayer, R. E. *Thinking and problem solving: An introduction to human cognition and learning.* Glenview, Ill.: Scott, Foresman, 1977.

Mayer, R. E. Can advance organizers influence meaningful learning? *Review of Educational Research,* 1979, *49,* 371–383.

Mayer, R. E., & Bromage, B. K. Different recall protocols for technical texts due to advance organizers. *Journal of Educational Psychology,* 1980, *72,* 209–225.

McAllister, L. W., Stachowiak, J. G., Baer, D. M., & Conderman, L. The application of operant conditioning techniques in a secondary school. *Journal of Applied Behavior Analysis,* 1969, *2,* 277–285.

McCall, R. B. Childhood IQ's as predictors of adult educational and occupational status. *Science,* 1977, *197,* 482–483.

McCall, W. A. A new kind of school examination. *Journal of Educational Research,* 1920, *1,* 33–46.

McCall, W. A. *How to measure in education.* New York: Macmillan, 1922.

McClelland, D. C. *The achieving society.* Princeton: Van Nostrand, 1961.

McClelland, D. C. Toward a theory of motive acquisition. *American Psychologist,* 1965, *20,* 321–333.

McClelland, D. C. *Motivational trends in society.* New York: General Learning Press, 1971.

McClelland, D. C., Atkinson, J. W., Clark, R. A., & Lowell, E. L. *The achievement motive.* New York: Appleton-Century-Crofts, 1953.

McClelland, D. C., & Winter, D. G. *Motivating economic achievement.* New York: Free Press, 1969.

McConkie, G. W., & Raynor, K. Identifying the span of the effective stimulus in reading: Literature review and theories of reading. In H. Singer & R. B. Ruddell (Eds.), *Theoretical models and processes of reading* (2nd ed.). Newark, Del.: International Reading Association, 1976.

McCrudden, T. *A contextualist analysis of adjunct aids in prose processing.* Unpublished doctoral dissertation, University of Nebraska, Lincoln, 1979.

McDaniel, T. R. Exploring alternatives to punishment: The keys to effective discipline. *Phi Delta Kappan,* 1980, *61*(7), 455 458.

McDougall, W. *Introduction to social psychology.* London: Methuen, 1908.

McGeoch, J. A. Forgetting and the law of disuse. *Psychological Review,* 1932, *39,* 352–370.

McGeoch, J. A., & McDonald, W. T. Meaningful relation and retroactive inhibition. *American Journal of Psychology,* 1931, *43,* 579–588.

McGraw, B., & Grotelueschen, A. Direction of the effect of questions in prose material. *Journal of Educational Psychology,* 1972, *63,* 580–588.

McKenzie, H. S., Clark, M., Wolf, M. M., Kothera, R., & Benson, C. Behavior modification of children with learning disabilities using tokens and allowances as back-up reinforcers. *Exceptional Children,* 1968, *34,* 745–752.

McKinnon, D. W. The nature and nurture of creative talent. *American Psychologist,* 1962, *16,* 484–495.

Meador, B. D., & Rogers, C. R. Client-centered therapy. In R. Corsini (Ed.), *Current psychotherapies.* Itasca, Ill.: Peacock, 1974.

Mednick, S. A. The associative basis of the creative process. *Psychological Review,* 1962, *69,* 220–232.

Mehrens, W. A., & Lehmann, I. J. *Measurement and evaluation in education and psychology* (2nd ed.). New York: Holt, Rinehart, & Winston, 1975.

Mehrens, W. A., & Lehmann, I. J. *Measurement and evaluation in education and psychology* (3rd ed.). New York: Holt, Rinehart, & Winston, 1978.

Meichenbaum, D. H. *Cognitive behavior modification.* New York: Plenum, 1977.

Meichenbaum, D. H., & Goodman, K. S. Training impulsive children to talk about themselves: A means of developing self-control. *Journal of Abnormal Psychology,* 1971, *77,* 115–126.

Melton, J. W. The science of learning and the technology of educational methods. *Harvard Educational Review,* 1959, *29,* 96–106.

Melton, J. W. Implications of short-term memory for a general theory of memory. *Journal of Verbal Learning and Verbal Behavior,* 1963, *2,* 1–21.

Melton, J. W., & Irwin, J. M. The influence of degree

on interpolated learning on retroactive inhibition and the overt transfer of specific responses. *American Journal of Psychology,* 1940, *53,* 173–203.

Melton, J. W., & Martin E. (Eds.). *Coding processes in human memory.* Washington, D.C.: Winston, 1972.

Mendonca, J. D., & Siess, T. F. Counseling for indecisiveness: Problem solving and anxiety management training. *Journal of Counseling Psychology,* 1976, *23*(4), 339–347.

Mercer, J. F. I.Q.: The lethal label. *Psychology Today,* 1972, *6*(4), 44–97.

Messick, S. (Ed.). *Individuality in learning. Implications of cognitive styles and creativity for human development.* San Francisco: Jossey-Bass, 1976.

Metfessel, N., Michael, W. B., & Kirsner, P. A. Instrumentation of Bloom's and Krathwohl's taxonomies for the writing of behavioral objectives. *Psychology in the Schools,* 1969, *6,* 227–231.

Meyer, B. J. F. *The organization of prose and its effects on recall.* Amsterdam: North-Holland, 1975.

Meyer, D. E. On the representation and retrieval of stored semantic information. *Cognitive Psychology,* 1970, *21,* 242–300.

Meyer, M. The grading of students. *Science,* 1908, *28,* 243–250.

Miller, G. A. The magical number seven, plus or minus two: Some limits on our capacity to process information. *Psychological Review,* 1956, *63,* 81–97.

Miller, G. A. Some psychological studies of grammar. *American Psychologist,* 1962, *17,* 748–762.

Miller, G. A. *Mathematics and psychology.* New York: Wiley, 1964.

Miller, G. A. Psychology as a means of promoting human welfare. *American Psychologist,* 1969, *24,* 1026–1075.

Miller, H. G., Williams, R. G., & Haladyna, R. M. *Beyond facts: Objective ways to measure thinking.* Englewood Cliffs, N.J.: Educational Technology Publications, 1978.

Miller, J. R., & Kintsch, W. Readability and recall of short prose passages: A theoretical analysis. *Journal of Experimental Psychology: Human Learning and Memory,* 1980, *6,* 335–353.

Miller, N. E., & Dollard, M. J. *Social learning and imitation.* New Haven: Yale University Press, 1941.

Miller, R. B. *Handbook in training and training equipment design.* Technical Report 53-137. Wright Patterson AFB, Ohio: Wright Air Development Center, 1953. (a)

Miller, R. B. *A method for man-machine task analysis.* Technical Report 53-136. Wright-Patterson AFB, Ohio: Wright Air Development Center, 1953. (b)

Miller, R. B. *A suggested guide to position-task description.* Technical Memorandum ASPRL-TM-56-6. Lackland AFB, Tex.: Air Force Personnel and Training Research Center, 1956.

Mischel, W. *Personality and assessment.* New York: Wiley, 1968.

Mitchell, P. B., & Erickson, D. K. The education of gifted and talented children: A status report. *Exceptional Children,* 1978, *45,* 12–16.

Moates, D. R., & Schumacher, G. M. *An introduction to cognitive psychology.* Belmont, Calif.: Wadsworth, 1980.

Monroe, W. S. Hazards in the measurement of achievement. *School and Society,* 1935, *41,* 38–49.

Monroe, W. S. Educational measurement in 1920 and 1945. *Journal of Educational Research,* 1945, *38,* 334–340.

Montgomery, J., & Bruning, R. H. *A field test of a rereading method of reading instruction.* Paper presented at the Annual Meeting of the American Educational Research Association, Toronto, 1978.

Morariu, J., & Bruning, R. H. *Differential cognitive processing by deaf and hearing high school students using printed English and American Sign Language passages.* Paper presented to the annual convention of the American Educational Research Association, New York City, March 1982.

Morgan, C. L. *Habit and instinct.* London: Arnold, 1896.

Morphett, M., & Washburne, C. When should children begin to read? *Elementary School Journal,* 1931, *31,* 496–503.

Morris, C. J., & Kimbrell, G. Performance and attitudinal effects of the Keller method in an introductory psychology course. *Psychological Record,* 1972, *22,* 523–530.

Morris, C. J. & Kimbrell, G. Individual differences and PSI: A reanalysis. *Journal of Personalized Instruction,* 1977, *2,* 47–49.

Morris, P. E., & Cook, N. When do first letter mnemonics aid recall? *British Journal of Educational Psychology,* 1978, *48,* 22–28.

Murray, F. S., & Rowe, F. B. Psychological laboratories in the United States prior to 1900. *Teaching of Psychology,* 1979, *6,* 19–21.

Murray, H. A. *Explorations in personality.* New York: Oxford University Press, 1938.

Myers, A. E., McConville, C., & Coffman, W. E. Simplex structure in the grading of essay tests. *Educational and Psychological Measurement,* 1966, *26,* 41–54.

Nairn, A., & Associates. *The reign of ETS: The corporation that makes up minds.* Washington, D.C., 1980.

National Society for the Study of Education. *Forty-fifth yearbook. Part I: Measurement of understanding.* Bloomington, Ill.: Public School Publishing Company, 1945.

Neisser, V. *Cognitive psychology.* New York: Appleton-

Century-Crofts, 1967.

Neisser, U. *Cognition and reality.* San Francisco: Freeman, 1976.

Neisser, U. *Memory observed: Remembering in natural contexts.* San Francisco: Freeman, 1982.

Nelson, D. L., & Archer, C. S. The first letter mnemonic. *Journal of Educational Psychology,* 1972, *63,* 482–486.

Newell, A., Shaw, J. C., & Simon, H. A. Report on a general problem-solving program for a computer. *Information processing: Proceedings of the International Conference on Information Processing.* Paris: UNESCO, 1960.

Newell, A., & Simon, H. A. The logic machine: A complex information processing system. *IRE Transactions on Information Theory,* 1956, *2,* 61–79.

Newell, A., & Simon, H. A. *Human problem solving.* Englewood Cliffs, N.J.: Prentice-Hall, 1972.

Newman, H. H., Freeman, F. N., & Holzinger, K. J. *Twins: A study of heredity and environment.* Chicago: University of Chicago Press, 1937.

Noble, C. E. An analysis of learning. *Psychological Review,* 1952, *59,* 421–430.

Noble, C. E. Meaningfulness and familiarity. In C. N. Cofer & B. S. Musgrave (Eds.), *Verbal behavior and learning: Problems and processes.* New York: McGraw-Hill, 1963.

Norman, D. A., & Bobrow, D. G. On data-limited and resource-limited processes. *Cognitive Psychology,* 1975, *7,* 44–64.

Norman, D. A., & Bobrow, D. G. Descriptions: An intermediate stage in memory retrieval. *Cognitive Psychology,* 1979, *11,* 107–123.

O'Connor, R. D. Relative efficacy of modeling, shaping and the combined procedures for modification of social withdrawal. In C. M. Franks & G. T. Wilson (Eds.), *Behavior therapy and practice.* New York: Brunner/Mazel, 1973.

O'Leary, K. D. Behavior modification in the classroom.: A rejoinder to Winnet and Winkler. *Journal of Applied Behavior Analysis,* 1972, *5,* 505–511.

O'Leary, K. D., & Becker, W. C. Behavioral modification of an adjustment class: A token reinforcement program. *Exceptional Children,* 1967, *3,* 637–642.

O'Leary, K. D., Becker, W. C., Evans, M. B., & Saundargas, R. A. A token reinforcement program in a public school: A replication and systematic analysis. *Journal of Applied Behavior Analysis,* 1969, *2,* 3–14.

O'Leary, K. D., Kaufman, K. F., Kass, R. C., & Drabman, R. S. The effects of loud and soft reprimands on the behavior of disruptive students. *Exceptional Children,* 1970, *57,* 145–155.

O'Leary, K. D., & O'Leary, S. G. *Classroom management: The successful use of behavior modification.* New York: Pergamon, 1972.

O'Leary, K. D., & Wilson, G. T. *Behavior therapy: Appliction and outcome.* Englewood Cliffs, N.J.: Prentice-Hall, 1975.

O'Leary, S. G., & Dubey, D. R. Applications of self-control procedures by children: A review. *Journal of Applied Behavior Analysis,* 1979, *12,* 449–466.

Orton, S. T. *Reading, writing and speech problems in children.* New York: Norton, 1937.

Osborne, J. G. Free time as a reinforcer in the management of classroom behavior. *Journal of Applied Behavior Analysis,* 1969, *2,* 113–118.

Owen, F. *Familial studies of learning disabled children.* Paper presented to the Interdisciplinary Institute on Reading and Child Development, Newark, Del., June 1974.

Owen, F. W. Learning disability—a familial study. *Bulletin of the Orton Society,* 1968, *18,* 33–39.

Packard, R. G. The control of "classroom attention": A group contingency for complex behavior. *Journal of Applied Behavior Analysis,* 1970, *3,* 13–28.

Page, E. B. Teacher comments and student performance: A seventy-four classroom experiment in school motivation. *Journal of Educational Psychology,* 1958, *49,* 173–181.

Paige, J. M., & Simon, H. A. Cognitive processes in solving algebra word problems. In B. Kleinmuntz (Ed.), *Problem solving: Research, method, and theory.* New York: Wiley, 1966.

Paivio, A. *Imagery and verbal processes.* New York: Holt, Rinehart, & Winston, 1971.

Paivio, A., & Desrochers, A. Mnemonic techniques in second language learning. *Journal of Educational Psychology,* 1981, *73,* 780–795.

Palmer, O. Some classic ways of grading dishonestly. *The English Journal,* 1962, *52,* 464–467.

Parish, T. S. The enhancement of altruistic behavior in children through the implementation of language conditioning procedures. *Behavior Modification,* 1977, *1,* 283–306.

Parnes, S. J., & Harding, H. F. (Eds.). *A sourcebook for creative thinking.* New York: Scribner, 1962.

Pavlov, I. P. [*Lectures on conditioned reflexes*] (W. H. Gantt, trans.). New York: International Press, 1928.

Payne, D. A. *The assessment of learning: Cognitive and affective.* Lexington, Mass.: Heath, 1974.

Peper, R. J., & Mayer, R. E. Note taking as a generative activity. *Journal of Educational Psychology,* 1978, *70,* 514–522.

Perl, E., & Lambert, W. E. The relation of bilingualism to intelligence. *Psychological Monographs,* 1962, *76,* 1–23.

Petersen, C. P. *Problem solving among the aged.* Unpublished doctoral dissertation, University of Nebraska, 1979.

Peterson, C. H., Glover, J. A., & Ronning, R. R. An

examination of three prose learning strategies on reading comprehension. *The Journal of General Psychology* (in press).

Pflaum, S. W., Walberg, H. J., Karegianes, M. L., & Rasher, S. P. Reading instruction: A quantitative analysis. *Educational Research,* 1980, *9,* 12–18.

Phares, E. J. *Locus of control in personality.* Morristown, N.J.: General Learning Press, 1976.

Phillips, J. L. *The origins of intellect: Piaget's theory* (2nd ed.). San Francisco: Freeman, 1975.

Piaget, J. [*The origins of intelligence in children*] (M. Cook, trans.). New York: International Universities Press, 1952.

Piaget, J. [*The mechanisms of perception*] (G. N. Seagrim, trans.). London: Routledge & Kegan Paul, 1969.

Piaget, J. [*The child's conception of movement and speed*] (M. J. MacKensie, trans.). London: Routledge & Kegan Paul, 1970. (a)

Piaget, J. Piaget's theory. In P. Mussen (Ed.), *Carmichael's manual of child psychology* (3rd ed.). New York: Wiley, 1970. (b)

Piaget, J. [*To understand is to invent: The future of education*] (G. Robers & A. Robers, trans.). New York: Grossman, 1973.

Piaget. J. *Le comportement moteur de l'évolution.* Paris: Gallimand, 1976.

Piaget, J. Problems of equilibration. In M. H. Appel & L. S. Goldberg (Eds.), *Topics in cognitive development* (Vol. 1). New York: Plenum, 1977.

Piaget, J. A summary of the theory of Jean Piaget. In D. K. Gardiner (Ed.), *Readings in developmental psychology.* New York: Holt, 1978.

Piaget, J., & Inhelder, B. [*The psychology of the child*] (H. Weaver, trans.). London: Routledge & Kegan Paul, 1969.

Piaget, J., & Inhelder, B. [*Memory and intelligence*] (A. J. Pomerans, trans.). London: Routledge & Kegan Paul, 1973.

Pichert, J. W., & Anderson, R. C. Taking different perspectives on a story. *Journal of Educational Psychology,* 1977, *69,* 309–315.

Plake, B. S. A comparison of a statistical and subjective procedure to ascertain item validity: One step in the test validation process. *Educational and Psychological Measurement,* 1980, *40,* 397–404.

Plummer, S., Baer, D. M., & LeBlanc, J. M. Functional considerations in the use of time-out and an effective alternative. *Journal of Applied Behavior Analysis,* 1977, *10,* 689–705.

Polya, G. *How to solve it.* Princeton: Princeton University Press, 1946.

Pope, L. M. *From theory to practice in bilingual education.* Paper presented to the annual convention of the American Educational Research Association, New York City, March 1982.

Popham, W. J. The case for criterion-referenced measurements. *Educational Researcher,* 1978, *7,* 6–10.

Popham, W. J., & Husek, T. F. Implications of criterion-referenced measurement. *Journal of Educational Measurement,* 1969, *6,* 1–9.

Porterfield, J. K., Herbert-Jackson, E., & Risely, T. R. Contingent observation: An effective and acceptable procedure for reducing disruptive behavior of young children in a group setting. *Journal of Applied Behavior Analysis,* 1976, *9,* 55–64.

Postman, L., Stark, K., & Henschel, D. Conditions of recovery after unlearning. *Journal of Experimental Psychology Monograph,* 1969, *81*(1, Pt. 2).

Postman, L., & Underwood, B. J. Critical issues in interference theory. *Memory and Cognition,* 1973, *1,* 19–40.

Prakesh, A. O. *Effects of modeling and social reinforcement on the racial preferences of children.* ERIC Document Reproduction Service, ED 086 357. Washington, D.C.: U.S. Government Printing Service, 1973.

Premack, D. Toward empirical behavioral laws: I. Positive reinforcement. *Psychological Review,* 1959, *66,* 219–233.

Premack, D. Reinforcement theory. In D. Levine (Ed.), *Nebraska Symposium on Motivation.* Lincoln: University of Nebraska Press, 1965.

Pressey, S. L. Concerning the nature and nurture of genius. *Scientific Monthly,* 1955, *81,* 123–129.

Pressey, S. L. An interview with S. L. Pressey. *Directive Teacher,* 1979, *2,* 1, 23–24.

Pressley, M., Levin, J. R., & Delaney, H. D. *The mnemonic keyword method.* Theoretical Paper No. 92. Madison, Wis.: Wisconsin Research and Development Center for Individualized Schooling, 1981.

Pribram, R. H. *The language of the brain.* Englewood Cliffs, N.J.: Prentice-Hall, 1971.

Proger, B. B., Carter, C. E., Mann, L., Taylor, R. G., Jr., Bayuk, R. J., Jr., Morris, V. R., & Reckless, D. E. Advance and concurrent organizers for detailed verbal passages used with elementary school pupils. *Journal of Educational Research,* 1973, *66,* 451–456.

Pryor, R. W., Haag, R., & O'Reilley, J. The creative porpoise: Training for novel behavior. *Journal of the Experimental Analysis of Behavior,* 1969, *12,* 653–661.

Rachlin, H. *Introduction to modern behaviorism* (2nd ed.). San Francisco: Freeman, 1976.

Radgowski, T. A., Allen, K. E., Ruggles, T. R., Schilmoeller, G., & LeBlanc, J. M. *Training of a foresight language in preschool children using a delayed presentation of feedback.* Paper presented at the Annual Convention of the Midwest Association for Behavior Analysis, Chicago, 1978.

Rayner, K. Eye movements in reading and information processing. *Psychological Review,* 1978. *85,* 618–660.

Rayner, K., & Bertera, J. H. Reading with a fovea. *Science,* 1979, *206,* 468–469.

Rayner, K., & McConkie, G. W. Perceptual processes in reading: The perceptual spans. In A. S. Reber & D. L. Scarborough (Eds.), *Toward a psychology of reading.* Hillsdale, N.J.: Erlbaum, 1977.

Reese, E. The analysis of human operant behavior (2nd ed.). Dubuque, Iowa: Brown, 1978.

Reese, H. W., & Parnes, S. J. Programming creative behavior. *Child Development,* 1972, *41,* 83–89.

Reeves, B., & Lometti, G. E. The dimensional structure of children's perceptions of television characters: A replication. *Human Communication Research,* 1979, *5,*(3), 247–256.

Reid, D. W., & Ware, E. Multidimensionality of internal versus external control: Addition of a third dimension and nondistinction of self versus others. *Canadian Journal of Behavioral Science,* 1974, *6,* 131–142.

Reid, H. P., Archer, M. B., & Friedman, R. M. Using the personalized system of instruction with low-reading ability middle school students: Problems and results. *Journal of Personalized Instruction,* 1977, *2,* 199–203.

Reitman, W. R. Heuristic decision procedures, open constraints, and the structure of ill-defined problems. In M. W. Shelly & G. L. Bryan (Eds.), *Human judgments and optimality.* New York: Wiley ,1964.

Remmers, H. H., Bloom, B. S., Krathwohl, D. R., Burros, O. K., Mowrer, O. H., & Stalnaker, J. M. *Symposium: The development of a taxonomy of educational objectives.* Fifty-ninth Annual Meeting of the American Psychological Association, Chicago, August 31–September 5, 1951.

Resnick, D. P. Testing in America: A supportive environment. *Phi Delta Kappan,* 1981, *62,* 625–628.

Resnick, L. B. Task analysis in instructional design: Some cases from mathematics. In D. Klahr (Ed.), *Cognition and instruction.* Hillsdale, N.J.: Erlbaum, 1976.

Resnick, L. B. Introduction: Research to inform a debate. *Phi Delta Kappan,* 1981, *62,* 623–624.

Resnick, L. B., & Wang, M. C. Approaches to the validation of learning hierarchies. *Proceedings of the Eighteenth Annual Regional Conference on Testing Problems.* Princeton: Educational Testing Service, 1969.

Reynolds, C. R. The problem of bias in psychological assessment. In C. R. Reynolds and T. B. Gutkin (Eds.), *A handbook for school psychologists.* New York: Wiley, 1981.

Reynolds, G. S. *A primer of operant conditioning* (2nd ed.). Glenview, Ill.: Scott, Foresman, 1975.

Reynolds, M. C., & Balow, B. Categories and variables in special education. *Exceptional Children,* 1972, *38,* 357–366.

Reynolds, M. C., & Birch, J. W. *Teaching exceptional children in all America's schools.* Reston, Va.: Council for Exceptional Children, 1977.

Reynolds, R. E., & Anderson, R. C. *Influence of questions on the allocation of attention during reading.* Technical Report No. 183, Center for the Study of Reading. Urbana-Champaign, Ill.: University of Illinois Press, 1980.

Reynolds, R. E., Standiford, S. M., & Anderson, R. C. Distribution of reading time when questions are asked about a restricted category of text information. *Journal of Educational Psychology,* 1979, *71,* 183–190.

Rice, J. M. The futility of the spelling grind. *Forum,* 1897, *23,* 163–172, 409–419.

Richards, C. S. Behavior modification of studying through study skills advice and self-control procedures. *Journal of Counseling Psychology,* 1975, *22,* 431–436.

Richards, C. S., Perri, M. G., & Gortney, C. Increasing the maintenance of self-control treatments through faded therapist contact and high information feedback. *Journal of Counseling Psychology,* 1976, *23,* 405–406.

Rickards, J. P., & DiVesta, F. S. Type and frequency of questions in processing textual material. *Journal of Educational Psychology,* 1974, *66,* 354–362.

Rincover, A., Cook, R., Peoples, A., & Packard, D. Sensory extinction and sensory reinforcement principles for programming multiple adaptive behavior change. *Journal of Applied Behavior Analysis,* 1979, *12,* 221–234.

Rips, L. J., Shoben, E. J., & Smith, E. E. Semantic distance and the verification of semantic relations. *Journal of Verbal Learning and Verbal Behavior,* 1973, *12,* 1–20.

Robinson, F. *Effective study.* New York: Macmillan, 1972.

Roediger, H. L. Output interference in the recall of categorized and paired-associate lists. *Journal of Experimental Psychology: Human Learning and Memory,* 1980, *6,* 91–105.

Rogers, C. R. *Counseling and psychotherapy.* Boston: Houghton Mifflin, 1942.

Rogers, C. R. *Client-centered therapy.* Boston: Houghton Mifflin, 1951.

Rogers, C. R. Client-centered therapy. In E. Shostrom (Ed.), *Three approaches to psychotherapy.* Santa Ana, Calif.: Psychological Films, 1965.

Rogers, C. R. *Freedom to learn: A view of what education might become.* Columbus, Ohio: Merrill, 1969.

Rogers-Warren, A., & Baer, D. M. The role of offer rates in controlling sharing by young children. *Journal of Applied Behavior Analysis,* 1976, *9,* 491–497.

Rosenbaum, M. S., & Drabman, R. S. Self-control training in the classroom: A review and critique. *Journal of Applied Behavior Analysis,* 1979, *12,* 467–486.

Rosenshine, B. *Teaching behaviors and student achievement.* London: National Foundation for Educational Research, 1971.

Ross, C. C. *Measurement in today's schools.* New York: Prentice-Hall, 1947.

Ross, E. A. *Social control.* New York: Macmillan, 1901.

Ross, E. A. *Social psychology.* New York: Macmillan, 1908.

Rothkopf, E. Z. Some theoretical experimental approaches to problems in written instruction. In J. D. Krumboltz (Ed.), *Learning and the educational process.* Chicago: Rand McNally, 1965.

Rothkopf, E. Z. Learning from written instructive materials: An exploration of the control of inspection behavior by test-like events. *American Educational Research Journal,* 1966, *3,* 241–249.

Rothkopf, E. Z. The concept of mathemagenic activities. *Review of Educational Research,* 1970, *40,* 325–336.

Rothkopf, E. Z. Variable adjunct question schedules, interpersonal interaction, and incidental learning from written material. *Journal of Educational Psychology,* 1972, *63,* 87–92.

Rothkopf, E. Z., & Bisbicos, E. E. Selective facilitation effects of interspersed questions on learning from written materials. *Journal of Educational Psychology,* 1967, *58,* 56–81.

Rothkopf, E. Z., & Bloom, R. D. Effects of interpersonal interaction in the instructional value of adjunct questions in learning from written material. *Journal of Educational Psychology,* 1970, *61,* 417–422.

Rothkopf, E. Z., & Kaplan, R. Exploration of the effect of density and specificity of instructional objectives on learning from text. *Journal of Educational Psychology,* 1972, *63,* 295–302.

Rotter, J. B. *Social learning and clinical psychology.* Englewood Cliffs, N.J.: Prentice-Hall, 1954.

Rotter, J. B. Generalized expectancies for internal versus external control of reinforcement. *Psychological Monographs,* 1966, *80*(1, Whole No. 609).

Royce, J. The psychology of invention. *Psychological Review,* 1898, *5,* 123–144.

Rozin, P., & Gleitman, L. R. The structure and acquisition of reading. II: The reading process and the acquisition of the alphabetic principle. In A. S. Reber & D. L. Scarborough (Eds.), *Toward a psychology of reading.* Hillsdale, N.J.: Erlbaum, 1977.

Rubin, A. M. Television use by children and adolescents. *Human Communication Research,* 1979, *5*(2), 109–120.

Ruch, G. M. *The improvement of the written examination.* Chicago: Scott, Foresman, 1924.

Ruch, G. M., & Stoddard, G. D. *Tests and measurements in high school instruction.* Yonkers, N.Y.: World Book, 1927.

Rumelhart, D. E., Lindsay, P. H., & Norman, D. A. A process for long-term memory. In E. Tulving & W. Donaldson (Eds.), *Organization of memory.* New York: Academic Press, 1972.

Russell, W. A. *Milestones in motivation: Contributions to the psychology of drive and purpose.* New York: Appleton-Century-Crofts, 1970.

Salmon-Cox, L. Teachers and standardized achievement tests: What's really happening? *Phe Delta Kappan,* 1981, *62,* 631–634.

Samuels, S. R. Introduction to theoretical models of reading. In W. Otto, C. W. Peters, & N. Peters (Eds.), *Reading problems: A multidisciplinary perspective.* Reading, Mass.: Addison-Wesley, 1977.

Sattler, J. M. *Assessment of children's intelligence.* Philadelphia: Saunders, 1974.

Satz, P. Reading problems in perspective. In W. Otto, C. W. Peters, & N. Peters (Eds,), *Reading problems: A multidisciplinary perspective.* Reading, Mass.: Addison-Wesley, 1977.

Sautter, F. J., & Glover, J. A. *Behavior, development and training of the dog.* New York: Arco, 1978. (a)

Sautter, F. J., & Glover, J. A. The relationship of perceived reinforcement potential on the production of creative behaviors. *The Journal of Genetic Psychology,* 1978, *131,* 129–136. (b)

Schnell, T. R. The effect of organizers on reading comprehension of community college freshmen. *Journal of Reading Behavior,* 1973, *5,* 169–176.

Schultz, D. *A history of modern psychology* (2nd ed.). New York: Academic Press, 1975.

Scriven, M. Some issues in the logic and ethics of mainstreaming. *Minnesota Education,* 1976, *2,* 61–67.

Sears, P. S. Levels of aspiration in academically successful and unsuccessful children. *Journal of Abnormal Social Psychology,* 1940, *35,* 498–536.

Sechenov, I. M. *Reflexes of the brain.* Moscow: Russian Academy of Sciences, 1863.

Seligman, M. E. P. Chronic fear produced by unpredictable shock. *Journal of Comparative and Physiological Psychology,* 1966, *66,* 402–411.

Semb, G. The effects of mastery criteria and assignment length on college student test performance. *Journal of Applied Behavior Analysis,* 1974, *7,* 61–69.

Semb, G. Building an empirical base for instruction. *Journal of Personalized Instruction,* 1976, *1,* 11–12.

Shannon, C. E., & Weaver, W. *The mathematical theory of communication.* Urbana, Ill.: University of Illinois Press, 1949.

Sheppard, E. M. The effect of quality of penmanship on grades. *Journal of Educational Research,* 1929, *19,* 102–105.

Sherman, J. A., & Bushell, D. Behavior modification as

Thurstone, L. L. Creative talent. In L. L. Thurstone (Ed.), *Applications of psychology.* New York: Harper, 1952.

Tierney, R. J., & Pearson, P. D. *Learning to learn from text: A framework for improving classroom practice.* Reading Education Report No. 30. Urbana-Champaign, Ill.: University of Illinois, Center for the Study of Reading, 1981.

Tinbergen, N. *The study of instinct.* New York: Oxford University Press, 1951.

Tinker, M. A. *Basis for effective reading.* Minneapolis: University of Minnesota Press, 1965.

Titchener, E. B. The postulates of a structural psychology. *Psychological Review,* 1898, *7,* 449–465.

Titchener, E. B. *Lectures on the experimental psychology of thought processes.* New York: Macmillan, 1909.

Todd, D. D., Scott, R. B., Boston, D. E., & Alexander, S. B. Modification of the excessive inappropriate classroom behavior of two elementary school students using home-based consequences and daily report card procedures. *Journal of Applied Behavior Analysis,* 1976, *9,* 106.

Tolman, E. C. *Purposive behavior in animals and man.* New York: Naiburg, 1932.

Tolman, E. C. The determiners of behavior at a choice point. *Psychological Review,* 1938, *45,* 1–41.

Torrance, E. P. *Guiding creative talent.* Englewood Cliffs, N.J.: Prentice-Hall, 1962.

Torrance, E. P. *Creativity in the classroom.* Englewood Cliffs, N.J.: Prentice-Hall, 1965.

Torrance, E. P. The Minnesota studies of creative behaviors: National and international extensions. *Journal of Creative Behavior,* 1967, *1*(2), 137–154.

Torrance, E. P. Torrance Test of Creative Thinking. Lexington, Mass.: Ginn, 1974.

Torrance, E. P. *The state of the art of education for the gifted and talented.* Presented to the first Annual Nebraska Symposium on the Education of Gifted Children, Lincoln, Nebr., June 1980.

Torrey, J. W. Reading that comes naturally: The early reader. In T. G. Waller & G. E. MacKinnon (Eds.), *Reading research: Advances in theory and practice* (Vol. 1). New York: Academic Press, 1979.

Touhey, J. C., & Villamez, W. J. Ability attribution as a result of variable effort and achievement motivation. *Journal of Personality and Social Psychology,* 1980, *38,* 211–216.

Trachtenburg, D. Student tasks in text material: What cognitive skills do they tap? *Peabody Journal of Education,* 1974, *52,* 54–57.

Traxler, A. E., & Anderson, H. A. The reliability of an essay examination in English. *School Review,* 1935, *43,* 534–539.

Trotter, R. J. This is going to hurt you more than it hurts me. *Science News,* 1972, *18,* 332.

Tuckman, B. W. *Measuring educational outcomes: Fundamentals of testing.* New York: Harcourt, Brace, Jovanovich, 1975.

Tulving, E. Episodic and semantic memory. In E. Tulving & W. Donaldson (Eds.), *Organization of memory.* New York: Academic Press, 1972.

Tulving, E. Relation between encoding specificity and level of processing. In L. S. Cermak & F. I. M. Craik (Eds.), *Levels of processing and human memory.* Hillsdale, N.J.: Erlbaum, 1979.

Tyler, R. W. General statement on evaluation. *Journal of Educational Research,* 1942, *35,* 492–501.

Underwood, B. J. Interference and forgetting. *Psychological Review,* 1957, *64,* 49–60.

United States Commission on Civil Rights. Report on the effectiveness of compensatory educational programs. Washington, D.C.: United States Commission on Civil Rights, 1967.

Urban, H. B., & Ford, D. H. Some historical and conceptual perspectives on psychotherapy and behavior change. In A. E. Bergin & S. L. Garfield (Eds.), *Handbook of psychotherapy and behavior change: An empirical analysis.* New York: Wiley, 1971.

Van Hoaten, R. V., Morrison, E., Jarvis, R., & McDonald, M. The effects of explicit timing and feedback on compositional response rate in elementary school children. *Journal of Applied Behavior Analysis,* 1974, *7,* 547–555.

Van Riper, C. *Speech correction: Principles and methods.* Englewood Cliffs, N.J.: Prentice-Hall, 1972.

Van Riper, C. *Speech correction: Principles and methods,* (6th ed.). Englewood Cliffs, N.J.: Prentice-Hall, 1978.

Vargas, J. S. *Writing worthwhile behavioral objectives.* New York: Harper & Row, 1972.

Vargas, J. S. *Behavioral psychology for teachers.* New York: Harper & Row, 1977.

Vellutino, F. R. Alternative conceptualizations of dyslexia: Evidence in support of a verbal deficit hypothesis. Harvard Educational Review, 1977, *47,* 112–221.

Venezky, R. L. Prereading skills: Theoretical foundations and practical applications. In T. A. Brigham, R. Hawkins, J. W. Scott, & T. F. McLaughlin (Eds.), *Behavior analysis in education: Self control and reading.* Dubuque, Iowa: Kendall/Hunt, 1975.

Wahler, R. G. Setting generality: Some specific and general effects of child behavior therapy. *Journal of Applied Behavior Analysis,* 1969, *2,* 239–246.

Waite, C. J., Blick, K. A., & Boltwood, C. E. Prior use of the first letter technique. *Psychological Reports,* 1971, *29,* 630.

Walker, J. E., & Shea, T. M. *Behavior modification: A practical approach for educators.* St. Louis, Mo.: Mosby, 1976.

Wallach, M. A., & Kogan, N. *Modes of thinking in young children: A study of the creativity-intelligence distinction.* New York: Holt, Rinehart, & Winston, 1965.

Waller, T. G. Children's recognition memory for written sentences: A comparison of good and poor readers. *Child Development,* 1976, *47,* 90–95.

Ward, H. M., & Baker, B. L. Reinforcement therapy in the classroom. *Journal of Applied Behavior Analysis,* 1968, *1,* 323–328.

Watson, D. L., & Tharp, R. G. *Self-directed behavior: Self-modification for personal adjustment* (2nd ed.). Monterey, Calif.: Brooks/Cole, 1977.

Watson, J. B. Psychology as the behaviorist views it. *Psychological Review,* 1913, *20,* 158–177.

Watson, J. B. *Psychological care of infant and child.* New York: Norton, 1928.

Watson, P. I.Q.: The racial gap. *Psychology Today,* 1972, 6(4), 48–99.

Waugh, N. C., & Norman, D. A. Primary memory. *Psychological Review,* 1965, *72,* 89–104.

Wechsler, D. *Manual for the Wechsler Intelligence Scale for Children.* New York: Psychological Corporation, 1949.

Wechsler, D. *Manual for the Wechsler Adult Intelligence Scale.* New York: Psychological Corporation, 1955.

Wechsler, D. *Manual for the Wechsler Preschool and Primary Scale of Intelligence.* New York: Psychological Corporation, 1967.

Wechsler, D. *Manual for the Wechsler Intelligence Scale for Children—revised manual.* New York: Psychological Corporation, 1974.

Wechsler, D. *Manual for the Wechsler Adult Intelligence Scale—revised.* New York: Psychological Corporation, 1981.

Weiner, B. *Theories of motivation.* Chicago: Rand McNally, 1972.

Weiner, B., & Kukla, A. An attributional analysis of achievement motivation. *Journal of Personality and Social Psychology,* 1970, *15,* 1–20.

Weiss, G., & Hechtman, L. The hyperactive child syndrome. *Science,* 1979, *205,* 1348–1354.

Wertheimer, M. *A brief history of psychology.* New York: Holt, Rinehart, & Winston, 1978.

Wesman A. G. Intelligent testing. In B. L. Kintz & J. L. Bruning (Eds.), *Research in psychology.* Glenview, Ill.: Scott, Foresman, 1970.

Whipple, G. M. *Manual of mental and physical tests.* Baltimore: Warwick & York, 1910.

Whipple, G. M. *The twenty-fourth yearbook of the National Society for the Study of Education. Part I. Report of the National Committee on Reading.* Bloomington, Ill.: Public School Publishing Company, 1925.

White, E. E. *The elements of pedagogy.* New York: American Book, 1886.

White, G. M. Immediate and deferred effects of model observation and guided and unguided rehearsal on donating and stealing. *Journal of Personality and Social Psychology,* 1972, *21,* 139–148.

White, R. T., & Gagné, R. M. Past and future research on learning hierarchies. *Educational Psychologist,* 1974, *11,* 19–28.

Wickelgren, W. A. *How to solve problems.* San Francisco: Freeman, 1974.

Wilde, O. *Intentions: The decay of lying, and other essays.* Portland, Maine: Mosher, 1904.

Willerman, L. *The psychology of individual and group differences.* San Francisco: Freeman, 1979.

Willerman, L., & Turner, R. G. *Readings about individual and group differences.* San Francisco: Freeman, 1979.

Williams, J. Building perceptual and cognitive strategies into a reading curriculum. In A. S. Reber & D. L. Scarborough (Eds.), *Toward a psychology of reading.* Hillsdale, N.J.: Erlbaum, 1977.

Williams, R. L., & Anadam, K. *Cooperative classroom management.* Columbus, Ohio: Merrill, 1973.

Winett, R. A., & Winkler, R. C. Current behavior modification in the classroom: Be still, be quiet, be docile. *Journal of Applied Behavior Analysis,* 1972, *5,* 499–504.

Winne, P. E. *Matching students' cognitive processing to text with instructional objectives or inserted questions.* Research Report No. 80-02. Burnaby, British Columbia: Simon Fraser University, 1981.

Witmer, L. Editorial. *Psychological Clinic,* 1907, *1,* 1–4.

Wittrock, M. C. Focus on educational psychology. *Educational Psychologist,* 1967, *4*(2), 17–20.

Wittrock, M. C. The cognitive movement in instruction. *Educational Researcher,* 1979, *8,* 5–11.

Wolf, M. M., Giles, D. K., & Hall, R. V. Experiments with token reinforcements in a remedial classroom. *Behavior Research and Therapy,* 1968, *6,* 51–64.

Wolf, R. L., & Simon, R. J. Does busing improve the racial interactions of children? *Educational Researcher,* 1975, *4,* 5–10.

Woodson, M. I. C. E. Seven aspects of teaching concepts. *Journal of Educational Psychology,* 1974, *66,* 184–188.

Woodworth, R. S. *Dynamic psychology.* New York: Columbia University Press, 1918.

Worthen, B., & Sanders, J. R. *Educational evaluation: Theory and practice.* Worthington, Ohio: Jones, 1973.

Yaroush, R., Sullivan, M. J., & Ekstrand, B. R. Effect of sleep on memory. II: Differential effect of the first and second half of the night. *Journal of Experimental Psychology,* 1971, *88,* 361–366.

Yoakam, G. A. *Basal reading instruction.* New York: McGraw-Hill, 1955.

Young, P. T. *Motivation of behavior.* New York: Wiley, 1936.

Zelnicker, T., & Jeffrey, W. E. Reflective and impulsive children: Strategies of information processing underlying differences in problem solving. *Monographs of the Society for Research,* 1976.

Zimmer, J. W. *A level of processing analysis of memory for prose.* Paper presented at the Annual Meeting of the American Educational Research Association, Toronto, 1978. (a)

Zimmer, J. W. *A processing activities approach to memory for prose.* Paper presented at the Annual Meeting of the American Psychological Association, Toronto, 1978. (b)

Zimmer, J. W. *A level of processing approach to memory for prose.* Paper presented at the Annual Meeting of the American Educational Research Association, Montreal, 1979.

Zimmer, J. W., & Glover, J. A. *Logical inferences and prose processing.* Paper presented at the Annual Meeting of the Western Psychological Association, San Diego, 1979.

Zimmer, J. W., Petersen, C. H., Ronning, R. R., & Glover, J. A. The effects of adjunct aids in prose processing: A re-examination. *Journal of Instructional Psychology,* 1978, *5,* 27–34.

Zimmerman, B. J., & Brody, G. H. Race and modeling on the interpersonal play patterns of boys. *Journal of Educational Psychology,* 1975, *67,* 591–598.

Zimmerman, B. J., & Pike, E. O. Effects of modeling and reinforcement on the acquisition and generalization of question asking behavior. *Child Development,* 1972, *43,* 892–907.

INDEX